EMILY DICKINSO

As She

EMILY DICKINSON'S

POEMS

As She Preserved Them

edited by Cristanne Miller

The Belknap Press of Harvard University Press

Cambridge, Massachusetts London, England 2016

Printed in the United States of America

Designed and typeset by Julie Fry

Third printing

Library of Congress Cataloging-in-Publication Data

Dickinson, Emily, 1830–1886, author.
Emily Dickinson's poems : as she preserved them / Emily Dickinson ; edited by Cristanne Miller.
pages cm
Includes bibliographical references and index.
ISBN 978-0-674-73796-9 (alk. paper)
1. Dickinson, Emily, 1830–1886—Criticism and interpretation. 2. Dickinson, Emily, 1830–1886—Manuscripts. 3. Poetry—Editing. I. Miller, Cristanne, editor. II. Title.
PS1541.Z5M483 2016
811'.4—dc23

2015030724

Contents

Preface

THIS IS the first edition of Emily Dickinson's poems to present in easily readable form Dickinson's own ordering of the poems she bound into forty handmade booklets between 1858 and 1864, and of the poems she copied onto unbound sheets between 1864 and 1875. It is also the first annotated reading edition of her poems. And it is the first edition to include the alternative words and phrases Dickinson wrote on the pages of many of the poems she retained. It presents the poet at work—beginning with her early copying of the poems she wanted to keep onto folded sheets of stationery, and progressing through her late poems, many of which were left in a state of chaotic draft or perhaps experimental fluidity. The reader can see at a glance, in this edition, the poems that Dickinson retained for herself, and arguably for posterity, in pristine condition and those that include possible substitutions for a concept or thought—sometimes a single alternative word in a poem of twenty or more lines and sometimes more than a score of alternatives for a single line. The reader can further observe which poems Dickinson left in an entirely fluid or unfinished state—a distinction disguised in other reading editions by editorial choices presenting a hypothesized clean or finished version. The poems presented here provide easily legible access to the full complexity of Dickinson's work and her working process.

This edition foregrounds the copies and versions of poems that Dickinson kept for herself during her lifetime, in the form in which she retained them—hence the title, *Emily Dickinson's Poems: As She Preserved Them.* While there is no clear evidence as to whether she retained some of the extant manuscripts, we know with certainty that she retained the more than 1,100 poems she either bound into booklets (called "fascicles" by Dickinson scholars) or copied systematically in fair hand onto unbound sheets and leaves of stationery. After 1875, Dickinson kept her poems in a more miscellaneous state—some cleanly written and signed as if to send to a correspondent, but then retained, and some on scraps of envelopes, wrapping paper, or drafts of letters. She also circulated almost one hundred fifty poems without retaining a copy for herself. Dickinson's retained poems provide both a record of what she chose to save and the best surviving evidence of her compositional practice: they show lines and poems the poet resolved entirely, poems she copied with isolated alternative possibilities for continued thinking, and lines or poems on which she was still considering multiple alternatives. Often Dickinson circulated a copy of a poem without alternatives and kept for her own records only the page showing the draft, or highly fluid, stage of her thinking and writing. For example, Dickinson circulated the poem "A little madness in the Spring" to two friends with a fifth line that read "This whole Experiment of Green"; in her retained copy, line 5, first written as "This sudden legacy of Green," has fifteen alternatives. This still fluid text is the source copy for the poem printed here.

This volume clarifies Dickinson's different modes of copying, retaining, and circulating her poems by dividing them into five sections: [1] "The Fascicles"—the poems Dickinson copied onto folded sheets of stationery, typically embossed and lightly ruled, and bound into booklets; [2] "Unbound Sheets"—the poems systematically copied onto sheets or leaves of stationery but left unbound; [3] "Loose Poems"—the poems Dickinson retained on paper of various sizes and shapes, not as part of her systematic copying and often in draft or fluid form, showing her process of deliberation between multiple alternatives; [4] "Poems Transcribed by Others"—the poems that remain to us only as transcribed by others because although Dickinson probably retained them, the manuscripts were lost after her death; and [5] "Poems Not Retained"—the poems we have in full only because they were sent to others who preserved them. Annotations appear as endnotes; circulation information appears at the foot of each page. The glossary provides the names of correspondents to whom Dickinson sent poems, and brief notes about them. The appendix indicates the correspondence between Ralph W. Franklin's "sets" and the unbound sheets as numbered here (Franklin was the most recent editor of a variorum edition of Dickinson's poems). With the exception of a few titles, mostly suggested in letters, Dickinson neither titled nor numbered her poems and I have neither titled nor numbered them here. The concluding index of first lines does, however, include cross-references to the poem numbers assigned by Thomas H. Johnson and Ralph W. Franklin in their 1955 and 1998 editions of Dickinson's poetry.

The introduction describes Dickinson's practices in copying and circulating poems, introduces the volume's annotations, summarizes some of the debates within Dickinson scholarship, and presents the editorial principles guiding the presentation of poems in this edition. The "Abbreviations and Reading Guide" provides examples of this edition's representation of the poems, especially Dickinson's alternative words and phrases, which can be challenging to decipher in relation to what is typically the initial text of the poem or, in the case of some chaotic manuscripts, a structurally logical rendering of the text. Every poem appears in clean form on the left side of the page; on the right, and sometimes in the space immediately following the poem, are the alternatives, if any were present on the manuscript used here as source text. My hope is that this edition provides new ways of thinking about Dickinson's poems by allowing the reader to see them in the groupings determined by the poet's own organization of her work. I also hope that it leads to new ways of thinking about the poet Emily Dickinson herself, by allowing the reader to see more fully her various processes of copying, circulating, and composing.

It has been a challenge and a joy to read Dickinson's manuscripts thoroughly and repeatedly, locating the patterns of her inscription and noting her varied deviations from those patterns. I have renewed appreciation and gratitude for the work of R. W. Franklin in his meticulous ordering, dating, and transcribing of the manuscripts, and for all previous editors of the poems. My debts to other scholars are also extensive. Domhnall Mitchell has provided touchstone advice, support, and a willingness to consult from the beginning. At various stages in the manuscript's preparation, Páraic Finnerty, Jennifer Leader, and Helen Vendler generously read every annotation for clarity, accuracy, or typographical error, and Páraic read a draft of the entire edition. Bonnie Costello, Paul Crumbley, Jane Eberwein, Alfred Habegger, Gunhild Kübler, Linda Leavell, Joel Myerson, Marjorie Perloff, Vivian Pollak, Eliza Richards, Christopher Ricks, Gary Stonum, and Marta Werner have all read sections or sample pages and provided valuable commentary; Martha Nell Smith corresponded helpfully about several aspects of Dickinson's manuscripts and transcription; and Judith Scholes provided information for annotation. Jane Wald and Cindy Dickinson of the Emily Dickinson Museum also convened a group that gave excellent feedback on an early draft of the page design. The volume *Open Me Carefully: Emily Dickinson's Intimate Correspondence to Susan Huntington*

Dickinson, edited by Martha Nell Smith, has been a useful resource, as have the Dickinson Electronic Archives and the digital text and archive Emily Dickinson's Correspondences. The Emily Dickinson Archive maintained by the Houghton Library, Harvard University, will simplify the work of all future editors of Dickinson's verse by making a great many manuscript images available. I am grateful to the editor-in-chief of Harvard University Press, Susan Wallace Boehmer, for her enthusiasm for this project from its first mention, and to editor John Kulka's keen eye for detail and sage advice throughout the final stages of preparing this edition. I alone am responsible for any mistakes and for interpretive decisions.

I could not have completed this edition without the superb assistance of librarians from several university and private collections: Harvard University's Houghton Library, Amherst College's Robert Frost Library, the Boston Public Library, Yale University's Beinecke Rare Book and Manuscript Library and Sterling Memorial Library, the Morgan Library & Museum in New York, the American Antiquarian Society in Worcester, Massachusetts, the Forbes Library in Northampton, Massachusetts, and the Jones Library in Amherst. In particular, I would like to thank Leslie Morris, Susan Halpert, and Heather Cole at the Houghton, and Michael Kelly and Margaret Dakin at the Frost, for their exceptional generosity and assistance. University at Buffalo SUNY graduate students Patricia Caroline Chaudron, Andrew Dorkin, and Daniel Schweitzer ably assisted in collecting and formatting information and proofreading, as did Elizabeth Miller. My research was supported by fellowships from the Fulbright Foundation and the American Council of Learned Societies and the leave time provided by the University at Buffalo SUNY.

EMILY DICKINSON'S POEMS

As She Preserved Them

Introduction

EMILY DICKINSON did not see any of her almost 1,800 poems through the process of publication, but she did copy more than 1,100 poems in fair hand onto folded sheets of stationery, binding the majority of the sheets into the booklets Dickinson scholars call fascicles. This is the first edition of Dickinson's poems to present her fascicle and unbound-sheet poems in the order in which she copied them, in easily readable form.[1] *Emily Dickinson's Poems: As She Preserved Them* presents one version of all her known poems. The emphasis, however, is on the copies that Dickinson herself retained—especially those retained after careful copying and binding into booklets, because these are the poems she took greatest care to ensure would survive during her lifetime and, arguably, for posterity. This is also the first annotated reading edition of Dickinson's poems, with brief notes on her quotations and allusions and on the contexts of her writing, and it is the first to present the alternative words and revisions Dickinson included on the texts she saved. It shows the poet at work through the varying stages of her writing life. *Emily Dickinson's Poems* is intended to provide a clear text of her poems for use in the classroom and for general readers. At the same time, it includes critical information of interest to scholars and advanced students of Dickinson or poetry studies in general.

Dickinson may have ordered the poems in her forty fascicles to develop a particular theme or idea. Or she may have constructed these booklets to create some order among the poems she had accumulated by the time she was twenty-seven, in 1858, when she apparently began this systematic copying: after carefully copying a poem, she discarded previous copies. For the next seven years, Dickinson recopied virtually everything that she wrote or that she wanted to save. Throughout this process, her primary unit for the copies was the folded sheet. To make a booklet, she stacked folded sheets of copied poems on top of one another, poked holes through the stack at the folded edges, and then bound them together with string. While she used a variety of types of paper for these hundreds of poems, most frequently she used embossed blue-lined or lightly lined stationery already folded by the stationer, most pages measuring about seven to eight inches by five inches.[2] She only twice continued onto a new sheet to finish a poem.[3] Because the sheet was her ordering unit, this edition identifies poems according to both the fascicle in which they were bound, as numbered by Ralph W. Franklin, and the sheet on which they were written. "Safe in their Alabaster Chambers –," for example, appears in its earliest extant version in what is now numbered Fascicle 6 on Sheet 3 (F6 Sh3) and appears with alternative second stanzas in Fascicle 10, Sheet 4 (F10 Sh4). Dickinson copied all but thirty-two of the more than 1,100 poems she had written and saved by 1866 onto a sheet, and most sheets were bound into fascicles.

Franklin hypothesized that Dickinson's unbound sheets were organized into groups that he called "sets." He based his determination of what constituted each set by correlating the date of the handwriting and the type of paper used, and also the state of the manuscripts when Dickinson's sister, Lavinia, passed them on to Mabel Loomis Todd to prepare for publication: four gatherings were connected by a brass fastener and others were grouped in what Todd called "packets." There is no evidence, however, that these gatherings were Dickinson's.[4] In the types of paper used, the apparently systematic nature of Dickinson's copying, and their inclusion of multiple poems per sheet (except in Franklin's Set 15), these unbound sheets are nonetheless distinct from the great majority of the loose poems found among Dickinson's papers after her death.[5]

Dickinson also circulated more than a quarter of her known compositions to family and friends, mostly in her later years. While she circulated many of the poems copied in fascicles and on unbound sheets, so far as we know the great majority of these poems remained private, perhaps out of self-censorship about subjects and feelings she did not wish to share during her lifetime. Judging from extant letters, Dickinson circulated relatively few of her poems about death, pain, and desire, and, before the late 1870s, few articulating religious doubt; among the almost 1,300 poems she kept entirely private are "Because I could not stop for death –," "I felt a Funeral, in my Brain," "After great pain, a formal feeling comes –," "Wild nights – Wild nights!," "Ourselves were wed one summer – dear –," "'Heaven' – is what I cannot reach!," and "This World is not conclusion." Interestingly, she also apparently never shared "This is my letter to the World" (F24 Sh4), suggesting that she may have regarded not just that poem but all her carefully copied poems as a "letter" that might be read after her death. Many of the poems she circulated were brief, or she circulated only a stanza or a few lines of a longer poem. Many were also occasional—sent in reference to a season of the year, an event in the recipient's life, or accompanying a gift. The smallest occasion, however, might give rise to profound speculation on human nature, theology, or the human relationship to the natural world.

This edition indicates if a poem was circulated, to whom it was sent, on what date, whether the circulated poem varied from the version printed in this edition, and other appropriate information—for example, whether Dickinson suggested a title for the poem or whether it accompanied a gift. "The Guest is gold and crimson –" includes the note: "Sent to SD (variant) c. late 1858, titled "'Navy' Sunset!"—in other words, Dickinson sent this poem to Susan Dickinson in a variant version around late 1858, with a title. If even a single punctuation mark or capitalization varies from the source text of this edition, the circulated copy is identified as "variant." Variant versions are not presented here, but variant first lines are listed. One coy 1862 poem begins, alternatively, "Going – to – Her!," "Going to them, happy letter!," and "Going to Him! Happy letter!" The reader will find "Going – to – Her!" in "Loose Poems"; in the circulation information at the bottom of that page, the reader will discover that "Going to them, happy letter!" was sent to Dickinson's Norcross cousins, Louisa and Frances, at about the same time that she copied the poem she retained. A note further informs the reader that she kept an additional copy of the poem written out later that year, beginning "Going to Him! Happy letter!"

After 1865, Dickinson's productivity dropped precipitously. While she apparently wrote more than 900 poems during the years of the Civil War (1861–1865), in the five years between 1866 and 1870 she seems to have written only 72 poems and copied none onto bifolium sheets. Although she returned sporadically to such copying between 1871 and 1875, after 1865 she also retained poems copied on single loose leaves or scraps of paper—some written out on stationery in fair hand and without alternatives, as if to be circulated; some with several alternatives or in draft, on brown wrapping paper, old envelopes, the back of drafts of letters or advertising flyers, and one on a wrapper from a packet of cooking chocolate.[6] This volume's section "Loose Poems" includes all the poems we have good reason to believe Dickinson retained for which we have extant manuscripts and that are not in fascicles or on systematically copied unbound sheets and leaves.

Around 1876, after Dickinson stopped copying poems onto folded sheets, she may have turned to correspondence as her preferred method of maintaining a record of her work—trusting that her friends would save her missives. This hypothesis is supported by two facts: first, she circulated a much higher proportion of her poems after she stopped systematically copying them, and, second, many of the poems she retained after 1875 were written on clean stationery, sometimes including a signature, as if they were intended to be circulated, but were not. Dickinson without doubt circulated more poems than we have records of; extant evidence, however, suggests it is unlikely that she circulated a great number of her poems before 1876.[7] Ninety of the around five hundred poems we know she circulated were sent to more than one person. Extant records and manuscripts indicate that Dickinson did not retain almost one hundred fifty poems in complete text (see "Poems Not Retained"). "Poems Transcribed by Others" presents poems probably retained by Dickinson but lost after her death—fortunately, after having been transcribed by someone else.

In several cases, we cannot know whether Dickinson circulated or retained a poem, especially in regard to her correspondence with Susan. Many manuscripts passed into her sister-in-law's possession after Dickinson's death.[8] Martha Nell Smith has been the primary proponent of the argument that Susan received more manuscripts during Dickinson's lifetime than Franklin acknowledges. In most cases, I find Franklin's representation of Dickinson's correspondence convincing, but I include in the poems' notes competing claims about whether a manuscript was circulated, and I represent every poem Franklin lists as even "apparently" or "perhaps" sent as circulated.

Around the summer of 1861, Dickinson began including alternative words on her pages, most often at the conclusion of a poem, usually marking with a small plus sign the word or phrase potentially being replaced. For example, in the last stanza of "My Life had stood – a Loaded Gun –" (F34 Sh4), Dickinson wrote, "For I have but the power to kill," marking the word "power" for an alternative and giving "art" as her potential substitution:

> Though I than He – may longer live
> He longer must – than I –
> For I have but the power to kill, [the] art
> Without – the power to die –

The alternative "art" for "power" introduces the possibility that one might feel like a loaded gun in the context of inspiration or creative endeavor. That she retained the poem with this alternative (and others) suggests that she wanted to keep a range of possible interpretations open, at least at the time she copied the poem.

Dickinson also revised fascicle poems by writing in margins or between lines, sometimes cancelling her first choice. By including Dickinson's alternative words, revisions, and cancellations in her record copies of a poem's text, this edition illuminates the degree to which she kept alternative choices in play for further resolution in other copies. While Dickinson revised a few poems first copied in 1859 and 1860, it is not until late in 1861, in Fascicle 11, that we see with any frequency alternative words added at the time that she copied the poem.[9] Dickinson did not circulate poems with alternatives, although she sent to Susan a few poems with an individual cancelled word.[10] I use the term "alternative" to indicate a potential substitution written on the page of a poem, as distinct from a "variant" word choice made in other copies of the same poem—for example, in a copy she circulated.

Including alternatives in writing out a poem was not a constant practice; well over half of Dickinson's poems contain no alternative words of any kind. Of the texts printed in this edition, around 60 percent contain no alternative words or revisions, and more than 75 percent contain two or fewer.[11] At the other end of the spectrum, some poems contain so many alternative words and phrases that it is difficult to identify a final direction to her thinking. There is a qualitative as well as quantitative difference between Dickinson's poems containing alternative substitutions for words or phrases in some number of a poem's lines and those containing so many potential substitutions that it is hard to get a sense of distinct progression in the poem. Whereas the former have the characteristics of a finished work, such as a capitalized word at the start of each poetic line, the latter often do not. I regard the latter poems as "in draft," although Marta Werner has persuasively argued that in her late years Dickinson may have developed a more fluidly disordered style of writing. "A Sparrow took a slice of Twig" is representative of such later poems in that it begins with apparently clear word choices and then has multiple, inconclusive options for its final lines. Even primarily resolved poems can present the reader (or the poet) with a dizzying range of choices: the twenty-six-line poem "Those fair – fictitious People –" (F18 Sh3) contains twenty-one alternatives, making for a possible 7,680 distinct ways of resolving the poem.

Although only a small minority of Dickinson's manuscripts contain a large number of alternatives or revisions, her recurring use of this compositional, revising, or copying method suggests that at the very least she thought of her poems as always open to new formulations of her thought, or new thinking. In this, she resembles her peer Walt Whitman, who frequently revised poems for later publication. Dickinson's variant versions of many of the poems she circulated also underline her sense of a poem's fluidity. Writing a poem without alternatives in one copy did not prevent her from later recasting that poem in an equally stable but variant form. Dickinson's alternatives resemble multiple performance options for a single production: variation is potentially unlimited, but when performing—in Dickinson's case, reading a poem aloud or circulating a text to a friend—the artist chooses a single version.

Dickinson's poems thus range along a continuum of resolution. This edition's inclusion of her alternatives, revisions, and cancellations allows readers to see at a glance which poems she left to us in a single copy without alternatives, which remain only in highly unresolved or draft form, and which lie in between. Readers may determine for themselves whether a poem has achieved its final shape or whether it remains a draft, or a piece of writing in which Dickinson is "choosing not choosing," as Sharon Cameron put it.[12] Readers who value uninterrupted reading pleasure above indeterminacy, and the insights that indeterminacy can provide into the mind of the poet at work, may restrict themselves to the unmarked text on the left side of the page. Others will enjoy following Dickinson's thinking process as she proposed alternatives—a process that in some cases requires thoughtful deciphering on the reader's part because of the sheer density of the potential substitutions or breadth of her range of conception.

Some scholars believe that Dickinson composed with attention not just to language but to the visual space of the page, and even to the kind and shape of paper she chose to write on. They read a poem as a visual structure in which the slants of her dashes, the placement and shape of words and letters across the space of her writing surface, and the material characteristics of each scrap of paper or embossed stationery page all signify as elements of the poetry. Consequently, each writing out of a set of words constitutes in effect a new poem. My own work with the manuscripts and poetry, in contrast, convinces me that while Dickinson took a real interest in writing out her poems, this was for her always an activity of secondary importance to her play with language.

Images of Dickinson's poetry manuscripts are now available online in the Emily Dickinson Archive (edickinson.org).[13] The archive gives readers the opportunity to explore the ways Dickinson might have played, brilliantly, with the space on a page or the shape or previous use of some reclaimed paper scrap. It may not have been accidental that Dickinson wrote a draft of "But that defeated accent" on an advertising sheet for the New York "Home Insurance Co.," with its announcement of "Cash Assets, over SIX MILLION DOLLARS," given that the poem ends with a reference to the "Affluence of time." Readers will also see that she typically wrote poems cleanly on sheets or leaves of stationery. This edition attempts to represent the full complexity of Dickinson's composing and copying without mirroring or accounting for a manuscript's visual properties.

It is my conviction that Dickinson's poems are separable from their handwritten artifacts, and that it is both useful and reasonable to reproduce them in print in the form she typically indicated she imagined them—namely, with initial capital letters in poetic lines that follow or depart meaningfully from metered patterns. As with any poet's manuscripts, a print transcription cannot retain the aura of a handwritten artifact, the idiosyncrasies of the poet's handwriting, or the perhaps playful use of the page. It does give us, however, everything essential to what I believe Dickinson conceived as the poem—even if not everything remarkable about particular presentations of a poem. The fact that when she made multiple copies of a poem she used different sizes and kinds of paper and varied several aspects of the physical presentation (stanzaic organization, punctuation, letter size, run-on rows of script for a poetic line) suggests that she also saw the poem as separable from any particular handwritten artifact. Although she wrote an early (eight-line) version of "The Mushroom is the Elf of Plants –" diagonally on the inside of an envelope, perhaps playfully alluding to the mushroom's pointy "Truffled Hut," she later revised and recopied the poem four times, in letters and on stationery, in ways that bear no visual resemblance to this early trial.

Dickinson knew by heart much of the Bible and many poems by her favorite authors. In some of her poems she quotes such sources exactly, with or without quotation marks. More frequently, she alludes to or echoes other work. The endnote annotations in this volume do not identify every allusion in Dickinson's poems; they do provide a general guide to works or events that may elucidate a poem's context. By far the majority of such references are to the Bible, especially the Christian New Testament. The most obvious (references to Adam and Eve, for example) are not annotated.

It is often impossible to know whether an allusion is intended: some apparent allusions involve sentiments common in Dickinson's day, and famous lines were often reworked or parodied by other writers whom she would have known. When she wrote "I died for Beauty" and then claimed Truth and Beauty "are One" (F21 Sh3), she apparently referred to John

Keats's "Ode on a Grecian Urn" (1820): "Beauty is truth, truth beauty." She may also, however, have been echoing more recent allusions to Keats's ode, for example, in Ralph Waldo Emerson's *Nature* (1836): "The true philosopher and the true poet are one, and a beauty, which is truth, and a truth, which is beauty, is the aim of both"; or Elizabeth Barrett Browning's "A Vision of Poets" (1844): "These were poets true / Who died for Beauty, as martyrs do / For truth – the ends being scarcely two"—lines marked in the Dickinson family copy of Barrett Browning's poems. After the Bible, the most frequent allusions in Dickinson's poems are to Shakespeare, Barrett Browning, Emerson, and other nineteenth-century British and American authors, although she also refers to popular culture and current events—including circuses, minstrel shows, and concerts she attended; literary or scientific textbooks read during her years at the Amherst Academy (1841–1847 and the fall of 1848) and Mount Holyoke Seminary for Women (1847–1848); and popular literature appearing in journals subscribed to by her family, such as the *Atlantic Monthly*.

I do not annotate general preconditions—for example, the several potential sources for Dickinson's posthumous-speaker poems or sentimental expressions. I also do not credit information to particular critics, although I am indebted to many Dickinson scholars for their identification of allusions in her poems—especially to Jack Capps (*Emily Dickinson's Reading*) and Helen Vendler (*Dickinson: Selected Poems and Commentaries*), Mary Loeffelholz and Páraic Finnerty (both for several recent publications), and Jennifer Leader (for her extensive familiarity with biblical scripture).[14] Critics are just beginning to discover the extent of Dickinson's allusions to literary and popular culture and events of her day. For example, Dickinson probably knew Harriet Prescott Spofford's story "The Amber Gods," which ends "I must have died at ten minutes past one" (*Atlantic Monthly*, 1860)—whether or not it influenced her own use of posthumous speakers.

Dickinson grew up in a period of active experimentation with poetic form, which encouraged her to experiment with metrical patterns, line length, and rhyme. The great majority of her poems are written in iambic or catalectic meter or in a popular beat-based rhythm, typically combining the rising rhythms of iambs and anapests.[15] Almost all her poems rhyme, albeit often irregularly or slant. Similarly, Dickinson's verse typically maintains a metrical base, even among its irregularities of rhythm, rhyme, line length, and stanzaic structure. Alternatives generally maintain a poem's meter, and where this is not the case, they may return the poem to a more regular stanzaic or metrical pattern than Dickinson's initial word choice.

Like many poets of her day, Dickinson at times used archaic poeticisms as a guide to metrical pronunciation. In the second stanza of "Trust in the Unexpected –" (F27 Sh5), for example, Dickinson writes "Discerned" as "Discern_ed," evidently underlining the *e* in order to mark "ed" as a pronounced syllable, to fill out the measure: in this edition, the stanza reads

Through this – the old Philosopher –
His Talismanic Stone
Discernèd – still witholden
To effort undivine –

While the seven syllables of "Discernèd – still witholden" still do not match the first line's eight syllables ("Through this – the old Philosopher –"), pronouncing the "ed" maintains the iambic meter and gives the quatrain a shape Dickinson used frequently: an 8676 syllable sequence.

In "'Twould ease – a Butterfly –" (F39 Sh6), Dickinson uses the elisions "'Twould" and "Thou'rt" to condense "It would" and "Thou art"—again in the service of an irregular stanzaic organization but regular iambic meter. The first stanza reads

'Twould ease – a Butterfly –
Elate – a Bee –
Thou'rt neither –
Neither – thy capacity –

Other such contractions appear frequently—for example, the one-syllable "ne'er" for "never" in "Success is counted sweetest / By those who ne'er succeed" (F5 Sh1). In contrast, in "There is a word," Dickinson does not mark the "ed" endings:

There is a word
Which bears a sword
Can pierce an armed man –
It hurls its barbed syllables
And is mute again –

Readers must decide for themselves whether this poem's rhythm follows an iambic meter requiring the pronunciations "armèd" and "barbèd," or a looser rhythm, in which spondees ("armed man," "barbed syll[ables]") disrupt the iambic measure.[16]

Despite the many colloquial elements of her verse, Dickinson also used some archaic diction. She often used the biblical pronouns "thee" and "thou" and occasionally used exclamations such as "Lo"; old-fashioned words, such as "aforetime" or "betimes"; and poeticized spellings such as "thro'" and "eno'" (for "through" and "enough")—spellings that do not change the words' number of syllables. All indicate that she was writing within conventions of nineteenth-century verse as well as pushing against them.

EDITORIAL PRINCIPLES

This is a reading edition, not a variorum. I have worked roughly from the principles of genetic editing, which assume that an author's work typically consists of a series of discrete and equally authoritative versions and that all such texts are both unstable, in that they exist as part of a process, and fixed, in and of themselves. A genetic edition does not present a "best" text or "the" poem but instead focuses on a moment or stage in a work's presentation or genesis. In the case of this edition, that moment is Dickinson's copying of the text that, to the best of our knowledge, she retained. Because Dickinson never saw her own poems into print, there can be no single correct or definitive printing of her poems. Moreover, Dickinson's use of alternatives in many poems and her writing out of variant versions suggest that *she* had a sense of her poems as both appropriately finished and potentially fluid, hence genetic criticism provides an excellent foundation for editing her poems. This edition seeks to complement, not replace, existing editions that offer other approaches to the poems.

This edition is "complete" in that it includes one representation of every poem. It does not include variant representations of a poem, except in the sixteen instances where a poem appears more than once in a fascicle or in her unbound sheets.[17] Twice Dickinson copied the same poem in quick succession: in 1860 she copied "Portraits are to daily faces" and then "Pictures are to daily faces" on Sheets 2 and 5 of Fascicle 8, and in 1865 she copied the three-line "Be Mine the Doom –" on Unbound Sheets 12 and 17.[18] She frequently used short poems to fill the space at the bottom of a page or the end of a sheet. I do not include "If I should see a single bird," which Franklin numbers as poem 1591; Martha Dickinson Bianchi reported that a poem beginning with this line was sent to her brother Gilbert, but no transcript or manuscript survives. A report of a first line is not, in my view, a poem.[19]

I also omit "Too few the mornings be," a text extant only in a transcription by Frances Norcross as prose, and "How slow the Wind –," a fourteen-syllable text extant only in a letter to Sarah Tuckerman that Franklin describes as "bordering prose and verse" but that seems to me distinctly written as prose (Franklin numbers 1,201 and 1,607). There are many passages of metered prose in Dickinson's letters, some of it including rhyme.

Editors and scholars do not agree as to what constitutes a "poem," a version of a poem, metered prose, a letter-poem, or even whether to call Dickinson's work "poems" (some prefer "manuscript writing"). I find that the great majority of Dickinson's manuscripts indicate clearly both whether she was writing poetry or prose and what she intended as the form of her poems, once one understands the patterns of her inscription, and assuming that her poems occur in poetic lines marked with an initial capital letter.[20] I take the typical Dickinson poem as my guide for editing, not her exceptions—although there is no denying the interest and even beauty of such exceptions. There is also a lyric grace in several of Dickinson's metered-prose messages, aphorisms, and textual fragments that might well lead readers to call them "poems" or to classify them as occupying an intergenre borderland. At the same time, much great prose has lyrical qualities, as do most of Dickinson's letters, but that does not make them poems.

Whereas the two previous inclusive editions of Dickinson's poems have been organized chronologically, this volume is only roughly chronological, in that between 1858 and 1865 Dickinson tended to copy poems onto sheets relatively soon after writing them, and she saved very few loose poems until she no longer engaged in such copying. The poems extant only in others' transcriptions and the great majority of poems she circulated and did not retain also seem to have been written relatively late. Readers seeking to follow Dickinson's writing in stricter chronological sequence will want to turn to Franklin's edition of the poems. Fragmentary phrases that also appear in poems are mentioned, and often quoted, in a poem's note. Readers seeking representation of Dickinson's fragments may turn to Marta Werner's *Radical Scatters*.[21]

Dickinson did not number her poems; nor does this edition. This edition does not provide comprehensive new dating of the poems, a new organization of the fascicles, or a new analysis of Dickinson's handwriting and punctuation. It provides a new, easily readable print organization, foregrounding Dickinson's own use and retention of her poems and showing the full range of the complexity of the texts she left to us in the different stages of her composing, copying, and circulating poems. Like all editions, it is an interpretation of the work the poet left to us, in the form in which she left it.

SOURCE AND ORGANIZATION OF TEXTS

Copy texts for this edition are, first, the poems now extant in fascicles or on Dickinson's unbound sheets and leaves; second, the poems she retained in loose form—always taking the most complete (preferably fair-hand) copy when more than one text survives, or the earliest copy if two extant texts are equally resolved or complete and in fair hand (or roughly written); and third, the poems she did not retain, again taking either the most complete or the earliest poem circulated if there is more than one copy. Where Dickinson's retained copy was transcribed and lost but an apparently equally complete copy of the poem survives as circulated, I use that copy as my source text and position the poem where the lost copy would have appeared (that is, in a fascicle, on an unbound sheet, or as a loose poem). Similarly, if a circulated but unretained copy was transcribed after Dickinson's death and then lost, the poem appears in "Poems Not Retained." Where appropriate, source texts are marked with the name of the transcriber, immediately following the poem. If there is any ambiguity as to a copy text, I identify it in a note.

Generalizations about Dickinson's copying and circulation practices cannot be entirely accurate because she was inconsistent, because too much remains unknown, and because many poems, or copies of poems, may be lost. R. W. Franklin's *The Editing of Emily Dickinson* and his introduction to the 1998 *Poems of Emily Dickinson* remain the best general sources of information on Dickinson's practices and the handling of the manuscripts after her death. An excellent supplemental resource is Domhnall Mitchell's *Measures of Possibility: Emily Dickinson's Manuscripts*.[22] Susan Howe, Martha Nell Smith, and Marta Werner have influentially interpreted the poems' material and visual aspects; under Smith's general direction, the digital sources Dickinson Electronic Archives and Emily Dickinson's Correspondences also provide useful information about several poems, and Smith and Hart's *Open Me Carefully* is invaluable for those interested in the poet's relationship with Susan.[23]

DATING THE POEMS

Poems in this edition are dated according to when they were copied or circulated, using Franklin's dates except in the few instances where scholars have persuasively challenged them.[24] The assigned date of copying is based on Dickinson's handwriting as it changed from year to year, the dating of paper sources, and, if appropriate, the date of circulation; the date of circulation comes from postmarks, internal references to events, notes made by recipients of the poems, handwriting, and paper sources. For this edition, I have not undertaken a systematic reexamination of Dickinson's handwriting or of poems' dates. To my knowledge, there are only three instances in which scholars have argued that a specific poem's date assigned by Franklin is wrong. It seems to me likely that some of the poems Dickinson copied into her earliest fascicles in 1858 and 1859 were written earlier; the retained date ("c. 1859") refers, like all dates in this edition, to the date of copying the source text, not the date of composition.[25] Because I generally follow Franklin's dating, I also mark the date of copying or circulation as tentative unless there is clear evidence for precision.

ALTERNATIVES AND REVISIONS

This edition does not visually distinguish alternatives from revisions; both appear either in the right margin or at the foot of the poem. Dickinson often repeated words when writing out alternatives—sometimes repeating words from the initial text and sometimes repeating alternatives themselves. I represent the vast majority of her repetitions to give a sense of her writing process but omit those meant to clarify handwriting, correct spelling, or reassert an isolated, otherwise unquestioned word choice, and I omit a few others for clarity of presentation. When Dickinson cancelled a word in her first writing of the text and underlined an alternative, I move the underlined word (unitalicized) into the text on the left and place the cancelled word in the right margin as an alternative. When she underlined an alternative without cancelling her previous choice, the alternative appears italicized in the margin. Following standard print practice, I represent all underscoring as italics. I do not indicate where Dickinson cancelled or underscored a word more than once. While I typically follow the order in which Dickinson presents alternatives, I alter her order at times to clarify the relationship between alternatives or to the line that was written first. Readers interested in the order of alternatives may turn to the manuscript images online in the Emily Dickinson Archive.

Some late poems do not distinguish alternatives as such. For example, in around 1883, Dickinson wrote a poem here represented as:

> The Summer that we did not prize
> Her treasures were so easy

Instructs us by departure now — [by] derision more
And recognition lazy –
Bestirs itself – puts on its Coat
and scans with fatal promptness — with what a fatal promptness
For Trains that moment out of sight — [Trains] serenely out of sight
Unconscious of his smartness – — Disdainful of his [smartness –]

Line 6, "with what a fatal promptness" (here presented in the right margin), was written flush left and was followed by "and scans with fatal promptness"—as if they were consecutive lines. Logically, in the poem's narrative the lines substitute for each other. Because the poem's concluding lines follow the sense of the latter, I place the initially written phrase in the margin as an alternative. Neither line begins with a capitalized word—a sign that this poem was still in draft, although Dickinson did not always capitalize alternatives for the capitalized first word of a line even in earlier, more fully resolved poems. When Dickinson marked the words beginning a line for transposition and the line initially began with a capital, I silently emend the newly designated first word to begin with a capital letter.

Dickinson also occasionally used the word "or" to mark an alternative. This occurs dramatically in "All overgrown by cunning moss," where she copied five stanzas, writing "or" in the space between stanzas 3 and 4. Interpreting "or" to mark an alternative, in their respective reading editions Johnson prints stanzas 1, 4, and 5, and Franklin prints stanzas 1, 2, and 3. Because it is impossible to tell how Dickinson meant her "or," I include all five stanzas, with the word "or" as she wrote it. In other instances, depending on the circumstances, this edition includes "or" in the margin with the alternative, or indicates in a note that Dickinson wrote "or" on her page. In "I noticed People disappeared," Dickinson wrote "or" before the alternatives for lines 5 and 8, then cancelled the alternatives and in line 8 also cancelled "or."

Some poems transcribed by others contain alternatives because Mabel Loomis Todd included alternative wording in her transcriptions of the poems. Susan Dickinson did not. Susan did apparently add hyphens to words Dickinson wrote without them: for example, in "A full fed Rose on meals of Tint" she transcribed "full-fed"; in another circulated (and still extant) manuscript, Dickinson wrote "full fed." Susan also typically wrote "to-day" and "to-morrow," which (like Franklin) I have silently emended to be consistent with Dickinson's spelling. Like Franklin, I correct spelling and handwriting errors in transcriptions. Unlike Franklin, I never emend transcriptions to be consistent with what one might presume were Dickinson's misspellings ("it's" for "its," "intrenched" for "entrenched," and so on). I do, however, represent transcribed dashes to look like the shorter dashes Dickinson generally produced, regardless of how they were drawn by the transcriber.

POETIC FORM AND LINEATION

Dickinson was inconsistent about the stanzaic organization of her poems—for example, she frequently circulated poems without stanzaic division that she copied in stanzas for her own keeping. Although she typically marked stanzas by leaving space between lines and often drew a horizontal line following a poem (or following its alternatives) to indicate its conclusion, she sometimes drew lines between stanzas. This was a relatively standard practice at the time; her sister Lavinia, for example, drew a line between stanzas in a poem she wrote for Emily after their mother's death.[26] Dickinson also occasionally indented a line or patterned series of lines—especially in her early fascicles (see "Papa above!" F7 Sh3). Similarly, she occasionally assigned titles to poems in her fascicles or letters, sometimes formally and sometimes indirectly: she wrote the title "Snow flakes" on her fascicle copy of "I counted till they danced so" and sent a copy of "Heart not so heavy as mine" to Catherine Scott Anthon, referring to it as "Whistling under my window –."

Although Dickinson's increasingly large handwriting caused her to use more run-on lines in her later years, it is in most cases obvious where Dickinson chose to begin a new poetic line.[27] She marked poetic lines by beginning with a capital letter written flush with the left margin (except where she indented to avoid a watermark or the tail of punctuation on the line above), often by leaving blank space at the end of the preceding row of script, and by syntax: Dickinson did not end poetic lines on an article ("the," "a") or minor preposition (such as "of").[28] The definitive use of such patterns in her more than eleven hundred fascicle and unbound-sheet poems, and her continuation of these patterns in presentation copies of her later poems, make it clear that for her these were norms.

Meter is not always a clear yardstick for poetic form because Dickinson at times unambiguously flouted the metrical presentation of a line. Her most typical variation of the metrical line is to split it into two poetic lines—for example, in "There is a word / Which bears a sword." Frequently such lines appear at the beginning of a poem, often to call attention to a rhyme or syntactic parallelism. For example, Dickinson split two lines to highlight parallel phrasing in "You'll know it – as you know 'tis Noon –" (F15 Sh3):

You'll know it – as you know 'tis Noon –
By Glory –
As you do the Sun –
By Glory –
As you will in Heaven –
Know God the Father – and the Son.

One hears a common-meter quatrain (8888 syllables) but the lines as written (835358) emphasize the poem's repetitions.

Far less frequently, Dickinson combined two metrical lines into a single poetic line, as, for example, in "I tried to think a lonelier Thing" (F25 Sh1). This poem's first two lines initiate what we might expect to be a standard 8686 meter. The third poetic line, however, combines two metrical lines—as Dickinson indicated by ending her row of script with "An"; were she making metrical and poetic lines coincide, "An" would have begun a row of print. The fourth poetic line of this clearly marked stanza is a seven-syllable line that one would expect to begin stanza 2—perhaps included as part of stanza 1 because it concludes the previous phrase: "An Omen . . . / Of Death's . . . nearness –." Consequently the poem's first stanza has a syllable count of 8, 6, 13, and then 7 syllables, and the second stanza has only three lines, with a 676 syllable pattern. One hears 8676 7676, but in this edition one sees:

I tried to think a lonelier Thing
Than any I had seen –
Some Polar Expiation – An Omen in the Bone
Of Death's tremendous nearness –

I probed Retrieveless things
My Duplicate – to borrow –
A Haggard comfort springs

When Dickinson ceased predictably capitalizing the first word of a new line, and when poems conclude in margins, upside down, or on the backs of pages, it becomes more difficult to tell whether she might have had such linear variation in mind.

I tried to think a Lonelier
Thing
Than any I had seen -
Some Polar Expiation - An
Omen in the Bone
Of Death's tremendous nearness -

I probed Retrieveless things
My Duplicate - to borrow -
A Haggard Comfort springs

From the belief that Somewhere
Within the Clutch of thought -
There dwells one other Creature
Of Heavenly Love - forgot -

I plucked at our Partition
As One should pry the Walls -
Between Himself - and Horror's
Twin -
Within Opposing Cells -

"I tried to think a lonelier Thing"

Even earlier, Dickinson's lineation is occasionally ambiguous. In "She staked Her Feathers – Gained an Arc –" (F38 Sh3), Dickinson began a new row of script with a new syntactic phrase and the capitalized "Gained." Because in the alternative for this line, "[She staked Her] Wings – and gained a Bush –," she did not capitalize "gained" and began a new row of script at "Bush –," and because nothing else in the single extant manuscript of this poem suggests patterned deviation from a metrical norm, I present the poem's first stanza as:

She staked Her Feathers – Gained an Arc – [Her] Wings – and gained a Bush –
Debated – Rose again –
This time – beyond the estimate [the] inference
Of Envy, or of Men –

In contrast, "The Sea said" (Unbound Sheet 90) presents the possibility of a distinct pattern of split metrical lines and syntax; Dickinson ended successive rows of script with "said" and put the sea or brook's speech on a new row of script. One might present this in print as:

The Sea said
"Come" to the Brook –
The Brook said
"Let me grow" –
The Sea said
"Then you will be a Sea" –
"I want a Brook –
Come now" –
The Sea said
"Go" to the Sea –
The Sea said
"I am he
You cherished" –
"Learned Waters –
Wisdom is stale to me" –

A presentation that assumes a three-beat metrical line (except in the longer line 3) would read like this:

The Sea said "Come" to the Brook –
The Brook said "Let me grow" –

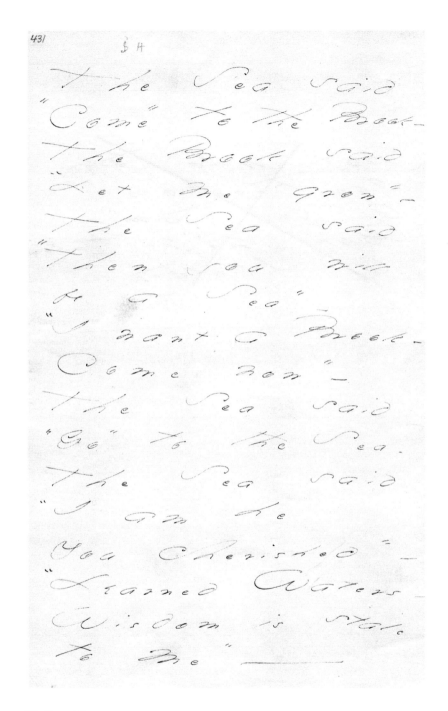
431 $ H

The Sea said
"Come" to the Brook -
The Brook said
"Let me grow" -
The Sea said
"Then you will
be a Sea"
"I want a Brook -
Come now" -
The Sea said
"Go" to the Sea.
The Sea said
"I am he
You cherished" -
"Learned Waters -
Wisdom is stale
to Me" ——

"The Sea said"

AMHERST 431; COURTESY OF AMHERST COLLEGE ARCHIVES AND SPECIAL COLLECTIONS

The Sea said "Then you will be a Sea" –
"I want a Brook – Come now" –
The Sea said "Go" to the Sea –
The Sea said "I am he
You cherished" – "Learned Waters –
Wisdom is stale to me" –

Both presentations are accurate in that they follow guidelines Dickinson herself implicitly established in writing out her poems. The first follows her splitting of metrical lines into patterned syntactic or rhetorical patterns; the second, her more frequent practice of writing metrical lines as run-ons when there was not adequate space to continue on a single row of script. A circulated copy does not break rows of script at "said" but leaves it ambiguous whether "Learned Waters –" might begin a new poetic line. This edition prints the poem following the pattern of lineation Dickinson used on the unbound sheet, as though that line splitting was deliberate, while acknowledging in a note the possibility of metrical lineation.

While I have more often than Franklin interpreted Dickinson to be splitting or combining metrical lines, like him I find that there must be strong indicators of such a pattern, given the prevalence of her use of run-on lines. To my mind, to present all Dickinson's run-on rows of script as though they were poetic lines ignores her repeated and typical indication that she has a more deliberate sense of the line. At the same time, several manuscripts demand interpretive judgment as to whether she splits a metrical line. Here, as with many aspects of transcribing Dickinson's poems, Emerson's prescription against a foolish consistency allows the most sensitive and sensible response. Where this edition differs from Franklin's (or Johnson's) presentation of a poem, it is because I [1] am using a different source text; [2] interpret aspects of the same source text differently; [3] see a word or punctuation mark missed by previous editors; or [4] have chosen differently to emend, or not emend, a spelling idiosyncrasy.

PUNCTUATION, CAPITALIZATION, AND SPELLING

Dickinson used dashes frequently and for various purposes—syntactic, rhetorical, and emphatic. Like most people who write by hand, however, her formation of punctuation and capital letters is inconsistent; moreover, her handwriting changed over time. Theodora Ward's 1951 chart of Dickinson's handwriting variations remains the best guide to her letter formation.[29] It would be useful to update this guide and to construct a similarly systematic guide to Dickinson's formation and placement of punctuation marks over the years, to conform with current editorial understanding.

Dickinson wrote dashes that were long, short, high, and low on the page and slanted in various directions, but most are very short. Occasionally she used a long dramatic dash, for example in the line "One's – Money — One's – the Mine –" in "Some – Work for Immortality –" (F28 Sh3). Because this edition does not attempt to replicate the look of Dickinson's pages, it standardizes representation of all dashes as short, straight, and midline. Franklin, I find, overestimates Dickinson's use of the dash, at times reading what more logically appear to be commas and periods as dashes.[30] Like many of her contemporaries, she probably often wrote elongated periods—in a kind of rolling stop. She also may have written commas both high within her row of script and slanting right rather than left. In this edition I present some individual punctuation marks differently from the Franklin edition, typically to agree with Johnson's or Hart and Smith's judgments, but I do not thoroughly revise earlier interpretations of these marks.

Dickinson was an erratic speller and, like all people who write extensively by hand, she made a number of graphic errors: she omitted letters or words and frequently wrote over letters to correct them. I silently emend accidental errors: "Bave" for "Brave," "clutcth" for "clutch," "fictitoius" for "fictitious," "verg" for "very," and so on. I also correct a few words she typically misspelled in all genres ("Febuary" and "opon") and a few she used rarely in poetry (such as "apparelled," "Mattrass," "Perrennial") because they seem to me to have no significance beyond pointing to the poet's indifferent spelling. Dickinson used some nineteenth-century spellings ("alway," "extasy," "vail") and some British spellings ("centre," "traveller," "practise") inconsistently; here I follow her inconsistencies. I also leave uncorrected the great majority of Dickinson's idiosyncratic spellings, both to give a sense of her idiosyncrasy and because some may have metrical or other significance: she may have written "sovreign" for "sovereign" because she pronounced it with two syllables, or "wo" for "woe" under the influence of Shakespearean spelling, or to emphasize the long *o*. Other of Dickinson's many idiosyncratic spellings include "Bethleem," "Boddice," "Bretheren," "Cimitar," "Develope," "nescessity," "teazing," and "withold"—with their various related forms ("unnescessary," "witheld"). Occasionally Dickinson corrected her own spelling: in "Left in immortal Youth" she emended "cancelled" to "canceled," and in a note to Higginson she remarked on her misspelling of "Ancle." All word coinages are left as Dickinson wrote them. It is perhaps also notable that because of handwriting idiosyncrasies, most instances of the words "where" and "there" closely resemble "when" and "then"; context and a slight difference in the shape of the letters enable one to distinguish *re* from *n*.

Misuse or absence of apostrophes has been corrected on two principles. First, Dickinson used apostrophes correctly in many words, although not entirely consistently—for example, in "o'er," "that's," "'twere," "'tis," "'twould," "sh'd," "I'll," "she'll," "he'd," and in nouns like "Maple's." Second, her use of an apostrophe to designate the possessive "its" as "it's," or "our's" or "her's," was acceptable in the late eighteenth and early nineteenth centuries, before spelling standardization was common in the United States. Her usage, then, appears to be old-fashioned but correct, and it is equally consistent in her prose—that is, she was not establishing a poetic variation. I emend her apostrophe use to make her syntax less ambiguous for current readers—for example, her consistent use of "cant" for "can't" does not indicate the noun for sanctimonious speech.[31] In their reading editions, Johnson and Franklin silently emend Dickinson's spelling of many words, including her archaic use or misuse of some apostrophes, although Franklin maintains some characteristic idiosyncrasies, most noticeably the absence or misplacement of apostrophes in contractions involving "not" ("wont," "cant," "did'nt," "would'nt"); her archaic representation of the possessive "its" as "it's"; and her spelling of "upon" as "opon"—a spelling she herself changed to "upon" around 1880.[32]

I do not reproduce the many instances in which Dickinson began a word and then cancelled or wrote over letters to change spelling, the word, or the placement of the word in relation to a poetic line. For example, in "Must be a Wo –" (F28 Sh4) she wrote "a" at the end of a row of script, then cancelled it and began the next row of script with the capitalized word "As"—apparently having changed her mind as to where a new poetic line should begin. I do indicate where Dickinson wrote a word and then cancelled it, for example, in "I think To Live – may be a Bliss" (F34 Sh1), where she wrote "So plausible ~~appears~~ becomes"; I put "~~appears~~" in the margin with other alternatives. Similarly, if Dickinson apparently inadvertently omitted a word, I include it within square brackets and comment on the addition in a note: in "Afraid! Of whom am I afraid?" (F16 Sh4), Dickinson omits "a" in the line "'Twere odd I fear [a] thing." These decisions, like all editorial decisions, are shaped by the edition's goal. My goal has been to provide clear, accurate texts for the general reader in the context of their use and circulation, while also indicating the range of Dickinson's practices in copying the poems and in marking a text's fluidity or irresolution at various stages of copying and composition.

Abbreviations and Reading Guide

The following abbreviations and symbols are used to indicate previous editions of Dickinson's writing, sources referred to in the notes, organizational features of this volume, and frequently mentioned correspondents and family members.

ABBREVIATIONS

AD	William Austin Dickinson, called Austin
Bianchi	Martha Dickinson Bianchi, editor of Emily Dickinson, *The Single Hound: Poems of a Lifetime* (Boston: Little, Brown, 1914); *The Complete Poems of Emily Dickinson* (Boston, MA: Little, Brown, 1924); *Emily Dickinson Face to Face* (Cambridge, MA: Riverside Press, 1932)
Bingham	Millicent Todd Bingham, author of *Ancestors' Brocades: The Literary Debut of Emily Dickinson* (New York: Harper & Brothers, 1945)
DEA	Dickinson Electronic Archives, Martha Nell Smith, executive editor; Lara Vetter, general editor; Ellen Louise Hart and Marta Werner, associate editors; http://archive.emilydickinson.org/working/csd.php
DIHOT	*Dickinson in Her Own Time*, edited by Jane Donahue Eberwein, Stephanie Farrar, and Cristanne Miller (Iowa City: University of Iowa Press, 2015)
ED	Emily Dickinson
EDC	*Emily Dickinson's Correspondences: A Born-Digital Textual Inquiry*, edited by Martha Nell Smith and Lara Vetter (Charlottesville: University of Virginia Press, 2008–); http://www.rotunda.upress.virginia.edu/edc/default.xqy
EH	Elizabeth Holland

F — Fascicle; a bound booklet of poems copied onto folded sheets

Fr — *The Poems of Emily Dickinson*, edited by Ralph W. Franklin, 3 vols. (Cambridge, MA: Belknap Press of Harvard University Press, 1998)

HHJ — Helen Hunt Jackson

L — "L" numbers cited in this volume refer to the numbers assigned to Dickinson's letters in *The Letters of Emily Dickinson*, edited by Thomas H. Johnson and Theodora Ward, 3 vols. (Cambridge, MA: Belknap Press of Harvard University Press, 1958)

Leyda — Jay Leyda, author of *The Years and Hours of Emily Dickinson*, 2 vols. (New Haven, CT: Yale University Press, 1960)

MLT — Mabel Loomis Todd, coeditor with Thomas Wentworth Higginson of Emily Dickinson's *Poems* and *Poems, Second Series* (Boston: Roberts Brothers, 1890 and 1891, respectively); editor of *Letters of Emily Dickinson* and *Poems, Third Series* (Boston: Roberts Brothers, 1894 and 1896)

Ns — Louisa and Frances Norcross

OMC — *Open Me Carefully: Emily Dickinson's Intimate Correspondence to Susan Huntington Dickinson*, edited by Ellen Louise Hart and Martha Nell Smith (Ashfield, MA: Paris Press, 1998)

RWF — Ralph W. Franklin, editor of *The Poems of Emily Dickinson* (1998); see "Fr"

SB — Samuel Bowles

SD — Susan Huntington Gilbert Dickinson

Sh — Sheet, a folded piece of stationery constituting two leaves, or four pages

ST — Sarah Tuckerman

THJ — Thomas H. Johnson, coeditor of *The Letters of Emily Dickinson* (1958)—see "L"—and editor of *The Poems of Emily Dickinson*, 3 vols. (Cambridge, MA: Belknap Press of Harvard University Press, 1955)

TWH — Thomas Wentworth Higginson

Webster's — Noah Webster, *American Dictionary of the English Language* (Amherst, MA: J. S. & C. Adams, 1844); the 1844 dictionary constituted bound sheets printed for the 1841 revised edition; ED used the 1844 Webster's

MARKS USED IN PRESENTATION OF POEMS

~ Indicates the end of a poem

[ ] A bracketed word precedes and positions the alternative or revision for a word in that line of the poem; when the alternative begins a line, the bracketed word follows the potential substitution. Typically, an alternative replaces a word or words of the same type and length; if it is unclear how many words an alternative replaces, I give the preceding word in brackets, the alternative, and the following word in brackets: [preceding word] alternative [following word]. Where there are no brackets, the alternative word or phrase replaces the entire line.

• Indicates that the following word or phrase is an alternative for what precedes it. For example:

Or Order, or Apparent Action – [Apparent] signal – • notice

indicates that either "signal –" or "notice" follows "Apparent" and might replace "Action."

1863 Dates refer to the date of copying, not the date of the composition of a poem

o Indicates a stanza break when the poem continues onto the following page

Example 1

I cannot dance upon my Toes –[1]
No Man instructed me –
But oftentimes, among my mind,
A Glee possesseth me,

That had I Ballet Knowledge –
Would put itself abroad
In Pirouette to blanch a Troupe –
Or lay a Prima, mad,

And though I had no Gown of Gauze –
No Ringlet, to my Hair,

Nor hopped for Audiences – like Birds,
One Claw upon the air –

Nor tossed my shape in Eider Balls,
Nor rolled on wheels of snow
Till I was out of sight, in sound,
The House encore me so –

Nor any know I know the Art
I mention – easy – Here –
Nor any Placard boast me –
It's full as Opera –

I cannot dance: *Sent to TWH (variant) c. August 1862*

SHEET TWO c. autumn 1862

1. I cannot dance: the terms "glee," "troupe," "prima," and "opera" were commonly used to refer to minstrel shows or houses, and dancing grotesquely like a bird might suggest the popular dance "Jim Crow." ED called herself "Mrs. Jim Crow" in an August 1860 letter (L223).

This poem occurs at the end of Sheet 1 in Fascicle 19 (c. autumn 1862), hence "Sheet Two" and a date follow the line designating the poem's end and its circulation information; fascicle numbers appear as a running header throughout this section of the text, marking this poem as part of Fascicle 19 (not shown here). It was sent to Thomas Wentworth Higginson, probably sometime before it was copied onto the page bound into a fascicle. There are no alternatives. The annotation (note 1) appears with other notes in the back of this book.

Example 2

SHEET TWO c. early 1862

I got so I could hear his name –[2] [could] think – • *take* –
Without – Tremendous gain –
That Stop-sensation – on my Soul –
And Thunder – in the Room –

o

I got so I could walk across
That Angle in the floor,
Where he turned so, and I turned – how – [I] let go –
And all our Sinew tore –

I got so I could stir the Box –
In which his letters grew
Without that forcing, in my breath –
As Staples – driven through –

Could dimly recollect a Grace – [a] Force
I think, they called it "God" –
Renowned to ease Extremity – [Renowned] to stir – Extremity –
When Formula, had failed – [When] Filament – had failed –

And shape my Hands –
Petition's way,
Tho' ignorant of a word
That Ordination – utters –

My Business – with the Cloud,
If any Power behind it, be,
Not subject to Despair – Supremer than – • Superior to – [Despair –]
It care – in some remoter way,
For so minute affair
As Misery –
Itself, too great, for interrupting – more – [too] *vast*

2. I got so: business "with the Cloud" refers to Exodus 13:21, "And the Lord went before them by day in a pillar of a cloud, to lead them the way."

This is the first poem on Sheet 2 in Fascicle 12 (as indicated by the new sheet number and date preceding the poem and a running header indicating the fascicle, not shown here), copied around early 1862; it was not circulated. In line 1, Dickinson proposed two alternatives ("think –" and "*take* –") as possible substitutes for "hear" (following "could"); that is, the line might read "I got so I could think his name –" or "I got so I could *take* his name –." Dickinson apparently underlined "take" to indicate her preference; with alternatives, underlining seems to indicate preference, not emphasis. Similarly, the underlined "vast" in the last line suggests a preference for the line to read: "Itself, too vast for interrupting – more –." Line 7 proposes "let go –" for "turned – how –," following the word "I." Line 13 proposes "Force" for "Grace –"; Dickinson linked punctuation to the preceding word; with "Force," the line would not end with a dash. In the sixth stanza, Dickinson gives alternatives that would begin the line, preceding "Despair"; this line might read "Supremer than – Despair –" or "Superior to – Despair –."

Example 3

Summer – we all have seen –
A few of us – believed –
A few – the more aspiring
Unquestionably loved –

But Summer does not care –
She takes her gracious way
As eligible as the Moon
To the Temerity – [To] a – • our –

Deputed to adore – ~~Contented~~ [to]
The Doom to be adored [The] ~~Lot~~
Unknown as to an Ecstasy
The Embryo endowed –

line 6: [She] *goes* [her] *spacious* [way] • her ample way – • She goes her sylvan way –
[She goes her] perfect • spacious • subtle • simple • mighty • gallant [way]
lines 7–8: ~~As undiverted as the Moon – from her Divinity~~ –
As unperverted as the Moon / By Our obliquity –
As eligible • unavailing – as the Moon – to our extremity – • Adversity –
lines 9–10: Created to adore – / The Affluence evolved – • conferred – • bestowed –
• involved –

c. 1876

This poem was kept among the loose poems and was not circulated. As is frequently the case, Dickinson resolved the beginning of the poem but not the end. Because there are so many alternatives, most appear at the foot of the poem. Here she cancelled some alternatives and underlined others.

Dickinson often provided alternatives in pairs or groups of lines. In this poem's line 6, Dickinson gave eight alternative words for "gracious," linking them to the alternative "goes" (substituting for "takes"), and she underlined both "goes" and "spacious," in addition to repeating both words. For lines 7 and 8, she provided three alternative paired lines, cancelling one; following the final paired alternative, she proposed two alternatives to its words: "unavailing –" for "eligible" and "Adversity –" for "extremity –." As my transcription shows, Dickinson did not consistently write paired alternatives as distinct poetic lines: in the alternatives for lines 7 and 8, "~~from~~" and "to" are not capitalized and do not begin a row of script, although they replace the "To" at the beginning of line 8. Lines 9 and 10 are similarly reimagined as a group, but with three alternatives to the proposed substitution's final word, "evolved –." The poem's last two stanzas might include any combination of these alternatives for lines 6 through 10. Few poems are this complex in their alternatives.

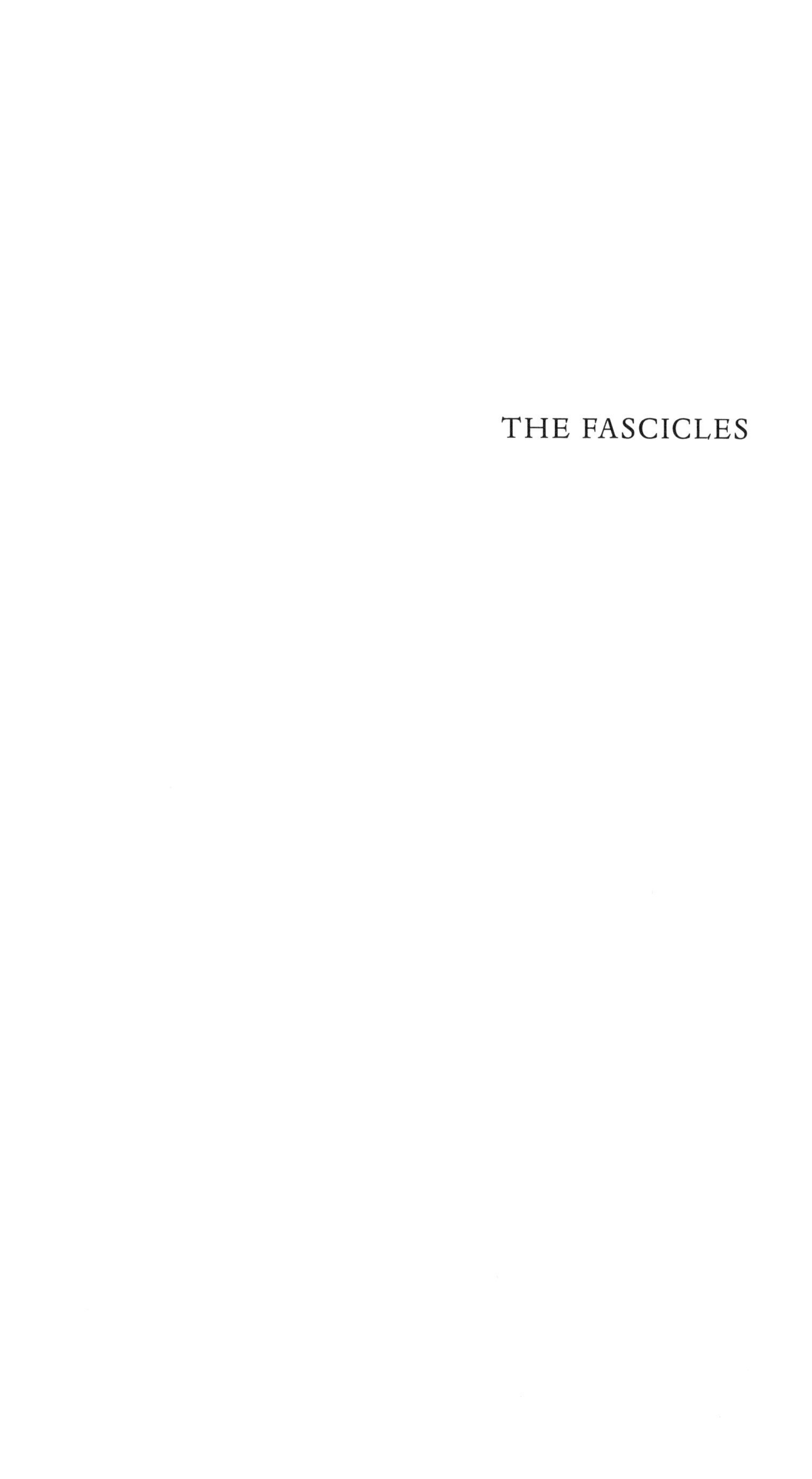

THE FASCICLES

The Gentian weaves her fringes –
The Maple's loom is red –
My departing blossoms
Obviate parade.

A brief, but patient illness –
An hour to prepare,
And one below, this morning
Is where the Angels are –
It was a short procession,
The Bobolink was there –
An aged Bee addressed us –
And then we knelt in prayer.
We trust that she was willing,
We ask that we may be.
Summer – Sister – Seraph!
Let us go with thee!

In the name of the Bee.
And of the Butterfly.
And of the Breeze. Amen!

"The Gentian weaves her fringes –"; "A brief, but patient illness –"; and "In the name of the Bee –"

FASCICLE ONE

SHEET ONE c. late summer 1858

The Gentian weaves her fringes –
The Maple's loom is red –
My departing blossoms
    Obviate parade.

~

A brief, but patient illness –
An hour to prepare –
And one below, this morning
Is where the angels are –
It was a short procession –
The Bobolink was there –
An aged Bee addressed us –
And then we knelt in prayer –
We trust that she was willing –
We ask that we may be –
Summer – Sister – Seraph!
Let us go with thee!

~

In the name of the Bee –[1]
And of the Butterfly –
And of the Breeze – Amen!

~

Frequently the woods are pink –
Frequently, are brown.
Frequently the hills undress
Behind my native town –
Oft a head is crested
I was wont to see –

Frequently the woods: *Sent to SD (variant) c. summer 1858*

And as oft a cranny
Where it used to be –
And the Earth – they tell me
On its axis turned!
Wonderful rotation –
By but *twelve* performed!

~

A sepal – petal – and a thorn[2]
Upon a common summer's morn –
A flask of Dew – A Bee or two –
A Breeze – a caper in the trees –
    And I'm a Rose!

~

Distrustful of the Gentian –[3]
And just to turn away,
The fluttering of her fringes
Chid my perfidy –
Weary for my ——
I will singing go –
I shall not feel the sleet – then –
I shall not fear the snow.

~

Flees so the phantom meadow
Before the breathless Bee –
So bubble brooks in deserts
On ears that dying lie –
Burn so the evening spires
To eyes that Closing go –
Hangs so distant Heaven –
To a hand below.

~

We lose – because we win –
Gamblers – recollecting which –
Toss their dice again!

~

All these my banners be.
I sow my – pageantry
In May –
It rises train by train –
Then sleeps in state again –
My chancel – all the plain
 Today.

~

To lose – if One can find again –[4]
To miss – if One shall meet –
The Burglar cannot rob – then –
The Broker cannot cheat.
So build the hillocks gaily –
Thou little spade of mine
Leaving nooks for Daisy
And for Columbine –
You and I the secret
Of the Crocus know –
Let us chant it softly –
"*There* is no more snow"!

~

To him who keeps an Orchis' heart –[5]
The swamps are pink with June.

~

SHEET TWO c. summer 1858

I had a guinea golden –[6]
I lost it in the sand –
And tho' the sum was simple
And pounds were in the land –
Still, had it such a value
Unto my frugal eye –
That when I could not find it –
I sat me down to sigh.

I had a crimson Robin –
Who sang full many a day

But when the woods were painted –
He – too – did fly away –
Time brought me other Robins –
Their ballads were the same –
Still, for my missing Troubadour
I kept the "house at hame".

I had a star in heaven –
One "Pleiad" was its name –
And when I was not heeding,
It wandered from the same –
And tho' the skies are crowded –
And all the night ashine –
I do not care about it –
Since none of them are mine.

My story has a moral –
I have a missing friend –
"Pleiad" its name – and Robin –
And guinea in the sand –
And when this mournful ditty
Accompanied with tear –
Shall meet the eye of traitor
In country far from here –
Grant that repentance solemn
May seize upon his mind –
And he no consolation
Beneath the sun may find.

There is a morn by men unseen –[7]
Whose maids upon remoter green
Keep their seraphic May –
And all day long, with dance and game,
And gambol I may never name –
Employ their holiday.

Here to light measure, move the feet
Which walk no more the village street –
Nor by the wood are found –
Here are the birds that sought the sun

When last year's distaff idle hung
And summer's brows were bound.

Ne'er saw I such a wondrous scene –
Ne'er such a ring on such a green –
Nor so serene array –
As if the stars some summer night
Should swing their cups of Chrysolite –
And revel till the day –

Like thee to dance – like thee to sing –
People upon that mystic green –
I ask, each new May morn.
I wait thy far – fantastic bells –
Announcing me in other dells –
Unto the different dawn!

~

As if I asked a common alms –[8]
And in my wondering hand,
A stranger pressed a kingdom –
And I – bewildered stand –
As if I asked the Orient
Had it for me a morn?
And it sh'd lift its purple dikes
And flood me with the Dawn!

~

She slept beneath a tree –[9]
Remembered but by me.
I touched her Cradle mute –
She recognized the foot –
Put on her Carmine suit
    And see!

~

SHEET THREE c. summer 1858

The feet of people walking home[10]
With gayer sandals go –
The crocus – till she rises –

As if I: *Sent to TWH (variant) 7 June 1862*
The feet of: *Apparently sent to SD (variant) c. early 1859*

The vassal of the snow –
The lips at Hallelujah
Long years of practise bore –
Till bye and bye, these Bargemen
Walked – singing – on the shore.

Pearls are the Diver's farthings,
Extorted from the sea –
Pinions – the Seraph's wagon –
Pedestrian once – as we –
Night is the morning's canvas –
Larceny – legacy –
Death – but our rapt attention
To immortality.

My figures fail to tell me
How far the village lies –
Whose peasants are the angels –
Whose cantons dot the skies –
My Classics vail their faces –
My faith that Dark adores –
Which from its solemn abbeys –
Such resurrection pours!

It's all I have to bring today –
This, and my heart beside –
This, and my heart, and all the fields –
And all the meadows wide –
Be sure you count – sh'd I forget
Some one the sum could tell –
This, and my heart, and all the Bees
Which in the Clover dwell.

Morns like these – we parted –
Noons like these – she rose –
Fluttering first – then firmer
To her fair repose.

○

Morns like these –: *Sent to Ns (lost, transcribed variant) and to SD (variant) c. summer 1858*

Never did she lisp it –
It was not for me –
She – was mute from transport –
I – from agony –

Till – the evening nearing
One the curtains drew –
Quick! A sharper rustling!
And this linnet flew!

~

So has a Daisy vanished
From the fields today –
So tiptoed many a slipper
To Paradise away –
Oozed so, in crimson bubbles
Day's departing tide –
Blooming – tripping – flowing –
Are ye then with God?

~

If those I loved were lost[11]
The Crier's voice w'd tell me –
If those I loved were found
The bells of Ghent w'd ring –
Did those I loved repose
The Daisy would impel me.
Philip – when bewildered
Bore his riddle in!

~

SHEET FOUR c. summer 1858

Adrift! A little boat adrift![12]
And night is coming down!
Will *no* one guide a little boat
Unto the nearest town?

So sailors say – on yesterday –
Just as the dusk was brown

One little boat gave up its strife
And gurgled down and down.

So angels say – on yesterday –
Just as the dawn was red
One little boat – o'erspent with gales –
Retrimmed its masts – redecked its sails –
And shot – exultant on!

~

Summer for thee, grant I may be
When Summer days are flown!
Thy music still, when Whippowil
And Oriole – are done!

For thee to bloom, I'll skip the tomb
And row my blossoms o'er!
Pray gather me –
    Anemone –
Thy flower – forevermore!

~

When Roses cease to bloom, Sir,[13]
And Violets are done –
When Bumblebees in solemn flight
Have passed beyond the Sun –
The hand that paused to gather
Upon this Summer's day
Will idle lie – in Auburn –
Then take my flowers – pray!

~

Oh if remembering were forgetting –
Then I remember not!
And if forgetting – recollecting –
How near I had forgot!
And if to miss – were merry –
And to mourn were gay,
How very blithe the maiden
Who gathered these today!

~

Oh if remembering: *Sent to SB (variant) c. summer 1859*

On this wondrous sea – sailing silently –[14]
Ho! Pilot! Ho!
Knowest thou the shore
Where no breakers roar –
Where the storm is o'er?

In the silent West
Many – the sails at rest –
The anchors fast.
Thither I pilot thee –
Land! Ho! Eternity!
Ashore at last!

Garlands for Queens, may be –[15]
Laurels – for rare degree
Of soul or sword –
Ah – but remembering me –
Ah – but remembering thee –
Nature in chivalry –
Nature in charity –
Nature in equity –
The Rose ordained!

Nobody knows this little Rose –[16]
It might a pilgrim be
Did I not take it from the ways
And lift it up to thee.
Only a Bee will miss it –
Only a Butterfly,
Hastening from far journey –
On its breast to lie –
Only a Bird will wonder –
Only a Breeze will sigh –
Ah Little Rose – how easy
For such as thee to die!

On this wondrous: *Sent to SD (variant) March 1853, with the comment "Write! Comrade, write!"*

FASCICLE TWO

SHEET ONE c. late 1858

There is a word
Which bears a sword
Can pierce an armed man –
It hurls its barbed syllables
And is mute again –
But where it fell
The saved will tell
On patriotic day,
Some epauletted Brother
Gave his breath away.

Wherever runs the breathless sun –
Wherever roams the day,
There is its noiseless onset –
There is its victory!
Behold the keenest marksman!
The most accomplished shot!
Time's sublimest target
Is a soul "forgot"!

Through lane it lay – thro' bramble –[17]
Through clearing and thro' wood –
Banditti often passed us
Upon the lonely road.

The wolf came peering curious –
The Owl looked puzzled down –
The serpent's satin figure
Glid stealthily along,

o

There is a: *Sent to SD (variant) c. late 1858*
Through lane it: *Sent to SD (variant) c. late 1858*

The tempests touched our garments –
The lightning's poinards gleamed –
Fierce from the Crag above us
The hungry Vulture screamed –

The Satyrs fingers beckoned –
The Valley murmured "Come" –
These were the mates –
This was the road
These Children fluttered home.

~

The Guest is gold and crimson –
An Opal guest, and gray –
Of ermine is his doublet –
His Capuchin gay –

He reaches town at nightfall –
He stops at every door –
Who looks for him at morning –
I pray him too – explore
The Lark's pure territory –
Or the Lapwing's shore!

~

Snow flakes.
I counted till they danced so
Their slippers leaped the town –
And then I took a pencil
To note the rebels down –
And then they grew so jolly
I did resign the prig –
And ten of my once stately toes
Are marshalled for a jig!

~

Before the ice is in the pools –
Before the skaters go,
Or any cheek at nightfall
Is tarnished by the snow –

o

The Guest is: *Sent to SD (variant) c. late 1858, titled "'Navy' Sunset!"*

Before the fields have finished –
Before the Christmas tree,
Wonder upon wonder –
Will arrive to me!

What we touch the hems of
On a summer's day –
What is only walking
Just a bridge away –

That which sings so – speaks so –
When there's no one here –
Will the frock I wept in
Answer me to wear?

~

By such and such an offering
To Mr So and So –
The web of life is woven –
So martyrs albums show!

~

SHEET TWO c. early 1859

It did not surprise me –
So I said – or thought –
She will stir her pinions
And the nest forgot,

Traverse broader forests –
Build in gayer boughs,
Breathe in Ear more modern
God's old fashioned vows –

This was but a Birdling –
What and if it be
One within my bosom
Had departed me?

This was but a story –
What and if indeed

There were just such coffin
In the heart – instead?

~

When I count the seeds
That are sown beneath –
To bloom so, bye and bye –

When I con the people
Lain so low –
To be received as high –

When I believe the garden
Mortal shall not see –
Pick by faith its blossom
And avoid its Bee,
I can spare this summer – unreluctantly.

~

Bless God, he went as soldiers,[18]
His musket on his breast –
Grant God, he charge the bravest
Of all the martial blest!

Please God, might I behold him
In epauletted white –
I should not fear the foe then –
I should not fear the fight!

~

If I should cease to bring a Rose
Upon a festal day,
'Twill be because *beyond* the Rose
I have been called away –

If I should cease to take the names
My buds commemorate –
'Twill be because *Death*'s finger
Clasps my murmuring lip!

~

One Sister have I in the house –[19]
And one a hedge away.
There's only one recorded –
But both belong to me.

One came the road that I came –
And wore my last year's gown –
The other, as a bird her nest
Builded our hearts among.

She did not sing as we did –
It was a different tune –
Herself to her a music
As Bumble bee of June.

Today is far from childhood,
But up and down the hills,
I held her hand the tighter –
Which shortened all the miles –

And still her hum
The years among,
Deceives the Butterfly;
And in her Eye
The Violets lie,
Mouldered this many May –

I spilt the dew,
But took the morn –
I chose this single star
From out the wide night's numbers –
Sue – forevermore!

SHEET THREE early 1859

"Lethe" in my flower,[20]
Of which they who drink,
In the fadeless Orchards
Hear the bobolink!

o

One Sister have: *Sent to SD (variant) c. late 1858, perhaps as a birthday greeting*

Merely flake or petal
As the Eye beholds
Jupiter! my father!
I perceive the rose!

⁓

To venerate the simple days
Which lead the seasons by –
Needs but to remember
That from you or I,
They may take the trifle
Termed *mortality!*

To invest existence with a stately air –
Needs but to remember
That the Acorn there
Is the egg of forests
For the upper Air!

⁓

I've got an arrow here.[21]
Loving the hand that sent it
I the dart revere.

Fell, they will say, in "skirmish"!
Vanquished, my soul will know
By but a simple arrow
Sped by an archer's bow. MLT

⁓

I robbed the Woods –[22]
The trusting Woods –
The unsuspecting Trees
Brought out their Burs and mosses
My fantasy to please –
I scanned their trinkets curious –
I grasped – I bore away –
What will the solemn Hemlock –
What will the Oak tree say?

⁓

A Day! Help! Help!
Another Day!
Your prayers – Oh Passer by!
From such a common ball as this
Might date a Victory!
From marshallings as simple
The flags of nations swang.
Steady – my soul! What issues
Upon thine arrow hang!

~

Could live – *did* live –
Could die – *did* die –
Could smile upon the whole
Through faith in one he met not –
To introduce his soul –

Could go from scene familiar
To an untraversed spot –
Could contemplate the journey
With unpuzzled heart –

Such trust had one among us –
Among us *not* today –
We who saw the launching
Never sailed the Bay!

~

If she had been the Mistletoe[23]
And I had been the Rose –
How gay upon your table
My velvet life to close!
Since I am of the Druid –
And she is of the dew –
I'll deck Tradition's buttonhole –
And send the Rose to you.

~

If she had: *Sent to SB (variant) September or October 1859, apparently with a rose*

SHEET FOUR c. spring 1859

My Wheel is in the dark!
I cannot see a spoke
Yet know its dripping feet
Go round and round.

My foot is on the Tide!
An unfrequented road –
Yet have all roads
A clearing at the end –

Some have resigned the Loom –
Some in the busy tomb
Find quaint employ –

Some with new – stately feet –
Pass royal thro' the gate –
Flinging the problem back
At you and I!

~

There's something quieter than sleep
Within this inner room!
It wears a sprig upon its breast –
And will not tell its name.

Some touch it, and some kiss it –
Some chafe its idle hand –
It has a simple gravity
I do not understand!

I would not weep, if I were they –
How rude in one to sob!
Might scare the quiet fairy
Back to her native wood!

While simple-hearted neighbors
Chat of the "Early dead" –
We – prone to periphrasis,
Remark that Birds have fled!

~

My Wheel is: *Sent to SD (variant) c. early 1859*

I keep my pledge.
I was not called –
Death did not notice me.
I bring my Rose –
I plight again –
By every sainted Bee –
By Daisy called from hillside –
By Bobolink from lane –
Blossom and I –
Her oath, and mine –
Will surely come again –

Heart! We will forget him!
You and I – tonight!
You may forget the warmth he gave –
I will forget the light!

When you have done, pray tell me
That I may straight begin!
Haste! lest while you're lagging
I remember him!

Once more, my now bewildered Dove[24]
Bestirs her puzzled wings.
Once more, her mistress, on the deep
Her troubled question flings –

Thrice to the floating casement
The Patriarch's bird returned –
Courage! My brave Columba!
There may yet be *Land!*

Baffled for just a day or two –
Embarrassed – not afraid –
Encounter in my garden
An unexpected Maid.

o

Baffled for just: *Sent to EH (variant) c. spring 1859, with a rosebud*

She beckons, and the woods start –
She nods, and all begin –
Surely, such a country
I was never in!

FASCICLE THREE

SHEET ONE c. spring 1859

Delayed till she had ceased to know –
Delayed till in its vest of snow
Her loving bosom lay –
An hour behind the fleeting breath –
Later by just an hour than Death –
Oh lagging Yesterday!

Could she have guessed that it w'd be –
Could but a crier of the joy
Have climbed the distant hill –
Had not the bliss so slow a pace
Who knows but this surrendered face
Were undefeated still?

Oh if there may departing be
Any forgot by Victory
In her imperial round –
Show them this meek apparreled thing
That could not stop to be a king –
Doubtful if it be crowned!

Some things that fly there be –
Birds – Hours – the Bumblebee –
Of these no Elegy.

Some things that stay there be –
Grief – Hills – Eternity –
Nor this behooveth me.

There are that resting, rise.
Can I expound the skies?
How still the Riddle lies!

Delayed till she: *Sent to SD (variant) c. spring 1859*

Within my reach!
I could have touched!
I might have chanced that way!
Soft sauntered thro' the village –
Sauntered as soft away!
So unsuspected Violets
Within the meadows go –
Too late for striving fingers
That passed, an hour ago!

~

So bashful when I spied her!
So pretty – so ashamed!
So hidden in her leaflets
Lest anybody find –

So breathless till I passed her –
So helpless when I turned
And bore her struggling, blushing,
Her simple haunts beyond!

For whom I robbed the Dingle –
For whom betrayed the Dell –
Many, will doubtless ask me –
But I shall never tell!

~

My friend must be a Bird –
Because it flies!
Mortal, my friend must be –
Because it dies!
Barbs has it, like a Bee!
Ah, curious friend!
Thou puzzlest me!

~

Went up a year this evening!
I recollect it well!
Amid no bells nor bravoes
The bystanders will tell!

Cheerful – as to the village –
Tranquil – as to repose –
Chastened – as to the Chapel
This humble Tourist rose!
Did not talk of returning!
Alluded to no time
When, were the gales propitious –
We might look for him!
Was grateful for the Roses
In life's diverse boquet –
Talked softly of new species
To pick another day;
Beguiling thus the wonder
The *wondrous* nearer drew –
Hands bustled at the moorings –
The crowd respectful grew –
Ascended from our vision
To countenances new!
A Difference – A Daisy –
Is all the rest I knew!

SHEET TWO c. spring 1859

Angels, in the early morning
May be seen the Dews among,
Stooping – plucking – smiling – flying –
Do the Buds to them belong?

Angels, when the sun is hottest
May be seen the sands among,
Stooping – plucking – sighing – flying –
Parched the flowers they bear along.

My nosegays are for Captives –
Dim – long expectant eyes –
Fingers denied the plucking,
Patient till Paradise –

To such, if they sh'd whisper
Of morning and the moor –

They bear no other errand,
And I, no other prayer.

~

Sexton! My Master's sleeping here.[25]
Pray lead me to his bed!
I came to build the Bird's nest –
And sow the early seed –

That when the snow creeps slowly
From off his chamber door –
Daisies point the way there –
And the Troubadour.

~

The rainbow never tells me[26]
That gust and storm are by –
Yet is she more convincing
Than Philosophy.

My flowers turn from Forums –
Yet eloquent declare
What Cato couldn't prove me
Except the *birds* were here!

~

One dignity delays for all –
One mitred afternoon –
None can avoid this purple –
None evade this crown!

Coach, it insures, and footmen –
Chamber, and state, and throng –
Bells, also, in the village
As we ride grand along!

What dignified attendants!
What service when we pause!
How loyally at parting
Their hundred hats they raise!

How pomp surpassing ermine
When simple You, and I,

Present our meek escutscheon
And claim the rank to die!

~

As by the dead we love to sit –
Become so wondrous dear –
As for the lost we grapple
Tho' all the rest are here –

In broken mathematics
We estimate our prize
Vast – in its fading ratio
To our penurious eyes!

~

New feet within my garden go –
New fingers stir the sod –
A Troubadour upon the Elm
Betrays the solitude.

New Children play upon the green –
New Weary sleep below –
And still the pensive Spring returns –
And still the punctual snow!

~

I hide myself within my flower[27]
That wearing on your breast –
You – unsuspecting, wear me too –
And angels know the rest!

~

SHEET THREE c. autumn 1858

I never told the buried gold[28]
Upon the hill – that lies –
I saw the sun – his plunder done
Crouch low to guard his prize.

He stood as near
As stood you here –

As by the: *Sent to EH (variant) 2 March 1859*
I never told: *Sent to SD (variant) c. autumn 1858*

A pace had been between –
Did but a snake bisect the brake
My life had forfeit been.

That was a wondrous booty –
I hope 'twas honest gained.
Those were the fairest ingots
That ever kissed the spade!

Whether to keep the secret –
Whether to reveal –
Whether as I ponder
"Kidd" will sudden sail –

Could a shrewd advise me
We might e'en divide –
Should a shrewd betray me –
Atropos decide!

~

I never lost as much but twice –
And that was in the sod.
Twice have I stood a beggar
Before the door of God!

Angels – twice descending
Reimbursed my store –
Burglar! Banker – Father!
I am poor once more!

~

I haven't told my garden yet –
Lest that should conquer me.
I haven't quite the strength now
To break it to the Bee –

I will not name it in the street
For shops w'd stare at me –
That one so shy – so ignorant
Should have the face to die.

○

The hillsides must not know it –
Where I have rambled so –
Nor tell the loving forests
The day that I shall go –

Nor lisp it at the table –
Nor heedless by the way
Hint that within the Riddle
One will walk today –

~

I often passed the Village[29]
When going home from school –
And wondered what they did there –
And why it was so still –

I did not know the year then,
In which my call would come –
Earlier, by the Dial,
Than the rest have gone.

It's stiller than the sundown.
It's cooler than the dawn –
The Daisies dare to come here –
And birds can flutter down –

So when you are tired –
Or – perplexed – or cold –
Trust the loving promise
Underneath the mould,
Cry "it's I," "take Dollie,"
And I will enfold!

~

SHEET FOUR c. autumn 1858

The morns are meeker than they were –
The nuts are getting brown –
The berry's cheek is plumper –
The Rose is out of town.

The maple wears a gayer scarf –
The field a scarlet gown –

The morns are: *Sent to SD (variant) c. autumn 1858, with a flower and ribbon*

Lest I sh'd be old fashioned
I'll put a trinket on.

Whether my bark went down at sea –
Whether she met with gales –
Whether to isles enchanted
She bent her docile sails –

By what mystic mooring
She is held today –
This is the errand of the eye
Out upon the Bay.

Taken from men – this morning –
Carried by men today –
Met by the Gods with banners –
Who marshalled her away –

One little maid – from playmates –
One little mind from school –
There must be guests in Eden –
All the rooms are full –

Far – as the East from Even –
Dim – as the border star –
Courtiers quaint, in Kingdoms
Our departed are.

Sleep is supposed to be[30]
By souls of sanity
The shutting of the eye.

Sleep is the station grand
Down wh', on either hand
The hosts of witness stand!

Morn is supposed to be
By people of degree
The breaking of the Day.

Sleep is supposed: *Sent to SD (variant) c. summer 1858*

Morning has not occurred!

That shall Aurora be –
East of Eternity –
One with the banner gay –
One in the red array –
That is the break of Day!

~

If I should die –[31]
And you should live –
And time sh'd gurgle on –
And morn sh'd beam –
And noon should burn –
As it has usual done –
If Birds should build as early
And Bees as bustling go –
One might depart at option
From enterprise below!
'Tis sweet to know that stocks will stand
When we with Daisies lie –
That Commerce will continue –
And Trades as briskly fly –
It makes the parting tranquil
And keeps the soul serene –
That gentlemen so sprightly
Conduct the pleasing scene!

~

By Chivalries as tiny,
A Blossom, or a Book,
The seeds of smiles are planted –
Which blossom in the dark.

~

FASCICLE FOUR

SHEET ONE c. summer 1859

Perhaps you'd like to buy a flower,[32]
But I could never sell –
If you would like to *borrow*,
Until the Daffodil

Unties her yellow Bonnet
Beneath the village door,
Until the Bees, from Clover rows
Their Hock, and sherry, draw,

Why, I will lend until just then,
But not an hour more!

~

Water, is taught by thirst.
Land – by the Oceans passed.
Transport – by throe –
Peace, by its battles told –
Love, by memorial mold –
Birds, by the snow.

~

Have you got a Brook in your little heart,
Where bashful flowers blow,
And blushing birds go down to drink –
And shadows tremble so –

And nobody knows, so still it flows,
That any brook is there,
And yet your little draught of life
Is daily drunken there –

o

Why – look out for the little brook in March,
When the rivers overflow,
And the snows come hurrying from the hills,
And the bridges often go –

And *later,* in *August* it may be,
When the meadows parching lie,
Beware, lest this little brook of life,
Some burning noon go dry!

Flowers – Well – if anybody[33]
Can the extasy define –
Half a transport – half a trouble –
With which flowers humble men:
Anybody find the fountain
From which floods so contra flow –
I will give him all the Daisies
Which upon the hillside blow.

Too much pathos in their faces
For a simple breast like mine –
Butterflies from St Domingo
Cruising round the purple line –
Have a system of aesthetics –
Far superior to mine.

Pigmy seraphs – gone astray –[34]
Velvet people from Vevay –
Belles from some lost summer day –
Bees exclusive Coterie –

Paris could not lay the fold
Belted down with emerald –
Venice could not show a cheek
Of a tint so lustrous meek –
Never such an ambuscade
As of briar and leaf displayed
For my little damask maid –

o

Pigmy seraphs – gone: *Sent to SD (variant) c. summer 1859*

I had rather wear her grace
Than an Earl's distinguished face –
I had rather dwell like her
Than be "Duke of Exeter" –
Royalty enough for me
To subdue the Bumblebee.

SHEET TWO c. summer 1859

Heart not so heavy as mine
Wending late home –
As it passed my window
Whistled itself a tune –

A careless snatch – a ballad –
A Ditty of the street –
Yet to my irritated ear
An anodyne so sweet –

It was as if a Bobolink
Sauntering this way
Carolled and mused, and carolled –
Then bubbled slow away –

It was as if a chirping brook
Upon a toilsome way
Set bleeding feet to minuets
Without the knowing why –

Tomorrow – night will come again –
Perhaps – tired and sore –
Oh Bugle, by the window
I pray you stroll once more!

Soul, Wilt thou toss again?
By just such a hazard
Hundreds have lost indeed,
But tens have won an all –

°

Heart not so: *Sent to Catherine Scott Turner (Anthon) (lost, transcribed variant), with the title "Whistling under my window –," and to Mary Bowles (variant) c. summer 1859*

Angels' breathless ballot
Lingers to record thee –
Imps in eager caucus
Raffle for my soul!

~

An altered look about the hills –[35]
A Tyrian light the village fills –
A wider sunrise in the morn –
A deeper twilight on the lawn –
A print of a vermillion foot –
A purple finger on the slope –
A flippant fly upon the pane –
A spider at his trade again –
An added strut in Chanticleer –
A flower expected everywhere –
An axe shrill singing in the woods –
Fern odors on untravelled roads –
All this and more I cannot tell –
A furtive look you know as well –
And Nicodemus' Mystery
Receives its annual reply!

~

Some, too fragile for winter winds[36]
The thoughtful grave encloses –
Tenderly tucking them in from frost
Before their feet are cold –

Never the treasures in her nest
The cautious grave exposes,
Building where schoolboy dare not look,
And sportsman is not bold.

This covert have all the children
Early aged, and often cold,
Sparrows, unnoticed by the Father –
Lambs for whom time had not a fold.

~

SHEET THREE c. summer 1859

Whose are the little beds – I asked[37]
Which in the valleys lie?
Some shook their heads, and others smiled –
And no one made reply.

Perhaps they did not hear – I said,
I will inquire again –
Whose are the beds – the tiny beds
So thick upon the plain?

'Tis Daisy, in the shortest –
A little further on –
Nearest the door – to wake the 1st,
Little Leontodon.

'Tis Iris, Sir, and Aster –
Anemone, and Bell –
Bartsia, in the blanket red,
And chubby Daffodil.

Meanwhile – at many cradles
Her busy foot she plied –
Humming the quaintest lullaby
That ever rocked a child.

Hush! Epigea wakens!
The Crocus stirs her lids –
Rhodora's cheek is crimson –
She's dreaming of the woods!

Then turning from them reverent –
Their bedtime 'tis, she said –
The Bumble bees will wake them
When April woods are red.

For every Bird a nest –
Wherefore in timid quest
Some little Wren goes seeking round –

Wherefore when boughs are free,

Households in every tree,
Pilgrim be found?

Perhaps a home too high –
Ah aristocracy!
The little Wren desires –

Perhaps of twig so fine –
Of twine e'en superfine,
Her pride aspires –

The Lark is not ashamed
To build upon the ground
Her modest house –

Yet who of all the throng
Dancing around the sun
Does so rejoice?

~

"They have not chosen me" – he said –[38]
"But I have chosen them"!
Brave – Broken hearted statement –
Uttered in Bethleem!

I could not have told it,
But since Jesus *dared*,
Sovreign, know a Daisy
Thy dishonor shared!

~

SHEET FOUR c. summer 1859

She bore it till the simple veins
Traced azure on her hand –
Till pleading, round her quiet eyes
The purple Crayons stand.

Till Daffodils had come and gone
I cannot tell the sum,
And then she ceased to bear it –
And with the Saints sat down.

o

"They have not: *Sent to Mary Bowles (variant) c. summer 1859*

No more her patient figure
At twilight soft to meet –
No more her timid bonnet
Upon the village street –

But crowns instead, and courtiers –
And in the midst so fair,
Whose but her shy – immortal face
Of whom we're whispering here?

~

We should not mind so small a flower[39]
Except it quiet bring
Our little garden that we lost
Back to the Lawn again.

So spicy her Carnations nod –
So drunken, reel her Bees –
So silver steal a hundred flutes
From out a hundred trees –

That whoso sees this little flower
By faith may clear behold
The Bobolinks around the throne
And Dandelions gold.

~

This heart that broke so long –
These feet that never flagged –
This faith that watched for star in vain,
Give gently to the dead –

Hound cannot overtake the Hare
That fluttered panting, here,
Nor any schoolboy rob the nest
Tenderness builded there.

~

On such a night, or such a night,
Would anybody care

We should not: *Sent to SD (variant) c. spring 1859*

If such a little figure
Slipped quiet from its chair,

So quiet – Oh how quiet,
That nobody might know
But that the little figure
Rocked softer – to and fro –

On such a dawn, or such a dawn –
Would anybody sigh
That such a little figure
Too sound asleep did lie

For Chanticleer to wake it –
Or stirring house below –
Or giddy bird in Orchard –
Or early task to do?

There was a little figure plump
For every little knoll,
Busy needles, and spools of thread –
And trudging feet from school –

Playmates, and holidays, and nuts –
And visions vast and small.
Strange that the feet so precious charged
Should reach so small a goal!

FASCICLE FIVE

SHEET ONE c. summer 1859

So from the mould
Scarlet and Gold
Many a Bulb will rise –
Hidden away, cunningly,
From sagacious eyes.

So from Cocoon
Many a Worm
Leap so Highland gay,
Peasants like me –
Peasants like Thee,
Gaze perplexedly!

~

Artists wrestled here!
Lo, a tint Cashmere!
Lo, a Rose!
Student of the Year!
For the Easel here
Say Repose!

~

Success is counted sweetest[40]
By those who ne'er succeed.
To comprehend a nectar
Requires sorest need.

Not one of all the purple Host
Who took the Flag today
Can tell the definition
So clear of Victory

○

So from the: *Sent to SD (variant) c. summer 1859*
Success is counted: *Sent to SD (variant) c. summer 1859 and to TWH (variant) July 1862*

As he defeated – dying –
On whose forbidden ear
The distant strains of triumph
Burst agonized and clear!

~

The Bee is not afraid of me.
I know the Butterfly –
The pretty people in the Woods
Receive me cordially –

The Brooks laugh louder
When I come –
The Breezes madder play;
Wherefore mine eye thy silver mists,
Wherefore, Oh Summer's Day?

~

Where bells no more affright the morn –[41]
Where scrabble never comes –
Where very nimble Gentlemen
Are forced to keep their rooms –

Where tired Children placid sleep
Thro' centuries of noon
This place is Bliss – this town is Heaven –
Please, Pater, pretty soon!

"Oh could we climb where Moses stood,
And view the Landscape o'er"
Not Father's bells – nor Factories –
Could scare us any more!

~

Ambition cannot find him –
Affection doesn't know
How many leagues of nowhere
Lie between them now!

Yesterday, undistinguished!
Eminent Today

Ambition cannot find: *Sent to SD (variant) c. summer 1859*

For our mutual honor,
Immortality!

~

Our share of night to bear –
Our share of morning –
Our blank in bliss to fill,
Our blank in scorning –

Here a star, and there a star,
Some lose their way!
Here a mist – and there a mist –
Afterwards – Day!

~

SHEET TWO c. summer 1859

"Good night," because we must!
How intricate the Dust!
I would *go* to know –
Oh Incognito!

Saucy, saucy Seraph,
To elude me so!
Father! they won't tell me!
Won't you tell them to?

~

South winds jostle them –[42]
Bumblebees come –
Hover – hesitate –
Drink, and are gone –

Butterflies pause
On their passage Cashmere –
I – softly plucking,
Present them here!

~

Low at my problem bending,
Another problem comes –

"Good night," because: *Sent to SB (variant) c. summer 1859*
South winds jostle: *Sent to Thomas Gilbert, SD's brother, (variant) and to Ns (lost) c. summer 1859, and to TWH (variant) 25 April 1862, with pressed flowers*
Low at my: *Sent to SD (variant) c. summer 1859*

Larger than mine – serener –
Involving statelier sums.

I check my busy pencil –
My figures file away –
Wherefore, my baffled fingers
Thy perplexity?

~

What Inn is this
Where for the night
Peculiar Traveller comes?
Who is the Landlord?
Where the maids?
Behold, what curious rooms!
No ruddy fires on the hearth –
No brimming tankards flow.
Necromancer! Landlord!
Who are these below?

~

I had some things that I called mine –[43]
And God, that he called his –
Till recently a rival claim
Disturbed these amities.

The property, my garden,
Which having sown with care –
He claims the pretty acre –
And sends a Bailiff there.

The station of the parties
Forbids publicity,
But Justice is sublimer
Than Arms, or pedigree.

I'll institute an "Action" –
I'll vindicate the law –
Jove! Choose your counsel –
I retain "Shaw"!

~

In rags mysterious as these
The shining Courtiers go,
Vailing the purple, and the plumes –
Vailing the ermine so.

Smiling, as they request an alms
At some imposing door –
Smiling when we walk barefoot
Upon their golden floor!

My friend attacks my friend!
Oh Battle picturesque!
Then I turn Soldier too,
And he turns Satirist!
How martial is this place!
Had I a mighty gun
I think I'd shoot the human race
And then to glory run!

SHEET THREE c. summer 1859

"Arcturus" is his other name –[44]
I'd rather call him "Star"!
It's very mean of Science
To go and interfere!

I slew a worm the other day,
A "Savan" passing by
Murmured "Resurgam" – "Centipede"!
"Oh Lord, how frail are we"!

I pull a flower from the woods –
A monster with a glass
Computes the stamens in a breath –
And has her in a "Class"!

Whereas I took the Butterfly
Aforetime in my hat,

"Arcturus" is his: *Sent to SD (variant) c. summer 1859*

He sits erect in "Cabinets" –
The Clover bells forgot!

What once was "Heaven"
Is "Zenith" now!
Where I proposed to go
When Time's brief masquerade was done
Is mapped, and charted too!

What if the "poles" should frisk about
And stand upon their heads!
I hope I'm ready for "the worst" –
Whatever prank betides!

Perhaps the "kingdom of Heaven's" changed.
I hope the "Children" there
Won't be "new fashioned" when I come –
And laugh at me – and stare!

I hope the Father in the skies
Will lift his little girl –
"Old fashioned"! naughty! everything!
Over the stile of "pearl"!

~

Talk with prudence to a Beggar[45]
Of "Potosi," and the mines!
Reverently, to the Hungry
Of your viands, and your wines!

Cautious, hint to any Captive
You have passed enfranchised feet!
Anecdotes of air, in Dungeons
Have sometimes proved deadly sweet!

~

If this is "fading"[46]
Oh let me immediately "fade"!
If this is "dying"
Bury – me, in such a shroud of red!
If this is "sleep,"

On such a night
How proud to shut the eye!
Good evening, gentle Fellow men!
Peacock presumes to die!

~

As Watchers hang upon the East –
As Beggars revel at a feast
By savory fancy spread –
As Brooks in Deserts, babble sweet
On Ear too far for the delight –
Heaven beguiles the tired.

As that same Watcher when the East
Opens the lid of Amethyst
And lets the morning go –
That Beggar, when an honored Guest –
Those thirsty lips to flagons pressed –
Heaven to us, if true.

~

Her breast is fit for pearls,[47]
But I was not a "Diver."
Her brow is fit for thrones –
But I had not a crest.
Her heart is fit for rest – [for] home –
I – a sparrow – build there
Sweet of twigs and twine
My perennial nest.

~

SHEET FOUR c. summer 1859

A something in a summer's Day
As slow her flambeaux burn away
Which solemnizes me.

A something in a summer's noon –
A depth – an Azure – a perfume –
Transcending extasy.

o

As Watchers hang: *Sent to SD (variant) c. summer 1859*
Her breast is: *Sent to SD (variant) c. summer 1859*

And still within a summer's night
A something so transporting bright
I clap my hands to see –

Then vail my too inspecting face
Lest such a subtle – shimmering grace
Flutter too far for me –

The wizard fingers never rest –
The purple brook within the breast
Still chafes its narrow bed –

Still rears the East her amber Flag –
Guides still the sun along the Crag
His Caravan of Red –

So looking on – the night – the morn
Conclude the wonder gay –
And I meet, coming thro' the dews
Another summer's Day!

~

A throe upon the features –
A hurry in the breath –
An extasy of parting
Denominated "Death" –

An anguish at the mention
Which when to patience grown –
I've known permission given
To rejoin its own.

~

Glowing is her Bonnet –
Glowing is her Cheek –
Glowing is her Kirtle –
Yet she cannot speak.

Better as the Daisy
From the summer hill
Vanish unrecorded
Save by tearful rill –

o

A throe upon: *Sent to SD (variant) c. summer 1859*
Glowing is her: *Sent to SD (variant) c. summer 1859*

Save by loving sunrise
Looking for her face.
Save by feet unnumbered
Pausing at the place.

⌁

Many cross the Rhine
In this cup of mine.
Sip old Frankfort air
From my brown Cigar.

⌁

In lands I never saw – they say
Immortal Alps look down –
Whose Bonnets touch the firmament –
Whose sandals touch the town;

Meek at whose everlasting feet
A myriad Daisy play –
Which, Sir, are you, and which am *I* –
Upon an August day?

⌁

For each extatic instant
We must an anguish pay
In keen and quivering ratio
To the extasy –

For each beloved hour
Sharp pittances of Years –
Bitter contested farthings –
And Coffers heaped with tears!

⌁

FASCICLE SIX

SHEET ONE c. early 1860

Who never lost, are unprepared
A Coronet to find!
Who never thirsted
Flagons, and Cooling Tamarind!

Who never climbed the weary league –
Can such a foot explore
The purple territories
On Pizarro's shore?

How many Legions overcome –
The Emperor will say?
How many *Colors* taken
On Revolution Day?

How many *Bullets* bearest?
Hast Thou the Royal scar?
Angels! Write "Promoted"
On this Soldier's brow!

A Lady red – amid the Hill
Her annual secret keeps!
A Lady white, within the Field
In placid Lily sleeps!

The tidy Breezes, with their Brooms –
Sweep vale – and hill – and tree!
Prithee, my pretty Housewives!
Who may expected be?

The neighbors do not yet suspect!
The woods exchange a smile!

Who never lost,: *Sent to SD (variant) c. early 1860, beginning "Who never lost, is unprepared"*
A Lady red –: *Sent to SD (variant) c. early 1860*

Orchard, and Buttercup, and Bird –
In such a little while!

And yet, how still the Landscape stands!
How nonchalant the Hedge!
As if the "Resurrection"
Were nothing very strange!

~

To fight aloud, is very brave –[48]
But *gallanter*, I know
Who charge within the bosom
The Cavalry of Wo –

Who win, and nations do not see –
Who fall – and none observe –
Whose dying eyes, no Country
Regards with patriot love –

We trust, in plumed procession
For such, the Angels go –
Rank after Rank, with even feet –
And Uniforms of snow.

~

'Houses' – so the Wise men tell me –[49]
'Mansions'! Mansions must be warm!
Mansions cannot let the tears in –
Mansions must exclude the storm!

'Many Mansions', by 'his Father' –
I don't know him; snugly built!
Could the children find the way there –
Some, would even trudge tonight!

~

SHEET TWO c. early 1860

Bring me the sunset in a cup –[50]
Reckon the morning's flagons up
And say how many Dew –

Bring me the: *Sent to SD (variant) c. early 1860*

Tell me how far the morning leaps –
Tell me what time the weaver sleeps
Who spun the breadths of blue!

Write me how many notes there be
In the new Robin's extasy
Among astonished boughs –
How many trips the Tortoise makes –
How many cups the Bee partakes,
The Debauchee of Dews!

Also, Who laid the Rainbow's piers,
Also, Who leads the docile spheres
By withes of supple blue?
Whose fingers string the stalactite –
Who counts the wampum of the night
To see that none is due?

Who built this little Alban House
And shut the windows down so close
My spirit cannot see?
Who'll let me out some gala day
With implements to fly away,
Passing Pomposity?

~

She died at play –
Gambolled away
Her lease of spotted hours,
Then sank as gaily as a Turk
Upon a Couch of flowers –

Her ghost strolled softly o'er the hill –
Yesterday, and Today –
Her vestments as the silver fleece –
Her countenance as spray –

~

Cocoon above! Cocoon below!
Stealthy Cocoon, why hide you so
What all the world suspect?

She died at: *Sent to SD (variant) c. early 1860*

An hour, and gay on every tree
Your secret, perched in extasy
Defies imprisonment!

An hour in chrysalis to pass –
Then gay above receding grass
A Butterfly to go!
A moment to interrogate,
Then wiser than a "Surrogate,"
The Universe to know!

~

Exultation is the going[51]
Of an inland soul to sea –
Past the Houses –
Past the Headlands –
Into deep Eternity –

Bred as we, among the mountains,
Can the sailor understand
The divine intoxication
Of the first league out from Land?

~

I never hear the word "Escape"[52]
Without a quicker blood,
A sudden expectation –
A flying attitude!

I never hear of prisons broad
By soldiers battered down,
But I tug childish at my bars
Only to fail again!

~

SHEET THREE c. late 1859

These are the days when Birds come back –[53]
A very few – a Bird or two –
To take a backward look.

o

Exultation is the: *Sent to SD (variant) c. early 1860*
I never hear: *Sent to SD (variant) c. early 1860*
These are the: *Sent to SD (variant) c. autumn 1859*

These are the days when skies resume
The old – old sophistries of June –
A blue and gold mistake.

Oh fraud that cannot cheat the Bee,
Almost thy plausibility
Induces my belief,

Till ranks of seeds their witness bear –
And softly thro' the altered air
Hurries a timid leaf.

Oh sacrament of summer days,
Oh Last Communion in the Haze –
Permit a child to join,

Thy sacred emblems to partake –
Thy consecrated bread to take
And thine immortal wine!

Besides the Autumn poets sing[54]
A few prosaic days
A little this side of the snow
And that side of the Haze –

A few incisive mornings –
A few Ascetic eves –
Gone – Mr Bryant's "Golden Rod" –
And Mr Thomson's "sheaves."

Still, is the bustle in the Brook –
Sealed are the spicy valves –
Mesmeric fingers softly touch
The eyes of many Elves –

Perhaps a squirrel may remain –
My sentiments to share –
Grant me, Oh Lord, a sunny mind –
Thy windy will to bear!

Besides the Autumn: *Sent to SD (variant) c. autumn 1859*

Safe in their Alabaster Chambers –[55]
Untouched by morning
And untouched by noon –
Sleep the meek members of the Resurrection –
Rafter of satin,
And Roof of stone.

Light laughs the breeze
In her Castle above them –
Babbles the Bee in a stolid Ear,
Pipe the sweet Birds in ignorant cadence –
Ah, what sagacity perished here!

A poor – torn heart – a tattered heart –
That sat it down to rest –
Nor noticed that the ebbing Day
Flowed silver to the west –
Nor noticed night did soft descend –
Nor Constellation burn –
Intent upon the vision
Of latitudes unknown.

The angels – happening that way
This dusty heart espied –
Tenderly took it up from toil
And carried it to God –
There – sandals for the Barefoot –
There – gathered from the gales –
Do the blue havens by the hand
Lead the wandering Sails.

SHEET FOUR c. late 1859

I bring an unaccustomed wine[56]
To lips long parching
Next to mine,
And summon them to drink;

○

Safe in their: *Sent to SD (lost) presumably c. late 1859 and twice (variant) c. 1861; sent to TWH (variant) 15 April 1862*
A poor – torn: *Sent to SD (variant) c. 1859, with two pictures cut from her father's copy of Charles Dickens's* Old Curiosity Shop *tied to the page*

Crackling with fever, they essay,
I turn my brimming eyes away,
And come next hour to look.

The hands still hug the tardy glass –
The lips I w'd have cooled, alas,
Are so superfluous Cold –

I w'd as soon attempt to warm
The bosoms where the frost has lain
Ages beneath the mould –

Some other thirsty there may be
To whom this w'd have pointed me
Had it remained to speak –

And so I always bear the cup
If, haply, mine may be the drop
Some pilgrim thirst to slake –

If, haply, any say to me
"Unto the little, unto me,"
When I at last awake –

As children bid the Guest "Good night"
And then reluctant turn –
My flowers raise their pretty lips –
Then put their nightgowns on.

As children caper when they wake –
Merry that it is Morn –
My flowers from a hundred cribs
Will peep, and prance again.

Going to Heaven![57]
I don't know when –
Pray do not ask me how!
Indeed I'm too astonished
To think of answering you!

Going to Heaven!: *Sent to SD (variant) c. late 1859*

Going to Heaven!
How dim it sounds!
And yet it will be done
As sure as flocks go home at night
Unto the Shepherd's arm!

Perhaps you're going too!
Who knows?
If you sh'd get there first
Save just a little place for me
Close to the two I lost –
The smallest "Robe" will fit me
And just a bit of "Crown" –
For you know we do not mind our dress
When we are going home –

I'm glad I don't believe it
For it w'd stop my breath –
And I'd like to look a little more
At such a curious Earth!
I am glad they did believe it
Whom I have never found
Since the mighty autumn afternoon
I left them in the ground.

Our lives are Swiss –[58]
So still – so Cool –
Till some odd afternoon
The Alps neglect their Curtains
And we look farther on!

Italy stands the other side!
While like a guard between –
The solemn Alps –
The siren Alps
Forever intervene!

Our lives are: *Sent to SD (variant) c. late 1859*

FASCICLE SEVEN

SHEET ONE c. early to spring 1860

A little East of Jordan,[59]
Evangelists record,
A Gymnast and an Angel
Did wrestle long and hard –

Till morning touching mountain –
And Jacob, waxing strong,
The Angel begged permission
To Breakfast – to return!

Not so, said cunning Jacob!
"I will not let thee go
Except thou bless me" – Stranger! [bless me" –] Signor
The which acceded to –

Light swung the silver fleeces
"Peniel" Hills beyond,
And the bewildered Gymnast
Found he had worsted God!

All overgrown by cunning moss,[60]
All interspersed with weed,
The little cage of "Currer Bell"
In quiet "Haworth" laid.

This Bird – observing others
When frosts too sharp became
Retire to other latitudes –
Quietly did the same –

But differed in returning –
Since Yorkshire hills are green –

A little East: *Sent to SD (lost, published variant) c. early 1860, with the first line "A little over Jordan,"*

Yet not in all the nests I meet –
Can Nightingale be seen –
    Or –
Gathered from many wanderings –
Gethsemane can tell
Thro' what transporting anguish
She reached the Asphodel!

Soft fall the sounds of Eden
Upon her puzzled ear –
Oh what an afternoon for Heaven,
When "Bronte" entered there!

~

A science – so the Savans say,[61]
"Comparative Anatomy" –
By which a single bone –
Is made a secret to unfold
Of some rare tenant of the mold –
Else perished in the stone –

So to the eye prospective led,
This meekest flower of the mead
Upon a winter's day,
Stands representative in gold
Of Rose and Lily, manifold,
And countless Butterfly!

~

Will there really be a "morning"?
Is there such a thing as "Day"?
Could I see it from the mountains
If I were as tall as they?

Has it feet like Water lilies?
Has it feathers like a Bird?
Is it brought from famous countries
Of which I have never heard?

Oh some Scholar! Oh some Sailor!
Oh some Wise Man from the skies!

Please to tell a little Pilgrim
Where the place called "morning" lies!

~

Great Caesar! Condescend[62]
The Daisy, to receive,
Gathered by Cato's Daughter,
With your majestic leave!

~

SHEET TWO c. spring 1860

I have a King, who does not speak –[63]
So – wondering – thro' the hours meek
I trudge the day away –
Half glad when it is night, and sleep,
If, haply, thro' a dream, to peep
In parlors, shut by day.

And if I do – when morning comes –
It is as if a hundred drums
Did round my pillow roll,
And shouts fill all my childish sky,
And Bells keep saying 'Victory'
From steeples in my soul!

And if I don't – the little Bird
Within the Orchard, is not heard,
And I omit to pray
'Father, thy will be done' today
For my will goes the other way,
And it were perjury!

~

Where I have lost, I softer tread –
I sow sweet flower from garden bed –
I pause above that vanished head
And mourn.

Whom I have lost, I pious guard
From accent harsh, or ruthless word –

Feeling as if their pillow heard,
    Though stone!

When I have lost, you'll know by this –
A Bonnet black – A dusk surplice –
A little tremor in my voice
    Like this!

Why, I have lost, the people know
Who dressed in frocks of purest snow
Went home a century ago
    Next Bliss!

~

She went as quiet as the Dew[64]
From an Accustomed flower. [From] a familiar
Not like the Dew, did she return
At the Accustomed hour!

She dropt as softly as a star
From out my summer's eve –
Less skillful than Le Verriere
It's sorer to believe!

~

To hang our head – ostensibly –
And subsequent, to find
That such was not the posture
Of our immortal mind –

Affords the sly presumption
That in so dense a fuzz –
You – too – take Cobweb attitudes
Upon a plane of Gauze!

~

The Daisy follows soft the Sun –[65]
And when his golden walk is done –
Sits shyly at his feet –
He – waking – finds the flower there –

Wherefore – Marauder – art thou here?
Because, Sir, love is sweet!

We are the Flower – Thou the Sun!
Forgive us, if as days decline –
We nearer steal to Thee!
Enamored of the parting West –
The peace – the flight – the amethyst –
Night's possibility!

~

SHEET THREE c. early 1860

Like her the Saints retire,
In their Chapeaux of fire,
Martial as she!

Like her the evenings steal
Purple and Cochineal
After the Day!

"Departed" – both – they say!
i.e, gathered away,
Not found,

Argues the Aster still –
Reasons the Daffodil
Profound!

~

Papa above![66]
Regard a mouse
O'erpowered by the Cat!
Reserve within thy kingdom
A "Mansion" for the Rat!

Snug in seraphic Cupboards
To nibble all the day,
While unsuspecting Cycles
Wheel solemnly away!

~

Like her the: *Sent to SD (variant) c. early 1860*
Papa above!: *Sent to SD (variant) c. early 1860*

'Twas such a little – little boat
That toddled down the bay!
'Twas such a gallant – gallant sea
That beckoned it away!

'Twas such a greedy, greedy wave
That licked it from the Coast –
Nor ever guessed the stately sails
My little craft was *lost!*

~

"Sown in dishonor"![67]
Ah! Indeed!
May *this* "dishonor" be?
If I were half so fine myself
I'd notice nobody!

"Sown in corruption"!
Not so fast!
Apostle is askew!
Corinthians 1. 15. narrates
A circumstance or two!

~

She died – *this* was the way she died.[68]
And when her breath was done
Took up her simple wardrobe
And started for the sun –
Her little figure at the gate
The Angels must have spied,
Since I could never find her
Upon the mortal side.

"Bernardine" Angels, up the hight
Her trudging feet Espied –

~

If pain for peace prepares[69]
Lo, what "Augustan" years
Our feet await!

If springs from winter rise.
Can the Anemones
Be reckoned up?

○

"Sown in dishonor"!: *Sent to SD (variant) c. early 1860*
If pain for: *Sent to SD (variant) c. early 1860*

If night stands first – *then* noon
To gird us for the sun –
What gaze!

When from a thousand skies
On our *developed* eyes
Noons blaze!

Surgeons must be very careful
When they take the knife!
Underneath their fine incisions
Stirs the Culprit – *Life!*

SHEET FOUR c. spring 1860

Some Rainbow – coming from the Fair![70]
Some Vision of the World Cashmere –
I confidently see!
Or else a Peacock's purple Train
Feather by feather – on the plain
Fritters itself away!

The dreamy Butterflies bestir!
Lethargic pools resume the whirr
Of last year's sundered tune!
From some old Fortress on the sun
Baronial Bees – march – one by one –
In murmuring platoon!

The Robins stand as thick today
As flakes of snow stood yesterday –
On fence – and Roof – and Twig!
The Orchis binds her feather on
For her old lover – Don the sun!
Revisiting the Bog!

Without Commander! Countless! Still!
The Regiments of Wood and Hill
In bright detachment stand!

Some Rainbow – coming: *Sent to SD (variant) c. spring 1860*

Behold, Whose multitudes are these?
The children of whose turbaned seas –
Or what Circassian Land?

~

By a flower – By a letter
By a nimble love –
If I weld the Rivet faster –
Final fast – above –

Never mind my breathless Anvil!
Never mind Repose!
Never mind the sooty faces
Tugging at the Forge!

~

I can't tell you – but you feel it –[71]
Nor can you tell me –
Saints, with ravished slate and pencil
Solve our April Day!

Sweeter than a vanished frolic
From a vanished green!
Swifter than the hoofs of Horsemen
Round a Ledge of dream!

Modest, let us walk among it
With our faces vailed –
As they say polite Archangels
Do in meeting God!

Not for me – to prate about it!
Not for you – to say
To some fashionable Lady
"Charming April Day"!

Rather – Heaven's "Peter Parley"!
By which children slow
To sublimer Recitation
Are prepared to go!

~

I can't tell: *Sent to SD (variant) c. April 1860*

FASCICLE EIGHT

SHEET ONE c. summer 1860

A *wounded* Deer – leaps highest –[72]
I've heard the Hunter tell –
'Tis but the extasy of *death* –
And then the Brake is still!

The *smitten* Rock that gushes!
The *trampled* Steel that springs!
A Cheek is always redder
Just where the Hectic stings!

Mirth is the mail of Anguish –
In which it cautious Arm,
Lest anybody spy the blood
And "you're hurt" exclaim!

~

The Sun kept stooping – stooping – low![73]
The Hills to meet him rose!
On his side, what Transaction!
On their side, what Repose!

Deeper and deeper grew the stain
Upon the window pane –
Thicker and thicker stood the feet
Until the Tyrian

Was crowded dense with Armies –
So gay – So Brigadier –
That *I* felt martial stirrings
Who once the Cockade wore –

Charged, from my chimney Corner –
But Nobody was there!

~

A *wounded* Deer –: *Sent to SD (lost) c. summer 1860*
The Sun kept: *Sent to SD (variant) c. summer 1860*

I met a King this Afternoon![74]
He had not on a Crown indeed –
A little Palm leaf Hat was all,
And he was barefoot, I'm afraid!

But sure I am he Ermine wore
Beneath his faded Jacket's blue –
And sure I am, the crest he bore
Within that Jacket's pocket too!

For 'twas too stately for an Earl –
A Marquis would not go so grand!
'Twas possibly a Czar petite –
A Pope, or something of that kind!

If I must tell you, of a Horse
My freckled Monarch held the rein –
Doubtless, an estimable Beast,
But not at all disposed to run!

And such a wagon! While I live
Dare I presume to see
Another such a vehicle
As then transported me!

Two other ragged Princes
His royal state partook!
Doubtless the first excursion
These sovreigns ever took!

I question if the Royal Coach
Round which the Footmen wait
Has the significance, on high,
Of this Barefoot Estate!

SHEET TWO c. summer 1860

To learn the Transport by the Pain –
As Blind Men learn the sun!
To die of thirst – suspecting
That Brooks in Meadows run!

o

To learn the: *Sent to SD (variant) c. summer 1860, beginning "To learn the transport thro' the pain –"*

To stay the homesick – homesick feet
Upon a foreign shore –
Haunted by native lands, the while –
And blue – beloved Air!

This is the sovreign Anguish!
This – the signal wo!
These are the patient "Laureates"
Whose voices – trained – below –

Ascend in ceaseless Carol –
Inaudible, indeed,
To us – the duller scholars
Of the Mysterious Bard!

~

If the foolish, call them *"flowers"* –[75]
Need the wiser, *tell*?
If the Savans "Classify" them
It is just as well!

Those who read the "Revelations"
Must not criticize
Those who read the same Edition –
With beclouded Eyes!

Could we stand with that Old "Moses" –
"Canaan" denied –
Scan like him, the stately landscape
On the other side –

Doubtless, we should deem superfluous
Many Sciences,
Not pursued by learned Angels
In scholastic skies!

Low amid that glad Belles lettres
Grant that we may stand –
Stars, amid profound *Galaxies* –
At that grand "Right hand"!

~

In Ebon Box, when years have flown[76]
To reverently peer –
Wiping away the velvet dust
Summers have sprinkled there!

To hold a letter to the light –
Grown Tawny, now – with time –
To con the faded syllables
That quickened us like Wine!

Perhaps a Flower's shrivelled cheek
Among its stores to find –
Plucked far away, some morning –
By gallant – mouldering hand!

A curl, perhaps, from foreheads
Our constancy forgot –
Perhaps, an antique trinket –
In vanished fashions set!

And then to lay them quiet back –
And go about its care –
As if the little Ebon Box
Were none of our affair!

Portraits are to daily faces[77]
As an Evening West,
To a fine – pedantic sunshine –
In a satin Vest!

SHEET THREE c. spring 1860

Wait till the Majesty of Death[78]
Invests so mean a brow!
Almost a powdered Footman
Might dare to touch it now!

Wait till in Everlasting Robes
This Democrat is dressed –

Then prate about "Preferment" –
And "Station," and the rest!

Around this quiet Courtier
Obsequious Angels wait!
Full royal is his Retinue!
Full purple is his state!

A Lord – might dare to lift the Hat
To such a modest Clay –
Since that My Lord – "the Lord of Lords"
Receives unblushingly!

~

'Tis so much joy! 'Tis so much joy![79]
If I should fail, what poverty!
And yet, as poor as I,
Have ventured all upon a throw!
Have gained! Yes! Hesitated so –
This side the Victory!

Life is but Life! And Death, but Death!
Bliss is but Bliss, and Breath but Breath!
And if indeed I fail,
At least, to know the worst, is sweet!
Defeat means nothing *but* Defeat,
No drearier, can befall!

And if I gain! Oh Gun at sea,
Oh Bells, that in the steeples be!
At first, repeat it slow!
For Heaven is a different thing,
Conjectured, and waked sudden in –
And might extinguish me!

~

A fuzzy fellow, without feet –
Yet doth exceeding run!
Of velvet, is his Countenance –
And his complexion, dun!

o

Sometime, he dwelleth in the grass!
Sometime, upon a bough,
From which he doth descend in plush
Upon the Passer-by!

All this in summer –
But when winds alarm the Forest Folk,
He taketh *Damask* Residence –
And struts in sewing silk!

Then, finer than a Lady,
Emerges in the spring!
A Feather on each shoulder!
You'd scarce recognize him!

By men, yclept Caterpillar!
By me! But who am I,
To tell the pretty secret
Of the Butterfly!

⁓

At last, to be identified![80]
At last, the lamps upon thy side
The rest of Life to *see!*

Past Midnight! Past the Morning Star!
Past Sunrise!
Ah, What leagues there *were*
Between our feet, and Day!

⁓

SHEET FOUR c. spring 1860

I have never seen 'Volcanoes' –
But, when Travellers tell
How those old – phlegmatic mountains
Usually so still –

Bear within – appalling Ordnance,
Fire, and smoke, and gun –
Taking Villages for breakfast,
And appalling Men –

○

If the stillness is Volcanic
In the human face
When upon a pain Titanic
Features keep their place –

If at length, the smouldering anguish
Will not overcome,
And the palpitating Vineyard
In the dust, be thrown?

If some loving Antiquary,
On Resumption Morn,
Will not cry with joy, "Pompeii"!
To the Hills return!

~

Dust is the only Secret.[81]
Death, the only One
You cannot find out all about
In his "native town."

Nobody knew "his Father" –
Never was a Boy –
Hadn't any playmates,
Or "Early history" –

Industrious! Laconic!
Punctual! Sedate!
Bold as a Brigand!
Stiller than a Fleet!

Builds, like a Bird, too!
Christ robs the Nest –
Robin after Robin
Smuggled to Rest!

~

I'm the little "Heart's Ease"![82]
I don't care for pouting skies!
If the Butterfly delay
Can I, therefore, stay away?

o

Dust is the: *Sent to SD (variant) c. spring 1860*

If the Coward Bumble Bee
In his chimney corner stay,
I, must resoluter be!
Who'll apologize for me?

Dear – Old fashioned, little flower!
Eden is old fashioned, too!
Birds are antiquated fellows!
Heaven does not change her blue.
Nor will I, the little Heart's Ease –
Ever be induced to do!

Ah, Necromancy Sweet!
Ah, Wizard erudite!
Teach me the skill,

That I instill the pain
Surgeons assuage in vain,
Nor Herb of all the plain
Can heal!

SHEET FIVE c. summer 1860

Except to Heaven, she is nought.
Except for Angels – lone.
Except to some wide-wandering Bee
A flower superfluous blown.

Except for winds – provincial.
Except by Butterflies
Unnoticed as a single dew
That on the Acre lies.

The smallest Housewife in the grass,
Yet take her from the Lawn
And somebody has lost the face
That made Existence – Home!

Except to Heaven,: *Sent to SD (variant) c. summer 1860*

Pictures are to daily faces[83]
As an Evening West
To a fine – pedantic Sunshine
In a satin Vest.

I cautious, scanned my little life –[84]
I winnowed what would fade
From what w'd last till Heads like mine
Should be a-dreaming laid.

I put the latter in a Barn –
The former, blew away.
I went one winter morning
And lo, my priceless Hay

Was not upon the "Scaffold" –
Was not upon the "Beam" –
And from a thriving Farmer –
A Cynic, I became.

Whether a Thief did it –
Whether it was the wind –
Whether Deity's guiltless –
My business is, to find!

So I begin to ransack!
How is it Hearts, with Thee?
Art thou within the little Barn
Love provided Thee?

If I could bribe them by a Rose
I'd bring them every flower that grows
From Amherst to Cashmere!
I would not stop for night, or storm –
Or frost, or death, or anyone –
My business were so dear!

If they w'd linger for a Bird
My Tamborin were soonest heard
Among the April Woods!

Unwearied, all the summer long,
Only to break in wilder song
When Winter shook the boughs!

What if they hear me!
Who shall say
That such an importunity
May not at last avail?
That, weary of this Beggar's face –
They may not finally say, Yes –
To drive her from the Hall?

As if some little Arctic flower
Upon the polar hem –
Went wandering down the Latitudes
Until it puzzled came
To continents of summer –
To firmaments of sun –
To strange, bright crowds of flowers –
And birds, of foreign tongue!
I say, As if this little flower
To Eden, wandered in –
What then? Why nothing,
Only, your *inference* therefrom!

FASCICLE NINE

SHEET ONE c. summer 1861

What shall I do – it whimpers so –[85]
This little Hound within the Heart –
All day and night – with bark and start –
And yet – it will not go?

Would you untie it – were you me –
Would it stop whining, if to Thee
I sent it – even now?

It should not teaze you – by your chair –
Or on the mat – or if it dare –
To climb your dizzy knee –

Or sometimes – at your side to run –
When you were willing –
May it come –
Tell Carlo – He'll tell me!

How many times these low feet staggered –[86]
Only the soldered mouth can tell –
Try – can you stir the awful rivet –
Try – can you lift the hasps of steel!

Stroke the cool forehead – hot so often –
Lift – if you care – the listless hair –
Handle the adamantine fingers
Never a thimble – more – shall wear –

Buzz the dull flies – on the chamber window –
Brave – shines the sun through the freckled pane –
Fearless – the cobweb swings from the ceiling –
Indolent Housewife – in Daisies – lain!

What shall I: *Sent to SB (variant) c. spring 1861*

Make me a picture of the sun –
So I can hang it in my room.
And make believe I'm getting warm
When others call it "Day"!

Draw me a Robin – on a stem –
So I am hearing him, I'll dream,
And when the Orchards stop their tune –
Put my pretense – away –

Say if it's really – warm at noon –
Whether it's Buttercups – that "skim" –
Or Butterflies – that "bloom"?
Then – skip – the frost – upon the lea –
And skip the Russet – on the tree –
Let's play those – never come!

Bound – a trouble –[87]
And lives can bear it!
Limit – how deep a bleeding go!
So – many – drops – of vital scarlet –
Deal with the soul
As with Algebra!

Tell it the Ages – to a cypher –
And it will ache – contented – on –
Sing – at its pain – as any Workman –
Notching the fall of the even sun!

LEAF TWO c. summer 1861

What is – "Paradise" –[88]
Who live there –
Are they "Farmers" –
Do they "hoe" –
Do they know that this is "Amherst" –
And that I – am coming – too –

o

Do they wear "new shoes" – in "Eden" –
Is it always pleasant – there –
Won't they scold us – when we're hungry – [we're] homesick
Or tell God – how cross we are –

You are sure there's such a person
As "a Father" – in the sky –
So if I get lost – there – ever –
Or do what the Nurse calls "die" –

I shan't walk the "Jasper" – barefoot –
Ransomed folks – won't laugh at me –
Maybe – "Eden" a'nt so lonesome
As New England used to be!

SHEET THREE c. spring 1861

The murmur of a Bee
A Witchcraft – yieldeth me –
If any ask me why –
'Twere easier to die –
Than tell –

The Red upon the Hill
Taketh away my will –
If anybody sneer –
Take care – for God is here –
That's all.

The Breaking of the Day
Addeth to my Degree –
If any ask me how –
Artist – who drew me so –
Must tell!

You love me – you are sure –[89]
I shall not fear mistake –
I shall not *cheated* wake –
Some grinning morn –

The murmur of: *Sent to SD (variant) c. early spring 1862, beginning "The Bumble of a Bee –"*

To find the Sunrise left –
And Orchards – unbereft –
And Dollie – gone!

I need not start – you're sure –
That night will never be –
When frightened – home to Thee I run –
To find the windows dark –
And no more Dollie – mark –
Quite none?

Be sure you're sure – you know –
I'll bear it better now –
If you'll just tell me so –
Than when – a little dull Balm grown –
Over this pain of mine –
You sting – again!

My River runs to Thee –[90]
Blue Sea – Wilt welcome me?

My River waits reply.
Oh Sea – look graciously!

I'll fetch thee Brooks
From spotted nooks –

Say Sea – take me?

It's such a little thing to weep –
So short a thing to sigh –
And yet – by Trades – the size of *these*
We men and women die!

He was weak, and I was strong – then –
So He let me lead him in –
I was weak, and He was strong then –
So I let him lead me – Home.

My River runs: *Sent to Mary Bowles (variant) c. August 1861*

'Twasn't far – the door was near –
'Twasn't dark – for He went – too –
'Twasn't loud, for He said nought –
That was all I cared to know.

Day knocked – and we must part –
Neither – was strongest – now –
He strove – and I strove – too –
We didn't do it – tho'!

SHEET FOUR   c. early spring 1861

The Skies can't keep their secret!
They tell it to the Hills –
The Hills just tell the Orchards –
And they – the Daffodils!

A Bird – by chance – that goes that way –
Soft overhears the whole –
If I should bribe the little Bird –
Who knows but *she* would tell?

I think I won't – however –
It's finer – not to know –
If Summer were *an axiom* –
What sorcery had *snow?*

So keep your secret – Father!
I would not – if I could –
Know what the Sapphire Fellows, do,
In your new-fashioned world!

Poor little Heart![91]
Did they forget thee?
Then dinna care! Then dinna care!

Proud little Heart!
Did they forsake thee?
Be debonnaire! Be debonnaire!

Frail little Heart!
I would not break thee –
Could'st credit *me*? Could'st credit me?

Gay little Heart –
Like Morning Glory!
Wind and Sun – wilt thee array!

~

I shall know why – when Time is over –[92]
And I have ceased to wonder why –
Christ will explain each separate anguish
In the fair schoolroom of the sky –

He will tell me what "Peter" promised –
And I – for wonder at his woe –
I shall forget the drop of anguish
That scalds me now – that scalds me now!

~

On this long storm the Rainbow rose –[93]
On this late morn – the sun –
The Clouds – like listless Elephants –
Horizons – straggled down –

The Birds rose smiling, in their nests –
The gales – indeed – were done –
Alas, how heedless were the eyes –
On whom the summer shone!

The quiet nonchalance of death –
No Daybreak – can bestir –
The slow – Archangel's syllables
Must awaken *her!*

~

SHEET FIVE c. late spring 1861

Musicians wrestle everywhere –[94]
All day – among the crowded air
I hear the silver strife –

Musicians wrestle everywhere –: *Sent to SD (variant) c. spring 1861, beginning "Musicians wrestling Everywhere!"*

And – waking – long before the morn –
Such transport breaks upon the town
I think it that "New life"!

It is not Bird – it has no nest –
Nor "Band" – in brass and scarlet – drest –
Nor Tamborin – nor Man –
It is not Hymn from pulpit read –
The "Morning Stars" the Treble led
On Time's first afternoon!

Some – say – it is "the Spheres" – at play!
Some say – that bright Majority
Of vanished Dames – and Men!
Some – think it service in the place
Where we – with late – celestial face –
Please God – shall ascertain!

~

For this – accepted Breath –[95]
Through it – compete with Death –
The fellow cannot touch this Crown –
By it – my title take –
Ah, what a royal sake
To my nescessity – stooped down!

No Wilderness – can be
Where this attendeth me –
No Desert Noon –
No fear of frost to come
Haunt the perennial bloom –
But Certain June!

Get Gabriel – to tell – the royal syllable –
Get saints – with new – unsteady tongue –
To say what trance below
Most like their glory show –
Fittest the Crown!

~

For this – accepted: *Sent to SB (second stanza, variant) c. spring 1861*

We don't cry – Tim and I –[96]
We are far too grand –
But we bolt the door tight
To prevent a friend –

Then we hide our brave face
Deep in our hand –
Not to cry – Tim and I –
We are far too grand –

Nor to dream – he and me –
Do we condescend –
We just shut our brown eye
To see to the end –

Tim – see Cottages –
But, Oh, so high!
Then – we shake – Tim and I –
And lest I – cry –

Tim – reads a little Hymn –
And we both pray,
Please, Sir, I and Tim –
Always lost the way!

We must die – by and by –
Clergymen say –
Tim – shall – if I – do –
I – too – if he –

How shall we arrange it –
Tim – was – so – shy?
Take us simultaneous – Lord –
I – "Tim" – and – me!

SHEET SIX c. spring 1861

Dying! Dying in the night![97]
Won't somebody bring the light
So I can see which way to go
Into the everlasting snow?

o

And "Jesus"! Where is *Jesus* gone?
They said that Jesus – always came –
Perhaps he doesn't know the House –
This way, Jesus, Let him pass!

Somebody run to the great gate
And see if Dollie's coming! Wait!
I hear her feet upon the stair!
Death won't hurt – now Dollie's here!

~

Morning – is the place for Dew –
Corn – is made at Noon –
After dinner light – for flowers –
Dukes – for setting sun!

~

An awful Tempest mashed the air –
The clouds were gaunt, and few –
A Black – as of a spectre's cloak
Hid Heaven and Earth from view –

The creatures chuckled on the Roofs –
And whistled in the air –
And shook their fists –
And gnashed their teeth –
And swung their frenzied hair –

The morning lit – the Birds arose –
The Monster's faded eyes
Turned slowly to his native coast –
And peace – was Paradise!

~

I'm "wife" – I've finished that –
That other state –
I'm Czar – I'm "Woman" now –
It's safer so –

How odd the Girl's life looks
Behind this soft Eclipse –

I think that Earth feels so
To folks in Heaven – now –

This being comfort – then
That other kind – was pain –
But Why compare?
I'm "Wife"! Stop there!

~

I stole them from a Bee –
Because – Thee –
Sweet plea –
He pardoned me!

~

Two swimmers wrestled on the spar –
Until the morning sun –
When One – turned smiling to the land –
Oh God! the Other One!

The stray ships – passing –
Spied a face –
Upon the waters borne –
With eyes in death – still begging raised –
And hands – beseeching – thrown!

~

My eye is fuller than my vase –
Her Cargo – is of Dew –
And still – my Heart – my eye outweighs –
East India – for you!

~

SHEET SEVEN c. late spring 1861

He forgot – and I – remembered –[98]
'Twas an everyday affair –
Long ago as Christ and Peter –
"Warmed them" at the "Temple fire".

○

I stole them: *Sent to SB (variant) c. spring 1861*
Two swimmers wrestled: *Sent to SB (variant) c. spring 1861*

"Thou wert with him" – quoth "the Damsel"?
"*No*" – said Peter – 'twasn't me –
Jesus merely "looked" at Peter –
Could I do aught else – to Thee?

A Slash of Blue! A sweep of Gray!
Some scarlet patches – on the way –
Compose an evening sky –

A little Purple – slipped between –
Some Ruby Trowsers – hurried on –
A Wave of Gold – a Bank of Day –
This just makes out the morning sky!

I should not dare to leave my friend,
Because – because if he should die
While I was gone – and I – too late –
Should reach the Heart that wanted me –

If I should disappoint the eyes
That hunted – hunted so – to see –
And could not bear to shut until
They "noticed" me – they noticed me –

If I should stab the patient faith
So sure I'd come – so sure I'd come –
It *listening* – listening – went to sleep –
Telling my tardy name –

My Heart would wish it broke before –
Since breaking then – since breaking then –
Were useless as next morning's sun –
Where midnight frosts – had lain!

The Flower must not blame the Bee –
That seeketh his felicity
Too often at her door –

o

A Slash of: *Sent to SD (variant) c. spring 1861*

But teach the Footman from Vevay –
Mistress is "not at home" – to say –
To people – any more!

Some – keep the Sabbath – going to church –[99]
I – keep it – staying at Home –
With a Bobolink – for a Chorister –
And an Orchard – for a Dome –

Some – keep the Sabbath, in Surplice –
I – just wear my wings –
And instead of tolling the bell, for church –
Our little Sexton – sings –

"God" – preaches – a *noted* Clergyman –
And the sermon is never long,
So – instead of getting to Heaven – at last –
I'm – going – all along!

Some – keep the: *Sent to TWH (variant) July 1861*

FASCICLE TEN

SHEET ONE c. second half of 1861

We – Bee and I – live by the quaffing –[100]
'Tisn't *all Hock* – with us –
Life has its *Ale* –
But it's many a lay of the Dim Burgundy –
We chant – for cheer – when the Wines – fail –

Do we "get drunk"?
Ask the jolly Clovers!
Do we "beat" our "Wife"?
I – never wed –
Bee – pledges *his* – in minute flagons –
Dainty – as the tress – on her deft Head –

While runs the Rhine –
He and I – revel –
First – at the Vat – and latest at the Vine –
Noon – our last Cup –
"Found dead" – "of Nectar" –
By a humming Coroner –
In a By-Thyme!

line 5: [it's] dim chat of Things Burgundy we know –

God permits industrious Angels –
Afternoons – to play –
I met one – forgot my schoolmates –
All – for Him – straightway –

God calls home – the Angels – promptly –
At the Setting Sun –

We – Bee and: *Sent to Ns (lost) c. 1861*

I missed mine – how *dreary* – *Marbles* –
After playing *Crown!*

The *Sun* – *just touched* the Morning
The *Morning* – Happy thing –
Supposed that He had come to *dwell* –
And Life would all be *Spring!*

She felt herself *supremer* –
A *Raised* – *Etherial Thing!*
Henceforth – for Her – *what Holiday!*
Meanwhile – Her wheeling King –
Trailed – slow – along the Orchards –
His *haughty* – *spangled* Hems –
Leaving a *new nescessity!*
The *want* of *Diadems!*

The Morning – *fluttered* – *staggered* –
Felt feebly – for Her *Crown* –
Her *unannointed forehead* –
Henceforth – Her *only* One!

The Lamp burns sure – within –
Tho' Serfs – supply the Oil –
It matters not the busy Wick –
At her phosphoric toil!

The Slave – forgets – to fill –
The Lamp – burns golden – on –
Unconscious that the oil is out –
As that the Slave – is gone.

SHEET TWO c. early 1861

Tho' my destiny be Fustian –[101]
Hers be damask fine –
Tho' she wear a silver apron –
I, a less divine –

○

Tho' my destiny: *Sent to EH (lost, transcribed variant) c. late summer 1860*

Still, my little Gipsey being
I would far prefer –
Still, my little sunburnt bosom
To her Rosier –

For, when Frosts, their punctual fingers
On her forehead lay,
You and I, and Dr Holland,
Bloom Eternally!

Roses of a steadfast summer
In a steadfast land –
Where no Autumn lifts her pencil –
And no Reapers stand!

Tho' I get home how late – how late –
So I get home – 'twill compensate –
Better will be the Extasy
That they have done expecting me –
When night – descending – dumb – and dark –
They hear my unexpected knock –
Transporting must the moment be –
Brewed from decades of Agony!

To think just how the fire will burn –
Just how long-cheated eyes will turn –
To wonder what myself will say,
And what itself, will say to me –
Beguiles the Centuries of way!

The Rose did caper on her cheek –
Her Boddice rose and fell –
Her pretty speech – like drunken men –
Did stagger pitiful –

Her fingers fumbled at her work –
Her needle would not go –
What ailed so smart a little maid –
It puzzled me to know –

Till opposite – I spied a cheek
That bore *another* Rose –
Just opposite – another speech
That like the Drunkard goes –

A Vest that like her Boddice, danced –
To the immortal tune –
Till those two troubled – little Clocks
Ticked softly into one.

⁓

With thee, in the Desert –
With thee in the thirst –
With thee in the Tamarind wood –
Leopard breathes – at last!

⁓

Faith is a fine invention[102]
For Gentlemen who *see* –
But *Microscopes* are prudent
In an Emergency!

⁓

The thought beneath so slight a film –
Is more distinctly seen –
As laces just reveal the surge –
Or Mists – the Appenine –

⁓

SHEET THREE c. early 1861

I'll tell you how the Sun rose –[103]
A Ribbon at a time!
The Steeples swam in Amethyst!
The news like squirrels ran!

The hills untied their Bonnets!
The Bobolinks begun!
Then I said softly to myself
"That must have been the sun"!

o

Faith is a: *Sent to SB (variant) c. early 1861*
I'll tell you: *Sent to TWH (variant) 15 April 1862*

But how he *set*, I know not!
There seemed a purple stile
Which little yellow boys and girls
Were Climbing all the while –

Till when they reached the other side,
A Dominie in gray
Put gently up the evening bars
And led the flock away!

~

A little Bread – A crust – a crumb –
A little trust – a demijohn –
Can keep the soul alive –
Not portly, mind! but breathing – warm –
Conscious – as old Napoleon,
The night before the crown!

A modest lot – A fame petite –
A brief Campaign of sting and sweet
Is plenty! Is enough!
A *Sailor's* business is *the shore!*
A *soldier's* – *balls!* Who asketh more,
Must seek the neighboring life!

~

Just lost, when I was saved![104]
Just felt the world go by!
Just girt me for the onset with Eternity,
When breath blew back,
And on the other side
I heard recede the disappointed tide!

Therefore, as One returned, I feel,
Odd secrets of the line to tell!
Some Sailor, skirting foreign shores –
Some pale Reporter, from the awful doors
Before the Seal!

Next time, to stay!
Next time, the things to see

A little Bread –: *Sent to SD (variant) c. second half of 1860*
Just lost, when: *Sent to SD (variant) c. late summer 1860*

By ear unheard –
Unscrutinized by eye –

Next time, to tarry,
While the Ages steal –
Slow tramp the Centuries,
And the Cycles wheel!

~

Come slowly – Eden![105]
Lips unused to Thee –
Bashful – sip thy Jessamines –
As the fainting Bee –

Reaching late his flower,
Round her chamber hums –
Counts his nectars –
Enters – and is lost in Balms.

~

Least Rivers – docile to some sea.[106]
My Caspian – thee.

~

SHEET FOUR c. second half of 1861

One life of so much consequence![107]
Yet I – for it – would pay –
My soul's *entire income* –
In ceaseless – salary –

One Pearl – to me – so signal – [*Pearl* –] Of such proportion
That I would instant dive –
Although – I *knew* – to *take* it –
Would *cost* me – *just a life!*

The Sea is full – I know it!
That – does not blur *my Gem!*
It burns – distinct from all the row –
Intact – in Diadem!

○

The life is thick – I know it!
Yet – not so dense a crowd –
But *Monarchs* – are *perceptible* –
Far down the dustiest Road!

~

You're right – "the way *is* narrow" –[108]
And "difficult the Gate" –
And "few there be" – Correct again –
That "enter in – thereat" –

'*Tis* Costly – So are *purples!*
'Tis just the price of *Breath* –
With but the "Discount" of *the Grave* –
Termed by the *Brokers* – *"Death"!*

And after *that* – there's Heaven –
The *Good* man's – *"Dividend"* –
And *Bad* men – "go to Jail" –
I guess –

~

Safe in their Alabaster chambers –[109]
Untouched by Morning –
And untouched by Noon –
Lie the meek members of the Resurrection –
Rafter of Satin – and Roof of Stone!

Grand go the Years – in the Crescent – above them –
Worlds scoop their Arcs –
And Firmaments – row –
Diadems – drop – and Doges – surrender –
Soundless as dots – on a Disc of snow –

—

Springs – shake the sills –
But – the Echoes – stiffen –
Hoar – is the window –
And – numb – the door –
Tribes – of Eclipse – in Tents – of Marble –
Staples – of Ages – have buckled – there –

—
o

Safe in their: *Sent to SD (lost) presumably c. late 1859 and twice (variant) c. 1861; sent to TWH (variant) 15 April 1862*

Springs – shake the seals –
But the silence – stiffens –
Frosts unhook – in the Northern Zones –
Icicles – crawl from polar Caverns –
Midnight in Marble –
Refutes – the Suns –

~

SHEET FIVE c. second half of 1861

The Court is far away –
No Umpire – have I –
My Sovreign is offended –
To gain his grace – I'd die!

I'll seek his royal feet –
I'll say – Remember – King –
Thou shalt – thyself – one day – a Child –
Implore a *larger* – thing –

That Empire – is of Czars –
As small – they say – as I –
Grant *me* – that day – the royalty –
To *intercede* – for *Thee* –

~

If *He dissolve* – then – there is *nothing* – *more* –[110]
Eclipse – at *Midnight* –
It was *dark* – *before* –

Sunset – at *Easter* –
Blindness – on the *Dawn* –
Faint Star of Bethleem –
Gone down!

Would but some *God* – *inform* Him –
Or it be *too late!*
Say – that the pulse *just lisps* –
The *Chariots wait* –

Say – that a *little life* – for *His* –
Is *leaking* – *red* –

His little Spaniel – tell Him!
Will He heed?

⁓

I think just how my shape will rise –[111]
When I shall be *"forgiven"* –
Till Hair – and Eyes – and timid Head –
Are *out of sight* – in Heaven –

I think just how my lips will weigh –
With shapeless – quivering – prayer –
That you – *so late* – *"consider" me* –
The *"sparrow"* of your care –

I mind me that of Anguish – sent –
Some drifts were moved away –
Before my simple bosom – broke –
And why not *this* – if *they?*

And so I con that thing – *"forgiven"* –
Until – delirious – borne –
By my long bright – and *longer* – *trust* –
I *drop* my Heart – *unshriven!*

⁓

I've nothing Else – to bring, You know –
So I keep bringing These –
Just as the Night keeps fetching Stars
To our familiar eyes –

Maybe, we shouldn't mind them –
Unless they didn't come –
Then – maybe, it would puzzle us
To find our way Home –

⁓

I've nothing Else –: *Sent to SB (variant) c. spring 1861*

FASCICLE ELEVEN

SHEET ONE c. late 1861

A Mien to move a Queen –[112]
Half Child – Half Heroine –
An Orleans in the Eye
That puts its manner by
For humbler Company
When none are near
Even a Tear –
Its frequent Visitor –

A Bonnet like a Duke –
And yet a Wren's Peruke
Were not so shy
Of Goer by –
And Hands – so slight,
They would elate a sprite
With merriment –

A Voice that alters – Low
And on the ear can go   [ear] doth
Like Let of Snow –
Or shift supreme –
As tone of Realm
On Subjects Diadem –
Too small – to fear –
Too distant – to endear –
And so Men Compromise –   And Men – too Brigadier –
And just – revere –

The Drop, that wrestles in the Sea –[113]
Forgets her own locality
As I, in Thee –

She knows herself an Offering small – [an] incense
Yet small, she sighs, if all, is all,
How larger – be?

The Ocean, smiles at her conceit –
But she, forgetting Amphitrite –
Pleads "Me"?

The Robin's my Criterion for Tune –[114]
Because I grow – where Robins do –
But, were I Cuckoo born –
I'd swear by him –
The ode familiar – rules the Noon –
The Buttercup's, my whim for Bloom –
Because, we're Orchard sprung –
But, were I Britain born,
I'd Daisies spurn – [I'd] Clovers – scorn –

None but the Nut – October fit –
Because – through dropping it,
The Seasons flit – I'm taught –
Without the Snow's Tableau
Winter, were lie – to me –
Because I see – New Englandly –
The Queen, discerns like me –
Provincially –

I've known a Heaven, like a Tent –[115]
To wrap its shining Yards –
Pluck up its stakes, and disappear –
Without the sound of Boards
Or Rip of Nail – Or Carpenter –
But just the miles of Stare –

The Drop, that: *Sent to SB (variant) c. second half of 1861*

That signalize a Show's Retreat –
In North America –

No Trace – no Figment – of the Thing
That dazzled, Yesterday,
No Ring – no Marvel –
Men, and Feats –
Dissolved as utterly –
As Bird's far Navigation
Discloses just a Hue –
A plash of Oars, a Gaiety –
Then swallowed up, of View.

LEAF TWO c. late 1861

I came to buy a smile – today –[116]
But just a single smile –
The smallest one upon your cheek – [your] face
Will suit me just as well –
The one that no one else would miss
It shone so very small –
I'm pleading at the counter – sir –
Could you afford to sell?

I've Diamonds – on my fingers!
You know what Diamonds – are!
I've Rubies – like the Evening Blood –
And Topaz – like the star!
'Twould be a bargain for a Jew!
Say? May I have it – Sir?

LEAF THREE c. late 1861

A Clock stopped –[117]
Not the Mantel's –
Geneva's farthest skill
Can't put the puppet bowing –
That just now dangled still –

o

I came to: *Sent to SB (variant) c. second half of 1861*

An awe came on the Trinket!
The Figures hunched – with pain –
Then quivered out of Decimals –
Into Degreeless noon –

It will not stir for Doctors –
This Pendulum of snow –
The Shopman importunes it –
While cool – concernless No –

Nods from the Gilded pointers – stares [from]
Nods from the Seconds slim –
Decades of Arrogance between
The Dial life –
And Him –

LEAF FOUR c. late 1861

I'm Nobody! Who are you?[118]
Are you – Nobody – too?
Then there's a pair of us!
Don't tell! they'd banish us – you know! [they'd] *advertise*

How dreary – to be – Somebody!
How public – like a Frog –
To tell your name – the livelong June – [To tell] *one's*
To an admiring Bog!

I held a Jewel in my fingers –
And went to sleep –
The day was warm, and winds were prosy –
I said "'Twill keep" –

I woke – and chid my honest fingers,
The Gem was gone –
And now, an Amethyst remembrance
Is all I own –

LEAF FIVE c. summer 1861

It is easy to work when the soul is at play –
But when the soul is in pain –
The hearing him put his playthings up
Makes work difficult – then –

It is simple, to ache in the Bone, or the Rind –
But Gimblets – among the nerve –
Mangle daintier – terribler –
Like a Panther in the Glove –

That after Horror – that 'twas *us* –
That passed the mouldering Pier –
Just as the Granite crumb let go –
Our Savior, by a Hair –

A second more, had dropped too deep
For Fisherman to plumb –
The very profile of the Thought
Puts Recollection numb –

The possibility – to pass
Without a moment's Bell –
Into Conjecture's presence –
Is like a Face of Steel –
That suddenly looks into ours
With a metallic grin –
The Cordiality of Death –
Who drills his Welcome in – [Who] nails

SHEET SIX c. late 1861

Ah, Moon, and Star![119]
You are very far –
But were no one
Farther than you –
Do you think I'd stop
For a Firmament –
Or a Cubit – or so?

That after Horror –: *Sent to TWH (third stanza, variant) c. late 1862*

I could borrow a Bonnet
Of the Lark –
And a Chamois' silver Boot –
And a stirrup of an Antelope –
And be with you – tonight!

But, Moon, and Star,
Though you're very far –
There is one – farther than you –
He – is more than a firmament – from me –
So I can never go!

Just so – Christ – raps –
He – doesn't weary –
First at the Knocker –
And then – at the Bell –
Then – on Divinest tiptoe standing –
Might he but spy the hiding soul!

When he – retires –
Chilled – or weary –
It will be ample time for me –
Patient – upon the steps – until then – [the] *mat*
Heart – I am knocking low
At thee!

Forever at His side to walk –
The smaller of the two!
Brain of His Brain –
Blood of His Blood –
Two lives – One Being – now –

Forever of His fate to taste –
If grief – the largest part –
If joy – to put my piece away
For that beloved Heart –

All life – to know each other
Whom we can never learn –

Just so – Christ –: *Sent to SD (variant) c. second half of 1861, beginning "Just so – Jesus – raps –"*

And bye and bye – a Change –
Called Heaven –
Rapt neighborhoods of men –
Just finding out – what puzzled us –
Without the lexicon!

~

It can't be "Summer"![120]
That – got through!
It's early – yet – for "Spring"!
There's that long town of White – to cross –
Before the Blackbirds sing!
It can't be "Dying"!
It's too Rouge –
The Dead shall go in white –
So Sunset shuts my question down
With Cuffs of Chrysolite!

~

SHEET SEVEN c. late 1861

What would I give to see his face?[121]
I'd give – I'd give my life – of course –
But *that* is not enough!
Stop just a minute – let me think!
I'd give my biggest Bobolink!
That makes *two* – *Him* – and *Life!*
You know who "*June*" is –
I'd give *her* –
Roses a day from Zinzebar –
And Lily tubes – like wells –
Bees – by the furlong –
Straits of Blue –
Navies of Butterflies – sailed thro' –
And dappled Cowslip Dells –

Then I have "shares" in Primrose "Banks" –
Daffodil Dowries – spicy "stocks" –
Dominions – broad as Dew –

It can't be: *Sent to Catherine Scott Turner (Anthon) (lost, transcribed variant) late October 1861, with three clover heads and some autumn leaves*

Bags of Doubloons – adventurous Bees
Brought me – from firmamental seas –
And Purple – from Peru –

Now – have I bought it –
"Shylock"? Say!
Sign me the Bond!
"I vow to pay
To Her – who pledges *this* –
One hour – of her Sovreign's face"!
Extatic Contract!
Niggard Grace!
My *Kingdom's worth* of Bliss!

Rearrange a "Wife's" Affection![122]
When they dislocate my Brain!
Amputate my freckled Bosom!
Make me bearded like a man!

Blush, my spirit, in thy Fastness –
Blush, my unacknowledged clay –
Seven years of troth have taught thee
More than Wifehood ever may!

Love that never leaped its socket –
Trust entrenched in narrow pain –
Constancy thro' fire – awarded –
Anguish – bare of anodyne!

Burden – borne so far triumphant –
None suspect me of the crown,
For I wear the "Thorns" till *Sunset* –
Then – my Diadem put on.

Big my Secret but it's *bandaged* –
It will never get away
Till the Day its Weary Keeper
Leads it through the Grave to thee.

Harriet Graves and MLT

SHEET EIGHT c. late 1861

Why – do they shut me out of Heaven?
Did I sing – too loud?
But – I can say a little "minor"
Timid as a Bird!

Wouldn't the Angels try me –
Just – once – more –
Just – see – if I troubled them –
But don't – shut the door!

Oh, if I – were the Gentleman
In the "White Robe" –
And they – were the little Hand – that knocked –
Could – I – forbid?

Wild nights – Wild nights!
Were I with thee
Wild nights should be
Our luxury!

Futile – the winds –
To a Heart in port –
Done with the Compass –
Done with the Chart!

Rowing in Eden –
Ah – the Sea!
Might I but moor – tonight –
In thee!

I shall keep singing!
Birds will pass me
On their way to Yellower Climes –
Each – with a Robin's expectation –
I – with my Redbreast –
And my Rhymes –

o

Late – when I take my place in summer –
But – I shall bring a fuller tune –
Vespers – are sweeter than matins – Signor –
Morning – only the seed – of noon –

Over the fence –
Strawberries – grow –
Over the fence –
I could climb – if I tried, I know –
Berries are nice!

But – if I stained my Apron –
God would certainly scold!
Oh, dear, – I guess if He were a Boy –
He'd – climb – if He could!

FASCICLE TWELVE

SHEET ONE c. early 1861

I taste a liquor never brewed –[123]
From Tankards scooped in Pearl –
Not all the Frankfort Berries
Yield such an Alcohol!

[the] Vats upon the Rhine

Inebriate of air – am I –
And Debauchee of Dew –
Reeling – thro' endless summer days –
From inns of molten Blue –

When "Landlords" turn the drunken Bee
Out of the Foxglove's door –
When Butterflies – renounce their "drams" –
I shall but drink the more!

Till Seraphs swing their snowy Hats –
And Saints – to windows run –
To see the little Tippler
From Manzanilla come!

Leaning against the – Sun –

Pine Bough.
A feather from the Whippowil
That everlasting sings –
Whose Galleries are Sunrise –
Whose Stanzas, are the Springs –

Whose Emerald Nest – the Ages spin –
With mellow – murmuring Thread –
Whose Beryl Egg, what School Boys hunt –
In "Recess", Overhead!

I taste a: *Sent to unidentified recipient, perhaps SD (lost) c. early 1861*
A feather from: *Sent to SB (variant) c. early 1861, with a sprig of white pine*

I lost a World – the other day![124]
Has Anybody found?
You'll know it by the Row of Stars
Around its forehead bound!

A Rich man – might not notice it –
Yet – to my frugal Eye,
Of more Esteem than Ducats –
Oh find it – Sir – for me!

If I shouldn't be alive
When the Robins come,
Give the one in Red Cravat,
A Memorial crumb –

If I couldn't thank you,
Being fast asleep,
You will know I'm trying
With my Granite lip!

I've heard an Organ talk, sometimes –
In a Cathedral Aisle,
And understood no word it said –
Yet held my breath, the while –

And risen up – and gone away,
A more Bernardine Girl –
Yet – knew not what was done to me
In that old Chapel Aisle.

A transport one cannot contain[125]
May yet, a transport be –
Though God forbid it lift the lid,
Unto its Extasy!

A Diagram – of Rapture!
A sixpence at a show –

With Holy Ghosts in Cages!
The *Universe* would go!

"Faith" is a fine invention[126]
For Gentlemen who *see!*
But Microscopes are prudent
In an Emergency!

SHEET TWO c. early 1862

I got so I could hear his name – [127] — [could] think – • *take* –
Without – Tremendous gain –
That Stop-sensation – on my Soul –
And Thunder – in the Room –

I got so I could walk across
That Angle in the floor,
Where he turned so, and I turned – how – — [I] let go –
And all our Sinew tore –

I got so I could stir the Box –
In which his letters grew
Without that forcing, in my breath –
As Staples – driven through –

Could dimly recollect a Grace – — [a] Force
I think, they called it "God" –
Renowned to ease Extremity – — [Renowned] to stir – Extremity –
When Formula, had failed – — [When] Filament – had failed –

And shape my Hands –
Petition's way,
Tho' ignorant of a word
That Ordination – utters –

My Business – with the Cloud,
If any Power behind it, be,
Not subject to Despair – — Supremer than – • Superior to – [Despair –]
It care – in some remoter way,
For so minute affair

"Faith" is a: *Sent to SB (variant) c. early 1861*

As Misery –
Itself, too great, for interrupting – more – [too] *vast*

~

A single Screw of Flesh
Is all that pins the Soul
That stands for Deity, to mine,
Upon my side the Vail –

Once witnessed of the Gauze –
Its name is put away
As far from mine, as if no plight
Had printed yesterday,

In tender – solemn Alphabet,
My eyes just turned to see,
When it was smuggled by my sight
Into Eternity –

More Hands – to hold – These are but Two –
One more new-mailed Nerve
Just granted, for the Peril's sake –
Some striding – Giant – Love –

So greater than the Gods can show,
They slink before the Clay,
That not for all their Heaven can boast
Will let its Keepsake – go

~

A Weight with Needles on the pounds –
To push, and pierce, besides –
That if the Flesh resist the Heft –
The puncture – Coolly tries –

That not a pore be overlooked
Of all this Compound Frame –
As manifold for Anguish –
As Species – be – for name.

~

SHEET THREE c. early 1862

Father – I bring thee – not myself –[128]
That were the little load –
I bring thee the departed Heart — [the] imperial
I had not strength to hold – — [not] power

The Heart I cherished in my own
Till mine – too heavy grew –
Yet – strangest – heavier – since it went –
Is it too large for you?

~

Where Ships of Purple – gently toss –
On Seas of Daffodil –
Fantastic Sailors – mingle –
And then – the Wharf is still!

~

This – is the land – the Sunset washes –[129]
These – are the Banks of the Yellow Sea –
Where it rose – or whither it rushes –
These – are the Western Mystery!

Night after Night
Her Purple traffic
Strews the landing – with Opal Bales –
Merchantmen – poise upon Horizons –
Dip – and vanish like Orioles!

~

The Doomed – regard the Sunrise
With different Delight –
Because – when next it burns abroad
They doubt to witness it –

The Man – to die – tomorrow –
Harks for the Meadow Bird – — Detects [the]
Because its Music stirs the Axe
That clamors for his head –

o

Father – I bring: *Sent to SD in a longer version c. early 1862, beginning "Savior! I've no one else to tell –"*

Jesus! thy Crucifix
Enable thee to guess
The smaller size!

Jesus! thy second face
Mind thee in Paradise
Of our's!

Did we disobey Him?
Just one time!
Charged us to forget Him,
But we couldn't learn!

Were Himself - such a Dunce -
What would we - do?
Love the dull lad - best -
Oh 'wouldn't you?

"Jesus! thy Crucifix" and "Did we disobey Him?"

Joyful – to whom the Sunrise
Precedes Enamored – Day –
Joyful – for whom the Meadow Bird
Has ought but Elegy!

~

Jesus! thy Crucifix
Enable thee to guess
The smaller size!

Jesus! thy second face
Mind thee in Paradise
Of ours!

~

Did we disobey Him?
Just one time!
Charged us to forget Him –
But we couldn't learn!

Were Himself – such a Dunce –
What would we – do?
Love the dull lad – best –
Oh, wouldn't you?

~

LEAF FOUR c. early 1862

Unto like Story – Trouble has enticed me –[130]
How Kinsmen fell –
Brothers and Sisters – who preferred the Glory –
And their young will
Bent to the Scaffold, or in Dungeons – chanted – [Dungeons –] waited –
Till God's full time – [God's] whole – will –
When they let go the ignominy – smiling –
And Shame went still – [And] Scorn [went] dumb.

Unto guessed Crests, my moaning fancy, leads me, [fancy] lures,
Worn fair
By Heads rejected – in the lower country –
Of honors there –

Jesus! thy Crucifix: *Sent to SB (variant) c. late 1861*

Such spirit makes her perpetual mention, Some – [spirit]
That I – grown bold – till [I]
Step martial – at my Crucifixion –
As Trumpets – rolled –

Feet, small as mine – have marched in Revolution
Firm to the Drum –
Hands – not so stout – hoisted them – in witness –
When Speech went numb –
Let me not shame their sublime deportments –
Drilled bright –
Beckoning – Etruscan invitation –
Toward Light – to – [Light –]

SHEET FIVE c. early 1862

One Year ago – jots what?
God – spell the word! I – can't –
Was't Grace? Not that –
Was't Glory? That – will do – [Glory?] 'Twas just you –
Spell slower – Glory –

Such anniversary shall be –
Sometimes – not often – in Eternity –
When farther Parted, than the common Wo – [When] sharper
Look – feed upon each other's faces – so –
In doubtful meal, if it be possible
Their Banquet's real – [Banquet's] *True*

I tasted – careless – then –
I did not know the Wine
Came once a World – Did you?
Oh, had you told me so –
This Thirst would blister – easier – now –
You said it hurt you – most –
Mine – was an Acorn's Breast –
And could not know how fondness grew
In Shaggier Vest –
Perhaps – I couldn't –
But, had you looked in –

A Giant – eye to eye with you, had been –
No Acorn – then –

So – Twelve months ago –
We breathed –
Then dropped the Air – [Then] lost
Which bore it best?
Was this – the patientest –
Because it was a Child, you know –
And could not value – Air?

If to be "Elder" – mean most pain –
I'm old enough, today, I'm certain – then –
As old as thee – how soon?
One – Birthday more – or Ten?
Let me – choose!
Ah, Sir, None!

~

It's like the Light –
A fashionless Delight –
It's like the Bee –
A dateless – Melody –

It's like the Woods –
Private – Like the Breeze –
Phraseless – yet it stirs
The proudest Trees –

It's like the morning –
Best – when it's done –
And the Everlasting Clocks –
Chime – Noon! Strike – [Noon!]

~

Alone, I cannot be –
The Hosts – do visit me – *for* – [Hosts]
Recordless Company –
Who baffle Key –

○

They have no Robes, nor Names –
No Almanacs – nor Climes –
But general Homes
Like Gnomes –

Their Coming, may be known
By Couriers within –
Their going – is not –
For they're never gone –

SHEET SIX c. early 1862

He put the Belt around my life –[131]
I heard the Buckle snap –
And turned away, imperial, — And left his process – satisfied –
My Lifetime folding up –
Deliberate, as a Duke would do
A Kingdom's Title Deed –
Henceforth – a Dedicated sort –
A Member of the Cloud –

Yet not too far to come at call – — Yet, near enough – [to]
And do the little Toils
That make the Circuit of the Rest –
And deal occasional smiles
To lives that stoop to notice mine – — [lives] As stoop –
And kindly ask it in –
Whose invitation, know you not — [invitation,] For this world –
For Whom I must decline?

The only Ghost I ever saw[132]
Was dressed in Mechlin – so –
He had no sandal on his foot – — [He] wore –
And stepped like flakes of snow –
His Mien, was soundless, like the Bird – — [His] Gait – [was soundless, like] a –
But rapid – like the Roe –
His fashions, quaint, Mosaic –
Or haply, Mistletoe –

o

His conversation – seldom –
His laughter, like the Breeze
That dies away in Dimples
Among the pensive Trees –   [the] smiling –

Our interview – was transient –
Of me, himself was shy –
And God forbid I look behind –
Since that appalling Day!

SHEET SEVEN c. early 1862

Doubt Me! My Dim Companion!   [My] faint Companion –
Why, God, would be content
With but a fraction of the Life –   [fraction] Of the love –
Poured thee, without a stint –
The whole of me – forever –
What more the Woman can,
Say quick, that I may dower thee   [quick,] so I can –
With last Delight I own!   [With] least Delight –

It cannot be my spirit –
For that was thine, before –
I ceded all of Dust I knew –
What Opulence the more
Had I – a freckled Maiden,
Whose farthest of Degree,
Was – that she might –
Some distant Heaven,
Dwell timidly – with thee!

Sift her, from Brow to Barefoot!
Strain till your last Surmise –   [till] ~~her~~
Drop, like a Tapestry, away,
Before the Fire's Eyes –
Winnow her finest fondness –
But hallow just the snow
Intact, in Everlasting flake –
Oh, Caviler, for you!

Many a phrase has the English language –[133]
I have heard but one –
Low as the laughter of the Cricket,
Loud, as the Thunder's Tongue –

Murmuring, like old Caspian Choirs,
When the Tide's a'lull –
Saying itself in new inflection –
Like a Whippowil –

Breaking in bright Orthography
On my simple sleep –
Thundering its Prospective –
Till I stir, and weep – [I] Grope – • start –

Not for the Sorrow, done me –
But the push of Joy – [the] Pain of joy –
Say it again, Saxon!
Hush – Only to me!

SHEET EIGHT c. early 1862

Of all the Sounds despatched abroad –
There's not a charge to me
Like that old measure in the Boughs
That phraseless Melody –
The Wind does – working like a Hand
Whose fingers brush the Sky – [fingers] *comb*
Then quiver down – with Tufts of Tune –
Permitted men – and me – [Permitted] *Gods*

Inheritance it is – to us –
Beyond the Art to Earn –
Beyond the trait to take away –
By Robber – since the Gain
Is gotten, not with fingers –
And inner than the Bone –
Hid golden – for the whole of Days –
And even in the Urn –
I cannot vouch the merry Dust

Of all the: *Sent to TWH (variant) 25 April 1862 and to SD (variant) c. early 1863*

Do not arise and play –
In some odd fashion of its own –
Some quainter Holiday –

When Winds go round and round, in Bands –
And thrum upon the Door –
And Birds take places – Overhead –
To bear them Orchestra –

I crave him grace – of Summer Boughs –
If such an Outcast be –
He never heard that fleshless Chant
Rise solemn, in the Tree –
As if some Caravan of sound
On Deserts, in the sky
Had broken Rank –
Then knit – and passed – [and] *swept*
In Seamless Company –

Her smile was shaped like other smiles –
The Dimples ran along –
And still it hurt you, as some Bird
Did hoist herself, to sing,
Then recollect a Ball, she got –
And hold upon the Twig,
Convulsive, while the Music crashed – [Music] *broke*
Like Beads – among the Bog –

A happy lip – breaks sudden –
It doesn't state you how
It contemplated – smiling –
Just consummated – now –
But this one, wears its merriment
So patient – like a pain –
Fresh gilded – to elude the eyes
Unqualified, to scan –

FASCICLE THIRTEEN

SHEET ONE c. early 1862

I know some lonely Houses off the Road
A Robber'd like the look of –
Wooden barred,
And Windows hanging low,
Inviting to –
A Portico,
Where two could creep –
One – hand the Tools –
The other peep –
To make sure all's asleep – [To] Guage the Sleep –
Old fashioned eyes –
Not easy to surprise!

How orderly the Kitchen'd look, by night –
With just a Clock –
But they could gag the Tick –
And Mice won't bark –
And so the Walls – don't tell –
None – will –

A pair of Spectacles ajar just stir –
An Almanac's aware –
Was it the Mat – winked,
Or a nervous Star?
The Moon – slides down the stair –
To see who's there!

There's plunder – where –
Tankard, or Spoon –
Earring – or Stone –
A Watch – Some Ancient Brooch [Some] Antique –

I know some: *Sent to SD (lost) c. 1862*

To match the Grandmama –
Staid sleeping – there –

Day – rattles – too –
Stealth's – slow –
The Sun has got as far
As the third Sycamore –
Screams Chanticleer
"Who's there"?

And Echoes – Trains away,
Sneer – "Where"!
While the old Couple, just astir,
Fancy the Sunrise – left the door ajar!

I can wade Grief –
Whole Pools of it –
I'm used to that –
But the least push of Joy
Breaks up my feet –
And I tip – drunken –
Let no Pebble – smile –
'Twas the New Liquor –
That was all!

Power is only Pain –
Stranded – thro' Discipline,
Till Weights – will hang –
Give Balm – to Giants –
And they'll wilt, like Men –
Give Himmaleh –
They'll carry – Him!

SHEET TWO c. early 1862

You see I cannot see – your lifetime –
I must guess –
How many times it ache for me – today – Confess –

How many times for my far sake
The brave eyes film –
But I guess guessing hurts –
Mine – get so dim!

Too vague – the face –
My own – so patient – covets –
Too far – the strength –
My timidness enfolds –
Haunting the Heart –
Like her translated faces –
Teazing the want –
It – only – can suffice!

~

"Hope" is the thing with feathers –[134]
That perches in the soul –
And sings the tune without the words –
And never stops – at all –

And sweetest – in the Gale – is heard –
And sore must be the storm –
That could abash the little Bird
That kept so many warm –

I've heard it in the chillest land –
And on the strangest Sea –
Yet – never – in Extremity,
It asked a crumb – of me.

~

To die – takes just a little while –
They say it doesn't hurt –
It's only fainter – by degrees –
And then – it's out of sight –

A darker Ribbon – for a Day –
A Crape upon the Hat –
And then the pretty sunshine comes –
And helps us to forget –

○

"Hope" is the: *Sent to Ns (lost) c. 1862*

The absent – mystic – creature –
That but for love of us –
Had gone to sleep – that soundest time –
Without the weariness –

~

If I'm lost – now –[135]
That I was found –
Shall still my transport be –
That once – on me – those Jasper Gates
Blazed open – suddenly –

That in my awkward – gazing – face –
The Angels – softly peered –
And touched me with their fleeces,
Almost as if they cared –
I'm banished – now – you know it –
How foreign that can be –
You'll know – Sir – when the Savior's face
Turns so – away from you –

~

SHEET THREE c. early 1862

Delight is as the flight –
Or in the Ratio of it,
As the Schools would say –
The Rainbow's way –
A Skein
Flung colored, after Rain,
Would suit as bright,
Except that flight
Were Aliment –

"If it would last"
I asked the East,
When that Bent Stripe
Struck up my childish
Firmament –

And I, for glee,
Took Rainbows, as the common way,
And empty skies
The Eccentricity –

And so with Lives –
And so with Butterflies –
Seen magic – through the fright
That they will cheat the sight –
And Dower latitudes far on –
Some sudden morn –
Our portion – in the fashion –
Done –

~

She sweeps with many-colored Brooms –
And leaves the shreds behind –
Oh Housewife in the Evening West –
Come back – and – dust the Pond!

You dropped a Purple Ravelling in –
You dropped an Amber thread –
And now you've littered all the East
With Duds of Emerald!

And still, she plies her spotted Brooms –
And still the Aprons fly,
Till Brooms fade softly into stars –
And then I come away –

~

Of Bronze – and Blaze –
The North – tonight –
So adequate – it forms –
So preconcerted with itself –
So distant – to alarms –
An Unconcern so sovreign
To Universe, or me –
Infects my simple spirit
With Taints of Majesty –

She sweeps with: *Sent to SD (variant) c. 1865*

Till I take vaster attitudes – [vaster] manners
And strut upon my stem –
Disdaining Men, and Oxygen,
For Arrogance of them –

My Splendors, are Menagerie –
But their Competeless Show
Will entertain the Centuries
When I, am long ago,
An Island in dishonored Grass – some – [Island]
Whom none but Daisies, know – [but] Beetles –

~

There's a certain Slant of light,
Winter Afternoons –
That oppresses, like the Heft
Of Cathedral Tunes –

Heavenly Hurt, it gives us –
We can find no scar,
But internal difference –
Where the Meanings, are –

None may teach it – Any –
'Tis the Seal Despair –
An imperial affliction
Sent us of the Air –

When it comes, the Landscape listens –
Shadows – hold their breath –
When it goes, 'tis like the Distance
On the look of Death –

~

SHEET FOUR c. early 1862

Blazing in Gold – and[136]
Quenching – in Purple!
Leaping – like Leopards to the sky – [Leopards] ~~in~~
Then – at the feet of the old Horizon –
Laying its spotted face – to die!

○

Blazing in Gold –: *Sent to SD (lost) c. 1862 and to TWH (variant) 9 June 1866*

Stooping as low as the kitchen window –
Touching the Roof –
And tinting the Barn –
Kissing its Bonnet to the Meadow –
And the Juggler of Day – is gone!

Good Night! Which put the Candle out?[137]
A jealous Zephyr – not a doubt –
Ah, friend, you little knew
How long at that celestial wick
The Angels – labored diligent –
Extinguished – now – for you!

It might – have been the Light House spark –
Some Sailor – rowing in the Dark –
Had importuned to see!
It might – have been the Waning lamp
That lit the Drummer from the Camp
To purer Reveille!

Read – Sweet – how others – strove –
Till we – are stouter –
What they – renounced –
Till we – are less afraid –
How many times they – bore the faithful witness –
Till we – are helped –
As if a Kingdom – cared!

Read then – of faith –
That shone above the fagot –
Clear strains of Hymn
The River could not drown –
Brave names of Men –
And Celestial Women –
Passed out – of Record
Into – Renown!

Put up my lute![138]
What of – my Music!
Since the sole ear I cared to charm –
Passive – as Granite – laps my music –
Sobbing – will suit – as well as psalm!

Would but the "Memnon" of the Desert –
Teach me the strain
That vanquished Him –
When He – surrendered to the Sunrise –
Maybe – that – would awaken – them!

SHEET FIVE c. early 1862

There came a Day – at Summer's full –[139]
Entirely for me –
I thought that such – were for the Saints –
Where Resurrections – be – [Where] Revelations

The Sun – as common – went abroad –
The Flowers – accustomed – blew –
As if no Soul the Solstice passed – ~~While our two Souls that~~ [Solstice]
That maketh all things new. ~~Which~~ [maketh]

The time was scarce profaned – by speech –
The symbol of a word [The] ~~falling~~ • ~~figure~~ –
Was needless – as at Sacrament –
The Wardrobe – of Our Lord –

Each was to each – the sealed church –
Permitted to commune – this time –
Lest we too awkward – show –
At "Supper of the Lamb."

The hours slid fast – as hours will –
Clutched tight – by greedy hands –
So – faces on two Decks – look back –
Bound to opposing Lands –

And so – when all the time had failed – [had] ~~leaked~~
Without external sound –

There came a: *Sent to Reverend Edward S. Dwight (last stanza, variant) c. early January 1862, to TWH (variant) 25 April 1862, and to SD (lost) c. probably early 1862*

Each – bound the other's Crucifix –
We gave no other bond –

Sufficient troth – that we shall rise –
Deposed – at length – the Grave –
To *that* New Marriage –
Justified – through Calvaries of Love!

∽

The lonesome for they know not What –
The Eastern Exiles – be –
Who strayed beyond the Amber line
Some madder Holiday –

And ever since – the purple Moat
They strive to climb – in vain –
As Birds – that tumble from the clouds
Do fumble at the strain –

The Blessed Ether – taught them –
Some Transatlantic Morn –
When Heaven – was too common – to miss –
Too sure – to dote upon!

∽

SHEET SIX c. early 1862

How the old Mountains drip with Sunset[140]
How the Hemlocks burn –
How the Dun Brake is draped in Cinder
By the Wizard Sun –

[Brake] Is tipped in Tinsel
By the Setting Sun –

How the old Steeples hand the Scarlet
Till the Ball is full –
Have I the lip of the Flamingo
That I dare to tell?

Then, how the Fire ebbs like Billows –
Touching all the Grass
With a departing – Sapphire – feature –
As a Duchess passed –

o

How a small Dusk crawls on the Village
Till the Houses blot
And the odd Flambeau, no men carry
Glimmer on the Street –

How it is Night – in Nest and Kennel –
And where was the Wood –
Just a Dome of Abyss is Bowing
Into Solitude –

These are the Visions flitted Guido – [the] Fashions – baffled –
Titian – never told –
Domenichino dropped his pencil –
Paralyzed, with Gold – Powerless to unfold –

line 19: [Just a Dome of Abyss is] nodding • [Just] Acres of Masts are standing
line 20: back of Solitude • At the • after – • unto • next to – [Solitude]

Of Tribulation, these are They,[141]
Denoted by the White –
The Spangled Gowns, a lesser Rank
Of Victors – designate –

All these – did Conquer –
But the ones who overcame most times –
Wear nothing commoner than snow –
No Ornament, but Palms –

Surrender – is a sort unknown –
On this superior soil –
Defeat – an outgrown Anguish –
Remembered, as the Mile

Our panting Ancle barely passed – [barely] gained
When Night devoured the Road –
But we – stood whispering in the House –
And all we said – was "Saved"!

Of Tribulation, these: *Sent to TWH (variant) July 1862*

If your Nerve, deny you –
Go above your Nerve –
He can lean against the Grave,
If he fear to swerve –

That's a steady posture –
Never any bend [Never] one – [bend]
Held of those Brass arms –
Best Giant made –

If your Soul seesaw – [Soul] stagger
Lift the Flesh door –
The Poltroon wants Oxygen –
Nothing more –

FASCICLE FOURTEEN

SHEET ONE c. early 1862

The maddest dream – recedes – unrealized – [The] nearest
The Heaven we chase –
Like the June Bee – before the Schoolboy –
Invites the Race –

Stoops to an Easy Clover –
Dips – Evades –
Teazes – deploys –
Then – to the Royal Clouds –

Spreads his light pinnace – lifts [his]
Heedless of the Boy –
Staring – defrauded – at the mocking sky – [Staring –] bewildered

Homesick for steadfast Honey –
Ah, the Bee
Flies not – that brews
That rare variety!

What if I say I shall not wait![142]
What if I burst the fleshly Gate –
And pass Escaped – to thee!

What if I file this mortal – off –
See where it hurt me – That's enough –
And step in Liberty! [And] *wade*

They cannot take me – any more! [take] us
Dungeons can call – and Guns implore – [Dungeons] may
Unmeaning – now – to me –

o

The maddest dream –: *Sent to TWH (variant) 15 April 1862*

As laughter – was – an hour ago –
Or Laces – or a Travelling Show –
Or who died – yesterday!

Ah, Moon – and Star![143]
You are very far –
But – were no one farther than you –
Do you think I'd stop for a firmament –
Or a cubit – or so?

I could borrow a Bonnet – of the Lark –
And a Chamois' silver boot –
And a stirrup of an Antelope –
And leap to you – tonight!

But – Moon – and Star –
Though you're very far –
There is one – farther than you –
He – is more than a firmament – from me –
And I cannot go!

A Shady friend – for Torrid days –[144]
Is easier to find –
Than one of higher temperature
For Frigid – hour of mind –

The Vane a little to the East –
Scares Muslin souls – away –
If Broadcloth Hearts are firmer [Broadcloth] Breasts
Than those of Organdy –

Who is to blame?
The Weaver?
Ah, the bewildering thread!
The Tapestries of Paradise
So notelessly – are made!

SHEET TWO c. early 1862

A solemn thing – it was – I said –[145]
A Woman – white – to be –
And wear – if God should count me fit –
Her blameless mystery –

A timid thing – to drop a life — [A] *hallowed*
Into the mystic well – — [the] *purple*
Too plummetless – that it come back – — [it] *return*
Eternity – until –

I pondered how the bliss would look –
And would it feel as big –
When I could take it in my hand –
As hovering – seen – through fog – — [As] glimmering

And then – the size of this "small" life –
The Sages – call it small –
Swelled – like Horizons – in my breast – — [my] *vest*
And I sneered – softly – "small"!

~

I breathed enough to take the Trick –
And now, removed from Air –
I simulate the Breath, so well –
That One, to be quite sure –

The Lungs are stirless – must descend
Among the cunning cells –
And touch the Pantomime – Himself,
How numb, the Bellows feels! — [How] cool –

~

Kill your Balm – and its Odors bless you –
Bare your Jessamine – to the storm –
And she will fling her maddest perfume –
Haply – your Summer night to Charm –

Stab the Bird – that built in your bosom –
Oh, could you catch her last Refrain –

Bubble! "forgive" – "Some better" – Bubble!
"Carol for Him – when I am gone"!

"Heaven" – is what I cannot reach![146]
The Apple on the Tree –
Provided it do hopeless – hang –
That – "Heaven" is – to Me!

The Color, on the cruising cloud –
The interdicted Land –
Behind the Hill – the House behind –
There – Paradise – is found!

Her teazing Purples – Afternoons –
The credulous – decoy –
Enamored – of the Conjuror –
That spurned us – Yesterday!

LEAF THREE c. late summer 1858

The feet of people walking home[147]
With gayer sandals go –
The Crocus – till she rises
The Vassal of the snow –
The lips at Hallelujah
Long years of practise bore
Till bye and bye these Bargemen
Walked singing on the shore.

Pearls are the Diver's farthings
Extorted from the sea –
Pinions – the Seraph's wagon
Pedestrian once – as we –
Night is the morning's Canvas
Larceny – legacy –
Death, but our rapt attention
To Immortality.

My figures fail to tell me
How far the village lies –

The feet of: *Sent to SD (variant) c. early 1859*

Whose peasants are the angels –
Whose Cantons dot the skies –
My Classics vail their faces –
My faith that Dark adores –
Which from its solemn abbeys
Such resurrection pours.

SHEET FOUR c. autumn 1862

Inconceivably solemn!
Things so gay [Things] too
Pierce – by the very Press
Of Imagery –

Their far Parades – order on the eye [Parades –] halt [on]
With a mute Pomp –
A pleading Pageantry –

Flags, are a brave sight –
But no true Eye
Ever went by One –
Steadily –

Music's triumphant –
But the fine Ear [But] a
Winces with delight aches [with]
Are Drums too near – The Drums to hear –

More Life – went out – when He went[148]
Than Ordinary Breath –
Lit with a finer Phosphor –
Requiring in the Quench –

A Power of Renowned Cold,
The Climate of the Grave
A Temperature just adequate
So Anthracite, to live –

For some – an Ampler Zero –
A Frost more needle keen

Is nescessary, to reduce
The Ethiop within.

Others – extinguish easier –
A Gnat's minutest Fan
Sufficient to obliterate
A Tract of Citizen –

Whose Peat life – amply vivid –
Ignores the solemn News
That Popocatapel exists –
Or Etna's Scarlets, Choose –

~

The Months have ends – the Years – a knot –
No Power can untie
To stretch a little further
A Skein of Misery –

The Earth lays back these tired lives
In her mysterious Drawers –
Too tenderly, that any doubt
An ultimate Repose –

The manner of the Children –
Who weary of the Day –
Themself – the noisy Plaything
They cannot put away –

~

Removed from Accident of Loss[149]
By Accident of Gain
Befalling not my simple Days –
Myself had just to earn –

Of Riches – as unconscious
As is the Brown Malay
Of Pearls in Eastern Waters –
Marked His – What Holiday

Would stir his slow conception –
Had he the power to dream

That but the Dower's fraction –
Awaited even – Him –

SHEET FIVE c. autumn 1862

Your Riches – taught me – Poverty.[150]
Myself – a Millionaire
In little Wealths, as Girls could boast
Till broad as Buenos Ayre –

You drifted your Dominions –
A Different Peru –
And I esteemed all Poverty
For Life's Estate with you –

Of Mines, I little know, myself –
But just the names, of Gems –
The Colors of the Commonest –
And scarce of Diadems –

So much, that did I meet the Queen –
Her Glory I should know –
But this, must be a different Wealth –
To miss it – beggars so –

I'm sure 'tis India – all Day –
To those who look on You –
Without a stint – without a blame,
Might I – but be the Jew –

I'm sure it is Golconda –
Beyond my power to deem –
To have a smile for mine – each Day,
How better, than a Gem!

At least, it solaces to know
That there exists – a Gold –
Altho' I prove it, just in time
Its distance – to behold –

Its far – far Treasure to surmise –
And estimate the Pearl –

Your Riches – taught: *Sent to SD (variant) c. 1862 and to TWH (variant) July 1862*

That slipped my simple fingers through –
While just a Girl at school.

A Toad, can die of Light –[151]
Death is the Common Right   [is the] mutual – • equal –
Of Toads and Men –
Of Earl and Midge
The privilege –
Why swagger, then?
The Gnat's supremacy is large as Thine –

Life – is a different Thing –   [is] Another [Thing –]
So measure Wine –
Naked of Flask – Naked of Cask –
Bare Rhine –
Which Ruby's mine?

There are two Ripenings –[152]
One – of Sight – whose Forces spheric round   [spheric] *wind*
Until the Velvet Product
Drop, spicy, to the Ground –

A Homelier – maturing –
A Process in the Bur –
Which Teeth of Frosts, alone disclose –   That Teeth [of]
In still October Air –   [In] far – • on far – [October]

SHEET SIX c. autumn 1862

It ceased to hurt me, though so slow
I could not see the trouble go –   [not] feel – [the] Anguish – [go]
But only knew by looking back –
That something – had obscured the Track –   [had] *benumbed*

Nor when it altered, I could say,
For I had worn it, every day,
As constant as the Childish frock –   [Childish] ~~Gown~~
I hung upon the Peg, at night.

o

There are two: *Sent to Catherine Scott Turner (Anthon) (lost, transcribed variant) c. 1862*

But not the Grief – that nestled Close
As Needles – ladies softly press
To Cushions Cheeks –
To keep their place –

Nor what consoled it, I could trace –
Except, whereas 'twas Wilderness –
It's better – almost Peace –

~

Give little Anguish,[153]
Lives will fret –
Give Avalanches,
And they'll slant,

Straighten – look cautious for their breath –
But make no syllable, like Death –
Who only shows his Granite face –
Sublimer thing – than Speech – [Sublimer] way –

~

Give little Anguish,: *Sent to SD (variant) c. early 1863*

FASCICLE FIFTEEN

SHEET ONE c. autumn 1862

The first Day's Night had come –
And grateful that a thing
So terrible – had been endured –
I told my Soul to sing –

She said her strings were snapt –
Her Bow – to atoms blown –
And so to mend her – gave me work
Until another Morn –

And then – a Day as huge
As Yesterdays in pairs,
Unrolled its horror in my face –
Until it blocked my eyes –

My Brain – begun to laugh –
I mumbled – like a fool –
And tho' 'tis Years ago – that Day –
My Brain keeps giggling – still.

And Something's odd – within –
That person that I was –
And this One – do not feel the same –
Could it be Madness – this?

The Color of the Grave is Green –[154]
The Outer Grave – I mean –
You would not know it from the Field –
Except it own a Stone –

To help the fond – to find it –
Too infinite asleep

To stop and tell them where it is –
But just a Daisy – deep –

The Color of the Grave is white –
The outer Grave – I mean –
You would not know it from the Drifts –
In Winter – till the Sun –

Has furrowed out the Aisles –
Then – higher than the Land
The little Dwelling Houses rise
Where Each – has left a friend –

The Color of the Grave within –
The Duplicate – I mean –
Not all the snows c'd make it white –
Not all the Summers – Green –

You've seen the Color – maybe –
Upon a Bonnet bound –
When that you met it with before –
The Ferret – Cannot find –

SHEET TWO c. autumn 1862

'Twas like a Maelstrom, with a notch,
That nearer, every Day,
Kept narrowing its boiling Wheel
Until the Agony

Toyed coolly with the final inch
Of your delirious Hem –
And you dropt, lost,
When something broke –
And let you from a Dream –

As if a Goblin with a Guage –
Kept measuring the Hours –
Until you felt your Second
Weigh, helpless, in his Paws –

o

And not a Sinew – stirred – could help,
And Sense was setting numb –
When God – remembered – and the Fiend
Let go, then, Overcome –

As if your Sentence stood – pronounced –
And you were frozen led
From Dungeon's luxury of Doubt
To Gibbets, and the Dead –

And when the Film had stitched your eyes
A Creature gasped "Reprieve"!
Which Anguish was the utterest – then –
To perish, or to live?

I gave myself to Him – [gave] Him all myself –
And took Himself, for Pay –
The solemn contract of a Life
Was ratified, this way –

The Wealth might disappoint –
Myself a poorer prove
Than this great Purchaser suspect,
The Daily Own – of Love

Depreciate the Vision –
But till the Merchant buy –
Still Fable – in the Isles of spice – How – • so – [Fable]
The subtle Cargoes – lie –

At least – 'tis Mutual – Risk –
Some – found it – Mutual Gain –
Sweet Debt of Life – Each Night to owe –
Insolvent – every Noon –

Sunset at Night – is natural –
But Sunset on the Dawn
Reverses Nature – Master –
So Midnight's – due – at Noon –

o

Eclipses be – predicted –
And Science bows them in –
But do One face us suddenly –
Jehovah's Watch – is wrong –

SHEET THREE c. autumn 1862

We grow accustomed to the Dark –[155]
When Light is put away –
As when the Neighbor holds the Lamp
To witness her Good bye –

A Moment – We uncertain step
For newness of the night –
Then – fit our Vision to the Dark –
And meet the Road – erect –

And so of larger – Darknesses –
Those Evenings of the Brain –
When not a Moon disclose a sign –
Or Star – come out – within –

The Bravest – grope a little –
And sometimes hit a Tree
Directly in the Forehead –
But as they learn to see –

Either the Darkness alters –
Or something in the sight
Adjusts itself to Midnight –
And Life steps almost straight.

You'll know it – as you know 'tis Noon –
By Glory –
As you do the Sun –
By Glory –
As you will in Heaven –
Know God the Father – and the Son.

o

By intuition, Mightiest Things
Assert themselves – and not by terms –
"I'm Midnight" – need the Midnight say –
"I'm Sunrise" – Need the Majesty?

Omnipotence – had not a Tongue –
His lisp – is Lightning – and the Sun –
His Conversation – with the Sea –
"How shall you know"?
Consult your Eye!

A Charm invests a face
Imperfectly beheld –
The Lady dare not lift her Vail
For fear it be dispelled –

But peers beyond her mesh –
And wishes – and denies –
Lest Interview – annul a want
That Image – satisfies –

SHEET FOUR c. autumn 1862

If I may have it, when it's dead,
I'll be contented – so – [contented –] now –
If just as soon as Breath is out
It shall belong to me –

Until they lock it in the Grave,
'Tis Bliss I cannot weigh – ['Tis] Right • Wealth I cannot weigh.
For tho' they lock Thee in the Grave,
Myself – can own the key – [can] hold

Think of it Lover! I and Thee
Permitted – face to face to be –
After a Life – a Death – we'll say –
For Death was That –
And This – is Thee –

o

A Charm invests: *Apparently sent to Maria Whitney* (*variant*) *c. autumn 1862*

I'll tell Thee All – how Bald it grew – [how] Blank –
How Midnight felt, at first – to me –
How all the Clocks stopped in the World –
And Sunshine pinched me – 'Twas so cold –

Then how the Grief got sleepy – some –
As if my soul were deaf and dumb –
Just making signs – across – to Thee – [signs –] it seemed [to]
That this way – thou could'st notice me – [could'st] speak to –

I'll tell you how I tried to keep
A smile, to show you, when this Deep
All Waded – We look back for Play,
At those Old Times – in Calvary.

Forgive me, if the Grave come slow – [Grave] seem
For Coveting to look at Thee – [For] eagerness –
Forgive me, if to stroke thy frost [to] touch • greet
Outvisions Paradise! [Out] fables –

I read my sentence – steadily –
Reviewed it with my eyes,
To see that I made no mistake
In its extremest clause –
The Date, and manner, of the shame –
And then the Pious Form
That "God have mercy" on the Soul
The Jury voted Him –
I made my soul familiar – with her extremity –
That at the last, it should not be a novel Agony –
But she, and Death, acquainted –
Meet tranquilly, as friends –
Salute, and pass, without a Hint –
And there, the Matter Ends –

SHEET FIVE c. autumn 1862

A Murmur in the Trees – to note –
Not loud enough – for Wind –

A star – not far enough to seek –
Nor near enough – to find –

A long – long Yellow – on the Lawn –
A Hubbub – as of feet –
Not audible – as Ours – to us –
But dapperer – more sweet –

A Hurrying Home of little Men
To Houses unperceived –
All this – and more – if I should tell –
Would never be believed –

Of Robins in the Trundle bed
How many I espy
Whose Nightgowns could not hide the Wings –
Although I heard them try –

But then I promised ne'er to tell –
How could I break My word?
So go your way – and I'll go Mine –
No fear you'll miss the Road.

It is dead – Find it –
Out of sound – Out of Sight –
"Happy"? Which is wiser –
You, or the Wind?
"Conscious"? Won't you ask that –
Of the low Ground?

"Homesick"? Many met it –
Even through them – This cannot testify –
Themself – as dumb –

Not in this World to see his face –
Sounds long – until I read the place
Where this – is said to be
But just the Primer – to a life –
Unopened – rare – Upon the Shelf –
Clasped yet – to Him – and me –

And yet – My Primer suits me so
I would not choose – a Book to know
Than that – be sweeter wise –
Might some one else – so learned – be –
And leave me – just my A – B – C –
Himself – could have the Skies –

~

I found the words to every thought [the] phrase
I ever had – but One –
And that – defies me –
As a Hand did try to chalk the Sun

To Races – nurtured in the Dark –
How would your Own – begin?
Can Blaze be shown in Cochineal – [be] done
Or Noon – in Mazarin?

~

SHEET SIX c. autumn 1862

I never felt at Home – Below –[156]
And in the Handsome skies
I shall not feel at Home – I know –
I don't like Paradise –

Because it's Sunday – all the time –
And Recess – never comes –
And Eden'll be so lonesome
Bright Wednesday Afternoons –

If God could make a visit –
Or ever took a Nap –
So not to see us – but they say
Himself – a Telescope

Perennial beholds us –
Myself would run away
From Him – and Holy Ghost – and all –
But there's the "Judgment Day"!

~

The Body grows without –[157] [grows] outside
The more convenient way –
That if the Spirit – like to hide
Its Temple stands, alway, [Its] Closet

Ajar – secure – inviting –
It never did betray
The Soul that asked its shelter
In solemn honesty [In] timid –

~

I had been hungry, all the Years –
My Noon had Come – to dine –
I trembling drew the Table near –
And touched the Curious Wine –

'Twas this on Tables I had seen –
When turning, hungry, Home
I looked in Windows, for the Wealth [the] Things
I could not hope – for Mine – [hope –] to earn

I did not know the ample Bread –
'Twas so unlike the Crumb
The Birds and I, had often shared
In Nature's – Dining Room –

The Plenty hurt me – 'twas so new –
Myself felt ill – and odd –
As Berry – of a Mountain Bush –
Transplanted – to the Road –

Nor was I hungry – so I found
That Hunger – was a way
Of persons Outside Windows – [Of] Creatures –
The entering – takes away –

~

FASCICLE SIXTEEN

SHEET ONE c. summer 1862

Before I got my eye put out –[158]
I liked as well to see
As other creatures, that have eyes –
And know no other way –

But were it told to me, Today,
That I might have the Sky
For mine, I tell you that my Heart
Would split, for size of me –

The Meadows – mine –
The Mountains – mine –
All Forests – Stintless stars –
As much of noon, as I could take –
Between my finite eyes –

The Motions of the Dipping Birds –
The Lightning's jointed Road – [The] Morning's Amber Road –
For mine – to look at when I liked,
The news would strike me dead –

So safer – guess – with just my soul
Upon the window pane
Where other creatures put their eyes –
Incautious – of the Sun –

Of nearness to her sundered Things
The Soul has special times –
When Dimness – looks the Oddity –
Distinctness – easy – seems –

o

Before I got: *Sent to TWH (variant) c. August 1862*

The Shapes we buried, dwell about,
Familiar, in the Rooms –
Untarnished by the Sepulchre,
The Mouldering Playmate comes – Our [Mouldering]

In just the Jacket that he wore –
Long buttoned in the Mold
Since we – old mornings, Children – played –
Divided – by a world –

The Grave yields back her Robberies –
The Years, our pilfered Things –
Bright Knots of Apparitions
Salute us, with their wings –

As we – it were – that perished –
Themself – had just remained till we rejoin them –
And 'twas they, and not ourself
That mourned –

SHEET TWO c. summer 1862

Tie the strings to my Life, My Lord,[159]
Then, I am ready to go!
Just a look at the Horses –
Rapid! That will do!

Put me in on the firmest side – [the] tightest • highest –
So I shall never fall –
For we must ride to the Judgment –
And it's partly, down Hill – And it's many a mile –

But never I mind the steepest – [the] Bridges
And never I mind the Sea –
Held fast in Everlasting Race –
By my own Choice, and Thee –

Good bye to the Life I used to live –
And the World I used to know –
And kiss the Hills, for me, just once – Here's a keepsake for the Hills
Then – I am ready to go! Now [I]

I like a look of Agony,[160]
Because I know it's true –
Men do not sham Convulsion,
Nor simulate, a Throe –

The eyes glaze once – and that is Death – ~~Death, comes~~
Impossible to feign
The Beads upon the Forehead
By homely Anguish strung.

~

I felt a Funeral, in my Brain,[161]
And Mourners to and fro
Kept treading – treading – till it seemed
That Sense was breaking through –

And when they all were seated,
A Service, like a Drum –
Kept beating – beating – till I thought
My mind was going numb –

And then I heard them lift a Box
And creak across my Soul [my] ~~Brain~~
With those same Boots of Lead, again,
Then Space – began to toll,

As all the Heavens were a Bell,
And Being, but an Ear,
And I, and Silence, some strange Race
Wrecked, solitary, here –

And then a Plank in Reason, broke,
And I dropped down, and down –
And hit a World, at every plunge, [every] Crash –
And Finished knowing – then – [And] Got through –

~

SHEET THREE c. summer 1862

'Tis so appalling – it exhilirates –
So over Horror, it half captivates – [Horror,] it dumb fascinates –
The Soul stares after it, secure –
To know the worst, leaves no dread more – A Sepulchre, fears frost, no more –

o

To scan a Ghost, is faint –
But grappling, conquers it –
How easy, Torment, now –
Suspense kept sawing so –

The Truth, is Bald – and Cold –
But that will hold –
If any are not sure –
We show them – prayer –
But we, who know,
Stop hoping, now –

Looking at Death, is Dying –
Just let go the Breath –
And not the pillow at your cheek
So slumbereth –

Others, can wrestle –
Yours, is done –
And so of Wo, bleak dreaded – come,
It sets the Fright at liberty –
And Terror's free –
Gay, Ghastly, Holiday!

How noteless Men, and Pleiads, stand,
Until a sudden sky
Reveals the fact that One is rapt
Forever from the eye –

Members of the Invisible,
Existing, while we stare,
In Leagueless Opportunity,
O'ertakeless, as the Air –

Why didn't we detain Them? [we] retain them – • it –
The Heavens with a smile,
Sweep by our disappointed Heads,
Without a syllable – But deign no syllable –

When we stand on the tops of Things –
And like the Trees, look down,
The smoke all cleared away from it –
And mirrors on the scene –

Just laying light – no soul will wink
Except it have the flaw –
The Sound ones, like the Hills – shall stand – [Hills –] stand up –
No lightning, scares away – [lightning,] drives –

The Perfect, nowhere be afraid –
They bear their dauntless Heads, [their] fearless – • tranquil –
Where others, dare not go at noon, [not] walk at noon –
Protected by their deeds –

The Stars dare shine occasionally
Upon a spotted World –
And Suns, go surer, for their Proof,
As if an axle, held – [As if] a muscle – held

SHEET FOUR c. summer 1862

'Twas just this time, last year, I died.[162]
I know I heard the Corn,
When I was carried by the Farms –
It had the Tassels on –

I thought how yellow it would look –
When Richard went to mill –
And then, I wanted to get out,
But something held my will.

I thought just how Red – Apples wedged
The Stubble's joints between –
And Carts went stooping round the fields
To take the Pumpkins in –

I wondered which would miss me, least,
And when Thanksgiving, came,
If Father'd multiply the plates –
To make an even Sum –

o

And would it blur the Christmas glee
My stocking hang too high
For any Santa Claus to reach
The altitude of me –

But this sort, grieved myself,
And so, I thought the other way,
How just this time, some perfect year –
Themself, should come to me –

Afraid! Of whom am I afraid?[163]
Not Death – for who is He?
The Porter of my Father's Lodge
As much abasheth me!

Of Life? 'Twere odd I fear [a] thing
That comprehendeth me
In one or two existences – [or] more –
Just as the case may be – As Deity decree –

Of Resurrection? Is the East
Afraid to trust the Morn
With her fastidious forehead?
As soon impeach my Crown!

He showed me Hights I never saw –
"Would'st Climb" – He said?
I said, "Not so" –
"With me –" He said – "With me"?

He showed me secrets – Morning's Nest –
The Rope the Nights were put across –
"And now, Would'st have me for a Guest"?
I could not find my "Yes" –

And then – He brake His Life – And lo,
A light for me, did solemn glow –
The steadier, as my face withdrew – [The] larger –
And could I further "No"?

He showed me: *Sent to SD (variant) c. summer 1862, beginning "I showed her Hights she never saw –"*

FASCICLE SEVENTEEN

SHEET ONE c. summer 1862

I dreaded that first Robin, so,
But He is mastered, now,
I'm some accustomed to Him grown,
He hurts a little, though –

I thought if I could only live
Till that first Shout got by –
Not all Pianos in the Woods
Had power to mangle me –

I dared not meet the Daffodils –
For fear their Yellow Gown
Would pierce me with a fashion
So foreign to my own –

I wished the Grass would hurry –
So when 'twas time to see –
He'd be too tall, the tallest one
Could stretch to look at me –

I could not bear the Bees should come,
I wished they'd stay away
In those dim countries where they go,
What word had they, for me?

They're here, though; not a creature failed –
No Blossom stayed away
In gentle deference to me –
The Queen of Calvary –

Each one salutes me, as he goes,
And I, my childish Plumes,
Lift, in bereaved acknowledgement
Of their unthinking Drums –

I would not paint – a picture – [164]
I'd rather be the One
Its bright impossibility [Its] fair
To dwell – delicious – on –
And wonder how the fingers feel
Whose rare – celestial – stir –
Evokes so sweet a torment – provokes [so]
Such sumptuous – Despair –

I would not talk, like Cornets –
I'd rather be the One
Raised softly to the Ceilings – [to] Horizons
And out, and easy on – [And] by –
Through Villages of Ether –
Myself endued Balloon [Myself] upborne • upheld • sustained
By but a lip of Metal –
The pier to my Pontoon –

Nor would I be a Poet –
It's finer – Own the Ear –
Enamored – impotent – content –
The License to revere,
A privilege so awful [A] luxury
What would the Dower be,
Had I the Art to stun myself
With Bolts – of Melody!

SHEET TWO c. summer 1862

He touched me, so I live to know [165]
That such a day, permitted so, [day,] Accepted so – • persuaded so –
I groped upon his breast – I dwelt – [upon] • I perished – [on]

It was a boundless place to me
And silenced, as the awful Sea
Puts minor streams to rest.

And now, I'm different from before,
As if I breathed superior air –
Or brushed a Royal Gown –

My feet, too, that had wandered so –
My Gypsy face – transfigured now –
To tenderer Renown –

Into this Port, if I might come,
Rebecca, to Jerusalem,
Would not so ravished turn –
Nor Persian, baffled at her shrine
Lift such a Crucifixal sign
To her imperial Sun.

~

I had the Glory – that will do –
An Honor, Thought can turn her to
When lesser Fames invite –
With one long "Nay" –
Bliss' early shape
Deforming – Dwindling – Gulphing up –
Time's possibility –

~

She sights a Bird – she chuckles –
She flattens – then she crawls –
She runs without the look of feet –
Her eyes increase to Balls –

Her Jaws stir – twitching – hungry – [Her] mouth stirs – longing – hungry
Her Teeth can hardly stand –
She leaps, but Robin leaped the first –
Ah, Pussy, of the Sand,

The Hopes so juicy ripening –
You almost bathed your Tongue –
When Bliss disclosed a hundred Toes – [hundred] wings –
And fled with every one –

~

They leave us with the Infinite.[166]
But He – is not a man –
His fingers are the size of fists –
His fists, the size of men –

o

And whom he foundeth, with his Arm
As Himmaleh, shall stand –
Gibraltar's everlasting Shoe
Poised lightly on his Hand,

So trust him, Comrade –
You for you, and I, for you and – me
Eternity is ample,
And quick enough, if true.

SHEET THREE c. summer 1862

I'm ceded – I've stopped being Theirs –[167]
The name They dropped upon my face
With water, in the country church
Is finished using, now,
And They can put it with my Dolls,
My childhood, and the string of spools,
I've finished threading – too –

Baptized, before, without the choice,
But this time, consciously, Of Grace –
Unto supremest name – [supremest] term
Called to my Full – The Crescent dropped –
Existence's whole Arc, filled up,
With one – small Diadem – [With] just one [Diadem –]

My second Rank – too small the first –
Crowned – Crowing – on my Father's breast –
A half unconscious Queen –
But this time – Adequate – Erect,
With Will to choose, [With] power
Or to reject,
And I choose, just a Crown – [a] Throne

line 12: [Existence's] ~~surmise~~ • [whole] ~~Rim~~ • [whole] Eye
line 15: [Crowned –] whimpering • dangling
line 16: [A] too unconscious [Queen] • An insufficient Queen

If Anybody's friend be dead
It's sharpest of the theme
The thinking how they walked alive –
At such and such a time –

Their costume, of a Sunday,
Some manner of the Hair –
A prank nobody knew but them
Lost, in the Sepulchre –

How warm, they were, on such a day,
You almost feel the date –
So short way off it seems –
And now – they're Centuries from that –

How pleased they were, at what you said! [they] looked
You try to touch the smile [to] reach
And dip your fingers in the frost – [And] mix
When was it – Can you tell –

You asked the Company to tea –
Acquaintance – just a few –
And chatted close with this Grand Thing
That don't remember you –

Past Bows, and Invitations –
Past Interview, and Vow –
Past what Ourself can estimate – [can] understand
That – makes the Quick of Wo!

SHEET FOUR c. summer 1862

It was not Death, for I stood up,[168]
And all the Dead, lie down –
It was not Night, for all the Bells
Put out their Tongues, for Noon.

It was not Frost, for on my Flesh [my] Knees
I felt Siroccos – crawl –
Nor Fire – for just my marble feet [just] two
Could keep a Chancel, cool –

And yet, it tasted, like them all,
The Figures I have seen
Set orderly, for Burial,
Reminded me, of mine –

As if my life were shaven,
And fitted to a frame,
And could not breathe without a key,
And 'twas like Midnight, some –

When everything that ticked – has stopped –
And space stares – all around –
Or Grisly frosts – first Autumn morns,
Repeal the Beating Ground –

But, most, like Chaos – Stopless – cool –
Without a Chance, or spar –
Or even a Report of Land –
To justify – Despair.

~

If you were coming in the Fall,[169]
I'd brush the Summer by
With half a smile, and half a spurn,
As Housewives do, a Fly.

If I could see you in a year,
I'd wind the months in balls –
And put them each in separate Drawers,
For fear the numbers fuse –

If only Centuries, delayed,
I'd count them on my Hand,
Subtracting, till my fingers dropped
Into Van Dieman's Land.

If certain, when this life was out –
That yours and mine, should be –
I'd toss it yonder, like a Rind,
And take Eternity – [And] taste

o

But, now, uncertain of the length
Of this, that is between,
It goads me, like the Goblin Bee –
That will not state – its sting.

SHEET FIVE c. summer 1862

I felt my life with both my hands
To see if it was there –
I held my spirit to the Glass,
To prove it possibler –

I turned my Being round and round
And paused at every pound
To ask the Owner's name –
For doubt, that I should know the sound –

I judged my features – jarred my hair –
I pushed my dimples by, and waited –
If they – twinkled back –
Conviction might, of me –

I told myself, "Take Courage, Friend –
That – was a former time –
But we might learn to like the Heaven,
As well as our Old Home"!

Perhaps I asked too large –
I take – no less than skies –
For Earths, grow thick as
Berries, in my native Town –

My Basket holds – just – Firmaments –
Those – dangle easy – on my arm,
But smaller bundles – Cram.

A Bird, came down the Walk –[170]
He did not know I saw –

A Bird, came: *Sent to TWH (lost, published variant) probably c. August 1862*

He bit an Angle Worm in halves [He] shook –
And ate the fellow, raw,

And then, he drank a Dew
From a convenient Grass –
And then hopped sidewise to the Wall
To let a Beetle pass –

He glanced with rapid eyes,
That hurried all abroad –
They looked like frightened Beads, I thought,
He stirred his Velvet Head. –

Like one in danger, Cautious,
I offered him a Crumb,
And he unrolled his feathers,
And rowed him softer Home –

Than Oars divide the Ocean,
Too silver for a seam,
Or Butterflies, off Banks of Noon,
Leap, plashless as they swim.

SHEET SIX c. summer 1862

The Soul has Bandaged moments –
When too appalled to stir –
She feels some ghastly Fright come up
And stop to look at her –

Salute her, with long fingers –
Caress her freezing hair –
Sip, Goblin, from the very lips
The Lover – hovered – o'er –
Unworthy, that a thought so mean
Accost a Theme – so – fair –

The soul has moments of escape –
When bursting all the doors –
She dances like a Bomb, abroad,
And swings upon the Hours,

o

As do the Bee – delirious borne –
Long Dungeoned from his Rose –
Touch Liberty – then know no more –
But Noon, and Paradise –

The Soul's retaken moments –
When, Felon led along,
With shackles on the plumed feet, [With] irons –
And staples, in the song, [And] rivets –

The Horror welcomes her, again,
These, are not brayed of Tongue –

Like Flowers, that heard the news of Dews, As – [Flowers]
But never deemed the dripping prize
Awaited their – low Brows –

Or Bees – that thought the Summer's name
Some rumor of Delirium,
No Summer – could – for Them –

Or Arctic Creatures, dimly stirred –
By Tropic Hint – some Travelled Bird
Imported to the Wood – imported – [to]

Or Wind's bright signal to the Ear –
Making that homely, and severe,
Contented, known, before –

The Heaven – unexpected come,
To Lives that thought the Worshipping
A too presumptuous Psalm –

FASCICLE EIGHTEEN

SHEET ONE c. autumn 1862

It's thoughts – and just One Heart –[171]
And Old Sunshine – about –
Make frugal – Ones – Content –
And two or three – for Company –
Upon a Holiday –
Crowded – as Sacrament –

Books – when the Unit –
Spare the Tenant – long eno' –
A Picture – if it Care –
Itself – a Gallery too rare – [a] Vatican – too rare –
For needing more –

Flowers – to keep the eyes – from going awkward –
When it snows –
A Bird – if they – prefer –
Though winter fire – sing clear as Plover –
To our – ear –

A Landscape – not so great
To suffocate the eye –
A Hill – perhaps –
Perhaps – the profile of a Mill
Turned by the wind –
Tho' *such* – are *luxuries* –

It's thoughts – and just two Heart –
And Heaven – about –
At least – a Counterfeit –
We would not have Correct –
And Immortality – can be almost –
Not quite – Content –

It's thoughts – and: *Sent to Ns (lost) c. 1862*

I know a place where Summer strives
With such a practised Frost –
She – each year – leads her Daisies back –
Recording briefly – "Lost" –

But when the South Wind stirs the Pools
And struggles in the lanes –
Her Heart misgives Her, for Her Vow –
And she pours soft Refrains

Into the lap of Adamant –
And spices – and the Dew –
That stiffens quietly to Quartz –
Upon her Amber Shoe –

~

As far from pity, as complaint –
As cool to speech – as stone –
As numb to Revelation
As if my Trade were Bone –

As far from Time – as History –
As near yourself – Today –
As Children, to the Rainbow's scarf –
Or Sunset's Yellow play

To eyelids in the Sepulchre –
How dumb the Dancer lies – [How] still
While Color's Revelations break –
And blaze – the Butterflies!

~

SHEET TWO c. autumn 1862

I know that He exists.
Somewhere – in silence –
He has hid his rare life
From our gross eyes.

'Tis an instant's play –
'Tis a fond Ambush –

Just to make Bliss
Earn her own surprise!

But – should the play
Prove piercing earnest –
Should the glee – glaze –
In Death's – stiff – stare –

Would not the fun   [the] "~~Joke~~"
Look too expensive!
Would not the jest –
Have crawled too far!

He strained my faith –[172]
Did he find it supple?
Shook my strong trust –
Did it then – yield?

Hurled my belief –
But – did he shatter – it?
Racked – with suspense –
Not a nerve failed!

Wrung me – with Anguish –
But I never doubted him –   Must be – I deserved – it –
'Tho' for what wrong
He did never say –

Stabbed – while I sued
His sweet forgiveness –
Jesus – it's your little "John"!
Don't you know – me?   Why – Slay – Me?

I tend my flowers for thee –
Bright Absentee!
My Fuschzia's Coral Seams
Rip – while the Sower – dreams –

Geraniums – tint – and spot –
Low Daisies – dot –

My Cactus – splits her Beard
To show her throat –

Carnations – tip their spice –
And Bees – pick up –
A Hyacinth – I hid –
Puts out a Ruffled Head –
And odors fall
From flasks – so small –
You marvel how they held –

Globe Roses – break their satin flake –
Upon my Garden floor –
Yet – thou – not there –
I had as lief they bore
No crimson – more –

Thy flower – be gay –
Her Lord – away!
It ill becometh me –
I'll dwell in Calyx – Gray –
How modestly – alway –
Thy Daisy –
Draped for thee!

SHEET THREE c. autumn 1862

I envy Seas, whereon He rides –[173] [Seas,] That bear Him
I envy Spokes of Wheels
Of Chariots, that Him convey –
I envy Crooked Hills [envy] speechless Hills

That gaze upon His journey – [That] grow along
How easy all can see
What is forbidden utterly [is] denied [utterly]
As Heaven – unto me! As Eden [unto]

I envy Nests of Sparrows –
That dot His distant Eaves;
The wealthy Fly, upon His Pane – [The] ~~happy~~
The happy – happy Leaves –

o

That just abroad His Window
Have Summer's leave to play –
The Ear Rings of Pizarro
Could not obtain for me –

I envy Light – that wakes Him –
And Bells – that boldly ring   [boldly] Come
To tell Him it is Noon, abroad –
Myself – be Noon to Him –

Yet interdict – my Blossom –
And abrogate – my Bee –
Lest Noon in everlasting night –   [Noon] down –
Drop Gabriel – and me –

Those fair – fictitious People –[174]   [Those] new
The Women – plucked away   [Women –] slipped away –
From our familiar Lifetime –
The Men of Ivory –

Those Boys and Girls, in Canvas –
Who stay upon the Wall   [Who] dwell
In everlasting Keepsake –   [In] Everlasting Childhood –
Can anybody tell?   Where are they – Can you tell –

We trust – in places perfecter –
Inheriting Delight
Beyond our faint Conjecture –   [our] small
Our dizzy Estimate –   [Our] scanty

Remembering ourselves, we trust –
Yet Blesseder – than we –
Through Knowing – where we only hope –   [only] guess
Receiving – where we – pray –   beholding [where]

Of Expectation – also –
Anticipating us
With transport, that would be a pain
Except for Holiness –

Esteeming us – as Exile –
Themself – admitted Home –
Through gentle Miracle of Death – [Through] curious • *easy* –
The Way ourself, must come –

line 3: [From our familiar] address – • gazing – • fingers – • [From our] familiar notice

SHEET FOUR c. autumn 1862

Within my Garden, rides a Bird[175]
Upon a single Wheel –
Whose spokes a dizzy music make
As 'twere a travelling Mill –

He never stops, but slackens
Above the Ripest Rose –
Partakes without alighting
And praises as he goes,

Till every spice is tasted –
And then his Fairy Gig [his] Microscopic Gig
Reels in remoter atmospheres –
And I rejoin my Dog,

And He and I, perplex us
If positive, 'twere we –
Or bore the Garden in the Brain
This Curiosity –

But He, the best Logician,
Refers my clumsy eye – [my] duller –
To just vibrating Blossoms!
An exquisite Reply!

Is Bliss then, such Abyss –
I must not put my foot amiss
For fear I spoil my shoe?

I'd rather suit my foot
Than save my Boot –

For yet to buy another Pair
Is possible,
At any store –

But Bliss, is sold just once.
The Patent lost
None buy it any more –
Say, Foot, decide the point!
The Lady cross, or not?
Verdict for Boot!

~

After great pain, a formal feeling comes –[176]
The Nerves sit ceremonious, like Tombs –
The stiff Heart questions 'was it He, that bore,'
And 'Yesterday, or Centuries before'?

The Feet, mechanical, go round –
A Wooden way
Of Ground, or Air, or Ought –
Regardless grown,
A Quartz contentment, like a stone –

This is the Hour of Lead –
Remembered, if outlived,
As Freezing persons, recollect the Snow –
First – Chill – then Stupor – then the letting go –

~

This World is not conclusion.[177]
A Species stands beyond – a sequel – [stands]
Invisible, as Music –
But positive, as Sound –
It beckons, and it baffles –
Philosophy, don't know –
And through a Riddle, at the last –
Sagacity, must go –
To guess it, puzzles scholars – [To] prove it –
To gain it, Men have borne

Contempt of Generations
And Crucifixion, shown –
Faith slips – and laughs, and rallies –
Blushes, if any see –
Plucks at a twig of Evidence –
And asks a Vane, the way –
Much Gesture, from the Pulpit –
Strong Hallelujahs roll – Sure – [Hallelujahs]
Narcotics cannot still the Tooth [the] Mouse –
That nibbles at the soul –

~

SHEET FIVE c. autumn 1862

It will be Summer – eventually.[178]
Ladies – with parasols –
Sauntering Gentlemen – with Canes –
And little Girls – with Dolls –

Will tint the pallid landscape –
As 'twere a bright Boquet –
Tho' drifted deep, in Parian –
The Village lies – today –

The Lilacs – bending many a year –
Will sway with purple load –
The Bees – will not despise the tune –
Their Forefathers – have hummed –

The Wild Rose – redden in the Bog –
The Aster – on the Hill
Her everlasting fashion – set –
And Covenant Gentians – frill –

Till Summer folds her miracle –
As Women – do – their Gown –
Or Priests – adjust the Symbols –
When Sacrament – is done –

~

My Reward for Being, was This –[179]
My premium – My Bliss –

It will be: *Sent lines 14–16 to SB (variant) c. early 1862*

An Admiralty, less –
A Sceptre – penniless –
And Realms – just Dross –

When Thrones accost my Hands –
With "Me, Miss, Me" –
I'll unroll Thee –
Dominions dowerless – beside this Grace –
Election – Vote –
The Ballots of Eternity, will show just that.

~

'Twas the old – road – through pain –
That unfrequented – One –
With many a turn – and thorn –
That stops – at Heaven –

This – was the Town – she passed –
There – where she – rested – last –
Then – stepped more fast –
The little tracks – close prest –
Then – not so swift –
Slow – slow – as feet did weary – grow –
Then – stopped – no other track!

Wait! Look! Her little Book –
The leaf – at love – turned back –
Her very Hat –
And this worn shoe just fits the track –
Herself – though – fled!

Another bed – a short one –
Women make – tonight –
In Chambers bright –
Too out of sight – though –
For our hoarse Good Night –
To touch her Head!

~

At least – to pray – is left – is left –[180]
Oh Jesus – in the Air –

'Twas the old –: *Sent to Ns (lost) c. 1862*

I know not which thy chamber is – [thy] palaces –
I'm knocking – everywhere –

Thou settest Earthquake in the South – [Thou] stirrest –
And Maelstrom, in the Sea –
Say, Jesus Christ of Nazareth –
Hast thou no arm for Me?

SHEET SIX c. autumn 1862

Better – than Music![181]
For I – who heard it –
I was used – to the Birds – before –
This – was different – 'Twas Translation –
Of all tunes I knew – and more –

'Twasn't contained – like other stanza –
No one could play it – the second time –
But the Composer – perfect Mozart –
Perish with him – that keyless Rhyme!

Children – so – told how Brooks in Eden – [Children –] assured that [Brooks]
Bubbled a better – melody –
Quaintly infer – Eve's great surrender –
Urging the feet – that would – not – fly –

Children – matured – are wiser – mostly – [Children –] grown up –
Eden – a legend – dimly told – [dimly] learned • crooned
Eve – and the Anguish – Grandame's story –
But – I was telling a tune – I heard –

Not such a strain – the Church – baptizes –
When the last Saint – goes up the Aisles –
Not such a stanza splits the silence –
When the Redemption strikes her Bells – [Redemption] shakes –

Let me not spill – its smallest cadence – [not] lose • waste –
Humming – for promise – when alone –
Humming – until my faint Rehearsal –
Drop into tune – around the Throne –

FASCICLE NINETEEN

SHEET ONE c. autumn 1862

The Grass so little has to do,
A Sphere of simple Green –
With only Butterflies, to brood,
And Bees, to entertain –

And stir all day to pretty tunes
The Breezes fetch along,
And hold the Sunshine, in its lap
And bow to everything,

And thread the Dews, all night, like Pearl,
And make itself so fine
A Duchess, were too common
For such a noticing,

And even when it die, to pass
In odors so divine,
As lowly spices, gone to sleep – [spices,] laid asleep • [laid] to sleep –
Or Amulets of Pine – [Or] Spikenards perishing.

And then to dwell in Sovreign Barns,
And dream the Days away,
The Grass so little has to do,
I wish I were a Hay –

All the letters I can write
Are not fair as this –
Syllables of Velvet –
Sentences of Plush,
Depths of Ruby, undrained,
Hid, Lip, for Thee –

The Grass so: *Sent to AD (variant) c. summer 1862*
All the letters: *Sent to Eudocia Converse Flynt (variant) c. 20 July 1862, with a flower*

Play it were a Humming Bird –
And just sipped – me –

I cannot dance upon my Toes –[182]
No Man instructed me –
But oftentimes, among my mind,
A Glee possesseth me,

That had I Ballet Knowledge –
Would put itself abroad
In Pirouette to blanch a Troupe –
Or lay a Prima, mad,

And though I had no Gown of Gauze –
No Ringlet, to my Hair,
Nor hopped for Audiences – like Birds,
One Claw upon the air –

Nor tossed my shape in Eider Balls,
Nor rolled on wheels of snow
Till I was out of sight, in sound,
The House encore me so –

Nor any know I know the Art
I mention – easy – Here –
Nor any Placard boast me –
It's full as Opera –

SHEET TWO c. autumn 1862

Good Morning – Midnight –
I'm coming Home –
Day – got tired of Me –
How could I – of Him?

Sunshine was a sweet place –
I liked to stay –
But Morn – didn't want me – now –
So – Good night – Day!

o

I cannot dance: *Sent to TWH (variant) c. August 1862*

I can look – can't I –
When the East is Red?
The Hills – have a way – then –
That puts the Heart – abroad –

You – are not so fair – Midnight –
I chose – Day –
But – please take a little Girl –
He turned away!

~

I like to see it lap the Miles –[183] [to] hear it –
And lick the Valleys up –
And stop to feed itself at Tanks –
And then – prodigious step

Around a Pile of Mountains –
And supercilious peer
In Shanties – by the sides of Roads –
And then a Quarry pare

To fit its sides [its] Ribs –
And crawl between
Complaining all the while
In horrid – hooting stanza –
Then chase itself down Hill –

And neigh like Boanerges – And, • then – [neigh]
Then – prompter than a Star [Then –] punctual as –
Stop – docile and omnipotent
At its own stable door –

~

It don't sound so terrible – quite – as it did –[184]
I run it over – "Dead", Brain – "Dead".
Put it in Latin – left of my school –
Seems it don't shriek so – under rule.

Turn it, a little – full in the face
A Trouble looks bitterest –
Shift it – just –

Say "When Tomorrow comes this way –
I shall have waded down one Day".

I suppose it will interrupt me some
Till I get accustomed – but then the Tomb
Like other new Things – shows largest – then –
And smaller, by Habit –

It's shrewder then
Put the Thought in advance – a Year –
How like "a fit" – then –
Murder – wear!

SHEET THREE c. autumn 1862

I'll clutch – and clutch –
Next – One – Might be the golden touch –
Could take it –
Diamonds – Wait –
I'm diving – just a little late –
But stars – go slow – for night –

I'll string you – in fine necklace –
Tiaras – make – of some –
Wear you on Hem –
Loop up a Countess – with you –
Make – a Diadem – and mend my old One –
Count – Hoard – then lose –
And doubt that you are mine –
To have the joy of feeling it – again –

I'll show you at the Court –
Bear you – for Ornament
Where Women breathe –
That every sigh – may lift you
Just as high – as I –

And – when I die –
In meek array – display you –
Still to show – how rich I go –
Lest Skies impeach a wealth so wonderful –
And banish me –

Taking up the fair Ideal,
Just to cast her down
When a fracture – we discover –
Or a splintered Crown –
Makes the Heavens portable –
And the Gods – a lie –
Doubtless – "Adam" – scowled at Eden –
For *his* perjury!

Cherishing – our poor Ideal –
Till in purer dress –
We behold her – glorified –
Comforts – search – like this –
Till the broken creatures –
We adored – for whole –
Stains – all washed –
Transfigured – mended –
Meet us – with a smile –

~

The Moon is distant from the Sea –
And yet, with Amber Hands –
She leads Him – docile as a Boy –
Along appointed Sands –

He never misses a Degree –
Obedient to Her eye –
He comes just so far – toward the Town –
Just so far – goes away –

Oh, Signor, Thine, the Amber Hand –
And mine – the distant Sea –
Obedient to the least command
Thine eye impose on me –

~

SHEET FOUR c. autumn 1862

It would never be Common – more – I said –
Difference – had begun –

Many a bitterness – had been –
But that old sort – was done –

Or – if it sometime – showed – as 'twill –
Upon the Downiest – morn –
Such bliss – had I – for all the years –
'Twould give an easier – pain –

I'd so much joy – I told it – Red –
Upon my simple Cheek –
I felt it publish – in my eye –
'Twas needless – any speak –

I walked – as wings – my body bore –
The feet – I former used –
Unnescessary – now to me –
As boots – would be – to Birds –

I put my pleasure all abroad –
I dealt a word of Gold
To every Creature – that I met –
And Dowered – all the World –

When – suddenly – my Riches shrank –
A Goblin – drank my Dew –
My Palaces – dropped tenantless –
Myself – was beggared – too –

I clutched at sounds –
I groped at shapes –
I touched the tops of Films –
I felt the Wilderness roll back
Along my Golden lines –

The Sackcloth – hangs upon the nail –
The Frock I used to wear –
But where my moment of Brocade –
My – drop – of India?

Me – Come! My dazzled face
In such a shining place!
Me – hear! My foreign Ear
The sounds of Welcome – there!

The Saints forget
Our bashful feet –

My Holiday, shall be
That They – remember me –
My Paradise – the fame
That They – pronounce my name –

Do People moulder equally,[185]
They bury, in the Grave?
I do believe a species
As positively live

As I, who testify it
Deny that I – am dead –
And fill my Lungs, for Witness –
From Tanks – above my Head –

I say to you, said Jesus,
That there be standing here –
A sort, that shall not taste of Death –
If Jesus was sincere –

I need no further Argue –
The statement of the Lord
Is not a controvertible –
He told me, Death was dead –

LEAF FIVE c. autumn 1862

Knows how to forget![186]
But – could she teach – it?
'Tis the Art, most of all,
I should like to know –

o

Long, at its Greek –
I – who pored – patient –
Rise – still the Dunce –
Gods used to know –

Mould my slow mind to this Comprehension –
Oddest of sciences – Book ever bore –

How to forget!
Ah, to attain it –
I would give *you* –
All other Lore –

SHEET SIX c. autumn 1862

We talked as Girls do –[187]
Fond, and late –
We speculated fair, on every subject, but the Grave –
Of ours, none affair –

We handled Destinies, as cool –
As we – Disposers – be –
And God, a Quiet Party
To our authority –

But fondest, dwelt upon Ourself
As we eventual – be –
When Girls, to Women, softly raised
We – occupy – Degree – [We –] too – partake –

We parted with a contract
To cherish, and to write [To] recollect – [to write]
But Heaven made both, impossible
Before another night.

Empty my Heart, of Thee –
Its single Artery – [Its] Giant –
Begin, and leave Thee out –
Simply Extinction's Date –

Much Billow hath the Sea –
One Baltic – They –
Subtract Thyself, in play,
And not enough of me
Is left – to put away –
"Myself" meant Thee –

Erase the Root – no Tree –
Thee – then – no me –
The Heavens stripped –
Eternity's vast pocket, picked. [Eternity's] wide

I cried at Pity – not at Pain –[188]
I heard a Woman say
"Poor Child" – and something in her voice
Convicted me – of me – Convinced ~~myself~~ of me –

So long I fainted, to myself
It seemed the common way,
And Health, and Laughter, curious things –
To look at, like a Toy –

To sometimes hear "Rich people" buy –
And see the Parcel rolled –
And carried, we suppose – to Heaven, [carried,] I [suppose]d
For children, made of Gold –

But not to touch, or wish for,
Or think of, with a sigh –
As so and so – had been to us, [to] me
Had God willed differently.

I wish I knew that Woman's name –
So when she comes this way,
To hold my life, and hold my ears
For fear I hear her say

She's "sorry I am dead" – again –
Just when the Grave and I –
Have sobbed ourselves almost to sleep,
Our only Lullaby –

LEAF SEVEN c. autumn 1862

The face I carry with me – last –[189]
When I go out of Time –
To take my Rank – by – in the West –
That face – will just be thine –

I'll hand it to the Angel –
That – Sir – was my Degree –
In Kingdoms – you have heard the Raised –
Refer to – possibly.

He'll take it – scan it – step aside –
Return – with such a crown
As Gabriel – never capered at –
And beg me put it on –

And then – he'll turn me round and round –
To an admiring sky –
As One that bore her Master's name –
Sufficient Royalty!

FASCICLE TWENTY

SHEET ONE c. autumn 1862

I took one Draught of Life –[190]
I'll tell you what I paid –
Precisely an existence –
The market price, they said.

They weighed me, Dust by Dust –
They balanced Film with Film,
Then handed me my Being's worth –
A single Dram of Heaven! MLT

A train went through a burial gate,[191]
A bird broke forth and sang,
And trilled, and quivered, and shook his throat
Till all the churchyard rang;

And then adjusted his little notes,
And bowed and sang again.
Doubtless, he thought it meet of him
To say good bye to men. MLT, *Poems* (1890)

The Morning after Wo –
'Tis frequently the Way –
Surpasses all that rose before –
For utter Jubilee –

As Nature did not Care –
And piled her Blossoms on –
The further to parade a Joy
Her Victim stared upon –

o

The Birds declaim their Tunes –
Pronouncing every word
Like Hammers – Did they know they fell
Like Litanies of Lead –

On here and there – a creature –
They'd modify the Glee
To fit some Crucifixal Clef –
Some key of Calvary –

Departed – to the Judgment –
A Mighty Afternoon –
Great Clouds – like Ushers – leaning – [Ushers –] placing
Creation – looking on –

The Flesh – Surrendered – Cancelled – [Surrendered –] Shifted
The Bodiless – begun –
Two Worlds – like Audiences – disperse –
And leave the Soul – alone –

line 7: the – [Worlds – like Audiences –] dissolve – • withdraw – • retire –

SHEET TWO c. autumn 1862

I think the Hemlock likes to stand[192]
Upon a Marge of Snow –
It suits his own Austerity –
And satisfies an awe

That men, must slake in Wilderness –
And in the Desert – cloy – Or [in]
An instinct for the Hoar, the Bald – [A] hunger [for the] drear –
Lapland's – nescessity –

The Hemlock's nature thrives – on cold –
The Gnash of Northern winds
Is sweetest nutriment – to him –
His best Norwegian Wines – [His] good

To satin Races – he is nought –
But children on the Don,
Beneath his Tabernacles, play,
And Dnieper Wrestlers, run.

~

Dare you see a Soul at the "White Heat"?[193]
Then crouch within the door –
Red – is the Fire's common tint –
But when the quickened Ore — [the] vivid

Has sated Flame's conditions – — [Has] vanquished
She quivers from the Forge — it [quivers]
Without a color, but the Light
Of unannointed Blaze –

Least Village, boasts its Blacksmith –
Whose Anvil's even ring
Stands symbol for the finer Forge
That soundless tugs – within –

Refining these impatient Ores
With Hammer, and with Blaze
Until the designated Light
Repudiate the Forge –

~

To hear an Oriole sing
May be a common thing –
Or only a divine.

It is not of the Bird
Who sings the same, unheard,
As unto Crowd –

The Fashion of the Ear
Attireth that it hear
In Dun, or fair –

So whether it be Rune –
Or whether it be none — [be] din –
Is of within.

○

Dare you see: *Sent to TWH (lost) probably c. August 1862*

The "Tune is in the Tree –"
The Skeptic – showeth me –
"No Sir! In Thee!"

I reason, Earth is short –
And Anguish – absolute –
And many hurt,
But, what of that?

I reason, we could die –
The best Vitality
Cannot excel Decay,
But, what of that?

I reason, that in Heaven –
Somehow, it will be even –
Some new Equation, given –
But, what of that?

SHEET THREE c. autumn 1862

To put this World down, like a Bundle –
And walk steady, away,
Requires Energy – possibly Agony –
'Tis the Scarlet way

Trodden with straight renunciation
By the Son of God –
Later, his faint Confederates
Justify the Road –

Flavors of that old Crucifixion –
Filaments of Bloom, Pontius Pilate sowed –
Strong Clusters, from Barabbas' Tomb –

Sacrament, Saints partook before us – [Saints] indorsed
Patent, every drop,
With the Brand of the Gentile Drinker [the] stamp [of]
Who indorsed the Cup – [Who] enforced

I reason, Earth: *Sent to SD (variant) c. mid-1862*

Although I put away his life –[194]
An Ornament too grand
For Forehead low as mine, to wear,
This might have been the Hand

That sowed the flower, he preferred –
Or smoothed a homely pain,
Or pushed the pebble from his path –
Or played his chosen tune –

On Lute the least – the latest –
But just his ear could know
That whatsoe'er delighted it,
I never would let go –

The foot to bear his errand –
A little Boot I know –
Would leap abroad like Antelope –
With just the grant to do –

His weariest Commandment –
A sweeter to obey,
Than "Hide and Seek" –
Or skip to Flutes –
Or all Day, chase the Bee –

Your Servant, Sir, will weary –
The Surgeon, will not come –
The World, will have its own – to do –
The Dust, will vex your Fame –

The Cold will force your tightest door
Some February Day,
But say my Apron bring the sticks
To make your Cottage gay –

That I may take that promise
To Paradise, with me –
To teach the Angels, avarice,
You, Sir, taught first – to me.

Over and over, like a Tune –[195]
The Recollection plays –
Drums off the Phantom Battlements
Cornets of Paradise –

Snatches, from Baptized Generations –
Cadences too grand
But for the Justified Processions
At the Lord's Right hand.

SHEET FOUR c. autumn 1862

One need not be a chamber – to be Haunted –[196]
One need not be a House –
The Brain – has Corridors surpassing
Material Place – Corporeal [Place –]

Far safer of a Midnight – meeting
External Ghost –
Than an Interior – confronting –
That cooler – Host – That Whiter Host.

Far safer, through an Abbey – gallop –
The Stones a'chase –
Than moonless – One's A'self encounter –
In lonesome place –

Ourself – behind Ourself – Concealed –
Should startle – most –
Assassin – hid in Our Apartment –
Be Horror's least –

The Prudent – carries a Revolver – The Body [carries] the
He bolts the Door –
O'erlooking a Superior Spectre –
More near –

lines 19–20: A Spectre – infinite – accompanying – / He fails to fear –
Maintaining a superior spectre – / None saw –

One need not: *Sent to SD (variant) c. early 1864*

Like Some Old fashioned Miracle –[197]
When Summertime is done –
Seems Summer's Recollection –
And the affairs of June –

As infinite Tradition – as [As] Bagatelles –
Cinderella's Bays –
Or little John – of Lincoln Green –
Or Blue Beard's Galleries

Her Bees – have an illusive Hum –
Her Blossoms – like a Dream
Elate us – till we almost weep –
So plausible – they seem – [So] exquisite

Her Memory – like Strains – enchant – [Her] Memories [like Strains –] Review –
Tho' Orchestra be dumb – [Orchestra] is
The Violin – in Baize – replaced –
And Ear, and Heaven – numb –

The Soul selects her own Society –[198]
Then – shuts the Door –
To her divine Majority – On [her]
Present no more – obtrude [no]

Unmoved – she notes the Chariots – pausing –
At her low Gate –
Unmoved – an Emperor be kneeling
Upon her Mat – On [her] Rush mat

I've known her – from an ample nation –
Choose One –
Then – close the Valves of her attention – [the] lids –
Like Stone –

SHEET FIVE c. autumn 1862

How sick – to wait – in any place – but thine –[199]
I knew last night – when some one tried to twine –

Like Some Old: *Sent to SD (variant) c. early 1863*

Thinking – perhaps – that I looked tired – or alone –
Or breaking – almost – with unspoken pain –

And I turned – ducal –
That right – was thine –
One port – suffices – for a Brig like *mine* –

Ours be the tossing – wild though the sea –
Rather than a mooring – unshared by thee.
Ours be the Cargo – *unladen – here* –
Rather than the *"spicy isles –"*
And thou – not there –

Mine – by the Right of the White Election!
Mine – by the Royal Seal!
Mine – by the sign in the Scarlet prison –
Bars – cannot conceal! Bolts [cannot]

Mine – here – in Vision – and in Veto!
Mine – by the Grave's Repeal –
Titled – Confirmed –
Delirious Charter! Good affidavit –
Mine – long as Ages steal! [Mine –] while [Ages]

She lay as if at play
Her life had leaped away –
Intending to return –
But not so soon –

Her merry Arms, half dropt –
As if for lull of sport –
An instant had forgot
The Trick to start –

Her dancing Eyes – ajar –
As if their Owner were
Still sparkling through
For fun – at you –

Her Morning at the door –
Devising, I am sure –
To force her sleep –
So light – so deep –

~

Heaven is so far of the Mind
That were the Mind dissolved –
The Site – of it – by Architect
Could not again be proved –

'Tis Vast – as our Capacity –
As fair – as our idea –
To Him of adequate desire
No further 'tis, than Here –

~

FASCICLE TWENTY-ONE

SHEET ONE c. late 1862

I – Years – had been – from Home –[200]
And now – before the Door –
I dared not open – lest a face
I never saw before

Stare vacant into mine –
And ask my Business there –
My Business – just a Life I left –
Was such – still dwelling there? [such –] Remaining there

I fumbled at my nerve –
I scanned the Windows o'er –
The Silence – like an Ocean rolled –
And broke against my Ear – [And] smote –

I laughed a Wooden laugh –
That I – could fear a Door –
Who Danger – and the Dead – had faced –
But never shook – before – [never] quaked –

I fitted to the Latch – my Hand –
With trembling Care –
Lest back the Awful Door should spring –
And leave me – in the Floor –

I moved my fingers off, as cautiously as Glass –
And held my Ears – and like a Thief
Stole – gasping – from the House. fled [gasping –]

You'll find – it when you try to die –
The easier to let go –

For recollecting such as went –
You could not spare – you know.

And though their places somewhat filled –
As did their Marble names
With Moss – they never grew so full –
You chose the newer names – [newer] times –

And when this World – sets further back –
As Dying – say it does –
The former love – distincter grows –
And supersedes the fresh –

And Thought of them – so fair invites –
It looks too tawdry Grace
To stay behind – with just the Toys
We bought – to ease their place –

SHEET TWO c. late 1862

I see thee better – in the Dark –
I do not need a Light –
The Love of Thee – a Prism be –
Excelling Violet –

I see thee better for the Years
That hunch themselves between – [That] pile themselves –
The Miner's Lamp – sufficient be –
To nullify the Mine –

And in the Grave – I see Thee best –
Its little Panels be
A'glow – All ruddy – with the Light
I held so high, for Thee –

What need of Day –
To Those whose Dark – hath so – surpassing Sun –
It deem it be – Continually –
At the Meridian?

I see thee: *Sent to Ns (lost) and to SD (lost, published variant) c. 1862*

Could – I do more – for Thee –
Wert Thou a Bumble Bee –
Since for the Queen, have I –
Nought but Boquet?

~

It would have starved a Gnat –
To live so small as I – [To] dine
And yet, I was a living child –
With Food's nescessity

Upon me – like a Claw –
I could no more remove
Than I could coax a Leech away – [could] modify [a Leech]
Or make a Dragon – move –

Nor like the Gnat – had I –
The privilege to fly
And seek a Dinner for myself – [And] gain
How mightier He – than I!

Nor like Himself – the Art
Upon the Window Pane
To gad my little Being out –
And not begin – again –

~

They shut me up in Prose –[201]
As when a little Girl
They put me in the Closet –
Because they liked me "still" –

Still! Could themself have peeped –
And seen my Brain – go round –
They might as wise have lodged a Bird
For Treason – in the Pound –

Himself has but to will
And easy as a Star
Look down upon Captivity – Abolish his – [Captivity –]
And laugh – No more have I –

~

SHEET THREE c. late 1862

This was a Poet –[202]
It is That
Distills amazing sense
From Ordinary Meanings –
And Attar so immense

From the familiar species
That perished by the Door –
We wonder it was not Ourselves
Arrested it – before –

Of Pictures, the Discloser –
The Poet – it is He –
Entitles Us – by Contrast –
To ceaseless Poverty –

Of Portion – so unconscious –
The Robbing – could not harm –
Himself – to Him – a Fortune –
Exterior – to Time –

In falling Timbers buried –[203] [In] crashing
There breathed a Man –
Outside – the spades – were plying – Without [the]
The Lungs – within –

Could He – know – they sought Him –
Could They – know – He breathed – [He] lived
Horrid Sand Partition –
Neither – could be heard –

Never slacked the Diggers –
But when spades had done –
Oh, Reward of Anguish, Recompense of [Anguish,]
It was dying – Then –

Many Things – are fruitless –
'Tis a Baffling Earth –
But there is no Gratitude
Like the Grace – of Death –

I died for Beauty – but was scarce[204]
Adjusted in the Tomb
When One who died for Truth, was lain
In an adjoining Room –

He questioned softly "Why I failed"?
"For Beauty", I replied –
"And I – for Truth – Themself are One –
We Bretheren, are", He said –

And so, as Kinsmen, met a Night –
We talked between the Rooms –
Until the Moss had reached our lips –
And covered up – Our names –

Dreams – are well – but Waking's better –
If One wake at Morn –
If One wake at Midnight – better –
Dreaming – of the Dawn –

Sweeter – the Surmising Robins –
Never gladdened Tree –
Than a Solid Dawn – confronting –
Leading to no Day –

SHEET FOUR c. late 1862

The Outer – from the Inner
Derives its magnitude –
'Tis Duke, or Dwarf, according
As is the central mood –

The fine – unvarying Axis
That regulates the Wheel –
Though Spokes – spin – more conspicuous
And fling a dust – the while.

The Inner – paints the Outer –
The Brush without the Hand –
Its Picture publishes – precise –
As is the inner Brand –

o

On fine – Arterial Canvas –
A Cheek – perchance a Brow –
The Star's whole secret – in the Lake –
Eyes were not meant to know.

~

At last – to be identified –[205]
At last – the Lamps upon your side –
The rest of life – to see –

Past Midnight – past the Morning Star –
Past Sunrise – Ah, What Leagues there were –
Between Our Feet – and Day!

~

The Malay – took the Pearl –[206]
Not – I – the Earl –
I – feared the Sea – too much
Unsanctified – to touch –

Praying that I might be
Worthy – the Destiny –
The Swarthy fellow swam –
And bore my Jewel – Home –

Home to the Hut! What lot
Had I – the Jewel – got –
Borne on a Dusky Breast –
I had not deemed a Vest
Of Amber – fit –

The Negro never knew
I – wooed it – too –
To gain, or be undone –
Alike to Him – One –

~

Love – thou art high –[207]
I cannot climb thee –
But, were it Two –
Who knows but we –

Taking turns – at the Chimborazo –
Ducal – at last – stand up by thee –

Love – thou art deep –
I cannot cross thee –
But, were there Two
Instead of One –
Rower, and Yacht – some sovreign Summer –
Who knows – but we'd reach the Sun?

Love – thou art Vailed –
A few – behold thee –
Smile – and alter – and prattle – and die –
Bliss – were an Oddity – without thee –
Nicknamed by God –
Eternity –

SHEET FIVE c. late 1862

Our journey had advanced –
Our feet were almost come
To that odd Fork in Being's Road –
Eternity – by Term –

Our pace took sudden awe –
Our feet – reluctant – led –
Before – were Cities – but Between –
The Forest of the Dead –

Retreat – was out of Hope –
Behind – a Sealed Route –
Eternity's White Flag – Before – [Eternity's] cool [Flag –] in front –
And God – at every Gate –

I rose – because He sank –[208]
I thought it would be opposite –
But when his power dropped – [power] bent
My Soul grew straight. [Soul] felt – • bent – • stood

○

I cheered my fainting Prince –
I sang firm – even – Chants – [sang] straight – steady chants –
I helped his Film – with Hymn – [I] stayed

And when the Dews drew off
That held his Forehead stiff –
I met him – [I] gave him –
Balm to Balm – Balm – for Balm

I told him Best – must pass
Through this low Arch of Flesh –
No Casque so brave
It spurn the Grave –

I told him Worlds I knew [told] A world
Where Emperors grew – [Where] Monarchs –
Who recollected us
If we were true –

And so with Thews of Hymn –
And Sinew from within –
And ways I knew not that I knew – till then –
I lifted Him –

It was given to me by the Gods –
When I was a little Girl –
They give us Presents most – you know –
When we are new – and small.
I kept it in my Hand –
I never put it down –
I did not dare to eat – or sleep –
For fear it would be gone –
I heard such words as "Rich" –
When hurrying to school –
From lips at Corners of the Streets –
And wrestled with a smile.
Rich! 'Twas Myself – was rich –
To take the name of Gold –
And Gold to own – in solid Bars –
The Difference – made me bold –

FASCICLE TWENTY-TWO

SHEET ONE c. late 1862

A Prison gets to be a friend –[209]
Between its Ponderous face
And Ours – a Kinsmanship express – [Kinsmanship] exist – • subsist – • arise
And in its narrow Eyes –

We come to look with gratitude [with] fondness – • pleasure
For the appointed Beam
It deal us – stated as Our food – [It] furnish [stated]
And hungered for – the same –

We learn to know the Planks –
That answer to Our feet –
So miserable a sound – at first –
Nor even now – so sweet –

As plashing in the Pools –
When Memory was a Boy –
But a Demurer Circuit – [Demurer] Measure –
A Geometric Joy –

The Posture of the Key
That interrupt the Day
To Our Endeavor – Not so real [so] true – • close – • near
The Cheek of Liberty –

As this Phantasm steel – [this] Companion
Whose features – Day and Night –
Are present to us – as Our Own –
And as escapeless – quite –

The narrow Round – the stint –
The slow exchange of Hope –

For something passiver – Content
Too steep for looking up –

The Liberty we knew
Avoided – like a Dream – [Avoided –] As
Too wide for any night but Heaven –
If That – indeed – redeem – [If] Even That – redeem –

~

Nature – sometimes sears a Sapling –
Sometimes – scalps a Tree –
Her Green People recollect it
When they do not die –

Fainter Leaves – to Further Seasons –
Dumbly testify –
We – who have the Souls –
Die oftener – Not so vitally –

~

SHEET TWO c. late 1862

She dealt her pretty words like Blades –
How glittering they shone –
And every One unbared a Nerve
Or wantoned with a Bone –

She never deemed – she hurt –
That – is not Steel's Affair –
A vulgar grimace in the Flesh –
How ill the Creatures bear –

To Ache is human – not polite –
The Film upon the eye
Mortality's old Custom –
Just locking up – to Die –

~

"Why do I love" You, Sir?[210]
Because –

Nature – sometimes sears: *Sent to SD (variant) c. late 1862*

The Wind does not require the Grass
To answer – Wherefore when He pass
She cannot keep Her place.

Because He knows – and
Do not You –
And We know not –
Enough for Us
The Wisdom it be so –

The Lightning – never asked an Eye
Wherefore it shut – when He was by –
Because He knows it cannot speak –
And reasons not contained – Of Talk –
There be – preferred by Daintier Folk –

The Sunrise – Sir – compelleth Me –
Because He's Sunrise – and I see –
Therefore – Then –
I love Thee –

~

The Himmaleh was known to stoop
Unto the Daisy low –
Transported with Compassion
That such a Doll should grow
Where Tent by Tent – Her Universe
Hung Out its Flags of Snow –

~

We Cover Thee – Sweet Face –
Not that We tire of Thee –
But that Thyself fatigue of Us –
Remember – as Thou go –
We follow Thee until
Thou notice Us – no more –
And then – reluctant – turn away
To Con Thee o'er and o'er –

And blame the scanty love
We were Content to show –

Augmented – Sweet – a Hundred fold –
If Thou would'st take it – now –

SHEET THREE c. late 1862

Of Being is a Bird
The likest to the Down
An Easy Breeze do put afloat
The General Heavens – upon –

It soars – and shifts – and whirls –
And measures with the Clouds
In easy – even – dazzling pace –
No different the Birds –

Except a Wake of Music
Accompany their feet –
As did the Down emit a Tune – [As] should
For Extasy – of it

A long – long Sleep – [A] vast – vast – • Brave – brave –
A famous – Sleep –
That makes no show for Morn –
By Stretch of Limb – or stir of Lid –
An independant One –

Was ever idleness like This? [ever] Arrogance
Upon a Bank of Stone Within a Hut of Stone.
To bask the Centuries away –
Nor once look up – for Noon?

Without this – there is nought –
All other Riches be
As is the Twitter of a Bird –
Heard opposite the Sea – Held [opposite]

I could not care – to gain
A lesser than the Whole –

For did not this include themself –
As Seams – include the Ball?

Or wished a way might be [a] sort
My Heart to subdivide –
'Twould magnify – the Gratitude –
And not reduce – the Gold –

~

The name – of it – is "Autumn" –[211]
The hue – of it – is Blood –
An Artery – upon the Hill –
A Vein – along the Road –

Great Globules – in the Alleys –
And Oh, the Shower of Stain –
When Winds – upset the Basin –
And spill the Scarlet Rain – [And] tip –

It sprinkles Bonnets – far below –
It gathers ruddy Pools –
Then – eddies like a Rose – away –
Upon Vermillion Wheels – And leaves me with the Hills.

line 10: [It] stands in – [ruddy] • makes Vermillion – [Pools –]

~

SHEET FOUR c. late 1862

I dwell in Possibility –[212]
A fairer House than Prose –
More numerous of Windows –
Superior – for Doors –

Of Chambers as the Cedars –
Impregnable of eye –
And for an everlasting Roof
The Gambrels of the Sky – [The] Gables –

Of Visitors – the fairest –
For Occupation – This –
The spreading wide my narrow Hands
To gather Paradise –

~

A Solemn thing within the Soul
To feel itself get ripe –
And golden hang – while farther up –
The Maker's Ladders stop –
And in the Orchard far below –
You hear a Being – drop –

A wonderful – to feel the sun
Still toiling at the cheek
You thought was finished –
Cool of eye, and critical of Work –
He shifts the stem – a little –
To give your Core – a look –

But solemnest – to know
Your chance in Harvest moves
A little nearer – Every sun
The single – to some lives.

Whole Gulfs – of Red, and Fleets – of Red –[213]
And Crews – of solid Blood –
Did place about the West – Tonight –
As 'twere specific Ground – ['twere] a signal Ground –

And They – appointed Creatures –
In Authorized Arrays –
Due – promptly – as a Drama –
That bows – and disappears –

My Garden – like the Beach –
Denotes there be – a Sea –
That's Summer –
Such as These – the Pearls
She fetches – such as Me

That first Day, when you praised Me, Sweet,
And said that I was strong –
And could be mighty, if I liked –
That Day – the Days among –

Glows central – like a Jewel
Between Diverging Golds –
The Minor One – that gleamed behind – [that] shone
And Vaster – of the World's. [And] this One – • different – [of the]

SHEET FIVE c. late 1862

To make One's Toilette – after Death
Has made the Toilette cool
Of only Taste we cared to please
Is difficult, and still –

That's easier – than Braid the Hair –
And make the Boddice gay –
When Eyes that fondled it are wrenched
By Decalogues – away –

'Tis good – the looking back on Grief – ['Tis] well
To re-endure a Day –
We thought the mighty Funeral – [the] monstrous
Of all conceived Joy –

To recollect how Busy Grass
Did meddle – one by one – [Did] tamper
Till all the Grief with Summer – waved [Summer –] blew –
And none could see the stone.

And though the Wo you have Today
Be larger – As the Sea
Exceeds its unremembered Drop – [its] undeveloped
They're Water – equally – they prove One Chemistry –

I was the slightest in the House –
I took the smallest Room –
At night, my little Lamp, and Book –
And one Geranium –

So stationed I could catch the mint
That never ceased to fall –
And just my Basket –
Let me think – I'm sure
That this was all –

I never spoke – unless addressed –
And then, 'twas brief and low –
I could not bear to live – aloud –
The Racket shamed me so –

And if it had not been so far –
And any one I knew
Were going – I had often thought
How noteless – I could die –

~

You love the Lord – you cannot see –
You write Him – every day –
A little note – when you awake –
And further in the Day,

An Ample Letter – How you miss –
And would delight to see –
But then His House – is but a step –
And mine's – in Heaven – You see –

~

SHEET SIX c. late 1862

Myself was formed – a Carpenter –[214]
An unpretending time
My Plane, and I, together wrought
Before a Builder came –

o

To measure our attainments –
Had we the Art of Boards
Sufficiently developed – He'd hire us
At Halves –

My Tools took Human – Faces –
The Bench, where we had toiled –
Against the Man, persuaded –
We – Temples build – I said –

~

We pray – to Heaven –
We prate – of Heaven –
Relate – when Neighbors die –
At what o'clock to Heaven – they fled –
Who saw them – Wherefore fly?

Is Heaven a Place – a Sky – a Tree?
Location's narrow way is for Ourselves –
Unto the Dead
There's no Geography –

But State – Endowal – Focus –
Where – Omnipresence – fly?

~

He fumbles at your Soul
As Players at the Keys –
Before they drop full Music on –
He stuns you by Degrees –

Prepares your brittle substance — [brittle] nature
For the etherial Blow
By fainter Hammers – further heard –
Then nearer – Then so – slow –

Your Breath – has chance to straighten – — [has] time
Your Brain – to bubble cool –
Deals One – imperial Thunderbolt –
That peels your naked soul – — [That] scalps

○

He fumbles at: *Sent to SD (variant) c. late 1862*

When Winds hold Forests in their Paws –
The Firmaments – are still – The Universe – is still

~

Just Once! Oh Least Request![215]
Could Adamant – refuse?
So small – a Grace – so scanty – put –
So agonized Urged? Such agonizing Terms –

Would not a God of Flint –
Be conscious of a sigh –
As down his Heaven – echoed faint – [Heaven –] dropt – remote –
"Just Once"! Sweet Deity!

~

Just Once! Oh: *Sent to SB (variant) c. 1863*

FASCICLE TWENTY-THREE

SHEET ONE c. late 1862

Because I could not stop for Death –[216]
He kindly stopped for me –
The Carriage held but just Ourselves –
And Immortality.

We slowly drove – He knew no haste
And I had put away
My labor and my leisure too,
For His Civility –

We passed the School, where Children strove
At Recess – in the Ring –
We passed the Fields of Gazing Grain –
We passed the Setting Sun –

Or rather – He passed Us –
The Dews drew quivering and Chill –
For only Gossamer, my Gown –
My Tippet – only Tulle –

We paused before a House that seemed
A Swelling of the Ground –
The Roof was scarcely visible –
The Cornice – in the Ground –

Since then – 'tis Centuries – and yet
Feels shorter than the Day
I first surmised the Horses' Heads
Were toward Eternity –

He fought like those[217]
Who've nought to lose –

Bestowed Himself to Balls — He gave himself [to Balls]
As One who for a further Life
Had not a further Use –

Invited Death – with bold attempt –
But Death was Coy of Him — [was] shy
As Other Men, were Coy of Death.
To Him – to live – was Doom –

His Comrades, shifted like the Flakes
When Gusts reverse the Snow –
But He – was left alive Because — [He –] remained
Of Greediness to die – — [Of] Urgency – • Vehemence

Fame of Myself, to justify,
All other Plaudit be
Superfluous – An Incense
Beyond Nescessity –

Fame of Myself to lack – Although
My Name be else supreme –
This were an Honor honorless –
A futile Diadem –

SHEET TWO c. late 1862

Wolfe demanded during Dying[218]
"Which controlled the Day?"
"General – the British" – "Easy"
Answered He – "to die" –

Montcalm – His opposing Spirit
Rendered with a smile –
"Sweet" said He, "My own Surrender
Liberty's – forestall –"

Most she touched me by her muteness –
Most she won me by the way

Wolfe demanded during: *Sent to SD (variant) c. late 1862*

She presented her small figure –
Plea itself – for Charity –

Were a Crumb my whole possession –
Were there famine in the land –
Were it my resource from starving –
Could I such a plea withstand – [a] face

Not upon her knee to thank me
Sank this Beggar from the Sky – [Sank] the
But the Crumb partook – departed –
And returned on High –

I supposed – when sudden
Such a Praise began
'Twas as Space sat singing
To herself – and men –

'Twas the Winged Beggar –
Afterward I learned
To her Benefactor
Making Gratitude paying [Gratitude]

From Blank to Blank –
A Threadless Way [Threadless] Course
I pushed Mechanic feet –
To stop – or perish – or advance –
Alike indifferent –

If end I gained [I] reached
It ends beyond
Indefinite disclosed –
I shut my eyes – and groped as well
'Twas lighter – to be Blind – ['Twas] firmer

SHEET THREE c. late 1862

The Whole of it came not at once –
'Twas Murder by degrees –

A Thrust – and then for Life a chance –
The Bliss to cauterize – The certain prey to teaze –

The Cat reprieves the mouse
She eases from her teeth
Just long enough for Hope to teaze – [to] stir
Then mashes it to death – [Then] crunches

'Tis Life's award – to die –
Contenteder if once –
Than dying half – then rallying [dying] part
For consciouser Eclipse – [For] totaller –

He told a homely tale
And spotted it with tears –
Upon his infant face was set
The Cicatrice of years –

All crumpled was the cheek
No other kiss had known
Than flake of snow, divided with [snow,] imprinted swift –
The Redbreast of the Barn – when hurrying to the town

If Mother – in the Grave –
Or Father – on the Sea –
Or Father in the Firmament –
Or Bretheren, had he –

If Commonwealth below,
Or Commonwealth above
Have missed a Barefoot Citizen – [Have] lost
I've ransomed it – alive – I've found it – 'tis alive –

Presentiment – is that long shadow – on the Lawn –
Indicative that Suns go down –

The notice to the startled Grass Monition – [to]
That Darkness – is about to pass –

You constituted Time –
I deemed Eternity
A Revelation of Yourself –
'Twas therefore Deity

The Absolute – removed [Absolute –] withdrew –
The Relative away –
That I unto Himself adjust
My slow idolatry –

SHEET FOUR c. late 1862

My Faith is larger than the Hills –
So when the Hills decay –
My Faith must take the Purple Wheel
To show the Sun the way –

'Tis first He steps upon the Vane – You see [He]
And then – upon the Hill –
And then abroad the World He go
To do His Golden Will –

And if His Yellow feet should miss –
The Bird would not arise – [The] Day
The Flowers would slumber on their Stems – [would] sleep upon – [their]
No Bells have Paradise –

How dare I, therefore, stint a faith
On which so vast depends –
Lest Firmament should fail for me – [Lest] Universe – • Deity –
The Rivet in the Bands

Rests at Night
The Sun from shining,
Nature – and some Men –
Rest at Noon – some Men –
While Nature
And the Sun – go on –

The World – feels Dusty
When We stop to Die –
We want the Dew – then –
Honors – taste dry –

Flags – vex a Dying face –
But the least Fan
Stirred by a friend's Hand –
Cools – like the Rain –

Mine be the Ministry
When thy Thirst comes –
Dews of Thessaly, to fetch –
And Hybla Balms –

~

To offer brave assistance[219]
To Lives that stand alone –
When One has failed to stop them – [When] You [have]
Is Human – but Divine

To lend an ample Sinew
Unto a Nameless Man –
Whose Homely Benediction
No other – stopped to earn – [other –] cared –

~

SHEET FIVE c. late 1862

When I hoped, I recollect
Just the place I stood –
At a Window facing West – In a Chamber [facing]
Roughest Air – was good –

Not a Sleet could bite me –
Not a frost could cool – No November cool
Hope it was that kept me warm –
Not Merino shawl –

When I feared – I recollect
Just the Day it was –

Worlds were lying out to Sun –
Yet how Nature froze –

Icicles upon my soul
Prickled Blue and cool – [Prickled] Raw and cool
Bird went praising everywhere –
Only Me – was still – Still Myself – • Me alone [was still –]

And the Day that I despaired –
This – if I forget
Nature will – that it be Night
After Sun has set – When the Sun is set
Darkness intersect her face – Dark shall overtake the Hill –
And put out her eye – Overtake the sky.
Nature hesitate – before
Memory and I –

line 11: Worlds were swimming in the Sun – • [Worlds were] lying [in the Sun –]

The Wind didn't come from the Orchard – today –
Further than that –
Nor stop to play with the Hay –
Nor threaten a Hat – [Nor] joggle –
He's a transitive fellow – very –
Rely on that –

If He leave a Bur at the door
We know He has climbed a Fir –
But the Fir is Where – Declare –
Were you ever there?

If He bring Odors of Clovers –
And that is His business – not Ours –
Then He has been with the Mowers –
Whetting away the Hours
To sweet pauses of Hay –
His Way – of a June Day –

If He fling Sand, and Pebble –
Little Boy's Hats – and stubble –
With an occasional steeple –

The Wind didn't: *Sent to SD (variant) c. summer 1862*

And a hoarse "Get out of the Way, I say",
Who'd be the fool to stay?
Would you – Say –
Would you be the fool to stay?

SHEET SIX c. late 1862

The Day undressed – Herself –
Her Garter – was of Gold –
Her Petticoat of Purple – just – [Purple –] plain –
Her Dimities as old

Exactly – as the World precisely [as]
And yet the newest Star
Enrolled upon the Hemisphere – [the] Firmament
Be wrinkled – much as Her –

Too near to God – to pray –
Too near to Heaven – to fear –
The Lady of the Occident
Retired without a Care – laid down – [without]

Her Candle so expire
The Flickering be seen
On Ball of Mast – in Foreign Port – [in] Bosporus –
And Spire – and Window Pane. And Dome – • Church – [and]

The Beggar Lad – dies early –[220]
It's Somewhat in the Cold –
And somewhat in the Trudging feet –
And haply, in the World –

The Cruel – smiling – bowing World –
That took its Cambric Way –
Nor heard the timid cry for "Bread –"
"Sweet Lady – Charity" –

Among Redeemed Children
If Trudging feet may stand –

The Day undressed –: *Sent to the Hollands (variant) c. late 1862*
The Beggar Lad –: *Sent to Ns (lost) c. late 1862*

The Barefoot time forgotten – so –
The Sleet – the bitter Wind –

The Childish Hands that teazed for Pence
Lifted adoring – then –
To Him whom never Ragged – Coat
Did supplicate in vain –

~

One and One – are One –
Two – be finished using –
Well enough for schools –
But for minor Choosing – [for] inner

Life – just – Or Death –
Or the Everlasting –
More – would be too vast Two – [would]
For the Soul's Comprising –

~

I lived on Dread –
To Those who know
The stimulus there is
In Danger – Other impetus
Is numb – and vitalless –

As 'twere a Spur – upon the Soul –
A Fear will urge it where
To go without the spectre's aid [spectre's] help –
Were challenging Despair.

~

FASCICLE TWENTY-FOUR

SHEET ONE c. spring 1863

It sifts from Leaden Sieves –[221]
It powders all the Field –
It fills with Alabaster Wool
The Wrinkles of the Road –

It makes an even face
Of Mountain – and of Plain –
Unbroken Forehead from the East
Unto the East – again –

It reaches to the Fence –
It wraps it, Rail by Rail,
Till it is lost in Fleeces –
It flings a Crystal Vail [It] deals celestial Vail –

On Stump – and Stack – and Stem –
The Summer's empty Room –
Acres of Joints – where Harvests were – Acres of Seams – [where]
Recordless – but for them –

It Ruffles Wrists of Posts –
As Ancles of a Queen –
Then stills its Artisans – like Swans – [its] Myrmidons [like] Ghosts –
Denying they have been –

Like Mighty Foot Lights – burned the Red
At Bases of the Trees –
The far Theatricals of Day
Exhibiting – to These –

'Twas Universe – that did applaud – [did] attend
While Chiefest – of the Crowd – [Chiefest –] in –

It sifts from: *Sent to SD (variant) c. late 1862; 12-line versions were sent to TWH c. 1871 and to Thomas Niles c. March 1883, called "the Snow"*

Enabled by his Royal Dress –
Myself distinguished God –

~

A Pit – but Heaven over it –[222]
And Heaven beside, and Heaven abroad;
And yet a Pit –
With Heaven over it.

To stir would be to slip –
To look would be to drop –
To dream – to sap the Prop
That holds my chances up.
Ah! Pit! With Heaven over it!

The depth is all my thought –
I dare not ask my feet –
'Twould start us where we sit
So straight you'd scarce suspect
It was a Pit – with fathoms under it
Its Circuit just the same
Whose Doom to whom
'Twould start them –
We – could tremble –
But since we got a Bomb –
And held it in our Bosom –
Nay – Hold it – it is calm –

Harriet Graves

~

A curious Cloud surprised the Sky,
'Twas like a sheet with Horns;
The sheet was Blue –
The Antlers Gray –
It almost touched the Lawns.

So low it leaned – then statelier drew –
And trailed like robes away;
A Queen adown a satin aisle,
Had not the majesty.

Harriet Graves

~

SHEET TWO c. spring 1863

Of Brussels – it was not –[223]
Of Kidderminster? Nay –
The Winds did buy it of the Woods –
They – sold it unto me   Then – sell it [unto]

It was a gentle price –
The poorest – could afford –
It was within the frugal purse
Of Beggar – or of Bird –

Of small and spicy Yards –   [spicy] Breadths –
In hue – a mellow Dun –
Of Sunshine – and of Sere – Composed –
But, principally – of Sun –

The Wind – unrolled it fast –
And spread it on the Ground –
Upholsterer of the Pines – is He –   [Upholsterer] Of the Sea • of the land – • Hills –
Upholsterer – of the Pond –

He found my Being – set it up –[224]
Adjusted it to place –
Then carved his name – upon it –   He wrote [his]
And bade it to the East   then – [bade]

Be faithful – in his absence –
And he would come again –
With Equipage of Amber –
That time – to take it Home –

Unto my Books – so good to turn –[225]
Far ends of tired Days –   [of] Homely –
It half endears the Abstinence –
And Pain – is missed – in Praise.   [Pain –] Forgets – for – [Praise.]

As Flavors – cheer Retarded Guests
With Banquettings to be –

Of Brussels – it: *Sent to Ns (lost) c. early 1863, with pine needle*

So Spices – stimulate the time
Till my small Library –

It may be Wilderness – without –
Far feet of failing Men –
But Holiday – excludes the night –
And it is Bells – within –

I thank these Kinsmen of the Shelf –
Their Countenances Kid
Enamor – in Prospective –
And satisfy – obtained –

~

The Spider holds a Silver Ball[226]
In unperceived Hands –
And dancing softly to Himself — [softly] as He knits
His Yarn of Pearl – unwinds –

He plies from nought to nought –
In unsubstantial Trade –
Supplants our Tapestries with His –
In half the period –

An Hour to rear supreme
His Continents of Light – — [His] theories
Then dangle from the Housewife's Broom – — [Then] perish by
His Boundaries – forgot – — [His] sophistries –

line 4: [His] Coil – [of Pearl –] expends – • Pursues his pearly strands –

~

SHEET THREE c. spring 1863

Three times – we parted –
Breath – and I –
Three times – He would not go –
But strove to stir the lifeless Fan — [the] flickering fan
The Waters – strove to stay.

Three times – the Billows threw me up – — [Billows] tossed
Then caught me – like a Ball –

Then made Blue faces in my face –
And pushed away a sail

That crawled Leagues off – I liked to see –
For thinking – While I die –
How pleasant to behold a Thing
Where Human faces – be –

The Waves grew sleepy –   The Ocean – tired – • wearied –
Breath – did not –
The Winds – like Children – lulled –
Then Sunrise kissed my Chrysalis –
And I stood up – and lived –

There is a pain – so utter –
It swallows substance up –   [swallows] Being
Then covers the Abyss with Trance –
So Memory can step
Around – across – upon it –
As One within a Swoon –
Goes safely – where an open eye –   [Goes] steady –
Would drop Him – Bone by Bone –   [Would] spill Him –

It troubled me as once I was –
For I was once a Child –
Concluding how an atom – fell –   Deciding [how]
And yet the Heavens – held –

The Heavens weighed the most – by far –   [Heavens] were the weightiest – far –
Yet Blue – and solid – stood –   [and] easy
Without a Bolt – that I could prove –
Would Giants – understand?   did – • might [Giants –]

Life set me larger – problems –
Some I shall keep – to solve   [shall] save [to] ~~prove~~
Till Algebra is easier –   where [Algebra]
Or simpler proved – above –

Then – too – be comprehended –
What sorer – puzzled me –
Why Heaven did not break away –
And tumble – Blue – on me –

A still – Volcano – Life – [still –] ~~Volcanic~~
That flickered in the night –
When it was dark enough to do [to] show
Without erasing sight – [Without] endangering

A quiet – Earthquake style –
Too subtle to suspect [Too] smouldering
By natures this side Naples –
The North cannot detect

The solemn – Torrid – Symbol –
The lips that never lie –
Whose hissing Corals part – and shut –
And Cities – ooze away – [Cities –] slip – • slide – • melt –

SHEET FOUR c. spring 1863

When I was small, a Woman died –[227]
Today – her Only Boy
Went up from the Potomac –
His face all Victory

To look at her – How slowly
The Seasons must have turned
Till Bullets clipt an Angle
And He passed quickly round – [He] went softly –

If pride shall be in Paradise –
Ourself cannot decide –
Of their imperial conduct –
No person testified –

But, proud in Apparition –
That Woman and her Boy

Pass back and forth, before my Brain
As even in the sky –

I'm confident, that Bravoes –
Perpetual break abroad
For Braveries, remote as this
In Yonder Maryland –

[Perpetual] be – • go –
[Braveries,] just proved – • sealed in
Scarlet [Maryland –]

This is my letter to the World
That never wrote to Me –
The simple News that Nature told –
With tender Majesty

Her Message is committed
To Hands I cannot see –
For love of Her – Sweet – countrymen –
Judge tenderly – of Me

God made a little Gentian –[228]
It tried – to be a Rose –
And failed – and all the Summer laughed –
But just before the Snows

There rose a Purple Creature –
That ravished all the Hill –
And Summer hid her Forehead –
And Mockery – was still –

The Frosts were her condition –
The Tyrian would not come
Until the North – invoke it –
Creator – Shall I – bloom?

My Reward for Being – was this –[229]
My Premium – My Bliss –
An Admiralty, less –
A Sceptre – penniless –
And Realms – just Dross –

When Thrones – accost my Hands –
With "Me – Miss – Me" –
I'll unroll – Thee –
Sufficient Dynasty –
Creation – powerless –
To Peer this Grace –
Empire – State –
Too little – Dust –
To Dower – so Great –

SHEET FIVE c. spring 1863

It always felt to me – a wrong[230]
To that Old Moses – done –
To let him see – the Canaan –
Without the entering –

And tho' in soberer moments –
No Moses there can be
I'm satisfied – the Romance
In point of injury –

Surpasses sharper stated –
Of Stephen – or of Paul –
For these – were only put to death –
While God's adroiter will

On Moses – seemed to fasten
With tantalizing Play — in [tantalizing]
As Boy – should deal with lesser Boy –
To prove ability – — [To] show supremacy

The fault – was doubtless Israel's –
Myself – had banned the Tribes –
And ushered Grand Old Moses
In Pentateuchal Robes

Upon the Broad Possession — [the] Lawful Manor –
'Twas little – He should see – — But titled Him – to see –
Old Man on Nebo! Late as this –
My justice bleeds – for Thee! — One – [justice]

I tie my Hat – I crease my Shawl –[231]
Life's little duties do – precisely –
As the very least
Were infinite – to me –

I put new Blossoms in the Glass –
And throw the Old – away –
I push a petal from my Gown
That anchored there – I weigh
The time 'twill be till six o'clock –
So much I have to do –
And yet – existence – some way back –
Stopped – struck – my ticking – through –

We cannot put Ourself away
As a completed Man
Or Woman – When the errand's done
We came to Flesh – upon –
There may be – Miles on Miles of Nought –
Of Action – sicker far –
To simulate – is stinging work –
To cover what we are
From Science – and from Surgery –
Too Telescopic eyes
To bear on us unshaded –
For their – sake – Not for Ours –

Therefore – we do life's labor –
Though life's Reward – be done –
With scrupulous exactness –
To hold our Senses – on –

~

SHEET SIX c. spring 1863

The Trees like Tassels – hit – and swung –[232]
There seemed to rise a Tune
From Miniature Creatures
Accompanying the Sun –

o

Far Psalteries of Summer –
Enamoring the Ear
They never yet did satisfy –
Remotest – when most fair [most] near –

The Sun shone whole at intervals –
Then Half – then utter hid –
As if Himself were optional
And had Estates of Cloud [And] owned

Sufficient to enfold Him
Eternally from view –
Except it were a whim of His
To let the Orchards grow –

A Bird sat careless on the fence –
One gossipped in the Lane
On silver matters charmed a Snake
Just winding round a stone –

Bright Flowers slit a Calyx
And soared upon a stem Or [soared]
Like Hindered Flags – Sweet hoisted –
With Spices – in the Hem –

'Twas more – I cannot mention –
How mean – to those that see –
Vandyke's Delineation
Of Nature's – Summer Day!

It feels a shame to be Alive –[233]
When Men so brave – are dead –
One envies the Distinguished Dust –
Permitted – such a Head –

The Stone – that tells defending Whom
This Spartan put away
What little of Him we – possessed
In Pawn for Liberty –

o

The price is great – Sublimely paid –
Do we deserve – a Thing –
That lives – like Dollars – must be piled
Before we may obtain?

Are we that wait – sufficient worth –
That such Enormous Pearl
As life – dissolved be – for Us –
In Battle's – horrid Bowl?

It may be – a Renown to live –
I think the Men who die –
Those unsustained – Saviors –
Present Divinity –

FASCICLE TWENTY-FIVE

SHEET ONE c. summer 1863

A precious – mouldering pleasure – 'tis –
To meet an Antique Book –
In just the Dress his Century wore –
A privilege – I think –

His venerable Hand to take –
And warming in our own –
A passage back – or two – to make –
To Times when he – was young –

His quaint opinions – to inspect –
His thought to ascertain
On Themes concern our mutual mind –
The Literature of Man –

What interested Scholars – most –
What Competitions ran –
When Plato – was a Certainty –
And Sophocles – a Man –

When Sappho – was a living Girl –
And Beatrice wore
The Gown that Dante – deified –
Facts Centuries before

He traverses – familiar –
As One should come to Town –
And tell you all your Dreams – were true –
He lived – where Dreams were born

His presence is enchantment –
You beg him not to go –
Old Volumes shake their Vellum Heads
And tantalize – just so –

A precious – mouldering: *Sent to SD (lost) presumably c. 1863*

I tried to think a lonelier Thing[234]
Than any I had seen –
Some Polar Expiation – An Omen in the Bone
Of Death's tremendous nearness –

I probed Retrieveless things
My Duplicate – to borrow –
A Haggard comfort springs

From the belief that Somewhere –
Within the Clutch of Thought –
There dwells one other Creature
Of Heavenly Love – forgot –

I plucked at our Partition –
As One should pry the Walls –
Between Himself – and Horror's Twin –
Within Opposing Cells –

I almost strove to clasp his Hand,
Such Luxury – it grew –
That as Myself – could pity Him –
Perhaps he – pitied me – He – too – could pity me –

SHEET TWO c. summer 1863

Two Butterflies went out at Noon –[235]
And waltzed upon a Farm –
Then stepped straight through the Firmament
And rested, on a Beam –

And then – together bore away
Upon a shining Sea –
Though never yet, in any Port –
Their coming, mentioned – be –

If spoken by the distant Bird –
If met in Ether Sea
By Frigate, or by Merchantman –
No notice – was – to me – Report was not – to me –

Two Butterflies went: *Sent to Ns (lost) c. summer 1863*

The Day came slow – till Five o'clock –
Then sprang before the Hills
Like Hindered Rubies – or the Light
A Sudden Musket – spills –

The Purple could not keep the East –
The Sunrise shook abroad
Like Breadths of Topaz – packed a night –
The Lady just unrolled –

The Happy Winds – their Timbrels took –
The Birds – in docile Rows
Arranged themselves around their Prince
The Wind – is Prince of Those –

The Orchard sparkled like a Jew –
How mighty 'twas – to be
A Guest in this stupendous place –
The Parlor – of the Day –

It was a quiet Way –[236]
He asked if I was His –
I made no answer of the Tongue,
But answer of the Eyes –

And then he bore me high
Before this mortal noise
With swiftness as of Chariots –
And distance – as of Wheels –

The World did drop away
As Counties – from the feet
Of Him that leaneth in Balloon –
Upon an Ether Street –

The Gulf behind – was not –
The Continents – were new –
Eternity – it was – before
Eternity was due –

o

The Day came: *Sent to Ns (lost) and to SD (variant) c. summer 1863*

No Seasons were – to us –
It was not Night – nor Noon –
For Sunrise – stopped upon the Place –
And fastened it – in Dawn –

~

I know lives, I could miss
Without a Misery –
Others – whose instant's wanting –
Would be Eternity –

The last – a scanty Number –
'Twould scarcely fill a Two –
The first – a Gnat's Horizon
Could easily outgrow –

~

SHEET THREE c. summer 1863

I'm saying every day[237]
"If I should be a Queen, Tomorrow" –
I'd do this way –
And so I deck, a little,

If it be, I wake a Bourbon,
None on me – bend supercilious –
With "This was she –
Begged in the Market place – Yesterday."

Court is a stately place –
I've heard men say –
So I loop my apron, against the Majesty
With bright Pins of Buttercup –
That not too plain –
Rank – overtake me –

And perch my Tongue
On Twigs of singing – rather high –
But this, might be my brief Term
To qualify –

o

Put from my simple speech all plain word –
Take other accents, as such I heard
Though but for the Cricket – just,
And but for the Bee –
Not in all the Meadow –
One accost me –

Better to be ready –
Than did next Morn
Meet me in Arragon –
My old Gown – on –

And the surprised Air
Rustics – wear –
Summoned – unexpectedly –
To Exeter –

The difference between Despair
And Fear – is like the One
Between the instant of a Wreck –
And when the Wreck has been –

The Mind is smooth – no Motion –
Contented as the eye
Upon the Forehead of a Bust –
That knows – it cannot see –

I went to Heaven –[238]
'Twas a small Town –
Lit – with a Ruby –
Lathed – with Down –

Stiller – than the fields
At the full Dew –
Beautiful – as Pictures –
No Man drew –
People – like the Moth –
Of Mechlin – frames –

The difference between: *Sent to SD (variant) c. 1864*
I went to: *Sent to Ns (lost) presumably c. 1863*

Duties – of Gossamer –
And Eider – names –
Almost – contented –
I – could be –
'Mong such unique
Society –

SHEET FOUR c. summer 1863

The Angle of a Landscape –
That every time I wake –
Between my Curtain and the Wall
Upon an ample Crack –

Like a Venetian – waiting –
Accosts my open eye –
Is just a Bough of Apples –
Held slanting, in the Sky –

The Pattern of a Chimney –
The Forehead of a Hill –
Sometimes – a Vane's Forefinger –
But that's – Occasional –

The Seasons – shift – my Picture –
Upon my Emerald Bough,
I wake – to find no – Emeralds –
Then – Diamonds – which the Snow

From Polar Caskets – fetched me –
The Chimney – and the Hill –
And just the Steeple's finger –
These – never stir at all –

The Soul unto itself[239]
Is an imperial friend –
Or the most agonizing Spy –
An Enemy – could send –

o

The Soul unto: *Sent to SD (variant) c. first half 1863 and to TWH (variant) c. 1863*

Secure against its own –
No treason it can fear –
Itself – its Sovreign – Of itself
The Soul should stand in Awe –

~

We see – Comparatively –[240]
The Thing so towering high
We could not grasp its segment — [its] Angle
Unaided – Yesterday –

This Morning's finer Verdict –
Makes scarcely worth the toil –
A furrow – Our Cordillera –
Our Appenine – a knoll –

Perhaps 'tis kindly – done us –
The Anguish – and the loss –
The wrenching – for His Firmament
The Thing belonged to us –

To spare these striding spirits — [these] shrinking – [spirits] • wincing natures –
Some Morning of Chagrin –
The waking in a Gnat's – embrace –
Our Giants – further on –

~

Of Course – I prayed –
And did God Care?
He cared as much as on the Air
A Bird – had stamped her foot –
And cried "Give Me" –
My Reason – Life –
I had not had – but for Yourself –
'Twere better Charity
To leave me in the Atom's Tomb –
Merry, and nought, and gay, and numb –
Than this smart Misery.

~

SHEET FIVE c. summer 1863

I'm sorry for the Dead – Today –
It's such congenial times [congenial] Way
Old neighbors have at fences –
It's time o'year for Hay,

And Broad – Sunburned Acquaintance
Discourse between the Toil –
And laugh, a homely species
That makes the Fences smile –

It seems so straight to lie away
From all the noise of Fields – [the] Sound
The Busy Carts – the fragrant Cocks –
The Mower's metre – Steals

A Trouble lest they're homesick –
Those Farmers – and their Wives –
Set separate from the Farming – Put quiet – [from]
And all the Neighbor's lives –

A Wonder if the Sepulchre
Don't feel a lonesome way –
When Men – and Boys – and Carts – and June, [and] Larks – [and June,]
Go down the Fields to "Hay" –

You cannot put a Fire out – No Man – [can put]
A Thing that can ignite
Can go, itself, without a Fan –
Upon the slowest night –

You cannot fold a Flood –
And put it in a Drawer –
Because the Winds would find it out –
And tell your Cedar Floor –

We dream – it is good we are dreaming –[241]
It would hurt us – were we awake –

But since it is playing – kill us, [since] They [are]
And we are playing – shriek –

What harm? Men die – Externally –
It is a truth – of Blood – [a] Fact
But we – are dying in Drama –
And Drama – is never dead – [is] seldom –

Cautious – We jar each other –
And either – open the eyes – [open] its
Lest the Phantasm – prove the mistake – [prove] just –
And the livid Surprise

Cool us to Shafts of Granite –
With just an age – and name –
And perhaps a phrase in Egyptian – [a] latin inscription –
It's prudenter – to dream –

line 1: We are dreaming [it is good we] should – [dream]

SHEET SIX c. summer 1863

If ever the lid gets off my head[242]
And lets the brain away
The fellow will go where he belonged –
Without a hint from me,

And the world – if the world be looking on –
Will see how far from home
It is possible for sense to live
The soul there – all the time. MLT

Some say good night – at night –
I say good night by day –
Good bye – the Going utter me –
Good night, I still reply –

For parting, that is night,
And presence, simply dawn –
Itself, the purple on the hight
Denominated morn. MLT

She's happy – with a new Content –
That feels to her – like Sacrament –
She's busy – with an altered Care –
As just apprenticed to the Air –

She's tearful – if she weep at all –
For blissful Causes – Most of all
That Heaven permit so meek as her – [so] faint
To such a Fate – to minister –

~

The Heart asks Pleasure – first – [asks] Blessing
And then – excuse from Pain –
And then – those little Anodynes
That deaden suffering –

And then – to go to sleep –
And then – if it should be
The will of its Inquisitor
The privilege to die – [The] liberty • luxury –

~

FASCICLE TWENTY-SIX

SHEET ONE c. summer 1863

They called me to the Window, for[243]
"'Twas Sunset" – Some one said –
I only saw a Sapphire Farm – [saw] an Amber –
And just a Single Herd –

Of Opal Cattle – feeding far
Upon so vain a Hill –
As even while I looked – dissolved –
Nor Cattle were – nor Soil –

But in their Room – a Sea – displayed – [their] stead –
And Ships – of such a size
As Crew of Mountains – could afford –
And Decks – to seat the Skies –

This – too – the Showman rubbed away –
And when I looked again –
Nor Farm – nor Opal Herd – was there –
Nor Mediterranean –

No Romance sold unto
Could so enthrall a Man –
As the perusal of
His individual One –

'Tis Fiction's – to dilute to plausibility [to] contract [to] credibility
Our – Novel. When 'tis small eno' [Our –] Romance
To credit – 'Tisn't true – [To] compass –

No Romance sold: *Sent to SD (variant) c. summer 1863*

I heard a Fly buzz – when I died –[244]
The Stillness in the Room
Was like the Stillness in the Air –
Between the Heaves of Storm –

The Eyes around – had wrung them dry –
And Breaths were gathering firm
For that last Onset – when the King
Be witnessed – in the Room –

I willed my Keepsakes – Signed away
What portion of me be
Assignable – and then it was
There interposed a Fly –

With Blue – uncertain – stumbling Buzz –
Between the light – and me –
And then the Windows failed – and then
I could not see to see –

The Soul that hath a Guest,
Doth seldom go abroad –
Diviner Crowd – at Home – [Crowd –] within
Obliterate the need –

And Courtesy forbids
The Host's departure – when
Upon Himself – be visiting
The Mightiest – of Men – The Emperor of Men –

SHEET TWO c. summer 1863

I watched the Moon around the House
Until upon a Pane –
She stopped – a Traveller's privilege – for Rest –
And there upon

I gazed – as at a Stranger, [I] turned
The Lady in the Town

The Soul that: *Sent to SD (variant) c. 1863*
I watched the: *Sent to Ns (lost, transcribed variant) presumably c. 1863*

Doth think no incivility
To lift her Glass – upon –

But never Stranger justified
The Curiosity
Like Mine – for not a Foot – nor Hand –
Nor Formula – had she –

But like a Head – a Guillotine
Slid carelessly away –
Did independent, Amber –
Sustain her in the sky –

Or like a Stemless Flower –
Upheld in rolling Air
By finer Gravitations –
Than bind Philosopher –

No Hunger – had she – nor an Inn –
Her Toilette – to suffice –
Nor Avocation – nor Concern
For little Mysteries

As harass us – like Life – and Death –
And Afterward – or Nay –
But seemed engrossed to Absolute –
With Shining – and the Sky –

The privilege to scrutinize
Was scarce upon my Eyes
When, with a Silver practise –
She vaulted out of Gaze –

And next – I met her on a Cloud –
Myself too far below
To follow her Superior Road – [Superior] pace
Or its Advantage – Blue –

When I hoped – I feared –
Since – I hoped – I dared

When I hoped –: *Sent to SD (variant) c. 1865 and to TWH (variant) c. November 1871*

Everywhere – alone –
As a church – remain –

Ghost – may not alarm –
Serpent – may not charm –
He is King of Harm –
Who hath suffered Him –

~

The Lightning playeth – all the while –[245]
But when He singeth – then –
Ourselves are conscious He exist –
And we approach Him – stern – [we] accost

With Insulators – and a Glove –
Whose short – sepulchral Bass
Alarms us – tho' His Yellow feet
May pass – and counterpass –

Upon the Ropes – above our Head –
Continual – with the News –
Nor We so much as check our speech –
Nor stop to cross Ourselves –

~

SHEET THREE c. summer 1863

Ourselves were wed one summer – dear –
Your Vision – was in June –
And when Your little Lifetime failed,
I wearied – too – of mine –

And overtaken in the Dark –
Where You had put me down –
By Some one carrying a Light –
I – too – received the Sign –

'Tis true – Our Futures different lay –
Your Cottage – faced the sun –
While Oceans – and the North must be – [North] did play
On every side of mine

o

'Tis true, Your Garden led the Bloom,
For mine – in Frosts – was sown –
And yet, one Summer, we were Queens – [were] wed –
But You – were crowned in June – but Yours was first – in June –

⁓

'Tis little I – could care for Pearls –
Who own the Ample sea –
Or Brooches – when the Emperor –
With Rubies – pelteth me –

Or Gold – who am the Prince of Mines –
Or Diamonds – when have I
A Diadem to fit a Dome –
Continual upon me –

⁓

The Brain – is wider than the Sky –
For – put them side by side –
The one the other will contain [will] include
With ease – and You – beside –

The Brain is deeper than the sea –
For – hold them – Blue to Blue –
The one the other will absorb –
As Sponges – Buckets – do –

The Brain is just the weight of God –
For – Heft them – Pound for Pound –
And they will differ – if they do –
As Syllable from Sound –

⁓

We do not play on Graves –
Because there isn't Room –
Besides – it isn't even – it slants
And People come –

And put a Flower on it –
And hang their faces so –

We're fearing that their Hearts will drop –
And crush our pretty play –

And so we move as far
As Enemies – away –
Just looking round to see how far
It is – Occasionally –

SHEET FOUR c. summer 1863

Her – last Poems –[246]
Poets ended –
Silver – perished – with her Tongue –
Not on Record – bubbled Other –
Flute – or Woman – so divine –

Not unto its Summer Morning – [Not] upon –
Robin – uttered half the Tune [Robin –] published • lavished
Gushed too full for the adoring –
From the Anglo-Florentine –

Late – the Praise – 'Tis dull – Conferring
On the Head too High – to Crown –
Diadem – or Ducal symbol – [Ducal] showing – • Token –
Be its Grave – sufficient Sign –

Nought – that We – No Poet's Kinsman –
Suffocate – with easy Wo –
What – and if Ourself a Bridegroom –
Put Her down – in Italy?

When Bells stop ringing – Church – begins –
The Positive – of Bells – [The] Transitive
When Cogs – stop – that's Circumference –
The Ultimate – of Wheels –

The Manner of its Death[247]
When Certain it must die –

Her – last Poems –: *Sent to SD (variant) c. 1863*

'Tis deemed a privilege to choose –
'Twas Major Andre's Way –

When Choice of Life – is past –
There yet remains a Love
Its little Fate to stipulate –

How small in those who live –

The Miracle to teaze
With Babble of the styles –
How "they are dying mostly – now" –
And Customs at "St James"!

~

The Red – Blaze – is the Morning –
The Violet – is Noon –
The Yellow – Day – is falling –
And after that – is None –

But Miles of Sparks – at Evening –
Reveal the Width that burned –
The Territory Argent – that never yet – consumed –

~

SHEET FIVE c. summer 1863

You'll know Her – by Her Foot –[248]
The smallest Gamboge Hand [The] finest
With Fingers – where the Toes should be –
Would more affront the sand –

Than this Quaint Creature's Boot –
Adjusted by a stem –
Without a Button – I c'd vouch –
Unto a Velvet Limb –

You'll know Her – by Her Vest –
Tight fitting – Orange – Brown –
Inside a Jacket duller –
She wore when she was born –

○

Her Cap is small – and snug –
Constructed for the Winds –
She'd pass for Barehead – short way off –
But as she closer stands –

So finer 'tis than Wool –
You cannot feel the seam –
Nor is it clasped unto of Band –
Nor held upon – of Brim – [Nor] has it any [Brim –]

You'll know Her – by Her Voice –
At first – a doubtful Tone –
A sweet endeavor – but as March
To April – hurries on –

She squanders on your Head [your] Ear
Such Threnodies of Pearl – [Such] Extacies – • Revenues – • *Arguments*
You beg the Robin in your Brain Deny she is a Robin – now –
To keep the other – still – And you're an Infidel –

I am alive – I guess –
The Branches on my Hand
Are full of Morning Glory –
And at my finger's end –

The Carmine – tingles warm –
And if I hold a Glass
Across my mouth – it blurs it –
Physician's – proof of Breath –

I am alive – because
I am not in a Room –
The Parlor – commonly – it is –
So Visitors may come –

And lean – and view it sidewise –
And add "How cold – it grew" –
And "Was it conscious – when it stepped
In Immortality"?

I am alive – because
I do not own a House –
Entitled to myself – precise –
And fitting no one else –

And marked my Girlhood's name –
So Visitors may know
Which Door is mine – and not mistake –
And try another Key –

How good – to be alive!
How infinite – to be
Alive – two-fold – The Birth I had –
And this – besides, in Thee!

SHEET SIX c. summer 1863

Except the smaller size –
No Lives – are Round –
These – hurry to a Sphere –
And show – and end –

The Larger – slower grow –
And later – hang –
The Summers of Hesperides [Summers] in
Are long –

Hugest of Core The Huge [of]
Present the awkward Rind –
Yield Groups of Ones –
No Cluster – ye shall find – [Cluster –] you

But far after Frost –
And Indian Summer Noon – [Summer] Sun –
Ships – offer These –
As West – Indian –

I think the longest Hour of all
Is when the Cars have come –

Except the smaller: *Sent first two stanzas to SD (variant) c. second half of 1863 and to TWH 17 March 1866*

And we are waiting for the Coach –
It seems as though the Time –

Indignant – that the Joy was come – Affronted [that]
Did block the Gilded Hands –
And would not let the Seconds by –
But slowest instant – ends –

The Pendulum begins to count –
Like little Scholars – loud –
The steps grow thicker – in the Hall –
The Heart begins to crowd –

Then I – my timid service done –
Tho' service 'twas, of Love –
Take up my little Violin –
And further North – remove –

~

So glad we are – a stranger'd deem
'Twas sorry – that we were –
For where the Holiday – should be –
There publishes – a Tear – [There] Bustles but

Nor how Ourselves be justified –
Since Grief and Joy are done
So similar – an Optizan
Could not discern between – [not] conclude – • decide –

~

A Night – there lay the Days between –
The Day that was Before –
And Day that was Behind – were One –
And now – 'twas Night – was here –

Slow – Night – that must be watched away –
As Grains upon a shore –
Too imperceptible to note –
Till it be Night – no more –

~

So glad we: *Sent to SB (variant) c. summer 1863*

FASCICLE TWENTY-SEVEN

SHEET ONE c. summer 1863

There's been a Death, in the Opposite House,
As lately as Today –
I know it, by the numb look
Such Houses have – alway –

The Neighbors rustle in and out –
The Doctor – drives away –
A Window opens like a Pod –
Abrupt – mechanically –

Somebody flings a Mattress out –
The Children hurry by –
They wonder if it died – on that –
I used to – when a Boy –

The Minister – goes stiffly in –
As if the House were His –
And He owned all the Mourners – now –
And little Boys – besides.

And then the Milliner – and the Man
Of the Appalling Trade –
To take the measure of the House –

There'll be that Dark Parade –

Of Tassels – and of Coaches – soon –
It's easy as a Sign –
The Intuition of the News –
In just a Country Town –

The Black Berry – wears a Thorn in his side –[249]
But no Man heard Him cry –
He offers His Berry, just the same
To Partridge – and to Boy –

[He] spices – • flavors –

He sometimes holds upon the Fence –
Or struggles to a Tree –
Or clasps a Rock, with both His Hands –
But not for sympathy –

We – tell a Hurt – to cool it –
This Mourner – to the Sky
A little further reaches – instead –
Brave Black Berry –

The One that could repeat the Summer Day –
Were Greater than Itself – though He –
Minutest of Mankind – should be –
And He – could reproduce the Sun –
At Period of Going down –
The Lingering – and the Stain – I mean –

[Mankind –] might – • could –

When Orient – have been outgrown –
And Occident – become Unknown –
His Name – Remain –

SHEET TWO c. summer 1863

I measure every Grief I meet
With narrow, probing, eyes –
I wonder if It weighs like Mine –
Or has an Easier size –

[With] Analytic eyes –

I wonder if They bore it long –
Or did it just begin –
I could not tell the Date of Mine –
It feels so old a pain –

I wonder if it hurts to live –
And if They have to try –

The One that: *Sent to SD (variant) c. summer 1863, beginning "The One who could repeat the Summer day –"*

And whether – could They choose between –
It would not be – to die –

I note that Some – gone patient long –
At length, renew their smile –
An imitation of a Light
That has so little Oil –

I wonder if when Years have piled –
Some Thousands – on the Harm –
That hurt them Early – such a lapse
Could give them any Balm –

Or would They go on aching still
Through Centuries of Nerve –
Enlightened to a larger Pain –
In Contrast with the Love –

The Grieved – are many – I am told –
There is the various Cause –
Death – is but one – and comes but once –
And only nails the Eyes –

There's Grief of Want – and Grief of Cold –
A sort they call "Despair" –
There's Banishment from native Eyes –
In sight of Native Air –

And though I may not guess the kind –
Correctly – yet to me
A piercing Comfort it affords
In passing Calvary –

To note the fashions – of the Cross –
And how they're mostly worn –
Still fascinated to presume
That Some – are like my own –

Conjecturing a Climate
Of unsuspended Suns –
Adds poignancy to Winter – gives [poignancy]
The shivering Fancy turns [The] freezing

o

To a fictitious Country
To palliate a Cold –
Not obviated of Degree –
Nor eased – of Latitude –

[fictitious] Summer – • Season –

SHEET THREE c. summer 1863

There is a Languor of the Life
More imminent than Pain –
'Tis Pain's Successor – When the Soul
Has suffered all it can –

A Drowsiness – diffuses –
A Dimness like a Fog
Envelopes Consciousness –
As Mists – obliterate a Crag.

The Surgeon – does not blanch – at pain –
His Habit – is severe –
But tell him that it ceased to feel –
The Creature lying there –

And he will tell you – Skill is late –
A Mightier than He –
Has ministered before Him –
There's no Vitality

When Diamonds are a Legend,
And Diadems – a Tale –
I Brooch and Earrings for Myself,
Do sow, and Raise for sale –

And tho' I'm scarce accounted,
My Art, a Summer Day – had Patrons –
Once – it was a Queen –
And once – a Butterfly –

I had not minded – Walls –
Were Universe – one Rock –
And far I heard his silver Call
The other side the Block –

I'd tunnel – till my Groove
Pushed sudden thro' to his –
Then my face take her Recompense –
The looking in his Eyes –

But 'tis a single Hair –
A filament – a law –
A Cobweb – wove in Adamant –
A Battlement – of Straw –

A limit like the Vail
Unto the Lady's face –
But every Mesh – a Citadel –
And Dragons – in the Crease –

A House upon the Hight –
That Wagon never reached –
No Dead, were ever carried down –
No Peddler's Cart – approached –

Whose Chimney never smoked –
Whose Windows – Night and Morn –
Caught Sunrise first – and Sunset – last –
Then – held an Empty Pane –

Whose fate – Conjecture knew –
No other neighbor – did –
And what it was – we never lisped –
Because He – never told –

SHEET FOUR c. summer 1863

It's Coming – the postponeless Creature –
It gains the Block – and now – it gains the Door –

Chooses its latch, from all the other fastenings –
Enters – with a "You know me – Sir"?

Simple Salute – and Certain Recognition –
Bold – were it enemy – Brief – were it friend –
Dresses each House in Crape, and Icicle –
And Carries one – out of it – to God –

I send Two Sunsets –
Day and I – in competition ran –
I finished Two – and several Stars –
While He – was making One –

His own was ampler – but as I
Was saying to a friend –
Mine – is the more convenient
To Carry in the Hand –

A Visitor in Marl –
Who influences Flowers –
Till they are orderly as Busts –
And Elegant – as Glass –

Who visits in the Night –
And just before the Sun –
Concludes his glistening interview –
Caresses – and is gone –

But whom his fingers touched –
And where his feet have run –
And whatsoever Mouth he kissed –
Is as it had not been –

Through the Dark Sod – as Education –[250]
The Lily passes sure –
Feels her White foot – no trepidation –
Her faith – no fear –

○

I send Two: *Sent to SD (variant) c. summer 1863*
Through the Dark: *Sent to Ns (lost) c. 1863*

Afterward – in the Meadow –
Swinging her Beryl Bell –
The Mold-life – all forgotten – now –
In Extasy – and Dell –

SHEET FIVE c. summer 1863

Did Our Best Moment last –
'Twould supersede the Heaven –
A few – and they by Risk – procure –
So this Sort – are not given –

Except as stimulants – in Cases of Despair –
Or Stupor – The Reserve –
These Heavenly moments are –

A Grant of the Divine –
That Certain as it Comes –
Withdraws – and leaves the dazzled Soul
In her unfurnished Rooms –

Trust in the Unexpected –[251]
By this – was William Kidd
Persuaded of the Buried Gold –
As One had testified –

Through this – the old Philosopher –
His Talismanic Stone
Discernèd – still witholden
To effort undivine –

'Twas this – allured Columbus –
When Genoa – withdrew — till [Genoa –]
Before an Apparition
Baptized America – — to wit [America –]

The Same – afflicted Thomas –
When Deity assured — [Deity] pronounced –
'Twas better – the perceiving not – — 'Twas blesseder – the seeing not –
Provided it believed –

'Twas Love – not me –[252]
Oh punish – pray –
The Real One died for Thee –
Just Him – not me –

Such Guilt – to love Thee – most!
Doom it beyond the Rest –
Forgive it – last –
'Twas base as Jesus – most!

Let Justice not mistake –
We Two – looked so alike –
Which was the Guilty Sake –
'Twas Love's – Now strike!

The Brain, within its Groove
Runs evenly – and true –
But let a Splinter swerve –
'Twere easier for You –

To put a Current back – [put] the Waters
When Floods have slit the Hills –
And scooped a Turnpike for Themselves –
And trodden out the Mills – [And] blotted out – • shoved away –

SHEET SIX c. summer 1863

She hideth Her the last –
And is the first, to rise –
Her Night doth hardly recompense
The Closing of Her eyes –

She doth Her Purple Work –
And putteth Her away
In low apartments in the sod –
As Worthily as We. [As] privately

To imitate Her life
As impotent would be [As] possible

As make of Our imperfect Mints,
The Julep – of the Bee –

line 11: [As] Mix • Brew from [Our] Uncomely – [Mints,]
As brew from our Obtuser Mints –

Reverse cannot befall
That fine Prosperity
Whose Sources are interior –
As soon – Adversity

A Diamond – overtake
In far – Bolivian Ground –
Misfortune hath no implement
Could mar it – if it found –

But little Carmine hath her face –
Of Emerald scant – her Gown –
Her Beauty – is the love she doth –
Itself – exhibit – mine – [Itself –] enable – • embolden –

It knew no Medicine –
It was not Sickness – then –
Nor any need of Surgery –
And therefore – 'twas not Pain –

It moved away the Cheeks –
A Dimple at a time –
And left the Profile – plainer –
And in the place of Bloom [the] stead

It left the little Tint
That never had a Name –
You've seen it on a Cast's face – [Cast's] cheek
Was Paradise – to blame –

If momently ajar – [If] Her sweet Door – ajar
Temerity – drew near –

Reverse cannot befall: *Sent to SD (lost, published variant) presumably c. 1863*
But little Carmine: *Apparently sent to Maria Whitney (variant) c. 1863*

And sickened – ever afterward
For Somewhat that it saw? [For] whatsoe'er – [it]

It knew no lapse, nor Diminution –
But large – serene –
Burned on – until through Dissolution – Glowed [on –]
It failed from Men –

I could not deem these Planetary forces
Annulled –
But suffered an Exchange of Territory – [But] Absent through Exchange –
Or World –

It knew no: *Sent to TWH (second stanza, as prose) c. 1863*

FASCICLE TWENTY-EIGHT

SHEET ONE c. spring 1863

My period had come for Prayer –
No other Art – would do –
My Tactics missed a rudiment –
Creator – Was it you?

God grows above – so those who pray
Horizons – must ascend –
And so I stepped upon the North   [I] stood –
To see this Curious Friend –   [To] Reach – • touch –

His House was not – no sign had He –
By Chimney – nor by Door –
Could I infer his Residence –
Vast Prairies of Air   Wide Prairies [of]

Unbroken by a Settler –
Were all that I could see –
Infinitude – Had'st Thou no Face
That I might look on Thee?

The Silence condescended –
Creation stopped – for me –   The Heavens paused – [for]
But awed beyond my errand –
I worshipped – did not "pray" –

I pay – in Satin Cash –
You did not state – your price –
A Petal, for a Paragraph
Is near as I can guess –

One Anguish – in a Crowd –
A minor thing – it sounds –
And yet, unto the single Doe
Attempted – of the Hounds

'Tis Terror as consummate
As Legions of Alarm
Did leap, full flanked, upon the Host –
'Tis Units – make the Swarm –

A small Leech – on the Vitals –
The sliver, in the Lung –
The Bung out – of an Artery – A leakage in [an]
Are scarce accounted – Harms – [scarce] computed

Yet mighty – by relation But [mighty –]
To that Repealless thing –
A Being – impotent to end – [to] stop –
When once it has begun –

'Tis not that Dying hurts us so –[253]
'Tis Living – hurts us more –
But Dying – is a different way –
A kind behind the Door –

The Southern Custom – of the Bird –
That ere the Frosts are due –
Accepts a better Latitude –
We – are the Birds – that stay.

The Shiverers round Farmer's doors –
For whose reluctant Crumb –
We stipulate – till pitying Snows
Persuade our Feathers Home

SHEET TWO c. spring 1863

A Dying Tiger – moaned for Drink –
I hunted all the Sand – [I] worried –

'Tis not that: *Sent to Ns (lost, transcribed variant); their father died 17 January 1863*
A Dying Tiger –: *Sent to Ns (lost) perhaps c. 1863*

I caught the Dripping of a Rock
And bore it in my Hand –

His mighty Balls – in death were thick –
But searching – I could see
A Vision on the Retina
Of Water – and of me –

'Twas not my blame – who sped too slow –
'Twas not his blame – who died
While I was reaching him –
But 'twas – the fact that He was dead –

He gave away his Life –
To Us – Gigantic Sum –
A trifle – in his own esteem – [his] estimate
But magnified – by Fame –

Until it burst the Hearts
That fancied they could hold –
When swift it slipped its limit – [When] quick
And on the Heavens – unrolled –

'Tis Ours – to wince – and weep –
And wonder – and decay
By Blossom's gradual process – [Blossom's] common
He chose – Maturity –

And quickening – as we sowed – [And] ripening –
Just obviated Bud –
And when We turned to note the Growth –
Broke – perfect – from the Pod –

We learned the Whole of Love –
The Alphabet – the Words –
A Chapter – then the mighty Book –
Then – Revelation closed –

But in each Other's eyes
An Ignorance beheld –

Diviner than the Childhood's
And each to each, a Child –

Attempted to expound
What neither – understood –
Alas, that Wisdom is so large –
And Truth – so manifold!

Did timidly expound –

The Winters are so short –[254]
I'm hardly justified
In sending all the Birds away –
And moving into Pod –

Myself – for scarcely settled –
The Phebes have begun –
And then – it's time to strike my Tent –
And open House – again –

It's mostly, interruptions –
My Summer – is despoiled –
Because there was a Winter – once –
And all the Cattle – starved –

And so there was a Deluge –
And swept the World away –
But Ararat's a Legend – now –
And no one credits Noah –

SHEET THREE c. spring 1863

I reckon – When I count at all –[255]
First – Poets – Then the Sun –
Then Summer – Then the Heaven of God –
And then – the List is done –

But, looking back – the First so seems
To Comprehend the Whole –
The Others look a needless Show –
So I write – Poets – All –

o

Their Summer – lasts a solid Year –
They can afford a Sun
The East – would deem extravagant –
And if the Further Heaven – [the] Other – • final

Be Beautiful as they prepare [they] Disclose
For Those who worship Them – to – [Those who] Trust in • ask of –
It is too difficult a Grace –
To justify the Dream –

~

How many Flowers fail in Wood –
Or perish from the Hill –
Without the privilege to know
That they are Beautiful –

How many cast a nameless Pod
Upon the nearest Breeze –
Unconscious of the Scarlet Freight –
It bear to other eyes –

~

It might be lonelier
Without the Loneliness –
I'm so accustomed to my Fate –
Perhaps the Other – Peace –

Would interrupt the Dark –
And crowd the little Room –
Too scant – by Cubits – to contain
The Sacrament – of Him –

I am not used to Hope –
It might intrude upon –
Its sweet parade – blaspheme the place –
Ordained to Suffering –

It might be easier
To fail – with Land in Sight –
Than gain – my Blue Peninsula –
To perish – of Delight –

~

How many Flowers: *Sent to Ns (lost) perhaps c. 1863, beginning "How many flowers fail in the wood"*

Some – Work for Immortality –
The Chiefer part, for Time –
He – Compensates – immediately –
The former – Checks – on Fame –

Slow Gold – but Everlasting –
The Bullion of Today –
Contrasted with the Currency
Of Immortality –

A Beggar – Here and There –
Is gifted to discern
Beyond the Broker's insight –
One's – Money – One's – the Mine –

SHEET FOUR c. spring 1863

I could die – to know – [I] would
'Tis a trifling knowledge –
News-Boys salute the Door –
Carts – joggle by –
Morning's bold face – stares in the window –
Were but mine – the Charter of the least Fly –

Houses hunch the House
With their Brick shoulders –
Coals – from a Rolling Load – rattle – how – near – [a] passing load
To the very Square – His foot is passing –
Possibly, this moment –
While I – dream – Here – [I –] wait,

Must be a Wo –
A loss or so –
To bend the eye
Best Beauty's way –

But – once aslant
It notes Delight [It] gains

As difficult — as clarified
As Stalactite – — [As] Violet –

A Common Bliss
Were had for less –
The price – is
Even as the Grace –

Our Lord – thought no
Extravagance
To pay – a Cross –

Delight – becomes pictorial –
When viewed through Pain –
More fair – because impossible
That any gain –

The Mountain – at a given distance –
In Amber – lies –
Approached – the Amber flits – a little – — possessed [the Amber] moves –
And That's – the Skies –

If What we could – were what we would –
Criterion – be small –
It is the Ultimate of Talk –
The Impotence to Tell –

The Test of Love – is Death –[256]
Our Lord – "so loved" – it saith –
What Largest Lover – hath –
Another – doth –

If Smaller Patience – be –
Through less Infinity –
If Bravo, sometimes swerve –
Through fainter Nerve –

○

If What we: *Sent to SD (variant) c. 1863*

Accept its Most – [its] Best
And overlook – the Dust –
Last – Least –
The Cross' – Request –

SHEET FIVE c. spring 1863

My first well Day – since many ill –
I asked to go abroad,
And take the Sunshine in my hands
And see the things in Pod –

A'blossom just – when I went in
To take my Chance with pain – [my] Risk
Uncertain if myself, or He,
Should prove the strongest One. [the] supplest – • lithest – • stoutest

The Summer deepened, while we strove –
She put some flowers away –
And Redder cheeked Ones – in their stead – [their] place
A fond – illusive way –

To Cheat Herself, it seemed she tried –
As if before a Child
To fade – Tomorrow – Rainbows held [To] die – [Tomorrow – Rainbows] thrust
The Sepulchre, could hide.

She dealt a fashion to the Nut – [dealt] the
She tied the Hoods to Seeds –
She dropped bright scraps of Tint, about –
And left Brazilian Threads

On every shoulder that she met – [shoulder] she could reach
Then both her Hands of Haze
Put up – to hide her parting Grace [to] hold
From our unfitted eyes – [our] unfurnished

My loss, by sickness – Was it Loss?
Or that Etherial Gain [that] seraphic gain,
One earns by measuring the Grave – One gets – [by]
Then – measuring the Sun –

My first well: *Sent to SB (last stanza, variant) c. mid-November 1862*

For Largest Woman's Heart I knew –
'Tis little I can do –
And yet the Largest Woman's Heart
Can hold an Arrow, too,
And so, instructed by my own –
I tenderer – turn me to –

Unit, like Death, for Whom?[257]
True, like the Tomb,
Who tells no secret
Told to Him –
The Grave is strict –
Tickets admit
Just two – the Bearer – and the Borne –
And seat – just One –
The Living – tell –
The Dying – but a syllable –
The Coy Dead – None –
No Chatter – here – No Tea –
So Babbler, and Bohea – stay there –
But Gravity – and Expectation – and Fear –
A tremor just, that all's not sure.

SHEET SIX c. spring 1863

"Heaven" has different Signs – to me –
Sometimes, I think that Noon
Is but a symbol of the Place –
And when again, at Dawn,

A mighty look runs round the World
And settles in the Hills –
An Awe if it should be like that
Upon the Ignorance steals –

The Orchard, when the Sun is on –
The Triumph of the Birds

For Largest Woman's: *Sent to SD (variant) c. early 1863*

When they together Victory make –
Some Carnivals of Clouds –

The Rapture of a finished Day — [of] Concluded Day –
Returning to the West –
All these – remind us of the place
That Men call "Paradise" –

Itself be fairer – we suppose –
But how Ourself, shall be
Adorned, for a Superior Grace –
Not yet, our eyes can see –

They dropped like Flakes –[258]
They dropped like stars –
Like Petals from a Rose –
When suddenly across the June
A Wind with fingers – goes –

They perished in the seamless Grass –
No eye could find the place –
But God can summon every face
On his Repealless – List.

I prayed, at first, a little Girl,[259]
Because they told me to –
But stopped, when qualified to guess
How prayer would feel – to me – — [would] sound

If I believed God looked around, — [I] supposed
Each time my Childish eye
Fixed full, and steady, on his own
In Childish honesty – — [In] solemn –

And told him what I'd like, today,
And parts of his far plan
That baffled me –
The mingled side — [The] under – • further [side]
Of his Divinity –

And often since, in Danger,
I count the force 'twould be
To have a God so strong as that
To hold my life for me [hold] the light

Till I could take the Balance [could] Catch my
That tips so frequent, now, [That] slips so easy [now,]
It takes me all the while to poise –
And then – it doesn't stay – It isn't steady – tho' –

FASCICLE TWENTY-NINE

SHEET ONE c. second half of 1863

From Cocoon forth a Butterfly
As Lady from her Door
Emerged – a Summer Afternoon –
Repairing Everywhere –

Without Design – that I could trace
Except to stray abroad
On miscellaneous Enterprise
The Clovers – understood –

Her pretty Parasol be seen
Contracting in a Field
Where Men made Hay –
Then struggling hard
With an opposing Cloud –

Where Parties – Phantom as Herself –
To Nowhere – seemed to go
In purposeless Circumference –
As 'twere a Tropic Show –

And notwithstanding Bee – that worked –
And Flower – that zealous blew –
This Audience of Idleness
Disdained them, from the Sky –

Till Sundown crept – a steady Tide –
And Men that made the Hay –
And Afternoon – and Butterfly –
Extinguished – in the Sea –

Her sweet Weight on my Heart a Night
Had scarcely deigned to lie –
When, stirring, for Belief's delight,
My Bride had slipped away –

If 'twas a Dream – made solid – just
The Heaven to confirm –
Or if Myself were dreamed of Her –
The power to presume – [the] wisdom

With Him remain – who unto Me –
Gave – even as to All –
A Fiction superseding Faith –
By so much – as 'twas real –

'Tis Opposites – Entice
Deformed Men – ponder Grace –
Bright fires – the Blanketless –
The Lost – Day's face –

The Blind – esteem it be
Enough Estate – to see –
The Captive – strangles new –
For deeming – Beggars – play –

To lack – enamor Thee –
Tho' the Divinity –
Be only
Me –

SHEET TWO c. second half of 1863

The Day that I was crowned
Was like the other Days –
Until the Coronation came –
And then – 'twas Otherwise –

As Carbon in the Coal
And Carbon in the Gem

Are One – and yet the former
Were dull for Diadem –

I rose, and all was plain –
But when the Day declined
Myself and It, in Majesty
Were equally – adorned –

The Grace that I – was chose –
To me – surpassed the Crown
That was the Witness for the Grace –
'Twas even that 'twas Mine –

~

'Twas warm – at first – like Us –
Until there crept upon
A Chill – like frost upon a Glass –
Till all the scene – be gone.

The Forehead copied stone –
The Fingers grew too cold
To ache – and like a Skater's Brook –
The busy eyes – congealed –

It straightened – that was all –
It crowded Cold to Cold –
It multiplied indifference –
As Pride were all it could –

And even when with Cords –
'Twas lowered, like a Weight – [a] Freight –
It made no Signal, nor demurred,
But dropped like Adamant.

~

God is a distant – stately Lover –[260]
Woos, as He states us – by His Son –
Verily, a Vicarious Courtship –
"Miles", and "Priscilla", were such an One –

But, lest the Soul – like fair "Priscilla"
Choose the Envoy – and spurn the 'Groom –

Vouches, with hyperbolic archness –
"Miles", and "John Alden" are Synonyme –

If any sink, assure that this, now standing –[261]
Failed like Themselves – and conscious that it rose –
Grew by the Fact, and not the Understanding
How Weakness passed – or Force – arose –

Tell that the Worst, is easy in a Moment –
Dread, but the Whizzing, before the Ball –
When the Ball enters, enters Silence –
Dying – annuls the power to kill –

SHEET THREE c. second half of 1863

The Night was wide, and furnished scant
With but a single Star –
That often as a Cloud it met –
Blew out itself – for fear –

The Wind pursued the little Bush –
And drove away the Leaves
November left – then clambered up
And fretted in the Eaves –

No Squirrel went abroad –
A Dog's belated feet
Like intermittent Plush, be heard
Adown the empty street –

To feel if Blinds be fast –
And closer to the fire –
Her little Rocking Chair to draw –
And shiver for the Poor – [And] recollect [the]

The Housewife's gentle Task –
How pleasanter – said she
Unto the Sofa opposite –
The Sleet – than May, no Thee –

To love thee Year by Year –
May less appear
Than sacrifice, and cease –
However, dear,
Forever might be short, I thought to show –
And so I pieced it, with a flower, now.

~

Did you ever stand in a Cavern's Mouth –
Widths out of the Sun –
And look – and shudder, and block your breath –
And deem to be alone

In such a place, what horror,
How Goblin it would be –
And fly, as 'twere pursuing you?
Then Loneliness – looks so –

Did you ever look in a Cannon's face –
Between whose Yellow eye –
And yours – the Judgment intervened –
The Question of "To die" –

Extemporizing in your ear
As cool as Satyr's Drums – distinct – [as Satyr's]
If you remember, and were saved
It's liker so – it seems –

~

Much Madness is divinest Sense –[262]
To a discerning Eye –
Much Sense – the starkest Madness –
'Tis the Majority
In this, as all, prevail –
Assent – and you are sane –
Demur – you're straightway dangerous –
And handled with a Chain –

~

To love thee: *Presumably sent to SD (lost, published variant) c. 1863*

SHEET FOUR c. second half of 1863

The Wind – tapped like a tired Man –
And like a Host – "Come in"
I boldly answered – entered then
My Residence within

A Rapid – footless Guest –
To offer whom a Chair
Were as impossible as hand
A Sofa to the Air –

No Bone had He to bind Him –
His Speech was like the Push
Of numerous Humming Birds at once
From a superior Bush –

His Countenance – a Billow –
His Fingers, as He passed
Let go a music – as of tunes
Blown tremulous in Glass –

He visited – still flitting –
Then like a timid Man
Again, He tapped – 'twas flurriedly –
And I became alone –

To interrupt His Yellow Plan
The Sun does not allow
Caprices of the Atmosphere –
And even when the Snow

Heaves Balls of Specks, like Vicious Boy
Directly in His Eye –
Does not so much as turn His Head –
Busy with Majesty –

'Tis His to stimulate the Earth –
And magnetize the Sea –
And bind Astronomy, in place,
Yet Any passing by

[Astronomy,] from blame

o

Would deem Ourselves – the busier
As the minutest Bee
That rides – emits a Thunder – [rides –] supports –
A Bomb – to justify –

~

Prayer is the little implement
Through which Men reach
Where Presence – is denied them –
They fling their Speech

By means of it – in God's Ear –
If then He hear –
This sums the Apparatus
Comprised in Prayer –

~

SHEET FIVE c. second half of 1863

What care the Dead, for Chanticleer –
What care the Dead for Day?
'Tis late your Sunrise vex their face –
And Purple Ribaldry – of Morning

Pour as blank on them
As on the Tier of Wall [the] Row
The Mason builded, yesterday,
And equally as cool –

What care the Dead for Summer?
The Solstice had no Sun
Could waste the Snow before their Gate – [Could] melt
And knew One Bird a Tune –

Could thrill their Mortised Ear [Could] penetrate [their Ear]
Of all the Birds that be –
This One – beloved of Mankind
Henceforward cherished be –

What care the Dead for Winter? Nor [care]
Themselves as easy freeze –

June Noon as January Night –
As soon the South – her Breeze
Of Sycamore – or Cinnamon –
Deposit in a Stone
And put a Stone to keep it Warm –
Give Spices – unto Men –

~

Forget! The lady with the Amulet
Forgot she wore it at her Heart
Because she breathed against
Was Treason twixt?

Deny! Did Rose her Bee –
For Privilege of Play
Or Wile of Butterfly
Or Opportunity – Her Lord away?

The lady with the Amulet – will fade –
The Bee – in Mausoleum laid –
Discard his Bride –
But longer than the little Rill –
That cooled the Forehead of the Hill –
While Other – went the Sea to fill –
And Other – went to turn the Mill –
I'll do thy Will –

~

Undue Significance a starving man attaches
To Food –
Far off – He sighs – and therefore – Hopeless –
And therefore – Good –

Partaken – it relieves – indeed –
But proves us
That Spices fly
In the Receipt – It was the Distance –
Was Savory –

~

SHEET SIX c. second half of 1863

I think I was enchanted[263]
When first a sombre Girl – [a] little Girl
I read that Foreign Lady –
The Dark – felt beautiful –

And whether it was noon at night –
Or only Heaven – at noon –
For very Lunacy of Light
I had not power to tell –

The Bees – became as Butterflies –
The Butterflies – as Swans – [Butterflies –] As Moons –
Approached – and spurned the narrow Grass – lit up the low – inferior Grass –
And just the meanest Tunes [the] faintest – • Common Tunes –

That Nature murmured to herself
To keep herself in Cheer –
I took for Giants – practising
Titanic Opera –

The Days – to Mighty Metres stept –
The Homeliest – adorned
As if unto a Jubilee [a] Sacrament
'Twere suddenly confirmed – [suddenly] ordained

I could not have defined the change –
Conversion of the Mind
Like Sanctifying in the Soul –
Is witnessed – not explained –

'Twas a Divine Insanity –
The Danger to be sane [The] Sorrow
Should I again experience –
'Tis Antidote to turn –

To Tomes of Solid Witchcraft –
Magicians be asleep –
But Magic – hath an element
Like Deity – to keep –

'Tis Customary as we part[264]
A Trinket – to confer –
It helps to stimulate the faith
When Lovers be afar –

'Tis various – as the various taste –
Clematis – journeying far –
Presents me with a single Curl
Of her Electric Hair –

The Battle fought between the Soul
And No Man – is the One
Of all the Battles prevalent –
By far the Greater One –

No News of it is had abroad –
Its Bodiless Campaign
Establishes, and terminates –
Invisible – Unknown –

Nor History – record it –
As Legions of a Night
The Sunrise scatters – These endure –
Enact – and terminate – [and] dissipate –

FASCICLE THIRTY

SHEET ONE c. second half of 1863

No Crowd that has occurred[265]
Exhibit – I suppose
That General Attendance
That Resurrection – does –

Circumference be full –
The long restricted Grave [long] subjected
Assert her Vital Privilege – [Assert] His Primogeniture
The Dust – connect – and live – [Dust –] adjust –

On Atoms – features place –
All Multitudes that were
Efface in the Comparison –
As Suns – dissolve a star – [Suns –] annul

Solemnity – prevail –
Its Individual Doom
Possess each – separate Consciousness –
August – Absorbed – Numb – [August –] Resistless – dumb

What Duplicate – exist –
What Parallel can be – [What] scenery
Of the Significance of This – [the] stupendousness
To Universe – and Me?

Beauty – be not caused – It Is –[266] [Beauty –] is
Chase it, and it ceases –
Chase it not, and it abides –

Overtake the Creases

In the Meadow – when the Wind
Runs his fingers thro' it – puts – [his]

Deity will see to it
That You never do it –

⁓

He parts Himself – like Leaves –
And then – He closes up –
Then stands upon the Bonnet
Of Any Buttercup –

And then He leans with all His Might
Upon a Buttercup –

And then He runs against
And oversets a Rose –
And then does Nothing –
Then away upon a Jib – He goes –

[And] overturns

And dangles like a Mote
Suspended in the Noon –
Uncertain – to return Below –
Or settle in the Moon –

indifferent – [to]

What come of Him at Night –
The privilege to say
Be limited by Ignorance –
What come of Him – That Day –

The liberty to say – • Authority – [to say –]

The Frost – possess the World –
In Cabinets – be shown –
A Sepulchre of quaintest Floss –
An Abbey – a Cocoon –

[Frost –] obtain the World –

⁓

SHEET TWO c. second half of 1863

I started Early – Took my Dog –[267]
And visited the Sea –
The Mermaids in the Basement
Came out to look at me –

And Frigates – in the Upper Floor
Extended Hempen Hands –
Presuming Me to be a Mouse –
Aground – upon the Sands –

o

But no Man moved Me – till the Tide
Went past my simple Shoe –
And past my Apron – and my Belt
And past my Boddice – too – [my] Bosom • Buckle

And made as He would eat me up –
As wholly as a Dew
Upon a Dandelion's Sleeve –
And then – I started – too –

And He – He followed – close behind –
I felt His Silver Heel
Upon my Ancle – Then My Shoes
Would overflow with Pearl –

Until We met the Solid Town –
No One He seemed to know – [No] man –
And bowing – with a Mighty look –
At me – The Sea withdrew –

~

"Morning" – means "Milking" – to the Farmer –
Dawn – to the Teneriffe –
Dice – to the Maid –
Morning means just Risk – to the Lover –
Just Revelation – to the Beloved –

Epicures – date a Breakfast – by it –
Brides – an Apocalypse –
Worlds – a Flood –
Faint-going Lives – Their lapse from Sighing –
Faith – The Experiment of Our Lord –

~

Endow the Living – with the Tears –[268]
You squander on the Dead, [You] spend upon –
And They were Men and Women – now,
Around Your Fireside –

Instead of Passive Creatures,
Denied the Cherishing

"Morning" – means "Milking" –: *Sent to SD (variant) c. 1861*

Till They – the Cherishing deny –
With Death's Etherial Scorn –

~

SHEET THREE c. second half of 1863

'Tis true – They shut me in the Cold –
But then – Themselves were warm
And could not know the feeling 'twas – [And] did
Forget it – Lord – of Them – [it –] Christ

Let not my Witness hinder Them [Witness] Them impair –
In Heavenly esteem –
No Paradise could be – Conferred
Through Their beloved Blame –

The Harm They did – was short – And since [was] brief
Myself – who bore it – do –
Forgive Them – Even as Myself –
Or else – forgive not me – Else – Savior – banish Me –

~

The Province of the Saved
Should be the Art – To Save – Exclusively – to Save –
Through Skill obtained in Themselves –
The Science of the Grave

No Man can understand
But He that hath endured
The Dissolution – in Himself –
That Man – be qualified

To qualify Despair
To Those who failing new –
Mistake Defeat for Death – Each time –
Till acclimated – to –

~

I took my Power in my Hand –[269]
And went against the World –
'Twas not so much as David – had –
But I – was twice as bold –

o

I aimed my Pebble – but Myself
Was all the one that fell –
Was it Goliah – was too large –
Or was myself – too small? [Or] just myself – • only me – • [only] I –

~

Some such Butterfly be seen
On Brazilian Pampas –
Just at noon – no later – Sweet – [later –] Than
Then – the License closes – [the] Vision – • Pageant

Some such Spice – express – and pass – [such] Rose
Subject to Your Plucking – present [to]
As the Stars – You knew last Night –
Foreigners – This Morning – Know not You – [This]

~

SHEET FOUR c. second half of 1863

I had no Cause to be awake –
My Best – was gone to sleep –
And Morn a new politeness took –
And failed to wake them up –
But called the others – clear –
And passed their Curtains by –
Sweet Morning – When I oversleep –
Knock – Recollect – to Me –

I looked at Sunrise – Once –
And then I looked at Them –
And wishfulness in me arose –
For Circumstance the same –

'Twas such an Ample Peace –
It could not hold a Sigh –
'Twas Sabbath – with the Bells divorced – [Bells] reversed
'Twas Sunset – all the Day – ['Twas] Sundown –

So choosing but a Gown –
And taking but a Prayer –
The Only Raiment I should need –
I struggled – and was There –

~

I fear a Man of frugal speech – [of] scanty
I fear a Silent Man –
Haranguer – I can overtake –
Or Babbler – entertain –

But He who weigheth – While the Rest –
Expend their furthest pound – [their] inmost –
Of this Man – I am wary –
I fear that He is Grand –

Rehearsal to Ourselves
Of a Withdrawn Delight –
Affords a Bliss like Murder –
Omnipotent – Acute –

We will not drop the Dirk –
Because We love the Wound
The Dirk Commemorate – Itself
Remind Us that We died –

The Martyr Poets – did not tell –
But wrought their Pang in syllable –
That when their mortal name be numb – [mortal] fame
Their mortal fate – encourage Some –
The Martyr Painters – never spoke –
Bequeathing – rather – to their Work –
That when their conscious fingers cease –
Some seek in Art – the Art of Peace – Men – [seek]

SHEET FIVE c. second half of 1863

I cross till I am weary
A Mountain – in my mind –
More Mountains – then a Sea –
More Seas – And then
A Desert – find –

o

And my Horizon blocks
With steady – drifting – Grains   [With] sudden – blinding
Of unconjectured quantity –
As Asiatic Rains –

Nor this – defeat my Pace –
It hinder from the West
But as an Enemy's salute
One hurrying to Rest –

What merit had the Goal –
Except there intervene
Faint Doubt – and far Competitor –
To jeopardize the Gain?

At last – the Grace in sight –   The Grace is just in sight
I shout unto my feet –
I offer them the Whole of Heaven   [them] the Half
The instant that we meet –

They strive – and yet delay –
They perish – Do we die –   [They] stagger –
Or is this Death's experiment –
Reversed – in Victory?

Answer July
Where is the Bee –
Where is the Blush –
Where is the Hay?

Ah, said July –
Where is the Seed –
Where is the Bud –
Where is the May –
Answer Thee – me –

Nay – said the May –
Show me the Snow –
Show me the Bells –
Show me the Jay!

Quibbled the Jay –
Where be the Maise –
Where be the Haze –
Where be the Bur?
Here – said the Year –

There is a Shame of Nobleness –
Confronting Sudden Pelf –
A finer Shame of Extasy –
Convicted of Itself –

A best Disgrace – a Brave Man feels –
Acknowledged – of the Brave –
One more – "Ye Blessed" – to be told –
But that's – Behind the Grave – But This – involves the Grave –

SHEET SIX c. second half of 1863

An ignorance a Sunset [An] impotence
Confer upon the Eye –
Of Territory – Color –
Circumference – Decay – [Circumference –] Array

Its Amber Revelation
Exhilirate – Debase –
Omnipotence' inspection [Omnipotence'] Analysis
Of Our inferior face –

And when the solemn features
Confirm – in Victory – Withdraw – [in]
We start – as if detected
In Immortality –

One Crucifixion is recorded – only –[270]
How many be
Is not affirmed of Mathematics –
Or History –

One Calvary – exhibited to stranger –
As many be
As Persons – or Peninsulas –
Gethsemane –

Is but a Province – in the Being's Centre – [the] Human Centre
Judea –
For Journey – or Crusade's Achieving –
Too near –

Our Lord – indeed – made Compound Witness – [indeed –] bore –
And yet –
There's newer – nearer Crucifixion
Than That –

The Sweetest Heresy received
That Man and Woman know –
Each Other's Convert –
Though the Faith accommodate but Two –

The Churches are so frequent –
The Ritual – so small –
The Grace so unavoidable –
To fail – is Infidel –

Take Your Heaven further on –
This – to Heaven divine Has gone –
Had You earlier blundered in
Possibly, e'en You had seen
An Eternity – put on –
Now – to ring a Door beyond
Is the utmost of Your Hand –
To the Skies – apologize –
Nearer to Your Courtesies
Than this Sufferer polite –
Dressed to meet You –
See – in White!

FASCICLE THIRTY-ONE

SHEET ONE c. second half of 1863

The Soul's Superior instants
Occur to Her – Alone –
When friend – and Earth's occasion
Have infinite withdrawn –

Or She – Herself – ascended
To too remote a Hight
For lower Recognition [lower] Interruption
Than Her Omnipotent –

This mortal Abolition
Is seldom – but as fair
As Apparition – subject
To Autocratic Air –

Eternity's disclosure
To a Revering – Eye To favorites – a few –
Of the Colossal substance
Of Immortality –

Me prove it now – Whoever doubt [now –] Whatever
Me stop to prove it – now –
Make haste – the Scruple! Death be scant Come near [the]
For Opportunity –

The River reaches to my feet –
As yet – My Heart be dry –
Oh Lover – Life could not convince –
Might Death – enable Thee –

The River reaches to My Breast –
Still – still – My Hands above

The Soul's Superior: *Sent to SD (variant) c. second half of 1863*

Proclaim with their remaining might –
Dost recognize the Love?

The River reaches to my Mouth –
Remember – when the Sea
Swept by my searching eyes – the last –
Themselves were quick – with Thee!

To lose One's faith – surpass
The loss of an Estate –
Because Estates can be
Replenished – faith cannot –

Inherited with Life –
Belief – but once – can be –
Annihilate a single clause –
And Being's – Beggary –

I saw no Way – The Heavens were stitched –
I felt the Columns close –
The Earth reversed her Hemispheres –
I touched the Universe –

And back it slid – and I alone –
A speck upon a Ball –
Went out upon Circumference –
Beyond the Dip of Bell –

SHEET TWO c. second half of 1863

Had I presumed to hope –
The loss had been to Me
A Value – for the Greatness' Sake –
As Giants – gone away – [Giants –] claimed

Had I presumed to gain
A Favor so remote –
The Failure but confirm the Grace
In further Infinite –

o

'Tis failure – not of Hope –
But Confident Despair – [But] diligent – • resolute –
Advancing on Celestial Lists –
With faint – Terrestrial power –

'Tis Honor – though I die –
For That no Man obtain
Till He be justified by Death –
This – is the Second Gain –

~

Sweet – You forgot – but I remembered[271]
Every time – for Two –
So that the Sum be never hindered [the] Love
Through Decay of You – [Through] Fatigue – • the Lapse –

Say if I erred? Accuse my Farthings –
Blame the little Hand [the] empty – • childish
Happy it be for You – a Beggar's –
Seeking more – to spend – Saving – [more –]

Just to be Rich – to waste my Guineas
On so Best a Heart –
Just to be Poor – for Barefoot Vision
You – Sweet – Shut me out –

~

It struck me – every Day –
The Lightning was as new
As if the Cloud that instant slit
And let the Fire through –

It burned Me – in the Night –
It Blistered to My Dream –
It sickened fresh upon my sight –
With every Morn that came –

I thought that Storm – was brief –
The Maddest – quickest by –
But Nature lost the Date of This –
And left it in the Sky –

~

Sweet – You forgot –: *Sent to SB (third stanza, variant) c. second half of 1863*

I went to thank Her –[272]
But She Slept –
Her Bed – a funneled Stone –
With Nosegays at the Head and Foot –
That Travellers – had thrown –

Who went to thank Her –
But She Slept –
'Twas Short – to cross the Sea –
To look upon Her like – alive –
But turning back – 'twas slow –

SHEET THREE c. second half of 1863

The Future never spoke –
Nor will he like the Dumb
Report by Sign a Circumstance — Reveal by sign a Syllable –
Of his profound To Come – — [his] Opaque –

But when the News be ripe
Presents it in the Act –
Forestalling Preparation –
Escape – or Substitute –

Indifferent to him
The Dower – as the Doom –
His Office but to execute
Fate's Telegram – to Him –

I gained it so –
By Climbing slow –
By catching at the Twigs that grow
Between the Bliss – and me –
It hung so high
As well the Sky
Attempt by Strategy –

I said I gained it –
This – was all –

The Future never: *Sent to SD (variant) c. second half of 1863*

Look, how I clutch it
Lest it fall –
And I a Pauper go –
Unfitted by an instant's Grace
For the Contented – Beggar's face
I wore – an hour ago –

~

Death sets a Thing significant[273]
The Eye had hurried by
Except a perished Creature
Entreat us tenderly

To ponder little workmanships
In Crayon – or in wool –
With "This was last Her fingers did" –
Industrious until –

The Thimble weighed too heavy –
The stitches stopped – themselves –
And then 'twas put among the Dust
Upon the Closet shelves –

A Book I have – a friend gave –
Whose Pencil – here and there –
Had notched the place that pleased Him –
At Rest – His fingers are –

Now – when I read – I read not –
For interrupting Tears –
Obliterate the Etchings
Too Costly for Repairs –

~

What I can do – I will –
Though it be little as a Daffodil –
That I cannot – must be
Unknown to possibility –

~

SHEET FOUR c. second half of 1863

There is a flower that Bees prefer –[274]
And Butterflies – desire –
To gain the Purple Democrat
The Humming Bird – aspire –

And Whatsoever Insect pass –
A Honey bear away
Proportioned to his several dearth
And her – capacity –

Her face be rounder than the Moon
And ruddier than the Gown
Of Orchis in the Pasture –
Or Rhododendron – worn –

She doth not wait for June –
Before the World be Green –
Her sturdy little Countenance
Against the Wind – be seen –

Contending with the Grass –
Near Kinsman to Herself –
For privilege of Sod and Sun –
Sweet Litigants for Life –

And when the Hills be full –
And newer fashions blow –
Doth not retract a single spice
For pang of jealousy –

Her Public – be the Noon –
Her Providence – the Sun –
Her Progress – by the Bee – proclaimed –
In sovreign – Swerveless Tune –

The Bravest – of the Host –
Surrendering – the last –
Nor even of Defeat – aware –
When cancelled by the Frost –

A Secret told –
Ceases to be a Secret – then –
A Secret – kept –
That – can appall but One –

Better of it – continual be afraid –
Than it –
And Whom you told it to – beside –

~

For Death – or rather
For the Things 'twould buy –
This – put away
Life's Opportunity –

The Things that Death will buy
Are Room –
Escape from Circumstances –
And a Name –

With Gifts of Life
How Death's Gifts may compare –
We know not –
For the Rates – lie Here –

~

SHEET FIVE c. second half of 1863

Exhiliration – is within –
There can no Outer Wine
So royally intoxicate
As that diviner Brand

The Soul achieves – Herself –
To drink – or set away
For Visitor – or Sacrament –
'Tis not of Holiday

To stimulate a Man
Who hath the Ample Rhine
Within his Closet – Best you can
Exhale in offering –

~

For Death – or: *Presumably sent to SD (lost, published variant) c. 1863*

'Tis One by One – the Father counts –[275]
And then a Tract between
Set Cypherless – to teach the Eye
The Value of its Ten –

Until the peevish Student
Acquire the Quick of Skill –
Then Numerals are dowered back –
Adorning all the Rule –

'Tis mostly Slate and Pencil –
And Darkness on the School
Distracts the Children's fingers –
Still the Eternal Rule

Regards least Cypherer alike
With Leader of the Band –
And every separate Urchin's Sum –
Is fashioned for his hand – [Is] fitted to –

To fill a Gap
Insert the Thing that caused it –
Block it up
With Other – and 'twill yawn the more –
You cannot solder an Abyss [cannot] Plug a Sepulchre –
With Air –

I've seen a Dying Eye
Run round and round a Room –
In search of Something – as it seemed – [of] Somewhat –
Then Cloudier become –
And then – obscure with Fog –
And then – be soldered down
Without disclosing what it be
'Twere blessed to have seen –

SHEET SIX c. second half of 1863

No Rack can torture me –
My Soul – at Liberty –
Behind this mortal Bone
There knits a bolder One –

You cannot prick with Saw –
Nor pierce with Cimitar –
Two Bodies – therefore be –
Bind One – The Other fly –

The Eagle of his Nest
No easier divest –
And gain the Sky
Than mayest Thou –

Except Thyself may be
Thine Enemy –
Captivity is Consciousness –
So's Liberty.

Death is potential to that Man
Who dies – and to his friend –
Beyond that – unconspicuous
To Anyone but God –

Of these Two – God remembers
The longest – for the friend –
Is integral – and therefore [Is] subsequent –
Itself dissolved – of God –

Smiling back from Coronation[276]
May be Luxury –
On the Heads that started with us –
Being's Peasantry –

Recognizing in Procession
Ones We former knew –

1 –

X

That I did always love
I bring thee Proof
That till I loved
I + never lived – Enough –

That I shall love alway –
I + argue thee
That love + is life –
And life hath Immortality –

This – dost thou doubt –
Sweet –
Then have I
Nothing to show
But Calvary –

+ did not live + Offer –
+ be.

(68)

"That I did always love"

When Ourselves were also dusty –
Centuries ago –

Had the Triumph no Conviction
Of how many be –
Stimulated – by the Contrast –
Unto Misery –

That I did always love[277]
I bring thee Proof
That till I loved
I never lived – Enough – [I] did not live

That I shall love alway –
I argue thee [I] offer –
That love is life – [love] be –
And life hath Immortality –

This – dost thou doubt – Sweet –
Then have I
Nothing to show
But Calvary –

FASCICLE THIRTY-TWO

SHEET ONE c. second half of 1863

Triumph – may be of several kinds –[278]
There's Triumph in the Room
When that Old Imperator – Death –
By Faith – be overcome –

There's Triumph of the finer mind
When Truth – affronted long –
Advance unmoved – to Her Supreme –
Her God – Her only Throng –

A Triumph – when Temptation's Bribe
Be slowly handed back –
One eye upon the Heaven renounced –
And One – upon the Rack –

Severer Triumph – by Himself
Experienced – who pass
Acquitted – from that Naked Bar –
Jehovah's Countenance –

Don't put up my Thread & Needle – [put] ~~down~~
I'll begin to Sow
When the Birds begin to whistle –
Better stitches – so –

These were bent – my sight got crooked –
When my mind – is plain
I'll do seams – a Queen's endeavor
Would not blush to own –

Hems – too fine for Lady's tracing
To the sightless knot –

Tucks – of dainty interspersion –
Like a dotted Dot –

Leave my Needle in the furrow –
Where I put it down –
I can make the zigzag stitches
Straight – when I am strong –

Till then – dreaming I am sowing   [then –] deeming
Fetch the seam I missed –
Closer – so I – at my sleeping –   [my] sighing –
Still surmise I stitch –

~

So well that I can live without –
I love thee – then How well is that?
As well as Jesus?
Prove it me
That He – loved Men –
As I – love thee –

~

At leisure is the Soul
That gets a staggering Blow –
The Width of Life – before it spreads   [it] runs
Without a thing to do –

It begs you give it Work –
But just the placing Pins –
Or humblest Patchwork – Children do –   [Children] may –
To still its noisy Hands –   [To] Help its Vacant Hands –

~

SHEET TWO c. second half of 1863

Sweet – safe – Houses –
Glad – gay – Houses –
Sealed so stately tight –
Lids of Steel – on Lids of Marble –
Locking Barefeet out –

o

Brooks of Plush – in Banks of Satin
Not so softly fall
As the laughter – and the whisper –
From their People Pearl –

No Bald Death – affront their Parlors –
No Bold Sickness come
To deface their stately Treasures –
Anguish – and the Tomb –

Hum by – in muffled Coaches –
Lest they – wonder Why –
Any – for the Press of Smiling –
Interrupt – to die –

~

Glee – The great storm is over –[279]
Four – have recovered the Land –
Forty – gone down together –
Into the boiling Sand –

Ring – for the scant Salvation –
Toll – for the bonnie Souls –
Neighbor – and friend – and Bridegroom –
Spinning upon the Shoals –

How they will tell the story –
When Winter shake the Door –
Till the Children urge – [Children] ask –
But the Forty –
Did they – Come back no more?

Then a silence – suffuse the story –
And a softness – the Teller's eye –
And the Children – no further question –
And only the Sea – reply –

~

It makes no difference abroad –[280]
The Seasons – fit – the same –
The Mornings blossom into Noons –
And split their Pods of Flame –

o

Wild flowers – kindle in the Woods –
The Brooks slam – all the Day – [Brooks] brag –
No Black bird bates His Banjo –
For passing Calvary –

Auto da Fe – and Judgment –
Are nothing to the Bee –
His separation from His Rose –
To Him – sums Misery –

I asked no other thing –
No other – was denied –
I offered Being – for it –
The Mighty Merchant sneered – [Merchant] smiled –

Brazil? He twirled a Button –
Without a glance my way –
"But – Madam – is there nothing else –
That We can show – Today"?

SHEET THREE c. second half of 1863

To know just how He suffered – would be dear –[281]
To know if any Human eyes were near
To whom He could entrust His wavering gaze –
Until it settled broad – on Paradise – [settled] full – • firm –

To know if He was patient – part content –
Was Dying as He thought – or different –
Was it a pleasant Day to die –
And did the Sunshine face His way –

What was His furthest mind –
Of Home – or God –
Or What the Distant say –
At News that He ceased Human Nature
Such a Day –

And Wishes – Had He any –
Just His Sigh – accented –

Had been legible – to Me –
And was He Confident until
Ill fluttered out – in Everlasting Well –

And if He spoke – What name was Best –
What last [What] first
What one broke off with
At the Drowsiest –

Was he afraid – or tranquil –
Might He know
How Conscious Consciousness – could grow –
Till Love that was – and Love too best to be –
Meet – and the Junction be Eternity [Junction] mean –

It was too late for Man –
But early, yet, for God –
Creation – impotent to help –
But Prayer – remained – Our side –

How excellent the Heaven –
When Earth – cannot be had –
How hospitable – then – the face
Of Our Old Neighbor – God – [Our] New

Forever – is composed of Nows –
'Tis not a different time –
Except for Infiniteness –
And Latitude of Home –

From this – experienced Here –
Remove the Dates – to These –
Let Months dissolve in further Months – [in] other –
And Years – exhale in Years –

Without Debate – or Pause – [Without] Certificate –
Or Celebrated Days –
No different Our Years would be As infinite – [Our]
From Anno Dominies –

SHEET FOUR c. second half of 1863

'Twas a long Parting – but the time
For Interview – had Come –
Before the Judgment Seat of God –
The last – and second time

These Fleshless Lovers met –
A Heaven in a Gaze –
A Heaven of Heavens – the Privilege
Of One another's Eyes –

No Lifetime set – on Them –
Appareled as the new
Unborn – except They had beheld –
Born infiniter – now – [Born] everlasting

Was Bridal – e'er like This?
A Paradise – the Host –
And Cherubim – and Seraphim –
The unobtrusive Guest – [The] most familiar –

Only God – detect the Sorrow –[282] [God –] Possess the secret –
Only God –
The Jehovahs – are no Babblers –
Unto God –

God the Son – confide it – [Son –] disclose it
Still secure –
God the Spirit's Honor –
Just as sure – Equal sure –

Like Eyes that looked on Wastes –
Incredulous of Ought
But Blank – and steady Wilderness –
Diversified by Night –

Just Infinites of Nought –
As far as it could see –

So looked the face I looked upon –
So looked itself – on Me –

I offered it no Help –
Because the Cause was Mine –
The Misery a Compact
As hopeless – as divine –

Neither – would be absolved –
Neither would be a Queen
Without the Other – Therefore –
We perish – tho' We reign –

A Tooth upon Our Peace
The Peace cannot deface –
Then Wherefore be the Tooth?
To vitalize the Grace –

The Heaven hath a Hell –
Itself to signalize –
And every sign before the Place –
Is Gilt with Sacrifice –

SHEET FIVE c. second half of 1863

I know Where Wells grow – Droughtless Wells –[283]
Deep dug – for Summer days –
Where Mosses go no more away –
And Pebble – safely plays –

It's made of Fathoms – and a Belt –
A Belt of jagged Stone –
Inlaid with Emerald – half way down –
And Diamonds – jumbled on –

It has no Bucket – were I rich
A Bucket I would buy –
I'm often thirsty – but my lips
Are so high up – You see –

o

I read in an Old fashioned Book
That People "thirst no more" –
The Wells have Buckets to them there –
It must mean that – I'm sure –

Shall We remember Parching – then?
Those Waters sound so grand –
I think a little Well – like Mine –
Dearer to understand –

~

The Tint I cannot take – is best –[284]
The Color too remote
That I could show it in Bazaar –
A Guinea at a sight –

The fine – impalpable Array –
That swaggers on the eye
Like Cleopatra's Company –
Repeated – in the sky –

The Moments of Dominion
That happen on the Soul
And leave it with a Discontent
Too exquisite – to tell –

The eager look – on Landscapes –
As if they just repressed
Some secret – that was pushing
Like Chariots – in the Vest – [Like] Columns – in the Breast –

The Pleading of the Summer –
That other Prank – of Snow –
That Cushions Mystery with Tulle, [That] Covers Mystery with Blonde –
For fear the Squirrels – know.

Their Graspless manners – mock us –
Until the Cheated Eye
Shuts arrogantly – in the Grave –
Another way – to see –

~

SHEET SIX c. second half of 1863

A Wife – at Daybreak – I shall be –[285]
Sunrise – Hast Thou a Flag for me?
At Midnight – I am yet a Maid –
How short it takes to make it Bride –
Then – Midnight – I have passed from Thee –
Unto the East – and Victory.

Midnight – Good night – I hear them Call –
The Angels bustle in the Hall –
Softly – my Future climbs the Stair –
I fumble at my Childhood's Prayer –
So soon to be a Child – no more –
Eternity – I'm coming – Sir –
Master – I've seen the Face – before –

Why make it doubt – it hurts it so –
So sick – to guess –
So strong – to know –
So brave – upon its little Bed
To tell the very last They said
Unto Itself – and smile – And shake –
For that dear – distant – dangerous – sake –
But – the Instead – the Pinching fear
That Something – it did do – or dare –
Offend the Vision – and it flee –
And They no more remember me –
Nor ever turn to tell me why –
Oh, Master, This is Misery –

I live with Him – I see His face –
I go no more away
For Visitor – or Sundown –
Death's single privacy

The Only One – forestalling Mine –
And that – by Right that He

Presents a Claim invisible –
No Wedlock – granted Me –

I live with Him – I hear His Voice –
I stand alive – Today –
To witness to the Certainty
Of Immortality –

Taught Me – by Time – the lower Way –
Conviction – every day –
That Life like This – is stopless –
Be Judgment – what it may –

The power to be true to You,
Until upon my face
The Judgment push His Picture –
Presumptuous of Your Place –

Of This – Could Man deprive Me –
Himself – the Heaven excel –
Whose invitation – Yours reduced
Until it showed too small –

FASCICLE THIRTY-THREE

SHEET ONE c. second half of 1863

The Way I read a Letter's – this – [Letter's –] so
'Tis first – I lock the Door –
And push it with my fingers – next –
For transport it be sure –

And then I go the furthest off
To counteract a knock –
Then draw my little Letter forth
And slowly pick the lock – [And] slily • softly

Then – glancing narrow, at the Wall –
And narrow at the floor [the] door
For firm Conviction of a Mouse
Not exorcised before –

Peruse how infinite I am
To no one that You – know –
And sigh for lack of Heaven – but not
The Heaven God bestow –

~

The Child's faith is new –
Whole – like His Principle –
Wide – like the Sunrise
On fresh Eyes –
Never had a Doubt –
Laughs – at a scruple –
Believes all sham
But Paradise –

Credits the World –
Deems His Dominion

Broadest of Sovreignties –
And Caesar – mean –
In the Comparison –
Baseless Emperor –
Ruler of nought,
Yet swaying all –

Grown bye and bye
To hold mistaken
His pretty estimates
Of Prickly Things
He gains the skill
Sorrowful – as certain –
Men – to anticipate   [to] propitiate –
Instead of Kings –

~

Except the Heaven had come so near –
So seemed to choose My Door –
The Distance would not haunt me so –
I had not hoped – before –

But just to hear the Grace depart –
I never thought to see –
Afflicts me with a Double loss –
'Tis lost – And lost to me –

~

To My Small Hearth His fire came –[286]
And all My House a'glow
Did fan and rock, with sudden light –
'Twas Sunrise – 'twas the Sky –

Impanelled from no Summer brief –
With limit of Decay –   [With] license
'Twas Noon – without the News of Night –   [without] Report of Night
Nay, Nature, it was Day –   'Twas further – [it]

~

SHEET TWO c. second half of 1863

My Portion is Defeat – today –[287]
A paler luck than Victory –
Less Paeans – fewer Bells –
The Drums don't follow Me – with tunes –
Defeat – a somewhat slower – means – [a] something dumber
More Arduous than Balls – [More] difficult –

'Tis populous with Bone and stain –
And Men too straight to stoop again – [to] bend
And Piles of solid Moan –
And Chips of Blank – in Boyish Eyes –
And scraps of Prayer – [And] shreds
And Death's surprise,
Stamped visible – in stone –

There's somewhat prouder, Over there – [There's] something
The Trumpets tell it to the Air –
How different Victory
To Him who has it – and the One
Who to have had it, would have been
Contenteder – to die –

I am ashamed – I hide –
What right have I – to be a Bride –
So late a Dowerless Girl –
Nowhere to hide my dazzled Face –
No one to teach me that new Grace –
Nor introduce – My soul –

Me to adorn – How – tell –
Trinket – to make Me beautiful –
Fabrics of Cashmere –
Never a Gown of Dun – more –
Raiment instead – of Pompadour –
For Me – My soul – to wear –

Fingers – to frame – my Round Hair
Oval – as Feudal Ladies wore –

Far Fashions – Fair –
Skill – to hold my Brow like an Earl –
Plead – like a Whippowil –
Prove – like a Pearl –
Then, for Character –

Fashion My Spirit quaint – white –
Quick – like a Liquor –
Gay – like Light –
Bring Me my best Pride –
No more ashamed –
No more to hide –
Meek – let it be – too proud – for Pride –
Baptized – this Day – A Bride –

SHEET THREE c. second half of 1863

I cannot live with You –[288]
It would be Life –
And Life is over there –
Behind the Shelf

The Sexton keeps the key to –
Putting up
Our Life – His Porcelain –
Like a Cup –

Discarded of the Housewife –
Quaint – or Broke –
A newer Sevres pleases –
Old Ones crack –

I could not die – with You –
For One must wait
To shut the Other's Gaze down –
You – could not –

And I – Could I stand by
And see You – freeze –
Without my Right of Frost –
Death's privilege?

o

Nor could I rise – with You –
Because Your Face
Would put out Jesus' –
That New Grace

Glow plain – and foreign
On my homesick eye –
Except that You than He
Shone closer by –

They'd judge Us – How –
For You – served Heaven – You know,
Or sought to –
I could not –

Because You saturated sight –
And I had no more eyes
For sordid excellence [sordid] consequence
As Paradise

And were You lost, I would be –
Though my name
Rang loudest
On the Heavenly fame –

And were You – saved –
And I – condemned to be
Where You were not
That self – were Hell to me –

So we must meet apart –
You there – I – here –
With just the Door ajar
That Oceans are – and Prayer –
And that White Sustenance – [White] exercise – • privilege –
Despair –

~

Size circumscribes – it has no room
For petty furniture –
The Giant tolerates no Gnat [Giant] entertains
For Ease of Gianture – [For] Simple Gianture – • Because of Gianture

o

Repudiates it, all the more –
Because intrinsic size
Ignores the possibility — Excludes [the]
Of Calumnies – or Flies – — [Of] Jealousies –

~

SHEET FOUR c. second half of 1863

They put Us far apart –
As separate as Sea
And Her unsown Peninsula –
We signified "These see" –

They took away our eyes –
They thwarted Us with Guns –
"I see Thee" Each responded straight
Through Telegraphic Signs –

With Dungeons – They devised –
But through their thickest skill –
And their opaquest Adamant –
Our Souls saw – just as well –

They summoned Us to die –
With sweet alacrity
We stood upon our stapled feet –
Condemned – but just – to see –

Permission to recant –
Permission to forget –
We turned our backs upon the Sun
For perjury of that –

Not Either – noticed Death –
Of Paradise – aware –
Each other's Face – was all the Disc
Each other's setting – saw –

~

Me from Myself – to banish –
Had I Art –

Invincible My Fortress
Unto All Heart –

impregnable [My]
To foreign Heart –

But since Myself – assault Me –
How have I peace
Except by subjugating
Consciousness?

And since We're Mutual Monarch
How this be
Except by Abdication –
Me – of Me – ?

Doom is the House without the Door –[289]
'Tis entered from the Sun –
And then the Ladder's thrown away,
Because Escape – is done –

'Tis varied by the Dream
Of what they do outside –
Where Squirrels play – and Berries dye –
And Hemlocks – bow – to God –

SHEET FIVE c. second half of 1863

I should have been too glad, I see –[290]
Too lifted – for the scant degree
Of Life's penurious Round –
My little Circuit would have shamed
This new Circumference – have blamed –
The homelier time behind –

I should have been too saved – I see –
Too rescued – Fear too dim to me
That I could spell the Prayer
I knew so perfect – yesterday –
That scalding one – Sabacthini –
Recited fluent – here –

o

I should have: *Sent to Ns (lost) and to SD (fourth stanza, variant) c. 1862*

Earth would have been too much – I see –
And Heaven – not enough for me –
I should have had the Joy
Without the Fear – to justify –
The Palm – without the Calvary –
So Savior – Crucify –

Defeat whets Victory – they say –
The Reefs in Old Gethsemane
Endear the shore beyond – [the] Coast
'Tis Beggars – Banquets best define –
'Tis Thirsting – vitalizes Wine –
Faith bleats to understand – [Faith] faints –

I meant to have but modest needs –[291]
Such as Content – and Heaven –
Within my income – these could lie
And Life and I – keep even –

But since the last – included both –
It would suffice my Prayer
But just for one – to stipulate –
And Grace would grant the Pair –

And so – upon this wise – I prayed –
Great Spirit – Give to me
A Heaven not so large as Yours,
But large enough – for me –

A Smile suffused Jehovah's face –
The Cherubim – withdrew –
Grave Saints stole out to look at me –
And showed their dimples – too –

I left the Place – with all my might –
I threw my Prayer away –
The Quiet Ages picked it up –
And Judgment – twinkled – too –
That one so honest – be extant –
It take the Tale for true –

That "Whatsoever Ye shall ask –
Itself be given You" –

But I, grown shrewder – scan the Skies
With a suspicious Air –
As Children – swindled for the first
All Swindlers – be – infer –

SHEET SIX c. second half of 1863

I could suffice for Him, I knew –
He – could suffice for Me –
Yet Hesitating Fractions – Both
Surveyed Infinity – delayed – • deferred – [Infinity –]

"Would I be Whole" He sudden broached –
My Syllable rebelled –
'Twas face to face with Nature – forced –
'Twas face to face with God –

Withdrew the Sun – to other Wests –
Withdrew the furthest Star
Before Decision – stooped to speech –
And then – be audibler

The Answer of the Sea unto
The Motion of the Moon –
Herself adjust Her Tides – unto –
Could I – do else – with Mine?

You left me – Sire – two Legacies – [me –] Sweet
A Legacy of Love
A Heavenly Father would suffice [would] content –
Had He the offer of –

You left me Boundaries of Pain –
Capacious as the Sea –
Between Eternity and Time –
Your Consciousness – and me –

No Man can compass a Despair –
As round a Goalless Road
No faster than a mile at once
The Traveller proceed –

Unconscious of the Width –
Unconscious that the Sun
Be setting on His progress –
So accurate the one

At estimating Pain –
Whose own – has just begun –
His ignorance – the Angel
That pilot Him along –

FASCICLE THIRTY-FOUR

SHEET ONE c. late 1863

Bereavement in their death to feel
Whom We have never seen –
A Vital Kinsmanship import
Our Soul and theirs – between –

For Stranger – Strangers do not mourn –
There be Immortal friends
Whom Death see first – 'tis news of this
That paralyze Ourselves –

Who – vital only to Our Thought –
Such Presence bear away
In dying – 'tis as if Our souls
Absconded – suddenly –

[Our] World – • selves – • Sun –

I think To Live – may be a Bliss
To those who dare to try –
Beyond my limit – to conceive –
My lip – to testify –

[a] Life
[those] allowed

I think the Heart I former wore
Could widen – till to me
The Other, like the little Bank
Appear – unto the Sea –

I think the Days – could every one
In Ordination stand –
And Majesty – be easier –
Than an inferior kind –

No numb alarm – lest Difference come –
No Goblin – on the Bloom –

No start in Apprehension's Ear, [No] click
No Bankruptcy – no Doom – [No] Sepulchre – • Wilderness

But Certainties of Sun – [of] Noon
Midsummer – in the Mind – Meridian [in]
A steadfast South – upon the Soul –
Her Polar time – behind – [Polar] Night

The Vision – pondered long –
So plausible becomes [So] tangible – • positive ~~appears~~
That I esteem the fiction – real – [fiction –] true
The Real – fictitious seems – [The] Truth

How bountiful the Dream –
What Plenty – it would be
Had all my Life but been Mistake [Life] been one • [been] bleak
Just rectified – in Thee [Just] qualified –

A little Road – not made of Man –
Enabled of the Eye –
Accessible to Thill of Bee –
Or Cart of Butterfly –

If Town it have – beyond itself – [have –] besides
'Tis that – I cannot say –
I only know – no Curricle that rumble there [only] sigh – [no] Vehicle
Bear me – hold – [me –]

SHEET TWO c. late 1863

Her Sweet turn to leave the Homestead
Came the Darker Way –
Carriages – Be Sure – and Guests – True – [Guests –] too
But for Holiday

'Twas more pitiful Endeavor
Than did Loaded Sea [did] swelling
O'er the Curls attempt to caper
It had cast away –

Never Bride had such Assembling –
Never kinsmen kneeled
To salute so fair a Forehead –
Garland be indeed –

Fitter Feet – of Her before us – fitter for the feet [before]
Than whatever Brow
Art of Snow – or Trick of Lily
Possibly bestow Ever could endow –

Of Her Father – Whoso ask Her – [Whoso] claim
He shall seek as high
As the Palm – that serve the Desert –
To obtain the sky –

Distance – be Her only Motion – [only] Signal
If 'tis Nay – or Yes –
Acquiescence – or Demurral –
Whosoever guess –

He – must pass the Crystal Angle first [must pass the Crystal] limit
That obscure Her face – [That] divide –
He – must have achieved in person
Equal Paradise –

⁓

Pain – has an Element of Blank –
It cannot recollect
When it begun – Or if there were
A time when it was not – [A] Day –

It has no Future – but itself –
Its Infinite contain
Its Past – enlightened to perceive
New Periods – Of Pain.

⁓

So much Summer
Me for showing
Illegitimate –
Would a Smile's minute bestowing
Too exorbitant [Too] extravagant – • importunate –

o

To the Lady
With the Guinea [Guinea]s
Look – if she should know
Crumb of Mine
A Robin's Larder
Would suffice to stow – Could – [suffice]

SHEET THREE c. late 1863

Promise This – When You be Dying –[292]
Some shall summon Me – Some one [summon]
Mine belong Your latest Sighing –
Mine – to Belt Your Eye –

Not with Coins – though they be Minted
From An Emperor's Hand –
Be my lips – the only Buckle
Your low Eyes – demand – [Your] meek –

Mine to stay – when all have wandered –
To devise once more
If the Life be too surrendered –
Life of Mine – restore –

Poured like this – My Whole Libation – [My] best
Just that You should see
Bliss of Death – Life's Bliss extol thro'
Imitating You –

Mine – to guard Your Narrow Precinct –
To seduce the Sun [To] entice – • persuade
Longest on Your South, to linger, latest [on]
Largest Dews of Morn newest – • freshest [Dews]

To demand, in Your low favor –
Lest the Jealous Grass
Greener lean – Or fonder cluster [Or] later linger
Round some other face –

Mine to supplicate Madonna –
If Madonna be

Could behold so far a Creature –
Christ – omitted – Me –

Just to follow Your dear feature – still [to]
Ne'er so far behind –
For My Heaven –
Had I not been Of All Her Glories –
Most enough – denied? Amplest – • Worthiest – to have gained –

lines 15–16: [Bliss of Death – Life's Bliss] surpass in / more resembling You

Bliss of Death – Life's Bliss excel in / More resembling You –

line 27: [Could] regard [so] small – • dim [a Creature –]

Could regard so scarce a Creature –

I had no time to Hate –
Because
The Grave would hinder me –
And Life was not so
Ample I
Could finish – Enmity –

Nor had I time to Love –
But since
Some Industry must be –
The little Toil of Love –
I thought
Be large enough for Me –

SHEET FOUR c. late 1863

My Life had stood – a Loaded Gun –[293]
In Corners – till a Day
The Owner passed – identified –
And carried Me away –

And now We roam in Sovreign Woods – [roam] the –
And now We hunt the Doe –
And every time I speak for Him
The Mountains straight reply –

o

And do I smile, such cordial light
Upon the Valley glow –
It is as a Vesuvian face
Had let its pleasure through –

And when at Night – Our good Day done –
I guard My Master's Head –
'Tis better than the Eider Duck's
Deep Pillow – to have shared – low [Pillow]

To foe of His – I'm deadly foe –
None stir the second time – [None] harm
On whom I lay a Yellow Eye –
Or An emphatic Thumb –

Though I than He – may longer live
He longer must – than I –
For I have but the power to kill, [the] art
Without – the power to die –

The Sunrise runs for Both –
The East – Her Purple Troth
Keeps with the Hill –
The Noon unwinds Her Blue
Till One Breadth cover Two –
Remotest – still –

Nor does the Night forget
A Lamp for Each – to set –
Wicks wide away –
The North – Her blazing Sign
Erects in Iodine –
Till Both – can see –

The Midnight's Dusky Arms
Clasp Hemispheres, and Homes
And so
Upon Her Bosom – One –
And One upon Her Hem –
Both lie –

No Bobolink – reverse His Singing[294]
When the only Tree
Ever He minded occupying
By the Farmer be –

Clove to the Root – [the] Core
His Spacious Future –
Best Horizon – gone – All [Horizon –] known –
Brave Bobolink –
Whose Music be His
Only Anodyne –

SHEET FIVE c. late 1863

One Blessing had I than the rest
So larger to my Eyes
That I stopped guaging – satisfied –
For this enchanted size –

It was the limit of my Dream –
The focus of my Prayer –
A perfect – paralyzing Bliss –
Contented as Despair –

I knew no more of Want – or Cold –
Phantasms both become fictitious [both]
For this new Value in the Soul – [new] fortune – • portion –
Supremest Earthly Sum –

The Heaven below the Heaven above –
Obscured with ruddier Blue – [with] nearer • comelier
Life's Latitudes leant over – full –
The Judgment perished – too –

Why Bliss so scantily disburse – [so] cautiously – express – • afford
Why Paradise defer – [Paradise] demur –
Why Floods be served to Us – in Bowls –
I speculate no more –

Victory comes late –[295]
And is held low to freezing lips –
Too rapt with frost
To take it –
How sweet it would have tasted –
Just a Drop –
Was God so economical?
His Table's spread too high for Us –
Unless We dine on Tiptoe –
Crumbs – fit such little mouths –
Cherries – suit Robins –
The Eagle's Golden Breakfast strangles – Them –
God keep His Oath to Sparrows –
Who of little Love – know how to starve –

~

The Mountains – grow unnoticed –
Their Purple figures rise
Without attempt – Exhaustion –
Assistance – or Applause –

In Their Eternal Faces
The Sun – with just delight [with] broad
Looks long – and last – and golden –
For fellowship – at night – [For] sympathy –

~

SHEET SIX c. late 1863

These – saw Visions –
Latch them softly – bind • Bar [them]
These – held Dimples –
Smooth them slow –
This – addressed departing accents –
Quick – Sweet Mouth – to miss thee so – soon [Sweet]

This – we stroked –
Unnumbered – Satin –
These – we held among our own – [we] fondled in
Fingers of the Slim Aurora –
Not so arrogant – this Noon –

o

Victory comes late –: *Sent to SB (variant) c. late 1861*

These – adjust – that ran to meet Us –
Pearl – for stocking – Pearl for Shoe – [Pearl –] the – [stocking – Pearl] the –
Paradise – the only Palace
Fit for Her reception – now –

~

Strong Draughts of Their Refreshing Minds
To drink – enables Mine
Through Desert or the Wilderness
As bore it sealed Wine –

To go elastic – Or as One
The Camel's trait – attained –
How powerful the stimulus
Of an Hermetic Mind –

~

We miss Her – not because We see –
The Absence of an Eye – [The] Journey
Except its Mind accompany –
Abridge Society impair • debar – • deprive – [Society]

As slightly as the Routes of Stars – [As] scarcely [as the] flights
Ourselves – asleep below –
We know that their superior Eyes
Include Us – as they go – Scan better – • Convey Us – [as]

~

Essential Oils – are wrung –[296]
The Attar from the Rose
Be not expressed by Suns – alone –
It is the gift of Screws –

The General Rose – decay –
But this – in Lady's Drawer
Make Summer – When the Lady lie
In Ceaseless Rosemary –

~

We miss Her –: *Sent to SD (variant) c. 1863*
Essential Oils – are: *Sent to SD (variant) c. 1863*

FASCICLE THIRTY-FIVE

SHEET ONE c. second half of 1863

The Sun kept setting – setting – still
No Hue of Afternoon –
Upon the Village I perceived –
From House to House 'twas Noon –

The Dusk kept dropping – dropping – still
No Dew upon the Grass –
But only on my Forehead stopped –
And wandered in my Face –

My Feet kept drowsing – drowsing – still
My fingers were awake –
Yet why so little sound – Myself
Unto my seeming – make?

How well I knew the Light before –
I could not see it now –
'Tis Dying – I am doing – but
I'm not afraid to know –

Shells from the Coast mistaking –
I cherished them for all –
Happening in After Ages
To entertain a Pearl –

Wherefore so late – I murmured –
My need of Thee – be done –
Therefore – the Pearl responded –
My Period begin

The Heaven vests for Each
In that small Deity
It craved the grace to worship
Some bashful Summer's Day –

Half shrinking from the Glory
It importuned to see
Till these faint Tabernacles drop
In full Eternity –

How imminent the Venture –
As One should sue a Star –
For His mean sake to leave the Row
And entertain Despair –

A Clemency so common –
We almost cease to fear –
Enabling the minutest –
And furthest – to adore –

~

The Spirit is the Conscious Ear –[297]
We actually Hear
When We inspect – that's audible –
That is admitted – Here –

For other Services – as Sound – [other] purposes
There hangs a smaller Ear [a] minor
Outside the Castle – that Contain – [the] Centre – • City [that] present –
The other – only – Hear –

~

SHEET TWO c. second half of 1863

If He were living – dare I ask –
And how if He be dead –
And so around the Words I went –
Of meeting them – afraid –

I hinted Changes – Lapse of Time –
The Surfaces of Years –
I touched with Caution – lest they crack – [they] slit –
And show me to my fears –

o

Reverted to adjoining Lives –
Adroitly turning out
Wherever I suspected Graves –
'Twas prudenter – I thought –

And He – I pushed – with sudden force –
In face of the Suspense –
"Was buried" – "Buried"! "He!"
My Life just holds the Trench –

~

As if the Sea should part
And show a further Sea –
And that – a further – and the Three
But a Presumption be –

Of Periods of Seas –
Unvisited of Shores –
Themselves the Verge of Seas to be –
Eternity – is Those –

~

"Nature" is what We see –[298]
The Hill – the Afternoon –
Squirrel – Eclipse – the Bumble bee –
Nay – Nature is Heaven –

"Nature" is what We hear –
The Bobolink – the Sea –
Thunder – the Cricket –
Nay – Nature is Harmony – [is] Melody

"Nature" is what We know –
But have no Art to say –
So impotent our Wisdom is [Wisdom] be –
To Her Sincerity –

~

Upon Concluded Lives
There's nothing cooler falls –
Than Life's sweet Calculations – [Life's] new
The mixing Bells and Palls –

o

"Nature" is what: *Sent to SD (variant) c. second half of 1863*

Makes Lacerating Tune –
To Ears the Dying side –
'Tis Coronal – and Funeral –
Saluting – in the Road – Confronting • Contrasting [in]

~

SHEET THREE c. second half of 1863

Have any like Myself
Investigating March,
New Houses on the Hill descried –
And possibly a Church –

That were not, We are sure –
As lately as the Snow –
And are Today – if We exist –
Though how may this be so?

Have any like Myself
Conjectured Who may be
The Occupants of these Abodes –
So easy to the Sky –

'Twould seem that God should be
The nearest Neighbor to –
And Heaven – a convenient Grace
For Show, or Company?

Have any like Myself
Preserved the Charm secure [the] Vision sure – • clear
By shunning carefully the Place [the] spot • site
All Seasons of the Year,

Excepting March – 'Tis then
My Villages be seen – the – [Villages]
And possibly a Steeple –
Not afterward – by Men –

~

Each Life converges to some Centre –
Expressed – or still –
Exists in every Human Nature
A Goal –

o

Embodied scarcely to itself – it may be – Admitted [scarcely]
Too fair
For Credibility's presumption [Credibility's] temerity
To mar – to dare –

Adored with caution – as a Brittle Heaven – Beheld [with]
To reach
Were hopeless, as the Rainbow's Raiment [as] a
To touch –

Yet persevered toward – surer – for the Distance – [toward –] stricter –
How high –
Unto the Saints' slow diligence – [slow] industry
The Sky –

Ungained – it may be – by a Life's low Venture – [be –] in –
But then –
Eternity enable the endeavoring
Again.

SHEET FOUR c. second half of 1863

Their Hight in Heaven comforts not –
Their Glory – nought to me –
'Twas best imperfect – as it was –
I'm finite – I can't see –

The House of Supposition –
The Glimmering Frontier that skirts the Acres of Perhaps –
To me – shows insecure –

The Wealth I had – contented me –
If 'twas a meaner size –
Then I had counted it until
It pleased my narrow Eyes –

Better than larger values –
That show however true –
This timid life of Evidence
Keeps pleading – "I don't know" –

Each Life converges: *Sent to SD (fifth stanza, variant) c. 1863, signed "Springfield"*

I could bring You Jewels – had I a mind to –[299]
But You have enough – of those –
I could bring You Odors from St Domingo –
Colors – from Vera Cruz –

Berries of the Bahamas – have I –
But this little Blaze
Flickering to itself – in the meadow –
Suits me – more than those –

Never a Fellow matched this Topaz –
And his Emerald Swing –
Dower itself – for Bobadilo –
Better – Could I bring?

~

Life – is what we make it –
Death – We do not know –
Christ's acquaintance with Him
Justify Him – though –

He – would trust no stranger –
Other – could betray –
Just His own endorsement –
That – sufficeth Me –

All the other Distance
He hath traversed first –
No new mile remaineth –
Far as Paradise –

His sure foot preceding –
Tender Pioneer –
Base must be the Coward
Dare not venture – now –

~

The Judge is like the Owl –[300]
I've heard my Father tell –
And Owls do build in Oaks –
So here's an Amber Sill –

o

That slanted in my Path –
When going to the Barn –
And if it serve You for a House –
Itself is not in vain –

About the price – 'tis small –
I only ask a Tune
At Midnight – Let the Owl select
His favorite Refrain.

SHEET FIVE c. second half of 1863

The Props assist the House –[301]
Until the House is Built –
And then the Props withdraw –
And adequate – Erect – [And] Conscious and

The House support itself – [House] sustain
And cease to recollect
The Scaffold, and the Carpenter – [The] Augur [and]
Just such a Retrospect
Hath the Perfected Life –
A Past of Plank – and Nail – [A] time – • state
And Slowness – then the Stagings drop – [the] scaffolds drop – • cleave
Affirming it – A Soul – pronouncing – [it]

You've seen Balloons set – Haven't You?[302]
So stately they ascend –
It is as Swans – discarded You,
For Duties Diamond –

Their Liquid Feet go softly out
Upon a Sea of Blonde –
They spurn the Air, as 'twere too mean
For Creatures so renowned –

o

Their Ribbons just beyond the eye –
They struggle – some – for Breath –
And yet the Crowd applaud, below –
They would not encore – Death –

o

The Props assist: *Sent to SD (variant) c. 1865*

The Gilded Creature strains – and spins –
Trips frantic in a Tree –
Tears open her imperial Veins –
And tumbles in the Sea –

The Crowd – retire with an Oath –
The Dust in Streets – go down –
And Clerks in Counting Rooms
Observe – "'Twas only a Balloon" –

~

The Zeros taught Us – Phosphorus –
We learned to like the Fire
By handling Glaciers – when a Boy –
And Tinder – guessed – by power

Of Opposite – to equal Ought –
Eclipses – Suns – imply –
Paralysis – our Primer dumb [Primer] numb –
Unto Vitality –

~

A Thought went up my mind today –
That I have had before –
But did not finish – some way back –
I could not fix the Year –

Nor Where it went – nor why it came
The second time to me –
Nor definitely, what it was –
Have I the Art to say –

But somewhere – in my soul – I know –
I've met the Thing before –
It just reminded me – 'twas all –
And came my way no more –

~

SHEET SIX c. second half of 1863

The Love a Life can show Below[303]
Is but a filament, I know,
Of that diviner thing

The Zeros taught: *Sent to SB (variant) c. 1862*

That faints upon the face of Noon –
And smites the Tinder in the Sun –
And hinders Gabriel's Wing –

'Tis this – in Music – hints and sways –
And far abroad on Summer days –
Distills uncertain pain –
'Tis this enamors in the East –
And tints the Transit in the West
With harrowing Iodine –

'Tis this – invites – appalls – endows –
Flits – glimmers – proves – dissolves –
Returns – suggests – convicts – enchants
Then – flings in Paradise –

~

A first Mute Coming –[304]
In the Stranger's House –
A first fair Going –
When the Bells rejoice –

A first Exchange – of
What hath mingled – been –
For Lot – exhibited to
Faith – alone –

~

Out of sight? What of that?
See the Bird – reach it!
Curve by Curve – Sweep by Sweep –
Round the Steep Air –
Danger! What is that to Her?
Better 'tis to fail – there –
Than debate – here –

Blue is Blue – the World through –
Amber – Amber – Dew – Dew –
Seek – Friend – and see –
Heaven is shy of Earth – that's all –
Bashful Heaven – thy Lovers small –
Hide – too – from thee –

~

No matter – now – Sweet –
But when I'm Earl –
Won't you wish you'd spoken
To that dull Girl?

Trivial a Word – just –
Trivial – a Smile –
But won't you wish you'd spared one
When I'm Earl?

I shan't need it – then –
Crests – will do –
Eagles on my Buckles –
On my Belt – too –

Ermine – my familiar Gown –
Say – Sweet – then
Won't you wish you'd smiled – just –
Me upon?

SHEET SEVEN c. second half of 1863

The Moon was but a Chin of Gold
A night or two ago –
And now she turns Her perfect Face
Upon the World below –

Her Forehead is of Amplest Blonde –
Her Cheek – a Beryl hewn –
Her Eye unto the Summer Dew
The likest I have known –

Her Lips of Amber never part –
But what must be the smile
Upon Her Friend she could confer   [could] bestow –
Were such Her silver will –

And what a privilege to be
But the remotest star –
For Certainty she take Her way
Beside Your Palace Door –   [Your] twinkling – • glimmering –

○

The Moon was: *Sent to Ns (lost) presumably c. 1863*

Her Bonnet is the Firmament –
The Universe – Her shoe – The Valleys – are Her shoe –
The Stars – the Trinkets at Her Belt –
Her Dimities – of Blue –

You said that I "was Great" – one Day –
Then "Great" it be – if that please Thee –
Or Small, or any size at all –
Nay – I'm the size suit Thee –

Tall – like the Stag – would that?
Or lower – like the Wren –
Or other hights of other ones
I've seen?

Tell which – it's dull to guess –
And I must be Rhinoceros
Or Mouse
At once – for Thee –

So say – if Queen it be –
Or Page – please Thee –
I'm that – or nought –
Or other thing – if other thing there be –
With just this stipulus – [this] Reservation –
I suit Thee –

I many times thought Peace had come
When Peace was far away –
As Wrecked Men – deem they sight the Land –
At Centre of the Sea –

And struggle slacker – but to prove
As hopelessly as I –
How many the fictitious Shores –
Or any Harbor be – Before the Harbor be –

FASCICLE THIRTY-SIX

SHEET ONE c. second half of 1863

No Other can reduce Our[305]
Mortal Consequence
Like the remembering it be Nought –
A Period from hence –

But Contemplation for
Cotemporaneous Nought –
Our Mutual Fame – that haply
Jehovah – recollect –

No Other can exalt Our
Mortal Consequence
Like the remembering it exist –
A period from hence –

Invited from Itself
To the Creator's House –
To tarry an Eternity –
His – shortest Consciousness –

Joy to have merited the Pain –[306]
To merit the Release –
Joy to have perished every step –
To Compass Paradise –

Pardon – to look upon thy face –
With these old fashioned Eyes –
Better than new – could be – for that –
Though bought in Paradise –

Because they looked on thee before –
And thou hast looked on them –

No Other can: *sent to SD (first two stanzas, variant) c. 1865*

Prove Me – My Hazel Witnesses — [My] swimming Witnesses –
The features are the same –

So fleet thou wert, when present –
So infinite – when gone –
An Orient's Apparition –
Remanded of the Morn –

The Hight I recollect –
'Twas even with the Hills –
The Depth upon my Soul was notched –
As Floods – on Whites of Wheels –

To Haunt – till Time have dropped
His last Decade away, — [His] slow Decades away –
And Haunting actualize – to last
At least – Eternity –

Bound a Trouble – and Lives will bear it –[307]
Circumscription – enables Wo –
Still to anticipate – Were no limit – — [to] conjecture
Who were sufficient to Misery? — [Who] could begin on – [Misery?]

State it the Ages – to a cipher –
And it will ache contented on –
Sing, at its pain, as any Workman –
Notching the fall of the even Sun –

SHEET TWO c. second half of 1863

On a Columnar Self –[308]
How ample to rely
In Tumult – or Extremity –
How good the Certainty

That Lever cannot pry –
And Wedge cannot divide
Conviction – That Granitic Base –
Though none be on our side –

o

Suffice Us – for a Crowd –
Ourself – and Rectitude –
And that Assembly – not far off
From furthest Spirit – God – [furthest] Faithful

lines 11–12: [And that] Companion – not far off / from furthest Good Man – God –

Nature – the Gentlest Mother is,
Impatient of no Child –
The feeblest – or the Waywardest – [The] dullest
Her Admonition mild –

In Forest – and the Hill –
By Traveller – be heard –
Restraining Rampant Squirrel –
Or too impetuous Bird –

How fair Her Conversation –
A Summer Afternoon –
Her Household – Her Assembly –
And when the Sun go down –

Her Voice among the Aisles
Incite the timid prayer
Of the minutest Cricket –
The most unworthy Flower –

When all the Children sleep –
She turns as long away
As will suffice to light Her lamps –
Then bending from the Sky – [Then] stooping –

With infinite Affection –
And infiniter Care –
Her Golden finger on Her lip –
Wills Silence – Everywhere –

No Prisoner be –[309]
Where Liberty –
Himself – abide with Thee –

Good Night – Which put the Candle Out?[310]
A jealous Zephyr – not a doubt –
Ah, friend, You little knew
How long at that celestial wick
The Angels – labored diligent –
Extinguished – now – for You –

It might have been the Light House Spark –
Some Sailor – rowing in the Dark –
Had importuned to see –
It might have been the waning Lamp
That lit the Drummer – from the Camp –
To purer Reveille –

SHEET THREE c. second half of 1863

Behind Me – dips Eternity –
Before Me – Immortality –
Myself – the Term between –
Death but the Drift of Eastern Gray,
Dissolving into Dawn away,
Before the West begin –

'Tis Kingdoms – afterward – they say –
In perfect – pauseless Monarchy –
Whose Prince – is Son of none –
Himself – His Dateless Dynasty –
Himself – Himself diversify –
In Duplicate divine –

'Tis Miracle before Me – then –
'Tis Miracle behind – between –
A Crescent in the Sea –
With Midnight to the North of Her –
And Midnight to the South of Her –
And Maelstrom – in the Sky –

She dwelleth in the Ground –[311]
Where Daffodils – abide –
Her Maker – Her Metropolis –
The Universe – Her Maid –

To fetch Her Grace – and Hue –
And Fairness – and Renown –
The Firmament's – To pluck Her –
And fetch Her Thee – be mine –

Sweet Mountains – Ye tell Me no lie –
Never deny Me – Never fly –
Those same unvarying Eyes
Turn on Me – When I fail – or feign,
Or take the Royal names in vain –
Their far – slow – Violet Gaze –

My Strong Madonnas – Cherish still –
The Wayward Nun – beneath the Hill –
Whose service – is to You –
Her latest Worship – When the Day
Fades from the Firmament away –
To lift Her Brows on You –

It tossed – and tossed –
A little Brig I knew – o'ertook by Blast –
It spun – and spun –
And groped delirious, for Morn –

It slipped – and slipped –
As One that drunken – stept –
Its white foot tripped –
Then dropped from sight –

Ah, Brig – Good Night
To crew and You –
The Ocean's Heart too smooth – too Blue –
To break for You –

She dwelleth in: *Sent to Ns (lost) c. 1863, "With a Crocus," and to SD (variant) and an unidentified recipient (variant) c. spring 1863, the latter apparently with a crocus*

SHEET FOUR c. second half of 1863

It's easy to invent a Life –
God does it – every Day –
Creation – but the Gambol
Of His Authority –

It's easy to efface it –
The thrifty Deity
Could scarce afford Eternity
To Spontaneity –

The Perished Patterns murmur –
But His Perturbless Plan
Proceed – inserting Here – a Sun –
There – leaving out a Man –

God gave a Loaf to every Bird –
But just a Crumb – to Me –
I dare not eat it – tho' I starve –
My poignant luxury –

To own it – touch it –
Prove the feat – that made the Pellet mine –
Too happy – for my Sparrow's chance – [happy –] in
For Ampler Coveting –

It might be Famine – all around –
I could not miss an Ear –
Such Plenty smiles upon my Board –
My Garner shows so fair –

I wonder how the Rich – may feel –
An Indiaman – An Earl –
I deem that I – with but a Crumb –
Am Sovreign of them all –

God gave a: *Sent to Ns (lost) presumably c. 1863*

Where Thou art – that – is Home –[312]
Cashmere – or Calvary – the same –
Degree – or Shame –
I scarce esteem Location's Name –
So I may Come –

What Thou dost – is Delight –
Bondage as Play – be sweet –
Imprisonment – Content –
And Sentence – Sacrament –
Just We two – meet –

Where Thou art not – is Wo –
Tho' Bands of Spices – row –
What Thou dost not – Despair –
Tho' Gabriel – praise me – Sir –

~

We thirst at first – 'tis Nature's Act –
And later – when we die –
A little Water supplicate –
Of fingers going by –

It intimates the finer want –
Whose adequate supply
Is that Great Water in the West –
Termed Immortality –

~

SHEET FIVE c. second half of 1863

Through the Straight Pass of Suffering[313]
The Martyrs even trod – [Martyrs] steady
Their feet upon Temptation –
Their foreheads – upon God – [Their] faces

A Stately – Shriven Company –
Convulsion playing round –
Harmless as Streaks of Meteor –
Upon a Planet's Bond –

o

Through the Straight: *Sent to SD (lost) and to SB (variant) c. 1861*

Their faith the Everlasting Troth –
Their Expectation – sure – [Expectation –] fair –
The Needle to the North Degree
Wades so – through Polar Air –

Precious to Me – She still shall be –
Though She forget the name I bear –
The fashion of the Gown I wear –
The very Color of My Hair –

So like the Meadows – now –
I dared to show a Tress of Theirs
If haply – She might not despise
A Buttercup's Array –

I know the Whole – obscures the Part –
The fraction – that appeased the Heart
Till Number's Empery –
Remembered – as the Milliner's flower
When Summer's Everlasting Dower –
Confronts the dazzled Bee –

Dropped into the Ether Acre –[314]
Wearing the Sod Gown –
Bonnet of Everlasting Laces –
Brooch – frozen on –

Horses of Blonde – and Coach of Silver –
Baggage a strapped Pearl – [Baggage] ~~of~~
Journey of Down – and Whip of Diamond –
Riding to meet the Earl –

Ah, Teneriffe – Receding Mountain –[315]
Purples of Ages halt for You –
Sunset reviews Her Sapphire Regiments –
Day – drops You His Red Adieu –

Dropped into the: *Sent to Ns (lost) and to SD (variant) c. 1862*
Ah, Teneriffe – Receding: *Sent to SD (variant) c. 1863*

Still clad in Your Mail of Ices –
Eye of Granite – and Ear of Steel –
Passive alike – to Pomp – and Parting –
Ah, Teneriffe – We're pleading still –

SHEET SIX c. second half of 1863

Grief is a Mouse –
And chooses Wainscot in the Breast
For His shy House –
And baffles quest –

Grief is a Thief – quick startled –
Pricks His Ear – report to hear
Of that Vast Dark –
That swept His Being – back –

Grief is a Juggler – boldest at the Play –
Lest if He flinch – the eye that way
Pounce on His Bruises – One – say – or Three –
Grief is a Gourmand – spare His luxury –

Best Grief is Tongueless – before He'll tell –
Burn Him in the Public square –
His Ashes – will [His] embers –
Possibly – if they refuse – How then know –
Since a Rack couldn't coax a syllable – now [coax] an answer –

Let Us play Yesterday –[316]
I – the Girl at School –
You – and Eternity – the untold Tale –

Easing my famine
At my Lexicon –
Logarithm – had I – for Drink –
'Twas a dry Wine –

Somewhat different – must be –
Dreams tint the Sleep –
Cunning Reds of Morning
Make the Blind – leap –

○

Still at the Egg-life –
Chafing the Shell –
When you troubled the Ellipse –
And the Bird fell –

Manacles be dim – they say –
To the new Free –
Liberty – commoner –
Never could – to me –

'Twas my last gratitude
When I slept – at night –
'Twas the first Miracle
Let in – with Light –

Can the Lark resume the Shell –
Easier – for the Sky –
Wouldn't Bonds hurt more
Than Yesterday?

Wouldn't Dungeons sorer grate
On the Man – free –
Just long enough to taste –
Then – doomed new –

God of the Manacle
As of the Free –
Take not my Liberty
Away from Me –

Alter! When the Hills do –
Falter! When the Sun
Question if His Glory
Be the Perfect One –

Surfeit! When the Daffodil
Doth of the Dew –
Even as Herself – Sir –
I will – Of You –

Alter! When the: *Sent to SD (first stanza, lost) presumably c. 1863*

FASCICLE THIRTY-SEVEN

SHEET ONE c. late 1863

Conscious am I in my Chamber –
Of a shapeless friend –
He doth not attest by Posture –
Nor confirm – by Word –

Neither Place – need I present Him –
Fitter Courtesy
Hospitable intuition
Of His Company –

Presence – is His furthest license –
Neither He to Me
Nor Myself to Him – by Accent –
Forfeit Probity –

Weariness of Him, were quainter
Than Monotony
Knew a Particle – of Space's
Vast Society –

Neither if He visit Other –
Do He dwell – or Nay – know I –
But Instinct esteem Him [Instinct] Report Him
Immortality –

~

You taught me Waiting with Myself –[317]
Appointment strictly kept –
You taught me fortitude of Fate –
This – also – I have learnt –

An Altitude of Death, that could
No bitterer debar

Conscious am I: *Sent to SD (lost in part, variant) c. late 1863*

Than Life – had done – before it –
Yet – there is a Science more –

The Heaven you know – to understand
That you be not ashamed
Of Me – in Christ's bright Audience — [bright] Latitude
Upon the further Hand –

Suspense – is Hostiler than Death –
Death – tho'soever Broad,
Is just Death, and cannot increase –
Suspense – does not conclude –

But perishes – to live anew –
But just anew to die –
Annihilation – plated fresh
With Immortality –

SHEET TWO c. late 1863

Drama's Vitallest Expression is the Common Day
That arise and set about Us –
Other Tragedy

Perish in the Recitation –
This – the best enact — [the] more exert
When the Audience is scattered
And the Boxes shut –

"Hamlet" to Himself were Hamlet –
Had not Shakespeare wrote –
Though the "Romeo" left no Record — ["Romeo"] leave
Of his Juliet,

It were infinite enacted — [were] tenderer –
In the Human Heart –
Only Theatre recorded
Owner cannot shut – — Never yet was shut –

Life, and Death, and Giants –
Such as These – are still –
Minor – Apparatus – Hopper of the Mill –
Beetle at the Candle –
Or a Fife's Fame –
Maintain – by Accident that they proclaim –

~

Four Trees – upon a solitary Acre –
Without Design
Or Order, or Apparent Action – [Apparent] signal – • notice
Maintain – Do reign –

The Sun – upon a Morning meets them –
The Wind –
No nearer Neighbor – have they –
But God –

The Acre gives them – Place –
They – Him – Attention of Passer by –
Of Shadow, or of Squirrel, haply –
Or Boy –

What Deed is Theirs unto the General Nature – [Deed] they bear
What Plan
They severally – retard – or further – [severally –] promote – or hinder –
Unknown –

~

The Grace – Myself – might not obtain –
Confer upon my flower –
Refracted but a Countenance –
For I – inhabit Her –

~

SHEET THREE c. late 1863

The Birds reported from the South –[318]
A News express to Me –
A spicy Charge, My little Posts – [little] friends –
But I am deaf – Today – [But] you must go away

o

The Flowers – appealed – a timid Throng –
I reinforced the Door – [I] only sealed
Go blossom to the Bees – I said –
And trouble Me – no More – [And] harass

The Summer Grace, for notice strove –
Remote – Her best Array –
The Heart – to stimulate the Eye
Refused too utterly –

At length, a Mourner, like Myself,
She drew away austere –
Her frosts to ponder – then it was
I recollected Her – [I] rose to comfort –

She suffered Me, for I had mourned –
I offered Her no word –
My Witness – was the Crape I bore – [the] Black –
Her – Witness – was Her Dead –

Thenceforward – We – together dwelt – [together] walked
She – never questioned Me – I never questioned Her –
Nor I – Herself –
Our Contract [Our] Compact –
A Wiser Sympathy [A] Wordless – • silent – • speechless –

Remorse – is Memory – awake –[319]
Her Parties all astir – [Her] Companies [astir –]
A Presence of Departed Acts –
At window – and at Door –

Its Past – set down before the Soul
And lighted with a match –
Perusal – to facilitate –
And help Belief to stretch – [to] reach • Of its Condensed Despatch

Remorse is cureless – the Disease
Not even God – can heal –
For 'tis His institution – and
The Adequate of Hell – [The] Complement –

Renunciation – is a piercing Virtue –
The letting go
A Presence – for an Expectation –
Not now –
The putting out of Eyes –
Just Sunrise –
Lest Day –
Day's Great Progenitor –
Outvie — Outshow • Outglow –
Renunciation – is the Choosing
Against itself –
Itself to justify
Unto itself –
When larger function –
Make that appear –
Smaller – that Covered Vision – Here – — [that] flooded – • sated –

SHEET FOUR c. late 1863

Never for Society[320]
He shall seek in vain –
Who His own acquaintance
Cultivate – Of Men
Wiser Men may weary – — [Wiser] One – • Ear
But the Man within

Never knew Satiety –
Better entertain — braver – [entertain]
Than could Border Ballad –
Or Biscayan Hymn –
Neither introduction
Need You – unto Him –

I sometimes drop it, for a Quick –
The Thought to be alive –
Anonymous Delight to know –
And madder – to conceive –

o

Consoles a wo so monstrous
That did it tear all Day,
Without an instant's Respite –
'Twould look too far – to Die –

Delirium – diverts the Wretch
For Whom the Scaffold neighs –
The Hammock's motion lulls the Heads
So close on Paradise –

A Reef – crawled easy from the Sea
Eats off the Brittle Line –
The Sailor doesn't know the Stroke –
Until He's past the Pain –

~

It dropped so low – in my Regard –[321]
I heard it hit the Ground –
And go to pieces on the Stones — [pieces] in the Ditch –
At bottom of my mind –

Yet blamed the Fate that fractured – less — [that] – *flung it* [*less*]
Than I reviled Myself, — [I] *denounced*
For entertaining Plated Wares
Upon my Silver Shelf –

~

Autumn – overlooked my Knitting –
Dyes – said He – have I –
Could disparage a Flamingo – — [Could] dishonor
Show Me them – said I – — Give them Me – [said]

Cochineal – I chose – for deeming
It resemble Thee – — That [resemble]
And the little Border – Dusker –
For resembling Me – — That – resemble Me –

~

SHEET FIVE c. late 1863

Bloom upon the Mountain stated –
Blameless of a name –

Bloom upon the: *Sent to Ns (lost, transcribed variant) and to SD (variant) c. summer 1863*

Efflorescence of a Sunset – Flower of a single Sunset –
Reproduced – the same –

Seed had I, my Purple Sowing
Should address the Day – [Should] endow – • reward
Not – a Tropic of a Twilight – [Not – a] Manner
Show itself away – shift [itself]

Who for tilling – to the Mountain
Come – and disappear –
Whose be her Renown – or fading – [be] this
Witness is not here –

While I state – the Solemn Petals –
Far as North – and East –
Far as South – and West expanding – [West] disclosing
Culminate – in Rest –

And the Mountain to the Evening
Fit His Countenance – Strain [His]
Indicating by no Muscle [no] feature
His Experience – the – [Experience –]

Publication – is the Auction
Of the Mind of Man –
Poverty – be justifying
For so foul a thing

Possibly – but We – would rather
From Our Garret go
White – unto the White Creator –
Than invest – Our Snow –

Thought belong to Him who gave it –
Then – to Him Who bear
Its Corporeal illustration – sell
The Royal Air –

In the Parcel – Be the Merchant
Of the Heavenly Grace –

But reduce no Human Spirit
To Disgrace of Price –

~

All but Death, Can be adjusted
Dynasties repaired –
Systems – settled in their Sockets –
Citadels – dissolved – Centuries removed

Wastes of Lives – resown with Colors
By Succeeding Springs – [By] supremer springs –
Death – unto itself – Exception –
Is exempt from Change –

~

SHEET SIX c. late 1863

Growth of Man – like Growth of Nature –[322]
Gravitates within –
Atmosphere, and Sun endorse it – [Sun] Confirm –
But it stir – alone –

Each – its difficult Ideal [its] absolute
Must achieve – Itself –
Through the solitary prowess
Of a Silent Life –

Effort – is the sole condition –
Patience of Itself –
Patience of opposing forces –
And intact Belief – [And] direct – • distinct

Looking on – is the Department
Of its Audience –
But Transaction – is assisted
By no Countenance –

~

My Worthiness is all my Doubt –
His Merit – all my fear –

Contrasting which, my quality
Do lowlier – appear –

Lest I should insufficient prove [insufficient] be
For His beloved Need –
The Chiefest Apprehension
Upon my thronging Mind – [my] crowded – • happy

'Tis true – that Deity to stoop
Inherently incline –
For nothing higher than Itself
Itself can rest upon – [can] lift – • base –

So I – the Undivine Abode
Of His Elect Content –
Conform my Soul – as 'twere a Church,
Unto Her Sacrament –

~

So the Eyes accost – and sunder
In an Audience –
Stamped – occasionally – forever – [Stamped –] in instances
So may Countenance [So] can –

Entertain – without addressing
Countenance of One
In a Neighboring Horizon –
Gone – as soon as known –

~

My Soul – accused Me – And I quailed –
As Tongues of Diamond had reviled [As] Throngs – • Eyes –
All Else accused Me – and I smiled – the World [accused]
My Soul – that Morning – was My friend –

Her favor – is the best Disdain
Toward Artifice of Time – or Men –
But Her Disdain – 'twere lighter bear ['twere] cooler
A finger of Enamelled Fire –

~

FASCICLE THIRTY-EIGHT

SHEET ONE c. early 1864

A Drop fell on the Apple Tree –[323]
Another – on the Roof –
A Half a Dozen kissed the Eaves –
And made the Gables laugh –

A few went out to help the Brook
That went to help the Sea – Who [went]
Myself Conjectured were they Pearls –
What Necklaces could be – [Necklaces] for Me –

The Dust replaced, in Hoisted Roads –
The Birds jocoser sung –
The Sunshine threw his Hat away –
The Bushes – spangles flung – [The] Orchards – • Meadows –

The Breezes brought dejected Lutes –
And bathed them in the Glee –
Then Orient showed a single Flag, The East • Nature put out a single Flag
And signed the Fete away – [the] Show –

Her final Summer was it –
And yet We guessed it not – Yet we suspected not
If tenderer industriousness
Pervaded Her, We thought

A further force of life [further] Fund
Developed from within –
When Death lit all the shortness up [the] limit – [up] • [the] brevity
It made the hurry plain –

We wondered at our blindness
When nothing was to see

A Drop fell: *Sent to SD (last eight lines, variant) c. 1873*

But Her Carrara Guide post –
At Our Stupidity –

When duller than our dullness
The Busy Darling lay –
So busy was she – finishing –
So leisurely – were We –

Who Giants know, with lesser Men
Are incomplete, and shy –
For Greatness, that is ill at ease — [is] ill composed
In minor Company – — With other quality –

A Smaller, could not be perturbed –
The Summer Gnat displays –
Unconscious that his single Fleet — [single] Bulk – • Sail –
Do not comprise the skies –

SHEET TWO c. early 1864

By my Window have I for Scenery[324]
Just a Sea – with a Stem –
If the Bird and the Farmer – deem it a "Pine" – — Grant [the Bird]
The Opinion will do – for them – — [will] *serve*

It has no Port, nor a "Line" – but the Jays –
That split their route to the Sky – — [That] Ply between it, and the Sky
Or a Squirrel, whose giddy Peninsula
May be easier reached – this way – — [be] Better attained – • easier gained –

For Inlands – the Earth is the under side –
And the upper side – is the Sun –
And its Commerce – if Commerce it have –
Of Spice – I infer from the Odors borne –

Of its Voice – to affirm – when the Wind is within –
Can the Dumb – define the Divine? — [Dumb –] divulge
The Definition of Melody – is –
That Definition is none –

It – suggests to our Faith –
They – suggest to our Sight –
When the latter – is put away
I shall meet with Conviction I somewhere met
That Immortality –

Was the Pine at my Window a "Fellow
Of the Royal" Infinity?
Apprehensions – are God's introductions –
To be hallowed – accordingly – Extended inscrutably –

Defrauded I a Butterfly –
The lawful Heir – for Thee –

"I want" – it pleaded – All its life –
I want – was chief it said
When Skill entreated it – the last –
And when so newly dead –

I could not deem it late – to hear
That single – steadfast sigh –
The lips had placed as with a "Please"
Toward Eternity –

SHEET THREE c. early 1864

It was a Grave – yet bore no Stone –[325]
Enclosed 'twas not – of Rail –
A Consciousness – its Acre – And
It held a Human Soul –

Entombed by whom – for what offence –
If Home or foreign – born –
Had I the Curiosity –
'Twere not appeased of Man –

Till Resurrection, I must guess –
Denied the small desire

It was a: *Sent to Ns (lost) c. 1864*

A Rose upon its Ridge – to sow –
Or sacrificial Flower – [Or] palliate a Briar –

⁓

She staked Her Feathers – Gained an Arc – [Her] Wings – and gained a Bush –
Debated – Rose again –
This time – beyond the estimate [the] inference
Of Envy, or of Men –

And now, among Circumference –
Her steady Boat be seen –
At home – among the Billows – As [At] ease
The Bough where she was born –

⁓

Despair's advantage is achieved
By suffering – Despair –
To be assisted of Reverse
One must Reverse have bore – [must] itself [have] • have previous

The Worthiness of Suffering like
The Worthiness of Death [The] Excellence – • quality
Is ascertained by tasting – [by] testing –

As can no other Mouth

Of Savors – make us conscious –
As did ourselves partake –
Affliction feels impalpable
Until Ourselves are struck –

⁓

Two – were immortal twice –[326]
The privilege of few –
Eternity – obtained – in Time – Eternity – in Time obtained –
Reversed Divinity –

That our ignoble Eyes
The quality conceive [quality] perceive –
Of Paradise superlative –
Through their Comparative.

⁓

Two – were immortal: *Sent to SD (variant) c. early 1864*

SHEET FOUR c. early 1864

I play at Riches – to appease
The Clamoring for Gold –
It kept me from a Thief, I think,
For often, overbold

With Want, and Opportunity –
I could have done a Sin [I] might
And been Myself that easy Thing [that] distant
An independent Man –

But often as my lot displays
Too hungry to be borne
I deem Myself what I would be –
And novel Comforting [And] so much comforting

My Poverty and I derive –
We question if the Man –
Who own – Esteem the Opulence –
As we – Who never Can –

Should ever these exploring Hands
Chance Sovreign on a Mine –
Or in the long – uneven term
To win, become their turn – [become] my

How fitter they will be – for Want – ’Tis [fitter] I shall be – by [Want –]
Enlightening so well –
I know not which, Desire, or Grant – [or] Right – • sight
Be wholly beautiful – [Be] chiefest • utmost

She rose to His Requirement – dropt[327]
The Playthings of Her Life
To take the honorable Work
Of Woman, and of Wife –

If ought She missed in Her new Day,
Of Amplitude, or Awe –
Or first Prospective – or the Gold
In using, wear away,

o

It lay unmentioned – as the Sea
Develope Pearl, and Weed,
But only to Himself – be known
The Fathoms they abide –

~

Time feels so vast that were it not
For an Eternity –
I fear me this Circumference
Engross my Finity –

To His exclusion, who prepare
By Processes of Size — [By] Rudiments – • Prefaces of size
For the Stupendous Vision — for the stupendous Volume
Of His Diameters –

~

SHEET FIVE c. early 1864

Who Court obtain within Himself[328]
Sees every Man a King –
And Poverty of Monarchy — so – • the [Poverty]
Is an interior thing –

No Man depose — [No] Fate depose
Whom Fate Ordain – — whom Trait – [Ordain –]
And Who can add a Crown
To Him who doth continual
Conspire against His Own — repudiate – [His]

~

No Notice gave She, but a Change –
No Message, but a sigh –
For Whom, the Time did not suffice — [not] remain
That she should specify. — [she] could

She was not warm, though Summer shone
Nor scrupulous of cold
Though Rime by Rime, the steady Frost
Upon Her Bosom piled – — [her] Petals – • softness

o

Of shrinking ways – she did not fright [ways –] Forebore her fright
Though all the Village looked –
But held Her gravity aloft –
And met the gaze – direct –

And when adjusted like a seed
In careful fitted Ground
Unto the Everlasting Spring
And hindered but a Mound

Her Warm return, if so she chose –
And We – imploring drew –
Removed our invitation by
As Some She never knew – [As] Us –

line 17: [Her] straight – • good – • quick – • safe [return, if so she] signed

They say that "Time assuages" –
Time never did assuage –
An actual suffering strengthens
As Sinews do, with Age –

Time is a Test of Trouble –
But not a Remedy –
If such it prove, it prove too
There was no Malady –

SHEET SIX c. early 1864

On the Bleakness of my Lot
Bloom I strove to raise –
Late – my Garden of a Rock [my] Acre of
Yielded Grape – and Maise –

Soil of Flint, if steady tilled [if] steadfast tilled
Will refund the Hand – [Will] reward – • repay –
Seed of Palm, by Lybian Sun
Fructified in Sand –

They say that: *Sent to TWH (second stanza, variant) 9 June 1866*
On the Bleakness: *Sent to SD (second stanza, variant) c. early 1864*

This Bauble was preferred of Bees –
By Butterflies admired [Butterflies] adored – • desired
At Heavenly – Hopeless Distances –
Was justified of Bird – Of Bird – was justified –

Did Noon – enamel – in Herself [Noon –] enable – • embellish
Was Summer to a Score
Who only knew of Universe –
It had created Her – [had] afforded –

~

A Plated Life – diversified
With Gold and Silver Pain
To prove the presence of the Ore
In Particles – 'tis when

A Value struggle – it exist – [A] nature
A Power – will proclaim
Although Annihilation pile
Whole Chaoses on Him – Oblivions – [on]

~

Expectation – is Contentment –
Gain – Satiety –
But Satiety – Conviction
Of Nescessity

Of an Austere trait in Pleasure –
Good, without alarm
Is a too established Fortune –
Danger – deepens Sum –

line 7: [Is a] too Contented Measure – • [Is a too] secure Possession –

~

FASCICLE THIRTY-NINE

LEAF ONE c. early 1864

None can experience stint[329]
Who Bounty – have not known –
The fact of Famine – could not be — Nor fact of Famine could exist –
Except for Fact of Corn –

Want – is a meagre Art
Acquired by Reverse –
The Poverty that was not Wealth – — It is that Poverty was Wealth –
Cannot be Indigence – — Enables Indigence –

~

The hallowing of Pain
Like hallowing of Heaven,
Obtains at a corporeal cost –
The Summit is not given

To Him who strives severe
At middle of the Hill – — [At] Bottom – • Centre
But He who has achieved the Top – — [the] Crest –
All – is the price of All –

~

SHEET TWO c. early 1864

Deprived of other Banquet,
I entertained Myself –
At first – a scant nutrition – — [a] plain Regaling
An insufficient Loaf – — An innutritious Loaf

But grown by slender addings
To so esteemed a size
'Tis sumptuous enough for me –
And almost to suffice

o

A Robin's famine – able – [Robin's] palate – • hunger –
Red Pilgrim, He and I –
A Berry from our table
Reserve – for Charity –

~

It is a lonesome Glee –
Yet sanctifies the Mind –
With fair association –
Afar upon the Wind remote – • astray – [upon]

A Bird to overhear –
Delight without a Cause –
Arrestless as invisible –
A Matter of the Skies.

~

If Blame be my side – forfeit Me –
But doom me not to forfeit Thee –
To forfeit Thee? The very name
Is sentence from Belief – and Home – [Is] exile –

~

Purple –
The Color of a Queen, is this –
The Color of a Sun
At setting – this and Amber –
Beryl – and this, at Noon –

And when at night – Auroran widths
Fling suddenly on Men –
'Tis this – and Witchcraft – nature keeps
A Rank – for Iodine –

lines 7–8: that's [this – and Witchcraft –] nature has respect to – [Iodine –]
• nature knows the rank of – [Iodine –] • nature has an awe of – [Iodine –]

~

To be alive – is Power –
Existence – in itself –

To be alive –: *Sent to SD (variant) c. early 1864*

Without a further function –
Omnipotence – Enough –

To be alive – and will! –
'Tis able as a God –
The Maker – of Ourselves – be what –
Such being Finitude!

SHEET THREE c. early 1864

The Loneliness One dare not sound –
And would as soon surmise
As in its Grave go plumbing [go] measuring
To ascertain the size – to register – [the]

The Loneliness whose worst alarm
Is lest itself should see –
And perish from before itself
For just a scrutiny – [For] simple scrutiny

The Horror not to be surveyed – [The] chasm –
But skirted in the Dark –
With Consciousness suspended –
And Being under Lock –

I fear me this – is Loneliness –
The Maker of the soul
Its Caverns and its Corridors
Illuminate – or seal – make populate – • [make] manifest

Least Bee that brew – a Honey's Weight
The Summer multiply –
Content Her smallest fraction help
The Amber Quantity –

This that would greet – an hour ago –
Is quaintest Distance – now – [quaintest] stiffness –

Least Bee that: *Sent to SD (lost in part, variant) c. early 1864*

Had it a Guest from Paradise –
Nor glow, would it, nor bow –

Had it a notice from the Noon   [a] summons
Nor beam, would it – nor Warm –
Match me the Silver Reticence –   [the] crystal
Match me the Solid Calm –

The Service without Hope –
Is tenderest, I think –
Because 'tis unsustained
By stint – Rewarded Work –   [By] end

Has impetus of Gain –
And impetus of Goal –
There is no Diligence like that
That knows not an Until –

SHEET FOUR c. early 1864

I meant to find Her when I Came –[330]
Death – had the same design –
But the Success – was His – it seems –
And the Discomfit – Mine –   [the] ~~Surrender~~

I meant to tell Her how I longed
For just this single time –   [just] this only • [For this] *specific* • peculiar
But Death had told Her so the first –   [Death] enamored [so]
And she had past, with Him –   [had] *fled* [with] • [had] *hearkened* • trusted

To wander – now – is my Repose –   [my] *Abode*
To rest – To rest would be
A privilege of Hurricane   [of] misery
To Memory – and Me –

line 10: [To] pause [To rest] • [To] pause – [To] dwell • [To] dwell – [To] stay [would be]

The Truth – is stirless –
Other force – may be presumed to move –

This – then – is best for confidence –
When oldest Cedars swerve –

And Oaks untwist their fists – [Oaks] unknot – • [un]knit – • [un]clinch
And Mountains – feeble – lean –
How excellent a Body, that [a] Giant
Stands without a Bone –

How vigorous a Force
That holds without a Prop –
Truth stays Herself – and every man
That trusts Her – boldly up –

A South Wind – has a pathos
Of individual Voice –
As One detect on Landings
An Emigrant's address –

A Hint of Ports – and Peoples –
And much not understood –
The fairer – for the farness –
And for the foreignhood –

To wait an Hour – is long –
If Love be just beyond –
To wait Eternity – is short –
If Love reward the end – [Love] Be at the end –

There is an arid Pleasure –
As different from Joy –
As Frost is different from Dew –
Like Element – are they –

Yet one – rejoices Flowers –
And one – the Flowers abhor –
The finest Honey – curdled –
Is worthless – to the Bee – Repels the healthy Bee –

SHEET FIVE c. early 1864

The Birds begun at Four o'clock –
Their period for Dawn –
A Music numerous as space – [Music] measureless as Noon –
But neighboring as Noon –

I could not count their Force –
Their Voices did expend [Their] numbers
As Brook by Brook bestows itself
To multiply the Pond. [To] magnify

Their Witnesses were not – [Their] Listener – was none
Except Occasional Man –
In homely industry arrayed – [industry] attired
To overtake the Morn –

Nor was it for applause – [for] Parade – • Result
That I could ascertain –
But independent Extasy
Of Deity, and Men – [Of] Universe

By Six, the Flood had done – [the] Gush
No tumult there had been
Of Dressing, or Departure –
And yet the Band – was gone – Yet all [the]

The Sun engrossed the East –
The Day controlled the World – [Day] Resumed –
The Miracle that introduced
Forgotten, as fulfilled.

Bereaved of all, I went abroad –
No less bereaved was I
Upon a New Peninsula –
The Grave preceded me –

Obtained my Lodgings, ere myself – engrossed [my]
And when I sought my Bed –
The Grave it was reposed upon
The Pillow for my Head –

o

The Birds begun: *Sent to Ns (lost, transcribed variant) perhaps c. 1863*

I waked, to find it first awake –
I rose – It followed me –
I tried to drop it in the Crowd – [to] shift
To lose it in the Sea –

In Cups of artificial Drowse
To steep its shape away –
The Grave – was finished – but the Spade
Remained in Memory –

They have a little Odor – that to me
Is metre – nay – 'tis melody – ['tis] Poesy –
And spiciest at fading – indicate – [fading –] celebrate –
A Habit – of a Laureate –

SHEET SIX c. early 1864

Severer Service of myself
I hastened to demand
To fill the awful Vacuum [awful] Longitude –
Your life had left behind –

I worried Nature with my Wheels
When Hers had ceased to run –
When she had put away Her Work
My own had just begun –

I strove to weary Brain and Bone –
To harass to fatigue
The glittering Retinue of nerves –
Vitality to clog

To some dull comfort Those obtain
Who put a Head away
They knew the Hair to –
And forget the color of the Day – [the] figure –

Affliction would not be appeased –
The Darkness braced as firm [The] trouble –

They have a: *Sent to Gertrude Vanderbilt (lost, transcribed variant) perhaps c. 1863*

As all my strategem had been
The Midnight to confirm –

No Drug for Consciousness – can be –
Alternative to die
Is Nature's only Pharmacy
For Being's Malady –

~

'Twould ease – a Butterfly –
Elate – a Bee –
Thou'rt neither –
Neither – thy capacity –

But, Blossom, were I,
I would rather be
Thy moment
Than a Bee's Eternity –

Content of fading
Is enough for me –
Fade I unto Divinity –

And Dying – Lifetime –
Ample as the Eye –
Her least attention raise on me –

~

Such is the Force of Happiness – [the] strength
The Least – can lift a ton
Assisted by its stimulus –

Who Misery – sustain –
No Sinew can afford –
The Cargo of Themselves –
Too infinite for Consciousness'
Slow capabilities – benumbed abilities –

~

'Twould ease – a: *Apparently sent to SD (last six lines, variant) c. early 1864*

FASCICLE FORTY

SHEET ONE c. early 1864

The only news I know[331]
Is Bulletins all Day
From Immortality.

The only Shows I see –
Tomorrow and Today –
Perchance Eternity – Three – with Eternity – • And some Eternity –

The only one I meet
Is God – The only Street –
Existence – This traversed [This] traverst

If other news there be –
Or admirabler show –
I'll tell it You – [I'll] Signify – • testify –

Wert Thou but ill – that I might show thee[332]
How long a Day I could endure
Though thine attention stop not on me
Nor the least signal, Me assure – [signal,] Mine

Wert Thou but stranger in ungracious country –
And Mine – the Door
Thou paused at, for a passing bounty – [a] doubtful
No More –

Accused – wert Thou – and Myself – Tribunal –
Convicted – sentenced – Ermine – not to Me
Half the Condition, thy Reverse – to follow – [the] distinction
Just to partake -- the infamy –

The only news: *Sent to TWH (first stanza, variant) early June 1864*

The Tenant of the narrow Cottage, wert Thou –
Permit to be
The Housewife in thy low attendance
Contenteth Me –

No Service hast Thou, I would not achieve it – [not] attempt
To die – or live –
The first – Sweet, proved I, ere I saw thee – [Sweet,] That was
For Life – be Love – [For] Life is – • [Life] means –

~

Midsummer, was it, when They died –
A full, and perfect time –
The Summer closed upon itself
In Consummated Bloom –

The Corn, her furthest Kernel filled
Before the coming Flail –
When These – leaned into Perfectness – [When] These Two – leaned in –
Through Haze of Burial –

~

SHEET TWO c. early 1864

The first Day that I was a Life[333]
I recollect it – How still –
The last Day that I was a Life
I recollect it – as well –

'Twas stiller – though the first
Was still –
'Twas empty – but the first
Was full –

This – was my finallest Occasion –
But then
My tenderer Experiment
Toward Men –

"Which choose I"?
That – I cannot say –

Midsummer, was it,: *Sent to Ns (lost) c. early 1864*

"Which choose They"?
Question Memory!

~

A nearness to Tremendousness –
An Agony procures –
Affliction ranges Boundlessness –
Vicinity to Laws

Contentment's quiet Suburb –
Affliction cannot stay
In Acres – Its Location — In Acre – or Location –
Is Illocality – — It rents Immensity –

~

"Unto Me"? I do not know you –[334]
Where may be your House?

"I am Jesus – Late of Judea –
Now – of Paradise" –

Wagons – have you – to convey me?
This is far from Thence –

"Arms of Mine – sufficient Phaeton –
Trust Omnipotence" –

I am spotted – "I am Pardon" –
I am small – "The Least
Is esteemed in Heaven the Chiefest –
Occupy my House" – — [my] Breast["] –

~

Denial – is the only fact
Perceived by the Denied –
Whose Will – a numb significance – — [a] Blank intelligence
The Day the Heaven died –

And all the Earth strove common round –
Without Delight, or Beam – — [or] aim –
What comfort was it Wisdom – was –
The spoiler of Our Home?

~

SHEET THREE c. early 1864

All forgot for recollecting [forgot] through –
Just a paltry One –
All forsook, for just a Stranger's
New Accompanying –

Grace of Wealth, and Grace of Station Grace of Rank – and – Grace of Fortune
Less accounted than
An unknown Esteem possessing – [unknown] content
Estimate – Who can –

Home effaced – Her faces dwindled –
Nature – altered small –
Sun – if shone – or Storm – if shattered –
Overlooked I all –

Dropped – my fate – a timid Pebble –
In thy bolder Sea –
Prove – me – Sweet – if I regret it – Ask – [me –]
Prove Myself – of Thee –

I hide myself – within my flower,[335]
That fading from your Vase –
You – unsuspecting – feel for me –
Almost – a loneliness –

Had I not This, or This, I said,
Appealing to Myself,
In moment of prosperity –
Inadequate – were Life –

"Thou hast not Me, nor Me" – it said,
In moment of Reverse –
"And yet Thou art industrious –
No need – had'st Thou – of us –"?

My need – was all I had – I said
The need did not reduce –

Because the food – exterminate –
The hunger – does not cease –

But diligence – is sharper –
Proportioned to the chance –
To feed upon the Retrogade –
Enfeebles – the Advance –

~

Between My Country – and the Others –
There is a Sea –
But Flowers – negotiate between us –
As Ministry.

~

SHEET FOUR c. early 1864

The Admirations – and Contempts – of time –[336]
Show justest – through an Open Tomb –
The Dying – as it were a Hight
Reorganizes Estimate
And what We saw not
We distinguish clear –
And mostly – see not
What We saw before –

'Tis Compound Vision –
Light – enabling Light –
The Finite – furnished
With the Infinite –
Convex – and Concave Witness –
Back – toward Time –
And forward –
Toward the God of Him –

~

Till Death – is narrow Loving –
The scantest Heart extant
Will hold you till your privilege
Of Finiteness – be spent –

o

But He whose loss procures you
Such Destitution that
Your Life too abject for itself
Thenceforward imitate –

Until – Resemblance perfect –
Yourself, for His pursuit
Delight of Nature – abdicate –
Exhibit Love – somewhat –

⁓

'Tis Sunrise – little Maid – Hast Thou
No Station in the Day?
'Twas not thy wont, to hinder so –
Retrieve thine industry –

'Tis Noon – My little Maid –
Alas – and art thou sleeping yet?
The Lily – waiting to be Wed –
The Bee – Hast thou forgot?

My little Maid – 'Tis Night – Alas
That Night should be to thee
Instead of Morning – Had'st thou broached
Thy little Plan to Die –
Dissuade thee, if I c'd not, Sweet,
I might have aided – thee –

⁓

Pain – expands the Time –
Ages coil within [Ages] lurk
The minute Circumference
Of a single Brain –

Pain contracts – the Time –
Occupied with Shot
Gammuts of Eternities Triplets [of]
Are as they were not – flit – • show – [as]

⁓

SHEET FIVE c. early 1864

Fitter to see Him, I may be[337]
For the long Hindrance – Grace – to Me –
With Summers, and with Winters, grow,
Some passing Year – a trait bestow   [a] charm

To make Me fairest of the Earth –
The Waiting – then – will seem so worth
I shall impute with half a pain
The blame that I was chosen – then –   [was] common

Time to anticipate His Gaze –   Time's [to]
Its first – Delight – and then – Surprise –   the [first]
The turning o'er and o'er my face
For Evidence it be the Grace –

He left behind One Day – So less
He seek conviction, That – be This –

I only must not grow so new
That He'll mistake – and ask for me   [That] ~~He~~ –
Of me – when first unto the Door
I go – to Elsewhere go no more

I only must not change so fair
He'll sigh – "The Other – She – is Where"?   ["The] ~~Real One~~ [She –]
The Love, tho', will array me right   [will] ~~instruct~~
I shall be perfect – in His sight –

If He perceive the other Truth –
Upon an Excellenter Youth –

How sweet I shall not lack in Vain –
But gain – thro' loss – Through Grief – obtain –   [Through] pain
The Beauty that reward Him most –   [Him] best
The Beauty of Demand – at Rest –   [of] Belief –

He who in Himself believes –
Fraud cannot presume –   Lie [cannot]
Faith is Constancy's Result –
And assumes – from Home –   [And] infers

Cannot perish, though it fail
Every second time –
But defaced Vicariously – When – • if – [defaced]
For Some Other Shame. [For] another shame –

SHEET SIX c. early 1864

Color – Caste – Denomination –[338]
These – are Time's Affair –
Death's diviner Classifying
Does not know they are –

As in sleep – all Hue forgotten –
Tenets – put behind –
Death's large – Democratic fingers
Rub away the Brand –

If Circassian – He is careless –
If He put away
Chrysalis of Blonde – or Umber –
Equal Butterfly –

They emerge from His Obscuring –
What Death – knows so well –
Our minuter intuitions –
Deem unplausible [Deem] incredible –

I make His Crescent fill or lack –
His Nature is at Full
Or Quarter – as I signify –
His Tides – do I control –

He holds superior in the Sky
Or gropes, at my Command
Behind inferior Clouds – or round
A Mist's slow Colonnade –

But since We hold a Mutual Disc –
And front a Mutual Day –

Which is the Despot, neither knows –
Nor Whose – the Tyranny –

Robbed by Death – but that was easy –
To the failing Eye [the] Dying – • clouding –
I could hold the latest Glowing –
Robbed by Liberty

For Her Jugular Defences –
This, too, I endured –
Hint of Glory – it afforded –
For the Brave Beloved – [the] bold

Fraud of Distance – Fraud of Danger,
Fraud of Death – to bear –
It is Bounty – to Suspense's
Vague Calamity –

Staking our entire Possession [our] divine –
On a Hair's result –
Then – Seesawing – coolly – on it –
Trying if it split – As to estimate

Unfulfilled to Observation –
Incomplete – to Eye –
But to Faith – a Revolution
In Locality –

Unto Us – the Suns extinguish –
To our Opposite –
New Horizons – they embellish – [they] Replenish
Fronting Us – with Night. Turning Us – their Night.

UNBOUND SHEETS

SHEET ONE c. second half of 1863

A Tongue – to tell Him I am true! [1]
Its fee – to be of Gold –
Had Nature – in Her monstrous House
A single Ragged Child –

To earn a Mine – would run
That Interdicted Way,
And tell Him – Charge Thee speak it plain –
That so far – Truth is True?

And answer What I do –
Beginning with the Day
That Night – begun –
Nay – Midnight – 'twas –
Since Midnight – happened – say –

If once more – Pardon – Boy –
The Magnitude thou may
Enlarge my Message – If too vast
Another Lad – help Thee –

Thy Pay – in Diamonds – be –
And His – in solid Gold –
Say Rubies – if He hesitate –
My Message – must be told –

Say – last I said – was This –
That when the Hills – come down –
And hold no higher than the Plain –
My Bond – have just begun –

And when the Heavens – disband –
And Deity conclude –

Then – look for me – Be sure you say –
Least Figure – on the Road –

~

I could not prove the Years had feet –
Yet confident they run
Am I, from symptoms that are past
And Series that are done –

I find my feet have further Goals –
I smile upon the Aims
That felt so ample – Yesterday –
Today's – have vaster claims – [vaster] forms

I do not doubt the Self I was
Was competent to me –
But something awkward in the fit – [something] odd about – [the]
Proves that – outgrown – I see –

~

What Soft – Cherubic Creatures –[2]
These Gentlewomen are –
One would as soon assault a Plush –
Or violate a Star –

Such Dimity Convictions –
A Horror so refined
Of freckled Human Nature –
Of Deity – ashamed –

It's such a common – Glory –
A Fisherman's – Degree –
Redemption – Brittle Lady –
Be so – ashamed of Thee –

~

SHEET TWO c. second half of 1863

You know that Portrait in the Moon –[3]
So tell me Who 'tis like –
The very Brow – the stooping eyes –
A-fog for – Say – Whose Sake?

o

The very Pattern of the Cheek –
It varies – in the Chin –
But – Ishmael – since we met – 'tis long –
And fashions – intervene –

When Moon's at full –
'Tis Thou – I say –
My lips just hold the name –
When crescent – Thou art worn – I note – [I] mind
But – there – the Golden Same –

And when – Some Night –
Bold – slashing Clouds
Cut Thee away from Me –
That's easier – than the other film
That glazes Holiday –

~

Funny – to be a Century –
And see the People – going by –
I – should die of the oddity –
But then – I'm not so staid – as He –

He keeps His Secrets safely – very –
Were He to tell – extremely sorry
This Bashful Globe of Ours would be –
So dainty of Publicity –

~

Not probable – The barest Chance –
A smile too few – a word too much
And far from Heaven as the Rest –
The Soul so close on Paradise –

What if the Bird – from journey far –
Confused by Sweets – as Mortals – are –
Forget the secret of His wing
And perish – but a Bough between –
Oh, Groping feet –
Oh Phantom Queen!

~

When Night is almost done –
And Sunrise grows so near
That We can touch the Spaces –
It's time to smooth the Hair –

And get the Dimples ready –
And wonder We could care
For that Old – faded Midnight –
That frightened – but an Hour –

SHEET THREE c. early 1864

Love – is that later Thing than Death –
More previous – than Life –
Confirms it at its entrance – And
Usurps it – of itself –

Tastes Death – the first – to hand the sing [to] pass – • prove
The Second – to its friend –
Disarms the little interval –
Deposits Him with God –

Then hovers – an inferior Guard –
Lest this Beloved Charge
Need – once in an Eternity – Miss [once]
A smaller than the Large – [A] lesser –

Struck, was I, nor yet by Lightning –
Lightning – lets away
Power to perceive His Process
With Vitality –

Maimed – was I – yet not by Venture –
Stone of Stolid Boy –
Nor a Sportsman's Peradventure –
Who mine Enemy?

Robbed – was I – intact to Bandit – [I –] yet met no Bandit –
All my Mansion torn –

Sun – withdrawn to Recognition –
Furthest shining – done –

Yet was not the foe – of any –
Not the smallest Bird
In the nearest Orchard dwelling – [Orchard] waiting
Be of Me – afraid –

Most – I love the Cause that slew Me –
Often as I die
Its beloved Recognition that [beloved]
Holds a Sun on Me –

Best – at Setting – as is Nature's –
Neither witnessed Rise [Neither] noticed –
Till the infinite Aurora
In the Other's Eyes –

line 7: [Nor a Sportsman's] ruthless pleasure – • wanton leisure

Patience – has a quiet Outer –
Patience – Look within –
Is an Insect's futile forces
Infinites – between –

'Scaping One – against the Other
Fruitlesser to fling –
Patience – is the Smile's exertion [the] Mouth's exertion – • Love's [exertion –]
Through the quivering –

lines 7–8: [Patience – is the] Mean of forces – stand by Her Wing –

SHEET FOUR c. early 1864

It bloomed and dropt, a Single Noon –[4]
The Flower – distinct and Red –
I, passing, thought another Noon
Another in its stead

Will equal glow, and thought no more
But came another Day

To find the Species disappeared –
The Same Locality –

The Sun in place – no other fraud
On Nature's perfect Sum –   [Nature's] General Sum
Had I but lingered Yesterday –
Was my retrieveless blame –

Much Flowers of this and further Zones
Have perished in my Hands
For seeking its Resemblance –   [its] similitude –
But unapproached it stands –

The single Flower of the Earth
That I, in passing by
Unconscious was – Great Nature's Face
Passed infinite by Me –   Went infinite by Me –

lines 19–20: Was ignorant that Nature closed / My Opportunity

---

This Merit hath the Worst –
It cannot be again –
When Fate hath taunted last
And thrown Her furthest Stone –

The Maimed may pause, and breathe,
And glance securely round –
The Deer attracts no further   [Deer] invites no longer –
Than it resists – the Hound –   than it evades – • eludes – [the]

We can but follow to the Sun –
As oft as He go down
He leave Ourselves a Sphere behind –
'Tis mostly – following –

We go no further with the Dust
Than to the Earthen Door –
And then the Panels are reversed –
And we behold – no more

SHEET FIVE c. 1864

This Dust, and its Feature –[5]
Accredited – Today –
Will in a second Future – [second] Being
Cease to identify –

This Mind, and its measure –
A too minute Area
For its enlarged inspection's
Comparison – appear –

This World, and its species [its] Nations – • Fashions – • symbols – • standards
A too concluded show
For its absorbed Attention's
Remotest scrutiny – Memorial – [scrutiny –]

I felt a Cleaving in my Mind –
As if my Brain had split –
I tried to match it – Seam by Seam –
But could not make them fit –

The thought behind, I strove to join [I] tried
Unto the thought before –
But Sequence ravelled out of Sound – [of] reach –
Like Balls – upon a Floor –

Fairer through Fading – as the Day
Into the Darkness dips away – [the] Twilight – • Evening –
Half Her Complexion of the Sun –
Hindering – Haunting – Perishing –

Rallies Her Glow, like a dying Friend – [Rallies] the West
Teazing, with glittering Amend – taunting – [with]
Only to aggravate the Dark Just to intensify [the]
Through an expiring – perfect – look – Nature's – [expiring –]

I felt a: *Sent to SD (second stanza, variant) c. early 1864*

What I see not, I better see –[6] When [I]
Through Faith – My Hazel Eye
Has periods of shutting –
But, No lid has Memory –

For frequent, all my sense obscured [For] often
I equally behold
As some one held a light unto [light] upon
The Features so beloved –
And I arise – and in my Dream –
Do Thee distinguished Grace –
Till jealous Daylight interrupt –
And mar thy perfectness –

SHEET SIX c. early 1864

A Coffin – is a small Domain,[7]
Yet able to contain
A Citizen of Paradise a Rudiment [of]
In its diminished Plane –

A Grave – is a restricted Breadth – [is] an inferior
Yet ampler than the Sun –
And all the Seas He populates –
And Lands He looks upon

To Him who on its small Repose [its] low
Bestows a single Friend – conferred – [a]
Circumference without Relief –
Or Estimate – or End –

I learned – at least – what Home could be –[8]
How ignorant I had been
Of pretty ways of Covenant –
How awkward at the Hymn [at] the Plan

Round our new Fireside – but for this –
This pattern – of the way –
Whose Memory drowns me, like the Dip
Of a Celestial Sea –

o

What Mornings in our Garden – guessed –
What Bees – for us – to hum –
With only Birds to interrupt [only] Bloom
The Ripple of our Theme –

And Task for Both –
When Play be done –
Your Problem – of the Brain – [Your] labor
And mine – some foolisher effect –
A Ruffle – or a Tune – [A] Thimble

The Afternoons – together spent –
And Twilight – in the Lanes –
Some ministry to poorer lives –
Seen poorest – thro' our gains –

And then Return – and Night – and Home – [Return – and] Trust

And then away to You to pass –
A new – diviner – Care –
Till Sunrise take us back to Scene – [Sunrise] call –
Transmuted – Vivider –

This seems a Home –
And Home is not –
But what that Place could be –
Afflicts me – as a Setting Sun –
Where Dawn – knows how to be –

SHEET SEVEN c. early 1865

Experience is the Angled Road
Preferred against the Mind
By – Paradox – the Mind itself –
Presuming it to lead

Quite Opposite – How complicate
The Discipline of Man –
Compelling Him to choose Himself
His Preappointed Pain –

'Twas awkward, but it fitted me –
An Ancient fashioned Heart –
Its only lore – its Steadfastness –
In Change – unerudite –

It only moved as do the Suns – [only] swerved –
For merit of Return –
Or Birds – confirmed perpetual
By Alternating Zone –

I only have it not Tonight
In its established place –
For technicality of Death –
Omitted in the Lease –

~

The Soul's distinct connection [9]
With immortality
Is best disclosed by Danger
Or quick Calamity –

As Lightning on a Landscape
Exhibits Sheets of Place – Developes [Sheets]
Not yet suspected – but for Flash – still unsuspected [but for] Fork
And Click – and Suddenness. [And] Bolt – [and]

~

Too little way the House must lie
From every Human Heart
That holds in undisputed Lease
A white inhabitant –

Too narrow is the Right between –
Too imminent the chance –
Each Consciousness must emigrate
And lose its neighbor once –

~

SHEET EIGHT c. early 1865

A Doubt if it be Us
Assists the staggering Mind

In an extremer Anguish
Until it footing find –

An Unreality is lent,
A merciful Mirage
That makes the living possible
While it suspends the lives.

~

Absence disembodies – so does Death
Hiding individuals from the Earth
Superstition helps, as well as love –
Tenderness decreases as we prove –

~

Split the Lark – and you'll find the Music –[10]
Bulb after Bulb, in Silver rolled –
Scantily dealt to the Summer Morning
Saved for your Ear, when Lutes be old –

Loose the Flood – you shall find it patent –
Gush after Gush, reserved for you –
Scarlet Experiment! Sceptic Thomas!
Now, do you doubt that your Bird was true?

~

Light is sufficient to itself –[11]
If Others want to see
It can be had on Window Panes
Some Hours in the Day.

But not for compensation –
It holds as large a Glow
To Squirrel in the Himmaleh
Precisely, as to you.

~

That Distance was between Us
That is not of Mile or Main –
The Will it is that situates –
Equator – never can –

~

Perhaps you think Me stooping
I'm not ashamed of that
Christ – stooped until He touched the Grave –
Do those at Sacrament

Commemorate Dishonor
Or love annealed of love
Until it bend as low as Death
Redignified, above?

SHEET NINE c. early 1865

That is solemn we have ended[12] [is] tender – • sacred
Be it but a Play
Or a Glee among the Garret
Or a Holiday

Or a leaving Home, or later,
Parting with a World
We have understood for better
Still to be explained – yet [to]

They ask but our Delight –
The Darlings of the Soil
And grant us all their Countenance
For a penurious smile –

Because the Bee may blameless hum[13]
For Thee a Bee do I become
List even unto Me –

Because the Flowers unafraid
May lift a look on thine, a Maid
Alway a Flower would be –

Nor Robins, Robins need not hide
When Thou upon their Crypts intrude
So Wings bestow on Me
Or Petals, or a Dower of Buzz

Perhaps you think: *Sent to SB (variant) c. early 1862*

That Bee to ride – or Flower of Furze
I that way worship Thee –

~

Finding is the first Act[14]
The second, loss,
Third, Expedition for the "Golden Fleece"

Fourth, no Discovery –
Fifth, no Crew –
Finally, no Golden Fleece –
Jason, sham, too –

~

Given in Marriage unto Thee[15]
Oh thou Celestial Host –
Bride of the Father and the Son
Bride of the Holy Ghost –

Other Betrothal shall dissolve –
Wedlock of Will, decay –
Only the Keeper of this Ring   [of] the Seal
Conquer Mortality –

~

SHEET TEN c. early 1865

As Frost is best conceived
By force of its Result –   [By] scanning its Result –
Affliction is inferred
By subsequent effect –

If when the Sun reveal,   [If] as
The Garden keep the Gash –   [The] Landscape show – • own – • hold
If as the Days resume   [Days] increase
The wilted countenance   [The] Blackened

Cannot correct the crease   [Cannot] efface –
Or counteract the stain –
Presumption is Vitality
Was somewhere put in twain –

~

Given in Marriage: *Sent to SD (first stanza, variant) c. 1864*

To my quick ear the Leaves – conferred –
The Bushes – they were Bells –
I could not find a Privacy
From Nature's sentinels –

In Cave if I presumed to hide
The Walls – begun to tell –
Creation seemed a mighty Crack –
To make me visible –

~

A Man may make a Remark – [may] drop
In itself – a quiet thing [a] tranquil
That may furnish the Fuse unto a Spark [furnish] ignition
In dormant nature – lain –

Let us divide – with skill – [us] deport
Let us discourse – with care – [us] disclose
Powder exists in Charcoal – [in] Elements – • sulphurets
Before it exists in Fire – [it] express

~

A Door just opened on a street – [Door] there opened – to a House –
I – lost – was passing by –
An instant's Width of Warmth disclosed –
And Wealth – and Company –

The Door as instant shut – And I – [as] sudden
I – lost – was passing by –
Lost doubly – but by contrast – most –
Informing – Misery – enlightening – • enabling – [Misery –]

~

SHEET ELEVEN c. early 1865

What shall I do when the Summer troubles –
What, when the Rose is ripe –
What when the Eggs fly off in Music
From the Maple Keep?

o

What shall I do when the Skies a'chirrup
Drop a Tune on Me –
When the Bee hangs all Noon in the Buttercup
What will become of Me?

Oh, when the Squirrel fills His Pockets
And the Berries stare
How can I bear their jocund Faces
Thou from Here, so far?

'Twouldn't afflict a Robin –
All His Goods have Wings –
I – do not fly, so Wherefore [I –] fly not [so]
My Perennial Things?

~

Drab Habitation of Whom?[16]
Tabernacle or Tomb –
Or Dome of Worm –
Or Porch of Gnome –
Or some Elf's Catacomb?

~

As One does Sickness over
In convalescent Mind,
His scrutiny of Chances
By blessed Health obscured –

As One rewalks a Precipice
And whittles at the Twig
That held Him from Perdition
Sown sidewise in the Crag

A Custom of the Soul [A] Habit
Far after suffering
Identity to question [to] handle –
For evidence 'thas been –

~

We met as Sparks – Diverging Flints
Sent various – scattered ways –

We parted as the Central Flint
Were cloven with an Adze –
Subsisting on the Light We bore
Before We felt the Dark –
We knew by change between itself
And that etherial Spark.

A Flint unto this Day – perhaps –
But for that single Spark.

SHEET TWELVE c. early 1865

Nature and God – I neither knew[17]
Yet Both so well knew Me
They startled, like Executors
Of My identity –

Yet Neither told – that I could learn –
My Secret as secure
As Herschel's private interest
Or Mercury's Affair –

Be Mine the Doom –[18]
Sufficient Fame –
To perish in Her Hand!

Each Scar I'll keep for Him[19]
Instead I'll say of Gem
In His long Absence worn
A Costlier One

But every Tear I bore
Were He to count them o'er
His own would fall so more
I'll missum them –

How well I knew her not
Whom not tò know – has been

Nature and God –: *Sent to SB (variant) c. early 1864*
How well I: *Sent to Maria Whitney (variant), perhaps acknowledging the death of her sister on 9 July 1864*

A Bounty in prospective, now
Next Door to mine the Pain –

⁓

Snow beneath whose chilly softness
Some that never lay
Make their first Repose this Winter
I admonish Thee

Blanket Wealthier the Neighbor
We so new bestow
Than thine Acclimated Creature
Wilt Thou, Austere Snow? [Thou,] Russian

⁓

I could not drink it, Sweet,
Till You had tasted first,
Though cooler than the Water was
The Thoughtfulness of Thirst.

⁓

The Sun is gay or stark
According to Our Deed –
If merry, He is merrier –
If eager for the Dead

Or an expended Day
He helped to make too bright
His mighty pleasure suits Us not
It magnifies Our Freight

⁓

SHEET THIRTEEN c. early 1865

They won't frown always – some sweet Day
When I forget to teaze –
They'll recollect how cold I looked
And how I just said "Please".

Then They will hasten to the Door
To call the little Girl

I could not: *Sent to SD (variant) c. 1864, beginning "I could not drink it, Sue,"*
They won't frown: *Sent to Ns (lost) perhaps c. 1865*

Who cannot thank Them for the Ice
That filled the lisping full.

~

On that dear Frame the Years had worn
Yet precious as the House
In which We first experienced Light
The Witnessing, to Us –

Precious! It was conceiveless fair
As Hands the Grave had grimed
Should softly place within our own
Denying that they died. Disputing [that]

~

The Lady feeds Her little Bird
At rarer intervals –
The little Bird would not dissent [not] demur
But meekly recognize

The Gulf between the Hand and Her
And crumbless and afar
And fainting, on Her yellow Knee
Fall softly, and adore –

~

Soto! Explore thyself![20]
Therein thyself shalt find
The "Undiscovered Continent" –
No Settler had the Mind.

~

I stepped from Plank to Plank
A slow and cautious way
The Stars about my Head I felt
About my Feet the Sea –

I knew not but the next
Would be my final inch –
This gave me that precarious Gait
Some call Experience –

~

Soto! Explore thyself!: *Sent to AD (variant) c. 1864*

SHEET FOURTEEN c. early 1865

Each Second is the last
Perhaps, recalls the Man
Just measuring unconsciousness
The Sea and Spar between –

To fail within a chance –
How terribler a thing
Than perish from the chance's list
Before the Perishing!

The Bird must sing to earn the Crumb
What merit have the Tune
No Breakfast if it guaranty

The Rose, content may bloom
To gain renown of Lady's Drawer
But if the Lady come
But once a Century, the Rose
Superfluous become –

I've none to tell me to but Thee
So when Thou failest, nobody –
It was a little tie –
It just held Two, nor those it held
Since Somewhere thy sweet Face has spilled
Beyond my Boundary –

If things were opposite – and Me
And Me it were, that ebbed from Thee
On some unanswering Shore –
Would'st Thou seek so – just say
That I the Answer may pursue
Unto the lips it eddied through –
So – overtaking Thee –

All I may, if small,
Do it not display

All I may,: *Sent to SD (variant) c. early 1864*

Larger for the Totalness –
'Tis Economy

To bestow a World
And withold a Star –
Utmost, is Munificence –
Less, tho' larger, poor –

~

SHEET FIFTEEN c. early 1865

The Poets light but Lamps –
Themselves – go out –
The Wicks they stimulate
If vital Light

Inhere as do the Suns –
Each Age a Lens
Disseminating their
Circumference –

~

An Everywhere of Silver
With Ropes of Sand
To keep it from effacing
The Track called Land –

~

Our little Kinsmen – after Rain
In plenty may be seen,
A Pink and Pulpy multitude
The tepid Ground upon.

A needless life, it seemed to me
Until a little Bird
As to a Hospitality
Advanced and breakfasted –

As I of He, so God of Me
I pondered, may have judged,
And left the little Angle Worm
With Modesties enlarged.

~

Of Tolling Bell I ask the cause?[21]
"A Soul has gone to Heaven"
I'm answered in a lonesome tone –
Is Heaven then a Prison?

That Bells should ring till all should know [all should] hear
A Soul had gone to Heaven
Would seem to me – the more the way
A Good News should be given –

~

These tested Our Horizon –
Then disappeared
As Birds before achieving
A Latitude.

Our Retrospection of Them
A fixed Delight,
But Our Anticipation
A Dice – a Doubt –

~

SHEET SIXTEEN c. early 1865

As imperceptibly as Grief[22]
The Summer lapsed away –
Too imperceptible at last
To feel like Perfidy –

A Quietness distilled –
As Twilight long begun –
Or Nature – spending with Herself
Sequestered Afternoon –

Sobriety inhered
Though gaudy influence
The Maple lent unto the Road
And graphic Consequence

Invested sombre place –
As suddenly be worn

Of Tolling Bell: *Sent to SD (stanza 2, variant) c. 1871*
As imperceptibly as: *Sent to TWH (stanzas 1, 2, 7, 8, variant) 9 June 1866 and apparently to SD (lost) c. 1865*

By sober Individual
A Homogeneous Gown –

Departed was the Bird –
And scarcely had the Hill
A flower to help His straightened face
In stress of Burial –

The Winds came closer up –
The Cricket spoke so clear
Presumption was – His Ancestors
Inherited the Floor –

The Dusk drew earlier in –
The Morning foreign shone –
The courteous – but harrowing Grace
Of Guest who would be gone –

And thus, without a Wing
Or Service of a Keel –
Our Summer made Her light Escape
Unto the Beautiful – into [the]

As Willing lid o'er Weary Eye
The Evening on the Day leans
Till of all our Nature's House
Remains but Balcony

Not all die early, dying young –
Maturity of Fate
Is consummated equally
In Ages, or a Night –

A Hoary Boy, I've known to drop
Whole statured – by the side
Of Junior of Fourscore – 'twas Act
Not Period – that died.

Not all die: *Sent to SD (variant) and to Josiah Holland (variant) c. early 1865*

SHEET SEVENTEEN c. 1865

Those who have been in the Grave the longest –
Those who begin Today –
Equally perish from our Practise –
Death is the other way – [the] further

Foot of the Bold did least attempt it –
It is the White Exploit –
Once to achieve, annuls the power
Once to communicate –

Be Mine the Doom[23]
Sufficient Fame
To perish in Her Hand.

It was a Grave, yet bore no Stone[24]
Enclosed 'twas not of Rail
A Consciousness its Acre, and
It held a Human Soul –

Entombed by whom, for what offence
If Home or Foreign born –
Had I the curiosity
'Twere not appeased of men

Till Resurrection, I must guess
Denied the small desire
A Rose upon its Ridge to sow
Or take away a Briar –

Impossibility, like Wine
Exhilirates the Man
Who tastes it; Possibility
Is flavorless – Combine

A Chance's faintest tincture
And in the former Dram

It was a: *Sent to Ns (lost) perhaps c. 1864*

Enchantment makes ingredient
As certainly as Doom –

~

So set its Sun in Thee
What Day be dark to me
What Distance far
So I the Ships may see
That touch how seldomly
Thy Shore?

~

How the Waters closed above Him
We shall never know –
How He stretched His anguish to us [His] Spirit –
That – is covered too –

Spreads the Pond Her Base of Lilies
Bold above the Boy
Whose unclaimed Hat and Jacket
Sum the History –

~

SHEET EIGHTEEN c. 1865

Always Mine!
No more Vacation!
Term of Light, this Day begun!
Failless as the fair rotation
Of the Seasons and the Sun –

Old the Grace, but new the Subjects –
Old, indeed, the East,
Yet upon His Purple Programme
Every Dawn, is first.

~

I cannot buy it – 'tis not sold –
There is no other in the World –
Mine was the only one

o

So set its: *Sent to SD (variant) c. 1865*

I was so happy I forgot
To shut the Door
And it went out
And I am all alone –

If I could find it Anywhere
I would not mind the journey there
Though it took all my store

But just to look it in the Eye –
"Did'st thou"? "Thou did'st not mean", to say,
Then, turn my Face away.

A Moth the hue of this
Haunts Candles in Brazil –
Nature's Experience would make
Our Reddest Second pale –

Nature is fond, I sometimes think,
Of Trinkets, as a Girl.

Good to hide, and hear 'em hunt!
Better, to be found,
If one care to, that is,
The Fox fits the Hound –

Good to know, and not tell –
Best, to know and tell,
Can one find the rare Ear
Not too dull –

SHEET NINETEEN c. 1865

Dying! To be afraid of thee[25]
One must to thine Artillery
Have left exposed a Friend –
Than thine old Arrow is a Shot
Delivered straighter to the Heart
The leaving Love behind –

o

Dying! To be: *Sent to Gertrude Vanderbilt (variant) and to Ns (lost) c. 1865*

Not for itself, the Dust is shy,
But, enemy, Beloved be
Thy Batteries divorce.
Fight sternly in a Dying eye
Two Armies, Love and Certainty
And Love and the Reverse –

I made slow Riches but my Gain
Was steady as the Sun
And every Night, it numbered more
Than the preceding One

All Days, I did not earn the same
But my perceiveless Gain
Inferred the less by Growing than
The Sum that it had grown.

Spring is the Period
Express from God –
Among the other seasons
Himself abide

But during March and April
None stir abroad
Without a cordial interview
With God –

Before He comes
We weigh the Time,
'Tis Heavy and 'tis Light.
When He depart, an Emptiness
Is the prevailing Freight –

Twice had Summer her fair Verdure
Proffered to the Plain –

Before He comes: *Sent to SB (variant) c. early 1865*

Twice – a Winter's Silver Fracture
On the Rivers been –

Two full Autumns for the Squirrel
Bounteous prepared –
Nature, Had'st thou not a Berry
For thy wandering Bird?

~

SHEET TWENTY c. 1865

Unable are the Loved to die
For Love is Immortality,
Nay, it is Deity –

Unable they that love – to die
For Love reforms Vitality
Into Divinity.

~

Finite – to fail, but infinite – to Venture –
For the one ship that struts the shore
Many's the gallant – overwhelmed Creature
Nodding in Navies Nevermore –

~

Just as He spoke it from his Hands
This Edifice remain –
A Turret more, a Turret less
Dishonor his Design –

According as his skill prefer
It perish, or endure –
Content, soe'er, it ornament
His Absent Character.

~

The good Will of a Flower
The Man who would possess
Must first present Certificate
Of minted Holiness.

~

Unable are the: *Sent to SD (first stanza, variant); her sister Harriet Cutler died on 8 March 1865*

I sing to use the Waiting,
My Bonnet but to tie
And shut the Door unto my House
No more to do have I

Till His best step approaching
We journey to the Day
And tell each other how We sung
To keep the Dark away.

~

Her Grace is all she has –
And that, so least displays –
One Art to recognize, must be,
Another Art, to praise –

~

When the Astronomer stops seeking[26]
For his Pleiad's Face –
When the lone British Lady
Forsakes the Arctic Race

When to his Covenant Needle
The Sailor doubting turns –
It will be amply early
To ask what treason means –

~

SHEET TWENTY-ONE c. 1865

Absent Place – an April Day –
Daffodils a'blow
Homesick curiosity
To the Souls that snow – Unto [Souls]

Drift may block within it
Deeper than without –
Daffodil delight but
Him it duplicate – Whom [it]

~

Her Grace is: *Sent to SD (variant) c. 1865*

Apology for Her
Be rendered by the Bee –
Herself, without a Parliament
Apology for Me –

~

The Heart has narrow Banks
It measures like the Sea — [It] paces
In mighty – unremitting Bass
And Blue monotony

Till Hurricane bisect
And as itself discerns
Its insufficient Area
The Heart convulsive learns

That Calm is but a Wall
Of Unattempted Gauze
An instant's Push demolishes
A Questioning – dissolves.

~

When One has given up One's life
The parting with the rest
Feels easy, as when Day lets go
Entirely the West

The Peaks, that lingered last
Remain in Her regret
As scarcely as the Iodine
Upon the Cataract –

~

The Veins of other Flowers
The Scarlet Flowers are
Till Nature leisure has for Terms
As "Branch", and "Jugular". — [As] Trunk

We pass, and she abides.
We conjugate Her Skill

The Veins of: *Sent to SD (second stanza, variant) c. early 1864*

While She creates and federates
Without a syllable –

SHEET TWENTY-TWO c. 1865

A Light exists in Spring
Not present on the Year
At any other period –
When March is scarcely here
A Color stands abroad
On Solitary Fields
That Science cannot overtake
But Human Nature feels.

It waits upon the Lawn,
It shows the furthest Tree
Upon the furthest Slope you know
It almost speaks to you.

Then as Horizons step
Or Noons report away
Without the Formula of sound
It passes and we stay –

A quality of loss
Affecting our Content
As Trade had suddenly encroached
Upon a Sacrament –

Banish Air from Air –
Divide Light if you dare –
They'll meet
While Cubes in a Drop
Or Pellets of Shape
Fit –
Films cannot annul
Odors return whole
Force Flame
And with a Blonde push

A Light exists: *Sent to SD (lost in part, variant) c. 1865*

Over your impotence
Flits Steam.

~

Like Men and Women Shadows walk
Upon the Hills Today
With here and there a mighty Bow
Or trailing Courtesy [Or] sweeping

To Neighbors doubtless of their own
Not quickened to perceive
Minuter Landscape as Ourselves
And Boroughs where We live [And] limits

~

How far is it to Heaven?
As far as Death this way –
Of River or of Ridge beyond Of Fathom or of League [beyond]
Was no discovery.

How far is it to Hell?
As far as Death this way –
How far left hand the Sepulchre
Defies Topography. Forbid that any know –

~

SHEET TWENTY-THREE c. 1865

Truth – is as old as God –
His Twin identity
And will endure as long as He
A Co-Eternity –

And perish on the Day
Himself is borne away
From Mansion of the Universe
A lifeless Deity.

~

A Death blow is a Life blow, to Some,
Who till they died, did not alive become

Like Men and: *Sent to SD (variant) c. 1865*
Truth – is as: *Sent to Josiah Holland (variant) c. early 1864*
A Death blow: *Sent to SD (variant) c. 1865, perhaps in response to her sister's death, and to TWH (variant) 17 March 1866*

Who had they lived had died, but when
They died, Vitality begun.

~

Two Travellers perishing in Snow
The Forests as they froze
Together heard them strengthening
Each other with the words [the] news

That Heaven if Heaven, must contain
What Either left behind
And then the cheer too solemn grew
For language, and the Wind

Long steps across the features took
That Love had touched that Morn
With reverential Hyacinth –
The taleless Days went on

Till Mystery impatient drew
And those They left behind
Led absent, were procured of Heaven [were] obtained

As Those first furnished, said –

~

Fame is the tint that Scholars leave
Upon their Setting Names –
The Iris not of Occident
That disappears as comes –

~

Escaping backward to perceive
The Sea upon our place –
Escaping forward, to confront
His glittering Embrace –

Retreating up, a Billow's hight
Retreating blinded down
Our undermining feet to meet
Instructs to the Divine.

~

SHEET TWENTY-FOUR c. 1865

The Mountain sat upon the Plain
In his tremendous Chair. [his] Eternal – • enormous –
His observation omnifold,
His inquest, everywhere –

The Seasons played around his knees
Like Children round a Sire –
Grandfather of the Days is He
Of Dawn, the Ancestor –

Peace is a fiction of our Faith –[27]
The Bells a Winter Night
Bearing the Neighbor out of Sound
That never did alight.

To this World she returned[28]
But with a tinge of that
A Compound manner as a Sod
Espoused a Violet –

That chiefer to the Skies
Than to Himself allied
Dwelt hesitating, half of Dust
And half of Day the Bride.

Not what We did, shall be the test
When Act and Will are done
But what Our Lord infers We would
Had We diviner been –

Death is a Dialogue between
The Spirit and the Dust.
"Dissolve" says Death,
The Spirit "Sir
I have another Trust" –

To this World: *Sent to Gertrude Vanderbilt (variant) c. September 1864*
Not what We: *Sent to SD (variant) c. 1865; SD mistakenly dated the MS as 1860*

Death doubts it –
Argues from the Ground – Reasons [from]
The Spirit turns away
Just laying off for evidence
An Overcoat of Clay.

~

The largest Fire ever known[29]
Occurs each Afternoon –
Discovered is without Surprise
Proceeds, without concern –

Consumes without Report to Men
An Occidental Town –
Rebuilt in time next Morning
To be burned down again.

line 7: [Rebuilt] Another Morning • Without insurance – • to the Horizon –

~

SHEET TWENTY-FIVE c. 1865

And this, of all my Hopes
This, is the silent end
Bountiful colored, My Morning rose
Early and sere, its end

Never Bud from a stem
Stepped with so gay a Foot
Never a Worm so confident
Bored at so brave a Root

~

Good to have had them lost[30]
For News that they be saved!
The nearer they departed Us
The nearer they, restored,

Shall stand to Our Right Hand –
Most precious – are the Dead –
Next precious, those that turned to go [that] rose
Then thought of Us, and stayed –

~

The largest Fire: *Sent to SD (variant) c. 1867*

Besides this May
We know
There is Another –
How fair
Our speculations of the Foreigner!

Some know Him whom [know] it
We knew –
Sweet Wonder –
A Nature be [A] Section
Where Saints, and our plain going Neighbor
Keep May!

I cannot be ashamed
Because I cannot see
The love you offer –
Magnitude
Reverses Modesty

And I cannot be proud
Because a Hight so high
Involves Alpine
Requirements
And services of Snow –

SHEET TWENTY-SIX c. 1865

Faith – is the Pierless Bridge
Supporting what We see
Unto the Scene that We do not –
Too slender for the eye

It bears the Soul as bold
As it were rocked in Steel
With Arms of steel at either side –
It joins – behind the Vail

To what, could We presume
The Bridge would cease to be

To Our far, vascillating Feet
A first Nescessity.

~

His Feet are shod with Gauze –[31]
His Helmet, is of Gold,
His Breast, a single Onyx
With Chrysophras, inlaid –

His Labor is a Chant –
His Idleness – a Tune –
Oh, for a Bee's experience
Of Clovers, and of Noon!

~

Love – is anterior to Life –
Posterior – to Death –
Initial of Creation, and
The Exponent of Earth –

~

Only a Shrine, but Mine –[32]
I made the Taper shine –
Madonna dim, to whom all Feet may come,
Regard a Nun –

Thou knowest every Wo –
Needless to tell thee – so –
But can'st thou do
The Grace next to it – heal?
That looks a harder skill to us –
Still – just as easy, if it be thy Will
To thee – Grant Me –
Thou knowest, though, so Why tell thee?

~

If I can stop one Heart from breaking
I shall not live in vain
If I can ease one Life the Aching
Or cool one Pain

o

Or help one fainting Robin
Unto his Nest again
I shall not live in vain.

~

SHEET TWENTY-SEVEN c. 1865

Bee! I'm expecting you!
Was saying Yesterday
To Somebody you know
That you were due –

The Frogs got Home last Week –
Are settled, and at work –
Birds mostly back –
The Clover warm and thick –

You'll get my Letter by
The Seventeenth; Reply
Or better, be with me –
Yours, Fly.

~

Satisfaction – is the Agent
Of Satiety –
Want – a quiet Comissary
For Infinity –

To possess, is past the instant
We achieve the Joy –
Immortality contented
Were Anomaly –

~

Here, where the Daisies fit my Head[33]
'Tis easiest to lie
And every Grass that plays outside
Is sorry, some, for Me –

~

Where I am not afraid to go
I may confide my Flower –
Who was not Enemy of Me
Will gentle be, to Her –

Nor separate, Herself and Me
By Distances become –
A single Bloom we constitute
Departed, or at Home –

Her little Parasol to lift[34]
And once to let it down
Her whole Responsibility –
To imitate, be Mine –

A Summer further I must wear,
Content if Nature's Drawer
Present Me from sepulchral Crease
As blemishless, as Her –

SHEET TWENTY-EIGHT c. 1865

Said Death to Passion
"Give of thine an Acre unto me".
Said Passion, through contracting Breaths
"A Thousand Times Thee Nay".

Bore Death from Passion
All His East
He – sovreign as the Sun
Resituated in the West
And the Debate was done

Air has no Residence, no Neighbor,
No Ear, no Door,
No Apprehension of Another
Oh, Happy Air!

o

Where I am: *Sent to Ns (lost) perhaps c. 1865*

Etherial Guest at e'en an Outcast's Pillow –
Essential Host, in Life's faint, wailing Inn,
Later than Light thy Consciousness accost Me
Till it depart, persuading Mine – [depart,] conveying

~

We'll pass without the parting
So to spare
Certificate of Absence –
Deeming where

I left Her I could find Her
If I tried –
This way, I keep from missing
Those that died.

~

His Bill an Augur is[35]
His Head, a Cap and Frill
He laboreth at every Tree
A Worm, His utmost Goal –

~

To undertake is to achieve[36]
Be Undertaking blent
With fortitude of obstacle
And toward Encouragement

That fine Suspicion Natures must
Permitted to revere
Departed Standards and the few
Criterion Natures – here –

~

SHEET TWENTY-NINE c. 1865

Three Weeks passed since I had seen Her –
Some Disease had vext
'Twas with Text and Village Singing [and] Antique
I beheld Her next

o

We'll pass without: *Sent to Maria Avery Howard (lost, transcribed variant) c. 1863, with oleander blossom tied with black ribbon, beginning "We'll pass without a parting –"*
To undertake is: *Sent to TWH (variant) 9 June 1866*

And a Company – Our pleasure
To discourse alone
Gracious now to me as any –
Gracious unto none –

Borne without dissent of Either — [of] any
To the Parish night –
Of the Separated Parties — [Separated] People
Which be out of sight?

~

A Sickness of this World it most occasions[37]
When Best Men die.
A Wishfulness their far Condition
To occupy.

A Chief indifference, as Foreign
A World must be
Themselves forsake – contented –
For Deity

~

Partake as doth the Bee –[38]
Abstemiously –
A Rose is an Estate — I know the Family
In Sicily – — in Tripoli.

~

He scanned it – Staggered –
Dropped the Loop
To Past or Period –
Caught helpless at a sense as if
His Mind were going blind –

Groped up, to see if God were there – — [God] was
Groped backward at Himself
Caressed a Trigger absently
And wandered out of Life –

~

Partake as doth: *Sent to Perez Dickinson Cowan (lost), received 26 April 1864, with a bouquet of flowers*

The missing All, prevented Me
From missing minor Things.
If nothing larger than a World's
Departure from a Hinge
Or Sun's Extinction, be observed
'Twas not so large that I
Could lift my Forehead from my work
For Curiosity.

~

SHEET THIRTY c. 1865

I heard, as if I had no Ear[39]
Until a Vital Word
Came all the way from Life to me
And then I knew I heard –

I saw, as if my Eye were on
Another, till a Thing
And now I know 'twas Light, because
It fitted them, came in.

I dwelt, as if Myself were out,
My Body but within
Until a Might detected me
And set my Kernel in –

And Spirit turned unto the Dust
"Old Friend, thou knowest Me",
And Time went out to tell the News
And met Eternity

~

Not so the infinite Relations – Below
Division is Adhesion's forfeit – On High
Affliction but a speculation – And Wo
A Fallacy, a Figment, We knew –

~

Somewhat, to hope for,
Be it ne'er so far
Is Capital against Despair –

o

The missing All,: *Sent to SD (variant) c. 1865*

Somewhat, to suffer,
Be it ne'er so keen –
If terminable, may be borne –

~

Spring comes on the World –
I sight the Aprils –
Hueless to me, until thou come
As, till the Bee
Blossoms stand negative,
Touched to Conditions
By a Hum –

~

Lest this be Heaven indeed
An Obstacle is given
That always guages a Degree
Between Ourself and Heaven.

~

Just to be Rich[40]
To waste my Guinea
On so broad a Heart!
Just to be Poor,
For Barefoot pleasure
You, Sir, shut me out!

~

SHEET THIRTY-ONE c. 1865

The Stimulus, beyond the Grave
His Countenance to see
Supports me like imperial Drams
Afforded Day by Day.

~

Aurora is the effort
Of the Celestial Face
Unconsciousness of Perfectness
To simulate, to Us.

~

Just to be: *Sent to SB (variant) c. second half of 1863*

Dying at my music!
Bubble! Bubble!
Hold me till the Octave's run!
Quick! Burst the Windows!
Ritardando!
Phials left, and the Sun!

~

There is no Silence in the Earth – so silent
As that endured
Which uttered, would discourage Nature
And haunt the World –

~

Bind me – I still can sing –
Banish – my mandolin
Strikes true, within –

Slay – and my Soul shall rise
Chanting to Paradise –
Still thine –

~

The first We knew of Him was Death –
The second, was Renown –
Except the first had justified
The second had not been –

~

Falsehood of Thee, could I suppose
'Twould undermine the Sill
To which my Faith pinned Block by Block
Her Cedar Citadel –

~

How still the Bells in Steeples stand
Till swollen with the Sky
They leap upon their silver Feet
In frantic Melody!

~

SHEET THIRTY-TWO c. 1865

I was a Phebe – nothing more –[41]
A Phebe – nothing less –
The little note that others dropt
I fitted into place –

I dwelt too low that any seek –
Too shy, that any blame –
A Phebe makes a little print
Upon the Floors of Fame –

Knows how to forget![42]
But could It teach it?
Easiest of Arts, they say
When one learn how

Dull Hearts have died
In the Acquisition
Sacrifice for Science
Is common, though, now –

I – went to School
But was not wiser
Globe did not teach it
Nor Logarithm Show

"How to forget"!
Say some Philosopher!
Ah, to be erudite
Enough to know!

Is it in a Book?
So, I could buy it –
Is it like a Planet?
Telescopes would know –

If it be invention
It must have a Patent –
Rabbi of the Wise Book
Don't you know?

'Tis Anguish grander than Delight –[43]
'Tis Resurrection Pain –
The meeting Bands of smitten Face
We questioned to, again –

'Tis Transport wild as thrills the Graves
When Cerements let go
And Creatures clad in Miracle
Go up by Two and Two.

SHEET THIRTY-THREE c. 1865

Crumbling is not an instant's Act
A fundamental pause
Dilapidation's processes
Are organized Decays –

'Tis first a Cobweb on the Soul
A Cuticle of Dust
A Borer in the Axis
An Elemental Rust –

Ruin is formal – Devil's work
Consecutive and slow –
Fail in an instant, no man did
Slipping – is Crashe's law –

Not to discover weakness is[44]
The Artifice of strength – [The] Mystery
Impregnability inheres
As much through Consciousness [through] Conscious faith

Of faith of others in itself of others in its ableness
As Pyramidal Nerve [As] elemental – • plupotential
Behind the most unconscious clock [most] Consummate
What skillful Pointers move – [What] Anxious

Best Things dwell out of Sight
The Pearl – the Just – Our Thought –

○

'Tis Anguish grander: *Sent to SD (last 3 lines, variant) c. 1861*

Most shun the Public Air
Legitimate, and Rare –

The Capsule of the Wind
The Capsule of the Mind

Exhibit here, as doth a Burr –
Germ's Germ be where?

~

No other can reduce[45]
Our mortal Consequence
Like the remembering it be nought
A period from hence

But Contemplation for
Cotemporaneous nought –
Our mutual fame, that haply
Jehovah recollect

Our only Competition
Jehovah's Estimate.

~

SHEET THIRTY-FOUR c. 1865

Superfluous were the Sun
When Excellence be dead
He were superfluous every Day
For every Day be said

That syllable whose Faith
Just saves it from Despair
And whose "I'll meet You" hesitates
If Love inquire "Where"?

Upon His dateless Fame
Our Periods may lie
As Stars that drop anonymous
From an abundant sky.

~

This was in the White of the Year –[46]
That – was in the Green –

No other can: *Sent to SD (variant) c. 1865*
This was in: *Sent to Louisa Norcross (lost, transcribed variant) c. March 1865*

Drifts were as difficult then to think
As Daisies now to be seen –

Looking back, is best that is left
Or if it be – before –
Retrospection is Prospect's half,
Sometimes, almost more –

⁓

The Fingers of the Light
Tapped soft upon the Town
With "I am great and cannot wait
So therefore let me in".

"You're soon", the Town replied,
"My Faces are asleep
But swear, and I will let you by
You will not wake them up".

The easy Guest complied
But once within the Town
The transport of His Countenance
Awakened Maid and Man

The Neighbor in the Pool
Upon His Hip elate
Made loud obeisance and the Gnat
Held up His Cup for Light.

⁓

Ideals are the Fairy Oil
With which We help the Wheel
But when the Vital Axle turns
The Eye rejects the Oil.

⁓

SHEET THIRTY-FIVE c. 1865

The Soul should always stand ajar[47]
That if the Heaven inquire
He will not be obliged to wait
Or shy of troubling Her

○

Ideals are the: *Sent to SD (variant) c. 1865*

Depart, before the Host have slid
The Bolt unto the Door [Bolt] upon
To search for the accomplished Guest, [To] seek
Her Visitor, no more –

~

Up Life's Hill with my little Bundle
If I prove it steep –
If a Discouragement withold me –
If my newest step

Older feel than the Hope that prompted –
Spotless be from blame
Heart that proposed as Heart that accepted
Homelessness, for Home –

~

She rose as high as His Occasion[48]
Then sought the Dust –
And lower lay in low Westminster
For Her brief Crest –

~

There is a Zone whose even Years
No Solstice interrupt –
Whose Sun constructs perpetual Noon
Whose perfect Seasons wait –

Whose Summer set in Summer, till Where [Summer]
The Centuries of June
And Centuries of August cease [August] fuse – • lapse – • blend
And Consciousness – is Noon –

~

Which is best? Heaven –
Or only Heaven to come
With that old Codicil of Doubt?
I cannot help esteem

The "Bird within the Hand"
Superior to the one

The "Bush" may yield me
Or may not –
Too late to choose again.

~

SHEET THIRTY-SIX c. 1865

A bold, inspiriting Bird[49]
Is the Jay –
Good as a Norseman's Hymn –
Brittle and brief in quality –
Warrant in every line –

Riding a Bough like a Brigadier –
Confident and straight –
Good is the look of Him in March
As a Benefit

~

Too scanty 'twas to die for you,
The merest Greek could that.
The living, Sweet, is costlier –
I offer even that –

The Dying, is a trifle, past,
But living, this include
The dying multifold – without
The Respite to be dead.

~

Did We abolish Frost
The Summer would not cease –
If Seasons perish or prevail
Is optional with Us –

~

Were it but Me that gained the Hight –
Were it but They, that failed!
How many things the Dying play
Might they but live, they would!

~

A bold, inspiriting: *Sent to SD (variant) c. 1872, beginning "A prompt – executive Bird is the Jay –"*

The Hills in Purple syllables
The Day's Adventures tell
To little Groups of Continents
Just going Home from School –

~

To die – without the Dying
And live – without the Life
This is the hardest Miracle
Propounded to Belief.

~

SHEET THIRTY-SEVEN c. 1865

Who saw no Sunrise cannot say
The Countenance 'twould be –
Who guess at seeing, guess at loss
Of the Ability –

The Emigrant of Light, it is
Afflicted for the Day –
The Blindness that beheld and blest –
And could not find its Eye.

~

I had a daily Bliss
I half indifferent viewed
Till sudden I perceived it stir –
It grew as I pursued

Till when around a Hight
It wasted from my sight
Increased beyond my utmost scope — enlarged [beyond]
I learned to estimate –

~

My Season's furthest Flower –
I tenderer commend
Because I found Her Kinsmanless –
A Grace without a Friend.

~

Trudging to Eden, looking backward,[50]
I met Somebody's little Boy
Asked him his name –
He lisped me "Trotwood" –
Lady, did He belong to thee?

Would it comfort – to know I met him –
And that He didn't look afraid?
I couldn't weep – for so many smiling
New Acquaintance – this Baby made –

Far from Love the Heavenly Father
Leads the Chosen Child,
Oftener through Realm of Briar
Than the Meadow mild.

Oftener by the Claw of Dragon
Than the Hand of Friend
Guides the Little One predestined
To the Native Land –

SHEET THIRTY-EIGHT c. 1865

I knew that I had gained
And yet I knew not how
By Diminution it was not
But Discipline unto

A Rigor unrelieved
Except by the Content
Another bear its Duplicate
In other Continent.

It rises – passes – on our South
Inscribes a simple Noon –
Cajoles a Moment with the Spires
And infinite is gone –

So large my Will
The little that I may
Embarrasses
Like gentle infamy –

Affront to Him
For whom the Whole were small
Affront to me
Who know His meed of all.

Earth at the best
Is but a scanty Toy –
Bought, carried Home
To Immortality

It looks so small
We chiefly wonder then
At our Conceit
In purchasing.

~

The Products of my Farm are these
Sufficient for my Own
And here and there a Benefit
Unto a Neighbor's Bin.

With Us, 'tis Harvest all the Year
For when the Frosts begin
We just reverse the Zodiac
And fetch the Acres in –

~

The Dying need but little, Dear,
A Glass of Water's all,
A Flower's unobtrusive Face
To punctuate the Wall,

A Fan, perhaps, a Friend's Regret
And Certainty that one
No color in the Rainbow
Perceive, when you are gone –

~

SHEET THIRTY-NINE c. 1865

Bloom – is Result – to meet a Flower
And casually glance
Would cause one scarcely to suspect [Would] scarcely cause [one]
The minor Circumstance

Assisting in the Bright Affair
So intricately done
Then offered as a Butterfly
To the Meridian –

To pack the Bud – oppose the Worm –
Obtain its right of Dew –
Adjust the Heat – elude the Wind –
Escape the prowling Bee –

Great Nature not to disappoint
Awaiting Her that Day –
To be a Flower, is profound
Responsibility –

My Heart upon a little Plate
Her Palate to delight
A Berry or a Bun, would be,
Might it an Apricot!

'Twas my one Glory –
Let it be
Remembered
I was owned of Thee –

Nor Mountain hinder Me
Nor Sea –
Who's Baltic
Who's Cordillera?

My Heart upon: *Sent to Ns (lost) perhaps c. 1865*

SHEET FORTY c. 1865

When they come back – if Blossoms do –
I always feel a doubt
If Blossoms can be born again
When once the Art is out –

When they begin, if Robins may,
I always had a fear
I did not tell, it was their last Experiment
Last Year,

When it is May, if May return,
Had nobody a pang
Lest in a Face so beautiful
He might not look again?

If I am there – One does not know
What Party – One may be
Tomorrow, but if I am there
I take back all I say –

~

Superiority to Fate
Is difficult to gain
'Tis not conferred of any
But possible to earn

A pittance at a time
Until to Her surprise
The Soul with strict economy
Subsist till Paradise.

~

Revolution is the Pod
Systems rattle from
When the Winds of Will are stirred
Excellent is Bloom

But except its Russet Base
Every Summer be

The entomber of itself,
So of Liberty –

Left inactive on the Stalk
All its Purple fled
Revolution shakes it for
Test if it be dead –

~

We learn in the Retreating
How vast an one
Was recently among us –
A Perished Sun

Endear in the departure
How doubly more
Than all the Golden presence
It was – before –

~

SHEET FORTY-ONE c. 1865

What Twigs We held by –[51]
Oh the View
When Life's swift River striven through
We pause before a further plunge
To take Momentum –
As the Fringe

Upon a former Garment shows
The Garment cast,
Our Props disclose
So scant, so eminently small
Of Might to help, so pitiful
To sink, if We had labored, fond
The diligence were not more blind

How scant, by everlasting Light
The Discs that satisfied our sight –
How dimmer than a Saturn's Bar
The Things esteemed, for Things that are!

~

We miss a Kinsman more
When warranted to see
Than when witheld of Oceans
From possibility

A Furlong than a League
Inflicts a pricklier pain,
Till We, who smiled at Pyrrhenees –
Of Parishes, complain.

Ended, ere it begun –[52]
The Title was scarcely told
When the Preface perished from Consciousness
The story, unrevealed –

Had it been mine, to print!
Had it been yours, to read!
That it was not our privilege
The interdict of God –

Myself can read the Telegrams
A Letter chief to me
The Stock's advance and retrograde
And what the Markets say

The Weather – how the Rains
In Counties have begun.
'Tis News as null as nothing,
But sweeter so, than none.

SHEET FORTY-TWO c. 1865

I am afraid to own a Body –
I am afraid to own a Soul –
Profound – precarious Property –
Possession, not optional –

Double Estate, entailed at pleasure
Upon an unsuspecting Heir –

Duke in a moment of Deathlessness
And God, for a Frontier.

~

The Well upon the Brook
Were foolish to depend –
Let Brooks – renew of Brooks –
But Wells – of failless Ground!

~

It was not Saint – it was too large –
Nor Snow – it was too small –
It only held itself aloof
Like something spiritual –

~

Because 'twas Riches I could own,
Myself had earned it – Me,
I knew the Dollars by their names –
It feels like Poverty

An Earldom out of sight, to hold,
An Income in the Air,
Possession – has a sweeter chink
Unto a Miser's Ear –

~

Themself are all I have –
Myself a freckled – be –
I thought you'd choose
A Velvet Cheek
Or one of Ivory –
Would you – instead of Me?

~

To Whom the Mornings stand for Nights,
What must the Midnights – be!

~

SHEET FORTY-THREE c. 1865

Could I but ride indefinite
As doth the Meadow Bee
And visit only where I liked
And no one visit me

And flirt all Day with Buttercups
And marry whom I may
And dwell a little everywhere [little] generally
Or better, run away

With no Police to follow
Or chase Him if He do
Till He should jump Peninsulas
To get away from me –

I said "But just to be a Bee"
Upon a Raft of Air
And row in Nowhere all Day long
And anchor "off the Bar"

What Liberty! So Captives deem
Who tight in Dungeons are.

Embarrassment of one another
And God
Is Revelation's limit, [Revelation's] caution
Aloud
Is nothing that is chief,
But still,
Divinity dwells under Seal –

While it is alive[53]
Until Death touches it
While it and I lap one Air
Dwell in one Blood
Under one Sacrament
Show me division can split or pare –

○

Love is like Life merely longer
Love is like Death, during the Grave
Love is the Fellow of the Resurrection
Scooping up the Dust and chanting "Live"!

~

To One denied to drink
To tell what Water is
Would be acuter, would it not
Than letting Him surmise?

To lead Him to the Well
And let Him hear it drip
Remind Him, would it not, somewhat
Of His condemned lip?

~

SHEET FORTY-FOUR c. 1865

Uncertain lease – developes lustre
On Time –
Uncertain Grasp, appreciation
Of Sum –

The shorter Fate – is oftener the chiefest
Because
Inheritors upon a tenure
Prize –

~

Noon – is the Hinge of Day –
Evening – the Tissue Door – [the] Folding
Morning – the East compelling the Sill
Till all the World is ajar –

~

This Chasm, Sweet, upon my life
I mention it to you,
When Sunrise through a fissure drop
The Day must follow too.

o

If we demur, its gaping sides
Disclose as 'twere a Tomb
Ourself am lying straight wherein
The Favorite of Doom –

When it has just contained a Life
Then, Darling, it will close
And yet so bolder every Day
So turbulent it grows

I'm tempted half to stitch it up
With a remaining Breath
I should not miss in yielding, though
To Him, it would be Death –

And so I bear it big about
My Burial – before
A Life quite ready to depart
Can harass me no more –

My best Acquaintances are those[54]
With Whom I spoke no Word –
The Stars that stated come to Town
Esteemed Me never rude
Although to their Celestial Call
I failed to make reply –
My constant – reverential Face
Sufficient Courtesy –

Though their repeated Grace
Elicit no reply.

SHEET FORTY-FIVE c. 1865

The Sun and Moon must make their haste –
The Stars express around
For in the Zones of Paradise
The Lord alone is burned –

His Eye, it is the East and West –
The North and South when He

Do concentrate His Countenance
Like Glow Worms, flee away –

Oh Poor and Far –
Oh Hindered Eye
That hunted for the Day –
The Lord a Candle entertains
Entirely for Thee –

~

As the Starved Maelstrom laps the Navies[55]
As the Vulture teazed
Forces the Broods in lonely Valleys
As the Tiger eased

By but a Crumb of Blood, fasts Scarlet
Till he meet a Man
Dainty adorned with Veins and Tissues
And partakes – his Tongue

Cooled by the Morsel for a moment
Grows a fiercer thing
Till he esteem his Dates and Cocoa
A Nutrition mean

I, of a finer Famine
Deem my Supper dry
For but a Berry of Domingo
And a Torrid Eye –

~

Ribbons of the Year –
Multitude Brocade –
Worn to Nature's Party once

Then, as flung aside
As a faded Bead
Or a Wrinkled Pearl –
Who shall charge the Vanity
Of the Maker's Girl?

~

Death leaves Us homesick, who behind,
Except that it is gone
Are ignorant of its Concern
As if it were not born.

Through all their former Places, we like Individuals go [all] its
Who something lost, the seeking for
Is all that's left them, now –

line 6: [Who something] dropt [the] looking [for]

SHEET FORTY-SIX c. 1865

Crisis is a Hair
Toward which forces creep
Past which – forces retrograde
If it come in sleep

To suspend the Breath
Is the most we can
Ignorant is it Life or Death
Nicely balancing –

Let an instant push
Or an Atom press
Or a Circle hesitate
In Circumference

It may jolt the Hand
That adjusts the Hair
That secures Eternity
From presenting – Here –

Under the Light, yet under,
Under the Grass and the Dirt,
Under the Beetle's Cellar
Under the Clover's Root, [Clover's] Foot

Further than Arm could stretch
Were it Giant long,

Further than Sunshine could
Were the Day Year long,

Over the Light, yet over,
Over the Arc of the Bird –
Over the Comet's chimney –
Over the Cubit's Head,

Further than Guess can gallop
Further than Riddle ride –
Oh for a Disc to the Distance
Between Ourselves and the Dead!

Away from Home are some and I –[56]
An Emigrant to be
In a metropolis of Homes
Is easy possibly – [Is] common –

The Habit of a Foreign Sky
We – difficult acquire
As Children, who remain in Face
The more their Feet retire.

A Burdock twitched my Gown[57]
Not Burdock's blame – but mine
Who went too near the Burdock's Den –

A Bog affronts my shoe.
What else have Bogs to do –
The only art they know [only] Trade
The splashing men?

'Tis Minnows – should despise –
An Elephant's calm eyes
Look further on.

SHEET FORTY-SEVEN c. 1865

Who occupies this House?
A Stranger I must judge

Away from Home: *Sent to EH or to both the Hollands (variant) c. 1864*
A Burdock twitched: *Sent to AD (variant) c. 1862, beginning "A Burdock – clawed my Gown –"*

Since No one knows His Circumstance –
'Tis well the name and age

Are writ upon the Door
Or I should fear to pause
Where not so much as Honest Dog
Approach encourages –

It seems a Curious Town –
Some Houses very old,
Some – newly raised this Afternoon,
Were I compelled to build

It should not be among
Inhabitants so still
But where the Birds assemble
And Boys were possible

Before Myself was born
'Twas settled, so they say,
A Territory for the Ghosts
And Squirrels, formerly.

Until a Pioneer, as Settlers often do
Liking the quiet of the Place
Attracted more unto –

And from a Settlement
A Capitol has grown
Distinguished for the gravity
Of every Citizen –

The Owner of this House
A Stranger He must be –
Eternity's Acquaintances
Are mostly so – to me –

The Chemical conviction[58]
That Nought be lost
Enable in Disaster
My fractured Trust –

o

The Faces of the Atoms
If I shall see
How more the Finished Creatures
Departed Me! Entrusted [Me!]

~

The Hollows round His eager Eyes
Were Pages where to read
Pathetic Histories – although
Himself had not complained. [had] hitherto concealed –
Biography to All who passed
Of Unobtrusive Pain
Except for the italic Face
Endured, unhelped – unknown – [Endured,] resigned –

~

SHEET FORTY-EIGHT c. 1865

A loss of something ever felt I –
The first that I could recollect
Bereft I was – of what I knew not
Too young that any should suspect

A Mourner walked among the children [Mourner] lurked
I notwithstanding went about [notwithstanding] stole
As one bemoaning a Dominion
Itself the only Prince cast out –

Elder, Today, A session wiser,
And fainter, too, as Wiseness is
I find Myself still softly searching
For my Delinquent Palaces –

And a Suspicion, like a Finger
Touches my Forehead now and then
That I am looking oppositely
For the Site of the Kingdom of Heaven –

~

Herein a Blossom lies –
A Sepulchre, between –

Cross it, and overcome the Bee –
Remain – 'tis but a Rind –

What did They do since I saw Them?[59]
Were They industrious?
So many questions to put Them
Have I the Eagerness

That could I snatch Their Faces
That could Their lips reply
Not till the last was answered
Should They start for the Sky –

Not if the Just suspect Me
And offer a Reward
Would I restore my Booty
To that Bold Person, God,

Not if Their Party were waiting,
Not if to talk with Me
Were to Them now, Homesickness
After Eternity –

As plan for Noon and plan for Night
So differ Life and Death
In positive Prospective –
The Foot upon the Earth

At Distance, and Achievement, strains,
The Foot upon the Grave
Makes effort at Conclusion
Assisted faint, of Love – [Assisted] slow

SHEET FORTY-NINE c. 1865

Of Consciousness, her awful mate
The Soul cannot be rid –
As easy the secreting her
Behind the eyes of God –

o

The deepest hid is sighted first
And scant to Him the Crowd –
What triple Lenses burn upon
The Escapade from God –

⁓

A Cloud withdrew from the Sky
Superior Glory be
But that Cloud and its Auxiliaries
Are forever lost to me

Had I but further scanned
Had I secured the Glow
In an Hermetic Memory
It had availed me now –

Never to pass the Angel
With a glance and a Bow
Till I am firm in Heaven
Is my intention, now –

⁓

Of Silken Speech and Specious Shoe[60]
A Traitor is the Bee
His service to the newest Grace
Present continually

His Suit a chance
His Troth a Term
Protracted as the Breeze
Continual Ban propoundeth He
Continual Divorce.

⁓

How fortunate the Grave –
All Prizes to obtain,
Successful certain, if at last,
First Suitor not in vain.

⁓

How happy I was if I could forget
To remember how sad I am
Would be an easy adversity
But the recollecting of Bloom

Keeps making November difficult
Till I who was almost bold
Lose my way like a little Child
And perish of the cold.

~

SHEET FIFTY c. 1865

Experiment to Me[61]
Is Every One I meet
If It contain a Kernel –
The figure of a Nut

Presents upon a Tree
Equally plausibly –
But Meat within is requisite
To Squirrels, and to Me –

~

That Such have died enable Us
The tranquiller to die –
That Such have lived,
Certificate for Immortality.

~

Sang from the Heart, Sire,[62]
Dipped my Beak in it,
If the Tune drip too much
Have a tint too Red

Pardon the Cochineal –
Suffer the Vermillion –
Death is the Wealth
Of the Poorest Bird.

o

Experiment to Me: *Sent to SD (variant) c. 1865*

Bear with the Ballad –
Awkward – faltering –
Death twists the strings –
'Twas'nt my blame –

Pause in your Liturgies –
Wait your Chorals –
While I repeat your [I] recite
Hallowed Name –

Fate slew Him, but He did not drop –
She felled – He did not fall –
Impaled Him on Her fiercest stakes –
He neutralized them all –

She stung Him – sapped His firm Advance –
But when Her Worst was done
And He – unmoved regarded Her –
Acknowledged Him a Man –

Who is the East?
The Yellow Man
Who may be Purple if He can
That carries in the Sun.

Who is the West?
The Purple Man
Who may be Yellow if He can
That lets Him out again.

SHEET FIFTY-ONE c. 1865

Nature rarer uses Yellow
Than another Hue –
Saves she all of that for Sunsets
Prodigal of Blue

o

Nature rarer uses: *Sent to Ns (lost) presumably c. 1865*

Spending Scarlet, like a Woman
Yellow she affords
Only scantly and selectly
Like a Lover's Words –

⁓

To help our Bleaker Parts
Salubrious Hours are given
Which if they do not fit for Earth –
Drill silently for Heaven – Arrange the Heart [for]

⁓

I've dropped my Brain –[63]
My Soul is numb –
The Veins that used to run
Stop palsied – 'tis Paralysis
Done perfecter in stone –

Vitality is Carved and cool –
My nerve in marble lies –
A Breathing Woman
Yesterday – endowed with Paradise.

Not dumb – I had a sort that moved –
A Sense that smote and stirred –
Instincts for Dance – a caper part –
An Aptitude for Bird –

Who wrought Carrara in me
And chiselled all my tune
Were it a witchcraft – were it Death –
I've still a chance to strain

To Being, somewhere – Motion – Breath –
Though Centuries beyond,
And every limit a Decade –
I'll shiver, satisfied.

⁓

The Opening and the Close
Of Being, are alike

Or differ, if they do,
As Bloom upon a Stalk –

That from an equal Seed
Unto an equal Bud
Go parallel, perfected
In that they have decayed –

SHEET FIFTY-TWO c. late 1865

This quiet Dust was Gentlemen and Ladies
And Lads and Girls –
Was laughter and ability and Sighing
And Frocks and Curls.

This Passive Place a Summer's nimble mansion
Where Bloom and Bees
Exist an Oriental Circuit
Then cease, like these –

There is a June when Corn is cut
And Roses in the Seed –
A Summer briefer than the first
But tenderer indeed

As should a Face supposed the Grave's
Emerge a single Noon
In the Vermillion that it wore
Affect us, and return –

Two Seasons, it is said, exist –
The Summer of the Just,
And this of ours, diversified
With Prospect – and with Frost –

May not our Second with its First
So infinite compare
That We but recollect the one
The other to prefer? [to] adore

This quiet Dust: *Sent to SD (variant) c. 1865*
There is a: *Sent to SD (first 2 lines, variant) c. June 1864*

To own the Art within the Soul
The Soul to entertain
With Silence as a Company
And Festival maintain

In an unfurnished Circumstance
Possession is to One
As an Estate perpetual
Or a reduceless Mine.

~

There is a finished feeling
Experienced at Graves –
A leisure of the Future –
A Wilderness of Size.

By Death's bold Exhibition
Preciser what we are
And the Eternal function
Enabled to infer.

~

SHEET FIFTY-THREE c. late 1865

The Robin is the One
That interrupt the Morn
With hurried – few – express Reports
When March is scarcely on –

The Robin is the One
That overflow the Noon
With her cherubic quantity –
An April but begun –

The Robin is the One
That speechless from her Nest
Submit that Home – and Certainty
And Sanctity, are best

~

'Twas Crisis – All the length had passed –
That dull – benumbing time

The Robin is: *Apparently sent to SD (lost) c. 1863 and to TWH (lost, published variant) spring 1863*

There is in Fever or Event –
And now the Chance had come –

The instant holding in its Claw
The privilege to live
Or Warrant to report the Soul [to] present
The other side the Grave.

The Muscles grappled as with leads [Muscles] struggled
That would not let the Will –
The Spirit shook the Adamant –
But could not make it feel – [it] tell –

The Second poised – debated – shot –
Another, had begun –
And simultaneously, a Soul
Escaped the House unseen –

We outgrow love, like other things
And put it in the Drawer –
Till it an Antique fashion shows –
Like Costumes Grandsires wore.

When I have seen the Sun emerge
From His amazing House –
And leave a Day at every Door
A Deed, in every place –

Without the incident of Fame
Or accident of Noise –
The Earth has seemed to me a Drum,
Pursued of little Boys

SHEET FIFTY-FOUR c. late 1865

A narrow Fellow in the Grass[64]
Occasionally rides –
You may have met Him – did you not
His notice sudden is –

o

A narrow Fellow: *Sent to unidentified recipient (published variant) c. 1865 and to SD (variant) c. late 1872*

The Grass divides as with a Comb –
A spotted shaft is seen –
And then it closes at your feet
And opens further on –

He likes a Boggy Acre
A Floor too cool for Corn
Yet when a Boy, and Barefoot –
I more than once at Noon
Have passed, I thought, a Whip lash
Unbraiding in the Sun
When stooping to secure it
It wrinkled, and was gone –

Several of Nature's People
I know, and they know me –
I feel for them a transport
Of cordiality –

But never met this Fellow
Attended, or alone
Without a tighter breathing
And Zero at the Bone –

Ashes denote that Fire was –
Revere the Grayest Pile — Respect [the]
For the Departed Creature's sake
That hovered there awhile –

Fire exists the first in light
And then consolidates
Only the Chemist can disclose
Into what Carbonates –

The Leaves like Women, interchange
Sagacious Confidence –
Somewhat of Nods and somewhat
Portentous inference –

o

The Leaves like: *Sent to SD (variant) c. 1865*

The Parties in both cases
Enjoining secrecy –
Inviolable compact
To notoriety.

~

SHEET FIFTY-FIVE c. late 1865

At Half past Three, a single Bird[65]
Unto a silent Sky
Propounded but a single term
Of cautious melody –

At Half past Four, Experiment
Had subjugated test
And lo, Her silver Principle
Supplanted all the rest –

At Half past Seven, Element
Nor Implement, be seen –
And Place was where the Presence was
Circumference between –

~

The last Night that She lived
It was a Common Night
Except the Dying – this to Us
Made Nature different

We noticed smallest things –
Things overlooked before
By this great light upon our minds
Italicized – as 'twere.

As We went out and in
Between Her final Room
And Rooms where Those to be alive
Tomorrow, were, a Blame

That others could exist
While She must finish quite

At Half past: *Sent to Josiah Holland (variant) c. 1865*

A Jealousy for Her arose
So nearly infinite –

We waited while She passed –
It was a narrow time –
Too jostled were Our Souls to speak
At length the notice came.

She mentioned, and forgot –
Then lightly as a Reed — [Then] softly
Bent to the Water, struggled scarce – — [Water,] shivered –
Consented, and was dead –

And We – We placed the Hair –
And drew the Head erect –
And then an awful leisure was
Belief to regulate – — With nought to – • Our faith to – [regulate –]

If Nature smiles – the Mother must
I'm sure, at many a whim
Of Her eccentric Family –
Is She so much to blame?

SHEET FIFTY-SIX c. late 1865

Dew – is the Freshet in the Grass –
'Tis many a tiny Mill
Turns unperceived beneath – our feet
And Artisan lies still – — [And] Small Estate stands – [still –]

We spy the Forests and the Hills
The Tents to Nature's Show
Mistake the Outside for the in
And mention what we saw.

Could Commentators on the Sign
Of Nature's Caravan
Obtain "admission" as a Child
Some Wednesday Afternoon.

Dew – is the: *Sent to SD (stanzas 2 and 3, variant) c. 1865*
Perception of an: *Sent to SD (variant) c. 1865*

Perception of an Object costs
Precise the Object's loss – more oft – [the]
Perception in itself a Gain
Replying to its price –

The Object absolute, is nought –
Perception sets it fair
And then upbraids a Perfectness
That situates so far – that 'tis so Heavenly far –

The Crickets sang[66]
And set the Sun
And Workmen finished one by one
Their Seam the Day upon –

The Bee had perished from the Scene
And distant as an Order done
And doubtful as Report upon
The Multitudes of Noon –

The low Grass loaded with the Dew
The Twilight leaned as Strangers do [Twilight] stood
With Hat in Hand, polite and new
To stay as if, or go –

A Vastness, as a Neighbor, came –
A Wisdom without Face or Name –
A Peace, as Hemispheres at Home
And so, the Night became –

Of the Heart that goes in, and closes the Door
Shall the Playfellow Heart complain
Though the Ring is unwhole, and the Company broke
Can never be fitted again? [be] matched –

The Crickets sang: *Sent, perhaps, to SB (three stanzas, variant) c. 1865 and to SD (three stanzas, variant) c. 1866*

SHEET FIFTY-SEVEN c. late 1865

These are the Signs to Nature's Inns –
Her invitation broad
To Whosoever famishing
To taste her mystic Bread –

These are the rites of Nature's House –
The Hospitality
That opens with an equal width
To Beggar and to Bee

For Sureties of her staunch Estate
Her undecaying Cheer
The Purple in the East is set
And in the North, the Star –

My Cocoon tightens – Colors teaze –
I'm feeling for the Air –
A dim capacity for Wings
Demeans the Dress I wear – Degrades [the]

A power of Butterfly must be –
The Aptitude to fly
Meadows of Majesty concedes [Majesty] implies –
And easy Sweeps of Sky –

So I must baffle at the Hint
And cipher at the Sign
And make much blunder, if at last
I take the clue divine –

The Bustle in a House
The Morning after Death
Is solemnest of industries
Enacted upon Earth –

The Sweeping up the Heart
And putting Love away
We shall not want to use again
Until Eternity –

The Sun went down – no Man looked on –
The Earth and I, alone,
Were present at the Majesty –
He triumphed, and went on –

The Sun went up – no Man looked on –
The Earth and I and One
A nameless Bird – a Stranger
Were Witness for the Crown –

SHEET FIFTY-EIGHT c. late 1865

One Day is there of the Series[67]
Termed Thanksgiving Day –
Celebrated part at Table
Part, in Memory –

Neither Patriarch nor Pussy
I dissect the Play –
Seems it to my Hooded thinking
Reflex Holiday –

Had there been no sharp Subtraction
From the early Sum –
Not an Acre or a Caption
Where was once a Room –

Not a mention, whose small Pebble
Wrinkled any Sea,
Unto Such, were such Assembly,
'Twere Thanksgiving Day.

The Luxury to apprehend[68]
The Luxury 'twould be
To look at Thee a single time
An Epicure of Me

In whatsoever Presence makes
Till for a further Food

One Day is: *Sent to SD (variant) c. 1867*
The Luxury to: *Sent to Ns (lost) and to SD (variant) c. 1864, and to TWH (variant) 16 July 1867*

I scarcely recollect to starve
So first am I supplied –

The Luxury to meditate
The Luxury it was
To banquet on thy Countenance
A Sumptuousness bestows

On plainer Days, whose Table far
As Certainty can see
Is laden with a single Crumb
The Consciousness of Thee.

⌒

The Robin for the Crumb
Returns no syllable
But long records the Lady's name
In Silver Chronicle.

⌒

He outstripped Time with but a Bout,
He outstripped Stars and Sun
And then, unjaded, challenged God
In presence of the Throne –

And He and He in mighty List
Unto this present, run,
The larger Glory for the less
A just sufficient Ring.

⌒

SHEET FIFTY-NINE c. late 1865

This is a Blossom of the Brain –
A small – italic Seed
Lodged by Design or Happening
The Spirit fructified –

Shy as the Wind of his Chambers [his] Lodgings
Swift as a Freshet's Tongue

The Robin for: *Sent to ED's Aunt Lucretia Bullard (variant) c. 1864*

So of the Flower of the Soul
Its process is unknown –

When it is found, a few rejoice
The Wise convey it Home
Carefully cherishing the spot
If other Flower become –

When it is lost, that Day shall be
The Funeral of God,
Upon his Breast, a closing Soul
The Flower of Our Lord –

~

All Circumstances are the Frame[69]
In which His Face is set –
All Latitudes exist for His
Sufficient Continent –

The Light His Action, and the Dark
The Leisure of His Will –
In Him Existence serve or set
A Force illegible.

~

A Shade upon the mind there passes
As when on Noon
A Cloud the mighty Sun encloses
Remembering

That some there be too numb to notice
Oh God
Why give if Thou must take away
The Loved?

~

It is an honorable Thought
And makes One lift One's Hat
As One met sudden Gentlefolk — [One] encountered [Gentlefolk]
Upon a daily Street

○

All Circustances are: *Sent to SD (variant) c. 1865*

That We've immortal Place
Though Pyramids decay
And Kingdoms, like the Orchard
Flit Russetly away

~

SHEET SIXTY c. late 1865

This Consciousness that is aware
Of Neighbors and the Sun
Will be the one aware of Death
And that itself alone

Is traversing the interval
Experience between
And most profound experiment
Appointed unto Men –

How adequate unto itself
Its properties shall be
Itself unto itself and None
Shall make discovery –

Adventure most unto itself
The Soul condemned to be –
Attended by a single Hound
Its own identity.

~

From Us She wandered now a Year,[70]
Her tarrying, unknown,
If Wilderness prevent her feet
Or that Etherial Zone

No Eye hath seen and lived
We ignorant must be –
We only know what time of Year
We took the Mystery.

~

This Consciousness that: *Sent to SD (final stanza, variant) c. 1864*
From Us She: *Sent to unidentified recipient (variant) c. early 1864*

The Sunset stopped on Cottages — [Sunset] dropped
Where Sunset hence must be
For treason not of His, but Life's,
Gone Westerly, Today –

The Sunset stopped on Cottages
Where Morning just begun – — [Where] Sunrise
What difference, after all, Thou mak'st
Thou Supercilious Sun?

Ample make this Bed
Make this Bed with Awe
In it wait till Judgment break
Excellent and Fair

Be its Mattress straight
Be its Pillow round
Let no Sunrise' Yellow noise
Interrupt this Ground.

SHEET SIXTY-ONE c. late 1865

Let down the Bars, Oh Death –[71]
The tired Flocks come in
Whose bleating ceases to repeat
Whose wandering is done –

Thine is the stillest night
Thine the securest Fold — [the] Paternal
Too near Thou art for seeking Thee
Too tender, to be told – — too willing, to be called

Reportless Subjects, to the Quick
Continual addressed –
But foreign as the Dialect
Of Danes, unto the rest.

Reportless Measures, to the Ear
Susceptive – stimulus –

Ample make this: *Perhaps sent to SD (variant) c. early 1864, to TWH (variant) 9 June 1866, and to Thomas Niles (variant) c. April 1883, referred to as "a Country Burial"*

But like an Oriental Tale
To others, fabulous –

The Definition of Beauty is
That Definition is none –
Of Heaven, easing Analysis,
Since Heaven and He are One.

Pain has but one Acquaintance
And that is Death –
Each one unto the other
Society enough –

Pain is the Junior Party
By just a Second's right –
Death tenderly assists Him
And then absconds from Sight –

Gratitude – is not the mention
Of a Tenderness,
But its still appreciation
Out of Plumb of Speech –

When the Sea return no Answer
By the Line and Lead
Proves it there's no Sea, or rather
A remoter Bed?

LEAF SIXTY-TWO c. 1871

Of Paul and Silas it is said[72]
They were in Prison laid
But when they went to take them out
They were not there instead.

Security the same insures
To our assaulted minds –

The Definition of: *Sent to SD (variant) c. early 1864*
Gratitude – is not: *Sent to Ns (first stanza, lost; transcribed by MLT as prose) and to SD (first stanza, variant) c. 1865*

The staple must be optional
That an Immortal binds.

~

LEAF SIXTY-THREE c. 1871

The Voice that stands for Floods to me
Is sterile borne to some –
The Face that makes the Morning mean
Glows impotent on them –

What difference in Substance lies
That what is Sum to me
By other Financiers be deemed
Exclusive Poverty!

~

LEAF SIXTY-FOUR c. 1871

"Remember me" implored the Thief![73]
Oh Hospitality!
My Guest "Today in Paradise"
I give thee guaranty.

That Courtesy will fair remain
When the Delight is Dust
With which we cite this mightiest case
Of compensated trust.

Of all we are allowed to hope
But Affidavit stands
That this was due where most we fear
Be unexpected Friends.

~

LEAF SIXTY-FIVE c. 1871

Somehow myself survived the Night
And entered with the Day –
That it be saved the Saved suffice
Without the Formula –

○

"Remember me" implored: *Sent to SD (variant) c. 1873*

Henceforth I take my living place
As one commuted led –
A Candidate for Morning Chance
But dated with the Dead.

LEAF SIXTY-SIX c. 1871

Because He loves Her[74]
We will pry and see if she is fair
What difference is on her Face
From Features others wear.

It will not harm her magic pace
That we so far behind –
Her Distances propitiate
As Forests touch the Wind

Not hoping for his notice vast
But nearer to adore
'Tis Glory's far sufficiency
That makes our trying poor.

'Tis Glory's overtakelessness
That makes our running poor.

LEAF SIXTY-SEVEN c. 1871

Some we see no more, Tenements of Wonder
Occupy to us though perhaps to them
Simpler are the Days than the Supposition
Their removing Manners
Leave us to presume.

That oblique Belief which we call Conjecture
Grapples with a Theme stubborn as sublime
Able as the Dust to equip its feature
Adequate as Drums to enlist the Tomb.

LEAF SIXTY-EIGHT c. 1871

Its Hour with itself
The Spirit never shows –

What Terror would enthrall the Street
Could Countenance disclose

The Subterranean Freight
The Cellars of the Soul –
Thank God the loudest Place he made
Is licensed to be still.

~

LEAF SIXTY-NINE c. 1871

My Triumph lasted till the Drums
Had left the Dead alone
And then I dropped my Victory
And chastened stole along
To where the finished Faces
Conclusion turned on me
And then I hated Glory
And wished myself were They.

What is to be is best descried
When it has also been –
Could Prospect taste of Retrospect
The Tyrannies of Men
Were Tenderer, diviner
The Transitive toward –
A Bayonet's contrition
Is nothing to the Dead –

~

LEAF SEVENTY c. 1871

Like Trains of Cars on Tracks of Plush
I hear the level Bee –
A Jar across the Flowers goes
Their Velvet Masonry

Withstands until the sweet Assault
Their Chivalry consumes –
While He, victorious tilts away
To vanquish other Blooms.

~

Not any higher: *Sent to TWH (variant) c. 1873*

LEAF SEVENTY-ONE c. 1871

Not any higher stands the Grave[75]
For Heroes than for Men –
Not any nearer for the Child
Than numb Three score and Ten –

This latest Castle equal holds — [latest] *Leisure* [equal] *lulls*
The Beggar and his Queen –
Propitiate this Democrat
A Summer's Afternoon!

LEAF SEVENTY-TWO c. 1871

The harm of Years is on him –
The infamy of Time –
Depose him like a Fashion
And give Dominion room –

Forget his Morning Forces –
The Glory of Decay
Is a minuter Pageant — Is a denuded Pageant
Than least Vitality. — Beside Vitality.

LEAF SEVENTY-THREE c. 1871

A Wind that rose though not a Leaf[76]
In any Forest stirred –
But with itself did cold commune — [cold] ~~engage~~
Beyond the realm of Bird.

A Wind that woke a lone Delight
Like Separation's Swell –
Restored in Arctic confidence
To the invisible.

A Wind that: *Sent to SD (variant, probably lost in part) c. early 1871 and to TWH (last stanza, variant) c. January 1874*

LEAF SEVENTY-FOUR c. 1871

I worked for chaff and earning Wheat
Was haughty and betrayed.
What right had Fields to arbitrate
In Matters ratified?

I tasted Wheat and hated Chaff
And thanked the ample friend –
Wisdom is more becoming viewed
At distance than at hand.

LEAF SEVENTY-FIVE c. 1871

The Bone that has no Marrow,[77]
What Ultimate for that?
It is not fit for Table
For Beggar or for Cat –

A Bone has obligations –
A Being has the same –
A Marrowless Assembly
Is culpabler than shame –

But how shall finished Creatures
A function fresh obtain?
Old Nicodemus' Phantom
Confronting us again!

LEAF SEVENTY-SIX c. 1871

Who goes to dine must take his Feast[78]
Or find the Banquet mean –
The Table is not laid without
Till it is laid within.

For Pattern is the Mind bestowed
That imitating her
Our most ignoble services
Exhibit worthier.

LEAF SEVENTY-SEVEN c. 1871

The Popular Heart is a Cannon first –
Subsequent a Drum –
Bells for an Auxiliary
And an Afterward of Rum –

Not a Tomorrow to know its name
Nor a Past to stare –
Ditches for Realms and a Trip to Jail
For a Souvenir.

LEAF SEVENTY-EIGHT c. 1871

It came at last but prompter Death
Had occupied the House –
His pallid Furniture arranged
And his metallic Peace –

Oh faithful Frost that kept the Date [faithful] Sleet
Had Love as punctual been
Delight had aggrandized the Gate
And blocked the coming in.

LEAF SEVENTY-NINE c. 1871

The pungent Atom in the Air
Admits of no debate –
All that is named of Summer Days
Relinquished our Estate –

For what Department of Delight
As positive are we
As Limit of Dominion
Or Dams – of Extasy –

LEAF EIGHTY c. 1871

Immortal is an ample word
When what we need is by
But when it leaves us for a time
'Tis a nescessity.

Of Heaven above the firmest proof
We fundamental know
Except for its marauding Hand
It had been Heaven below –

LEAF EIGHTY-ONE c. 1871

Are Friends Delight or Pain?
Could Bounty but remain
Riches were good –

But if they only stay
Ampler to fly away — Bolder – [to]
Riches are sad.

LEAF EIGHTY-TWO c. 1871

The Mountains stood in Haze –
The Valleys stopped below
And went or waited as they liked
The River and the Sky.

At leisure was the Sun –
His interests of Fire
A little from remark withdrawn –
The Twilight spoke the Spire.

So soft upon the Scene — [the] Place
The Act of evening fell
We felt how neighborly a thing
Was the Invisible.

Immortal is an: *Sent (last stanza, variant) to TWH, whose brother died on 9 March 1872*

LEAF EIGHTY-THREE c. 1871

Somewhere upon the general Earth
Itself exist Today –
The Magic passive but extant
That consecrated me –

Indifferent Seasons doubtless play
Where I for right to be – [to] go –
Would pay each Atom that I am [Would] pawn –
But Immortality –

Reserving that but just to prove
Another Date of Thee –
Oh God of Width, do not for us
Curtail Eternity! contract [Eternity!]

SHEET EIGHTY-FOUR c. 1871

Step lightly on this narrow spot –[79]
The broadest Land that grows
Is not so ample as the Breast
These Emerald Seams enclose.

Step lofty, for this name be told
As far as Cannon dwell
Or Flag subsist or Fame export
Her deathless syllable.

I cannot want it more –
I cannot want it less –
My Human Nature's fullest force
Expends itself on this.

And yet it nothing is
To him who easy owns –
Is Worth itself or Distance
He fathoms who obtains.

Step lightly on: *Sent to SD (first stanza, variant) c. 1871 and to TWH (variant) November 1871*

SHEET EIGHTY-FIVE c. 1871

The Days that we can spare[80]
Are those a Function die
Or Friend or Nature – stranded then
In our Economy

Our Estimates forsook [Estimates] *a scheme*
Our Affluence a Whim [Our] *ultimates* [a] *sham*
We let go all of Time without
Arithmetic of him

~

'Twas fighting for his Life he was –[81]
That sort accomplish well –
The Ordnance of Vitality
Is frugal of its Ball.

It aims once – kills once – conquers once –
There is no second War
In that Campaign inscrutable
Of the Interior.

~

Frigid and sweet Her parting Face –
Frigid and fleet my Feet –
Alien and vain whatever Clime
Acrid whatever Fate –

Given to me without the Suit
Riches and Name and Realm –
Who was She to withold from me
Penury and Home? Hemisphere [and]

~

An honest Tear
Is durabler than Bronze –
This Cenotaph
May each that dies –

○

The Days that: *Sent to TWH (variant) c. November 1871*

Reared by itself –
No Deputy suffice –
Gratitude bears
When Obelisk decays.

⸻

SHEET EIGHTY-SIX c. 1871

I should not dare to be so sad
So many Years again –
A Load is first impossible
When we have put it down –

The Superhuman then withdraws
And we who never saw
The Giant at the other side
Begin to perish now.

⸻

Remembrance has a Rear and Front.[82]
'Tis something like a House –
It has a Garret also
For Refuse and the Mouse –

Besides the deepest Cellar
That ever Mason laid –
Leave me not ever there alone
Oh thou Almighty God!

Look to it by its Contents • Fathoms
Ourselves be not pursued!

⸻

Because my Brook is fluent[83]
I know 'tis dry –
Because my Brook is silent
It is the Sea –

And startled at its swelling
I try to flee
To where the Strong assure me
Is "no more Sea" –

[its] *rising*

⸻

Remembrance has a: *Sent to Ns (lost, transcribed variant) c. 1871 and to TWH (variant) c. November 1871*

SHEET EIGHTY-SEVEN c. 1871

A little Dog that wags his tail[84]
And knows no other joy
Of such a little Dog am I
Reminded by a Boy

Who gambols all the living Day
Without an earthly cause
Because he is a little Boy
I honestly suppose –

The Cat that in the Corner dwells
Her martial Day forgot
The Mouse but a Tradition now
Of her desireless Lot

Another class remind me
Who neither please nor play
But not to make a "bit of noise"
Beseech each little Boy –

Oh Shadow on the Grass![85]
Art thou a step or not?
Go make thee fair, my Candidate –
My nominated Heart!

Oh Shadow on the Grass!
While I delayed to dress [to] guess
Some other thou did'st consecrate –
Oh unelected Face!

To make Routine a Stimulus
Remember it can cease –
Capacity to terminate
Is a specific Grace –
Of Retrospect the Arrow
That power to repair

A little Dog: *Sent to Ned Dickinson (last 8 lines, published variant, lost) presumably c. 1871*

Departed with the torment
Become, alas, more fair –

SHEET EIGHTY-EIGHT c. 1871

To disappear enhances –[86]
The Man who runs away   [Man] *that*
Is gilded for an instant   [Is] *tinctured*
With Immortality

But yesterday a Vagrant
Today in Memory lain
With superstitious value –   [superstitious] merit • *moment*
We tamper with again

But Never – far as Honor
Removes the paltry Thing   withdraws [the] worthless one
And impotent to cherish
We hasten to adorn –

Of Death the sternest feature   [the] sharpest function
That just as we discern
The Quality defies us –   [The] excellence
Securest gathered then

The Fruit perverse to plucking
But leaning to the Sight
With the extatic limit
Of unobtained Delight.

So much of Heaven has gone from Earth
That there must be a Heaven
If only to enclose the Saints
To Affidavit given –

The Missionary to the Mole
Must prove there is a Sky
Location doubtless he would plead   [would] urge
But what excuse have I?

o

To disappear enhances –: *Sent to SD (last 8 lines, variant) c. 1871 and to TWH (variant) late 1872*

Too much of Proof affronts Belief
The Turtle will not try
Unless you leave him – then return –
And he has hauled away.

SHEET EIGHTY-NINE c. 1872

So I pull my Stockings off[87]
Wading in the Water
For the Disobedience' Sake
Boy that lived for "Ought to" [for] "or'ter"

Went to Heaven perhaps at Death
And perhaps he didn't
Moses wasn't fairly used –
Ananias wasn't –

What we see we know somewhat
Be it but a little –
What we don't surmise we do
Though it shows so fickle

I shall vote for Lands with Locks
Granted I can pick 'em –
Transport's doubtful Dividend
Patented by Adam.

The Past is such a curious Creature
To look her in the Face
A Transport may receipt us [Transport] might –
Or a Disgrace –

Unarmed if any meet her
I charge him fly [him] flee –
Her faded Ammunition [Her] Rusty
Might yet reply. [Might] still – destroy –

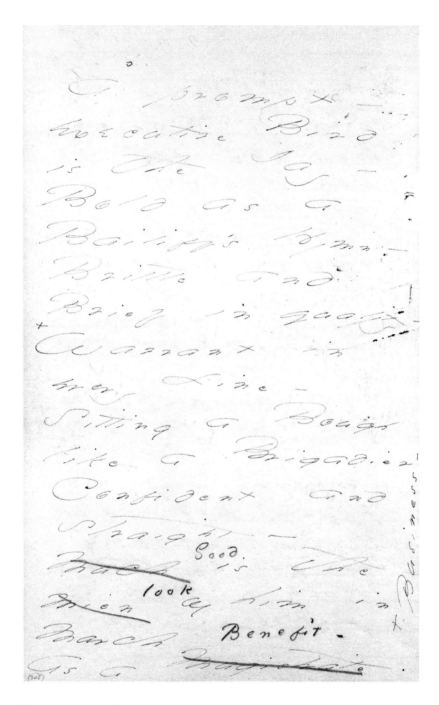

"A prompt – executive Bird is the Jay –"

A prompt – executive Bird is the Jay –[88]
Bold as a Bailiff's Hymn –
Brittle and Brief in quality –
Warrant in every Line – Business – [in]
Sitting a Bough like a Brigadier
Confident and straight –
Good is the look of him in March ~~Much~~ [is the] ~~mien~~
As a Benefit – [a] ~~Magistrate~~.

SHEET NINETY c. 1872

Now I knew I lost her –[89]
Not that she was gone –
But Remoteness travelled
On her Face and Tongue.

Alien, though adjoining
As a Foreign Race –
Traversed she though pausing
Latitudeless Place.

Elements Unaltered –
Universe the same
But Love's transmigration –
Somehow this had come –

Henceforth to remember
Nature took the Day
I had paid so much for –
His is Penury
Not who toils for Freedom
Or for Family
But the Restitution
Of Idolatry.

The Sea said[90]
"Come" to the Brook –
The Brook said
"Let me grow" –

A prompt – executive: *Sent to SD (variant) c. 1872*
The Sea said: *Apparently sent to SD (first stanza, lost, transcribed variant) perhaps c. 1872 and to TWH (variant) late 1872*

The Sea said
"Then you will be a Sea" –
"I want a Brook –
Come now" –
The Sea said
"Go" to the Sea –
The Sea said
"I am he
You cherished" –
"Learned Waters –
Wisdom is stale to me" –

LEAF NINETY-ONE c. 1873

September's Baccalaureate
A combination is
Of Crickets – Crows – and Retrospects
And a dissembling Breeze

That hints without assuming –
An Innuendo sear
That makes the Heart put up its Fun –
And turn Philosopher.

SHEET NINETY-TWO c. 1874

The Way to know the Bobolink[91]
From every other Bird
Precisely as the Joy of him –
Obliged to be inferred.

Of impudent Habiliment
Attired to defy,
Impertinence subordinate
At times to Majesty –

Of Sentiments seditious
Amenable to Law –

As Heresies of Transport
Or Puck's Apostacy –

Extrinsic to Attention
Too intimate with Joy –
He compliments Existence
Until allured away

By Seasons or his Children –
Adult and urgent grown –
Or unforeseen Aggrandizement
Or, happily, Renown – [Or,] possibly

By Contrast certifying
The Bird of Birds is gone –
How nullified the Meadow –
Her Sorcerer withdrawn!

~

Not with a Club, the Heart is broken[92]
Nor with a Stone –
A Whip so small you could not see it
I've known

To lash the Magic Creature
Till it fell,
Yet that Whip's Name
Too noble then to tell.

Magnanimous as Bird
By Boy descried –
Singing unto the Stone
Of which it died –

Shame need not crouch
In such an Earth as Ours –
Shame – stand erect –
The Universe is yours.

~

SHEET NINETY-THREE c. 1874

The Mushroom is the Elf of Plants –[93]
At Evening, it is not –
At Morning, in a Truffled Hut
It stop upon a Spot

As if it tarried always
And yet its whole Career
Is shorter than a Snake's Delay – [Snake's] Event –
And fleeter than a Tare –

'Tis Vegetation's Juggler –
The Germ of Alibi –
Doth like a Bubble antedate
And like a Bubble, hie –

I feel as if the Grass was pleased
To have it intermit –
This surreptitious Scion
Of Summer's circumspect.

Had Nature any supple Face
Or could she one contemn –
Had Nature an Apostate –
That Mushroom – it is Him!

A Bee his Burnished Carriage[94]
Drove boldly to a Rose –
Combinedly alighting –
Himself – his Equipage. [his] Carriage is – • was –

The Rose received his Visit
With frank tranquility,
Witholding not a Crescent
To his cupidity.

Their Moment consummated
Remained for him – to flee –
Remained for her, of Rapture
But the Humility.

The Mushroom is: *Sent to Ns (lost, transcribed variant) c. 1874 and to TWH (fourth stanza, variant) c. late May or early June 1874*

SHEET NINETY-FOUR c. 1875

A Dew sufficed itself –[95]
And satisfied a Leaf –
And felt "How vast a Destiny"! [And] ~~thought~~
"How trivial is Life"!

The Sun went out to work –
The Day went out to play –
But not again that Dew be seen
By Physiognomy –

Whether by Day abducted –
Or emptied by the Sun
Into the Sea – in passing –
Eternally unknown.

Attested to this Day
That awful Tragedy
By Transport's instability In Transport's Exegesis –
And Doom's celerity. And Hope's Necrology.

~

The Spider as an Artist
Has never been employed –
Though his surpassing Merit
Is freely certified

By every Broom and Bridget
Throughout a Christian Land –
Neglected Son of Genius
I take thee by the Hand –

~

Winter is good – his Hoar Delights
Italic flavor yield –
To Intellects inebriate
With Summer, or the World –

Generic as a Quarry
And hearty – as a Rose –

A Dew sufficed: *Sent to SD (variant) c. 1875*

Invited with asperity
But welcome when he goes.

~

SHEET NINETY-FIVE c. 1875

Delight's Despair at setting
Is that Delight is less
Than the sufficing Longing
That so impoverish.

Enchantment's Perihelion
Mistaken oft has been
For the Authentic orbit
Of its Anterior Sun.

~

Which is the best – the Moon or the Crescent?
Neither – said the Moon –
That is best which is not – Achieve it –
You efface the Sheen –

Not of detention is Fruition –
Shudder to attain.
Transport's decomposition follows –
He is Prism born.

~

A Rat surrendered here
A brief career of Cheer
And Fraud and Fear.

Of Ignominy's due
Let all addicted to
Beware –

The most obliging Trap
Its tendency to snap
Cannot resist –

Temptation is the Friend
Repugnantly resigned
At last.

~

This dirty – little – Heart
Is freely mine –
I won it with a Bun –
A Freckled shrine –

But eligibly fair
To him who sees
The Visage of the Soul
And not the knees.

SHEET NINETY-SIX c. 1875

How News must feel when travelling[96]
If News have any Heart
Alighting at the Dwelling — Advancing on the Transport
'Twill enter like a Dart! — 'Twill riddle like a Shot.

What News must think when pondering
If News have any Thought
Concerning the stupendousness
Of its perceiveless freight!

What News will do when every Man
Shall comprehend as one — [Shall] scrutinize.
And not in all the Universe
A thing to tell remain?

SHEET NINETY-SEVEN c. 1875

The last of Summer is Delight[97]
Deterred by Retrospect –
'Tis Ecstasy's revealed Review –
Enchantment's Syndicate.

To meet it – nameless as it is
Without celestial Mail –
Audacious as without a knock
To walk within the Vail.

The last of: *Sent to TWH (variant) January 1876*

The Heart is the Capital of the Mind[98]
The Mind is a single State –
The Heart and the Mind together make
A single Continent –

One – is the Population –
Numerous enough –
This ecstatic Nation
Seek – it is Yourself.

Not any more to be lacked –[99]
Not any more to be known –
Denizen of Significance
For a span so worn –

Even Nature herself
Has forgot it is there –
Sedulous of her Multitudes
Notwithstanding Despair –

Too elate of her Multitudes –
To retain Despair.

Of the Ones that pursued it
Suing it not to go
Some have solaced the longing
To accompany –

Some – rescinded the Wrench –
Others – Shall I say
Plated the residue of Adz
With Monotony.

SHEET NINETY-EIGHT c. 1875

After all Birds have been investigated[100]
And laid aside
Nature imparts the little Blue Bird –
Assured
Her conscientious voice
Will soar unmoved
Above ostensible vicissitude –

o

The Heart is: *Sent to TWH (variant) January 1876*
After all Birds: *Sent to SB (last 3 lines, variant) c. summer 1877 and to TWH (variant) August 1877, referred to as "a Blue Bird"*

First at the March
Competing with the Wind –
Her zealous Note
Delights it to ascend –
Last at the Scene
When Summer swerves away –
Fortitude – flanked with Melody.

~

The Mind lives on the Heart[101]
Like any Parasite –
If that is full of Meat
The Mind is fat –

But if the Heart omit –
Emaciate the Wit –
The Aliment of it
So absolute.

~

That sacred Closet when you sweep –
Entitled "Memory" –
Select a reverential Broom –
And do it silently –

'Twill be a Labor of surprise –
Besides Identity
Of other Interlocutors
A probability –

August the Dust of that Domain –
Unchallenged – let it lie –
You cannot supersede itself,
But it can silence you.

~

The Mind lives: *Sent to TWH (variant) January 1876*

LOOSE POEMS

Mute – thy coronation –
Meek – my Vive le roi, low – [my]
Fold a tiny courtier
In thine ermine, Sir,
There to rest revering
Till the pageant by,
I can murmur broken,
Master, It was I –

c. second half of 1860

Did the Harebell loose her girdle
To the lover Bee
Would the Bee the Harebell *hallow*
Much as formerly?

Did the "Paradise" – *persuaded* –
Yield her moat of pearl –
Would the Eden *be* an Eden,
Or the Earl – an *Earl?*

c. second half of 1860

If it had no pencil,[1]
Would it try mine –
Worn – now – and *dull* – sweet,
Writing much to thee.
If it had no word –
Would it make the Daisy,
Most as big as I was –
When it plucked me?

c. early 1861

No Rose, yet felt myself a'bloom,[2]
No Bird – yet rode in Ether –

c. summer 1861

Again – his voice is at the door –[3]
I feel the old *Degree* –
I hear him ask the servant
For such an one – as me –
  I take a *flower* – as I go –
My face to *justify* –
He never *saw* me – in *this life* –
I might *surprise* his eye! [might] not please
  I cross the Hall with *mingled* steps –
I – silent – pass the door – [I –] speechless
I look on all this world *contains* –
Just his face – nothing more!
  We talk in *careless* – and in *toss* – [talk in] venture
A kind of *plummet* strain –
Each – sounding – shily –
Just – how – deep –
The *other's* one – had been – [*other's*] foot had been
  We *walk* – I leave my Dog – at home – [Dog –] behind
A *tender* – *thoughtful* Moon
Goes with us – just a little way –
And – then – we are *alone* –
  Alone – if *Angels* are "alone" –
First time they *try* the *sky!*
Alone – if those "vailed faces" – be –
We cannot *count* – That murmur so – • [That] chant so – far –
On High!
I'd give – to live that hour – *again* –
The *purple* – *in my Vein* –
But *He* must *count the drops* – *himself* – [*He*] should
My price for *every stain!*

c. early 1862

Civilization – spurns – the Leopard!
Was the Leopard – bold?
Deserts – never rebuked her Satin –
Ethiop – her Gold –
Tawny – her Customs –
She was Conscious –
Spotted – her Dun Gown –
This was the Leopard's nature – Signor –
Need – a keeper – frown?

Pity – the Pard – that left her Asia!
Memories – of Palm –
Cannot be stifled – with Narcotic –
Nor suppressed – with Balm –

c. early 1862

Going – to – Her![4]
Happy – Letter! Tell Her –
Tell Her – the page I never wrote!
Tell Her, I only said – the Syntax –
And left the Verb and the Pronoun – out!
Tell Her just how the fingers – hurried –
Then – how they – stammered – slow – slow –
And then – you wished you had eyes – in your pages –
So you could see – what moved – them – so –

Tell Her – it wasn't a practised Writer –
You guessed –
From the way the sentence – toiled –
You could hear the Boddice – tug – behind you –
As if it held but the might of a Child!
You almost pitied – it – you – it worked so –
Tell Her – No – you may quibble – there –
For it would split Her Heart – to know it –
And then – you and I – were silenter!

Tell Her – Day – finished – before we – finished –
And the old Clock kept neighing – "Day"!

Going – to – Her!: *Sent to Ns (lost) c. early 1862, beginning "Going to them, happy letter!"*

And you – got sleepy –
And begged to be ended –
What could – it hinder so – to say?
Tell Her – just how she sealed – you – Cautious!
But – if she ask "where you are hid" – until the evening –
Ah! Be bashful!
Gesture Coquette –
And shake your Head!

c. early 1862

Of all the Souls that stand create –
I have Elected – One –
When Sense from Spirit – files away –
And Subterfuge – is done –
When that which is – and that which was –
Apart – intrinsic – stand –
And this brief Tragedy of Flesh – [brief] *Drama in the flesh*
Is shifted – like a Sand –
When Figures show their royal Front –
And Mists – are carved away,
Behold the Atom – I preferred –
To all the lists of Clay!

c. early 1862

The World – stands – solemner – to me –
Since I was wed – to Him –
A modesty – befits the soul
That bears another's – name –
A doubt – if it be fair – indeed –
To wear that perfect – pearl –
The Man – upon the Woman – binds –
To clasp her soul – for all –
A prayer, that it more angel – prove –
A Whiter Gift – within –
To that munificence, that chose –
So unadorned – a Queen –

A Gratitude – that such be true –
It had esteemed the Dream –
Too beautiful – for Shape to prove –
Or posture – to redeem!

c. early 1862

Me, change! Me, alter!
Then I will, when on the Everlasting Hill
A Smaller Purple grows –
At Sunset, or a lesser glow
Flickers upon Cordillera –
At Day's superior close!

c. 1862

We play at Paste –[5]
Till qualified for Pearl –
Then, drop the Paste –
And deem Ourself a fool –
The Shapes, tho', were similar,
And our new Hands
Learned Gem Tactics
Practising Sands –

c. 1865

The Wind begun to rock the Grass
With threatening Tunes and low –
He threw a Menace at the Earth –
A Menace at the Sky –

The Leaves unhooked themselves from Trees –
And started all abroad
The Dust did scoop itself like Hands
And throw away the Road.

o

We play at: *Sent to TWH (variant) 15 April 1862*
The Wind begun: *Sent to EH or the Hollands (variant) c. 1864, to SD (variant) c. 1866, to TWH (lost, transcribed variant) c. 1873, and to Thomas Niles (variant) April 1883, called "a Thunder Storm"*

The Wagons quickened on the Streets
The Thunder hurried slow –
The Lightning showed a Yellow Beak
And then a livid Claw –

The Birds put up the Bars to Nests –
The Cattle fled to Barns – [Cattle] ~~flung~~
There came one drop of Giant Rain
And then as if the Hands

That held the Dams had parted hold
The Waters wrecked the Sky –
But overlooked my Father's House –
Just quartering a Tree –

c. 1873

I never saw a Moor.[6]
I never saw the Sea –
Yet know I how the Heather looks
And what a Billow be –

I never spoke with God
Nor visited in Heaven –
Yet certain am I of the spot
As if the Checks were given –

c. early 1864

As Sleigh Bells seem in Summer[7] [Bells] sound
Or Bees, at Christmas show –
So fairy – so fictitious – [So] foreign [so]
The individuals do
Repealed from Observation –
A Party that we knew – [Party] whom
More distant in an instant
Than Dawn in Timbuctoo – [Dawn] on

c. early 1864

The spry Arms of the Wind ~~The long Arms~~ [of]
If I could crawl between
I have an errand imminent
To an adjoining Zone –
I should not care to stop,
My Process is not long
The Wind could wait without the Gate
Or stroll the Town among.
To ascertain the House
And is the Soul at Home [And] if [the] soul's within
And hold the Wick of mine to it
To light, and then return –

c. early 1864

These Strangers, in a foreign World,[8]
Protection asked of me –
Befriend them, lest Yourself in Heaven
Be found a Refugee –

c. early 1864

Love reckons by itself – alone –[9]
"As large as I" – relate the Sun
To One who never felt it blaze –
Itself is all the like it has –

c. 1864

Fame's Boys and Girls, who never die
And are too seldom born –

c. 1865

The Overtakelessness of Those[10]
Who have accomplished Death –
Majestic is to me beyond
The Majesties of Earth –

The Overtakelessness of: *Sent to SD (variant) c. 1865*

The Soul her "Not at Home"
Inscribes upon the Flesh,
And takes a fine aerial gait
Beyond the Writ of Touch.

c. 1865

~

Further in Summer than the Birds[11]
Pathetic from the Grass
A minor Nation celebrates
Its unobtrusive Mass

No Ordinance be seen
So gradual the Grace
A pensive Custom it becomes
Enlarging Loneliness.

Antiquest felt at Noon [Antique]F
When August burning low
Arise this spectral Canticle
Repose to typify.

Remit as yet no Grace
No Furrow on the Glow
Yet a Druidic – Difference
Enhances Nature now

c. early 1866

~

Purple – is fashionable twice –
This season of the year,
And when a soul perceives itself
To be an Emperor.

c. 1865

~

She sped as Petals of a Rose[12]
Offended by the Wind –

Further in Summer: *Sent to Gertrude Vanderbilt (variant) c. late summer 1865, to Ns (lost) perhaps c. 1865, to TWH (variant) 27 January 1866, to Thomas Niles (variant) March 1883, called "My Cricket," and to MLT (variant) later in 1883, with a cricket*

She sped as: *Sent (variant) to SD, whose niece died 3 November 1865*

A frail Aristocrat of Time
Indemnity to find –
Leaving on nature – a Default
As Cricket or as Bee –
But Andes, in the Bosoms where
She had begun to lie –

c. 1865

The Sky is low – the Clouds are mean.
A Travelling Flake of Snow
Across a Barn or through a Rut
Debates if it will go –
A Narrow Wind complains all Day
How some one treated him — How Parties treated him –
Nature, like Us is sometimes caught
Without her Diadem –

c. 1866

I cannot meet the Spring, unmoved –
I feel the old desire –
A Hurry with a lingering, mixed,
A Warrant to be fair –

A Competition in my sense
With something, hid in Her –
And as she vanishes, Remorse
I saw no more of Her –

c. 1866

Between the form of Life and Life
The difference is as big
As Liquor at the Lip between
And liquor in the Jug
The latter – excellent to keep – — [to] have
But for extatic need

The Sky is: *Sent to EH (lost) c. 1866*
I cannot meet: *Sent to SD (stanza 2, variant) c. 1866*

The corkless is superior –	~~Give me the corkless~~
I know for I have tried	

c. 1866

Paradise is of the Option.	
Whosoever will	
Dwell in Eden notwithstanding	*Own in* [Eden]
Adam and Repeal –	

c. 1866

His Bill is clasped – his Eye forsook	[is] locked [his Eye] estranged
His Feathers wilted low –	
The Claws that clung, like lifeless Gloves	
Indifferent hanging now –	[Indifferent] gathered
The Joy that in his happy Throat	
Was waiting to be poured	Assembled [to]
Gored through and through with Death, to be	
Assassin of a Bird	
Resembles to my outraged mind	
The firing in Heaven,	
On Angels – squandering for you	
Their Miracles of Tune –	[Their] unsuspecting • [unsus]picious [Tune –]

c. 1866

After the Sun comes out[13]	
How it alters the World –	
Wagons like messengers hurry about	
Yesterday is old –	Liverpool is old –
All men meet as if	Men express as if • [All men] pass – • haste [as if]
Each foreclosed a news –	
Fresh as a Cargo from Balize	
Nature's qualities –	

c. 1866

Paradise is of: *Sent to TWH (variant) 9 June 1866*
His Bill is: *Sent to Ns (lost) presumably c. 1866, beginning "His bill is locked, his eye estranged,"*

I fit for them –[14]
I seek the Dark
Till I am thorough fit.
The labor is a sober one
With the austerer sweet –

That abstinence of mine produce [of] me
A purer food for them, if I succeed,
If not I had
The transport of the Aim –

line 5: [With] an – • this – [austerer sweet –] • With this sufficient Sweet

c. 1866

The Frost of Death was on the Pane –[15]
"Secure your Flower" said he.
Like Sailors fighting with a Leak
We fought Mortality –

Our passive Flower we held to Sea –
To mountain – to the Sun –
Yet even on his Scarlet shelf
To crawl the Frost begun –

We pried him back
Ourselves we wedged
Himself and her between –
Yet easy as the narrow Snake
He forked his way along

Till all her helpless beauty bent
And then our wrath begun –
We hunted him to his Ravine
We chased him to his Den –

We hated Death and hated Life
And nowhere was, to go –
Than Sea and continent there is
A larger – it is Woe

c. 1866

The Frost of: *Sent to Ns (lost, transcribed variant) and to SD c. 1866*

A Diamond on the Hand[16]   ~~The~~ • a [Diamond]
To Custom Common grown
Subsides from its significance
The Gem were best unknown –
Within a Seller's shrine
How many sight and sigh
And cannot, but are mad with fear   [mad] for
That any other buy –

line 8: lest some one else should [buy –] • Lest Richer people buy –

c. 1867

Some Wretched creature, savior take
Who would exult to die
And leave for thy sweet mercy's sake   [sweet] patience'
Another Hour to me

line 4: [My] human Life [to me] • My earthly Hour to me

c. 1867

There is a strength in proving that it can be borne[17]   [a] good [in] knowing
Although it tear –
What are the sinews of such cordage for
Except to bear
The ship might be of satin had it not to fight –
To walk on seas requires cedar Feet   [on] tides

c. 1867

The Merchant of the Picturesque[18]
A Counter has and sales
But is within or negative
Precisely as the calls –
To Children he is small in price   [is] least
And large in courtesy –   [And] most
It suits him better than a check
Their artless currency –

Of Counterfeits he is so shy
Do one advance so near [one] obtain
As to behold his ample flight – [his] gentle –

c. 1867

None who saw it ever told it[19] they [who]
'Tis as hid as Death
Had for that specific treasure
A departing breath –
Surfaces may be invested [Surfaces] can [be] related
Did the Diamond grow
General as the Dandelion ~~Gentle~~ [as]
Would you serve it so? [you] seek

c. 1867

Soul, take thy risk,[20] [thy risk]s • chance
With Death to be
Were better than be not with thee

c. 1867

Too cold is this[21]
To warm with Sun –
Too stiff to bended be.
To joint this Agate were a work – [a] feat –
Outstaring Masonry –

How went the Agile Kernel out
Contusion of the Husk
Nor Rip, nor wrinkle indicate
But just an Asterisk.

line 5: Defying – • Appalling – • Abashing [Masonry –] • Beyond machinery –

c. 1867

There is another Loneliness
That many die without –
Not want of friend occasions it
Or circumstance of Lot

But nature, sometimes, sometimes thought
And whoso it befall
Is richer than could be revealed
By mortal numeral –

c. 1867

We do not know the time we lose –[22]
The awful moment is
And takes its fundamental place
Among the certainties –

A firm appearance still inflates
The card – the chance – the friend –
The spectre of solidities
Whose substances are sand –

c. 1867

The Lightning is a yellow Fork
From Tables in the Sky
By inadvertent fingers dropt
The awful Cutlery [The] solemn

Of mansions never quite disclosed
And never quite concealed
The Apparatus of the Dark
To ignorance revealed –

c. 1867

The murmuring of Bees has ceased[23]
But murmuring of some

There is another: *Apparently sent to SD (lost, published variant) perhaps c. 1867*
The murmuring of: *Sent to SD (variant) c. 1867*

Posterior, prophetic
Has simultaneous come –

The lower metres of the Year
When Nature's Laugh is done –
The Revelations of the Book
Whose Genesis was June

Appropriate Creatures to her change
The typic mother sends –
As Accent fades to interval   [Accent] ~~wanes~~
With separating Friends

Till what we speculate has been
And thoughts we will not show
More intimate with us become
Than Persons that we know –

line 13: [Till what we] ~~could not see, has come~~ • [could not] ~~choose~~ • ~~prove~~ • ~~name~~ • ~~face~~

c. 1867

The smouldering embers blush –[24]
Oh Cheek within the Coal   [Oh] *Heart*
Hast thou survived so many nights?   [many] *years*
The smouldering embers smile –

Soft stirs the news of Light   [Soft] stir the Flakes
The stolid Rafters glow   [stolid] Hours • instants • *centres* • *seconds*
One requisite has Fire that lasts
Prometheus never knew –

lines 7–8: [One requisite has] earthly • mortal • thorough Fire / [Prometheus] did not know
This requisite has Fire that lasts / It must at first be true –

c. 1868

Paradise is that old mansion[25]
Many owned before –
Occupied by each an instant
Then reversed the Door –

Bliss is frugal of her Leases
Adam taught her Thrift
Bankrupt once through his excesses –

c. 1868

In thy long Paradise of Light
No moment will there be
When I shall long for Earthly Play
And mortal Company –

c. 1868

Soft as the massacre of Suns   [massacre]s
By Evening's sabres slain   [Evening's] sabre

c. 1868

The Bird did prance – the Bee did play –[26]
The Sun ran miles away
So blind with joy he could not choose   [So] ~~full of~~
Between his Holiday –   the [Holiday –]

The morn was up – the meadows out
The Fences all but ran –
Republic of Delight, I thought
Where each is Citizen –

From Heavy laden Lands to thee   [laden] Climes
Were seas to cross to come
A Caspian were crowded –
Too near thou art for Fame –   [Too] close

c. 1868

Tell as a Marksman – were forgotten[27]
Tell – this Day endures   [Tell –] till now

Ruddy as that Coeval Apple
The Tradition bears – [The] Heroism

Fresh as Mankind that humble story new [as]
Though a statelier Tale while [a]
Grown in the Repetition hoary [Grown] by
Scarcely would prevail – [Scarcely] could

Tell had a son – The ones that knew it [that] heard
Need not linger here – [not] tarry
Those who did not to Human nature [Those] that do
Will subscribe a Tear – Would [subscribe]

Tell would not bare his Head
In Presence
Of the Ducal Hat –
Threatened for that with Death – by Gessler –
Tyranny bethought

Make of his only Boy a Target
That surpasses Death –
Stolid to Love's supreme entreaty [Love's] sublime
Not forsook of Faith – [Not] forgot

Mercy of the Almighty begging – Power [of the Almighty] asking
Tell his Arrow sent –
God it is said replies in Person
When the Cry is meant

c. 1868

After a hundred years
Nobody knows the Place [Nobody] knew
Agony that enacted there
Motionless as Peace

Weeds triumphant ranged
Strangers strolled and spelled
At the lone Orthography
Of the Elder Dead

Winds of Summer Fields
Recollect the way –

Instinct picking up the Key
Dropped by memory –

c. 1868

~

These are the Nights that Beetles love –[28]   [Nights] ~~the Beetle loves~~
From Eminence remote
Drives ponderous perpendicular
His figure intimate –   this [figure]
The terror of the Children   [The] transport
The merriment of men   [The] jeopardy
Depositing his Thunder
He hoists abroad again –
A Bomb upon the Ceiling
Is an improving thing –
It keeps the nerves progressive   [nerves] ~~in progress~~
Conjecture flourishing –
Too dear the Summer evening   [dear] ~~were s~~[ummer]
Without discreet alarm –
Supplied by Entomology
With its remaining charm   [With] a

c. 1868

~

'Tis my first night beneath the Sun
If I should spend it here –   [I] ~~shall~~
Above him is too low a hight
For his Barometer
Who Airs of expectation breathes
And takes the Wind at prime –
But Distance his Delights confides
To those who visit him

c. 1868

~

The Wind took up the Northern Things
And piled them in the South –   [And] showed them to

Then gave the East unto the West   [Then] bent – • bowed
And opening his mouth   [opening] its
The Four Divisions of the Earth
Did make as to devour   Presumed as to [devour]
While everything to corners slunk
Behind the awful power –   Like Worms beneath • before [the]

The Wind unto his Chamber went   [unto] its [Chamber]s
And nature ventured out –
Her subjects scattered into place
Her systems ranged about   [systems] stole

Again the smoke from Dwellings rose   [Dwellings] curled
The Day abroad was heard –   [The Day] resumed abroad
How intimate, a Tempest past   [How] orderly the
The Transport of the Bird –   [The] Rapture – • Triumph • Riot of the Bird –

c. 1868

I noticed People disappeared[29]
When but a little child –
Supposed they visited remote
Or settled Regions wild –
Now know I – They both visited   ~~I know now~~
And settled Regions wild –
But did because they died   [But] ~~vaster~~ • ~~vaster, that~~
A Fact witheld the little child –   ~~the~~ [Fact witheld] a

c. 1869

The Snow that never drifts –
The transient, fragrant snow
That comes a single time a Year
Is softly driving now –

So thorough in the Tree
At night beneath the star   [night] below
That it was February's Foot   [February's] Face • self
Experience would swear –   [Experience] ~~could~~

o

Like Winter as a Face
We stern and former knew
Repaired of all but Loneliness
By Nature's Alibi –

Were every Storm so spice — [every] Gale • snow [so] fair • sweet
The Value could not be –
We buy with contrast –
Pang is good
As near as memory –

c. 1869

That odd old man is dead a year –
We miss his stated Hat –
'Twas such an evening bright and stiff
His faded lamp went out –

Who miss his antiquated Wick – — [antiquated] Light –
Are any hoar for him? — [any] bleak
Waits any indurated mate
His wrinkled coming Home?

Oh Life, begun in fluent Blood
And consummated dull –
Achievement, contemplating thee – — [contemplating] this – • here
Feels transitive and cool.

c. 1869

Exhiliration is the Breeze[30]
That lifts us from the Ground
And leaves us in another place
Whose statement is not found –

Returns us not, but after time
We soberly descend
A little newer for the term
Upon Enchanted Ground –

c. 1869

Best Witchcraft is Geometry[31]
To the magician's mind –
His ordinary acts are feats
To thinking of mankind –

c. 1869

The duties of the Wind are few –[32]
To cast the ships, at Sea,
Establish March, the Floods escort,
And usher Liberty.

The pleasures of the Wind are broad,
To dwell Extent among,
Remain, or wander,
Speculate, or Forests entertain –

The kinsmen of the Wind, are Peaks
Azof – the Equinox,
Also with Bird and Asteroid
A bowing intercourse –

The limitations of the Wind
Do he exist, or die,
Too wise he seems for Wakelessness,
However, know not I –

c. 1869

The Day grew small, surrounded tight[33]
By early, stooping Night –
The Afternoon in Evening deep
Its Yellow shortness dropt –
The Winds went out their martial ways
The Leaves obtained excuse –
November hung his Granite Hat
Upon a nail of Plush –

c. 1869

Best Witchcraft is: *Sent to SD (first 2 lines, variant) c. 1869*
The duties of: *Sent to SD (stanza 1, variant) c. 1869*
The Day grew: *Sent to SD c. 1869*

Great Streets of silence led away
To Neighborhoods of Pause –
Here was no Notice – no Dissent
No Universe – no Laws –

By Clocks, 'twas Morning, and for Night
The Bells at Distance called –
But Epoch had no basis here
For Period exhaled.

c. 1870

Some Days retired from the rest[34]
In soft distinction lie
The Day that a Companion came
Or was obliged to die

c. 1870

Of Nature I shall have enough
When I have entered these
Entitled to a Bumble bee's
Familiarities –

c. 1870

The Suburbs of a Secret
A Strategist should keep –
Better than on a Dream intrude
To scrutinize the Sleep –

c. 1870

The incidents of love
Are more than its Events –

Great Streets of: *Sent to Ns (lost) c. spring 1870 and to SD (variant) c. 1870*
Some Days retired: *Apparently sent to SD (variant) c. 1870*
The Suburbs of: *Apparently sent to SD c. 1870*
The incidents of: *Sent to SD (variant) c. 1870*

Investment's best Expositor
Is the minute Per Cents –

c. 1870

Alone and in a Circumstance[35] [and] of
Reluctant to be told
A spider on my reticence
Assiduously crawled deliberately • determinately • impertinently [crawled]

And so much more at Home than I
Immediately grew
I felt myself a visitor [myself] the
And hurriedly withdrew – [And] hastily

Revisiting my late abode with articles of claim
I found it quietly assumed as a Gymnasium [assumed] for
Where Tax asleep and Title off
The inmates of the Air [The] Peasants
Perpetual presumption took [Perpetual] complacence
As each were special Heir – [were] only • lawful
If any strike me on the street
I can return the Blow –
If any take my property [any] seize
According to the Law
The Statute is my Learned friend
But what redress can be
For an offence nor here nor there [offence] ~~not~~ [here nor there] • [not] anywhere
So not in Equity –
That Larceny of time and mind
The marrow of the Day
By spider, or forbid it Lord
That I should specify –

c. 1870

Contained in this short Life[36]
Are magical extents
The soul returning soft at night
To steal securer thence

As Children strictest kept
Turn soonest to the sea
Whose nameless Fathoms slink away
Beside infinity

c. 1870

Nature affects to be sedate — [Nature] was known
Upon Occasion, grand
But let our observation shut — [observation] *halt*
Her practises extend — [Her] qualities
To Necromancy and the Trades
Remote to understand — astute • obscure [to]
Behold our spacious Citizen — [Behold] my • this
Unto a Juggler turned –

c. 1870

Where every Bird is bold to go
And Bees abashless play
The Foreigner before he knocks
Must thrust the Tears away –

c. 1870

The Riddle that we guess[37]
We speedily despise –
Not anything is stale so long
As Yesterday's Surprise.

c. October 1870

Experiment escorts us last – — [Experiment] ~~accosts~~
His pungent company
Will not allow an Axiom
An Opportunity –

c. October 1870

Too happy Time dissolves itself
And leaves no remnant by –
'Tis Anguish not a Feather hath
Or too much weight to fly –

c. October 1870

We introduce ourselves
To Planets and to Flowers
But with ourselves
Have etiquettes
Embarrassments
And awes

c. 1870

Had we known the Ton she bore — [the] ~~weight~~ • ~~Load~~
We had helped the terror
But she straighter walked for Freight
So be hers the error –

lines 3–4: Smiled too brave for the detecting • our detection / Till arrested here • [Till] Discovered here –

c. 1870

Oh Sumptuous moment[38]
Slower go
That I may gloat on thee – — ~~Till I~~ • Till [I] can [gloat]
'Twill never be the same to starve
Now I abundance see – — since that [abundance]
Which was to famish, then or now –
The difference of Day
Ask him unto the Gallows led – — to [him unto the Gallows] called
With morning in the sky — By [morning]

c. 1870

376

That this should
feel the need
of Death
the same as those
that lives
Is such a stroke
Hight - treat - pass-
of Irony
As never was
achieved.
As makes one
hide its head-
hang

not satisfied to
ape the Great in
his simplicity
the small must
die, the same
as he. as well as He.

What a Pomposity.
an absurdity.
Perversity.
Oh the pom
posity
Oh the Audacity.

"That this should feel the need of Death"

AMHERST 375–376, BOX 5, FOLDERS 16, 17 (2 PP.); COURTESY OF AMHERST COLLEGE ARCHIVES AND SPECIAL COLLECTIONS

A great Hope fell[39]
You heard no noise   [no] crash
The Ruin was within   [The] havoc • damage
Oh cunning Wreck
That told no Tale
And let no Witness in

The mind was built for mighty Freight
For dread occasion planned
How often foundering at Sea
Ostensibly, on Land

c. 1870

A not admitting of the wound[40]
Until it grew so wide
That all my Life had entered it
And there were troughs beside –   [there] was space • room

A closing of the simple lid that opened to the sun   [simple] Gate
Until the tender Carpenter   [the] sovereign • unsuspecting Carpenters
Perpetual nail it down –

c. 1870

That this should feel the need of Death
The same as those that lived
Is such a Feat of Irony   [a] ~~stroke~~ • ~~Hight –~~ • ~~pass~~
As never was achieved –

Not satisfied to ape the Great in his simplicity
The small must die, the same as he –   [must] ~~do~~ • [must die,] as well as He –
Oh the audacity –

line 4: [As never was] ~~beheld~~ – • ~~As makes one hide its head~~ – • hang [~~its head –~~]
line 7: ~~What a Pomposity~~ – • ~~an absurdity~~ – • ~~Perversity~~ – • ~~Oh the pomposity~~

c. 1870

The Frost was never seen –[41]
If met, too rapid passed,
Or in too unsubstantial Team –
The Flowers notice first

A Stranger hovering round
A Symptom of alarm
In Villages remotely set
But search effaces him

Till some retrieveless night
Our Vigilance at waste
The Garden gets the only shot
That never could be traced.

Unproved is much we know –
Unknown the worst we fear –
Of Strangers is the Earth the Inn
Of Secrets is the Air – [Of] Travellers the [Air –]

To Analyze perhaps
A Philip would prefer
But Labor vaster than myself
I find it to infer.

c. 1870

We like March – his Shoes are Purple –[42]
He is new and high –
Makes he Mud for Dog and Peddler –
Makes he Forest dry –
Knows the Adder's Tongue his coming
And begets her Spot.
Stands the Sun so close and mighty
That our Minds are hot –
News is he of all the others –
Bold it were to die
With the Blue Birds buccaneering
On his British Sky.

c. 1878

We like March –: *Sent to SD (variant) c. 1871 and perhaps to MLT (last stanza) c. 1883, signed "March"*

Society for me my misery
Since Gift of Thee –

c. 1871

Safe Despair it is that raves –
Agony is frugal.
Puts itself severe away
For its own perusal.

Garrisoned no Soul can be
In the Front of Trouble –
Love is one, not aggregate –
Nor is Dying double –

c. 1871

We never know how high we are
Till we are asked to rise [are] called
And then if we are true to plan [to] growth
Our statures touch the skies –

The Heroism we recite
would be a normal thing [a] daily
Did not ourselves the Cubits warp
For fear to be a King –

c. 1871

This slow Day moved along –
I heard its axles go
As if they could not hoist themselves
They hated motion so –

I told my soul to come –
It was no use to wait –
We went and played and came again
And it was out of sight

c. 1871

Safe Despair it: *Sent to SD (variant) c. 1871*

A soft Sea washed around the House
A Sea of Summer Air
And rose and fell the magic Planks
That sailed without a care –
For Captain was the Butterfly
For Helmsman was the Bee   ~~How gracious~~ [was] • [For] steersman [was]
And an entire universe
For the delighted Crew –

c. 1871

Whatever it is – she has tried it –[43]   [it] be [she]
Awful Father of Love –   [Awful] ~~Founder~~
Is not Ours the chastising –
Do not chastise the Dove –

Not for Ourselves, petition –
Nothing is left to pray –
When a subject is finished –   [is] ended –
Words are handed away –   Language is driven – [away –]

Only lest she be lonely
In thy beautiful House
Give her for her Transgression
License to think of us –   [to] ~~cherish us~~

lines 7–8: When the subject is taken / The words are withered away
[When the subject] is stolen / [The] speech is [withered away]

c. 1871

On the World you colored
Morning painted rose –
Idle his Vermillion
Aimless crept the Glows   [Aimless] stole
Over Realms of Orchards
I the Day before
Conquered with the Robin –
Misery – how fair

Till your wrinkled Finger
Shoved the Sun away — pushed [the]
Midnight's awful Pattern
In the Goods of Day –

c. 1871

Lest they should come – is all my fear
When sweet incarcerated – here

c. 1871

All men for Honor hardest work
But are not known to earn –
Paid after they have ceased to work
In Infamy or Urn –

c. 1871

Shall I take thee, the Poet said
To the propounded word?
Be stationed with the Candidates
Till I have finer tried – — [have] further • vainer

The Poet searched Philology — [Poet] probed
And was about to ring — [And] just • when [about]
for the suspended Candidate
There came unsummoned in – — Advanced [unsummoned]
That portion of the Vision
The Word applied to fill
Not unto nomination
The Cherubim reveal –

c. 1872

Fly – fly – but as you fly –[44]
Remember – the second pass you by –

The Second is pursuing the Century
The Century is chasing Eternity –
Ah the Responsibility –
No wonder that the little Second flee –
Out of its frightened way –

line 5: ~~Such a Responsibility~~ • ~~What a~~ – • *what a* [Responsibility]

c. 1872

Like Rain it sounded till it curved[45] [it] swelled
And then I knew 'twas Wind – [then] *we*
It walked as wet as any Wave
But swept as dry as Sand –
When it had pushed itself away
To some remotest Plain
A coming as of Hosts was heard
That was indeed the Rain –
It filled the Wells, it pleased the Pools
It warbled in the Road –
It pulled the spigot from the Hills
And let the Floods abroad –
It loosened acres, lifted seas
The sites of Centres stirred
Then like Elijah rode away
Upon a Wheel of Cloud –

c. 1872

The Clouds their Backs together laid[46]
The North begun to push
The Forests galloped till they fell
The Lightning played like mice [Lightning] skipped

The Thunder crumbled like a stuff
How good to be in Tombs [How] safe • firm • calm
Where nature's Temper can not reach [Temper] ~~could~~ [not]
Nor missile ever comes [Nor] vengeance

c. 1872

We like a Hairbreadth 'scape I [like]
It tingles in the Mind
Far after Act or Accident
Like paragraphs of Wind [Like] ~~Articles~~

If we had ventured less [If] I
The Gale were not so fine [The] *Breeze*
That reaches to our utmost Hair
Its Tentacles divine. [Its] Resonance

c. 1872

The Sun and Fog contested
The Government of Day –
The Sun took down his Yellow Whip
And drove the Fog away –

c. 1872

Had I not seen the Sun
I could have borne the shade
But Light a newer Wilderness
My Wilderness has made –

c. 1872

If my Bark sink[47]
'Tis to another Sea –
Mortality's Ground Floor [Mortality's] ~~first~~
Is Immortality –

c. 1872

Look back on Time with kindly Eyes –[48]
He doubtless did his best –
How softly sinks that trembling Sun [sinks] his
In Human Nature's West –

c. 1872

Risk is the Hair that holds the Tun
Seductive in the Air –
That Tun is hollow – but the Tun –   [the] one
With Hundred Weights – to spare –
Too ponderous to suspect the snare
Espies that fickle chair
And seats itself to be let go   [And] mounts to be to atoms hurled –
By that perfidious Hair –

The "foolish Tun" the Critics say –
While that delusive Hair   [that] obliging – • enchanting –
Persuasive as Perdition,
Decoys its Traveller   [its] Passenger

c. 1872

Let my first knowing be of thee
With morning's warming Light –
And my first Fearing, lest Unknowns
Engulph thee in the night –

c. 1872

Fortitude incarnate
Here is laid away
In the swift Partitions
Of the awful Sea –   [the] ~~swinging~~

Babble of the Happy   ~~Carol~~ – [of]
Cavil of the Bold
Hoary the Fruition   ~~wrinkled~~ – • ~~arid~~ – • ~~shrunken~~ • ~~Evil~~ • ~~rigid~~ [the Fruition]
But the Sea is old   [the] ~~Deep~~

Edifice of Ocean   ~~Architect~~ • ~~Edifice~~ [of]
Thy tumultuous Rooms
Suit me at a venture
Better than the Tombs   ~~Rather than~~ [the]

line 11: ~~please~~ [me at a venture] • ~~Fit me for a Lodging~~ • ~~suit~~ [~~me for a Lodging~~]

c. 1872

The Clover's simple Fame[49]
Remembered of the Cow –
Is better than enameled Realms
Of notability.
Renown perceives itself
And that degrades the Flower – [that] profanes
The Daisy that has looked behind
Has Compromised its power –

c. 1872

A Sparrow took a slice of Twig[50]
And thought it very nice
I think, because his empty Plate
Was handed Nature twice –

Invigorated fully – sprang lightly to the sky
As an accustomed stirrup –
And boldly rode away –

lines 5–7: [Invigorated fully –] Absconded daintily – • *fluently* / The Epicure of Courtesy • Purposes / As of Amenity – • Propriety
[Invigorated fully –] Rose softly in the sky / As a familiar Stirrup / To mount Immensity –
[Invigorated fully –] As speculations flee / By no Conclusion • Derision hindered / ~~Left~~ – • Rose surreptitiously –
[Invigorated fully –] Turned easy in the sky / As a familiar saddle – / And rode immensity
lines 6–7: The Epicure of Firmaments / As of Frugality – • The Epicure of Vehicles / As of Velocity.
line 7: And rode Immensity • And rode deriding by – • And gaily galloped by –

c. 1872

A Stagnant pleasure like a Pool
That lets its Rushes grow
Until they heedless tumble in
And make the Water slow

o

A Sparrow took: *Sent to SD (variant) c. 1872*

Impeding navigation bright   impede the [navigation] fair
Of Shadows going down   [Of] Ripples
Yet even this shall rouse itself   [shall] stir
When Freshets come along –

c. 1872

As old as Woe –[51]
How old is that?
Some Eighteen thousand years –
As old as Bliss   [as] Joy –
How old is that   or The age of that
They are of equal years –

Together chiefest they are found   [Together] chiefly
But seldom side by side –   Tho' [seldom]
From neither of them tho' he try   ~~not~~ [neither]
Can Human nature hide   may [Human]

c. 1872

Is Heaven a Physician?
They say that He can heal –
But Medicine Posthumous
Is unavailable –
Is Heaven an Exchequer?
They speak of what we owe –
But that negotiation
I'm not a Party to –

c. 1872

The Lilac is an ancient Shrub[52]
But ancienter than that
The Firmamental Lilac
Upon the Hill Tonight –
The Sun subsiding on his Course
Bequeathes this final plant

To Contemplation – not to Touch – To spectacle, but not to Touch
The Flower of Occident.

Of one Corolla is the West –
The Calyx is the Earth –
The Capsule's burnished Seeds the Stars –
The Scientist of Faith
His research has but just begun –
Above his Synthesis
The Flora unimpeachable
To Time's Analysis –
"Eye hath not seen" may possibly
Be current with the Blind
But let not Revelation
By Theses be detained – [be] profaned –

c. 1872

Until the Desert knows
That Water grows
His Sands suffice
But let him once suspect
That Caspian Fact
Sahara dies

Utmost is relative –
Have not or Have
Adjacent Sums
Enough – the first Abode
On the familiar Road
Galloped in Dreams –

line 6: Contentment dies • Creation dies • His status dies • Standard denies

c. 1872

Tell all the truth but tell it slant –
Success in Circuit lies
Too bright for our infirm Delight [Too] bold
The Truth's superb surprise

As Lightning to the Children eased
With explanation kind
The Truth must dazzle gradually — [dazzle] moderately
Or every man be blind –

c. 1872

Like Time's insidious wrinkle
On a beloved Face –
We clutch the Grace the tighter
Though we resent the Crease — but • while [we]
The Frost himself so comely — [Frost] ~~itself~~
Dishevels every prime
Asserting from his Prism
That none can punish him

line 1: [Time's] invading • presuming • appointed • foreclosing – • repealing • appointed –

c. 1872

Through what transports of Patience
I reached the stolid Bliss
To breathe my Blank without thee
Attest me this and this – — Remit me this and this
By that bleak exultation
I won as near as this
Thy privilege of dying
Abbreviate me this

c. 1872

He preached about Breadth till it argued him narrow
The Broad are too broad to define
And of Truth until it proclaimed him a Liar
The Truth never flaunted a sign – — [never] ~~hoisted~~
Simplicity fled from his counterfeit presence
As Gold the Pyrites would shun — [Gold] – a [Pyrites]

He preached about: *Sent to TWH (variant) late 1872, beginning "He preached upon 'Breadth' till it argued him narrow –"*

What confusion would cover the innocent Jesus
To meet so Religious a man –

line 1: [He preached] *upon* [Breadth till] ~~we knew he was~~ [narrow]
line 8: at meeting • [to meet] so accomplished • [so] ~~learned~~ • enabled • discerning • accoutred • established • conclusive [a man –]

c. 1872

A Word dropped careless on a Page[53]
May stimulate an Eye — [May] consecrate
When folded in perpetual seam
The Wrinkled Maker lie — [Wrinkled] Author

Infection in the sentence breeds
We may inhale Despair — ~~And~~ [we inhale]
At distances of Centuries
From the Malaria –

c. 1872

I thought that nature was enough[54]
Till Human nature came
But that the other did absorb — ~~And~~ [that]
As Parallax a Flame – — [As] Firmament

Of Human nature just aware
There added the Divine
Brief struggle for capacity –
The power to contain
Is always as the contents
But give a Giant room
And you will lodge a Giant — [you] shall [lodge a Giant] • A Giant is your Tenant
And not a smaller man — [a] lesser –

c. 1872

The Show is not the Show[55]
But they that go –

A Word dropped: *Sent to Ns (first stanza, lost, published variant) c. late 1872*
The Show is: *Sent to TWH (2 lines, variant) c. December 1872*

Menagerie to me
My Neighbor be –
Fair Play –
Both went to see –

c. 1872

"Was Not" was all the statement.[56]
The Unpretension stuns –
Perhaps – the Comprehension –
They wore no Lexicons –

But lest our Speculation
In inanition die
Because "God took him" mention –
That was Philology –

c. 1873

So proud she was to die[57]
It made us all ashamed
That what we cherished, so unknown
To her desire seemed –
So satisfied to go
Where none of us should be
Immediately – that Anguish stooped
Almost to Jealousy –

c. 1873

The things we thought that we should do[58]
We other things have done
But those peculiar industries
Have never been begun –

The Lands we thought that we should seek –
When large enough to run –
By Speculation ceded
To Speculation's Son –

o

The things we: *Sent to TWH c. spring 1876*

The Heaven in which we hoped to pause
When discipline was done –
Untenable to Logic
But possibly the one –

c. 1876

~

Who were "the Father and the Son"[59]
We pondered when a child – ~~I~~ [pondered]
And what had they to do with us [with] ~~me~~
And when portentous told [when] ~~in terror~~

With inference appalling [inference] ~~alarming~~
By childhood fortified [By] ~~Distance~~
We thought, at least they are no worse ~~I~~ [thought]
Than they have been described.

Who are "the Father and the Son"
Did we demand Today [Did] ~~I~~
"The Father and the Son" himself
Would doubtless specify – [doubtless] ~~answer me~~ –

But had they the felicity ~~had~~ [they the] ~~readiness~~
When we desired to know, [When] ~~I~~
We better Friends had been, perhaps,
Than time ensue to be –

We start – to learn that we believe
But once – entirely –
Belief, it does not fit so well
When altered frequently –

We blush – that Heaven if we achieve – [if we] ~~behold~~
Event ineffable –
We shall have shunned until Ashamed
To own the Miracle –

lines 5–6: ~~Through Accents terrible as Death / To one that never died –~~

c. 1873

~

Who were "the: *Sent to TWH (lost, transcribed variant) c. 1873*

Could Hope inspect her Basis — [inspect] its
Her Craft were done –
Has a fictitious Charter — Her Charter is fictitious
Or it is none – — [Or] she ~~has~~

Balked in the vastest instance
But to renew –
Felled by but one assassin –
Prosperity –

c. 1873

I know Suspense – it steps so terse
And turns so weak away –
Besides – Suspense is neighborly
When I am riding by –

Is always at the Window
Though lately I descry
And mention to my Horses
The need is not of me – — The Fact • Look is not for me –

c. 1873

The most triumphant Bird[60]
I ever knew or met
Embarked upon a Twig Today
And till Dominion set
I perish to behold another such a might
And sang for nothing in the World — [nothing] scrutable
But competent Delight – — [But] absolute • impudent
Retired and resumed
His transitive estate
To what delicious accident
Does finest Glory fit –

line 5: [I perish to behold] so delicate • so adequate [a might] • so competent a sight

c. 1873

The most triumphant: *Sent to Ns (lost, transcribed variant) c. 1873 and to EH (variant) c. early summer 1873*

There is no Frigate like a Book[61]
To take us Lands away [take] one
Nor any Coursers like a Page
Of prancing Poetry –
This Travel may the poorest take [This] Traverse
Without offence of Toll – [Without] *oppress*
How frugal is the Chariot
That bears the Human Soul –

c. 1873

Power is a familiar growth –
Not distant – not to be – [Not] *foreign*
Beside us like a bland Abyss
In every company –
Escape it – there is but a chance –
When consciousness and clay
Lean forward for a final glance
Disprove that, and you may – Dispel that and you may –

c. 1873

Elijah's wagon had no thill –[62]
Was innocent of wheel –
Elijah's Horses as unique
As was his Vehicle –
Elijah's Journey – to portray
With him the skill remain [the] Right – • art –
Who justified Elijah
In that uncommon scene – [that] consummate

line 2: Was ignorant of wheel • was not enforced of wheel – • [was] un[enforced of wheel –]

lines 6–8: with him remain the skill / [Who justified Elijah] • Who Justified Elijah in his eccentric style • [Who Justified] the former [in his eccentric style] • [Who] authorized [Elijah in his] peculiar [style]

c. 1873

There is no: *Sent to Ns (lost, transcribed variant) c. 1873*

Left in immortal Youth
On that low Plain
That hath nor Retrospection [nor] Peradventure
Nor Again –
Ransomed from years –
Sequestered from Decay
Canceled like Dawn
In comprehensive Day –

c. 1873

Yesterday is History,
'Tis so far away –
Yesterday is Poetry – 'tis Philosophy –
Yesterday is mystery –
Where it is Today
While we shrewdly speculate [we] sage • shrewd investigate
Flutter both away

c. 1873

The Beggar at the Door for Fame
Were easily supplied
But Bread is that Diviner thing [that] Majestic thing
Disclosed to be denied displayed to be – [denied]

c. 1873

In this short Life that only lasts an hour [that] merely
How much – how little – is within our power

c. 1873

A Deed knocks first at Thought
And then – it knocks at Will –
That is the manufactoring spot
And Will at Home and well

o

It then goes out an Act
Or is entombed so still
That only to the Ear of God
Its Doom is audible –

c. 1873

I think that the Root of the Wind is Water –[63]
It would not sound so deep
Were it a Firmamental Product –
Airs no Oceans keep –
Mediterranean intonations –
To a Current's Ear –
There is a maritime conviction
In the Atmosphere –

c. 1873

Not one by Heaven defrauded stay –[64]
Although he seem to steal
He restitutes in some sweet way
Secreted in his will –

c. 1873

A Single Clover Plank   [Single] Clover Spar
Was all that saved a Bee   Alone sustained – • upheld – [a Bee]
A Bee I personally knew
From sinking in the sky –   In crisis in the sky – • in Hazard [in]

Twixt Firmament above
And Firmament below
The Billows of Circumference
Were sweeping him away –

The idly swaying Plank
Responsible to nought
A sudden Freight of Wind assumed   A sudden Freight • weight of wind took on –
And Bumble Bee was not –

This harrowing event
Transpiring in the Grass
Did not so much as wring from him
A wandering "Alas" –

c. 1873

Longing is like the Seed
That wrestles in the Ground,
Believing if it intercede
It shall at length be found –

The Hour, and the Clime, [and the] *Zone*
Each Circumstance unknown –
What Constancy must be achieved
Before it see the Sun!

c. 1873

The Day She goes
Or Day she stays
Are equally supreme –
Existence has a stated width
Departed, or at Home –

c. 1873

The Butterfly in honored Dust[65]
Assuredly will lie
But none will pass the Catacomb [pass] man's
So chastened as the Fly –

c. 1873

Recollect the Face of me[66]
When in thy Felicity,
Due in Paradise today
Guest of mine assuredly –

Longing is like: *Sent to TWH (variant) and to EH (variant) c. 1873*

Other Courtesies have been –
Other Courtesy may be –
We commend ourselves to thee
Paragon of Chivalry –

c. 1873

Warm in her Hand these accents lie
While faithful and afar
The Grace so awkward for her sake
Its fond subjection wear –

c. 1873

To break so vast a Heart
Required a Blow as vast –
No Zephyr felled this Cedar straight –
'Twas undeserved Blast –

c. 1873

Lain in Nature – so suffice us
The enchantless Pod
When we advertise existence
For the missing Seed –

Maddest Heart that God created
Cannot move a sod
Pasted by the simple summer
On the Longed for Dead – [the] soldered – [Dead –]

c. 1873

Had we our senses
But perhaps 'tis well they're not at Home Tho' [perhaps]
So intimate with Madness
He's liable with them That's • 'Tis [liable]

○

Had we the eyes within our Head –   [Head]s –
How well that we are Blind –   [How] prudent [we]
We could not look upon the Earth –   [the] World
So utterly unmoved –

c. 1873

Art thou the thing I wanted?[67]
Begone – my Tooth has grown –
Supply the minor Palate   invite • Endow some [minor]
That has not starved so long –   [That] was
I tell thee while I waited
The mystery of Food
Increased till I abjured it
And dine without   [And] grow
Like God –

c. 1873

'Twas later when the summer went
Than when the Cricket came –
And yet we knew that gentle Clock
Meant nought but Going Home –
'Twas sooner when the Cricket went
Than when the Winter came
Yet that pathetic Pendulum
Keeps Esoteric Time.

c. 1873

Because that you are going[68]
And never coming back
And I, however accurate,   [however] absolute
May overlook your track,   [May] ~~misconceive~~ • misinfer
Because that Death is Treason   [is] *final* • different
However true it be –   [However] due • just • first
This instant be abolished   This instant be suspended
To all but Fealty –   Above mortality

o

Because that you: *Sent to TWH (variant) January 1874*

Significance, that each has lived — Omnipotence [that]
The other to detect –
Discovery, not God himself
Could now annihilate –
Eternity, presumption,
The instant I perceive
That you, who were existence
Yourself forgot to live –

"The Life that is", will then have been
A thing I never knew,
As Paradise, fictitious,
Until the Realm of you.
The "Life that is to be" to me
A Residence too plain
Unless in my Redeemer's Face
I recognize your own –

Of Immortality who doubts
He may exchange with me — [may] confer
Curtailed by your obscuring Face — [your] removing
Of everything but he,
Of Heaven and Hell I also yield
The Right to reprehend
To whoso would commute this Face
For his less priceless Friend –

If "God is Love" as he admits,
We think that he must be
Because he is a jealous God
He tells us certainly –
If "All is possible" with him
As he besides concedes –
He will refund us finally
Our confiscated Gods –

c. January 1874

There's the Battle of Burgoyne –[69] — That's [the]
Over, every Day,

By the Time that Man and Beast
Put their work away –
"Sunset" sounds majestic –
But that solemn War
Could you comprehend it
You would chastened stare –

c. 1874

While we were fearing it, it came –[70]
But came with less of fear
Because that fearing it so long
Had almost made it fair –

There is a Fitting – a Dismay –
A Fitting – a Despair –
'Tis harder knowing it is Due
Than knowing it is Here.

The Trying on the Utmost
The Morning it is New
Is terribler than wearing it
A whole existence through –

c. 1874

Our little secrets slink away –
Beside God's shall not tell – [God's] will
He kept his word a Trillion years
And might we not as well –
But for the niggardly delight
To make each other stare
Is there no sweet beneath the sun
With this that may compare –

c. 1874

The Notice that is called the Spring
Is but a month from here – [month] ~~away~~ –

Put up my Heart thy Hoary work
And take a Rosy Chair –

Not any House the Flowers keep –
The Birds enamor Care –
Our salary the longest Day
Is nothing but a Bier –

c. 1874

~

Dear March – Come in –[71]
How glad I am –
I hoped for you before – [I] looked
Put down your Hat –
You must have walked –
How out of Breath you are –
Dear March, how are you, and the Rest –
Did you leave Nature well –
Oh March, Come right up stairs with me –
I have so much to tell –

I got your Letter, and the Birds –
The Maples never knew that you were coming –
I declare – how Red their Faces grew – till I called [how Red]
But March, forgive me – and [March,]
All those Hills you left for me to Hue –
There was no Purple suitable –
You took it all with you –

Who knocks? That April –
Lock the Door –
I will not be pursued –
He stayed away a Year to call
When I am occupied –
But trifles look so trivial
As soon as you have come the instant that [you]

That Blame is just as dear as Praise
And Praise as mere as Blame –

c. 1874

~

Go slow, my soul, to feed thyself[72]
Upon his rare Approach –
Go rapid, lest Competing Death
Prevail upon the Coach –
Go timid, lest his final eye – [timid,] *should* [his] testing • blazing • lofty
Determine thee amiss –
Go boldly – for thou paid'st his price — But [boldly –]
Redemption – for a Kiss – — Thy Total – • [Thy] Being – [for]

c. 1874

The vastest earthly Day[73]
Is shrunken small — Is chastened • shrivelled • dwindled small
By one Defaulting Face — By one heroic Face
Behind a Pall – — that owned it all –

c. 1874

Surprise is like a thrilling – pungent –
Upon a tasteless meat.
Alone – too acrid – but combined
An edible Delight –

c. 1874

I never hear that one is dead — [hear] that one has died –
Without the chance of Life
Afresh annihilating me
That mightiest Belief,

Too mighty for the Daily mind
That tilling its abyss,
Had Madness, had it once or, Twice
The yawning Consciousness, — [The] Consciousness of this.

Beliefs are Bandaged, like the Tongue
When Terror were it told
In any Tone commensurate
Would strike us instant Dead –

Go slow, my: *Sent to Ns (lost, transcribed variant) c. spring 1874*

I do not know the man so bold
He dare in lonely Place   [in] lonesome Place – • secret Place
That awful stranger – Consciousness
Deliberately face –   look squarely in the Face.

c. 1874

How many schemes may die[74]
In one short Afternoon
Entirely unknown
To those they most concern –
The man that was not lost   [not] robbed • killed • wrecked
Because by accident   Because ~~he was detained~~ –
He varied by a Ribbon's width
From his accustomed route –
The Love that would not try
Because beside the Door   [Because] before
Some unsuspecting Horse was tied
Surveying his Despair

c. 1874

The Symptom of the Gale –
The Second of Dismay –
Between its Rumor and its Face –
Is almost Revelry –   [almost] ecstasy –

The Houses firmer root –
The Heavens cannot be found –   [The] Trees – • Sky – • Field –
The Upper Surfaces of things
Take covert in the Ground –

The Mem'ry of the Sun
Not Any can recall –
Although by Nature's sterling Watch
So scant an interval –

And when the Noise is caught
And Nature looks around –

"We dreamed it"? she interrogates –
"Good Morning" – we propound?

c. 1874

The Butterfly's Assumption Gown[75]
In Chrysoprase Apartments hung
This Afternoon put on –

How condescending to descend
And be of Buttercups the friend
In a New England Town –

c. 1874

When a Lover is a Beggar
Abject is his Knee –
When a Lover is an Owner
Different is he –

What he begged is then the Beggar –
Oh disparity –
Bread of Heaven resents bestowal
Like an obloquy [an] obloquy –

c. 1874

My Heart ran so to thee
It would not wait for me
And I affronted grew [I] discouraged
And drew away
For whatsoe'er my pace
He first achieve thy Face – [first] espouse
How general a Grace
Allotted two –

Not in malignity
Mentioned I this to thee –
Had he obliquity
Soonest to share [to] spare

But for the Greed of him – [the] like • vaunt
Boasting my Premium – wooing [my]
Basking in Bethleem winning [in]
Ere I be there –

c. 1874

Abraham to kill him[76]
Was distinctly told – [Was] directly –
Isaac was an Urchin –
Abraham was old –

Not a hesitation –
Abraham complied –
Flattered by Obeisance
Tyranny demurred –

Isaac – to his Children
Lived to tell the tale –
Moral – with a Mastiff
Manners may prevail. will – [prevail.]

c. 1874

Knock with tremor –[77]
These are Caesars –
Should they be at Home
Flee as if you trod unthinking
On the Foot of Doom –

These seceded from your summons
Centuries ago –
Should they rend you with "How are you"
What have you to show?

line 6: [These seceded from your] ~~summits~~ • ~~subjects~~ • ~~substance~~ • summons
[These] receded to *accostal*

c. 1874

Whether they have forgotten   [Whether] it has
Or are forgetting now
Or never remembered –
Safer not to know

Miseries of conjecture
Are a softer wo
Than a Fact of Iron   [a] news
Hardened with I know –   ~~Fastened~~ [with]

c. 1874

Floss won't save you from an Abyss
But a Rope will –
Notwithstanding a Rope for a Souvenir   To be sure – [a Rope]
Is not beautiful –   does not look as well –

But I tell you every step is a Trough –   [a] sluice
And every stop a well –
Now will you have the Rope or the Floss?
Prices reasonable –   Fate has both to sell –

c. 1874

Elisabeth told Essex[78]
That she could not forgive   Herself [could]
The clemency of Deity
However – might survive –
That secondary succor
We trust that she partook
When suing – like her Essex
For a reprieving Look –

c. 1874

The Pile of Years is not so high[79]
As when you came before
But it is rising every Day   [is] higher – • further
From recollection's Floor

And while by standing on my Heart — [by] stepping
I still can reach the top — [can] touch
Efface the burden with your face
And catch me ere I drop

line 7: [Efface the] *mountain* • monster • stature • spectre • trouble – [with your face]
line 8: or [catch me] when • as [I drop] • [And catch me ere I] ~~softly climb~~

c. 1874

Time does go on –
I tell it gay to those who suffer now –
They shall survive –
There is a Sun –
They don't believe it now –

c. 1874

From his slim Palace in the Dust
He relegates the Realm,
More loyal for the exody
That has befallen him.

c. 1874

Without a smile –[80]
Without a throe
A Summer's soft assemblies go — Do • our – Nature's soft [assemblies]
To their entrancing end
Unknown – for all the times we met –
Estranged, however intimate –
What a dissembling Friend –

c. 1874

As Summer into Autumn slips[81]
And yet we sooner say

As Summer into: *Sent to Ns (transcribed variant) c. 1874 and to SB (variant) c. October 1874*

The Summer than the Autumn – lest
We turn the Sun away [the] spell

And count it almost an Affront
The Presence to concede
Of one however lovely – not
The one that we have loved

So we evade the Charge of Years
On one attempting shy
The Circumvention of the *Shaft* [the] ~~Thought~~ • ~~site~~ – • ~~Fact~~ –
Of Life's Declivity –

c. 1874

To flee from memory
Had we the Wings
Many would fly [would] soar
Inured to slower things [to] other
Birds with dismay [with] *surprise*
Would scan the mighty Van
Of men escaping
From the mind of man

line 6: [Would scan the] eager • breathless • thrilling • hurrying van • fluttering Van • *cowering Van*

c. 1874

The Infinite a sudden Guest
Has been assumed to be –
But how can that stupendous come
Which never went away?

c. 1874

The most pathetic thing I do[82]
Is play I hear from you –
I make believe until my Heart
Almost believes it too

But when I break it with the news
You knew it was not true [knew] that
I wish I had not broken it –
Goliah – so would you –

c. 1874

I send you a decrepit flower[83]
That nature sent to me
At parting – she was going south
And I designed to stay –

Her motive for the souvenir [Her] object in [the] souvenir
If sentiment for me [sentiment] it be
Or circumstance prudential
Witheld invincibly – Secreted utterly – • reserved [utterly –]

c. 1874

Wonder – is not precisely knowing
And not precisely knowing not –
A beautiful but bleak condition
He has not lived who has not felt –

Suspense – is his maturer Sister –
Whether Adult Delight is Pain [Delight] be
Or of itself a new misgiving – [itself] the
This is the Gnat that mangles men –

c. 1874

How soft this Prison is[84]
How sweet these sullen bars
No Despot but the King of Down
Invented this repose

Of Fate if this is all
Has he no added Realm

How soft this: *Sent to EH (stanza 1, variant) late January 1875, beginning "How soft his Prison is –"*

A Dungeon but a Kinsman is
Incarceration – Home.

c. 1875 SD

His Mansion in the Pool[85]
The Frog forsakes –
He rises on a Log
And statements makes –
His Auditors two Worlds
Deducting me –
The Orator of April
Is hoarse Today –
His Mittens at his Feet
No Hand hath he – [Hand] has
His eloquence a Bubble
As Fame should be –
Applaud him to discover
To your chagrin
Demosthenes has vanished
In Waters Green – [In] Forums –

c. 1875

A little madness in the Spring[86]
Is wholesome even for the King
But God be with the Clown
Who ponders this Tremendous scene
This sudden legacy of Green
As if it were his own –

line 5: [This] gay • bright • *quick* • whole • swift – • fleet • sweet • whole [legacy of Green] [This] fair *Apocalypse* of Green – • This whole Apocalypse of Green – • [This whole] Experience – • Astonishment – • Periphery – • *Experiment* • wild Experiment [of Green]

c. 1875

A little madness: *Sent to SD (variant) and to EH (variant) c. 1875*

Pink – small – and punctual –[87]
Aromatic – low –
Covert in April –
Candid – in May –

Dear to the Moss –
Known of the Knoll –
Next to the Robin
In every Human Soul –

Bold little Beauty –
Bedecked with thee
Nature forswears
Antiquity –

c. 1875

You Cannot take itself
From any Human soul – [any] living –
That indestructible estate
Enable him to dwell – [Enable] each • it
Impregnable as Light
That every man behold [That] All the world behold
But take away as difficult
As undiscovered Gold –

line 5: Extravagant as Light • As opulent [as Light] • Luxurious • Abundant as the [Light]
line 7: [But] take away as easily – • take away as impotent

c. 1875

Luck is not chance –
It's Toil – or 'Tis Toil –
Fortune's expensive smile
Is earned –
The Father of the Mine
Is that old fashioned Coin
We spurned – Disowned –

c. 1875

Pink – small – and: *Sent to SD (variant) and to TWH (variant) c. 1875*

Let me not mar that perfect Dream
By an Auroral stain
But so adjust my daily Night
That it will come again.

Not when we know, the Power accosts –
The Garment of Surprise
Was all our timid Mother wore
At Home – in Paradise.

c. 1875

Lift it – with the Feathers ~~Launch it~~
Not alone we fly –
Launch it – the aquatic
Not the only sea –
Advocate the Azure
To the lower Eyes –
He has obligation
Who has Paradise –

c. 1875

That short – potential stir
That each can make but once –
That Bustle so illustrious
'Tis almost Consequence –

Is the eclat of Death –
Oh – thou unknown Renown
That not a Beggar would accept
Had he the power to spurn –

c. 1875

Escape is such a thankful Word[88]
I often in the Night

Let me not: *Apparently sent to SD (stanza 2, variant) c. 1875*

Consider it unto myself
No spectacle in sight [No] Monster then in sight • [No] Citadel [in]

Escape – it is the Basket
In which the Heart is caught
When down some awful Battlement
The rest of Life is dropt –

'Tis not to sight the savior –
It is to be the saved –
And that is why I lay my Head
Upon this trusty word –

c. 1875

Crisis is sweet and yet the Heart[89]
Upon the hither side
Has Dowers of Prospective
Surrendered by the Tried –

Inquire of the proudest Rose [the] fullest • *closing*
Which rapture – she preferred [Which] Hour – • Triumph • moment
And she will tell you sighing –
The transport of the Bud –

line 4: Witheld to the arrived – • Debarred – • denied [to the arrived] • *To Denizen denied*
line 7: [And she] ~~would~~ answer [sighing –] • [And she] will point undoubtedly • And she will point you fondly • longingly • *sighing*
line 8: [The] rapture [of the Bud –] • *The Hour of her Bud* – • [The] session of [her Bud –] To her surrendered Bud • *To her rescinded Bud* • [To her] rescinded • Departed – • Expended • receding • Receipted Bud

c. 1875

I'd rather recollect a Setting
Than own a rising Sun
Though one is beautiful forgetting [beautiful] Secession
And true the other one.

o

Because in going is a Drama
Staying cannot confer – [Staying] could not
To die divinely once a twilight – [once] an evening • [a] Limit
Than wane is easier – [Than] live

line 4: [And] real • bland the newer • [new]est • And best the newest one – • [And] fine • fair [the newest one –]

c. 1875

An antiquated Grace[90] it's [antiquated]
Becomes that cherished Face [that] magic
As well as prime *better than* [prime]
Enjoining us to part
We and our plotting Heart
Good friends with time

line 5: [We and our] scheming • Tinsel • gaudy Heart • We and our *pouting Heart*

c. 1875

Upon a Lilac Sea
To toss incessantly
His Plush Alarm
Who fleeing from the Spring
The Spring avenging fling
To Dooms of Balm –

c. 1875

The Rat is the concisest Tenant.[91]
He pays no Rent.
Repudiates the Obligation –
On Schemes intent

Balking our Wit
To sound or circumvent –
Hate cannot harm
A Foe so reticent –

Upon a Lilac: *Sent to HHJ (last 3 lines) upon her marriage to William Sharpless Jackson, 22 October 1875*
The Rat is: *Sent to SD c. 1875 and to TWH (variant) c. January 1876*

Neither Decree prohibit him –
Lawful as Equilibrium.

c. 1875

Unto the Whole – how add?
Has "All" a further Realm –
Or Utmost an Ulterior?
Oh, Subsidy of Balm!

c. 1875

"Faithful to the end" amended[92]
From the Heavenly clause –
Constancy with a Proviso
Constancy abhors –

"Crowns of Life" are servile Prizes
To the stately Heart,
Given for the Giving, solely, [for] the Majesty –
No Emolument –

c. early 1876

I suppose the time will come[93]
Aid it in the coming
When the Bird will crowd the Tree
And the Bee be booming –

I suppose the time will come
Hinder it a little
When the Corn in Silk will dress [in] Gilt
And in Chintz the Apple [in] Red – • Pink –

I believe the Day will be
When the Jay will giggle
At his new white House the Earth
That, too, halt a little –

c. 1876

"Faithful to the: *Sent to TWH (variant) c. January 1876 and to SD (stanza 1, variant) c. early 1876*

Those Cattle smaller than a Bee
That herd upon the Eye –
Whose tillage is the passing Crumb – [Whose] pasture [is the] wandering
Those Cattle are the Fly –
Of Barns for Winter – blameless – [Winter –] ignorant
Extemporaneous stalls
They found to our objection – [our] abhorrence
On Eligible Walls –
Reserving the presumption
To suddenly descend
And gallop on the Furniture –
Or odiouser offend – [Or] otherwise • fataller –
Of their peculiar calling
Unqualified to judge
To Nature we remand them
To justify or scourge –

c. 1876

The Butterfly's Numidian Gown[94]
With spots of Burnish – roasted on
Is proof against the Sun –
But prone to shut its spotted Fan Though – • yet – [prone to shut] his
And panting on a Clover lean
As if it were undone –

c. 1876

Of his peculiar light[95]
We keep one ray –
To clarify the sight
To seek him by –

c. 1876

How firm eternity must look
To crumbling men like me – [like] thee

Of his peculiar: *Sent to TWH (variant) c. August 1876, beginning "Of their peculiar light"*

The only adamant Estate
In all Identity –

How mighty to the insecure – momentous [to]
Thy Physiognomy
To whom not any Face cohere – [Face] present – • propound
Unless concealed in thee.

line 8: [Unless] affixed to thee – • intrenched • inlaid in thee

c. 1876

Gathered into the Earth,
And out of story –
Gathered to that strange Fame –
That lonesome Glory
That hath no omen here – but Awe –

c. 1876

The Sun is one – and on the Tare
He doth as punctual call
As on the conscientious Flower
And estimates them all –

c. 1876

The worthlessness of Earthly things[96]
The Ditty is that Nature Sings –
And then – enforces their delight
Till Synods are inordinate –

c. 1876

Dreams are the subtle Dower
That make us rich an Hour –
Then fling us poor
Out of the Purple Door

Into the Precinct raw — Into the minute raw
Possessed before – — We owned before – • Abhorred [before –]

c. 1876

His Heart was darker than the starless night[97]
For that there is a morn — [For that] somewhere is morn
But in this black Receptacle
Can be no Bode of Dawn
Can be no bode of Dawn

c. 1876

Touch lightly Nature's sweet Guitar
Unless thou know'st the Tune
Or every Bird will point at thee
Because a Bard too soon –

line 4: That wert a Bard too soon • The Bard to silence born –

c. 1876

In many and reportless places[98]
We feel a Joy –
Reportless, also, but sincere as Nature
Or Deity –

It comes, without a consternation –
Dissolves – the same – — abates – • Exhales – [the]
But leaves a sumptuous Destitution – — [a] blissful
Without a Name –

Profane it by a search – we cannot – — [by] pursuit
It has no home –
Nor we who having once inhaled it – thereafter roam. — [once] *waylaid it*

c. 1876

Long Years apart – can make no[99]
Breach a second cannot fill –
The absence of the Witch does not
Invalidate the spell –

The embers of a Thousand Years — [Thousand] years
Uncovered by the Hand
That fondled them when they were Fire
Will gleam and understand — [Will] *stir*

lines 3–4: Dim – • Far – [absence of] a [Witch] cannot / [Invalidate] a [spell –]
Who says the Absence of a Witch / Invalidates his spell?

c. 1876

Praise it – 'tis dead –
It cannot glow – — [cannot] thrill – • blush –
Warm this inclement Ear
With the encomium it earned
Since it was gathered here – — [was] tethered –
Invest this alabaster Zest
In the Delights of Dust – — [the] Awards
Remitted – since it flitted it
In recusance august.

c. 1876

A Saucer holds a Cup[100]
In sordid human Life
But in a Squirrel's estimate
A Saucer holds a Loaf –

A Table of a Tree
Demands the little King — [Demands] my
And every Breeze that run along
His Dining Room do swing – — [Room do]th

His Cutlery – he keeps
Within his Russet Lips – — between [his]

To see it flashing when he dines
Do Birmingham eclipse – [Do] Manchester

Convicted – could we be
Of our Minutiae
The smallest Citizen that flies
Is heartier than we – Has more integrity.

c. 1876

The Bat is dun, with wrinkled Wings –
Like fallow Article –
And not a song pervade his Lips –
Or none perceptible.

His small Umbrella quaintly halved
Describing in the Air
An Arc alike inscrutable
Elate Philosopher.

Deputed from what Firmament –
Of what Astute Abode –
Empowered with what malignity
Auspiciously withheld –

To his adroit Creator
Ascribe no less the praise –
Beneficent, believe me,
His eccentricities –

c. 1876

Death warrants are supposed to be [are] believed to be • [believed to] ~~me~~
An enginery of Equity
A merciful mistake [A] hazardous
A pencil in an Idol's Hand [in a] dainty
A Devotee has oft consigned [has] cool – • bland
To Crucifix or Block [or] stake

c. 1876

Summer laid her simple Hat[101]
On its boundless shelf –
Unobserved – a Ribin slipt
Fasten it – yourself. ~~Summon~~ • ~~Sanction~~ [it]

Summer laid her supple Glove
In its silvan Drawer –
Wheresoe'er – as was she – [Where] ~~she is~~ • [Wheresoe'er –] or
The Affair of Awe – an [Affair] • The Demand of Awe

c. 1876

Summer – we all have seen –
A few of us – believed –
A few – the more aspiring
Unquestionably loved –

But Summer does not care –
She takes her gracious way
As eligible as the Moon [As] unavailing –
To the Temerity – To] a – • our –

Deputed to adore – ~~Contented~~ [to]
The Doom to be adored [The] ~~Lot~~
Unknown as to an Ecstasy
The Embryo endowed –

line 6: [She] *goes* [her] *spacious* [way] • her ample way – • She goes her sylvan way – • [She goes her] perfect • spacious • subtle • simple • mighty • gallant [way]
lines 7–8: ~~As undiverted as the Moon – from her Divinity~~ – • As unperverted as the Moon / By Our obliquity – • As eligible as the Moon – to our extremity – • Adversity –
lines 9–10: Created to adore – / The Affluence evolved – • conferred – • bestowed – • involved –

c. 1876

How fits his Umber Coat
The Tailor of the Nut?

Summer laid her: *Sent to EH (stanza 1, variant) c. October 1876 and to TWH (stanza 2, variant) c. late October 1876*

Combined without a seam
Like Raiment of a Dream –

Who spun the Auburn Cloth?
Computed how the girth?
The Chestnut aged grows
In those primeval Clothes –

We know that we are wise –
Accomplished in Surprise –
Yet by this Countryman –
This nature – how undone!

c. 1876

A wild Blue sky abreast of Winds
That threatened it – did run
And crouched behind his Yellow Door
Was the defiant sun – sat [the]
Some conflict with those upper friends
So genial in the main
That we deplore peculiarly
Their arrogant Campaign – this [arrogant]

c. 1877

A Field of Stubble – lying sere
Beneath the second sun
Its toils to Brindled People tost [Its] corn – [to Brindled] nations *thrust* • cast –
Its triumphs – to the Bin – [Its] Pumpkin to –

Accosted by a timid Bird With usually • generally a sober Bird –
Irresolute of Alms – Revisiting for Alms –
Is often seen – but seldom felt
On our New England Farms –

c. 1877

A Field of: *Sent to Ned Dickinson (variant) c. March 1877, called "a Portrait of the Parish," with maple sugar*

How much the present moment means
To those who've nothing more –
The Fop – the Carp – the Atheist – [The] Dog – the Tramp – [the]
Stake an entire store
Upon a moment's shallow Rim [moment's] fickle
While their commuted Feet
The Torrents of Eternity [The] waters
Do all but inundate – [Do] almost – [inundate –]

c. 1877

Of Paradise' existence
All we know
Is the uncertain certainty –
But its vicinity, infer,
By its Bisecting Messenger –

c. 1877

March is the Month of Expectation.[102]
The things we do not know –
The transports of prognostication
Are coming now –
We try to show becoming firmness
But pompous Joy
Reports us, as his first Betrothal
Betrays a Boy –

line 3: [The] *Persons* • *Treasures* [of prognostication] • [The] *aspects of prognostication*
We feel it by the fluctuation

c. 1877

The inundation of the Spring[103]
Enlarges every Soul – submerges [every]
It sweeps the – tenement – away [tenement]s
But leaves the Water whole –

o

March is the: *Sent to SD (variant) c. 1877*

In which the Soul at first estranged – [first] alarmed • submerged
Seeks faintly for its Shore –
But acclimated – pines no more [acclimated –] Loses sight
For that Peninsula – [Of] ~~its~~ • Of aught Peninsular –

line 6: Seeks furtive for its shore • gropes [faintly] • [Seeks] softly [for its Shore –]

c. 1877

Hope is a strange invention –
A Patent of the Heart –
In unremitting action
Yet never wearing out –

Of this electric adjunct
Not anything is known
But its unique momentum
Embellish all we own –

c. 1877

Bees are Black, with Gilt Surcingles –[104]
Buccaneers of Buzz –
Ride abroad in ostentation
And subsist on Fuzz –

Fuzz ordained – not Fuzz contingent –
Marrows of the Hill –
Jugs a Universe's Fracture [Universe's] rupture
Could not jar or spill –

c. 1877

Lay this Laurel on the one[105]
Triumphed and remained unknown –
Laurel – fell your futile Tree –
Such a Victor could not be –

Hope is a: *Sent to Mary Channing Higginson (stanza 2, variant) c. March or April 1877*
Bees are Black,: *Sent to EH (variant) c. late May 1877*
Lay this Laurel: *Sent to TWH (last 4 lines, variant) June 1877*

Lay this Laurel on the one
Too intrinsic for Renown –
Laurel – vail your deathless Tree –
Him you chasten – that is he –

c. 1877

I shall not murmur if at last[106]
The ones I loved below
Permission have to understand
For what I shunned them so –
Divulging it would rest my Heart
But it would ravage theirs –
Why, Katie, Treason has a Voice –
But mine – dispels – in Tears.

c. 1877

We shun because we prize her Face
Lest sight's ineffable disgrace   [Lest] proof's
Our Adoration stain   [Adoration] mar • flaw

c. 1877

Such are the inlets of the mind –[107]   These [are]
His outlets – would you see   [you] know
Ascend with me the eminence   [the] Table Land
Of Immortality –

c. June 1877

I have no life but this[108]   [life] ~~to live~~
To lead it here   ~~But~~ [lead]
Nor any Death but lest
Abased from there –   dispelled • Withheld – • deprived from there –

I have no: *Sent to SB (variant) c. 29 June 1877 and to TWH (variant) c. August 1877, as "a Word to a Friend"*

Nor Plea for World to come — Nor tie to [World]s [to come]
Nor Wisdoms new
Except through this extent — [this] expanse –
The loving you –

c. 1877

What mystery pervades a well![109]
The water lives so far –
A neighbor from another world
Residing in a jar

Whose limit none have ever seen,
But just his lid of glass – — [his] lip
Like looking every time you please
In an abyss's face!

The grass does not appear afraid,
I often wonder he
Can stand so close and look so bold
At what is awe to me. — [is] dread

Related somehow they may be,
The sedge stands next the sea
Where he is floorless
And does no timidity betray – — And of fear no evidence gives he

But nature is a stranger yet;
The ones that cite her most
Have never passed her haunted house,
Nor simplified her ghost.

To pity those that know her not
Is helped by the regret
That those who know her, know her less
The nearer her they get.

c. 1877 — MLT

What mystery pervades: *Sent to SD (final 2 stanzas, variant) c. 1877, beginning "But Susan is a stranger yet –"*

To the stanch Dust[110]
We safe commit thee –
Tongue if it hath,
Inviolate to thee –
Silence – denote –
And Sanctity – enforce thee –
Passenger – of Infinity –

c. 1877

Shame is the shawl of Pink
In which we wrap the Soul
To keep it from infesting Eyes –
The elemental Veil
Which helpless Nature drops
When pushed upon a scene
Repugnant to her probity –
Shame is the tint divine –

c. 1877

Sweet skepticism of the Heart –
That knows – and does not know –
And tosses like a Fleet of Balm –
Affronted by the snow –
Invites and then retards the truth
Lest Certainty be sere
Compared with the delicious throe
Of transport thrilled with Fear –

c. 1877

Unworthy of her Breast
Though by that scathing test
What Soul survive?
By her exacting light

To the stanch: *Sent to SD c. 1877*

How counterfeit the white
We chiefly have!

c. 1877

How Human Nature dotes
On what it can't detect –
The moment that a Plot is plumbed
Its meaning is extinct – [Its] import – • *Prospective is extinct.*

Prospective is the friend
Reserved for us to know
When Constancy is clarified
Of Curiosity –

Of subjects that resist
Redoubtablest is this
Where go we –
Go we anywhere
Creation after this?

c. 1877

How lonesome the Wind must feel Nights –[111]
When People have put out the Lights
And everything that has an Inn
Closes the shutter and goes in – [Closes] his
How pompous the Wind must feel Noons
Stepping to incorporeal Tunes
Correcting errors of the sky
And clarifying scenery
How mighty the Wind must feel Morns
Encamping on a thousand Dawns –
Espousing each and spurning all [Espousing] one
Then soaring to his Temple Tall – [his] Turret

c. 1877

It was a quiet seeming Day –
There was no harm in earth or sky –
Till with the setting sun [the] *closing sun*
There strayed an accidental Red
A strolling Hue, one would have said
To westward of the Town – To upper [of]

But when the Earth begun to jar
And Houses vanished with a roar
And Human Nature hid [and] Population fled
We comprehended by the Awe [We] postulated • recollected
As those that Dissolution saw
The Poppy in the Cloud – [The] warrant

lines 10–11: [We comprehended by] The Flash • Flare – • Glare – • Blare – between the Crevices of Crash –

c. 1877

The fairest Home I ever knew
Was founded in an Hour
By Parties also that I knew
A spider and a Flower –
A manse of mechlin and of Floss – [of] Gloss – • sun –

c. 1877

The pretty Rain from those sweet Eaves
Her unintending Eyes –
Took her own Heart, including ours,
By innocent Surprise –

The wrestle in her simple Throat
To hold the feeling down
That vanquished her – defeated Feat –
Was Fervor's sudden Crown –

line 4: [By] eloquent – • hallowed – • heavenly – • diffident – [Surprise –]

c. 1877

To earn it by disdaining it
Is Fame's consummate Fee –
He loves what spurns him – [He] seeks [what] shuns
Look behind – He is pursuing thee –

So let us gather – every Day –
The Aggregate of Life's Bouquet
Be Honor and not shame –

c. 1877

~

Water makes many Beds
For those averse to sleep –
Its awful chamber open stands –
Its Curtains blandly sweep –
Abhorrent is the Rest
In undulating Rooms
Whose Amplitude no end invades – [no] clock
Whose Axis never comes

line 8: [Whose] owner [never comes] • morning never hums –

c. 1877

~

Who never wanted – maddest Joy
Remains to him unknown –
The Banquet of Abstemiousness
Defaces that of Wine – debases – • surpasses [that]

Within its reach, though yet ungrasped [its] hope and – just [ungrasped]
Desire's perfect Goal –
No nearer – lest the Actual –
Should disenthrall thy soul –

line 7: [No nearer – lest] Reality – • its penury – • the possible • Vicinity –

c. 1877

~

With Pinions of Disdain
The soul can farther fly

Than any feather specified — [feather] ratified • certified
in – Ornithology – — by – [Ornithology –]
It wafts this sordid Flesh
Beyond its dull – control — [its] slow
And during its electric gale – — [electric] spell • stay – • might – • act – • span
The Body is – a soul –
instructing by the same – — [by] itself
How little work it be – — What little act it be
To put off filaments like this
for immortality –

c. 1877

One Joy of so much anguish[112] — [One] sound
Sweet Nature has for me –
I shun it as I do Despair
Or dear iniquity –
Why Birds, a Summer morning
Before the Quick of Day
Should Stab my ravished Spirit
With Dirks of Melody
Is part of an inquiry — [part] of an inquiry
That will receive reply — Delaying its reply
When Flesh and Spirit sunder — till Flesh [and]
In Death's immediately –

line 6: [Before the] ripe • peal • Drum • Bells • Bomb • tick • shouts • Drums of Day –
• Burst of Day • Flags of Day – • step of Day • Bells of Day • Pink of Day
• Red of Day • Blade of Day

c. 1877

No Passenger was known to flee[113]
That lodged a night in memory –
That wily – subterranean Inn
Contrives that none go out again –

c. 1877

No Passenger was: *Sent to Josiah Holland c. 1877*

Incredible the Lodging
But limited the Guest

c. 1877

She laid her docile Crescent down[114]
And this mechanic Stone
Still states to Dates that have forgot
The News that she is gone –
So constant to its stolid Trust
The shaft that never knew
It shames the Constancy that fled
Before its Emblem flew –

c. 1877

It sounded as if the Streets were running –[115]
And then the Streets stood still –
Eclipse – was all we could see at the Window,
And Awe – was all we could feel –

By and by – the boldest stole out of his Covert
To see if Time was there –
Nature was in an Opal Apron,
Mixing fresher Air.

c. 1877

Perhaps they do not go so far[116]
As we who stay, suppose –
Perhaps come closer, for the lapse [the] ~~flight~~ • lapse –
Of their corporeal clothes –

It may be, know so certainly
How short we have to fear

She laid her: *Sent to EH (variant) c. 1877, with newspaper clippings of a star and crescent and of tombstones leaning against each other; to TWH (variant) c. August 1877, called "an Epitaph"*
It sounded as: *Sent to TWH (variant) August 1877, called "a Gale"*
Perhaps they do: *Sent to Harriet Austin Dickinson and Mary Taylor Dickinson as prose with flowers c. 1876, and to TWH (stanza 1, variant) after his wife's death on 2 September 1877, beginning "Perhaps she does not go so far"*

That Comprehension antedates   [Comprehension] fluctuates • ~~enforces~~
And estimates us there

line 8: [And] ~~Replevys~~ • ~~confiscates~~ [us there] • [And] There – ~~commences~~ – ~~Here~~ –

c. 1876 or 1877

Could mortal Lip divine[117]
The elemental Freight   [the] undeveloped
Of a delivered Syllable –   [Of] its
'Twould crumble with the weight –

The Prey of Unknown Zones –   In spans in Unknown Zones –
The Pillage of the Sea   Irreverenced – in the Sea –
The Tabernacles of the Minds
That told the Truth to me –   [the] News –

c. 1877

Summer has two Beginnings –
Beginning once in June –
Beginning in October
Affectingly again –

Without, perhaps, the Riot
But graphicer for Grace –
As finer is a going
Than a remaining Face –
Departing then – forever –   [Departing] next
Forever – until May –
Forever is deciduous –   [is] recurrent
Except to those who die –

c. 1877

The Gentian has a parched Corolla –
Like Azure dried
'Tis Nature's buoyant juices
Beatified –
Without a vaunt or sheen

Could mortal Lip: *Sent to SB (stanza 1, variant) c. 1877*

As casual as Rain — [As] odorless – • innocent
And as benign –

When most is past – it comes –
Nor isolate it seems –
Its Bond its Friend –
To fill its Fringed career — [Fringed] sphere
And aid an aged Year
Abundant end – — A fervent end – • [A] loyal • gracious • an ample [end –]

Its lot – were it forgot –
This truth endear – — [truth] declare
Fidelity is gain
Creation o'er –

c. 1877

Two Butterflies went out at Noon[118]
And waltzed upon a Farm
And then espied Circumference — Then overtook – [Circumference]
And caught a ride with him – — and took a Bout with him –
Then lost themselves and found themselves
In eddies of the sun
Till Rapture missed Peninsula –
And Both were wrecked in Noon – — [were] Drowned – • quenched – • Whelmed –
To all surviving Butterflies
Be this Fatuity — [Be] this Biography –
Example – and monition
To entomology –

line 5: Then chased themselves and caught themselves

lines 5–6: Then staked themselves and lost themselves in Gambols with the sun –

line 6: [in] Frenzy • [in Fren]zies • for Frenzy of the Sun • [for] gambols [of] • antics in the sun • [antics] with [the sun] • In Rapids of the Sun • [In] Fathoms in [the sun]

line 7: [Till Rapture] missed her footing – • Until a Zephyr pushed them • chased • flung • spurned [them] • Till Gravitation foundered • grumbled • [Till] *Gravitation* [*missed*] *them* • chased [*them*]

lines 7–8: Until a Zephyr scourged them / And they were hurled from noon
Till Gravitation humbled – ejected them from noon –

c. 1878

Two Butterflies went: *Sent to Ns (lost) c. summer 1863*

Upon what brittle Piers – [what] fickle – • trifling
Our Faith doth daily tread –
No Bridge below doth totter so
Yet – none hath such a Crowd – and [none]
It is as old as God –
Indeed – 'twas built by him –
He sent his son to test the Plank
And he pronounced it firm –

c. 1878

Brother of Ingots – Ah Peru –
Empty the Hearts that purchased you –

c. 1878

My Maker – let me be[119]
A World or two from thee –
But nearer this –
I more should miss –

c. 1878

Behold this little Bane –
The Boon of all alive –
As common as it is unknown
The name of it is Love –

To lack of it is Woe –
To own of it is Wound –
Not elsewhere – if in Paradise
Its Tantamount be found –

c. 1878

Upon what brittle: *Sent to Maria Whitney (variant) perhaps early 1878 and to TWH (variant) c. June 1878, both beginning "How brittle are the Piers"*
Brother of Ingots –: *Sent to SD (variant) with a flower, beginning "Sister of Ophir – Ah Peru –" c. 1878 and to ST (variant), beginning "Brother of Ophir" c. December 1880*
My Maker – let: *Sent to SD (variant) c. 1878*

How ruthless are the gentle –[120]
How cruel are the kind –
God broke his contract to his Lamb
To qualify the Wind –

c. 1878

These Fevered Days – to take them to the Forest
Where Waters cool around the mosses crawl –
And shade is all that devastates the stillness
Seems it sometimes this would be all –

c. 1878

To mend each tattered Faith
There is a needle fair
Though no appearance indicate –
'Tis threaded in the Air –

And though it do not wear
As if it never Tore
'Tis very comfortable indeed
And specious as before –

c. 1878

A Chilly Peace infests the Grass   [A] lonesome – • warning –
The Sun respectful lies –
Not any Trance of industry
These shadows scrutinize –   The [shadows]

Whose Allies go no more astray   [more] abroad –
For service or for Glee –   [For] Honor – • welcome
But all mankind deliver here
From whatsoever Sea –

line 7: though [all mankind] cruise softly here • row • sail [softly here] • do anchor – [here]

c. 1878

Death is the supple Suitor[121]
That wins at last –
It is a stealthy Wooing
Conducted first
By pallid innuendoes
And dim approach
But brave at last with Bugles
And a bisected Coach
It bears away in triumph
To Troth unknown
And Kinsmen as divulgeless
As throngs of Down –

lines 11–12: And Pageants as impassive / As Porcelain
[And] Kindred as responsive – / [As] *Clans* of Down

c. 1878

His Mind like Fabrics of the East –
Displayed to the despair — Unrolled – [to]
Of everyone but here and there
An humble Purchaser –
For though his price was not of Gold – — [though] the
More arduous there is –
That one should comprehend the worth,
Was all the price there was – — [the] terms

c. 1878

How good his Lava Bed,
To this laborious Boy –
Who must be up to call the World — that [must]
And dress the sleepy Day – — [And] curl

c. 1878

I thought the Train would never come –
How slow the whistle sang –

I don't believe a peevish Bird
So whimpered for the Spring –
I taught my Heart a hundred times
Precisely what to say –
Provoking Lover, when you came
Its Treatise flew away
To hide my strategy too late
To wiser be too soon –   [wiser] grow
For miseries so halcyon
The happiness atone –

c. 1878

The Road was lit with Moon and star –   [lit] ~~by~~
The Trees were bright and still –
Descried I – by – the distant Light   [I –] in [the] *gaining*
A traveller on a Hill –   [A] Horseman
To magic Perpendiculars   in [magic]
Ascending, though terrene –
Unknown his shimmering ultimate –   [his] giddy – • dazzling
But he indorsed the sheen –   [the] scene –

c. 1878

Whoever disenchants
A single Human soul
By failure or irreverence
Is guilty of the whole –

As guileless as a Bird
As graphic as a Star
Till the suggestion sinister
Things are not what they are –

line 7: Till Treason lightly propagates • [Till] Caviler insinuates • [Till] Perjury – [insinuates]

c. 1878

Your thoughts don't have words every day[122]
They come a single time
Like signal esoteric sips
Of the communion Wine [Of] sacramental
Which while you taste so native seems
So easy so to be
You cannot comprehend its price – [its] worth • the stint
Nor its infrequency nor the divinity

line 5: [Which while you taste] adjacent [seems] • so ample seems • [so] bounteous [seems] • so ample seems

line 6: [So] kindred [so to be] • So fully [so to be] • so intimate *so free* • *[so] affable* • affluent • gracious [*so free*]

c. 1878

One note from One Bird
Is better than a Million Word –
A scabbard has – but one sword [scabbard] holds • needs

c. 1878

A little Snow was here and there
Disseminated in her Hair –
Since she and I had met and played
Decade had hastened to Decade – [had] hurried • *gathered*

But Time had added, not obtained
Impregnable the Rose invincible – • inviolate – • illustrious the Rose –
For summer too indelible –
Too obdurate – for Snows – [Too] competent –

lines 6–8: Impregnable the Rose / For Summer too inscrutable / Too sumptuous for snows –

c. 1878

Forbidden Fruit a flavor has
That lawful Orchards mocks – [lawful] Damsons

How luscious lies within the Pod
The Pea that Duty locks –

c. 1879

Summer is shorter than any one –
Life is shorter than Summer –
Seventy Years is spent as quick
As an only Dollar –

Sorrow – now – is polite – and stays – Aroma – [now –] is courteous and stays –
See how well we spurn him – [spurn] ~~her~~ –
Equally to abhor Delight –
Equally retain him –

c. 1879

Blue Bird –
Before you thought of Spring[123]
Except as a Surmise
You see – God bless his Suddenness
A Fellow in the Skies
Of independent Hues
A little weather worn
Inspiriting habiliments
Of Indigo and Brown –
With specimens of song
As if for you to choose –
Discretion in the interval –
With gay delays he goes
To some superior Tree
Without a single Leaf
And shouts for joy to nobody
But his seraphic Self –

c. 1879

Before you thought: *Sent to Ns (lost, transcribed variant), to ST (variant), and to HHJ (lost) c. 1879, and perhaps to Thomas Niles 1883*

Belshazzar had a Letter –[124]
He never had but one –
Belshazzar's Correspondent
Concluded and begun
In that immortal Copy
The Conscience of us all
Can read without its Glasses
On Revelation's Wall –

c. 1879

One of the ones that Midas touched[125]
Who failed to touch us all
Was that confiding Prodigal
The reeling Oriole –

So drunk he disavows it
With badinage divine –
So dazzling we mistake him
For an alighting Mine –

A Pleader – a Dissembler –
An Epicure – a Thief –
Betimes an Oratorio –
An Ecstasy in chief –

The Jesuit of Orchards
He cheats as he enchants
Of an entire Attar
For his decamping wants –

The splendor of a Burmah
The Meteor of Birds,
Departing like a Pageant
Of Ballads and of Bards –

I never thought that Jason sought
For any Golden Fleece
But then I am a rural Man
With thoughts that make for Peace –

Belshazzar had a: *Sent to Ned Dickinson c. 1879*
One of the: *Sent to Ns (lost, transcribed variant) and to HHJ (lost) c. 1879*

But if there were a Jason,
Tradition bear with me
Behold his lost Aggrandizement
Upon the Apple Tree –

c. 1879

A Route of Evanescence[126]
With a delusive wheel — [a] dissembling • renewing – • dissolving wheel –
A Resonance of Emerald
A Rush of Cochineal
And every Blossom on the Bush
Adjusts its tumbled Head –
The Mail from Tunis – probably –
An easy morning's ride –

c. 1879

Its little Ether Hood
Doth sit upon its Head –
The millinery supple
Of the sagacious God –

Till when it slip away — And then doth [slip]
A nothing at a time –
And Dandelion's Drama
Expires in a stem.

c. 1879

To see the Summer Sky
Is Poetry, though never in a Book it lie –
True Poems flee –

c. 1879

A Route of: *Sent to HHJ (variant) and to Ns (lost, transcribed variant) c. 1879; to ST (variant) c. January 1880; to TWH (variant) c. November 1880; to MLT (variant) c. autumn 1882; and to Thomas Niles (variant) c. April 1883; in all copies, ED calls or signs the poem as a "Humming Bird" or "Humming bird"*

Ferocious as a Bee without a wing
The Prince of Honey and the Prince of Sting
So plain a flower presents her Disk to thee

c. 1879

Hope is a subtle Glutton –
He feeds upon the Fair –
And yet – inspected closely
What Abstinence is there –

His is the Halcyon Table –
That never seats but One –
And whatsoever is consumed
The same amount remain –

c. 1879

"Secrets" is a daily word[127]
Yet does not exist –
Muffled – it remits surmise – Mortised – [it] resists –
Murmured – it has ceased –
Dungeoned in the Human Breast
Doubtless secrets lie –
But that Grate inviolate –
Comes nor goes away
Nothing with a Tongue or Ear – [Nothing] with an Ear or Tongue –
Secrets stapled there
Will emerge but once – and dumb – [Will] decamp – [but once – and] armed –
To the Sepulchre –

c. 1879

A winged spark doth soar about –[128]
I never met it near
For Lightning it is oft mistook
When nights are hot and sere –

o

Its twinkling Travels it pursues
Above the Haunts of men –
A speck of Rapture – first perceived
By feeling it is gone –

[Rapture –] Rekindled
by some action quaint

c. 1879

If wrecked upon the Shoal of Thought[129]
How is it with the Sea?
The only Vessel that is shunned
Is safe – Simplicity –

c. 1879

The Sweets of Pillage, can be known[130]
By no one but the Thief –
Compassion for Integrity
Is his divinest Grief –

c. 1879

Their Barricade against the Sky[131]
The martial Trees withdraw
And with a Flag at every turn
Their Armies are no more –
What Russet Halts in Nature's March
They indicate or cause
An inference of Mexico
Effaces the Surmise –

Recurrent to the After Mind
That Massacre of Air –
The Wound that was not Wound nor Scar –
But Holidays of War –

c. 1879

The Sweets of: *Sent to SD (variant) c. 1879*
Their Barricade against: *Apparently sent to MLT (variant) c. 1883*

We talked with each other about each other[132]
Though neither of us spoke –
We were listening to the Second's Races
And the Hoofs of the Clock –
Pausing in Front of our Palsied Faces
Time compassion took –
Arks of Reprieve he offered to us –
Ararats – we took –

c. 1879

~

Fame is the one that does not stay –
Its occupant must die
Or out of sight of estimate
Ascend incessantly –
Or be that most insolvent thing
A Lightning in the Germ –
Electrical the embryo
But we demand the Flame — – or – findless is the [Flame]

c. 1879

~

His voice decrepit was with Joy –
Her words did totter so
How old the News of Love must be — [Love] should
To make Lips elderly
That purled a moment since with Glee –
Is it Delight or Woe –
Or Terror – that do decorate — [do] celebrate • generate –
This livid – interview –

c. 1879

~

How destitute is he[133]
Whose Gold is firm –
Who finds it every time
The same stale Sum –
When Love with but a Pence
Will so display — [so] array

As he had no esteem — You'd think • swear he took a Deed
For India – — Of India –

c. 1879

The Devil – had he fidelity[134]
Would be the best friend –
Because he has ability –
But Devils cannot mend –
Perfidy is the virtue
That would but he resign
The Devil – without question — [Devil –] so amended –
Were thoroughly divine — Were durably divine –

c. 1879

The fascinating chill that Music leaves[135] — [chill] of music
Is Earth's corroboration
Of Ecstasy's impediment –
'Tis Rapture's germination
In timid and tumultuous soil
A fine – estranging creature –
To something upper wooing us
But not to our Creator –

c. 1879

The way Hope builds his House
It is not with a sill –
Nor Rafter – has that Edifice — [Rafter –] mars – • knows
But only Pinnacle –

Abode in as supreme
This superficies
As if it were of Ledges smit
Or mortised with the Laws – — And [mortised]

c. 1879

'Tis whiter than an Indian Pipe –[136]
'Tis dimmer than a Lace –
No stature has it, like a Fog
When you approach the place –
Not any voice imply it here   [voice] denote
Or intimate it there –   [Or] designate –
A spirit – how doth it accost –
What function hath the Air?   What customs – [hath]
This limitless Hyperbole
Each one of us shall be –
'Tis Drama – if Hypothesis   ~~This~~ [Drama]
It be not Tragedy –

line 9: And this – this unsurmised thing – • [And this –] Apocalyptic thing –

c. 1879

Estranged from Beauty – none can be –
For Beauty is Infinity –
And power to be finite ceased
Before Identity was creased –   [was] leased – • When Fate incorporated us –

c. 1879

One thing of thee I covet –[137]
The power to forget –
The pathos of the Avarice
Defrays the Dross of it –

One thing of thee I borrow
And promise to return –
The Booty and the Sorrow
Thy sweetness to have known –

c. 1879

Glass was the Street – in Tinsel Peril
Tree and Traveller stood.

One thing of: *Sent to TWH (variant) December 1879, beginning "One thing of it we borrow"*

Filled was the Air with merry venture
Hearty with Boys the Road.

Shot the lithe Sleds like Shod vibrations
Emphasized and gone
It is the Past's supreme italic
Makes the Present mean – Makes next • *this* moment mean

c. 1880

It came his turn to beg –[138]
The begging for the life
Is different from another Alms
'Tis Penury in Chief –
I scanned his narrow Realm [narrow] ~~Grant~~
I gave him leave to live I gave him leave to live
Lest Gratitude revive the snake [revive] my ~~thought~~
Though – smuggled my – Reprieve [smuggled] his

c. 1880

The Face in Evanescence lain[139]
Is more distinct than ours –
And ours surrendered for its sake
As Capsules are for Flower's –

Or is it the confiding Sheen
Dissenting to be won – defying – [to]
Consenting to enamor us descending • established • imparted – [to]
Of Detriment divine?

c. 1880

How soft a Caterpillar steps –[140]
I find one on my Hand
From such a Velvet world it comes – [it] came • *came*
Such plushes at command

The Face in: *Sent to TWH (variant) mid-March 1880 and to Maria Whitney (stanza 1, lost, transcribed variant) c. 1880*

Its soundless travels just arrest
my slow – terrestrial eye –
Intent upon its own career – [own] circuit
What use has it for me –

lines 4–6: ~~Its journey never wakes my Hand / Till poising for a turn / its traverse~~
line 7: Intent upon its mission quaint • circuit quaint

c. 1880

The Road to Paradise is plain
And holds scarce one –
Not that it has not room
But we presume
A florid Road
Is more preferred –

The Guests of Paradise are few –
Not me, nor you –
But unsuspected things –
Mines have no Wings –

c. 1880

Her spirit rose to such a hight
Her countenance it did inflate
Like one that fed on awe.
More prudent to assault the dawn
Than merit the etherial scorn
That effervesced from her.

c. 1880 MLT

The Thrill came slowly like a Boon for Centuries delayed[141] [a] Light
Its fitness growing like the Flood
In sumptuous solitude –
The desolation only missed
While Rapture changed its Dress

The Road to: *Sent to Ns (lost, transcribed variant) c. 1880 and to EH (variant) July 1880*
Her spirit rose: *Sent to SD (variant, last 3 lines) c. 1880*

And stood arrayed before the change
In ravished Holiness –   In simple Holiness – • dazzling Holiness

line 6: [And stood arrayed before the] Boon • news • [And stood] before the suddenness

c. 1880

All that I do
Is in review
To his enamored mind
I know his eye
Where e'er I ply
Is pushing close behind

Not any Port
Not any flight   [any] Pause
But he doth there preside   Where he does not ~~first~~ preside
What omnipresence lies in wait
For her to be a Bride   [For] one • [For] an impending Bride

line 6: [Is] staring • plodding • is roaming • is ambling • ambling close behind

c. 1880

Facts by our side are never sudden
Until they look around
And then they scare us like a spectre   but [then]
Protruding from the Ground –

The hight of our portentous Neighbor   [our] unknowing
We never know –
Till summoned to his recognition
By an Adieu –
Adieu for whence the sage cannot Conjecture   [Adieu] till when [the] wise
The bravest die
As ignorant of their resumption
As you or I –   [As] Cowards do –

c. 1880

I saw the wind within her –[142]
I knew it blew for me –
But she must buy my shelter   But she must pay for succor
I asked Humility   my price Humility –

I watched the fluttering spirit
That would not intercede
Gibraltar could surrender   The Universe was needy
But not this little maid –   but not my little maid
Precisely how it ended –   ~~Precisely is it known~~
Redemption is the one
Of whom the explanation
Is hitherto unknown –

The saved have no remembrance   [saved] left • Nor have the saved – remembrance
In our competing Days
'Tis still an assistance   it is [an] • it is a timid Bulwark –
But theirs forget in praise   superfluous in theirs –

line 5: [I] bought [the] vanquished [spirit] • I watched the precious Beggar • subtle Beggar
lines 11–12: [Of whom the] exposition is prudently • Principally unknown
Of whom the exposition / Not one of us will own

c. 1880

More than the Grave is closed to me –
The Grave and that Eternity
To which the Grave adheres –
I cling to nowhere till I fall –
The Crash of nothing, yet of all –   A [Crash of nothing,] and [of all –]
How similar appears –

c. 1880

Of whom so dear
The name to hear
illumines with a Glow   ~~Suffuses~~ [with]
As intimate – as fugitive   [As] magical
As Sunset on the snow –

c. 1880

I do not care – why should I care[143]
And yet I fear I'm caring
To rock a fretting truth to sleep – [a] crying • wailing
Is short security [Is] no • frail • poor
The terror it will wake
persistent as perdition
Is harder than to face
the frank adversity –
There is an awful yes in every constitution

c. 1880

She could not live upon the Past
The Present did not know her
And so she sought this sweet at last
And nature gently owned her [nature] softly
The mother that has not a Knell
for either Duke or Robin

c. 1880

You cannot make Remembrance grow[144]
When it has lost its Root –
The tightening the Soil around
And setting it upright
Deceives perhaps the Universe
But not retrieves the Plant –
Real Memory, like Cedar Feet
Is shod with Adamant –
Nor can you cut Remembrance down
When it shall once have grown –
Its Iron Buds will sprout anew [sprout] afresh –
However overthrown –
Disperse it – slay it –

c. 1880

"And with what Body do they come?"[145]
Then they *do* come, Rejoice!
What Door – what Hour – Run – run – My Soul!
Illuminate the House!
"Body"! Then real – a Face – and Eyes –
To know that it is them! –
Paul knew the Man that knew the News –
He passed through Bethlehem –

early October 1880

The Savior must have been[146]
A docile Gentleman,
To come so far, so cold a Day,
For Little "Fellow men."

The Road to Bethlehem
Since he and I were Boys,
Was leveled, but for that 'twould be
A rugged Billion Miles –

c. late 1880

Mine Enemy is growing old –[147]
I have at last Revenge –
The Palate of the Hate departs –
If any would avenge

Let him be quick –
The Viand flits –
It is a faded Meat –
Anger as soon as fed – is dead –
'Tis Starving makes it fat –

c. late 1880

"And with what: *Sent to Perez Dickinson Cowan early October 1880*
The Savior must: *Sent to TWH (variant) November 1880, designated as "Christ's Birthday," and apparently to her brother's family at Christmas, with an iced cake (lost)*
Mine Enemy is: *Sent to TWH (variant) November 1880, designated as "Cupid's Sermon"*

An Antiquated Tree
Is cherished by the Crow. [cherished] of the Crow –
Because that Junior Foliage
Is disrespectful now

To venerable Birds
Whose Corporation Coat [Whose] unsuspecting Coat – • well intentioned Coat –
Would decorate Oblivion's
Fantastic Consulate – Most gracious – • dusky – • pompous [Consulate –]

c. 1881

A Pang is more conspicuous in Spring[148]
In contrast with the things that sing [with] those –
Not Birds entirely – but Minds –
And Winds – Minute Effulgencies
When what they sung for is undone
Who cares about a Blue Bird's Tune –
Why, Resurrection had to wait
Till they had moved a Stone –

c. 1881

We never know we go when we are going –
We jest and shut the Door –
Fate – following – behind us bolts it –
And we accost no more – [And] we know

c. 1881

His little Hearse like Figure[149]
Unto itself a Dirge
To a delusive Lilac
The vanity divulge

Of industry and ethics
And every founded thing

An Antiquated Tree: *Sent to EH (variant) c. early spring 1881*
We never know: *Sent to Ns (lost, transcribed variant) c. 1881*
His little Hearse: *Sent to Gilbert Dickinson (variant) c. 1881, titled "The Bumble Bee's Religion," apparently with a dead bee*

For the divine Perdition
Of idleness and spring –

c. 1881

A faded Boy – in sallow Clothes[150]
Who drove a lonesome Cow
To pastures of Oblivion –
A statesman's Embryo –

The Boys that whistled are extinct –
The Cows that fed and thanked
Remanded to a Ballad's Barn
Or Clover's Retrospect –

c. 1881

Oh give it motion – deck it sweet
With Artery and Vein –
Upon its fastened Lips lay words –
Affiance it again
To that Pink stranger we call Dust –
Acquainted more with that
Than with this horizontal one
That will not lift its Hat –

c. 1881

'Tis Seasons since the Dimpled War
In which we each were Conqueror
And each of us were slain
And Centuries 'twill be and more
Another Massacre before
So modest and so vain –
Without a Formula we fought
Each was to each the Pink Redoubt –

c. 1881

Above Oblivion's Tide there is a Pier
And an effaceless "Few" are lifted there – [And] the
Nay – lift themselves –
Fame has no Arms –
And but one Smile – that meagres Balms –

line 5: [And but one Smile – that] humbles – [Balms –] • And a chill
• bleak smile inlaid with Balms –

lines 2–5: [And] the [effaceless "Few"] are scattered there –
Scattered – I say –
To place them side by side [To] seat
Enough will not be found
When all have died –

c. 1881

From all the Jails the Boys and Girls
Ecstatically leap –
Beloved only Afternoon
That Prison doesn't keep –

They storm the Earth
And stun the Air,
A Mob of solid Bliss –
Alas – that Frowns should lie in wait [that] ~~Dusk~~
For such a Foe as this –

line 8: [For such a] ~~Sweet~~ • Bud – • Glee – • Dawn – • Scene – • Dew – • Joy – [as this –]

c. 1881

On that specific Pillow[151]
Our projects flit away –
The Night's tremendous Morrow
And whether sleep will stay
Or usher us – a stranger –
To situations new [To] exhibition – • comprehension
The effort to comprise it [effort] of comprising
Is all the soul can do –

c. 1881

The Life that tied too tight escapes
Will ever after run
With a prudential look behind
And spectres of the Rein –
The Horse that scents the living Grass
And sees the Pastures smile [And] spies –
Will be retaken with a shot
If he is caught at all –

lines 7–8: has views of Bridles and of Barns / That would expand us all – • betray us all –

c. 1881

The Bird her punctual music brings
And lays it in its place –
Its place is in the Human Heart
And in the Heavenly Grace –
What respite from her thrilling toil
Did Beauty ever take –
But work might be Electric Rest
To those that Magic make –

c. 1881

How fleet – how indiscreet an one – how always wrong is Love –[152]
The joyful little Deity
We are not scourged to serve –

c. 1881

The Blood is more showy than the Breath [more] gaudy
But cannot dance as well –

c. 1881

There comes a warning like a spy There came [a]
A shorter breath of Day

A stealing that is not a stealth — [A] symptom that is not a sound
And summer is away – — [summer] passed away • *And Summers are away*

c. 1881

His oriental heresies[153]
Exhilirate the Bee,
And filling all the Earth and Air
With gay apostasy

Fatigued at last, a Clover plain
Allures his jaded Eye
That lowly Breast where Butterflies
Have felt it meet to die –

c. late 1881

The Things that never can come back, are several –
Childhood – some forms of Hope – the Dead –
But Joys like men may sometimes make a Journey
And still abide –

We do not mourn for Traveler or Sailor –
Their Routes are fair –
But think – enlarged – of all that they will tell us –
Returning here –

"Here"! There are typic Heres –
Foretold Locations –
The Spirit does not stand –
Himself – at whatsoever Fathom
His Native Land –

c. 1881

Echo has no Magistrate – — Unobtrusive Blossom
Catch a Drop of Dew — Trap – • Bind [a]
And the Sun will free it — [will] *loose him* –
With a sneer at you –

o

The Things that: *Sent to EH (variant) c. October 1881; her husband died 12 October 1881*
Echo has no: *Sent to SD (stanza 2, variant) c. 1882*

Follow fine Orion till you furl your Eye –
Dazzlingly decamping
He is still more high –   [is] *just as high*

line 5: [Follow] Wise Orion till you waste your Eye – • lame [your Eye –]

c. 1882

~

How happy is the little stone   Invincible the little stone –
That rambles in the Road alone
And doesn't care about careers –
And Exigencies never – fears
Whose Coat of elemental Brown
A passing Universe put – on
And independent as the sun   *Who* [independent]
Associates – or basks alone –   associates – or links with none – • [or] glows alone –
Fulfilling absolute Decree   [Fulfilling] ~~some express~~ Decree
In casual simplicity –   [In] competent simplicity

c. 1882

~

He lived the Life of Ambush[154]
And went the way of Dusk
And now against his subtle name
There stands an Asterisk
As confident of him as we –
Impregnable we are –
The whole of Immortality
intrenched within a star –   secreted in [a]

c. 1882

~

Come show thy Durham Breast
To her who loves thee best   [loves] ~~you~~
Delicious Robin –

How happy is: *Sent to SD (variant), to Ns (lost), and perhaps to HHJ (lost) c. 1882; to Thomas Niles (variant) late April 1882; and to TWH (variant) c. summer 1882*
He lived the: *Sent to Samuel Bowles the younger (variant) 16 July 1882, with a spray of jasmine, beginning "Who abdicated Ambush"*
Come show thy: *Sent to TWH (first six lines, variant) c. summer 1882*

And if it be not me
At least within my Tree [within] ~~thy~~
Do the avowing –
Thy Nuptial so minute
Perhaps is more astute
Than vaster suing –
For so to soar away
Is our propensity
The Day ensuing –

c. 1882

The Moon upon her fluent Route
Defiant of a Road
The Star's Etruscan Argument
Substantiate a God –
How archly spared the Heaven "to come" –
If such prospective be –
By superseding Destiny
And dwelling there Today –

c. 1882

Diagnosis of the Bible, by a Boy –
The Bible is an untold Volume[155]
Written by unknown Men –
By the direction of hallowed Spectres –
Subjects – Bethlehem –

Genesis – Bethlehem's Ancestor –
Satan – the Brigadier –
Judas – the first Defaulter – [the] great
David – the Troubadour –

Sin – a distinguished Precipice –
But I must desist –
Boys that believe – are very lonesome –
Other Boys – are lost –

The Moon upon: *Sent to SD (variant) and perhaps to TWH (lost, transcribed variant) c. 1882*
The Bible is: *Sent to Ned Dickinson (variant) c. 1882, beginning "The Bible is an antique Volume –"*

Had but the Tale a thrilling Teller
All the Boys would come –
Orpheu's Sermon captivated –
It did not condemn –

line 11: [Boys that believe – are] bastinadoed – • ~~Boys that "believe" – Why – Boys are friendly~~ –
line 13: [Had but the Tale a] typic – • hearty – • bonnie – • breathless – • spacious – • tropic – • warbling – • ardent – • friendly – • magic – • pungent – • warbling – • winning • mellow – [Teller]

c. 1882

Meeting by Accident,[156]
We hovered by design –
As often as a Century
An error so divine
Is ratified by Destiny,
But Destiny is old
And economical of Bliss
As Midas is of Gold –

c. 1882

My Wars are laid away in Books –
I have one Battle more –
A Foe whom I have never seen
But oft has scanned me o'er –
And hesitated me between
And others at my side,
But chose the best – Neglecting me – till
All the rest have died –
How sweet if I am not forgot
By Chums that passed away –
Since Playmates at threescore and ten
Are such a scarcity –

c. 1882

The pattern of the sun
Can fit but him alone
For sheen must have a Disk
To be a sun –

c. 1882

Those – dying then,[157]
Knew where they went –
They went to God's Right Hand –
That Hand is amputated now
And God cannot be found –

The abdication of Belief
Makes the Behavior small –
Better an ignis fatuus
Than no illume at all –

c. 1882

Within thy Grave![158]
Oh no, but on some other flight –
Thou only camest to mankind
To rend it with Good night –

c. 1882

Bliss is the Plaything of the child –[159] [the] trinket –
The Secret of the man
The sacred stealth of Boy and Girl The happy guilt of Boy and Girl –
Rebuke it if we can

c. 1882

"Go tell it" – What a Message –[160]
To whom – is specified –

Not murmur – not endearment –
But simply – we obeyed –
Obeyed a Lure – a Longing?
Oh Nature – none of this –
To Law – said Sweet Thermopylae — [Sweet] Thermopolae –
I give my dying Kiss – — I send – • Convey my dying Kiss –

c. 1882

I groped for him before I knew
With solemn nameless need
All other bounty sudden chaff — [other] Bounty niggardly
For this foreshadowed Food — [this] unsullied
Which others taste and spurn and sneer – — [spurn and] slight
Though I within suppose
That consecrated it could be
The only Food that grows

c. 1882

Image of Light, Adieu – — Fellow [of]
Thanks for the interview –
So long – so short –
Preceptor of the whole –
Coeval Cardinal –
Impart – Depart –

c. 1882

Lives he in any other world
My faith cannot reply
Before it was imperative
'Twas all distinct to me – — All was distinct [to me –]

c. 1882

Of Death I try to think like this,[161]
The Well in which they lay us
Is but the Likeness of the Brook
That menaced not to slay us,
But to invite by that Dismay
Which is the Zest of sweetness
To the same Flower Hesperian, — [same] flower
Decoying but to greet us –

I do remember when a Child
With bolder Playmates straying
To where a Brook that seemed a Sea
Withheld us by its roaring
From just a Purple Flower beyond
Until constrained to clutch it
If Doom itself were the result, — Were Doom itself the penalty –
The boldest leaped, and clutched it – — [The] bravest

c. 1882

Tried always and Condemned by thee
Permit me this reprieve — Allow – • bestow – [me]
That dying I may earn the look — [the] gaze
For which I cease to live –

c. 1882

Cosmopolites without a plea[162] — [Cosmopolites] Without a Care –
Alight in every Land
The Compliments of Paradise
From these within my Hand — [From] *those*
Their dappled Journey – to themselves
A compensation fair – — [compensation] gay – • A competence so gay
Knock and it shall be opened
is their Theology — [their] Philosophy –

c. October 1882

He ate and drank the precious Words –
His Spirit grew robust –
He knew no more that he was poor,
Nor that his frame was Dust –
He danced along the dingy Days
And this Bequest of Wings
Was but a Book – What Liberty
A loosened Spirit brings – the [loosened]

c. late 1882

Pompless no Life can pass away –[163]
The lowliest career
To the same Pageant wends its way
As that exalted here –

How cordial is the mystery!
The hospitable Pall
A "this way" beckons spaciously –
A Miracle for all!

c. late 1882

No Brigadier throughout the Year[164]
So civic as the Jay –
A Neighbor and a Warrior too
With shrill felicity
Subduing Winds that censure us pursuing [Winds that] ~~sunder~~
A January Day – [A] February Day –
The Brother of the Universe
Was never blown away –
The Snow and he are intimate –
I've often seen them play
When Heaven looked upon us all
With such severity
I felt apology were due
To an insulted sky
Whose pompous frown was Nutriment
To their temerity –

No Brigadier throughout: *Sent to SD (variant) perhaps February 1883 and to TWH (variant) April 1883, with a clipping about birds*

The Pillow of this daring Head
Is pungent Evergreens –
His Larder – terse and Militant
Unknown – refreshing things –
His character – a Tonic –
His Future a Dispute – [His] Doctrines – • Dogmas • Chances a Redoubt –
Unfair an Immortality
That leaves this Neighbor out – [this] Major out

c. early 1883

To see her is a Picture –[165]
To hear her is a Tune –
To know her, a disparagement of every other Boon –
To know her not, Affliction –
To own her for a Friend
A warmth as near as if the Sun
Were shining in your Hand –

c. early 1883

The Clock strikes One[166]
That just struck Two –
Some Schism in the Sum –
A Vagabond from Genesis
Has wrecked the Pendulum –

c. 1883

A Sloop of Amber slips away[167]
Upon an Ether Sea
And wrecks in peace a Purple Tar –
The Son of Ecstasy – A Woe of Ecstasy –

c. 1883

To see her: *Sent to EH (variant) c. early 1883*
The Clock strikes: *Sent to EH (variant) 3 March 1883, to ST (variant) May 1883, and to Samuel Bowles the younger (variant) probably c. June 1884*

Forever honored be the Tree whose Apple winter-worn –[168]
Enticed to Breakfast from the Sky
Two Gabriels Yester Morn –
They registered in Nature's Book
As Robins, Sire and Son –
But Angels have that modest way
To screen them from renown –

c. March 1883

To be forgot by thee
Surpasses Memory
Of other minds
The Heart cannot forget
Unless it contemplate — Until [it]
What it declines
I was regarded then — [was] considered
Raised from oblivion
A single time — [a] royal – • signal – • hallowed
To be remembered what –
Worthy to be forgot
My low renown — is my renown • [My] one – • meek – • wan [renown]

lines 4–5: for one must recollect before it can forget

c. 1883

Not at Home to Callers
Says the Naked Tree –
Bonnet due in April – — Jacket [due]
Wishing you Good Day –

c. 1883

Lad of Athens faithful be to thyself and mystery –[169]
All the rest is perjury –

c. 1883

Forever honored be: *Sent to EH (variant) c. March 1883*
To be forgot: *Sent to HHJ (last 3 lines, variant) 10 April 1883, with harebells*
Not at Home: *Probably sent to Gilbert Dickinson (lost, published variant) spring of 1883*

Who has not found the Heaven – below –[170]
Will fail of it above –
For Angels rent the House next ours,
Wherever we remove –

c. 1883

Where Roses would not dare to go,
What Heart would risk the way, ~~could find~~
And so I send my Crimson Scouts
To sound the Enemy – ~~test~~

c. 1883

Witchcraft was hung, in History,
But History and I
Find all the Witchcraft that we need
Around us, Every Day –

c. 1883

The Lassitudes of Contemplation[171]
Beget a force –
They are the spirit's still vacation
That him refresh – [that] make him fresh
The Dreams
Consolidate
in action –
What mettle fair

c. 1883

It would not know if it were spurned,
This gallant little flower –
How therefore safe to be a flower
If one would tamper there.

o

Who has not: *Sent to Martha Dickinson and Sally Jenkins c. 1883*

To enter, it would not aspire –
But may it not despair
That it is not a Cavalier,
To dare and perish there?

c. 1883

This Me – that walks and works – must die[172]
Some fair or stormy Day –
Adversity if it may be
Or wild prosperity
The Rumor's Gate was shut so tight
Before my mind was born
Not even a Prognostic's push
Can make a Dent thereon – Could [make]

c. 1883

To her derided Home[173]
A weed of Summer came –
She did not know her station low
Nor ignominy's Name –
Bestowed a Summer long
Upon a fameless Flower –
Then swept as lightly from Disdain
As Lady from her Bower –
The Dandelion's Shield
Is valid as a Star –
The Buttercup's Escutcheon – Leontodon's Escutcheon
Sustains him anywhere – [sustains] her • Sustains him anywhere –

c. summer 1883

There came a Wind like a Bugle –
It quivered through the Grass [It] bubbled in –
And a Green Chill upon the Heat
So ominous did pass

This Me – that: *Sent to Maria Whitney (variant, last 6 lines) c. summer 1883*

We barred the Windows and the Doors
As from an Emerald Ghost –
The Doom's Electric Moccasin
That very instant passed –
On a strange Mob of panting Trees — Upon a Mob – [of]
And Fences fled away
And Rivers where the Houses ran
Those looked that lived – that Day – — The Living looked that Day –
The Bell within the steeple wild
The flying tidings told –
How much can come
And much can go,
And yet abide the World! — [yet] remain

c. 1883

The Bobolink is gone – the Rowdy of the Meadow –
And no one swaggers now but me –
The Presbyterian Birds can now resume the Meeting
He gaily interrupted that overflowing Day — [He] boldly
When opening the Sabbath in their afflictive Way
He bowed to Heaven instead of Earth
And shouted — and bubbled let us pray –
Let us pray –

line 5: When supplicating mercy / In a portentous way, • portentous way
line 6: [He bowed] to every Heaven above • to all the Saints he knew • [to] every God he knew
He recognized his maker – • [He] overturned the Decalogue –
lines 6–8: He swung upon the Decalogue / And shouted / Let us pray –
Gay from an unannointed Twig / He gurgled – • bubbled / Let us pray –
Sweet from a surreptitious Twig and bubbled let us pray –

c. 1883

The Summer that we did not prize[174]
Her treasures were so easy
Instructs us by departure now — [by] derision more
And recognition lazy –

Bestirs itself – puts on its Coat
and scans with fatal promptness — with what a fatal promptness
For Trains that moment out of sight — [Trains] serenely out of sight
Unconscious of his smartness – — Disdainful of his [smartness –]

c. 1883

To try to speak, and miss the way,
And ask it of the Tears,
Is Gratitude's sweet poverty,
The Tatters that he wears –

A better Coat if he possest,
Would help him to conceal,
Not subjugate, the Mutineer
Discreetly called "the Soul" –

January 1884

A Drunkard cannot meet a Cork[175]
Without a Revery –
And so encountering a Fly
This January Day
Jamaicas of Remembrance stir — [of] Prospective
That send me reeling in – — [reeling] on –
The moderate drinker of Delight
Does not deserve the Spring – — Has never Tasted spring –
Of Juleps, part are in the Jug
And more are in the Joy –
Your connoisaeur in Liquors consults the Bumble Bee –

c. 1884

'Tis not the swaying frame we miss –[176]
It is the steadfast Heart,
That had it beat a thousand years,
With Love alone had bent – — [alone] were

To try to: *Sent to ST (variant) January 1884*

Its fervor the electric Oar,
That bore it through the Tomb –
Ourselves, denied the privilege,
Consolelessly presume –

c. 1884

Arrows enamored of his Heart –[177] [his] Breast
Forgot to rankle there [to] enter
And Venoms he mistook for Balms the [Venoms]
disdained to rankle there – refused [to] • renounced their character

lines 3–4: Of injury too innocent / To know it when it passed

c. early 1884

Circumference thou Bride of Awe
Possessing thou shalt be
Possessed by every hallowed Knight reformed to nothing but Delight
That dares – to Covet thee which fears [to] • [That] ~~bends a Knee to thee~~ –

c. April 1884

Declaiming Waters none may dread,
But Waters that are still,
Are so for that most mighty cause
In Nature – they are full –

c. 1884

Few, yet enough,[178]
Enough is One –
To that etherial throng
Have not each one of us the right
To stealthily belong?

c. 1884

Circumference thou Bride: *Sent to Daniel Chester French (variant) c. April 1884*
Declaiming Waters none: *Sent to SD (variant) c. 1884*
Few, yet enough,: *Sent to SD c. 1884*

Though the great Waters sleep,[179]
That they are still the Deep,
We cannot doubt,
No vacillating God
Ignited this Abode
To put it out –

c. 1884

A World made penniless by that departure[180]
Of minor fabrics begs
But sustenance is of the spirit
The Gods but Dregs –

c. 1884

We send the Wave to find the Wave –
An Errand so divine,
The Messenger enamored too,
Forgetting to return,
We make the wise distinction still,
Soever made in vain,
The sagest time to dam the sea is when the sea is gone –

c. 1884

Sunset that screens, reveals[181]
Retarding what we see
By obstacles of swarthy gold
And amber mystery – [And] opal • purple

c. 1884

Though the great: *Sent to SD (variant) c. 1884, to Catherine Sweetser (lost, transcribed variant) c. November 1884, to Benjamin Kimball (variant) first half of 1885, and to Abigail Cooper (lost, transcribed variant) c. 1886*
We send the: *Sent to Ns (lost, transcribed variant) c. 1884*
Sunset that screens,: *Sent to MLT (variant) c. 1884*

Not knowing when the Dawn will come,[182]
I open every Door,
Or has it Feathers, like a Bird,
Or Billows, like a Shore –

c. 1884

A Flower will not trouble her, it has so small a Foot,
And yet if you compare the Lasts,
Hers is the smallest Boot –

c. 1884

Back from the Cordial Grave I drag thee
He shall not take thy Hand
Nor put his spacious Arm around thee
That none can understand

c. 1884

The pedigree of Honey[183]
Does not concern the Bee,
Nor lineage of Ecstasy
Delay the Butterfly
On spangled journeys to the peak
Of some perceiveless Thing –
The right of way to Tripoli
A more essential thing –

c. 1884

As from the Earth the light Balloon — [the] fair [Balloon]
Asks nothing but release – — [but] its flight
Ascension that for which it was,
Its soaring, Residence. — Its rapture – residence –

Not knowing when: *Sent to TWH (variant) spring 1886, beginning "Not knowing when Herself may come"*
The pedigree of: *Sent to MLT (lines 1–4, variant) c. 1884*

The spirit looks upon the Dust   its [spirit] turns upon – • gazes at • glances [at]
That fastened it so long
With indignation,
As a Bird
Defrauded of its Song.

c. 1884

Oh Future! thou secreted peace
Or subterranean Wo –   [Or] unsuspected
Is there no wandering route of grace
That leads away from thee –
No circuit sage of all the course   [circuit] ~~soft~~ [of all the] lines
Descried by cunning men
To balk thee of thy sacred Prey –
Advancing to thy Den –   Deputed to thy Den –

line 7: [To balk thee of] The [sacred Prey –] • the innocence • the myriads

c. 1884

So give me back to Death –
The Death I never feared
Except that it deprived of thee –
And now, by Life deprived,
In my own Grave I breathe
And estimate its size –
Its size is all that Hell can guess –   [Hell] surmise –
And all that Heaven was –

c. 1884

Still own thee – still thou art
What Surgeons call alive –
Though slipping – slipping – I perceive
To thy reportless Grave –

Which question shall I clutch –
What answer wrest from thee   [What] tidings –

Before thou dost exude away   [dost] dissolve away –
In the recallless sea?   in – [the]

c. 1884

Talk not to me of Summer Trees[184]
The foliage of the mind
A Tabernacle is for Birds
Of no corporeal kind
And winds do go that way at noon   [at] times
To their Etherial Homes   ~~Whose Homes~~
Whose Bugles call the least of us   [Bugles] bear
To undepicted Realms   [To] unreported [Realms] • Receipted with encores

c. 1884

The Sun in reining to the West
Makes not as much of sound
As Cart of man in road below
Adroitly turning round
That Whiffletree of Amethyst   his [Whiffletree]

c. 1884

Betrothed to Righteousness might be
An Ecstasy discreet
But Nature relishes the Pinks
Which she was taught to eat –

c. 1884

I held it so tight that I lost it
Said the Child of the Butterfly   [Said the] Boy
Of many a vaster Capture
That is the Elegy –

c. 1884

But that defeated accent
is louder now than him
Eternity may imitate
The Affluence of time [The] ~~Ecstasy~~ of time

lines 1–2: But that suspended • arrested syllable – / Is wealthier than him
But Love's dispelled Emolument / Finds no Abode in him – • Has [no Abode in him –]
• Has no retrieve in him

c. 1884

Upon his Saddle sprung a Bird[185] [Saddle] sprang the Bird,
And crossed a thousand Trees
Before a Fence without a Fare
His Fantasy did please
And then he lifted up his Throat
And squandered such a Note
A Universe that overheard A Universe's utter Art
Is stricken by it yet – Could not it imitate –

c. 1884

The farthest Thunder that I heard[186]
Was nearer than the Sky
And rumbles still, though torrid Noons
Have lain their Missiles by –
The Lightning that preceded it
Struck no one but myself –
But I would not exchange the Bolt
For all the rest of Life –
Indebtedness to Oxygen
The Happy may repay,
But not the obligation
To Electricity –
It founds the Homes and decks the Days
And every clamor bright

Upon his Saddle: *Sent to HHJ (last 4 lines, variant) September 1884*
The farthest Thunder: *Sent to SD (first 4 lines, variant) c. 1884 and to HHJ (variant, two lines as prose) September 1884*

Is but the gleam concomitant
Of that waylaying Light –
The Thought is quiet as a Flake –
A Crash without a Sound,
How Life's reverberation
Its Explanation found –

c. 1884

Apparently with no surprise[187]
To any happy Flower
The Frost beheads it at its play –
In accidental power –
The blonde Assassin passes on –
The Sun proceeds unmoved
To measure off another Day
For an Approving God –

c. 1884

The Jay his Castanet has struck[188]
Put on your muff for Winter — [your] *Bells*
The Tippet that ignores his voice — The [Tippet] that resists his voice
is impudent to nature — Teneriffe's Adventure
Of Swarthy Days he is the close — [the] ~~knell~~
His Lotus is a chestnut
The Cricket drops a sable line
No more from yours at present

lines 3–4: The Tippet that does not arise / Is ~~infidel~~ • ablative to Nature • [is] renegade to nature

c. 1884

Take all away from me, but leave me Ecstasy[189]
And I am richer then, than all my Fellow men.
Is it becoming me to dwell so wealthily

Take all away: *Sent to Mary and Eben Jenks Loomis (variant) 2 January 1885, perhaps to HHJ (lost) c. March 1885, and to Elizabeth and Samuel Bowles the younger (variant) 1885*

When at my very Door are those possessing more,
In abject poverty?

c. March 1885

Of God we ask one favor, that we may be forgiven –[190]
For what, he is presumed to know –
The Crime, from us, is hidden –
Immured the whole of Life
Within a magic Prison
We reprimand the Happiness
That too competes with Heaven –

c. March 1885

Some one prepared this mighty show[191]
To which without a Ticket go   [without] Delay
The nations and the Days –
Displayed before the simplest Door   Pass slow before the humblest Door
That all may examine them – and more   [examine] it – • [may] witness it [and]

line 3: The – of summer Days – • [The] pomp • ~~soul~~ of summer Days • the Ethiopian Days

c. 1885

The Ditch is dear to the Drunken man
for is it not his Bed – his Advocate – his Edifice –   [Edifice –] ~~The~~
How safe his fallen Head
In her disheveled Sanctity –
Above him is the sky –   ~~Beneath~~ [him]
Oblivion bending over him
And Honor leagues away –   [And] Doom a fallacy –

lines 6–7: [Oblivion] enfolding him with tender infamy –

c. 1885

Of God we: *Perhaps sent to HHJ (lost) c. March 1885*

The Ecstasy to guess,
Were a receipted Bliss
If Grace could talk –

c. 1885

"Red Sea," indeed! Talk not to me[192]
Of purple Pharaoh –
I have a Navy in the West
Would pierce his Columns thro' –
Guileless, yet of such Glory fine
That all along the Line
Is it, or is it not, marine –
Is it, or not, divine –
The Eye inquires with a sigh
That Earth sh'd be so big –
What Exultation in the Woe –
What Wine in the fatigue!

c. 1885

Extol thee – could I – Then I will[193]
by saying nothing new
But just the fair – averring –
That thou art heavenly –
Perceiving thee is evidence
That we are of the sky
Partaking thee a guaranty of immortality

line 3: [But just the] truest truth • fairest – • tritest – • sweetest • brightest truth –
lines 3–4: [But just] that tritest Eulogy / That thou art heavenly

c. 1885

Why should we hurry – Why indeed [should] I
When every way we fly

we are molested equally
by immortality
no respite from the inference [the] mightiness
that this which is begun [that] *tragedy* [begun]
though where its labors lie
A bland uncertainty
Besets the sight
This mighty night

c. 1885

The Immortality she gave,[194]
We borrowed at her Grave –
For just one Plaudit famishing,
The might of Human Love –

c. April 1886

The Immortality she: *Sent to TWH (variant) c. April 1886*

POEMS TRANSCRIBED BY OTHERS

No man saw awe, nor to his house[1]
Admitted he a man
Though by his awful residence
Has human nature been.

Not deeming of his dread abode
Till laboring to flee
A grasp on comprehension laid
Detained vitality.

Returning is a different route
The Spirit could not show
For breathing is the only work
To be enacted now.

"Am not consumed," old Moses wrote,
"Yet saw Him face to face" –
That very physiognomy
I am convinced was this

c. 1874 MLT

What tenements of clover
Are fitting for the bee?
What edifices azure
For butterflies and me?

What residences nimble
Arise and evanesce,
Without a bright suspicion, [a] wizard rumor
Or an assaulting guess!

c. 1875 MLT

What tenements of: *Sent to Olive Stearns (lost, transcribed variant) c. 1875*

My country need not change her gown,[2]
Her triple suit as sweet
As when 'twas cut at Lexington,
And first pronounced "a fit."

Great Britain disapproves "the stars;"
Disparagement discreet, –
There's something in their attitude
That taunts her bayonet.

c. 1880 MLT

Drowning is not so pitiful[3]
As the attempt to rise.
Three times, 'tis said, a sinking man
Comes up to face the skies,
And then declines forever
To that abhorred abode,
Where hope and he part company –
For he is grasped of God.
The Maker's cordial visage,
However good to see,
Is shunned, we must admit it,
Like an adversity.

c. 1880? MLT

The gleam of an heroic act
Such strange illumination
The Possible's slow fuse is lit
By the Imagination SD

Beauty crowds me till I die
Beauty mercy have on me
But if I expire today
Let it be in sight of thee – SD

My country need: *Sent to TWH (lost) November 1880, called "My Country's Wardrobe," and to Ns (lost) c. 1880*

Endanger it, and the Demand
Of tickets for a sigh
Amazes the Humility
Of Credibility –

Recover it to nature
And that dejected Fleet
Find Consternation's carnival
Divested of its meat SD

~

To tell the Beauty would decrease
To state the spell demean
There is a syllableless Sea
Of which it is the sign
My will endeavors for its word
And fails, but entertains
A Rapture as of Legacies –
Of introspective mines – SD

~

The Blunder is in estimate
Eternity is there
We say as of a Station
Meanwhile he is so near
He joins me in my Ramble
Divides abode with me
No Friend have I that so persists
As this Eternity SD

~

Volcanoes be in Sicily[4]
And South America
I judge from my Geography
Volcano nearer here
A Lava step at any time
Am I inclined to climb
A Crater I may contemplate
Vesuvius at Home SD

~

Of this is Day composed
A morning and a noon
A Revelry unspeakable
And then a gay unknown
Whose Pomps allure and spurn
And dower and deprive
And penury for Glory
Remedilessly leave SD

~

Summer begins to have the look
Peruser of enchanting Book
Reluctantly but sure perceives
A gain upon the backward leaves

Autumn begins to be inferred
By millinery of the cloud
Or deeper color in the shawl
That wraps the everlasting hill

The eye begins its avarice
A meditation chastens speech
Some Dyer of a distant tree
Resumes his gaudy industry

Conclusion is the course of all
Almost to be perennial
And then elude stability
Recalls to immortality – SD

~

Speech is one symptom of affection[5]
And Silence one –
The perfectest communication
Is heard of none

Exists and its indorsement
Is had within –
Behold said the Apostle
Yet had not seen! SD

~

Summer begins to: *Sent to Ns (lost), beginning "Summer begins to have a look"*

I see thee clearer for the Grave
That took thy face between
No mirror could illumine thee
Like that impassive stone –

I know thee better for the act
That made thee first unknown
The stature of the empty nest
Attests the Bird that's gone SD

There is a solitude of space[6]
A solitude of sea
A solitude of Death, but these
Society shall be
Compared with that profounder site
That polar privacy
A soul admitted to itself – SD

The ones that disappeared are back
The Phebe and the crow
Precisely as in March is heard
The curtness of the Jay –
Be this an Autumn or a Spring
My wisdom loses way
One side of me the nuts are ripe
The other side is May. SD

Lightly stepped a yellow star
To its lofty place
Loosed the Moon her silver hat
From her lustral Face
All of evening softly lit
As an Astral Hall
Father I observed to Heaven
You are punctual – SD

Peril as a Possession
'Tis good to bear
Danger disintegrates satiety
There's Basis there –
Begets an awe
That searches Human Nature's creases
As clean as Fire SD

Glory is that bright tragic thing
That for an instant
Means Dominion
Warms some poor name
That never felt the Sun
Gently replacing
In oblivion – SD

The butterfly obtains
But little sympathy
Though favorably mentioned
In Entomology –

Because he travels freely
And wears a proper coat
The circumspect are certain
That he is dissolute

Had he the homely scutcheon
Of modest Industry
'Twere fitter certifying
For Immortality – SD

Fame is a fickle food[7]
Upon a shifting plate
Whose table once a
Guest but not
The second time is set

Whose crumbs the crows inspect
And with ironic caw
Flap past it to the
Farmer's corn
Men eat of it and die SD

~

The wind drew off[8]
Like hungry dogs
Defeated of a bone
Through fissures in
Volcanic cloud
The yellow lightning shone –
The trees held up
Their mangled limbs
Like animals in pain
When Nature falls upon herself
Beware an Austrian SD

~

I know of people in the Grave
Who would be very glad
To know the news I know tonight
If they the chance had, had
'Tis this expands the least event
And swells the scantest deed
My right to walk upon the Earth
If they this moment had SD

~

These are the days that Reindeer love
And pranks the northern star
This is the Sun's objective
And Finland of the year SD

~

Today or this noon
She dwelt so close
I almost touched her

Tonight she lies
Past neighborhood
And bough and steeple
Now past surmise SD

Judgment is justest
When the Judged
His action laid away
Divested is of every Disk
But his sincerity

Honor is then the safest hue
In a posthumous Sun
Not any color will endure
That scrutiny can burn. SD

I did not reach Thee[9]
But my feet slip nearer every day
Three Rivers and a Hill to cross
One Desert and a Sea
I shall not count the journey one
When I am telling thee

Two deserts but the year is cold
So that will help the sand
One desert crossed –
The second one
Will feel as cool as land
Sahara is too little price
To pay for thy Right hand

The Sea comes last – Step merry feet
So short we have to go
To play together we are prone
But we must labor now
The last shall be the lightest load
That we have had to draw

o

The Sun goes crooked –
That is Night
Before he makes the bend
We must have passed the Middle Sea
Almost we wish the End
Were further off
Too great it seems
So near the Whole to stand

We step like Plush
We stand like snow
The water murmur new
Three rivers and the Hill are passed
Two deserts and the Sea!
Now Death usurps my Premium
And gets the look at Thee – SD

The Sun retired to a cloud
A Woman's shawl as big
And then he sulked in mercury
Upon a scarlet log –
The drops on Nature's forehead stood
Home flew the loaded bees
The South unrolled a purple fan
And handed to the trees SD

I watched her face to see which way
She took the awful news
Whether she died before she heard
Or in protracted bruise
Remained a few slow years with us
Each heavier than the last
A further afternoon to fail
As Flower at fall of Frost – SD

He went by sleep that drowsy route
To the surmising Inn –
At daybreak to begin his race
Or ever to remain – SD

~

Witchcraft has not a pedigree
'Tis early as our Breath
And mourners meet it going out
The moment of our death – SD

~

With sweetness unabated
Informed the hour had come
With no remiss of triumph
The autumn started home –
Her home to be with Nature
As competition done
By influential kinsmen
Invited to return
In supplements of Purple
An adequate repast
The heavenly reviewing
Her residue be past – SD

~

In snow thou comest
Thou shalt go with the resuming ground
The sweet derision of the crow
And Glee's advancing sound

In fear thou comest
Thou shalt go at such a gait of joy
That men anew embark to live
Upon the depth of thee – SD

~

A word made Flesh is seldom[10]
And tremblingly partook
Nor then perhaps reported
But have I not mistook
Each one of us has tasted
With ecstasies of stealth
The very food debated
To our specific strength –

A word that breathes distinctly
Has not the power to die
Cohesive as the Spirit
It may expire if He –

"Made Flesh and dwelt among us"
Could condescension be
Like this consent of Language
This loved Philology SD

That she forgot me was the least
I felt it second pain
That I was worthy to forget
Was most I thought upon

Faithful was all that I could boast
But Constancy became
To her, by her innominate
A something like a shame SD

Guest am I to have
Light my northern room
Why to cordiality so averse to come
Other friends adjourn
Other bonds decay
Why avoid so narrowly
My fidelity – SD

Rather arid delight
If Contentment accrue
Make an abstemious ecstasy
Not so good as joy –

But Rapture's Expense
Must not be incurred
With a tomorrow knocking
And the Rent unpaid – SD

'Tis easier to pity those when dead
That which pity previous
Would have saved
A Tragedy enacted
Secures applause
That Tragedy enacting
Too seldom does SD

Winter under cultivation
Is as arable as Spring SD

Down Time's quaint stream
Without an oar
We are enforced to sail
Our Port a secret
Our Perchance a Gale
What Skipper would
Incur the Risk
What Buccaneer would ride
Without a surety from the Wind
Or schedule of the Tide – SD

Nature can do no more
She has fulfilled her Dyes

Whatever Flower fail to come
Of other Summer days
Her crescent reimburse
If other Summers be
Nature's imposing negative
Nulls opportunity – SD

As we pass Houses musing slow
If they be occupied
So minds pass minds
If they be occupied SD

The event was directly behind Him
Yet He did not guess
Fitted itself to Himself like a Robe
Relished His ignorance
Motioned itself to drill
Loaded and Levelled
And let His Flesh
Centuries from His soul SD

If I could tell how glad I was
I should not be so glad –
But when I cannot make the Force
Nor mould it into word
I know it is a sign
That new Dilemma be
From mathematics further off
Than from Eternity SD

The right to perish might be tho't[11]
An undisputed right
Attempt it, and the Universe
Upon the opposite

Will concentrate its officers –
You cannot even die
But nature and mankind must pause
To pay you scrutiny – SD

Sometimes with the Heart
Seldom with the soul
Scarcer once with the might
Few – love at all SD

The Hills erect their Purple Heads
The Rivers lean to see
Yet man has not of all the Throng
A Curiosity SD

To do a magnanimous thing
And take one's self by surprise
If one's self is not in the habit of him
Is precisely the finest of Joys –

Not to do a magnanimous thing
Notwithstanding it never be known
Notwithstanding it cost us existence once
Is Rapture herself spurn – SD

His mind of man, a secret makes
I meet him with a start
He carries a circumference
In which I have no part

Or even if I deem I do
He otherwise may know
Impregnable to inquest
However neighborly – SD

The Look of thee, what is it like
Hast thou a hand or Foot
Or mansion of Identity
And what is thy Pursuit

Thy fellows are they realms or Themes
Hast thou Delight or Fear
Or Longing – and is that for us
Or values more severe –

Let change transfuse all other Traits
Enact all other Blame
But deign this least certificate
That thou shalt be the same – SD

They talk as slow as Legends grow
No mushroom is their mind
But foliage of sterility
Too stolid for the wind –

They laugh as wise as Plots of Wit
Predestined to unfold
The point with bland precision
Portentously untold SD

Of Yellow was the outer Sky[12]
In Yellower Yellow hewn
Till Saffron in vermillion slid
Whose seam could not be shown – SD

Eden is that old fashioned House
We dwell in every day
Without suspecting our abode
Until we drive away

How fair on looking back the Day
We sauntered from the Door

Unconscious our returning
But discover it no more SD

~

A – Cap of Lead across the sky
Was tight and surly drawn
We could not find the mighty Face
The Figure was Withdrawn –

A Chill came up as from a shaft
Our noon became a well
A Thunder storm combines the charms
Of Winter and of Hell SD

~

Advance is Life's condition
The Grave but a Relay
Supposed to be a terminus
That makes it hated so –

The Tunnel is not lighted
Existence with a wall
Is better we consider
Than not exist at all – SD

~

When we have ceased to care
The Gift is given
For which we gave the Earth
And mortgaged Heaven
But so declined in worth
'Tis ignominy now
To look upon – SD

~

Not any sunny tone
From any fervent zone
Find entrance there
Better a grave of Balm
Toward human nature's home
And Robins near

Than a stupendous Tomb
Proclaiming to the gloom
How dead we are – SD

Conferring with myself
My stranger disappeared
Though first upon a berry fat
Miraculously fared
How paltry looked my cares
My practise how absurd
Superfluous my whole career
Beside this travelling Bird SD

'Twas comfort in her Dying Room
To hear the living Clock
A short relief to have the wind
Walk boldly up and knock
Diversion from the Dying Theme
To hear the children play
But wrong the more
That these could live
And this of ours must *die* SD

A lane of Yellow led the eye[13]
Unto a Purple Wood
Whose soft inhabitants to be
Surpasses solitude
If Bird the silence contradict
Or flower presume to show
In that low summer of the West
Impossible to know – SD

In Winter in my Room
I came upon a Worm
Pink lank and warm

But as he was a worm
And worms presume
Not quite with him at home
Secured him by a string
To something neighboring
And went along –

A Trifle afterward
A thing occurred
I'd not believe it if I heard
But state with creeping blood
A snake with mottles rare
Surveyed my chamber floor
In feature as the worm before
But ringed with power
The very string with which
I tied him – too
When he was mean and new
That string was there –

I shrank – "How fair you are"!
Propitiation's Claw –
"Afraid he hissed
Of me"?
"No Cordiality" –
He fathomed me –
Then to a Rhythm *Slim*
Secreted in his Form
As Patterns swim
Projected him.

That time I flew
Both eyes his way
Lest he pursue
Nor ever ceased to run
Till in a distant Town
Towns on from mine
I set me down
This was a dream – SD

On my volcano grows the Grass[14]
A meditative spot –
An acre for a Bird to choose
Would be the general thought –

How red the Fire rocks below
How insecure the sod
Did I disclose
Would populate with awe my solitude SD

~

To their apartment deep
No ribaldry may creep
Untumbled this abode
By any man but God – SD

~

Unto a broken heart
No other one may go
Without the high prerogative
Itself hath suffered too SD

~

As subtle as tomorrow
That never came,
A warrant, a conviction,
Yet but a name. MLT

~

By a departing light [a] retreating • Absconding light
We see acuter, quite, [see] distincter • Sincerer quite.
Than by a wick that stays. [by] the
There's something in the flight
That clarifies the sight
And decks the rays [And] brims • fills • And swells the rays

MLT & Millicent Todd

~

Consulting summer's clock,
But half the hours remain.
I ascertain it with a shock –
I shall not look again.
The second half of joy
Is shorter than the first.
The truth I do not dare to know
I muffle with a jest.

MLT

Did life's penurious length
Italicize its sweetness,
The men that daily live
Would stand so deep in joy
That it would clog the cogs
Of that revolving reason
Whose esoteric belt
Protects our sanity.

MLT

God is indeed a jealous God –[15]
He cannot bear to see
That we had rather not with Him
But with each other play.

That we desire with ourselves
And not with Him to play.

MLT

Had I known that the first was the last[16]
I should have kept it longer.
Had I known that the last was the first
I should have mixed it stronger.
Cup, it was your fault,
Lip was not the liar.
No, lip it was yours,
Bliss was most to blame.

[have] drunk

MLT

He was my host – he was my guest,
I never to this day
If I invited him could tell,
Or he invited me.

So infinite our intercourse [our] interview
So intimate, indeed,
Analysis as capsule seemed [Analysis] like
To keeper of the seed.

MLT

~

Her face was in a bed of hair,[17]
Like flowers in a plot –
Her hand was whiter than the sperm
That feeds the sacred light. [the] central
Her tongue more tender than the tune [more] timid • magic [than the] tone
That totters in the leaves –
Who hears may be incredulous,
Who witnesses, believes. MLT

~

If all the griefs I am to have[18]
Would only come today,
I am so happy I believe
They'd laugh and run away.

If all the joys I am to have
Would only come today,
They could not be so big as this
That happens to me now. MLT

~

Is Immortality a bane
That men are so oppressed? MLT

~

Love can do all but raise the Dead
I doubt if even that

From such a giant were withheld [a] beggar
Were flesh equivalent [Were] Dust –

But love is tired and must sleep,
And hungry and must graze
And so abets the shining Fleet
Till it is out of gaze. Millicent Todd

One crown that no one seeks[19] [crown] not any seek
And yet the highest head Although [the]
Its isolation coveted
Its stigma deified [Its] forfeit

While Pontius Pilate lives
In whatsoever hell
That coronation pierces him
He recollects it well. MLT

Proud of my broken heart, since thou didst break it,[20]
Proud of the pain I did not feel till thee,

Proud of my night, since thou with moons dost slake it,
Not to partake thy passion, *my* humility.

Thou can't not boast, like Jesus, drunken without companion
Was the strong cup of anguish brewed for the Nazarene

Thou can't not pierce tradition with the peerless puncture,
See! I usurped *thy* crucifix to honor mine! MLT

That it will never come again
Is what makes life so sweet.
Believing what we don't believe
Does not exhilarate.

That if it be, it be at best
An ablative estate – [ablative] delight

This instigates an appetite
Precisely opposite. MLT

~

The joy that has no stem nor core,
Nor seed that we can sow,
Is edible to longing,
But ablative to show.

By fundamental palates
Those products are preferred
Impregnable to transit
And patented by pod. MLT

~

The mob within the heart
Police cannot suppress
The riot given at the first
Is authorized as peace

Uncertified of scene — Not certified [of]
Or signified of sound
But growing like a hurricane
In a congenial ground. MLT

~

The most important population
Unnoticed dwell.
They have a heaven each instant — [each] minute
Not any hell.

Their names, unless you know them,
'Twere useless tell.
Of bumble-bees and other nations
The grass is full. MLT

~

The parasol is the umbrella's daughter,
And associates with a fan

While her father abuts the tempest
And abridges the rain.

The former assists a siren
In her serene display;
But her father is borne and honored, [But] the latter, her sire, [is honored,]
And borrowed to this day.

MLT

The waters chased him as he fled,
Not daring look behind;
A billow whispered in his Ear,
"Come home with me, my friend;
My parlor is of shriven glass,
My pantry has a fish
For every palate in the Year," –
To this revolting bliss
The object floating at his side
Made no distinct reply.

MLT

The words the happy say
Are paltry melody
But those the silent feel
Are beautiful –

Millicent Todd

There comes an hour when begging stops,[21]
When the long interceding lips
Perceive their prayer is vain.
"Thou shalt not" is a kinder sword
Than from a disappointing God
"Disciple, call again."

MLT

This docile one inter
While we who dare to live
Arraign the sunny brevity
That sparkled to the Grave [That] sparkles in

On her departing span — of [her]
No wilderness remain — [wilderness] retain
As dauntless in the House of Death
As if it were her own – — MLT & Millicent Todd

line 7: As playful in the Porch of Death
[As] fearless • Contented [in the] Door • door [of Death]
As happy in her crib of dust • [her] bed [of dust]

~

Through those old grounds of memory,
The sauntering alone
Is a divine intemperance
A prudent man would shun.
Of liquors that are vended
'Tis easy to beware
But statutes do not meddle
With the internal bar.
Pernicious as the sunset
Permitting to pursue
But impotent to gather,
The tranquil perfidy
Alloys our firmer moments
With that severest gold
Convenient to the longing
But otherwise withheld. — MLT

~

'Twas here my summer paused
What ripeness after then
To other scene or other soul — [or] any
My sentence had begun.

To winter to remove
With winter to abide
Go manacle your icicle
Against your Tropic Bride — MLT & Millicent Todd

~

Softened by Time's consummate plush,
How sleek the woe appears
That threatened childhood's citadel
And undermined the years.

Bisected now, by bleaker griefs,
We envy the despair
That devastated childhood's realm,
So easy to repair.

[So] supple • pliant

MLT

~

My life closed twice before its close;[22]
It yet remains to see
If Immortality unveil
A third event to me,

So huge, so hopeless to conceive
As these that twice befel.
Parting is all we know of heaven,
And all we need of hell.

MLT

~

A face devoid of love or grace,
A hateful, hard, successful face,
A face with which a stone
Would feel as thoroughly at ease
As were they old acquaintances –
First time together thrown.

MLT

~

Upon the gallows hung a wretch,
Too sullied for the hell
To which the law entitled him.
As nature's curtain fell
The one who bore him tottered in, –
For this was woman's son.
"'Twas all I had," she stricken gasped –
Oh, what a livid boon!

What an appalling boon!

MLT

~

The reticent volcano keeps
His never slumbering plan;
Confided are his projects pink
To no precarious man.

If nature will not tell the tale
Jehovah told to her
Can human nature not proceed — [not] survive
Without a listener?

Admonished by her buckled lips
Let every prater be — [every] babbler
The only secret neighbors keep — [secret] people shun
Is Immortality.

MLT

~

To lose thee – sweeter than to gain
All other hearts I knew. — [other] things
'Tis true the drought is destitute,
But then, I had the dew!

The Caspian has its realms of sand,
Its other realm of sea.
Without the sterile perquisite,
No Caspian could be.

MLT

~

High from the earth I heard a bird;
He trod upon the trees
As he esteemed them trifles,
And then he spied a breeze,
And situated softly
Upon a pile of wind
Which in a perturbation
Nature had left behind.
A joyous going fellow
I gathered from his talk
Which both of benediction
And badinage partook.

Without apparent burden
I subsequently learned
He was the faithful father
Of a dependent brood.
And this untoward transport
His remedy for care, –
A contrast to our respites.
How different we are!

MLT

~

To make a prairie it takes a clover and one bee,
One clover, and a bee,
And revery.
The revery alone will do,
If bees are few.

MLT

~

Sweet is the swamp with its secrets,
Until we meet a snake;
'Tis then we sigh for houses,
And our departure take
At that enthralling gallop
That only childhood knows.
A snake is nature's treason, [is] summer's drama
And awe is where it goes. [And] guile

MLT

~

The distance that the dead have gone
Does not at first appear;
Their coming back seems possible
For many an ardent year.

And then, that we have followed them,
We more than half suspect,
So intimate have we become
With their dear retrospect.

MLT

line 4: For many a fruitless year. • That first abandoned year. • That first absconded year.

~

How dare the robins sing,
When men and women hear
Who since they went to their account
Have settled with the year! –
Paid all that life had earned
In one consummate bill.
And now, what life or death can do
Is immaterial.
Insulting is the sun
To him whose mortal light
Beguiled of immortality
Bequeath him to the night.
Extinct be every hum
In deference to him
Whose garden wrestled with the dew,
At daybreak overcome! MLT

Death is like the insect
Menacing the tree,
Competent to kill it,
But decoyed may be.

Bait it with the balsam
Seek it with the saw,
Baffle, if it cost you
Everything you are.

Then, if it have burrowed
Out of reach of skill –
Wring the tree and leave it.
'Tis the vermin's will. MLT

The grave my little cottage is,
Where "keeping house" for thee
I make my parlor orderly
And lay the marble tea.

For two divided, briefly,
A cycle, it may be,

Till everlasting life unite [everlasting] rite
In strong society. [In] one

MLT

Sweet hours have perished here,
This is a timid room –
Within its precincts hopes have played
Now fallow in the tomb. [Now] shadows

MLT

Were nature mortal lady[23]
Who had so little time
To pack her trunk and order
The great exchange of clime –

How rapid, how momentous –
What exigencies were –
But nature will be ready
And have an hour to spare.

To make some trifle fairer
That was too fair before –
Enchanting by remaining,
And by departure more.

Unknown

Fame is a bee.[24]
It has a song –
It has a sting –
Ah, too, it has a wing.

Unknown

The saddest noise, the sweetest noise,[25]
The maddest noise that grows, –
The birds, they make it in the spring,
At night's delicious close,

o

Between the March and April line –
That magical frontier
Beyond which summer hesitates,
Almost too heavenly near.

It makes us think of all the dead
That sauntered with us here,
By separation's sorcery
Made cruelly more dear.

It makes us think of what we had,
And what we now deplore.
We almost wish those siren throats
Would go and sing no more.

An ear can break a human heart
As quickly as a spear.
We wish the ear had not a heart
So dangerously near.

Unknown

POEMS NOT RETAINED

Valentine week.

Awake ye muses nine, sing me a strain divine,[1]
unwind the solemn twine, and tie my Valentine!

——— ——— ———

Oh the Earth was *made* for lovers, for damsel, and hopeless swain,
for sighing, and gentle whispering, and *unity* made of *twain,*
all things do go a courting, in earth, or sea, or air,
God hath made nothing single but *thee* in his world so fair!
The *bride*, and then the *bridegroom*, the *two*, and then the *one*,
Adam, and Eve, his consort, the moon, and then the sun;
the life doth prove the precept, who obey shall happy be,
who will not serve the sovreign, be hanged on fatal tree.
The high do seek the lowly, the great do seek the small,
none cannot find who *seeketh* on this terrestrial ball;
The bee doth court the flower, the flower his suit receives,
and they make a merry wedding, whose guests are hundred leaves;
the wind doth woo the branches, the branches they are won,
and the father fond demandeth the maiden for his son.
The storm doth walk the seashore humming a mournful tune,
the wave with eye so pensive, looketh to see the moon,
their spirits meet together, they make them solemn vows,
no more he singeth mournful, her sadness she doth lose.
The *worm* doth woo the *mortal*, death claims a living bride,
night unto day is married, morn unto eventide;
Earth is a merry damsel, and *Heaven* a knight so true,
and Earth is quite coquettish, and he seemeth in vain to sue.
Now to the *application*, to the reading of the roll,
to bringing thee to justice, and marshalling thy soul;
thou art a *human* solo, a being cold, and lone,
wilt have no kind companion, thou *reap'st* what thou hast *sown*.
Hast never silent hours, and minutes all too long,
and a deal of sad reflection, and *wailing* instead of song?

Awake ye muses: *Sent to Elbridge G. Bowdoin 4 March 1850, as dated by ED*

There's *Sarah*, and *Eliza,* and *Emeline* so fair,
and *Harriet*, and *Susan*, and she with *curling hair*!
Thine eyes are sadly blinded, but yet thou mayest see
six true, and comely maidens sitting upon the tree;
approach that tree with caution, then up it boldly climb,
and seize the one thou lovest, nor care for *space*, or *time*!
Then bear her to the greenwood, and build for her a bower,
and give her what she asketh, jewel, or bird, or flower;
and bring the fife, and trumpet, and beat upon the drum –
and bid the world Goodmorrow, and go to glory home!

4 March 1850

Sic transit gloria mundi[2]
"How doth the busy bee"
Dum vivamus vivamus
I stay mine enemy! –

Oh veni vidi vici!
Oh caput cap-a-pie!
And oh "memento mori"
When I am far from thee

Hurrah for Peter Parley
Hurrah for Daniel Boone
Three cheers sir, for the gentleman
Who first observed the moon –

Peter put up the sunshine!
Pattie arrange the stars
Tell Luna, tea is waiting
And call your brother Mars –

Put down the apple Adam
And come away with me
So shalt thou have a pippin
From off my Father's tree!

I climb the "Hill of Science"
I "view the Landscape o'er"

Sic transit gloria: *Sent to William Howland (lost, published variant) c. 1852*

Such transcendental prospect
I ne'er beheld before! –

Unto the Legislature
My country bids me go,
I'll take my india rubbers
In case the wind should blow.

During my education
It was announced to me
That gravitation stumbling
Fell from an apple tree –

The Earth upon its axis
Was once supposed to turn
By way of a gymnastic
In honor to the sun –

It was the brave Columbus
A sailing o'er the tide
Who notified the nations
Of where I would reside

Mortality is fatal
Gentility is fine
Rascality, heroic
Insolvency, sublime

Our Fathers being weary
Laid down on Bunker Hill
And though full many a morn'g
Yet they are sleeping still

The trumpet sir, shall wake them
In streams I see them rise
Each with a solemn musket
A marching to the skies!

A coward will remain, Sir,
Until the fight is done;
But an immortal hero
Will take his hat and run.

∘

Good bye Sir, I am going
My country calleth me
Allow me Sir, at parting
To wipe my weeping e'e

In token of our friendship
Accept this "Bonnie Doon"
And when the hand that pluck'd it
Hath passed beyond the moon

The memory of my ashes
Will consolation be
Then farewell Tuscarora
And farewell Sir, to thee.

c. 1852 Eudocia Converse/Jay Leyda

I have a Bird in spring[3]
Which for myself doth sing –
The spring decoys.
And as the summer nears –
And as the Rose appears,
Robin is gone.

Yet do I not repine
Knowing that Bird of mine
Though flown –
Learneth beyond the sea
Melody new for me
And will return.

Fast in a safer hand
Held in a truer Land
Are mine –
And though they now depart,
Tell I my doubting heart
They're thine.

In a serener Bright,
In a more golden light
I see

I have a: *Sent to SD c. 1854 and to Elizabeth and Josiah Holland (stanza 2, lost) 26 November 1854*

Each little doubt and fear,
Each little discord here
Removed.

Then will I not repine,
Knowing that Bird of mine
Though flown
Shall in a distant tree
Bright melody for me
Return.

c. 1854

Whose cheek is this?[4]
What rosy face
Has lost a blush today?
I found her – 'pleiad' – in the woods
And bore her safe away –

Robins, in the tradition
Did cover such with leaves,
But which the cheek –
And which the pall
My scrutiny deceives –

c. early 1859

When Katie walks, this Simple pair accompany her side,
When Katie runs unwearied they follow on the road,
When Katie kneels, their loving hands still clasp her pious knee –
Ah! Katie! Smile at Fortune, with *two* so *knit to thee!*

c. late 1859 Catherine Scott Turner (Anthon)

"Mama" never forgets her birds –[5]
Though in another tree.

Whose cheek is: *Sent to SD c. early 1859, with a flower and a tiny picture of a bird cut from the* New England Primer

When Katie walks,: *Sent to Catherine Scott Turner (Anthon) (lost) perhaps c. late 1859, with a pair of garters ED had knit*

"Mama" never forgets: *Sent to Louisa Norcross (lost) c. April 1860, on the death of her mother, ED's Aunt Lavinia*

She looks down just as often
And just as tenderly,
As when her little mortal nest
With cunning care she wove –
If either of her "sparrows fall",
She "notices" above.

c. April 1860 Frances Norcross

~

The Juggler's *Hat* her Country is –
The Mountain Gorse – the *Bee's* –

c. 1861

~

Could *I* – then – shut the door –
Lest *my* beseeching face – at last –
Rejected – be – of *Her*?

c. 1861

~

Is it true, dear Sue?[6]
Are there *two*?
I shouldn't like to come
For fear of joggling Him!
If you could shut him up
In a Coffee Cup,
Or tie him to a pin
Till I got in –
Or make him fast
To "Toby's" fist –
Hist! Whist! I'd come!

19 June 1861

~

"*Speech*" – is a prank of *Parliament* –
"*Tears*" – a trick of the *nerve* –

The Juggler's *Hat*: *Sent to SB c. 1861*
Could *I* – then –: *Sent to SD c. 1861*
Is it true,: *Sent to SD 19 June 1861, on the birth of her and Austin's first child, Edward (Ned)*
"*Speech*" – is a: *Sent to SB and to Ns (lost, transcribed variant) c. 1861*

But the Heart with the heaviest freight on –
Doesn't – always – move –

c. 1861

Title divine – is mine![7]
The Wife – without the Sign!
Acute Degree – conferred on me –
Empress of Calvary!
Royal – all but the Crown!
Betrothed – without the swoon
God sends us Women –
When you – hold – Garnet to Garnet –
Gold – to Gold –
Born – Bridalled – Shrouded –
In a Day –
"My Husband" – women say –
Stroking the Melody –
Is *this* – the way?

c. 1861

I'll send the feather from my Hat!
Who knows – but at the sight of *that*
My Sovreign will relent?
As trinket – worn by faded Child –
Confronting eyes long – comforted –
Blisters the Adamant!

c. 1861

Baby –
Teach Him – when He makes the *names* –[8]
Such an one – to say –
On his babbling – Berry – lips –
As should sound – to me –

Title divine – is: *Sent to SB c. 1861 and to SD (variant) 1865*
I'll send the: *Sent to SB c. 1861*
Teach Him – when: *Sent to Mary Bowles c. December 1861, after the birth of Charles Allen Bowles*

Were my Ear – as near his nest –
As my *thought* – today –
As should sound –
"Forbid us not" –
Some like "Emily."

c. December 1861

Would you like Summer? Taste of ours – Spices? Buy – here![9]
Ill! We have Berries, for the parching!
Weary! Furloughs of Down!
Perplexed! Estates of Violet – Trouble ne'er looked on!
Captive! We bring Reprieve of Roses!
Fainting! Flasks of Air!
Even for Death – A Fairy medicine –
But, which is it – Sir?

early February 1862

[Sh]ould you but fail [at] Sea –
[In] sight of me –
[Or] doomed lie –
[Ne]xt Sun – to die –
[O]r rap – at Paradise – unheard –
I'd *harass God* –
Until He let [you] in!

c. early 1862

A word is dead, when it is said
Some say –
I say it just begins to live
That day

probably early 1862 Frances Norcross

Would you like: *Sent to SB early February 1862*
Should you but: *Sent to SB c. early 1862 (text in brackets is supplied conjecturally; the page is torn)*
A word is: *Sent to Ns (lost) probably early 1862*

Let others – show this Surry's Grace –
Myself – assist his Cross –

late November or early December 1862

Best Gains – must have the Losses' test –
To constitute them – Gains.

c. 1863

Not "Revelation" – 'tis – that waits,
But our unfurnished eyes –

c. 1863

Life is death we're lengthy at,
Death the hinge to life.

c. 30 May 1863 Frances Norcross

The lovely flowers embarrass me,
They make me regret I am not a Bee –

c. late spring 1864

Her sovreign People
Nature knows as well
And is as fond of signifying
As if fallible –

c. 1865

Let others – show: *Sent to SB c. late November or early December 1862*
Best Gains – must: *Sent to TWH c. 1863, who was then commander of a Union regiment in South Carolina*
Not "Revelation" – 'tis –: *Sent to TWH c. 1863 and perhaps to SD (lost, transcribed as prose)*
Life is death: *Sent to Ns (lost) c. 30 May 1863*
The lovely flowers: *Sent to ED's Aunt Lucretia Bullard c. late spring 1864, in response to a gift of wisteria*
Her sovreign People: *Sent to SD c. 1865, perhaps with a flower, addressed "Rare to the Rare –"*

An Hour is a Sea
Between a few, and me –
With them would Harbor be –

c. late 1865

Count not that far that can be had[11]
Though sunset lie between
Nor that adjacent that beside
Is further than the sun.

early May 1866 MLT

Distance – is not the Realm of Fox
Nor by Relay of Bird
Abated – Distance is
Until thyself, Beloved.

c. 1866

A full fed Rose on meals of Tint
A Dinner for a Bee
In process of the Noon became –
Each bright mortality
The Forfeit is of Creature fair
Itself, adored before
Submitting for our unknown sake
To be esteemed no more

c. 1867

The longest day that God appoints
Will finish with the sun.

An Hour is: *Sent to SD c. late 1865*
Count not that: *Sent to EH early May 1866 (lost); SD transcribed another MS from c. spring 1866 (lost, transcribed variant)*
Distance – is not: *Sent to SD c. 1866*
A full fed: *Sent to SD c. 1867; SD transcribed another MS from c. 1867 (lost, transcribed variant)*
The longest day: *Sent to Ns (lost) c. 1868 (?)*

Anguish can travel to its stake,
And then it must return.

c. 1868 (?) Frances Norcross/MLT

The Work of Her that went,
The Toil of Fellows done –
In Ovens green Our Mother bakes,
By Fires of the Sun –

c. 1869

When Etna basks and purrs
Naples is more afraid
Than when she shows her Garnet Tooth –
Security is loud –

c. 1869

A Mine there is no Man would own[12]
But must it be conferred,
Demeaning by exclusive wealth
A Universe beside –

Potosi never to be spent
But hoarded in the mind
What Misers wring their hands tonight
For Indies in the Ground!

c. 1869

A Spider sewed at Night
Without a Light
Upon an Arc of White –

o

The Work of: *Apparently sent to SD c. 1869*
When Etna basks: *Apparently sent to SD c. 1869*
A Mine there: *Sent to SD c. 1869*
A Spider sewed: *Sent to SD and to Ns (lost, transcribed variant) c. 1869*

If Ruff it was of Dame
Or Shroud of Gnome
Himself himself inform –

Of Immortality
His strategy
Was physiognomy –

c. 1869

Were it to be the last
How infinite would be
What we did not suspect was marked
Our final interview.

c. late February 1870

I bet with every Wind that blew
Till Nature in chagrin
Employed a Fact to visit me
And scuttle my Balloon –

c. 1870

My God – He sees thee –
Shine thy best –
Fling up thy Balls of Gold
Till every Cubit play with thee
And every Crescent hold –
Elate the Acre at his feet –
Upon his Atom swim –
Oh Sun – but just a Second's right
In thy long Race with him!

c. 1870

Were it to: *Sent to ED's Aunt Catherine Sweetser c. late February 1870, after the 17 February death of her son*
I bet with: *Perhaps sent to SD c. 1870*
My God – He: *Sent to SD c. 1870*

He is alive, this morning –[13]
He is alive – and awake –
Birds are resuming for Him –
Blossoms – dress for His sake –
Bees – to their Loaves of Honey
Add an Amber Crumb
Him – to regale – Me – Only –
Motion, and am dumb.

c. June 1870

Trust adjusts her "Peradventure" –
Phantoms entered "and not you."

26 September 1870

The Life we have is very great.[14]
The Life that we shall see
Surpasses it, we know, because
It is Infinity.
But when all space has been beheld
And all Dominion shown
The smallest Human Heart's extent
Reduces it to none.

c. early October 1870

Lest any doubt that we are glad that they were born Today
Whose having lived is held by us in noble Holiday
Without the date, like Consciousness or Immortality –

December 1870

He is alive,: *Given to Samuel and Mary Bowles c. June 1870*
Trust adjusts her: *Sent to TWH 26 September 1870, following his August visit to ED*
The Life we: *Sent to EH c. early October 1870*
Lest any doubt: *According to Bianchi, sent to SD for her fortieth birthday, 19 December 1870, with flowers*

God made no act without a cause – nor heart without an aim –[15]
Our inference is premature, our premises to blame.

c. Christmas 1870 Frances Norcross

White as an Indian Pipe[16]
Red as a Cardinal Flower
Fabulous as a Moon at Noon
February Hour –

c. 1871

Of so divine a Loss
We enter but the Gain,
Indemnity for Loneliness
That such a Bliss has been.

c. September 1871

Like Brooms of Steel
The Snow and Wind
Had swept the Winter Street –
The House was hooked
The Sun sent out
Faint Deputies of Heat –
Where rode the Bird
The Silence tied
His ample – plodding Steed
The Apple in the Cellar snug
Was all the one that played.

c. early 1872

The Stars are old, that stood for me –
The West a little worn –

God made no: *Sent to Ns (lost, transcribed variant) c. Christmas 1870*
White as an: *Apparently sent to SD c. 1871*
Of so divine: *Sent to SD c. September 1871*
Like Brooms of: *Sent to SD c. early 1872*
The Stars are: *Sent to SD c. 1872 and to TWH (last 4 lines, variant) c. January 1874*

Yet newer glows the only Gold
I ever cared to earn –
Presuming on that lone result
Her infinite disdain
But vanquished her with my defeat
'Twas Victory was slain.

c. 1872

It is the Meek that Valor wear
Too mighty for the Bold.

c. late August 1872

Our own possessions – though our own –
'Tis well to hoard anew –
Remembering the Dimensions
Of Possibility.

c. 1872

I cannot see my soul, but know 'tis there –
Nor ever saw his house, nor furniture –
Who has invited me with him to dwell;
But a confiding guest, consult as well,
What raiment honor him the most,
That I be adequately dressed –
For he insures to none
Lest men specifical adorn –
Procuring him perpetual drest
By dating it a sudden feast.

c. 1873 (?) Frances Norcross

It is the: *Sent to EH, who had undergone eye surgery, c. late August 1872*
Our own possessions –: *Sent to SD c. 1872 and to TWH (variant) late 1872*
I cannot see: *Sent to Ns (lost) c. 1873 (?)*

Had this one Day not been,
Or could it cease to be
How smitten, how superfluous,
Were every other Day!

Lest Love should value less
What Loss would value more
Had it the stricken privilege,
It cherishes before.

c. 1873

This is the place they hoped before,[17]
Where I am hoping now.
The seed of disappointment grew
Within a capsule gay,
Too distant to arrest the feet
that walk this plank of balm,
Before them lies escapeless sea
The way is closed they came.

c. late May 1873 Frances Norcross

The Face we choose to miss –
Be it but for a Day
As absent as a Hundred Years,
When it has rode away –

c. 1873

Dominion lasts until obtained –
Possession just as long –
But these – endowing as they flit
Eternally belong.

How everlasting are the Lips
Known only to the Dew –

Had this one: *Sent to SD c. 1873*
This is the: *Sent to Frances Norcross (lost) c. late May 1873*
The Face we: *Perhaps sent to SD c. 1873*
Dominion lasts until: *Sent to TWH c. 1873*

These are the Brides of permanence –
Supplanting me and you.

c. 1873

Silence is all we dread.[18]
There's Ransom in a Voice –
But Silence is Infinity.
Himself have not a face.

c. autumn 1873

When Memory is full
Put on the perfect Lid –
This Morning's finest syllable
Presumptuous Evening said –

c. autumn 1873

Confirming All who analyze
In the Opinion fair
That Eloquence is when the Heart
Has not a Voice to spare –

c. 1873

I saw that the Flake was on it[19]
But plotted with Time to dispute –
"Unchanged" I urged with a candor
That cost me my honest Heart –

But "you" – she returned with valor
Sagacious of my mistake
"Have altered – Accept the pillage
For the progress' sake" –

c. 1873

Silence is all: *Sent to SD c. autumn 1873*
When Memory is: *Sent to EH c. autumn 1873*
Confirming All who: *Apparently sent to SD c. 1873*
I saw that: *Sent to SD c. 1873*

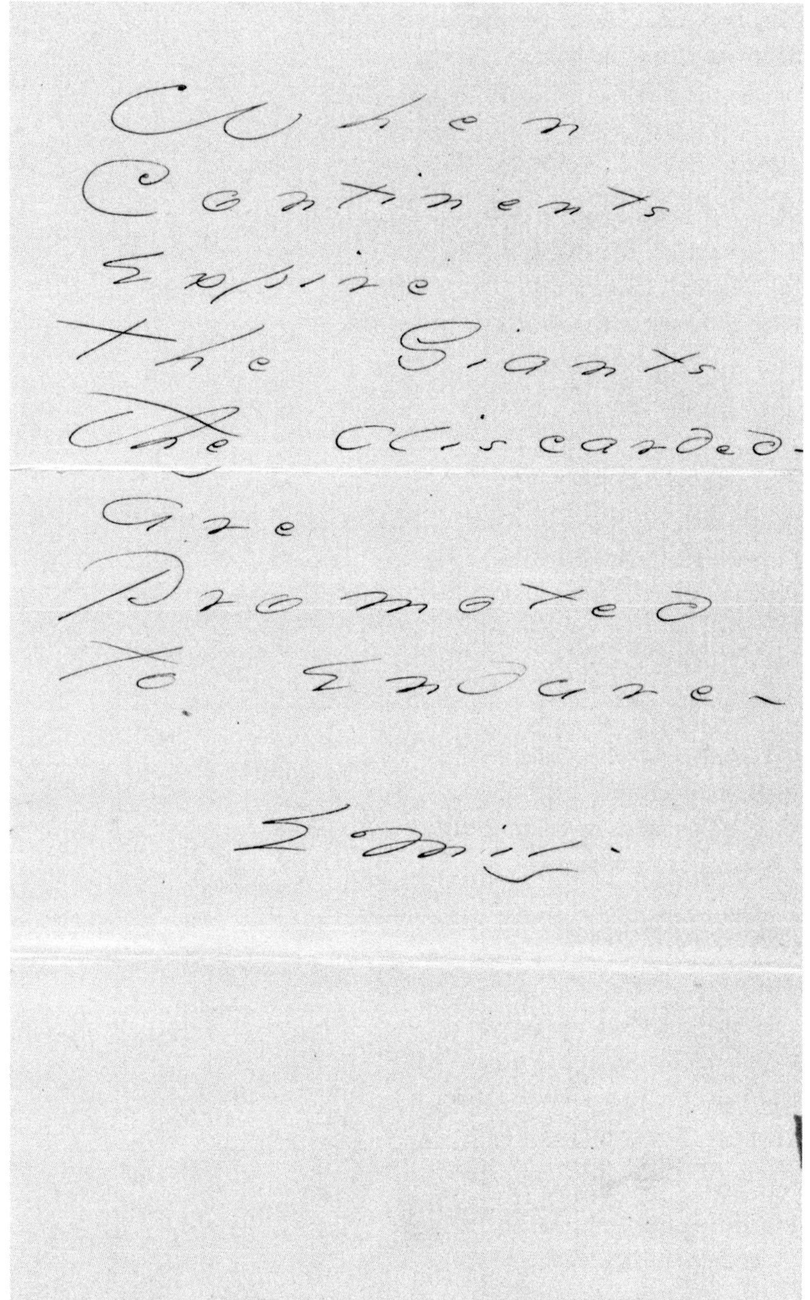

When
Continents
expire
the Giants
they discarded -
are
Promoted
to endure -

Emily.

"When Continents expire"

Death's Waylaying not the sharpest
Of the Thefts of Time –
There marauds a sorer Robber –
Silence – is his name –
No Assault, nor any menace
Doth betoken him.
But from Life's consummate Cluster,
He supplants the Balm.

c. 1874

When Continents expire[20]
The Giants they discarded – are
Promoted to endure –

March 1874

Of Life to own –[21]
From Life to draw –
But never touch the Reservoir –

c. late May 1874

To pile like Thunder to its close[22]
Then crumble grand away
While everything created hid
This – would be Poetry –

Or Love – the two coeval come –
We both and neither prove –
Experience either and consume –
For none see God and live –

c. 1875

Death's Waylaying not: *Sent to ED's Aunt Catherine Sweetser, whose husband walked out of their house and disappeared on 21 January 1874*
When Continents expire: *Sent to Sarah Jenkins with reference to Charles Sumner, who died 11 March 1874*
Of Life to: *Sent to TWH c. late May 1874*
To pile like: *Sent to Ns (lost) and to SD c. 1875*

Two Lengths has every Day –[23]
Its absolute extent
And Area superior
By Hope or Horror lent –

Eternity will be
Velocity or Pause
At Fundamental Signals
From Fundamental Laws.

To die is not to go –
On Doom's consummate Chart
No Territory new is staked –
Remain thou as thou Art.

c. 1875

Nature assigns the Sun –
That – is Astronomy –
Nature cannot enact a Friend –
That – is Astrology.

c. 1875

To his simplicity
To die – was little Fate –
If Duty live – contented
But her Confederate.

c. January 1876

The Treason of an accent[24]
Might Ecstasy transfer –
Of her effacing Fathom
Is no Recoverer –

February 1876

Two Lengths has: *Sent to SD c. 1875*
Nature assigns the: *Sent to EH c. 1875*
To his simplicity: *Sent to TWH c. January 1876, following a reference to her father's grave, and to Reverend Jonathan L. or Sarah Jenkins (variant) c. 1876*
The Treason of: *Sent to TWH February 1876 and to SD (variant) early 1876*

Take all away –
The only thing worth larceny
Is left – the Immortality –

c. spring 1876

I sued the News – yet feared – the News[25]
That such a Realm could be –
"The House not made with Hands" it was –
Thrown open wide – to me –

c. spring 1876

Love's stricken "why"
Is all that love can speak –
Built of but just a syllable,
The hugest hearts that break.

c. June 1876 MLT

The long sigh of the Frog
Upon a Summer's Day
Enacts intoxication
Upon the Passer by.

But his receding Swell
Substantiates a Peace
That makes the Ear inordinate
For corporal release –

c. early summer 1876

The Flake the Wind exasperate[26]
More eloquently lie

Take all away –: *Sent to TWH c. spring 1876, following a reference to her father's death* (*in 1874*)
I sued the: *Sent to TWH c. spring 1876*
Love's stricken "why": *Sent to Olive Stearns* (*lost*) *on the 8 June 1876 death of her husband William, president of Amherst College*
The long sigh: *Sent to TWH c. early summer 1876 and apparently to SD* (*variant*) *c. 1876*
The Flake the: *Sent to Mary Channing Higginson c. late summer 1876, with a fern leaf*

Than if escorted to its Down
By Arm of Chivalry.

c. late summer 1876

How know it from a Summer's Day?[27]
Its Fervors are as firm –
And nothing in the Countenance
But scintillates the same –
Yet Birds examine it and flee –
And Vans without a name
Inspect the Admonition
And sunder as they came –

c. autumn 1876

Trusty as the stars
Who quit their shining working
Prompt as when I lit them
In Genesis' new house,
Durable as dawn
Whose antiquated blossom
Makes a world's suspense
Perish and rejoice.

c. November 1876 Frances Norcross/MLT

These held their Wick above the west –[28]
Till when the Red declined –
Or how the Amber aided it –
Defied to be defined –

Then waned without disparagement
In a dissembling Hue

How know it: *Sent to Mary Channing Higginson c. autumn 1876, with oak leaves tied with a pink ribbon*
Trusty as the: *Sent to Ns (lost) c. November 1876*
These held their: *Sent to SD (last 4 lines, variant) with flower in late 1876, to TWH (last 4 lines, variant) January 1877, and to Josiah Holland c. early 1878*

That would not let the Eye decide
Did it abide or no –

c. early 1878

~

"Tomorrow" – whose location[29]
The Wise deceives
Though its hallucination
Is last that leaves –
Tomorrow, thou Retriever
Of every tare –
Of Alibi art thou
Or ownest where?

c. early February 1877

~

They might not need me, yet they might –[30]
I'll let my Heart be just in sight –
A smile so small as mine might be
Precisely their necessity –

c. early spring 1877

~

Whose Pink career may have a close[31]
Portentous as our own, who knows?
To imitate these neighbors fleet
In Awe and innocence, were meet.

c. June 1877

~

The Fact that Earth is Heaven –
Whether Heaven is Heaven or not
If not an Affidavit
Of that specific Spot

"Tomorrow" – whose location: *Sent to EH c. early February 1877*
They might not: *Sent to Mary Channing Higginson c. early spring 1877*
and to the Jonathan Jenkins family c. May 1877
Whose Pink career: *Sent to TWH c. June 1877*
The Fact that: *Probably sent to AD c. 1877, headed "Oliver," one of her brother's nicknames*

Not only must confirm us
That it is not for us
But that it would affront us
To dwell in such a place –

c. 1877

To own a Susan of my own
Is of itself a Bliss –
Whatever Realm I forfeit, Lord,
Continue me in this!

c. 1877

Ourselves – we do inter – with sweet derision
The channel of the Dust – who once achieves –
Invalidates the Balm of that Religion
That doubts – as fervently as it believes –

c. 1877

Than Heaven more remote,
For Heaven is the Root,
But these the flitted Seed,
More flown indeed,
Than Ones that never were,
Or those that hide, and are –

What madness, by their side,
A Vision to provide
Of future Days
They cannot praise –

My Soul – to find them – come –
They cannot call – they're dumb –
Nor prove – nor Woo –
But that they have Abode –

To own a: *Sent to SD c. 1877*
Ourselves – we do: *Sent to SB c. 1877*
Than Heaven more: *Sent to Maria Whitney after the death of SB, who died on 16 January 1878*

Is absolute as God –
And instant – too –

c. 1878

~

Not that he goes – we love him more who led us while he stayed.[32]
Beyond Earth's trafficking frontier, for what he moved, he made.

c. early 1878 MLT

~

The healed Heart shows its shallow scar
With confidential moan –
Not mended by Mortality
Are Fabrics truly torn –
To go its convalescent way
So shameless is to see
More genuine were perfidy
Than such Fidelity –

c. 1878

~

Go not too near a House of Rose –[33]
The depredation of a Breeze
Or inundation of a Dew
Alarm its Walls away –
Nor try to tie the Butterfly,
Nor climb the Bars of Ecstasy –
In insecurity to lie
Is Joy's insuring quality –

July 1878

~

We knew not that we were to live –[34]
Nor when we are to die –
Our ignorance our Cuirass is –
We wear Mortality

Not that he: *Sent to Mary Bowles (lost) c. early 1878 after the death of SB*
The healed Heart: *Sent to SD c. 1878*
Go not too: *Sent to ST July 1878*
We knew not: *Sent to Maria Whitney c. 1878 and to TWH (variant) c. December 1878*

As lightly as an Option Gown
Till asked to take it off –
By his intrusion, God is known –
It is the same with Life –

c. 1878

Spurn the temerity –[35]
Rashness of Calvary –
Gay were Gethsemane
Knew we of thee –

c. 1879

Those not live yet[36]
Who doubt to live again –
"Again" is of a twice
But this – is one –
The Ship beneath the Draw
Aground – is he?
Death – so – the Hyphen of the Sea –
Deep is the Schedule
Of the Disk to be –
Costumeless Consciousness,
That is he –

c. April 1879

Opinion is a flitting thing,
But Truth, outlasts the Sun –
If then we cannot own them both –
Possess the oldest one –

c. 1879

Spurn the temerity –: *Sent to HHJ c. 1879*
Those not live: *Sent to SD c. April 1879, signed "Easter"*
Opinion is a: *Sent to SD c. 1879*

So gay a Flower
Bereaves the mind
As if it were a Woe –
Is Beauty an Affliction – then?
Tradition ought to know –

c. 1879

~

It stole along so stealthy
Suspicion it was done
Was dim as to the wealthy
Beginning not to own –

c. 1879

~

Time's wily Chargers will not wait
At any Gate but Woe's –
But there – so gloat to hesitate
They will not stir for blows –

c. 1879

~

His Cheek is his Biographer –
As long as he can blush
Perdition is Opprobrium –
Past that, he sins in peace –

c. 1879

~

"Heavenly Father" – take to thee[37]
The supreme iniquity
Fashioned by thy candid Hand
In a moment contraband –
Though to trust us – seem to us
More respectful – "We are Dust" –

So gay a: *Sent to SD c. 1879*
It stole along: *Sent to SD c. 1879*
Time's wily Chargers: *Sent to Ned Dickinson c. 1879, signed "Dick" and "Jim," the names of family horses*
His Cheek is: *Probably sent to Ned Dickinson c. 1879, signed "Thief"*
"Heavenly Father" – take: *Sent to Ned Dickinson c. 1879*

We apologize to thee
For thine own Duplicity –

c. 1879

A little overflowing word
That any, hearing, had inferred
For Ardor or for Tears,
Though Generations pass away,
Traditions ripen and decay,
As eloquent appears –

c. 1879

A Counterfeit – a Plated Person –[38]
I would not be –
Whatever Strata of Iniquity
My Nature underlie –
Truth is good Health – and Safety, and the Sky –
How meagre, what an Exile – is a Lie,
And Vocal – when we die –

c. 1879

We shall find the Cube of the Rainbow –[39]
Of that – there is no doubt –
But the Arc of a Lover's conjecture
Eludes the finding out –

5 January 1880

The Robin is a Gabriel[40]
In humble circumstances –
His Dress denotes him socially,
Of Transport's Working Classes –
He has the punctuality
Of the New England Farmer –

A little overflowing: *Sent to SD c. 1879*
A Counterfeit – a: *Apparently sent to SD c. 1879*
We shall find: *Sent to ST 5 January 1880*
The Robin is: *Sent to ST c. March 1880 and to Ns (lost, transcribed variant) c. 1880*

The same oblique integrity,
A Vista vastly warmer –
A small but sturdy Residence,
A Self denying Household,
The Guests of Perspicacity
Are all that cross his Threshold –
As covert as a Fugitive,
Cajoling Consternation
By Ditties to the Enemy
And Silvan Punctuation –

c. 1880

A Dimple in the Tomb[41]
Makes that ferocious Room
A Home –

c. spring 1880

Could that sweet darkness where they dwell[42]
Be once disclosed to us,
The clamor for their loveliness
Would burst the loneliness.

c. June 1880 MLT

Love is done when Love's begun,
Sages say –
But have Sages known?
Truth adjourn your Boon
Without Day.

c. 1880

Birthday of but a single pang
That there are less to come –

A Dimple in: *Sent to TWH, with reference to his infant daughter, who died March 1880*
Could that sweet: *Sent to Maria Whitney (lost) c. June 1880*
Love is done: *Sent to ST c. 1880*
Birthday of but: *Sent to SD for her fiftieth birthday, 19 December 1880*

Afflictive is the Adjective
But affluent the doom –

December 1880

The Stem of a departed Flower[43]
Has still a silent rank –
The Bearer from an Emerald Court
Of a Despatch of Pink.

1 January 1881

All things swept sole away[44]
This – is immensity –

c. 1881

The Butterfly upon the Sky
That doesn't know its Name
And hasn't any Tax to pay
And hasn't any Home
Is just as high as you and I,
And higher, I believe,
So soar away and never sigh
And that's the way to grieve –

c. August 1881

"Go traveling with us"!
Her Travels daily be
By routes of ecstasy
To Evening's Sea –

c. autumn 1881

The Stem of: *Sent to ST as a New Year's greeting 1 January 1881*
All things swept: *Sent to TWH c. 1881*
The Butterfly upon: *Sent to Sally Jenkins and Martha Dickinson c. August 1881, addressed as "Little Women"*
"Go traveling with: *Sent to TWH, whose daughter Margaret was born 25 July 1881*

No Autumn's intercepting Chill[45]
Appalls this Tropic Breast –
But African Exuberance
And Asiatic Rest –

c. 1881

~

The Dandelion's pallid Tube
Astonishes the Grass –
And Winter instantly becomes
An infinite Alas –
The Tube uplifts a signal Bud
And then a shouting Flower –
The Proclamation of the Suns
That sepulture is o'er –

8 November 1881

~

Not seeing, still we know –[46]
Not knowing, guess –
Not guessing, smile and hide
And half caress –
And quake – and turn away,
Seraphic fear –
Is Eden's innuendo
"If you dare"?

c. late 1881

~

How much of Source escapes with thee –
How chief thy sessions be –
For thou hast borne a universe
Entirely away.

c. Christmas 1881 MLT

~

No Autumn's intercepting: *Sent to SD c. 1881 and to EH (variant) late November 1881*
The Dandelion's pallid: *Sent to ST 8 November 1881, with a pressed dandelion and scarlet ribbon*
Not seeing, still: *Sent to ST c. late 1881*
How much of: *Sent to EH (lost) c. Christmas 1881, with reference to her deceased husband*

Sweet Pirate of the Heart,
Not Pirate of the Sea –
What wrecketh thee?
Some Spice's Mutiny –
Some Attar's perfidy?
Confide in me –

January 1882

Obtaining but our own extent
In whatsoever Realm –
'Twas Christ's own personal Expanse
That bore him from the Tomb –

c. summer 1882

Now I lay thee down to Sleep –[47]
I pray the Lord thy Dust to keep –
And if thou live before thou wake –
I pray the Lord thy Soul to make –

c. 1882

No matter where the Saints abide,
They make their Circuit fair
Behold how great a Firmament
Accompanies a Star.

c. 1882

Elysium is as far as to[48]
The very nearest Room
If in that Room a Friend await
Felicity or Doom –

○

Sweet Pirate of: *Sent to ST January 1882 with thanks for a New Year's gift*
Obtaining but our: *Sent to TWH c. summer 1882 and to James Clark* (*variant*) *c. 1882, beginning "Obtaining but his own extent"*
Now I lay: *Apparently sent to SD c. 1882*
No matter where: *Sent to SD c. 1882*
Elysium is as: *Probably sent to MLT c. 1882*

What fortitude the Soul contains,
That it can so endure
The accent of a coming Foot –
The opening of a Door –

c. 1882

We shun it ere it comes,
Afraid of Joy,
Then sue it to delay
And lest it fly,
Beguile it more and more,
May not this be
Old Suitor Heaven,
Like our dismay at thee?

c. early 1883

Her Losses make our Gains ashamed.[49]
She bore Life's empty Pack
As gallantly as if the East
Were swinging at her Back –
Life's empty Pack is heaviest,
As every Porter knows –
In vain to punish Honey –
It only sweeter grows –

c. 1883

To the bright east she flies,
Brothers of Paradise
Remit her home
Without a change of wings
Or Love's convenient things
Enticed to come.

We shun it: *Sent to Joseph K. Chickering c. early 1883*
Her Losses make: *Sent to Thomas Niles c. 1883 and to SD (variant) c. 1883, beginning "His Losses made our Gains ashamed –"*
To the bright: *Sent to Maria Whitney (lost) c. spring 1883, following mention of ED's deceased mother*

Fashioning what she is,
Fathoming what she was,
We deem we dream –
And that dissolves the days
Through which existence strays
Homeless at home.

c. spring 1883 MLT

No ladder needs the bird but skies[50]
To situate its wings,
Nor any leader's grim baton
Arraigns it as it sings.
The implements of bliss are few –
As Jesus says of *Him*,
'Come unto me' the moiety
That wafts the cherubim.

c. May 1883 MLT

Candor – my tepid friend –[51]
Come not to play with me –
The Myrrhs, and Mochas, of the Mind
Are its iniquity –

c. 1883

By homely gifts and hindered words
The human heart is told
Of nothing –
"Nothing" is the force
That renovates the World –

c. 1883

Blossoms will run away –[52]
Cakes reign but a Day,

No ladder needs: *Sent to Maria Whitney (lost) c. May 1883*
Candor – my tepid: *Sent to SD c. 1883*
By homely gifts: *Sent to SD c. 1883*
Blossoms will run: *Sent to Cornelia Sweetser c. summer 1883, perhaps with cake and flowers*

But Memory like Melody,
Is pink eternally –

c. summer 1883

~

We wear our sober Dresses when we die,
But Summer, frilled as for a Holiday
Adjourns her Sigh –

August 1883

~

Morning is due to all –[53]
To some – the Night –
To an imperial few –
The Auroral Light –

c. autumn 1883

~

The Heart has many Doors –
I can but knock –
For any sweet "Come in"
Impelled to hark –
Not saddened by repulse,
Repast to me
That somewhere, there exists,
Supremacy –

c. late 1883

~

Pass to thy Rendezvous of Light,[54]
Pangless except for us –
Who slowly ford the Mystery
Which thou hast leaped across!

c. October 1883

~

We wear our: *Sent to ST August 1883*
Morning is due: *Sent to Samuel Bowles the younger upon his engagement, c. autumn 1883*
The Heart has: *Sent to SD after the death of her and AD's youngest son, Gilbert, on 5 October 1883*
Pass to thy: *Sent to SD c. October 1883, after Gilbert's death on 5 October, and to TWH February 1885, alluding to George Eliot*

Expanse cannot be lost –[55]
Not Joy, but a Decree
Is Deity –
His Scene, Infinity –
Whose rumor's Gate was shut so tight
Before my Beam was sown,
Not even a Prognostic's push
Could make a Dent thereon –

The World that thou hast opened
Shuts for thee,
But not alone,
We all have followed thee –
Escape more slowly
To thy Tracts of Sheen –
The Tent is listening,
But the Troops are gone!

c. October 1883

Climbing to reach the costly Hearts
To which he gave the worth,
He broke them, fearing punishment
He ran away from Earth –

late 1883

The Spirit lasts – but in what mode –[56]
Below, the Body speaks,
But as the Spirit furnishes –
Apart, it never talks –
The Music in the Violin
Does not emerge alone
But Arm in Arm with Touch, yet Touch
Alone – is not a Tune –
The Spirit lurks within the Flesh
Like Tides within the Sea

Expanse cannot be: *Sent to SD c. October 1883, after Gilbert's death*
Climbing to reach: *Sent to SD c. late 1883, after Gilbert's death, and to TWH (as prose, variant) spring 1884, in memory of his infant daughter's death 4 years earlier, beginning "Who 'meddled' with the costly Hearts"*
The Spirit lasts –: *Sent to Charles Clark mid-October 1883*

That make the Water live, estranged
What would the Either be?
Does that know – now – or does it cease –
That which to this is done,
Resuming at a mutual date
With every future one?
Instinct pursues the Adamant,
Exacting this Reply,
Adversity if it may be, or wild Prosperity,
The Rumor's Gate was shut so tight
Before my Mind was sown,
Not even a Prognostic's Push
Could make a Dent thereon –

mid-October 1883

Immured in Heaven![57]
What a Cell!
Let every Bondage be,
Thou sweetest of the Universe,
Like that which ravished thee!

c. late 1883

Quite empty, quite at rest,
The Robin locks her Nest, and tries her Wings –
She does not know a Route
But puts her Craft about
For *rumored* springs –
She does not ask for Noon –
She does not ask for Boon –
Crumbless and homeless, of but one request –
The Birds she lost –

c. March 1884

Immured in Heaven!: *Sent to SD c. late 1883, after the death of Gilbert*
Quite empty, quite: *Sent to EH, following mention of Otis Lord, who died 13 March 1884*

Within that little Hive
Such Hints of Honey lay
As made Reality a Dream
And Dreams, Reality –

c. March 1884

Each that we lose takes part of us;[58]
A crescent still abides,
Which like the moon, some turbid night,
Is summoned by the tides.

c. late March 1884 Frances Norcross/MLT

There are two Mays[59]
And then a Must
And after that a Shall
How infinite the compromise
That indicates I will

c. May 1884 Elizabeth Dickerman the younger

Who is it seeks my Pillow Nights,[60]
With plain inspecting face.
"Did you" or "Did you not," to ask –
'Tis "Conscience," Childhood's Nurse –

With Martial Hand she strokes the Hair
Upon my wincing Head –
"All" Rogues "shall have their part in" what –
The Phosphorous of God –

c. 1884

Morning, that comes but once,
Considers coming twice –

Within that little: *Sent to EH c. March 1884*
Each that we: *Sent to Ns (lost) c. late March 1884, following mention of the death of Otis Lord*
There are two: *Sent to Elizabeth Dickerman (lost), perhaps in a May basket, and to Ellen Mather (lost, transcribed variant) with an arbutus basket, c. May 1884*
Who is it: *Sent to SD c. 1884*
Morning, that comes: *Sent to MLT c. 1884*

Two Dawns upon a Single Morn
Make Life a sudden price –

c. 1884

~

The Auctioneer of Parting[61]
His "Going, going, gone"
Shouts even from the Crucifix,
And brings his Hammer down –
He only sells the Wilderness,
The prices of Despair
Range from a single human Heart
To Two – not any more –

c. 1884

~

Show me Eternity, and I will show you Memory –
Both in one package lain
And lifted back again –

Be Sue, while I am Emily –
Be next, what you have ever been, Infinity –

c. 1884

~

Not Sickness stains the Brave,[62]
Nor any Dart,
Nor Doubt of Scene to come,
But an adjourning Heart –

19 July 1884

~

The going from a world we know[63]
To one a wonder still
Is like the child's adversity
Whose vista is a hill,

The Auctioneer of: *Sent to MLT c. 1884*
Show me Eternity,: *Sent to SD c. 1884*
Not Sickness stains: *Sent to MLT 19 July 1884*
The going from: *Sent to Ns (lost) early August 1884, mentioning Gilbert's death and her own illness*

Behind the hill is sorcery
And everything unknown,
But will the secret compensate
For climbing it alone?

early August 1884 *Letters* (1894)

In other Motes,[64]
Of other Myths
Your requisition be.
The Prism never held the Hues,
It only heard them play –

c. September 1884

Some Arrows slay but whom they strike,[65]
But this slew all *but* him,
Who so appareled his Escape,
Too trackless for a Tomb –

c. October 1884

Parting with Thee reluctantly,
That we have never met,
A Heart sometimes a Foreigner,
Remembers it forgot –

c. autumn 1884

Oh what a Grace is this –
What Majesties of Peace –
That having breathed
The fine – ensuing Right
Without Diminuet Proceed!

19 November 1884

In other Motes,: *Sent to HHJ c. September 1884*
Some Arrows slay: *Sent to SD c. October 1884, with reference to Gilbert, who died in October 1883*
Parting with Thee: *Sent to Mary and Eben Jenks Loomis, who were about to leave Amherst, c. autumn 1884*
Oh what a: *Sent to Mary and Eben Jenks Loomis 19 November 1884, acknowledging a gift*

A Letter is a joy of Earth –
It is denied the Gods –

2 January 1885

~

Go thy great way![66]
The Stars thou meetst
Are even as thyself,
For what are Stars but Asterisks
To point a human Life?

c. February 1885

~

Is it too late to touch you, Dear?[67]
We this moment knew –
Love Marine and Love Terrene –
Love celestial too –

2 March 1885

~

A chastened Grace is twice a Grace –
Nay, 'tis a Holiness.

1 May 1885

~

Their dappled importunity
Disparage or dismiss –
The Obloquies of Etiquette
Are obsolete to Bliss –

c. 1885

~

Of Glory not a Beam is left[68]
But her Eternal House –

A Letter is: *Sent to Mary and Eben Jenks Loomis 2 January 1885, acknowledging a Christmas greeting, and to Charles Clark (variant) 19 January 1885*
Go thy great: *Sent to Benjamin Kimball c. February 1885 and to Abigail Cooper (variant) c. 1885*
Is it too: *Sent to Mary Warner Crowell 2 March 1885*
A chastened Grace: *Sent to ST 1 May 1885, with wishes for "a sweet May Day"*
Their dappled importunity: *Sent to MLT c. 1885*
Of Glory not: *Sent to TWH c. April 1886*

The Asterisk is for the Dead,
The Living, for the Stars –

c. April 1886

Those final Creatures, – who they are –[69]
That faithful to the close
Administer her ecstasy,
But just the Summer knows.

n.d. Bianchi

That Love is all there is[70]
Is all we know of Love,
It is enough, the freight should be
Proportioned to the groove.

n.d. Bianchi

Which misses most –[71]
The hand that tends
Or heart so gently borne,
'Tis twice as heavy as it was
Because the hand is gone?
Which blesses most
The lip that can,
Or that that went to sleep
With "if I could" endeavoring
Without the strength to shape?

n.d. Frances Norcross

Those final Creatures,: *Presumably sent to SD (lost) n.d.*
That Love is: *Sent to SD (lost) n.d.*
Which misses most –: *Sent to Ns (lost) n.d.*

Notes

Glossary of Correspondents

Appendix: Unbound Sheets

Index of First Lines

Notes

INTRODUCTION

1. Although the fascicle bindings were cut after Dickinson's death and the poems dispersed, Ralph W. Franklin has convincingly reassembled the order of the poems within these booklets to the extent that it can now be known. For his explanation of how he recreated the order of the booklets and the unbound sheets he calls sets, see Franklin, *The Editing of Emily Dickinson: A Reconsideration* (Madison: University of Wisconsin Press, 1967), and his introduction to *The Poems of Emily Dickinson*, ed. Ralph W. Franklin, 3 vols. (Cambridge, MA: Belknap Press of Harvard University Press, 1998). I have found no evidence to dispute his ordering of the poems within a fascicle or the ordering of the fascicles themselves. In January 1854, Dickinson reported having sent "two little volumes of mine" to Henry V. Emmons, perhaps early fascicle-style booklets that no longer survive. *The Letters of Emily Dickinson*, ed. Thomas H. Johnson and Theodora Ward, 3 vols. (Cambridge, MA: Belknap Press of Harvard University Press, 1958), L150. For print facsimile images of the fascicles and unbound sheets, see R. W. Franklin, ed., *The Manuscript Books of Emily Dickinson*, 2 vols. (Cambridge, MA: Belknap Press of Harvard University Press, 1981).

2. For a description of the paper used for each fascicle and sheet, see Franklin, *Manuscript Books*.

3. ED continues on a second sheet with the poems "One Sister have I in the house –" (F2 Sh2–3) and "I meant to have but modest needs –" (F33 Sh5–6). In the few other cases where a poem overflowed a sheet, she finished it on a leaf or small rectangle of paper that she attached to the sheet.

4. For the argument that Dickinson did not herself combine the unbound sheets into packets or sets, see Alexandra Socarides, *Dickinson Unbound: Paper, Process, Poetics* (New York: Oxford University Press, 2012). As Socarides also notes, although Franklin explains clearly his rationale for grouping the poems as he does, from another perspective the sets seem logically inconsistent: their order is not chronological (Franklin's Set 7 was copied earlier than Set 6) and the size of the sets varies dramatically (Set 7 contains twenty-six sheets; Set 15 contains one leaf with one poem).

5. As is so often the case with Dickinson, this generalization has some exceptions: Franklin's entire Set 15 has one poem; Sheet 3 in Set 14 has one poem; Sets 8a and 8b are made up of individual leaves. While these might be categorized as loose poems, they are written in ink, on the same paper, or the same kind of paper, used for other sets, and they resemble in style the other poems systematically copied onto sheets. See the appendix for more information on the unbound sheets.

6. Dickinson apparently used whatever kind of paper came to hand when she was working through poems or copying unsystematically and not for circulation. Paper was a precious resource, and even scraps and envelopes were apparently saved for reuse, as was true in other nineteenth-century households.

7. Friends and neighbors claimed to have received several poems from Dickinson, now lost, but in many cases there is no record of what they may have received—and as Dickinson became famous, some exaggerated their closeness to the poet. Many faulty memories appear in memoirs involving Dickinson written after her death.

8. Ellen Louise Hart and Martha Nell Smith argue that several poems Franklin regards as having come to Susan only after Dickinson's death were circulated to her during Dickinson's lifetime. See Hart and Smith, eds., *Open Me Carefully: Emily Dickinson's Intimate Correspondence to Susan Huntington Dickinson* (Ashfield, MA: Paris Press, 1998), hereafter cited as OMC; and the Dickinson Electronic Archives, Martha Nell Smith, executive editor; Lara Vetter, general editor; Ellen Louise Hart and Marta Werner, associate editors; http://archive.emilydickinson.org/working/csd.php; hereafter cited as DEA.

9. The earliest revision appears c. 1859 in Fascicle 5 Sheet 3, "Her breast is fit for pearls"; the first alternative apparently included at the time Dickinson copied the poem into a fascicle appears in summer 1861, Fascicle 9 Leaf 2, "What is – 'Paradise' –." "Again – his voice is at the door –," kept among Dickinson's loose poems, was copied c. early 1862 with several alternatives; perhaps it was not copied for a fascicle because it was still in draft.

10. In OMC, Hart and Smith argue that Emily and Susan engaged in an ongoing "workshop" exchange of poems in early stages of composition; the debate hinges largely on which texts one believes Susan to have received directly from Emily. That Dickinson sent no poems containing alternatives to any other correspondent is undisputed.

11. These figures may be too low because they include later revisions of what Dickinson initially wrote as a text without alternatives. Annotations indicate where alternatives probably were added in a later process of revision, although such a distinction is often unclear. At the same time, these figures do not include the variant words in other copies Dickinson made of a poem—changes she only sometimes noted on her cleanest or sheet copy. Most variations in her copying are in punctuation, capitalization, or poetic structure.

12. Sharon Cameron, *Choosing Not Choosing: Dickinson's Fascicles* (Chicago: University of Chicago Press, 1992).

13. Organizers of this site hope eventually to include images of all of Dickinson's writing.

14. Jack Capps, *Emily Dickinson's Reading: 1836–1886* (Cambridge, MA: Harvard University Press, 1966); Helen Vendler, *Dickinson: Selected Poems and Commentaries* (Cambridge, MA: Belknap Press of Harvard University Press, 2010).

15. Iambic meter has a rising rhythm: an unstressed followed by a stressed syllable; a catalectic line also alternates weak and strong stresses but both begins and ends with a stressed syllable; anapests have two unstressed syllables followed by a single stronger beat.

16. In poetic scansion, a spondee refers to two consecutive relatively stressed syllables, for example, "blue bird" or "armed man."

17. The exception to this rule is the highly revised "Two Butterflies went out at Noon –," which appears both in Fascicle 25 Sheet 2 (1863) and in "Loose Poems" (1875). In other cases of extreme revision, I describe the extent of the change in a note—for example, Dickinson reduced "It sifts from Leaden Sieves –" from twenty lines in 1862 to twelve lines in 1865, and she included three stanzas in the earliest extant copy of "Further in Summer than the Birds" (1865) that she dropped from her 1866 and 1883 copies.

18. When a poem is included twice, it is listed in the index of first lines under the formatting of its earlier copy; if the title begins with a different word in the later copy, the title appears twice in the index.

19. On the other hand, it would be important to include this poem if one is counting the number of poems Dickinson is known to have written or to have circulated.

20. In the 1850 "Awake ye muses nine," however, Dickinson does not use line-initial capital letters for its six-beat lines.

21. Marta Werner, *Radical Scatters: Emily Dickinson's Late Fragments and Related Texts, 1870–1886* (Ann Arbor: University of Michigan Press, 1999), http://jetson.unl.edu:8080/cocoon/radicalscatters/.

22. Domhnall Mitchell, *Measures of Possibility: Emily Dickinson's Manuscripts* (Amherst: University of Massachusetts Press, 2005).

23. Susan Howe, *My Emily Dickinson* (Berkeley, CA: North Atlantic Books, 1985; reissued New York: New Directions, 2007); Werner, *Radical Scatters*; Emily Dickinson's Correspondences: A Born-Digital Textual Inquiry, edited by Martha Nell Smith and Lara Vetter (Charlottesville: University of Virginia Press, 2008–), http://www.rotunda.upress.virginia.edu/edc/default.xqy, hereafter cited as EDC. My reservations about the interpretive perspectives and practices of previous editors are published elsewhere; see, e.g., "The Sound of Shifting Paradigms, or Hearing Emily Dickinson," in *A Historical Guide to Emily Dickinson*, ed. Vivian Pollak, 201–234 (New York: Oxford University Press, 2004).

24. Franklin is a conservative dater, often preferring to give a season or year as approximate even when his evidence points to a more precise dating—for example, he dates "March is the Month of Expectation" as c. 1877 rather than c. March 1877; in a few cases, I indicate the logically more precise date.

25. My thanks to Margaret Freeman for correspondence on this topic. There has been frequent innuendo about problems with Franklin's dating, but very little evidence of errors has been either published or shared with me in response to widespread requests. Alfred Habegger and Domhnall Mitchell have generously shared with me information on their dating of letters sent to Samuel Bowles and Maria Whitney, respectively.

26. See Lavinia Dickinson, "Poem for Emily" (1882), in *Dickinson in Her Own Time*, ed. Jane Donahue Eberwein, Stephanie Farrar, and Cristanne Miller (Iowa City: University of Iowa Press, 2015), hereafter cited as DIHOT.

27. This nomenclature distinguishes between the handwritten row of script on the page, the metrical line one hears, and the poetic line—which usually but not always coincides with the metrical line.

28. Susan transcribed "Fame is a fickle food" as including a line ending on "a" and another on "the"; meter and syntax suggest, however, that she mistook a capitalized letter at the beginning of a new row of script for a new poetic line. I leave Susan's lineation but indicate the more logical transcription in a note.

29. Theodora Ward, *Emily Dickinson's Letters to Dr. and Mrs. Josiah Holland* (Cambridge, MA: Harvard University Press, 1951), appendix D.

30. Like Franklin and Mitchell, I find no system in Dickinson's use of capitalization or dashes; she uses the same habits of handwriting in writing lists or letters as in poems. Many nineteenth-century writers make frequent use of capitals and dashes, although to my knowledge none as extensively or idiosyncratically as Dickinson. See Mitchell, *Measures of Possibility*.

31. Franklin emends transcriptions by Todd, Susan Dickinson, and others to make them consistent with Emily Dickinson's typical practice, for example, changing the possessive "its" to "it's" or "yours" to "your's."

32. Franklin lists (almost all) his emendations to Dickinson's spelling in an appendix to his 1998 *Poems*.

FASCICLES

1. In the name: echoes Matthew 28:19, "Go ye therefore, and teach all nations, baptizing them in the name of the Father, and of the Son, and of the Holy Ghost." These lines may point back toward the preceding poem's summer death. THJ regards the first three poems of F1 as a single poem because they are separated by white space, not a drawn line. RWF prints three poems.

2. A sepal – petal: RWF silently emends ED's phrase "a caper" to "a'caper," assuming it to be a verb.

3. Distrustful of the: Dickinson may have left a long dash in line 5 to be discreet, or because the space could be filled with various names or references. There is no other copy of this poem or evidence it was circulated. THJ prints this and "Flees so the phantom meadow" as one poem because they are separated by white space, not a drawn line.

4. To lose – if: according to Amherst Academy textbook *Familiar Lectures on Botany*, by Almira H. Lincoln (1815), the crocus was "dedicated to Saint Valentine" and therefore "peculiarly sacred to affection" because it often blooms in mid-February, when snow is still on the ground. The daisy and columbine bloom midspring.

5. To him who: probably refers to grass pink (*Calopogon pulchellus*), which has magenta-pink flowers and is found in bogs and marshy areas. ED included fourteen species of orchid in her herbarium.

6. I had a: quotes Robert Burns in two lines: "I set me down and sigh" from "Despondency" (1786) and "We're a'noddin at our house at hame" from "Gude'en To You, Kimmer" (1796). The Pleiades star cluster is also known as the "Seven Sisters." Because only six stars are easily visible, one Pleiad is said to be lost.

7. There is a: chrysolite is a gemstone mentioned several times in the Bible, including in Revelation. ED tells TWH that she reads "For prose, Mr. Ruskin, Sir Thomas Browne, and the Revelations" (L261).

8. As if I: additional copy retained c. 1884 (variant), written in fourteeners.

9. She slept beneath: MLT titles this poem "The Tulip" (*Poems*, 1896).

10. The feet of: also in F14 Leaf 3 (variant); ED wrote out and retained two additional copies (variant) in late summer 1858; one was on a leaf that she bound into F14 in 1862.

11. If those I: the hero of Sir Henry Taylor's 1834 dramatic romance *Philip van Artevelde* (a book owned by both ED and her brother) dies in Ghent while puzzling over the fact and mode of his dying. Additional copy retained c. summer 1858.

12. Adrift! A little: several aspects of this poem appear in the paintings *Manhood* and *Old Age* by Thomas Cole, part of his allegorical series *The Voyage of Life* (1842), widely distributed as engravings. In 1859, ED signed herself "Cole" in a letter (L214).

13. When Roses cease: refers to Mount Auburn Cemetery in Cambridge, which she visited August 1846.

14. On this wondrous: may allude to Thomas Cole's allegorical series of paintings *The Voyage of Life* (1842), widely distributed as engravings.

15. Garlands for Queens,: according to Amherst Academy textbook *Familiar Lectures on Botany*, by Almira H. Lincoln (1815), the Rose "on account of its beauty...is often dignified with the title of 'queen of flowers.'"

16. Nobody knows this: a lost copy (perhaps sent to Elizabeth Holland) was the source for the poem's 2 August 1858 *Springfield Daily Republican* publication, titled "To Mrs. —, with a Rose." Additional copy retained (variant) c. early 1861.

17. Through lane it: may allude to John Bunyan's *Pilgrim's Progress* (1678), in which Pilgrim must descend through woods and a tempest, resisting serpents, to arrive in his heavenly home.

18. Bless God, he: the pages of F2 Sh2 and Sh3 have been torn and cut so that watermarks and pinholes are missing. "One Sister have I in the house –," was also thoroughly mutilated by ink scribbles. Remaining evidence suggests that the poems follow the sequence represented here; the tears leave this poem and the following, "If I should cease to bring a Rose," fully intact.

19. One Sister have: after MLT transcribed the fascicle, the leaves on which ED wrote this poem were cut out of the fascicle, torn, and mutilated. Although the words of the poem are scribbled over, many are still legible; missing sections are supplied by the copy sent to SD. ED numbered stanzas to indicate the place of stanza 4, which she copied out of sequence.

20. "Lethe" in my: Aeneas's father explains to him that a drink from the Lethe "frees from care / In long forgetfulness" (Virgil, 70–19 BCE); ED studied the *Aeneid* at Amherst Academy. In Keats's "Ode to a Nightingale" (1819) the speaker feels "as though [I]... Lethe-wards had sunk... being too happy in thine [the nightingale's] happiness." The mutilated leaf beginning what was initially Sh3 of F2 started with the last lines of "One Sister have I in the house –"; it was cut so that only two lines of "'Lethe' in my flower" survive; missing text is supplied from MLT's transcript. Some scholars hypothesize a copy of this poem was sent to SD.

21. I've got an: perhaps a valentine; written on the portion of the mutilated leaf (lost) containing the end of "'Lethe' in my flower." Extant transcript was made by MLT when the fascicle was still intact.

22. I robbed the: in Wordsworth's "Nutting" (1800), the speaker gathers nuts "with crash / And merciless ravage" from "silent trees" in a "shady nook." Additional copy retained (variant) c. 1861, beginning "Who robbed the Woods –."

23. If she had: In *Evangeline* (1847), Longfellow writes of branches of "mystic mistletoe... Such as the Druids cut down"; ED read this popular epic poem in 1848. RWF regards this as the earliest manuscript ED sent to SB, dating it c. early 1859; Alfred Habegger dates it September or October 1859.

24. Once more, my: in Genesis 8:8–12, Noah sent forth a dove from his ark three times to discover land; having found land, however, it did not return the third time.

25. Sexton! My Master's: may allude to Mary Magdalene's visit to the tomb of Jesus, her "Master" (John 20:16), given the common association of spring with resurrection.

26. The rainbow never: Cato the Younger was a noted orator (95–46 BCE). In "Great Caesar! Condescend" (F7 Sh1), the speaker is "Cato's Daughter."

27. I hide myself: also copied in F40 Sh3 (variant), c. early 1864; additional copy retained (variant) c. 1863, with pinholes as if for sending with a flower.

28. I never told: William Kidd (1645–1701), aka Captain Kidd, a Scottish privateer, was arrested in Boston and transported to England, where he was executed for piracy. Atropos, in Greek mythology the eldest of the three Fates, cut the thread of life for each mortal.

29. I often passed: a copy may have been sent to SD (lost); "Dollie" was a nickname for SD used by her family, which ED adopted.

30. Sleep is supposed: copy in the letter to SD follows the ironic dedication: "To my Father – to whose untiring efforts in my behalf, I am indebted for my *morning – hours* – viz – 3. AM. to 12. PM. these grateful lines are inscribed by his aff Daughter" (L198). ED writes in another letter that her father typically "rapped on my door to wake me" (L175).

31. If I should: the Panic of 1857 bankrupted, among other "enterprise[s]," the railroad company in which ED's father and the town of Amherst were deeply invested.

32. Perhaps you'd like: "Hock" refers to German wine, from Hochheim in the Rheingau.

33. Flowers – Well – if: a lost copy was the source for this poem's 2 March 1864 publication in *Drum Beat*, with the title "Flowers"; *Drum Beat* was a fund-raising publication for the Union army, edited by a friend of the Dickinson family. Reprinted in the *Springfield Daily Republican* (9 March 1864), *Springfield Weekly Republican* (12 March 1864), and the *Boston Post* (16 March 1864).

34. Pigmy seraphs – gone: Jesus questioned, "And why take ye thought for raiment? Consider the lilies of the field . . . even Solomon in all his glory was not arrayed like one of these" (Matthew 6:28–29).

35. An altered look: in John 3:1–21, Jesus instructs the incredulous Nicodemus that "except a man be born again, he cannot see the kingdom of God."

36. Some, too fragile: Matthew 10:29–31, "Are not two sparrows sold for a farthing? and one of them shall not fall on the ground without your Father"; Luke 12:6, "Are not five sparrows sold for two farthings, and not one of them is forgotten before God?"

37. Whose are the: refers to several varieties of spring flowers; Leontodon is related to the daisy, aster, and dandelion; epigea and rhodora are wildflowers native only to North America. ED knew Emerson's poem "The Rhodora" (1847), in which the "fresh Rhodora in the woods" inspires the reflection that "Beauty is its own excuse for being" and "the self-same Power" created the speaker and the flower.

38. "They have not: in John 15:16, Jesus says, "Ye have not chosen me, but I have chosen you, and ordained you, that ye should go and bring forth fruit"; Daisy is a nickname ED used for herself in relation to a figure she called "Master." In line 5, ED wrote "have not" and marked the words for transposition; here they are transposed.

39. We should not: in Revelation 4:4, the elders "round about the throne . . . had on their heads crowns of gold."

40. Success is counted: a lost copy or a transcript from SD was the source for the *Brooklyn Daily Union*'s 27 April 1864 publication of this poem. Reprinted in *A Masque of*

Poets (Boston, 1878), in an 1878 review of the *Masque* published by Helen Hunt Jackson in the *Denver Daily Tribune*, and in the *Amateur Journal* (Judsonia, Arkansas, November 1882).

41. Where bells no: quotes from Isaac Watts's hymn "There Is a Land of Pure Delight" (1707), which ends: "Could we but climb where Moses stood, / And view the landscape o'er, / Not Jordan's stream, nor death's cold flood / Should fright us from the shore."

42. South winds jostle: additional copy retained (variant), c. early 1861.

43. I had some: Lemuel Shaw, Whig jurist and chief justice of the Massachusetts Supreme Court (1830–1860); Henry Shaw was the name of a day laborer hired to work in the Dickinsons' garden.

44. "Arcturus" is his: "Resurgam": Latin, "I shall rise again." In the Linnaean system—largely outdated by the late 1850s, as ED would have known—one counted stamens and pistils to classify flowers. The association of heaven with children alludes to Matthew 19:14, "Suffer little children, and forbid them not . . . for of such is the kingdom of heaven"; in Revelation 21:21, heaven's gates are of "solid pearl."

45. Talk with prudence: Potosí, Bolivia, was famous for the silver mines in the nearby mountains; the word's metrical placement indicates that ED probably pronounced it "Po-TO-si."

46. If this is: ED refers to herself as a peacock and addresses Louisa Norcross as "Dear Peacock" (L177, L228). She may also have known that the peacock is a symbol of the sun in Asia.

47. Her breast is: alternative added later; ED used the alternative "home" in her letter to SD.

48. To fight aloud,: may respond to Alfred Lord Tennyson's popular "The Charge of the Light Brigade" (1854); Tennyson's "In Memoriam" (1850) also repeats "we trust" and "I trust" in relation to an afterlife and human understanding.

49. 'Houses' – so the: John 14:2, "In my Father's house are many mansions."

50. Bring me the: revises God's questions to Job, such as "Who hath divided a watercourse for the overflowing of waters. . . . Who can number the clouds in wisdom? . . . Who provideth for the raven his food?" (Job 38).

51. Exultation is the: this manuscript page was cut; end punctuation for two lines is taken from the copy to SD.

52. I never hear: this manuscript page was cut; "bar" is filled in as "bars" based on the copy sent to SD.

53. These are the: a lost copy was the source for the poem's 11 March 1864 publication in *Drum Beat* (a Union army fund-raising publication), under the title "October." Two additional copies retained: of first two stanzas, c. 1883, and one that MLT gave away in 1904 (lost).

54. Besides the Autumn: alludes to William Cullen Bryant's phrase "the golden-rod" in "The Death of the Flowers" (1825), in which a squirrel is also mentioned; it also refers

to Scottish poet James Thomson's *The Seasons* (1730), required reading at the Amherst Academy and Mount Holyoke.

55. Safe in their: the first copy to SD is probably the lost source for the 1 March 1862 publication in the *Springfield Republican*, titled "The Sleeping." ED repeatedly revised this poem's second stanza, twice in response to SD's comments. ED recorded all alternative second stanzas in F10 Sh4, in the second half of 1861.

56. I bring an: Matthew 25:40, "Inasmuch as ye have done it unto one of the least of these my brethren, ye have done it unto me."

57. Going to Heaven!: alludes to Psalm 23, "The Lord is my shepherd," or perhaps John 10, which presents Jesus as shepherd; references to wearing a robe and crown in heaven are from Revelation (6:11, 2:10), although such descriptions of heavenly attire are also popular in hymns.

58. Our lives are: in "Beyond" (1861), Rose Terry Cooke (1827–1892) also presents Italy as a promised land "past the Alpine summits of great pain." Cooke could not have known ED's poem.

59. A little East: the Jacob story is told in Genesis 32, including reference to "Peniel" as the place where Jacob wrestled with the angel; Henry Vaughan wrote of Jacob wrestling with God, "let him not go / Until thou hast a blessing," in "Rules and Lessons" (1650, reprinted 1847). In 1886, ED refers to Jacob as "Pugilist and Poet" (L1042). The alternative "Signor" was added later.

60. All overgrown by: may acknowledge the anniversary of the death of Charlotte Brontë (d. 31 March 1855), who published as "Currer Bell" and lived in Haworth. Line 1 echoes Brontë's "Mementos" (1846): "All in this house is mossing over." Gethsemane is the garden where Jesus prayed on the night before his crucifixion; asphodel flowers are associated with the Greek underworld, e.g., in *The Odyssey*. The "Or" between stanzas 3 and 4 may indicate that stanzas 4 and 5 are alternatives. In their single-volume editions, THJ prints stanzas 1, 4, 5, and RWF prints stanzas 1, 2, 3.

61. A science – so: may allude to Wordsworth's "To the Small Celandine" (1807) in which he praises as "modest" the "Little, humble Celandine!" The celandine poppy, or wood poppy, a bright yellow spring wildflower native to North America, resembles the European celandine.

62. Great Caesar! Condescend: according to Plutarch, Portia, wife of Brutus and Cato's daughter, was "addicted to philosophy" and mutilated herself to prove that she was worthy of her husband's confidence. Bianchi claimed this poem was sent to AD (*Emily Dickinson Face to Face*).

63. I have a: the Lord's Prayer, central to Christian liturgy, includes the lines "Our Father which art in Heaven" and "Thy will be done" (Luke 11:2); Jesus also prays "thy will be done" before he is crucified (Matthew 26:42).

64. She went as: through mathematical calculations, Urbain Le Verrier (1811–1877) helped discover the planet Neptune in 1846; the alternative was added later.

65. The Daisy follows: ED wrote "shily" then added a tail to her "i" to correct the spelling to "shyly"; the dot over her "i" remains. ED often wrote over letters to correct spelling when copying her poems.

66. Papa above!: John 14:2, "In my Father's house are many mansions."

67. "Sown in dishonor!": 1 Corinthians 15:42–43 contrasts the mortal and resurrected body: it is "sown in corruption; it is raised in incorruption: It is sown in dishonor; it is raised in glory: it is sown in weakness; it is raised in power."

68. She died – *this*: by "Bernardine," ED may simply mean Catholic; her speaker is a "Bernardine Girl" in "I've heard an Organ talk, sometimes –," F12 Sh1. Alternatives were written later, following the word "Or."

69. If pain for: refers to the Pax Augusta (also called Pax Romana) that reigned in the first and second centuries CE.

70. Some Rainbow – coming: the Circassians were considered to be the original race from which all humans descended, and also considered extremely beautiful (e.g., see TWH, "Barbarism and Civilization," *Atlantic Monthly*, January 1861). From the northwest Caucasus, including Chechnya, Circassians were in the news because the final years of the Russian-Circassian War (1763–1864) involved their massacre and forced emigration. Many Circassian women were sold as slaves in Turkey.

71. I can't tell: Isaiah 6:2 describes seraphim as covering their faces with their wings; in Exodus 26:33, a "vail" separates the Holy of Holies from the rest of the inner sanctuary. ED frequently mentions veiling one's face before God or natural splendor. Under the pseudonym "Peter Parley," Boston publisher Samuel Griswold Goodrich (1793–1860) issued and himself wrote tales for the moral instruction of children.

72. A *wounded* Deer –: Numbers 20:11, "And Moses lifted up his hand, and with his rod he smote the rock twice: and the water came out abundantly."

73. The Sun kept: cockades were worn by the Continental army during the American Revolution; they have also been worn by the British, the French, and people of other nations to show allegiance to a particular political faction.

74. I met a: L. M. Hills ran a palm-leaf hat manufacturing company in Amherst that hired primarily Amherst natives.

75. If the foolish,: Moses was forbidden to enter the promised land (Numbers 20:12); in Revelation 1:16–20, Christ holds seven stars in his right hand, and there are several biblical references to the saved standing on God's right hand; this was also a common reference in hymns. Here, as in other poems, ED compares ways of reading the book of nature ("flowers")—through the Bible, the idiom of science, and personal experience.

76. In Ebon Box,: may allude to George Herbert's "The Flower" (1633): "Who could have thought my shrivelled heart / Could have recovered greenness?"

77. Portraits are to: also copied in F8 Sh5 as "Pictures are to daily faces," c. summer 1860.

78. Wait till the: Deuteronomy 10:17, "For the Lord your God is God of gods, and Lord of lords."

79. 'Tis so much: TWH titles this poem "Rouge Gagne," after a poem by Julia Ward Howe about a woman gambling for love; Howe's poem was not published until about six years after ED copied this one.

80. At last, to: also copied in F21 Sh4 (variant) c. late 1862.

81. Dust is the: legends associate robins with Jesus and with selfless service: in one, the robin warms the baby Jesus by fanning a dying fire with its wings, thereby burning its breast red.

82. I'm the little: the name pansy ("Heart's Ease") may be a corruption of the French *pensez a moi* (think of me); it was associated with remembrance or steadfastness in love.

83. Pictures are to: also copied in F8 Sh2 as "Portraits are to daily faces," c. summer 1860.

84. I cautious, scanned: may allude to the parable about a rich man building ever larger "barns" for his goods, followed by Jesus's instruction to "Consider the ravens . . . which neither have storehouse nor barn" and "provide yourselves . . . a treasure in the heavens that faileth not, where no thief approacheth" (Luke 12:16–33).

85. What shall I: Carlo is ED's dog.

86. How many times: perhaps alludes to Byron's "The Giaour," "He who hath bent him o'er the dead" (1813).

87. Bound – a trouble –: also copied in F36 Sh1 (variant) c. 1863. In Wordsworth's "The Solitary Reaper," a "Maiden sang . . . at her work" (1807).

88. What is – "Paradise" –: alludes to Revelation 7:16–17 and 21:19, which claim the saved shall neither hunger nor thirst and that the "first foundation" of the wall of the new Jerusalem is garnished with jasper.

89. You love me –: may have been sent to SD (lost); "Dollie" was a nickname for SD.

90. My River runs: additional copy retained (variant), c. early 1861.

91. Poor little Heart!: "dinna care" is quoted from Robert Burns's "Here's to thy health, my bonie lass" (1780).

92. I shall know: Peter promised Jesus, "Though I should die with thee, yet will I not deny thee," but then denied him three times, as Jesus prophesied (Matthew 26:34–35).

93. On this long: traditionally the rainbow is a sign of hope, as in Genesis 9:13, where it is a "token" of Noah's "covenant" with God.

94. Musicians wrestle everywhere –: in Job 38:7, the "morning stars sang together and all the sons of God shouted for joy" when God created the earth; "Morning Star" (1830) is also a tune by Lowell Mason. Jesus's resurrection is associated with new life, as in Romans 6:4, and the phrase was used frequently in hymns. ED heard several bands perform, e.g., the Germania Serenade Band in 1853 (L118), and her sheet music collection included tunes that minstrel groups typically performed with tambourine percussion. Jenny Lind, whom she also heard perform, often sang a selection called "Bird Song."

95. For this – accepted: Gabriel is the heavenly messenger associated with "glad tidings" and blessings (e.g., Luke 1:19).

96. We don't cry –: "high" "Cottages" may allude to John 14:2, "In my Father's house are many mansions." Tim could refer to Tiny Tim in Dickens's *A Christmas Carol* (1843).

97. Dying! Dying in: may have been sent to SD (lost); "Dollie" was a nickname for SD.

98. He forgot – and: Peter promised Jesus to be loyal but then denied knowing him three times, as Jesus had prophesied (Matthew 26:34–35).

99. Some – keep the: a lost copy was the source for the 12 March 1864 publication in the *Round Table*, titled "My Sabbath." In "Wood Worship" (1861), by Rose Terry Cooke, the speaker similarly prefers to observe the Sabbath in the woods and hear her "sermons from a flower!"

100. We – Bee and: revision added later. Many comic poems involving broad puns were published in the *Springfield Republican*, the Dickinsons' daily newspaper.

101. Tho' my destiny: may allude to Emerson's "The Romany Girl" (*Atlantic Monthly*, November 1857), whose speaker asserts the superiority of her naturalness over "Pale Northern girls!" Dr. Holland is EH's husband.

102. Faith is a: also copied in F12 Sh1 c. early 1862, as "'Faith' is a fine invention."

103. I'll tell you: "Dominie" is a Scottish term for schoolmaster; "Dominus" (Latin) means lord or master. In Psalm 23, God leads the flock. ED drew a line between stanzas 2 and 3 in her F10 copy but the copy to TWH clarifies that this is a single poem.

104. Just lost, when: echoes "Eye hath not seen, nor ear heard, neither have entered into the heart of man, the things which God hath prepared for them that love him" (1 Corinthians 2:9).

105. Come slowly – Eden!: "Jessamines" (jasmine) symbolized passion, according to *Familiar Lectures on Botany* by Almira H. Lincoln (1815); ED included jasmine in her herbarium.

106. Least Rivers – docile: The Caspian Sea was romanticized in orientalist literature, such as in the popular long poem *Lalla Rookh* (1817) by Thomas Moore, which AD owned and in which someone (perhaps ED) marked passages.

107. *One life* of: Matthew 13:45–46 compares the "kingdom of heaven" to a "pearl of great price," for which the merchant was willing to sell all he had.

108. You're right – "the: in Matthew 7:14, "Strait is the gate, and narrow is the way, which leadeth unto life, and few there be that find it." See also Luke 13:24.

109. Safe in their: the first copy to SD was probably the lost source for the 1 March 1862 publication in the *Springfield Republican*, titled "The Sleeping." The second stanza of this poem was repeatedly revised, twice in response to SD's comments. This copy includes three of ED's trial second stanzas, including one she did not send SD; she drew a line between the second stanzas to mark them as alternatives—replicated here. The earliest extant copy of this poem is in F6 Sh3, (variant) c. late 1859.

110. If *He dissolve* –: the star of Bethlehem led three wise men to the city where Jesus was born (Matthew 2:1–2). In *A Midsummer Night's Dream*, Helena says to Demetrius, "I am your spaniel; and . . . [t]he more you beat me, I will fawn on you."

111. I think just: Matthew 10:29–31, "Are not two sparrows sold for a farthing? and one of them shall not fall on the ground without your Father," and other biblical passages indicate God's concern for the least of earthly creatures (a "sparrow").

112. A Mien to: may allude to Jenny Lind (1820–1887), whom ED heard perform in Northampton, Massachusetts, July 1851; Queen Victoria famously attended one of Lind's concerts in 1847. "Orleans": from 1709 until the French Revolution, the dukes of Orléans were high in the order of succession to the French throne. Joan of Arc is also referred to as the Maid of Orléans.

113. The Drop, that: in Greek mythology, Amphitrite, a sea goddess and wife of Neptune, was sometimes considered the personification of the sea.

114. The Robin's my: the cuckoo appears frequently in English poetry as a sign of spring.

115. I've known a: traveling circuses and menageries came through Amherst and the surrounding towns.

116. I came to: this and several poems in Fascicle 11 were written on cut leaves of stationery, not folded sheets.

117. A Clock stopped –: the anonymous poem "The Life Clock" (*Hampshire Gazette*, 4 August 1846) also uses the clock-as-heart metaphor. ED quotes from it in L60.

118. I'm Nobody! Who: the anonymous poem "Nobody by Somebody" includes the line "Sign yourself 'nobody,' quick as you can" (*Hampshire and Franklin Express*, 4 April 1856).

119. Ah, Moon, and: also copied in F14 Sh1 (variant) c. early 1862.

120. It can't be: chrysolite is an apple- or yellow-green gemstone mentioned several times in the Bible.

121. What would I: Shylock is a Jew in *The Merchant of Venice* who persuades Antonio, a Christian, to pledge a pound of flesh for his bond and then vows to make him uphold his pledge when Antonio defaults on repayment.

122. Rearrange a "Wife's": the second leaf of Sheet 7 (containing this poem) was lost after 1891, when MLT recorded it as part of this fascicle.

123. I taste a: in "Bacchus" (1847) and "The Poet" (1844), Emerson writes of intoxication independent of alcohol, calling poetry "God's wine." A lost copy of ED's poem was the source for the 4 May 1861 publication in the *Springfield Daily Republican*, titled "The May-Wine."

124. I lost a: the head of Liberty depicted on copper one-cent and half-cent coins during the first half of the nineteenth century was surrounded by thirteen stars, for the original colonies.

125. A transport one: nineteenth-century circus cars often had biblical figures or narratives painted on them, and the sideshow with exceptional creatures was a main attraction.

126. "Faith" is a: also copied in F10 Sh2 (variant) c. early 1861.

127. I got so: business "with the Cloud" refers to Exodus 13:21, "And the Lord went before them by day in a pillar of a cloud, to lead them the way."

128. Father – I bring: the copy to SD contains four additional lines.

129. This – is the: Tennyson's "Locksley Hall" (1842) describes a sunset as "the heavens fill[ing] with commerce, argosies of magic sails, / Pilot of the purple twilight, dropping down with costly bales."

130. Unto like Story –: as in other poems, ED points toward the Civil War's battling "Kinsmen" through biblical allusion; in Hebrews 11:32–12:2, the faithful endure torments, "not accepting deliverance; that they might obtain a better resurrection," a passage concluding with reference to the crucifixion: "for the joy that was set before him [Jesus] endured the cross, despising the shame, and is set down at the right hand of the throne of God."

131. He put the: the phrase "Member of the Cloud" perhaps alludes to Hebrews 12:1: "Wherefore seeing we also are compassed about with so great a cloud of witnesses, let us lay aside . . . sin."

132. The only Ghost: Mechlin is one of the best-known and most delicate Flemish laces, popular for women's clothing.

133. Many a phrase: ED repeats "the English language –" as an alternative (not repeated here).

134. "Hope" is the: Emily Brontë also represents hope as a song bird, in "Hope was but a timid friend" (1846).

135. If I'm lost –: heavenly Jerusalem has twelve gates and walls of jasper (Revelation 21:12–18).

136. Blazing in Gold –: Perez Dickinson Cowan claims to have received a copy of this poem from SD in 1862; this lost manuscript is the likely source for the 29 February 1864 publication, titled "Sunset," in *Drum Beat*, a Civil War fund-raising paper for the Union troops.

137. Good Night! Which: also included in F36 Sh2 (variant) c. 1863.

138. Put up my: the Colossi of Memnon are huge ruined statues in Egypt at the entrance gate of a mortuary temple. After the northern colossus was damaged (27 BCE), it produced a strange musical sound at sunrise. Early Greek and Roman tourists named the statue Memnon after a Trojan hero who sang to his mother at dawn.

139. There came a: in Revelation 21:5 God says, "Behold, I make all things new"; Revelation 19:9 refers to "the marriage supper of the Lamb." May also have been inspired by Tennyson's "Love and Duty," a poem ED alludes to in L801. Cancellations and some alternatives added much later. Additional fair copy retained (variant) c. early 1862.

140. How the old: refers to Italian painters Guido Reni (1575–1642), Titian (1488–1576), and Domenichino (1581–1641), well known to nineteenth-century Americans.

141. Of Tribulation, these: Revelation 7:13–14 and 12:11 identify those "arrayed in white robes" as having come "out of great tribulation.... And they overcame [the accuser of our brethren] by the blood of the Lamb . . . and they loved not their lives unto the death." In the copy sent to TWH, ED writes "I spelled Ankle – wrong."

142. What if I: may respond to Hamlet's reflections on "shuffl[ing] off this mortal coil" in his "To be or not to be" speech.

143. Ah, Moon – and: also copied in F11 Sh6 (variant) c. late 1861.

144. A Shady friend –: muslin and organdy (a type of muslin) are light, thin fabrics usually worn by women; broadcloth is dense, heavy, and more often used for men's clothing.

145. A solemn thing –: section nine of Elizabeth Barrett Browning's "Isobel's Child" begins "A solemn thing it is to me / To look upon a babe that sleeps." There is a pencil mark (perhaps ED's) by these lines in SD's copy of Browning's *Poems* (1852).

146. "Heaven" – is what: "interdicted Land" may refer to God's preventing Moses from entering the promised land (Numbers 20:12, Deuteronomy 3:23–28).

147. The feet of: also copied in F1 Sh2 (variant) c. summer 1858; additional copy retained (variant) c. late summer 1858. The F14 leaf was copied in 1858 but not bound until 1862.

148. More Life – went: "Anthracite" may allude to Donald Grant Mitchell's distinction in *Reveries of a Bachelor* (published under the name Ik Marvell, 1850) between "sea-coal" and "anthracite" people; a character declares the ideal woman to be "anthracite," with an "angel face" and a steady, profound sensibility. By the mid-nineteenth century, "Ethiop" was synonymous with African; there was no U.S. slave trade with Ethiopia.

149. Removed from Accident: the Malay or Southeast Asian pearl diver was a popular figure in periodical literature; in orientalist stereotypes, the Malay was indolent and without initiative. Poets Dickinson admired also used pearl divers as figurative types, including George Herbert ("Vanity [1]," 1633) and Robert Browning (*Paracelsus*, 1835).

150. Your Riches – taught: in *Religio Medici* (1642), Sir Thomas Browne writes, "I have not *Peru* in my desires.... He is rich, who hath enough to be charitable"; Golconda is a thirteenth-century fort in India where the priceless Kohinoor diamond was found. In the final stanza, "Its far – far Treasure to surmise –" logically continues in syntactic parallel to "Its distance – to behold –" in a single two-stanza sentence, paraphrased as: at least it's a solace to know that a gold exists, although I prove it just in time to behold its distance, surmise its treasure, and estimate the pearl that slipped through my fingers when I was a girl. Following this logic, I emend "It's" to "Its" in lines 28 and 29.

151. A Toad, can: President Lincoln's September 1862 announcement of the pending Emancipation Proclamation may have stimulated ED to think about intrinsic human worth ("Naked of Flask – Naked of Cask –").

152. There are two: retained additional copy (variant) c. summer 1862. Most alternatives in F14 copy probably added later.

153. Give little Anguish,: There may be missing poems at the end of this fascicle; ED's writing runs across the torn edge of the final sheet, suggesting that the now-missing second leaf was at the time still attached. It would have been unusual for her to have torn off the second leaf after writing on the first. There is no record of this missing leaf or what might have been written on it.

154. The Color of: may respond to William Cullen Bryant's popular "June" (1826), which asserts that "his grave is green"; ED quotes Bryant's poem in a letter to Benjamin Kimball after the death of Otis Lord (1885, L967).

155. We grow accustomed: the lamp of life was a common idiom (e.g., in Tennyson's "Xantippe,"1880, and Maria Susanna Cummins's 1854 novel, *The Lamplighter*), associating light with divinity (as in John 1:5 and 8:12).

156. I never felt: retained additional copy (lost after 1923, transcribed variant) c. 1862.

157. The Body grows: may allude to 1 Corinthians 6:19–20: "Know ye not that your body is the temple of the Holy Ghost which is in you, which ye have of God, . . . therefore glorify God in your body, and in your spirit, which are God's."

158. Before I got: blind characters appear in Barrett Browning's *Aurora Leigh* (1856) and Charlotte Brontë's *Jane Eyre* (1847), books ED cherished.

159. Tie the strings: in *Aurora Leigh* Aurora reports that before her departure Romney "[touched] My hatstrings tied for going." Atypically, ED wrote the alternative "Now" immediately following "Then –" (Then – Now"), marking both words for potential substitution.

160. I like a: between lines 4 and 5, ED wrote and then ancelled "Death, comes," apparently after revising the line so that those words no longer fit its syntax.

161. I felt a: may revise Longfellow's famous "A Psalm of Life" (1838), in which "hearts, though stout and brave, / Still, like muffled drums, are beating / Funeral marches to the grave."

162. 'Twas just this: Christmas was primarily a religious holiday in the nineteenth century, although Clement Moore's 1822 poem "A Visit from St. Nicholas" ("'Twas the night before Christmas") helped popularize customs involving Santa Claus; in 1874, ED wrote that her father had "frowned upon Santa Claus – and all such prowling gentlemen" (L425). Thanksgiving was not declared a national holiday until 1863.

163. Afraid! Of whom: ED omitted the implied "a" in line 5: "Of Life? 'Twere odd I fear thing."

164. I would not: ED would have known several poems linking the arts of painting, music, and poetry (e.g., Keats's "Ode to a Nightingale," 1819). "Ether" generally meant sky or spirit, but ED may have known about the 1846 use of ether as an anesthetic at Massachusetts General Hospital; it was a great advance in surgical technology.

165. He touched me,: in the popular orientalist poem *Lalla Rookh* (1817), Thomas Moore writes of Persians lifting their hands in prayer; someone (perhaps ED) marked three passages in AD's copy of this poem. Rebecca was the wife of Isaac, mother of Jacob and Esau (Genesis 24–28).

166. They leave us: additional copy retained (variant) c. first half of 1862.

167. I'm ceded – I've: 1 Corinthians 13:11, "When I became a man, I put away childish things." ED's baptism as an infant in the First Congregational Church in Amherst followed her mother's conversion in July 1831. Her father did not become a converted member until 1850, and ED never became a converted member, although she attended church at least occasionally until she was around thirty years old.

168. It was not: the sirocco is a hot, dry wind that blows off the Sahara and across the Mediterranean. Planed wood being fit to a frame makes shavings. Alternatives added later.

169. If you were: When "Van Diemen's Land" became a self-governing British colony in 1856, it was renamed Tasmania—that is, ED refers to a country that no longer exists. The island was used as a penal colony until 1853.

170. A Bird, came: additional copy retained (variant) c. summer 1862.

171. It's thoughts – and: responds to Oliver Wendell Holmes's 1858 "Contentment," which revised John Quincy Adams's famous "The Wants of Man" (1841), itself a response to Oliver Goldsmith's 1765 ballad, "The Hermit." ED probably knew all three poems.

172. He strained my: the alternative for line 10 is preceded by "Or"—marking it as an option: ED wrote "Or – Must be – I deserved – it –." Here ED writes all alternatives flush left, like her other lines. "[L]ittle 'John'" may refer to John, the disciple "whom Jesus loved" (John 13:23). Both apostrophes on "'Tho'" (line 11) are ED's.

173. I envy Seas,: Francisco Pizarro (1471?–1541) was a Spanish conquistador who conquered the Inca empire; Inca elders wore huge gold earrings. ED also identifies herself with the archangel Gabriel in other poems.

174. Those fair – fictitious: some alternatives added in later revision.

175. Within my Garden,: line 10 with the alternative might read either "[H]is Microscopic Gig" or "And his Microscopic Gig."

176. After great pain,: lines 5–8, copied in the order 5, 7, 6, 8, were marked for transposition with underlined numbers; they are presented here as transposed.

177. This World is: in 1844 Karl Marx wrote, "Religion . . . is the opium of the people"; the Marquis de Sade and Novalis made similar statements in the 1790s; it is unknown whether ED was familiar with them.

178. It will be: "Parian" refers to a white, flawless marble from the Greek island of Paros, or to a fine-textured white ceramic substitute for the marble, first produced in England in 1842. The "Covenant" that "Gentians – [will] frill –" may allude playfully to

God's covenant with Noah that he would not again destroy the earth with water—or, perhaps, snow (Genesis 9:11).

179. My Reward for: also copied in F24 Sh4 (variant) c. early 1863.

180. At least – to: alludes to Mark 10:16, where Jesus "took [the children] up in his arms, put his hands upon them, and blessed them." With the alternative, line 3 presumably reads "I know not which thy palaces –."

181. Better – than Music!: line 10 was copied as "So – Children" and marked for transposition; presented here as transposed.

182. I cannot dance: the terms "glee," "troupe," "prima," and "opera" were commonly used to refer to minstrel shows or houses, and dancing grotesquely like a bird might suggest the popular dance Jump Jim Crow, first performed in 1828. ED called herself "Mrs. Jim Crow" in an 1860 letter (L223).

183. I like to: a railroad station was opened in Amherst in 1853, thanks to ED's father's efforts; Jesus called his disciples James and John "Boanerges," meaning "sons of Thunder" (Mark 3:17). Alternatives for line 14 were written with "or": "And, or then –."

184. It don't sound: responds to the death of Lieutenant Frazar A. Stearns, a friend of AD's, who was killed in the battle of New Bern, North Carolina, in March 1862. ED wrote to SB, "Austin is chilled by Frazar's murder. He says his brain keeps saying over 'Frazar is killed' – 'Frazar is killed,' just as Father told it – to Him" (L256). Several poems of this period may respond to Frazar's death.

185. Do People moulder: in Matthew 16:28 Jesus says, "There be some standing here, which shall not taste of death, till they see the Son of man coming in his kingdom"; in 1 Corinthians 54–55: when "this mortal shall have put on immortality, then shall be brought to pass the saying that... Death is swallowed up in victory. O death, where is thy sting? O grave, where is thy victory?"

186. Knows how to: also copied with two additional stanzas on Sh32 (variant) c. 1865.

187. We talked as: line 14, with the alternative, may read "To recollect – and write" rather than "To recollect – to write."

188. I cried at: revisions and the cancellation added later.

189. The face I: OMC presents this manuscript as sent to SD; RWF states that sewing holes, pin impression, and matching stationery indicate that although it was addressed to SD ("Sue"—later erased) it was bound into F19 as the concluding leaf.

190. I took one: in 1929, Bianchi gave the first leaf of this fascicle, containing this and the next poem, to Herbert F. Jenkins (lost); the second leaf of Sh1 was retained. Jenkins's transcription establishes the order of the poems, but the text here is taken from MLT's transcript.

191. A train went: in 1929, Bianchi gave the first leaf of this fascicle to Herbert F. Jenkins (lost); Jenkins' transcription establishes the order of the poems, but the text for this poem comes from *Poems* (1890).

192. I think the: logically, the article preceding "hunger" (line 7, alternative) would be "A," not "An," as suggested here in brackets.

193. Dare you see: may allude to Longfellow's "The Village Blacksmith" (1840) or to Harriet Spofford's story "The South Breaker" (May/June 1862), in which a character reflects that for the spirit "there's . . . a moment when the dross strikes off, and the impurities, . . . and there comes out the great white diamond," like ore "forged in the furnace and beaten to a blade fit for the hands of archangels." Additional copy retained (variant) c. summer 1862.

194. Although I put: may allude to Wordsworth's "Goody Blake and Harry Gill" (1798): Goody pulls "Stick after stick . . . Till she had filled her apron full," although Harry is unkind and old Goody Blake curses him.

195. Over and over,: the theological debate over whether the individual is "justified" by works or by faith was at the heart of the Protestant Reformation and continued into the nineteenth century; ED begs the question by stating that the resurrected "Processions" are "Justified." To stand at the right hand of God is to stand in a place of honor.

196. One need not: may echo Harriet Beecher Stowe's reflection in *Uncle Tom's Cabin* (1851–1852), "[A] human soul is an awful ghostly, unquiet possession. . . . What a fool is he who locks his door to keep out spirits, who has in his own bosom a spirit he dares not meet alone."

197. Like Some Old: Cinderella's "Bays" may refer to the mice transformed into her horses. Blue Beard, according to legend, had "Galleries" of murdered wives. Little John is a member of Robin Hood's band.

198. The Soul selects: additional copy of first stanza retained (variant) c. early 1864; OMC claims these lines were sent to SD.

199. How sick – to: Shelley's *Queen Mab* (1813) mentions "fragrant zephyrs . . . from spicy isles."

200. I – Years – had: additional copy retained (variant) c. 1872.

201. They shut me: may allude to Longfellow's "Pegasus in Pound" (1850), in which the "poet's wingèd steed" is put in the pound by "wise men, in their wisdom" but effortlessly flies away to the stars at night; ED misquotes the title as "Pegasus in the pound" in a letter (1851, L56).

202. This was a: in "Letter to a Young Contributor" (*Atlantic Monthly*, April 1862), TWH writes: "Literature is attar of roses, one distilled drop from a million blossoms"; ED first wrote TWH in response to this publication.

203. In falling Timbers: may allude to the January 1862 Hartley Collier disaster, which entombed hundreds of miners in England and resulted in the deaths of 204 men, most of whom died for want of oxygen.

204. I died for: echoes Keats's "Ode on a Grecian Urn" (1820): "Beauty is truth, truth beauty" but perhaps also refers to more recent allusions to this ode, for example, in

Emerson's "Nature" (1836) or Barrett Browning's "A Vision of Poets" (1844). The latter reads: "These were poets true / Who died for Beauty, as martyrs do / For truth—the ends being scarcely two," lines marked, perhaps by ED, in SD's copy.

205. At last – to: also copied in F8 Sh1 (variant) c. spring 1860.

206. The Malay – took: there were many mid-nineteenth-century articles and stories on pearl divers. Some refer to the divers as "Negro" or dark-skinned; most are set in India or other parts of Asia. George Herbert ("Vanity [1]," 1633) and Robert Browning (*Paracelsus*, 1835) used pearl divers as figurative types.

207. Love – thou art: after Alexander von Humboldt's 1802 exploration of Chimborazo, this inactive volcano in the Andes became a symbol of the sublime; Emerson used it as a figure for the true poet's exceptionalism ("The Poet," 1844). ED's poem may allude to Romans 8:38–39—"neither death, nor life, nor angels, nor principalities, nor powers, nor things present, nor things to come, nor height, nor depth, nor any other creature, shall be able to separate us from the love of God."

208. I rose – because: at the end of *Jane Eyre*, Jane returns to the now-blind Rochester: "He relapsed again into gloom. I, on the contrary, became more cheerful.... [A]ll I said or did seemed either to console or revive him." The poem may borrow other images from this much-admired novel; and ED may have named her dog "Carlo" after St. John Rivers's dog.

209. A Prison gets: may allude to Lord Byron's "The Prisoner of Chillon" (1816), which claims "My very chains and I grew friends"; ED mentioned this poem in a letter: "You remember the Prisoner of Chillon did not know Liberty when it came, and asked to go back to Jail" (1864, L293).

210. "Why do I: may allude to Barrett Browning's Sonnet 43 in *Sonnets from the Portuguese* (1850), beginning "How do I love thee?"

211. The name – of: may respond to poems such as John Greenleaf Whittier's "The Battle Autumn of 1862," which sees nature as unchanging in her "gladness" despite war's "hell": "She mocks with tint of flower and leaf / The war-field's crimson stain" (*Atlantic Monthly*, October 1862).

212. I dwell in: TWH figures poetry as a dwelling in his "Letter to a Young Contributor" (*Atlantic Monthly*, April 1862): "There may be phrases which shall be palaces to dwell in, treasure-houses to explore; a single word may be a window from which one may perceive all the kingdoms of the earth."

213. Whole Gulfs – of: there were numerous Civil War battles in late 1862, starting with the Battle of Antietam in September; the poem refers to no "specific [battle] Ground."

214. Myself was formed –: Jesus is called a carpenter (Mark 6:3); in Matthew, he is a carpenter's son (13:55).

215. Just Once! Oh: additional copy retained (variant) c. 1866.

216. Because I could: the popular death-journey metaphor appears in Robert Browning's "The Last Ride Together" (1835), which ED quoted in a letter (1885, L1015), and in an elegy commemorating the death of a family friend, Jacob Holt, in the *Hampshire and Franklin Express*, 25 May 1848. ED copied a poem by Holt onto a flyleaf of her Bible. ED also knew of a cousin who died while on a drive in 1847. A tippet is a long scarf worn over the shoulders; tulle is a lightweight netting.

217. He fought like: the minie ball was the most frequently used type of small ammunition during the Civil War; a relatively new invention, this conical, grooved lead bullet could be loaded quickly and fired accurately, and hence changed the nature of warfare.

218. Wolfe demanded during: in 1759 the British defeated the French in a battle outside Quebec that claimed the lives of both Major General James Wolfe and the Marquis de Montcalm. The narrative of ED's poem follows that of her Mount Holyoke textbook *Elements of History, Ancient and Modern*, by J. E. Worcester (1828). Additional copy (variant) retained c. 1866.

219. To offer brave: with the alternative "You" for "One," ED implies the change of verb from "has" to "have," suggested here in brackets.

220. The Beggar Lad –: many stories indicate Jesus's charity to children and the needy; in his Sermon on the Mount (Matthew 5:5), Jesus says, "Blessed are the meek: for they shall inherit the earth."

221. It sifts from: may respond to TWH's article "Snow" in the *Atlantic Monthly* (February 1862), which praises several poems on snow, especially Emerson's "The Snow-Storm" and James Russell Lowell's "The First Snowfall." Additional copy retained (variant) c. 1865, which reduces the poem's twenty lines to twelve; only the first four and the final lines are common (albeit at times variant) to all five copies. In the copy to SD, ED spelled "Ankles" correctly. ED also retained a line from Emerson's poem, copied as a fragment c. 1884: "Tumultuous privacy of Storm."

222. A Pit – but: the second leaf of Sh1, containing most of this poem and the next, was torn off and lost; ED finished copying this poem on a leaf also containing the end of "I tie my Hat – I crease my Shawl –," bound into the fascicle between Sh5 and Sh6, after the latter poem. The first sixteen lines of the poem come from Graves's transcription; the last five, from the extant leaf. Because I do not include notice of leaves or slips on which ED completes poems, the leaf containing the ends of these two poems is not enumerated here.

223. Of Brussels – it: Brussels and Kidderminster were famous for the quality of their carpets in the early nineteenth century.

224. He found my: Revelation 3:12, "Him that overcometh will I make a pillar in the temple of my God... and I will write upon him the name of my God, and the name of the city of my God, which is new Jerusalem, ... and I will write upon him my new name."

225. Unto my Books –: resembles other war-time poems grateful for the comfort of art, such as Whittier's "To E. W." (1863) and Oliver Wendell Holmes's "Shakespeare, Tercentennial Celebration, April 23, 1864."

226. The Spider holds: culturally dominant motifs regarded the spider as noxious or demonic, as in the hymnist Mary Howitt's nursery rhyme "The Spider and the Fly" (1829) or Jonathan Edwards's sermon "Sinners in the Hands of an Angry God" (1741). In Greek mythology, Athena competes with the expert weaver Arachne to see who has the most skill; when Arachne wins the contest, Athena turns her into a spider.

227. When I was: no death of a Dickinson acquaintance fits the details of this poem; there were no soldiers from the Amherst area in Maryland. Francis H. Dickinson (of Belchertown, Massachusetts) was killed a year and a half earlier at Ball's Bluff, Virginia, on the Potomac River (21 October 1861). Alternatives suggest that lines 19 and 20 may be combined, as: "For Braveries, just sealed in Scarlet Maryland –" (or "proved" for "sealed").

228. God made a: may respond to William Cullen Bryant's 1832 "To the Fringed Gentian" and Hans Christian Andersen's "The Ugly Duckling" (1843; translated into English 1846).

229. My Reward for: also copied in F18 Sh5 (variant) c. autumn 1862.

230. It always felt: Moses was forbidden to enter the promised land, which he viewed from Mount Nebo (Numbers 20:12, Deuteronomy 3:23–27). For Stephen's stoning, see Acts 7:59; Christian tradition holds that Paul was beheaded in Rome.

231. I tie my: ED marked the words of line 10, initially written "I have so much to do," for transposition as "so much I have to do"; presented here as transposed; "so" is changed to "So" to fit her pattern of line-initial capitalization.

232. The Trees like: Anthony van Dyck (1599–1641), a Flemish painter, known as an innovator of landscape painting in watercolor and for his courtly portraits.

233. It feels a: after the battle at Thermopylae, the heroism of the Spartans was inscribed on a stone (as described in ED's Mount Holyoke textbook *Elements of History, Ancient and Modern*, by J. E. Worcester, 1828). ED may also allude to the March 1863 Union draft law, which caused riots in New York City in July: draftees could pay a substitute to take their place, as AD and others from Amherst did the following year, in 1864. Emerson used a similar metaphor in "The Boston Hymn": the slave owner "goes in pawn to his victim" (*Atlantic Monthly*, February 1863).

234. I tried to: Sir John Franklin's 1845 failed polar expedition to find a northwest passage was a popular subject; search parties were sent to the arctic in 1850, 1854, and 1859. ED may also allude to Emerson's "Fate" (1860): "[Man] helps himself on each emergency by copying or duplicating his own structure."

235. Two Butterflies went: additional copy retained with extensive revision c. 1878; only the first two lines remain the same (see "Loose Poems").

236. It was a: additional copy retained (variant) c. 1865.

237. I'm saying every: the Bourbons were a European noble family whose members ruled in France, Spain, and parts of Italy between the sixteenth and nineteenth centuries. In 1863 a Bourbon held the throne of Spain. The Crown of Aragon was a confederation of kingdoms that ruled parts of modern France, Spain, Italy, and Greece in the fifteenth century.

238. I went to: Mechlin lace was one of the best-known Flemish laces, fine and transparent—used for women's hair styling and clothing.

239. The Soul unto: may echo Sir Thomas Browne's *Christian Morals*, III (1716), "Unthinking Heads, who have not learn'd to be alone, are in a Prison to themselves"; instead one should "delight to be alone and single with Omnipresency."

240. We see – Comparatively –: a cordillera is an extensive chain of mountains, often used to refer to the various mountain ranges of the Andes in South America. The Apennine Range stretches along peninsular Italy.

241. We dream – it: the alternative "should" in line 1 requires "dream," not "dreaming."

242. If ever the: the leaf containing this and the following poem was detached from the sheet and lost; MLT's transcript does not specify the order in which ED copied them.

243. They called me: may respond to noted Hudson River painter John F. Kensett's *Sunset with Cows* (1857), which SD owned; this subject was common to painters of the period.

244. I heard a: in Barrett Browning's *Aurora Leigh* (1856), a dying woman claims that "something came between" her and the man she loved, "catching every fly of doubt / To hold it buzzing at the window-pane." Sentimental death scenes were popular in the nineteenth century.

245. The Lightning playeth –: the telegraph was invented and developed during ED's lifetime; the first telegram sent in the United States was in 1838; by 1861 telegraph lines connected the East and West Coasts.

246. Her – last Poems –: Elizabeth Barrett Browning's *Last Poems* was published in 1862, following her death on 29 June 1861 in Florence, her primary home since 1847. Additional copy (variant) retained.

247. The Manner of: Major André, Benedict Arnold's accomplice in treason during the American Revolutionary War, pleaded to be executed by firing squad as a soldier rather than hanged as a spy, but was hanged; according to an October 1851 article in *Harper's*, "the *manner* of his death disturbed his spirit." St. James's Palace was the primary residence of the British monarch until early in the nineteenth century. ED wrote "to Choose" at the end of the first metrical line and then cancelled it, perhaps because she thought the syntax would be clearer if "to choose" followed "a privilege" in line 3, or because she wanted a 6686 stanza pattern throughout the poem.

248. You'll know Her –: a threnody is a song or poem of mourning. ED would have known Emerson's "Threnody" (1846) in memory of his son and perhaps Dryden's *Threnodia Augustalis* (1685), on the death of Charles II.

249. The Black Berry –: Women sold berries and herbs door to door. Lydia Louisa Anna Very presents an impoverished berry woman as a Christian martyr in "The Berry Woman" (*Poems*, 1856). In 1866, ED mentions that Lavinia is "trad[ing] blackberries with a Tawny Girl" (L320).

250. Through the Dark: in Psalm 23, the speaker's faith, "though I walk through the valley of the shadow of death," prevents all "fear." In Revelation 21:20, beryl is a stone used in the foundation of the New Jerusalem.

251. Trust in the: William Kidd (1645–1701), aka Captain Kidd, a Scotsman executed for piracy; in John 20:29 Jesus says, "Thomas, because thou hast seen me, thou hast believed: blessed are they that have not seen, and yet have believed." ED underlined the final *e* in "Discerned," here rendered as "Discernèd."

252. 'Twas Love – not: the sense of line 8 requires the possessive ("Jesus['s] – most!"), assuming the comparison is between the speaker's (or Love's) "Guilt" and Jesus's. ED may have omitted the possessive to maintain a six-syllable line.

253. 'Tis not that: ED may have misplaced the apostrophe on "Farmer's" (line 9); the copy to the Norcross cousins was transcribed as "farmers'."

254. The Winters are: Ararat is the mountain range on which Noah's ark landed after the great Flood (Genesis 8:4).

255. I reckon – When: Shakespeare's sonnet "Shall I compare thee to a summer's day" concludes: "thy eternal summer shall not fade" as long as his poem survives.

256. The Test of: quotes John 3:16, "For God so loved the world, that he gave his only begotten Son, that whosoever believeth in him should not perish, but have everlasting life."

257. Unit, like Death –: Barrett Browning's Aurora Leigh speaks of a "good neighbor," who "cuts your morning up / To mince-meat of the very smallest talk, / Then helps to sugar her bohea at night / With your reputation" (1856).

258. They dropped like: lists of dead soldiers were printed in daily newspapers following each Civil War battle.

259. I prayed, at: ED's alternative "under[side]" suggests Sir Thomas Browne's comment that "we are ignorant of the back-parts or lower side of His Divinity" (*Religio Medici*, 1643), echoing Exodus 33:23, "And I will take away mine hand, and thou shalt see my back parts: but my face shall not be seen."

260. God is a: ED knew Longfellow's narrative poem *The Courtship of Miles Standish* (1858), in which Alden wins Priscilla's love while courting her on Standish's behalf. ED wrote over "were" to make "are" in the final line.

261. If any sink,: during the Civil War the minie ball was the most frequently used type of small ammunition; a relatively new invention, this conical, grooved lead bullet could be loaded quickly and fired accurately.

262. Much Madness is: may allude to Polonius's remark in *Hamlet*, "Though this be madness, yet there is method in 't."

263. I think I: written in memory of Elizabeth Barrett Browning, who died on 29 June 1861.

264. 'Tis Customary as: the flower clematis is known as "traveler's joy."

265. No Crowd that: may recall Sir Thomas Browne's description in *Religio Medici* (1643) of "our separated dust . . . at the voice of God" joining again to "make up their primary and predestinate forms." The poem meditates on descriptions of resurrection (e.g., Revelation 20:11–13) that assume God made humanity from dust (Genesis 2:7).

266. Beauty – be not: Emerson writes that "beauty is its own excuse for being" ("The Rhodora," *Poems*, 1847); ED marked this poem in her volume.

267. I started Early –: a "stay mouse" is a nautical term for a bulge built into a sailing vessel's standing rigging (when the stays were still made of natural fibers) to prevent the rope from slipping.

268. Endow the Living –: additional copy perhaps retained or perhaps sent to an unidentified recipient (lost), c. 1863.

269. I took my: for the story of David and Goliath, see 1 Samuel 17:23–50.

270. One Crucifixion is: Calvary is the hill outside Jerusalem where Jesus was crucified (Luke 23:33); Gethsemane is the garden where Jesus and his disciples prayed the night before his crucifixion. Judea is the biblical name for territory with shifting boundaries within Israel and the West Bank, including Jerusalem.

271. Sweet – You forgot –: third stanza (variant) also included on Sh30 as "Just to be Rich," c. 1865.

272. I went to: memorializes Elizabeth Barrett Browning's death in Italy (29 June 1861).

273. Death sets a: may mark the tenth anniversary of the death of Benjamin Franklin Newton (d. 24 March 1853); in 1850 Newton gave ED a copy of Emerson's *Poems*; she referred to him as her "Preceptor" (L153).

274. There is a: published in 1890 with the title "Purple Clover." ED knew Darwinian theories of the survival of the fittest, represented here in the clover's struggle to survive and reproduce. In a memoir, MacGregor Jenkins writes that ED "loved . . . especially the grass and clover blossoms" ("A Child's Recollections of Emily Dickinson," 1891).

275. 'Tis One by: several biblical passages indicate that the lowly are equal to the mighty, e.g., "for he that is least among you all, the same shall be great" (Luke 9:48) and "many that are first shall be last; and the last shall be first" (Matthew 19:30).

276. Smiling back from: "Coronation" probably refers to passages in Revelation such as 2:10, "be thou faithful unto death, and I will give thee a crown of life," and 20:4, "And I saw thrones, and they sat upon them . . . and they lived and reigned with Christ a thousand years"; according to Genesis 3:19, God created humans from dust.

277. That I did: Calvary is the name of the hill outside Jerusalem on which Jesus was crucified.

278. Triumph – may be: Judgment Day is frequently represented as standing before the face of God; the word "overcome" also appears frequently in Revelation's description of resurrection, e.g., "He that overcometh shall not be hurt of the second death" (2:11); "triumph" also has religious resonance, e.g., "Now thanks be unto God, which always causeth us to triumph in Christ" (2 Corinthians 2:14).

279. Glee – The great: many popular ballads related community disasters as told to "Children"; "bonnie" echoes Scottish ballads. ED marked "softness" and "silence" in lines 14 and 15 for transposition; presented here as transposed.

280. It makes no: under the Spanish Inquisition, auto-da-fé (Portuguese, "act of the faith") was the ritual of public penance demanded of condemned heretics before they were executed, most often by burning; "Judgment" may refer to the Inquisition's trials or to the Last Judgment.

281. To know just: in its first stanzas, the poem rehearses questions typically asked in the nineteenth century about a loved one's death; ED herself asked such questions in her letters.

282. Only God – detect: refers to the Christian Trinity, God as Father, Son, and Holy Ghost (Matthew 28:19).

283. I know Where: in the story of Jesus and the woman at the well, Jesus says, "Whosoever drinketh of this water shall thirst again: But whosoever drinketh of the water that I shall give him shall never thirst" (John 4:13–14). Several hymns use the phrase "thirst no more," e.g., Isaac Watts's "Now in the Galleries of His Grace" (1837) and Charles Wesley's "Who Are These Arrayed in White" (1745).

284. The Tint I: several allusions suggest Shakespeare's portrayal of Cleopatra, in her enigmatic "Dominion" over Antony and the "exquisite" desire and "Discontent" she, or her "Company," inspires.

285. A Wife – at: two earlier copies retained (variant) c. spring 1861 and c. summer 1862.

286. To My Small: ED wrote "aglow," emended here to "a'glow."

287. My Portion is: the minie ball was the most frequently used type of small ammunition during the Civil War. Significant battles with high casualty numbers early in the second half of 1863 include Vicksburg, Gettysburg, and Chickamauga.

288. I cannot live: Sèvres is a French porcelain that dominated the market in the early nineteenth century with its diverse originality and quality. "I cannot live with You –" may respond to a tradition of carpe diem poems such as Christopher Marlowe's "The Passionate Shepherd to His Love" ("Come live with me and be my love"; 1589).

289. Doom is the: THJ mistakenly reads "Berries die" rather than "dye."

290. I should have: the last words Jesus spoke were "Eli, Eli, lama sabachthani?" or "My God, my God, why hast thou forsaken me?" (Matthew 27:46); Gethsemane is the garden in which Jesus prayed the night before his crucifixion.

291. I meant to: Matthew 7:7–8 begins, "Ask, and it shall be given you; seek, and ye shall find," a promise repeated in other gospels.

292. Promise This – When: alternatives cover two-thirds of a page at the end of this poem: included here are most but not all of ED's repetitions in writing out alternatives.

293. My Life had: a poem published anonymously during the Civil War, "The Gun," also uses a first-person speaker taking the perspective of an artillery piece (*Harper's Weekly*, 4 July 1863).

294. No Bobolink – reverse: ED wrote lines 9, 10, and 8 in that order and marked them for transposition; the lines are transposed here.

295. Victory comes late –: God's "Oath to Sparrows" is that they shall not "fall" without God's notice or be forgotten by God (Matthew 10:29–31 and Luke 12:6). In line 8, ED wrote "His' Table's"; the first apostrophe is omitted here.

296. Essential Oils – are: in Josiah Holland's *Bitter-Sweet* (1858), a poet states "Hearts, like apples, are hard and sour / Till crushed by Pain's resistless power / And yield their juices rich and bland / To none but Sorrow's heavy hand." Keats expresses the same popular romantic sentiment in his "Ode on Melancholy" (1820).

297. The Spirit is: Matthew twice refers to the need for spiritual hearing: "Who hath ears to hear, let him hear" (Matthew 13:43; also 11:15). In "Ode on a Grecian Urn" (1820), Keats urges pipes to play "not to the sensual ear, but . . . to the spirit ditties of no tone."

298. "Nature" is what: echoes ideas Emerson develops in "Nature" (1836); ED called a book of Emerson's essays "a little granite book . . . to lean on!" (L481).

299. I could bring: Francisco de Bobadilla (?–1502) accumulated vast wealth while governor of the Indies (Hispaniola).

300. The Judge is: may refer flirtatiously to Otis Lord, at this point a close friend of her father's and a judge on the Massachusetts Superior Court; the northeastern long-eared owl is named *Asio otus*.

301. The Props assist: Jesus is called a carpenter's son in Matthew 13:55 and a carpenter in Mark 6:3.

302. You've seen Balloons: in *Aurora Leigh* (1856), Barrett Browning describes hope as "some fallen balloon, / Which, whether caught by blossoming tree or bare, / Is torn alike."

303. The Love a: additional copy retained (variant) c. 1862, addressed to "Dollie" (a nickname for SD) and beginning "The Love a Child can show – below –"; OMC claims this copy was sent to SD.

304. A first Mute: in Genesis 19, Lot demonstrates faith by entertaining strangers, who prove to be angels and warn him to flee with his family before Sodom and Gomorrah are destroyed. A more metrically and syntactically probable rendering of this poem would be in two couplets (four lines of iambic pentameter) but ED used distinct capitalization and new rows of script, as represented here.

305. No Other can: the first two stanzas (variant) are copied on Sh33, c. 1865. In the Sh33 and circulated copies of this poem, the metrical presentation of lines 1 and 2 is regularized: "Our" appears at the beginning of line 2 ("No Other can reduce / Our . . .").

306. Joy to have: ED tells Higginson her eyes are "like the sherry in the glass, that the guest leaves" (L268), in other words they are hazel.

307. Bound a Trouble –: in Wordsworth's "The Solitary Reaper" (1807), the "Maiden" is "singing at her work," "a melancholy strain"; also copied in F9 Sh1 (variant) c. summer 1861.

308. On a Columnar: may respond to Emerson's essay "Self-Reliance" (1841) and borrow "Assembly" from Hebrews 12:22–23, where Moses says "ye are come . . . [t]o the general assembly and church of the firstborn, which are written in heaven, and to God the Judge of all."

309. No Prisoner be –: In *Emily Dickinson Face to Face*, Bianchi presents this poem as sent to SD, but RWF finds no evidence that another copy existed.

310. Good Night – Which: also included (variant) in F13, c. early 1862.

311. She dwelleth in: the crocus is a very early spring flower that grows from a bulb, like the daffodil.

312. Where Thou art –: echoes Ruth 1:16, "whither thou goest, I will go; and where thou lodgest, I will lodge"; in announcing Mary's pregnancy to her, Gabriel praised her as "blessed . . . among women" (Luke 1:28).

313. Through the Straight: perhaps suggested by an article in the *Springfield Republican*, titled "Our Martyrs and Their Resurrection," on writers who were celebrated only after their death (29 March 1863).

314. Dropped into the: in the 1880s, ED added the alternative "a" for "of."

315. Ah, Teneriffe – Receding: Tenerife, the largest of the Canary Islands, is home to the third largest volcano in the world; it is known as the "Island of Eternal Spring" because of its moderate climate.

316. Let Us play: some of the vocabulary here suggests contemporary issues of emancipation ("manacles," "liberty," "new Free"); "dungeons" does not.

317. You taught me: may echo 1 John 2:28, "And now, little children, abide in him; that, when he shall appear, we may have confidence, and not be ashamed before him at his coming."

318. The Birds reported: "She – never questioned Me –" appears to replace "I never questioned Her –" given the logic of the following line ("Nor I – Herself –"); ED wrote both lines flush left and marked both as having an alternative.

319. Remorse – is Memory –: "Companies" may replace only "Parties," in which case line 2 with alternative reads "[Her] companies all [astir]."

320. Never for Society: Scottish ("Border") and Basque ("Biscayan") ballads were popular in the United States during the early nineteenth century, as was the eighteenth-century English ballad "The Bay of Biscay."

321. It dropped so: alternatives were added and "less" (line 5) was underlined c. 1880. ED may have underlined "less" to show continuity with the evidently preferred revision, also underlined: "flung it"; she does not rewrite the word.

322. Growth of Man: God's face is frequently called his "countenance" in the Bible; see, e.g., Numbers 6:26, "The Lord lift up his countenance upon thee, and give thee peace."

323. A Drop fell: two copies of lines 7 and 8 (variant) were retained as fragments, c. 1864 and c. 1873.

324. By my Window: there was a Royal Society for Improving Natural Knowledge, founded 1660, and a Royal Academy of Music, founded 1822. In line 4, "serve" was underlined in later revision.

325. It was a: also included (variant) on Sh17, c. 1865.

326. Two – were immortal: Enoch and Elijah were taken to heaven without dying first (Genesis 5:24 and Hebrews 11:5).

327. She rose to: Caroline A. Howard's "By the Shore" uses a similar metaphor: "For thy murmuring voice . . . Sings soothingly unto me / Of things deep-buried, thoughts only known / To Him who the heart can see," identifying "Him" with the "boundless sea!" (*Springfield Republican*, 11 January 1862).

328. Who Court obtain: by writing the alternatives to lines 5 and 6 continuously and without a capital on "whom," ED indicates that the alternative version would have a four-line second stanza, with line 5 reading: "No Fate depose whom Trait – Ordain –."

329. None can experience: the first leaf of this sheet in Fascicle 39 was torn off, perhaps by ED, in part roughly; there is no evidence of which poems, or how many, may have been copied on the missing leaf.

330. I meant to: alternatives and cancellation are from the mid-1870s.

331. The only news: ED wrote this poem in Cambridge, Massachusetts, where she was undergoing eye treatment, hence seeing very little; TWH was with his Union regiment in the South. "[T]raverst" is sloppily underlined, apparently in a different hand, in pencil, near other stray marks on the page—perhaps not ED's marking or not intentional.

332. Wert Thou but: because a judge's robe was traditionally lined with ermine, the word "ermine" was used frequently to mean "judge."

333. The first Day: may allude to Philippians 1:21–23: "For to me to live is Christ, and to die is gain. But if I live in the flesh, this is the fruit of my labour: yet what I shall choose I wot not. For I am in a strait betwixt two, having a desire to depart, and to be with Christ."

334. "Unto Me"? I: echoes several biblical passages, including "Today shalt thou be with me in paradise" (Luke 23:43), references to the "mighty arm" of the Lord (e.g., Psalm 98:1), and the repeated idea that "the last shall be first" (e.g., Matthew 19:30).

335. I hide myself: also copied in F3 Sh2 (variant) c. spring 1859; additional fair copy retained (variant) with pinholes as if to send with a flower, c. 1863.

336. The Admirations – and: perhaps alludes to "For now we see through a glass, darkly; but then face to face" (1 Corinthians 13:12).

337. Fitter to see: cancellations made at a later date, perhaps not by ED.

338. Color – Caste – Denomination: perhaps a response to the issue of slavery or to the Emancipation Proclamation of 1 January 1863.

UNBOUND SHEETS

Some of the pages RWF identifies as Sets were held together in what MLT called "packets," joined with a brass fastener. Because it is unlikely that Dickinson herself created these groupings, I identify these poems, written in fair hand on unbound sheets or leaves during Dickinson's periods of systematic copying, by Sheet or Leaf, numbered chronologically, not as "sets." For the correspondence between the Sheet and Leaf numbers and RWF's Sets, see the appendix.

1. A Tongue – to: may echo Shakespeare's diction in various passages in which a lover charges a third person to relay extravagant proof of love or loyalty to a beloved.

2. What Soft – Cherubic: Hebrews 11:16, "But now they desire a better country, that is, an heavenly: wherefore God is not ashamed to be called their God: for he hath prepared for them a city."

3. You know that: Ishmael (son of Abraham and his wife Sarah's handmaiden Hagar) often represents a social outcast; ED may have been familiar with Melville's use of this name in *Moby Dick* (1851). By "A-fog" ED may mean "A'fog"; RWF makes this emendation.

4. It bloomed and: the speaker of Emerson's "Days" "hastily" takes only a few of the Day's proffered gifts, which then disappear; the poem ends "I, too late, / Under [Day's] solemn fillet saw the scorn" (*Atlantic Monthly*, November 1857).

5. This Dust, and: echoes Genesis 3:19, in which God says to Adam, "for dust thou art, and unto dust shalt thou return."

6. What I see: may allude to Shakespeare's sonnet 43, "When most I wink, then do mine eyes best see," which also claims that absence of the beloved makes days into "nights" but "nights bright days when dreams do show thee me." ED had hazel eyes. She may have combined the last eight lines into one stanza to fit the poem onto this sheet.

7. A Coffin – is: additional copy retained (lost), copied presumably c. 1864.

8. I learned – at: although not in the Bible, the word "covenant" has been associated with marriage for centuries, as in, for example, the 1549 *Book of Common Prayer*.

9. The Soul's distinct: photography and lightning were associated in the mid-nineteenth century, as they both combined the mystical or spiritual and the scientific in their illuminations. Several words in this poem ("quick," "Flash," "Click," "Developes") suggest the new technology of photography.

10. Split the Lark –: see John 20:24–25 for the story of doubting Thomas.

11. Light is sufficient: in Emerson's "Fable" (*Poems*, 1847), a squirrel asserts its equal importance in quarreling with a mountain; in a letter, ED describes a child as "deathless as Emerson's 'Squirrel'" (L794). Additional copy retained (variant) c. 1863.

12. That is solemn: according to Webster's, a "glee" may be either a "joy" or a "song sung in parts."

13. Because the Bee: furze (also called gorse) is a thorny evergreen shrub with striking yellow flowers and a very long blooming season. According to an old adage, "When gorse is out of bloom, kissing is out of season" or, alternatively, "When the furze is in bloom, my love's in tune."

14. Finding is the: in Greek mythology, Jason finds and claims the Golden Fleece, the skin of a winged ram, in order to assert his authority as rightful king of Thessaly.

15. Given in Marriage: traditionally, the church (or, by association, the Christian) is the bride of Christ, based on biblical passages such as "Let us be glad and rejoice, and give honour to him: for the marriage of the Lamb is come, and his wife hath made herself ready" (Revelation 19:7).

16. Drab Habitation of: In *Complete Poems*, Bianchi lists a copy of this poem as sent "with a cocoon" to Ned; RWF finds no evidence that such a copy existed.

17. Nature and God –: Sir William Herschel (1738–1822) was a composer and musician whose interest in music led him to astronomy; he discovered Uranus, two of its moons, and two moons of Saturn.

18. Be Mine the: also copied (variant) on Sh17, later in 1865; perhaps written to accompany a gift of flowers.

19. Each Scar I'll: THJ emends "missum" to "mis sum."

20. Soto! Explore thyself!: the Spanish conquistador Hernando de Soto (c. 1496–1542) was an early explorer of what is now the southeastern United States, and was the first European documented as having crossed the Mississippi River. Additional copy retained (variant) c. 1864.

21. Of Tolling Bell: there was perhaps an additional copy (lost), date unknown, transcribed variant by MLT.

22. As imperceptibly as: the copy sent to SD was lost after 1929 and never transcribed; two additional fair copies were retained c. 1866 and c. 1882. Like the copy sent to TWH, they consist of stanzas 1, 2, 7, and 8 (variant).

23. Be Mine the: also copied (variant) on Sh12, earlier in 1865.

24. It was a: included (variant) in F38 Sh3 c. early 1864.

25. Dying! To be: Gertrude Vanderbilt had recently recovered from a bullet wound, after being shot by her maid's rejected suitor on 20 March 1864.

26. When the Astronomer: the Pleiades star cluster is regarded in Greek mythology as representing the Pleiades, or Seven Sisters (the daughters of Atlas). One of the seven is "invisible," having hidden her face for reasons variously ascribed. Sir John Franklin (1786–1847) embarked on an unsuccessful Arctic exploration in 1845; Lady Jane Franklin financed repeated search parties in an effort to find his missing ship. In 1859 it was determined that all 129 men had died. This failed voyage was the subject of many ballads, novels, and artistic works.

27. Peace is a: the Civil War officially ended with General Robert E. Lee's surrender on 9 April 1865, followed less than a week later by the assassination of President Abraham Lincoln. Yet federal soldiers continued to be attacked by former Confederates in many parts of the South.

28. To this World: wounded by her maid's rejected suitor, Gertrude Vanderbilt was not expected to survive. ED received news of her recovery in September 1864.

29. The largest Fire: ED studied astronomy at Mount Holyoke Female Seminary and would have known that in 1838 Friedrich Bessel determined how to measure accurately the distance and movement of a star, thereby confirming that the earth orbits the sun and that the sun itself is a star.

30. Good to have: standing on the "Right Hand" usually refers to Jesus, or the holiest of the resurrected dead, standing in a place of honor beside God, e.g., in Mark 16:19, Luke 22:69, and Matthew 26:64. Additional copy retained (variant), beginning "Sweet, to have had them lost," c. 1864.

31. His Feet are: chrysoprase is a rare and valuable leek- or apple-green type of chalcedony reputed to have properties that alleviate feelings of depression and anxiety; it is mentioned in the Bible.

32. Only a Shrine,: anti-Catholicism was at a peak in the United States in the mid-nineteenth century because of the influx of Catholic immigrants from Ireland and Germany; ED here allies herself with Catholic worship.

33. Here, where the: THJ combines this poem with the next, "Where I am not afraid to go," perhaps because ED did not draw a line beneath these four lines, which end at the bottom of a leaf. She was inconsistent about drawing such lines, especially when a poem ended at the bottom of a page.

34. Her little Parasol: in *Ancestors' Brocades*, Bingham notes of this poem that "Mamma [MLT] says 'Morning Glory.'"

35. His Bill an: published in *Poems* (1896) as "The Woodpecker."

36. To undertake is: additional copy retained (variant) c. 1866.

37. A Sickness of: possibly alludes to the assassination of Abraham Lincoln on 14 April 1865.

38. Partake as doth: additional copy retained (variant) c. early 1864.

39. I heard, as: in Luke 22:34, Jesus tells Peter that he will "thrice deny that thou knowest me"; in most biblical uses of "thou knowest," an individual addresses God; in 1 Corinthians 15:37–44 Paul preaches that each body has its appropriate "seed" and that the resurrected body, although "sown in corruption," shall be "raised a spiritual body." Additional copy retained (last stanza, variant) c. October 1870.

40. Just to be: this is the last stanza of "Sweet – You forgot – but I remembered," copied (variant) in F31 Sh2, c. second half of 1863.

41. I was a: the eastern phoebe (common in the northeastern United States) is dull in coloration and has a raspy, brief, two-part song.

42. Knows how to: the first Jewish congregation in Massachusetts was established in Boston in the 1840s; there was no Jewish presence in Amherst during ED's lifetime. ED's knowledge of rabbis is likely to have been literary. Included (variant) as a four-stanza poem in F19 Leaf 5, c. autumn 1862.

43. 'Tis Anguish grander: in the letter to SD, the lines of the poem are preceded by metered prose: "I'm thinking on that other morn –."

44. Not to discover: ED writes the alternatives to lines 4 and 5 as continuous: "[As much through] Conscious faith of others in its ableness," perhaps indicating that she contemplated making this a single poetic line and making no stanza division.

45. No other can: included (variant) as stanzas 1 and 2 of a longer poem in F36 Sh1, c. second half of 1863.

46. This was in: in her letter to Louisa, ED refers to this poem as a "little hymn. I had hoped to express more. Love more I never can . . ." (L307).

47. The Soul should: Revelation 3:20, "Behold, I stand at the door, and knock: if any man hear my voice, and open the door, I will come in to him, and will sup with him, and he with me."

48. She rose as: may refer to Westminster Abbey; it was one of Britain's highest honors to be buried there.

49. A bold, inspiriting: also copied (variant) on Sh89 c. 1872, beginning "A prompt – executive Bird is the Jay –."

50. Trudging to Eden,: Trotwood is a nickname for the title character, an orphan with a pitiful childhood, in Charles Dickens's *David Copperfield* (1849–1850).

51. What Twigs We: new observations regarding the number and composition of Saturn's rings were made frequently in the mid-nineteenth century and some scientists observed dark bands ("bars"?) on the planet. ED studied astronomy at Mount Holyoke Female Seminary.

52. Ended, ere it: in *Emily Dickinson Face to Face*, Bianchi lists a copy of this poem as sent to SD; no such copy is known.

53. While it is: additional copy retained (variant) c. 1862.

54. My best Acquaintances: this is one of the unusual instances in which ED's alternative (line 5) changes her meter—in this case, from 8686 syllables to 6686, or from common to short meter.

55. As the Starved: Santo Domingo (in the Dominican Republic) underwent several changes of government through revolts against occupations by Spain, France, and Haiti during the first half of the nineteenth century; in 1865 the Dominicans again won independence from Spain. Santo Domingo was known for producing a variety of tropical fruits and for melons (a species of berry), although here it may signify tropical lushness.

56. Away from Home: ED mentions emigrating or exile in several poems, placing her "I" in the position of the emigrant. In the mid-nineteenth century, Irish immigration to Massachusetts was at a peak; Hampshire County had a nearly 10 percent foreign-born population in 1850; Boston had 45 percent. The Dickinsons hired Irish-born servants. Additional copy retained (variant) c. 1864, beginning "Away from Home, are They and I –." THJ and DEA describe the copy sent to EH or the Hollands as sent to SD.

57. A Burdock twitched: ED was apparently teasing AD about an encounter with Ithamar Francis Conkey, an Amherst lawyer and a political rival of the Dickinsons. To AD, ED commented, "Father said Frank Conkey – touched you –" (L240).

58. The Chemical conviction: in chemistry classes at Mount Holyoke, ED learned about the principle of the conservation of matter—that is, that matter changes but is not lost. Mary Lyon, the founder of Mount Holyoke Female Seminary, was trained as a chemist.

59. What did They: ED copied stanzas 1, 2, and 4, inserting stanza 3 by writing it on a slip of paper and pinning it into place.

60. Of Silken Speech: additional copy retained (variant) c. 1865.

61. Experiment to Me: additional copy retained (variant) c. 1866.

62. Sang from the: in Keats's "Ode to a Nightingale" (1820), the speaker hears the bird's "plaintive anthem" and comments, "Thou wast not born for death, immortal Bird!"

63. I've dropped my: since ancient times, Carrara marble has been valued for its complexity of light and its white and blue-gray tones.

64. A narrow Fellow: copy to unidentified recipient is the lost source for the *Springfield Daily Republican*'s 14 February 1866 publication, titled "The Snake"; the recipient may have been SD (as DEA indicates), in which case ED sent her the poem twice. Concerned that TWH might think she had approved the publication after telling him she "did not print," ED sent him a clipping with the poem on 17 March 1866, saying "it was robbed of me" (L316).

65. At Half past: additional copy retained (variant) c. 1866.

66. The Crickets sang: ED may have retained the copy that Leyda describes as possibly sent to SB.

67. One Day is: Thanksgiving was first declared a national holiday in 1863.

68. The Luxury to: additional copy retained (variant) c. 1866.

69. All Circumstances are: Paul teaches that God "dwelleth not in temples made with hands . . . seeing he giveth to all life, and breath, and all things . . . for in him we live, and move, and have our being" (Acts 17:24–28).

70. From Us She: in many cultures, one cannot see a god and live; see Exodus 33:20, "And he said, Thou canst not see my face: for there shall no man see me, and live."

71. Let down the: Jesus says, "I am the good shepherd: the good shepherd giveth his life for the sheep" (John 10:11).

72. Of Paul and: combines two accounts of the apostles Paul and Silas; in one, they were released by angels (Acts 5:23); in the second, they were still present when jailors came to fetch them (Acts 16:40). This and the following several poems were written on single leaves of paper; because the paper is of the same size and type as that ED used for fascicles and unbound sheets and because these pages were categorized soon after ED's death as belonging to a "packet," they are included in this section.

73. "Remember me" implored: a penitent thief crucified beside Jesus requested, "Jesus, Lord, remember me when thou comest into thy kingdom," and Jesus responded, "Today shalt thou be with me in paradise" (Luke 23:42–43). Retained copy of lines 2–3 (variant) c. 1873.

74. Because He loves: retained final two lines (variant) c. October 1870 in a draft of a letter to TWH and two copies of stanzas 2 and 3 (one variant; one lost, transcribed variant) c. late 1870.

75. Not any higher: alternatives underlined in later revision.

76. A Wind that: cancellation and substitution added later; additional copy retained (variant) c. 1871, on a sheet dated "December 5th," no year.

77. The Bone that: Jesus explains to the Pharisee Nicodemus, "That which is born of the flesh is flesh; and that which is born of the Spirit is spirit . . . Ye must be born again" to enter the Kingdom of God (John 3:6–7).

78. Who goes to: additional copy retained (variant) c. 1871.

79. Step lightly on: in January 1871 a statue of Abraham Lincoln by Vinnie Ream was unveiled in Washington, D.C. In September 1871, Lincoln's remains were moved to a monument in Springfield, Illinois, and another statue (by Randolph Rogers) was dedicated in Philadelphia. ED knew that TWH would be aware of these events, as a former colonel in the Union army. Retained copy of last two lines (variant) c. 1871.

80. The Days that: underlining added in later revision. Additional copy retained (variant) c. 1871, on a sheet dated "December 5th," no year.

81. 'Twas fighting for: although the Civil War officially ended in 1865, violence against federal soldiers and African Americans continued in the South. In April 1871 Congress passed the Third Enforcement Act, authorizing the president to declare

martial law and use military force to suppress the Ku Klux Klan, which he did. "Ball" is common shorthand for "minie ball," the type of small-arms ammunition most frequently used during the war.

82. Remembrance has a: at some point, ED cancelled lines 7 and 8 and the alternative "Contents" but then erased the cancellation. Additional copy lost (variant as transcribed by SD) c. 1871; DEA presents the lost copy as sent to SD.

83. Because my Brook: quotes Revelation 21:1, "And I saw a new heaven and a new earth: for the first heaven and the first earth were passed away; and there was no more sea."

84. A little Dog: in a note sent to SD five years earlier, ED writes about Ned: "Grandma 'hoped' characteristically 'he would be a very good Boy.' . . . Obtuse ambition of Grandmamas!" In 1895, in a letter to his mother, Ned refers to "Aunt Emily's cat 'with her desireless lot'!!!!"

85. Oh Shadow on: additional copy perhaps retained (variant) c. 1872; MLT claims that ED sent her this copy, but MLT did not move to Amherst until 1881, nearly a decade after it was apparently written and signed.

86. To disappear enhances –: the "Fruit perverse to plucking" is that forbidden to Adam and Eve in Eden (Genesis 2:16–17); underlining and some alternatives added later.

87. So I pull: Ananias was struck dead instantly after Peter accused him of a deceptive transaction (Acts 5:1–5). Moses freed the Jewish people from Egyptian enslavement but was not able to enter the land of Canaan; ED also refers in other poems to God's treatment of Moses as unjust.

88. A prompt – executive: by "Bailiff's Hymn," ED may mean the cry "Oyez, oyez, oyez," used to open court sessions. This poem is also copied (variant) on Sh36 c. 1865, beginning "A bold, inspiriting Bird." Cancellations and most alternatives were added in 1873 or 1874, returning to words used in the earlier copy.

89. Now I knew: ED copied this poem on the first leaf of a sheet and then she (or someone else) apparently rejected it: the first leaf is torn off and the poem's last four lines (at the top of the second leaf) are cancelled. Additional copy retained provides source text here; last four lines presented here vary from those cancelled in one capitalization and one punctuation mark.

90. The Sea said: as explained in the Introduction (pages 18–20), this poem might also logically be presented in longer, 3- or 4-beat lines.

91. The Way to: in English legend, Puck is a magical sprite or fairy; in *A Midsummer Night's Dream*, Shakespeare uses the name for a woodland sprite who mischievously mixes up the delivery of potions, creating temporary havoc among the lovers.

92. Not with a: fragment retained with the line "Shame need not crouch," c. 1874.

93. The Mushroom is: in her letter to TWH, ED wrote, "Today, I slew a Mushroom –" (L413). Additionally, retained earlier copies of lines 5–8, lines 1–8, and the complete poem (variant), c. 1874.

94. A Bee his: additional copy retained (variant) c. 1874.

95. A Dew sufficed: "thought" cancelled and "felt" added in revision c. 1878; ED retained one copy (three stanzas, variant) c. 1875 and two copies (variant) c. 1878. MLT claimed that ED gave her a copy of this poem, but the MS in question predated her arrival in Amherst by around six years.

96. How News must: ED began but did not complete "The last of Summer is Delight" on this sheet; the remaining two pages of the sheet are left blank.

97. The last of: to be within the veil is to be in the most holy place: "The vail shall divide unto you between the holy place and the most holy" (Exodus 26:33); additionally, ED retained copies of line 2 ("Revised to Retrospect –"), the first two lines (beginning "The last of Summer is Result –"), and the complete poem (beginning "The last of Summer is a Time") c. 1875. When first copying the poem onto a sheet, ED wrote the first seven words, then stopped and copied the entire poem on a new sheet.

98. The Heart is: additional copy (variant) retained c. 1875.

99. Not any more: an adz is an axe-like tool with a curved edge, used for shaping wood. On a fragment, ED wrote alternatives for the last line of this poem, c. 1875.

100. After all Birds: additionally, ED retained one copy of the second stanza, a copy of the final three lines (variant), and a copy of three lines from stanza 2 (variant) c. 1877.

101. The Mind lives: additionally, retained two copies (variant) and the final line as a fragment ("So absolute –") c. 1877.

LOOSE POEMS

This section includes the poems ED retained that were not included in fascicles or on unbound sheets (what RWF designated "Sets"). It does not include fragments that ED retained as part of longer, more complete poems. References to such fragments and to additional retained copies of poems appear in the notes. The poems in this section are organized chronologically, by the (usually hypothesized) date of the earliest extant copy.

1. If it had: see Alfred Habegger, *My Wars Are Laid Away in Books: The Life of Emily Dickinson* (New York: Random House, 2001), for the argument that this poem was not sent to SB, as RWF indicates. It was at some point pinned around the stub of a pencil.

2. No Rose, yet: added at the end of a draft letter addressed to "Master" (L233).

3. Again – his voice: in this poem ED seems to indent as a way of marking stanzas, rather than leaving a blank space; she neither indents nor leaves a space before the last four lines.

4. Going – to – Her!: ED wrote this poem with two variations in pronoun address, as "Going to them, happy letter!" to the Ns (c. early 1862) and "Going to Him! Happy letter!" on an additional retained copy (c. late summer 1862).

5. We play at: copy to TWH apparently responds to his "Letter to a Young Contributor," just published in the *Atlantic Monthly* (April 1862).

6. I never saw: the word "checks" was used colloquially to mean railroad tickets; one gave one's checks to the conductor.

7. As Sleigh Bells: Timbuktu, a city in Mali on the southern edge of the Sahara, flourished as a center of civilization between the twelfth and sixteenth centuries owing to trade in salt, gold, ivory, and slaves.

8. These Strangers, in: in Matthew 25:34–40, Jesus says, "Come, ye blessed of my Father, inherit the kingdom prepared for you from the foundation of the world: For I was an hungred, and ye gave me meat: I was thirsty, and ye gave me drink: I was a stranger, and ye took me in.... Inasmuch as ye have done it unto one of the least of these my brethren, ye have done it unto me."

9. Love reckons by: DEA claims this was sent to SD.

10. The Overtakelessness of: source copy for this text is from the letter to SD, since the apparently retained copy was lost (transcribed by SD as variant from the copy definitely sent to her). DEA presents both copies as sent to SD.

11. Further in Summer: in "Daisies" (1861) by Rose Terry Cooke, the speaker remarks to her flowers, "I alone am left to celebrate your mass." Earliest copy (to Gertrude Vanderbilt) concluded with five stanzas not appearing in any other extant manuscript; in the other extant copies, ED substituted some version of the final two stanzas given here.

12. She sped as: retained additional copy (variant) c. 1865, beginning "She sped as Petals from a Rose –."

13. After the Sun: Belize was administered by Great Britain after Central American emancipation from Spain in 1836 and was declared a Crown Colony (British Honduras) in 1862. ED could have read about Belize in her father's copy of *Incidents of Travel in Central America* (1841) by John L. Stephens, which represents it as a model of racial "practical amalgamation." Liverpool was a center of the transatlantic slave trade and remained one of the largest trading centers in Western Europe.

14. I fit for: according to OMC, this was sent to SD.

15. The Frost of: apparently retained copy from c. 1866 (lost) was transcribed by SD; source text here is copy sent to SD, which varies from her transcript of the lost poem.

16. A Diamond on: according to OMC, this was sent to SD.

17. There is a: alludes to the miracle of Jesus and Peter walking on water (Matthew 14:25–32).

18. The Merchant of: there is no evidence of a drafted final line, although there is room for at least one more line on the advertising flyer on which ED wrote the poem; syntax, meter, and rhyme suggest the poem is unfinished.

19. None who saw: the first alternative suggests that "ever" must change to "never": "they who saw it never told it."

20. Soul, take thy: a detailed penciled drawing of a tombstone in tall grass appears on the reverse side of the small rectangle of notepaper on which this poem is written.

21. Too cold is: according to OMC, this was sent to SD; RWF describes this manuscript as given to SD by Lavinia after ED's death.

22. We do not: according to OMC, this was sent to SD.

23. The murmuring of: cancellations and some alternatives were apparently added later.

24. The smouldering embers: the immortal Prometheus gave fire to humans; to punish him, Zeus ordered Prometheus bound to a rock where each day an eagle would come and eat out his liver, which then grew back over night. ED wrote line 3 as "So many nights hast thou survived?" and marked the phrases for transposition (transposed here, including assumed emendation of capital letters).

25. Paradise is that: may allude to Wordsworth's "Ode: Intimations of Immortality" (1807), which presents human beings at birth as "trailing clouds of glory do we come / From God, who is our home." This manuscript may be incomplete or the poem may be unfinished.

26. The Bird did: additional copy retained (variant) c. 1868; this manuscript allows us to see an incomplete draft with multiple cancellations on one side of a leaf and a more resolved version of the complete poem on the other.

27. Tell as a: William Tell was a major figure representing Swiss patriotism and independence in the early to mid-nineteenth century. Albrecht Gessler, a tyrannical representative of the Habsburg dynasty in the early 1300s, hung his hat on a pole and ordered townsfolk to bow before it. According to legend, Tell refused, was arrested, and then was made to shoot an apple off his own son's head. He later assassinated Gessler, thereby sparking a rebellion that led to Swiss independence. This story was the basis for theatrical and musical works by Schiller and Rossini and was popular in the United States; after assassinating Lincoln, John Wilkes Booth claimed that he had done "what made Tell a hero."

28. These are the: June bugs (*Phyllophaga* beetles) are nocturnal; they are attracted to lights and fly erratically, often crashing into ceilings, walls, and objects.

29. I noticed People: ED wrote "or" before the alternatives for lines 5 and 8, then cancelled the second "or" and both alternatives; cancellations and some alternatives added later.

30. Exhiliration is the: according to OMC, this was sent to SD.

31. Best Witchcraft is: OMC regards both copies of this poem as sent to SD. RWF claims the leaf containing this poem and "Exhiliration is the Breeze" came into SD's possession after ED's death.

32. The duties of: the Sea of Azov (also called the Maeotian Sea) dates back to 5600 BCE; connected by a narrow strait to the Black Sea, it has been associated with myths of prehistoric floods.

33. The Day grew: retained copy was lost after being transcribed by MLT; source text here is from the copy to SD.

34. Some Days retired: DEA claims that both extant copies of the poem were sent to SD.

35. Alone and in: poem written on a page with a three-cent stamp attached midpage and two clippings from a May 1870 *Harper's Magazine* sticking out of it like horns, bearing the words "George Sand" and "Mauprat," the title of one of Sand's novels (1837). ED wrote around the attachments.

36. Contained in this: two earlier drafts of this poem (variant) were written on the same leaf as this version.

37. The Riddle that: commercially printed c. 1870 (variant), from a lost manuscript; additional copy retained (variant) c. late 1870, beginning "The Riddle we can guess." This and the next two poems were written in the draft of a letter intended for TWH.

38. Oh Sumptuous moment: placement of alternatives for line 5 is ambiguous; the line might read "since [I abundance see –]," "that [I abundance see –]," or "[Now] that [I abundance see –]."

39. A great Hope: may allude to Longfellow's frequently quoted "The Building of the Ship" (1850), in which the master's ship, "Built for freight," is compared with the "Ship of State! / Sail on, O Union, strong and great!"

40. A not admitting: THJ combined this with "A great Hope fell" as one poem, although the handwriting is distinct and they are on different pages (the insides of envelopes). ED initially wrote "And Troughs there," then cancelled "Troughs" to change the line to "And there were troughs beside –." The alternative "unsuspecting Carpenters" would require other changes to the line were ED to retain her 8686 meter.

41. The Frost was: in John 14:8–9, Philip desires to be shown "the Father" to assuage his doubt.

42. We like March: two additional copies retained (variant) and also a fragment with the final two lines, c. 1878.

43. Whatever it is –: may respond to the death of ED's cousin Eliza Coleman Dudley, 3 June 1871.

44. Fly – fly – but: THJ categorizes these lines as "raw material for a poem" in his appendix "Prose Fragments" (*Poems of Emily Dickinson*, PF75).

45. Like Rain it: the prophet Elijah ascends into heaven when a chariot of fire lifts him off the ground in a whirlwind; this follows his having divided the River Jordan so that he and Elisha could cross on dry land (2 Kings 2:8–11).

46. The Clouds their: the alternative "skipped" may have been inspired by Psalms 114:4, "The mountains skipped like rams."

47. If my Bark: first two lines repeat the final line of "A Poet's Hope" (1843) by William Ellery Channing: "If my bark sinks, 'tis to another sea."

48. Look back on: may allude to the death of Margaret Kelly on 27 July 1872; ED addressed the fragment of envelope on which she wrote the poem to "Little Maggie."

49. The Clover's simple: two additional copies retained, c. 1872: one containing only the final quatrain (variant), and the other containing only the first quatrain (variant), beginning "A Clover's simple Fame."

50. A Sparrow took: the copy to SD contains a completely new second stanza: "Invigorated, waded / In all the deepest Sky / Until his little Figure / Was forfeited away –."

51. As old as: ED, who knew Darwin's theory of evolution, here represents the creation of humanity as in approximately 16,000 BCE; in another poem ("Our little secrets slink away –") she dates the creation of the world as "a Trillion years" ago. In line 5, "or" marks the following words as alternatives; in line 9, the cancelled "not" would presumably have been followed by "either" rather than "neither."

52. The Lilac is: 1 Corinthians 2:9, "Eye hath not seen, nor ear heard... the things which God have prepared for them that love him."

53. A Word dropped: in line 6, ED cancelled "And" in the phrase "And we inhale" and inserted "may," implying an initial capital for "we," as presented here.

54. I thought that: parallax is the apparent change of place in an object caused by its being viewed from different points; in 1838, Friedrich Bessel was the first to measure the distance to a star other than the sun, using the method of parallax—as ED would have known from her studies in astronomy at Mount Holyoke Female Seminary.

55. The Show is: in the 14 September 1864 *Springfield Republican*, "Straws, Jr." (Kate Field) published an account of Newport, Rhode Island, titled "A Human Menagerie"; TWH had moved to Newport in June. Additional copy retained (variant) c. 1872. The fair copy was reportedly sent to MLT, but Todd arrived in Amherst almost a decade after this manuscript was copied and signed.

56. "Was Not" was: Genesis 5:24, "And Enoch walked with God: and he *was* not; for God took him"; additional copy retained (variant) c. 1873.

57. So proud she: two other copies (variant) retained c. 1873, beginning "So pleased she was to die" and "So fain she was to die."

58. The things we: additional copy retained (variant) c. 1873; ED apparently also retained alternatives for lines 11 and 12 (lost, transcribed variant) c. 1873.

59. Who were "the: all alternatives and cancellations added in later revision; text presented as revised, including the marked transposition of "time to be ensue" (reordered as "time ensue to be"). OMC claims manuscript was sent to SD.

60. The most triumphant: ED bracketed the alternatives "so adequate," "scrutable," and "impudent," perhaps to indicate a preference; RWF reads the bracket as underlining. Additional copy (lost, transcribed variant) c. 1873.

61. There is no: fragment retained containing the words "Was never Frigate like" c. 1873; additional copy contained only last four lines (lost, transcribed variant).

62. Elijah's wagon had: Elijah ascended into heaven in a chariot of fire and with horses of fire (2 Kings 2:11); ED does not specify with which version of lines 7 and 8 the alternatives "authorized" and "peculiar" might be used. Additional copy (lost, transcribed variant) c. 1873.

63. I think that: OMC claims manuscript was sent to SD.

64. Not one by: fragment retained containing the words "Not one by Heaven defrauded," c. 1873. OMC claims quatrain was sent to SD.

65. The Butterfly in: earlier copy retained (variant) c. 1873. OMC claims later manuscript was sent to SD.

66. Recollect the Face: one of the malefactors crucified with Jesus said, "Lord, remember me when thou comest into thy kingdom," to which Jesus responded, "Today shalt thou be with me in paradise" (Luke 23:42–43).

67. Art thou the: additional copy retained (variant) c. 1873.

68. Because that you: quotes from or alludes to several biblical passages: Matthew 19:26, "with God all things are possible" (also in Mark); 1 Timothy 4:8, "godliness is profitable unto all things, having promise of the life that now is, and of that which is to come"; 1 John 4:26, "God is love"; and Exodus 20:5, "For I the Lord thy God am a jealous God"—or any of the many passages calling God "jealous." Additional copy retained (lines 1–29, variant) c. January 1874.

69. There's the Battle: the British general John Burgoyne (1722–1792) surrendered at Saratoga in 1777, a defeat regarded as a turning point in the American War of Independence.

70. While we were: additional copy retained (variant) c. 1874.

71. Dear March – Come: the alternative "the instant that" may assume a contraction to complete the line metrically: "the instant that [you've come]" or "the instant that [you come]."

72. Go slow, my: to the Ns, ED wrote, "Infinite March is here, and I 'hered' a blue bird. Of course I am standing on my head!" (L410), followed by the poem. The poem may allude to Judas, who betrayed Jesus with a kiss (Luke 22:47–48).

73. The vastest earthly: alternative to the final line is preceded by "or": "or that owned it all –."

74. How many schemes: ED wrote "~~Some~~ It must be Competitions" between lines 10 and 11, apparently a false start for the last two lines; similarly, "~~That~~" between lines 11 and 12 appears to be a false start.

75. The Butterfly's Assumption: chrysoprase (a variety of chalcedony) is a greenish-gold gemstone, mentioned in Revelation 21:20 as the tenth foundational stone of the wall of Jerusalem. Additional copy retained (lost, transcribed variant) c. 1874.

76. Abraham to kill: God commanded Abraham to kill his son Isaac; when he prepared to do so, God relented (Genesis 22:1–20).

77. Knock with tremor: referring to tribute money, Jesus says, "Render . . . unto Caesar the things which are Caesar's; and unto God the things that are God's" (Matthew 22:21). Written on the back of a leaf containing only the words "Dear Father –" and "Emily," this may have accompanied a note or object; ED's father died 16 June 1874. Cancellations and most revisions were added later.

78. Elisabeth told Essex: Queen Elizabeth failed to grant her desired pardon for the Earl of Essex's death sentence because of the Countess of Nottingham's negligence; when learning of the countess's neglect she allegedly exclaimed, "God may forgive you, but I never can." Here Elizabeth apparently addresses Essex.

79. The Pile of: ED underscored "standing," her first choice in line 5, to mark her preference of this word over "stepping," written immediately underneath it.

80. Without a smile –: the alternatives "Do" and "our –" might be read as preceding either "Summer's" or "Nature's" in line 3; another possibility is that the line read "A Nature's soft assemblies go."

81. As Summer into: ED wrote some version of "shaft" on the page four times, twice underlining the word three times.

82. The most pathetic: "Goliah" may have been a common form of allusion to Goliath, in the biblical story of the battle of David and Goliath (1 Samuel 17). In a famous American hoax orchestrated by George Hull, in October 1869 a ten-and-a-half-foot petrified man (called "Goliah") was discovered in Onondaga County, New York. The "Cardiff Giant" was created in response to Genesis 6:4, which states that giants once walked the earth. P. T. Barnum's exhibit of a replica of the giant was extremely popular, giving rise to the remark, "There's a sucker born every minute." ED wrote the poem on a signed flyleaf from her father's 1824 edition of Washington Irving's *Sketch Book of Geoffrey Crayon, Gent.* (1819).

83. I send you: written on a signed flyleaf from her father's copy of Washington Irving's *Sketch Book of Geoffrey Crayon*; the 1824 edition was in two volumes and hence had two flyleaves; Edward Dickinson signed both of them.

84. How soft this: copy to EH follows mention of the death of ED's father. The complete copy of this poem was lost after being transcribed by SD.

85. His Mansion in: Demosthenes (384–322 BCE) was a Greek orator and statesman of great rhetorical ability, who made his living as a professional speechwriter.

86. A little madness: may allude to spring frolics such as April Fool's Day; the copies to EH and SD are identical and give "This whole Experiment of Green –" for line 5.

87. Pink – small – and: additional copy (variant) retained c. 1875, signed "Arbutus." In 1890, this poem was titled "May-Flower," a plant more often known as trailing arbutus. Emily Fowler Ford writes in a memoir that "for years it was [ED's] habit to send me the first buds of the arbutus which we had often hung over together in the woods, joying in its fresh fragrance as the very breath of coming spring" (DIHOT).

88. Escape is such: on the reverse side of this page ED wrote and then cancelled the first two lines of this poem, (variant) c. 1875.

89. Crisis is sweet: some alternatives and the underlining and cancellation were added later; OMC includes this manuscript as sent to SD.

90. An antiquated Grace: the alternative "it's" in line 1 might be meant as the possessive pronoun "its" ("its antiquated Grace"); ED typically used an apostrophe for both "it's" and "its," as did others in the early and mid-nineteenth century.

91. The Rat is: the apparently retained manuscript (lost) was transcribed by SD; source text here is the copy sent to SD.

92. "Faithful to the: quotes from Revelation 2:10, "Be thou faithful unto death, and I will give thee a crown of life." ED retained two earlier copies (variant) c. early 1876; only lines 1 and 2 from these copies recur in her later three texts.

93. I suppose the: written on the back of an 1850 invitation to a "Candy Pulling!!" sent by George Gould when he and Austin were seniors at Amherst College.

94. The Butterfly's Numidian: additional copy retained (variant) c. 1876.

95. Of his peculiar: on an unsent and cancelled two-page note containing thanks for a book; ED used the verso of both pages to write other poems.

96. The worthlessness of: "synod" typically refers to the governing body of a particular church, although it may refer to any meeting or council; additional copy retained (variant) c. 1876.

97. His Heart was: it is unclear whether ED intended the repetition of the final line to serve as an alternative (RWF's interpretation).

98. In many and: ED concludes this poem by writing vertically in the margin, without marking a new line at "thereafter," where a new metrical line might be expected to begin.

99. Long Years apart –: someone has drawn an almost circular curved leafing branch, vaguely in the shape of a heart, on the back of this envelope, where the poem concludes. It is possible that no line break was intended after "no," so the poem would begin with a fourteen-syllable first line: "Long Years apart – can make no Breach a second cannot fill –."

100. A Saucer holds: since 1824, the Birmingham Assay Office in England held a regional monopoly on hallmarking silver and gold; the gold and silver electroplating industry was also founded there, in the 1840s. Manchester first achieved city status in 1853, thanks to an industrial boom.

101. Summer laid her: the 1844 Webster's gives "rib'in" as "a narrow web of silk used for an ornament . . . or for fastening some part of female dress" with no listing for "ribbon," a spelling ED used in one copy of this poem. Additional two copies (variant) retained of first stanza c. October 1876.

102. March is the: a curved drawn line may signify that some words are alternatives

rather than serving to underscore them; "Persons," however, is clearly underlined. Additional copy retained (variant) c. 1877.

103. The inundation of: ED wrote "or" before "s" ("or [tenement]s"), then cancelled both; she also retained part of the final two lines (variant) c. 1877. According to OMC, the longer copy was sent to SD.

104. Bees are Black,: a surcingle is either "a belt, band, or girth which passes over a saddle" or "the girdle of a cassock," according to Webster's. ED refers, in this poem, to a centuries-old theological debate as to whether the death of Jesus was divinely "ordained" or historically "contingent."

105. Lay this Laurel: in her letter to TWH, ED mentioned rereading his poem "Decoration" (1874), in which the speaker lays flowers on a woman's grave, calling her (not soldiers) the "bravest of the brave." TWH wrote MLT that ED composed this poem "after re-reading my 'Decoration.' It is the condensed essence of that and so far finer." Decoration Day was first celebrated in 1866; it was made a national holiday, called Memorial Day, by Congress in 1971. Additional copy retained (variant) c. 1877.

106. I shall not: "Katie" is Catherine Scott Anthon, who visited Amherst in 1877; the next poem, written on the same sheet of paper, may also refer, or be addressed, to Anthon. Anthon does not report having received either poem.

107. Such are the: poem is preceded by the sentence "I feel Barefoot all over as the Boys say –."

108. I have no: to SB, ED wrote: "I went to the Room as soon as you left, to confirm your presence – recalling the Psalmist's sonnet to God, beginning" (L515)—followed by the poem.

109. What mystery pervades: additional copy retained (variant) c. 1877, consisting of the last stanza and an additional four new lines. The only complete copy of this poem is in MLT's transcript.

110. To the stanch: retained manuscript (lost) was transcribed by MLT in two versions (variant), one beginning "To the unwilling dust." Source text is the extant manuscript sent to SD.

111. How lonesome the: additional manuscript (lost, transcribed variant), beginning "How spacious the wind must feel morns," has a different stanza order, progressing from morning to night.

112. One Joy of: RWF reads the alternative for line 11 as "like Flesh"; ED does not cross the *t* in "till."

113. No Passenger was: additional copy retained (variant) c. 1877.

114. She laid her: one of the clippings pasted on the copy to EH was from a 12 December 1856 copy of the *Hampshire and Franklin Express*, suggesting that ED had a collection of clippings and other items that interested her, keeping some for several years. Additional copy retained (variant) c. 1877, begins "He laid his docile Crescent down."

115. It sounded as: additional two copies retained (variant) c. 1877, one beginning "It sounded as if the Air were running."

116. Perhaps they do: according to their nephew, ED's distant cousins Harriet and Mary Dickinson surprised her in her garden in the summer of 1876; she fled but then sent them this poem shortly thereafter, with flowers; RWF dates the poem in 1877. Most cancellations and all revisions are later and were written so that it is unclear what verbs belong to line 7 or line 8; ED wrote out the final two lines (as represented here), in whole or part, three times.

117. Could mortal Lip: EDC regards this manuscript as sent to SD.

118. Two Butterflies went: additional copy retained in F25 Sh2, c. 1863; only the first two lines remain the same in this later revision.

119. My Maker – let: additional copy retained (variant) c. 1878.

120. How ruthless are: Jesus is described as "the Lamb of God, which taketh away the sin of the world" (John 1:29). Christians understand God to have made a "new covenant" through Jesus, as, for example, in Ephesians 2:12–13: "at that time ye were without Christ . . . and strangers from the covenants of promise, having no hope, and without God in the world: But now in Christ Jesus ye who sometimes were far off are made nigh by the blood of Christ."

121. Death is the: Edward Young's *Night Thoughts* (1742–1745) claims that Death can "Lay by his horrors, and put on smiles," become a "well-fashion'd figure" and "dreadful masquerader." Young's blank-verse poem was a textbook at Amherst Academy.

122. Your thoughts don't: one alternative is not easily decipherable; like RWF and THJ, I have represented it as "So fully" (line 6). This rough copy also leaves ambiguous whether some alternatives potentially replace words or phrases in line 5 or line 6.

123. Before you thought: ED wrote "Blue Bird –" on the recto of this copy; the Ns transcript begins "The Blue bird," and HHJ wrote, "I know your 'Blue bird' by heart." The repetition suggests that this designation functioned as a title. This may be the poem ED sent to Thomas Niles in 1883: she responded in April to a letter (lost), "I am glad if the Bird seemed true" (L814).

124. Belshazzar had a: "Mene, Mene, Tekel, Upharsin" appeared in handwriting on the wall of King Belshazzar; no one could interpret it but Daniel, who read it to mean that the king had displeased God and his rule was ended: "Thou art weighed in the balances, and art found wanting" (Daniel 5:27). ED's note in the copy sent to Ned ("Suggested by our Neighbor –", L1459) points to an Amherst legal case: in 1876 Mary Lothrop, the daughter of Reverend Charles D. Lothrop, accused her father of mistreating her mother and herself. Lothrop sued the *Springfield Republican* for libel but the court decided against him (April 1879). "A Counterfeit – a Plated Person –" also alludes to this case. Additional copy retained (variant) c. 1879.

125. One of the: may have been written in response to HHJ's request, "What should

you think of trying your hand on the oriole?" after she praised ED's "Blue bird." ED refers to the legend of King Midas, who turned everything he touched into gold, and the Greek mythological hero Jason's quest for the Golden Fleece, which would authorize his kingship. Conspiracy theories against the Jesuits representing them as treacherous were popular in the early nineteenth century. Additional copy retained (variant) of last ten lines of the poem c. 1879.

126. A Route of: ED wrote "Humming Bird" below this poem, as a signature or a title. All circulated copies use "revolving" in line 2 rather than any of the alternatives ED gives here and are identical to each other in wording. ED promised this and three other poems to the Mission Circle's sale for the benefit of children in foreign lands; her letter to TWH asks for his approval and review of the poems; the other poems were apparently written closer to the date of the Mission Circle's sale, 30 November 1880.

127. "Secrets" is a: ED wrote "Goes nor comes away" and marked it for transposition, repeating "Comes nor goes away" in the margin to confirm this choice; presented as transposed here.

128. A winged spark: THJ reads the alternative words as an additional line to the poem: "Rekindled by some action quaint"; ED did not mark the presence of an alternative, but in late poems she often included alternatives for a word or line without marking them as alternatives.

129. If wrecked upon: additional copy retained (variant) c. 1879, beginning "If wrecked upon the Wharf of Thought."

130. The Sweets of: manuscript torn so that only three lines remain; line 1 here is taken from copy to SD.

131. Their Barricade against: two wars were fought between the United States and Mexico when ED was between four and eighteen years old: the Texas Revolution (1835–1836) and the Mexican-American War (1846–1848). Two widely reported massacres during the former (at the Alamo and Goliad, both in 1836) gave Mexicans a reputation for brutality in the popular American imagination. ED may also refer to the brilliant colors of Mexico's tropical vegetation.

132. We talked with: Mount Ararat, the highest peak in Turkey, is where Noah's ark allegedly came to rest after the Flood (Genesis 8:4). Additional copy and fragment with two lines retained (variant) c. 1879. Because ED wrote "Second's Races" on her earlier copy, I add the apostrophe here.

133. How destitute is: additional copy (lost, transcribed variant) c. 1879.

134. The Devil – had: OMC claims manuscript was sent to SD.

135. The fascinating chill: the alternative "of music" assumes the omission of "leaves," changing the first line from ten to nine syllables.

136. 'Tis whiter than: ED wrote MLT that the Indian pipe is "the preferred flower of life" (L769).

137. One thing of: in the copy to TWH, ED's "it" refers to his recently published *Short Studies of American Authors*; she writes immediately preceding the poem: "Remorse for the brevity of a Book is a rare emotion, though fair as Lowell's 'Sweet Despair' in the Slipper Hymn –" (that is, James Russell Lowell's "After the Burial," *Atlantic Monthly*, May 1868; L622).

138. It came his: ED wrote out line 6 twice, turning the envelope upside down and beginning again after cancelling her first attempt toward lines 7 and 8: "~~Curtail so mean a luxury I could not~~."

139. The Face in: sent to TWH, apparently after ED saw the announcement of his infant daughter's death in the *Springfield Republican*, 21 March 1880.

140. How soft a: alternative cancelled for lines 4–6 is unfinished—that is, it is unclear how line 6 ("its traverse") might end. At this point (c. 1880), ED starts regularly writing "upon," not "opon" (see introduction).

141. The Thrill came: THJ reads the alternative "news" as "Morns" (line 6).

142. I saw the: ED repeats several words and the entire line 13, not transcribed here; "~~How~~" follows "~~Precisely is it known~~" but does not fit the direction of further composition. THJ reads line 15 as "'Tis still is an assistance," reading only "it" rather than "it is" as the alternative. The lines are so roughly written that certain reconstruction is impossible.

143. I do not: RWF regards the final line as probably prose and does not include it, although it provides an end rhyme ("perdition" / "constitution").

144. You cannot make: because this poem is written cleanly and fills a page, it may have been completed on a different leaf, now lost.

145. "And with what: Perez Dickinson Cowan notes that ED sent him the poem "after receiving [a] copy of 'The Lamb Folded,'" a brochure in memory of his daughter; ED quotes from 1 Corinthians 15:35. Retained copy (lost, transcribed variant) c. 1880; source text here is the copy to Cowan.

146. The Savior must: ED promised this and three other poems to the Mission Circle's sale for the benefit of children in foreign lands; her letter to TWH asks for his approval and review of the poems. The other three poems are "Mine Enemy is growing old –," "My country need not change her gown," and "A Route of Evanescence" (c. 1879).

147. Mine Enemy is: also considered for donation to the Mission Circle's sale for the benefit of children in foreign lands; additional copy retained (variant) c. late 1880.

148. A Pang is: in Matthew 28:2, an angel rolls away the stone before Jesus's tomb. For lines 3 and 4, ED wrote "Effulgen-cies" on two rows of print, with "cies" following the words "And Winds –," as though she first wrote "but Minds / And Winds" and interlineated "Minute Effulgencies." THJ represents line 4 as "Minute Effulgencies and Winds –." Additional copy of the last quatrain was retained (variant) c. 1881, following

five lines that perhaps relate to the poem: "As if a Drum went on and on / To captivate the slain – // I dare not write until I hear – / Intro without my Trans – // When what they sung for is undone."

149. His little Hearse: ED concluded her note to her nephew Gilbert with: "'All Liars shall have their part' – Jonathan Edwards – 'And let him that is athirst come' – Jesus –." The attribution to Edwards is in part facetious; "all liars, shall have their part in the lake which burneth with fire and brimstone" comes originally from Revelation 21:8; it is also used as the text for *L* in the *New-England Primer* alphabet. The phrase attributed to Jesus is from Revelation 22:17.

150. A faded Boy –: may elegize a statesman (such as Daniel Webster or Abraham Lincoln) who grew up on a farm; Lincoln made much of his farming boyhood during his 1860 presidential campaign.

151. On that specific: the penultimate line with alternative might read either "The effort of comprising" or "The effort of comprising it"; the former fits the poem's established meter.

152. How fleet – how: in the draft of a letter apparently to Otis Lord, the first line is written as a fourteener and begins in the middle of a row of script in prose.

153. His oriental heresies: additional copy (lost, transcribed variant) was composed of four stanzas rather than two.

154. He lived the: additional copy retained last four lines (variant) c. 1882.

155. The Bible is: according to Greek legend, Orpheus was so gifted a poet and singer that he could charm wild beasts and stones with his music. The copy to Ned begins "'Sanctuary Privileges' for Ned, as he is unable to attend –"—presumably because he was too ill to attend church (L753). Additional copy apparently retained (lost, transcribed variant).

156. Meeting by Accident,: in Greek mythology, the greedy King Midas wished for a golden touch; obtaining his wish, he turned everything he touched to gold, including his food and his daughter.

157. Those – dying then,: in a letter in 1877, ED wrote TWH that she heard a minister ask, "Is the Arm of the Lord shortened that it cannot save?" alluding to Isaiah 50:2; the "doubt of Immortality . . . besets me still," she continued (L503). In Christian idiom, "God's right hand" signifies heaven, or a privileged place in heaven. An "ignis fatuus" is a phosphorescent light that can appear over marshy ground at night and is associated with spirits or false hope.

158. Within thy Grave!: 1 Corinthians 15:54–55 says that, after Jesus's resurrection, "then shall be brought to pass the saying that is written, Death is swallowed up in victory. O death, where is thy sting? O grave, where is thy victory?"

159. Bliss is the: additional copy (lost, transcribed variant), beginning "Bliss is the sceptre of the child."

160. "Go tell it" –: refers to the Battle of Thermopylae, in which vastly outnumbered Spartans held off the Persian army for seven days before being annihilated. According to Dickinson's Mount Holyoke textbook, Worcester's *Elements of History, Ancient and Modern* (1827), an inscribed monument for the Greeks read: "O stranger! tell it at Lacedaemon that we died here in obedience to her laws." In a letter, ED wrote, "We die, said the Deathless of Thermopylae, in obedience to Law" (L906), followed by the poem "Not Sickness stains the Brave."

161. Of Death I: in Greek mythology, the Hesperides are nymphs, the daughters of the Evening Star (Hesperus), who tend a beautiful, heavenlike garden far in the West; in another myth, this is Hera's garden, from which Hercules steals golden apples that give the eater immortality.

162. Cosmopolites without a: Matthew 7:7, "Ask, and it shall be given you; seek, and ye shall find; knock, and it shall be opened unto you." ED wrote and cancelled "And of whoever ask their way –" between lines 2 and 3.

163. Pompless no Life: ED wrote "No Life can Pompless" and marked the words for transposition; additional copy retained (variant) begins with these words in transposed order (as they are here); she also retained a fragment with drafts toward two lines of the poem; both are c. late 1882.

164. No Brigadier throughout: ED cancelled but also triple underlined the word "censure" in line 5; the underlining may mean she still considered the word viable. THJ and RWF speculate that ED sent this poem to Thomas Niles in April 1883, but it is more likely she sent a more seasonal poem about a blue bird ("Before you thought of Spring").

165. To see her: additional copy (variant) retained c. early 1883; additional copy was lost (transcribed variant).

166. The Clock strikes: exiles in the book of Genesis who could be imagined as "A Vagabond" include Adam, Cain, and Abraham. The image of "Two" turning (back) to "One" may allude to Jesus's reference to God's creation of "male and female.... For this cause shall a man leave his father and mother, and cleave to his wife; and they twain shall be one flesh" (Mark 10:6–9). ED's note to EH commented on a picture of her daughters, one of whom was recently married, and she probably wrote to the younger Samuel Bowles in response to his marriage.

167. A Sloop of: additional copy retained (variant) c. 1883, following the request "Please accept a Sunset –"; fragment also retained with a version of the last line: "A Woe of Ecstasy."

168. Forever honored be: ED frequently wrote of angels as emissaries in the form of birds; Gabriel, in particular, was associated with praise. Additional copy (lost, transcribed variant) begins "Forever cherished be the tree."

169. Lad of Athens: echoes Polonius's advice to Laertes in *Hamlet*: "to thine own self be true, / And it must follow, as the night the day, / Thou canst not then be false to any

man." Additional copy retained (variant) in a drafted letter, c. 1883, follows the remark "That you have answered this Prince Question to your own delight, is joy to us all –."

170. Who has not: ED's retained copy was lost after having been transcribed (variant), ending "God's residence is next to mine, / His furniture is love"; source text here is the copy sent to the teenage girls Martha Dickinson and Sally Jenkins.

171. The Lassitudes of: written on a narrow strip of paper twenty-one inches long, with vertical lines apparently indicating line divisions, as represented here.

172. This Me – that: additional two copies (variant, incomplete) retained c. 1883; lines from this poem also appear in "Expanse cannot be lost –" and "The Spirit lasts – but in what mode –," c. October 1883.

173. To her derided: additional copy retained, c. summer 1883, in which ED substituted lines from "No ladder needs the bird but skies" for last four lines.

174. The Summer that: ED wrote "with what a fatal promptness," followed by the alternative "and scans with fatal promptness"; her concluding lines follow the sense of the latter. For this reason, it appears here as the primary line.

175. A Drunkard cannot: additional copy (variant) retained, first six lines.

176. 'Tis not the: perhaps written in reference to the death of Otis Lord, 13 March 1884; OMC claims manuscript was sent to SD.

177. Arrows enamored of: written on a fragment of a letter apparently intended for Otis Lord.

178. Few, yet enough,: ED's copy was lost (transcribed variant); source text here is the manuscript sent to SD.

179. Though the great: additional two copies (variant) retained c. 1884; one contains only the first three lines.

180. A World made: additional copy (variant) retained c. 1884, beginning "A World made penniless by his departure."

181. Sunset that screens,: an unusually long dash precedes "mystery," evidently indicating a blank space to be filled; ED wrote "amber," "opal," and "purple" below this line.

182. Not knowing when: additional copy (variant) retained c. 1884; copy to TWH refers to HHJ, who died the preceding August.

183. The pedigree of: additional copy retained (variant) of lines 1–4, c. 1884, identical to the copy sent to MLT but for one comma; in these copies, ED wrote lines 3 and 4 as "A Clover, any time, to him, / Is Aristocracy –," omitting the comma after "him" in the copy to MLT.

184. Talk not to: the rejected trial "~~Whose Homes~~" (beginning of line 6) does not fit the revised line.

185. Upon his Saddle: in her note to HHJ, ED refers to her as a bird: "From [your Crutch to Cane] to your Wings is but a stride –" (L937); HHJ was recovering from a fractured leg.

186. The farthest Thunder: additional copy retained (variant) c. 1884.

187. Apparently with no: Job 14:1–2, "Man . . . cometh forth like a flower, and is cut down."

188. The Jay his: ED made a mark after line 3, drew a line across the page, wrote "Teneriffe's Adventure," and then on the next row of script made another mark preceding "is impudent to nature," apparently indicating that the words should follow the mark preceding her drawn line; this suggests that "Teneriffe's Adventure" is an alternative. The sense and syntax of the rest of the poem and additional alternatives follow "is impudent to nature." THJ regards the phrase "Teneriffe's Adventure" as written between two stanzas, interpreting ED's line as a stanza break.

189. Take all away: source text is from a drafted letter to HHJ; three additional copies (variant) retained c. early 1885, one beginning "Take all I have away" and two in additional drafts to HHJ (variant).

190. Of God we: additional copy (variant) retained c. March 1885, first two lines; both copies are in drafts of a letter to HHJ.

191. Some one prepared: in the alternative for line 3, the blank space between "The" and "– of" is ED's.

192. "Red Sea," indeed!: Exodus 14 tells the story of God leading the Jews out of slavery in Egypt: Moses parts the Red Sea so his people may cross on dry land and then releases the waters, destroying the pharaoh's army.

193. Extol thee – could: ED wrote the false start "~~anti~~" before "fair" in line 3.

194. The Immortality she: copy to TWH acknowledged the publication of his sonnet on Helen Hunt Jackson; the retained copy is in a draft to TWH.

POEMS TRANSCRIBED BY OTHERS

This section includes poems for which there are no extant complete manuscripts in ED's hand but which ED apparently retained until her death. Poems extant only as transcribed by another's hand that we know ED bound into a fascicle or retained on an unbound sheet or circulated without retaining appear in the sections containing fascicles, unbound sheets, or poems not retained. The poems included here were apparently transcribed after ED's death and then given away or otherwise lost. Except in the few cases in which a circulated (lost) copy was dated or MLT dated a poem on the transcript, these poems cannot be dated; RWF believes that they are relatively late. SD apparently did not record ED's alternative words; MLT did. Dashes in these poems are represented consistently with others in this edition, not as transcribed (or, in a few cases, published).

1. No man saw: God appears to Moses in a burning bush "and, behold . . . the bush was not consumed" (Exodus 3:2); later in Exodus, "the Lord spake unto Moses face to face, as a man speaketh unto his friend" (Exodus 33:11). ED retained a fragment with

trial or alternative lines for 4 and 5: "Has Human Nature gone – / Unknowing of his dread abode –" (c. 1874).

2. My country need: the first battle of the American Revolutionary War began in Lexington, Massachusetts; the stars in the U.S. flag stand for its individual states, a design adopted in 1777, during the war. ED sent this poem to TWH asking for his approval to send it to a charity. MLT had a copy of this poem in 1891 and transcribed it, but both manuscript and transcript are now lost; source text here is *Poems* (1891).

3. Drowning is not: ED retained a fragment of line 8 (variant): "Grasped by God –" (c. 1880?).

4. Volcanoes be in: Vesuvius erupted several times during ED's lifetime: in 1834, 1839, 1850, 1855, 1861, 1868, and 1872; Sicily's Mount Etna, the tallest active volcano in Europe, was especially active from 1878 to 1886. ED's geography textbooks at Amherst Academy indicated that there were local volcanoes, in the Mount Holyoke range.

5. Speech is one: the Apostle Paul never saw Jesus in the flesh; in 1 Corinthians 15:51 he describes resurrection in part by saying "Behold, I shew you a mystery." The Apostle Peter commended members of the early church for their faith in Jesus, "Whom having not seen, ye love" (1 Peter 1:8).

6. There is a: in *The Single Hound* (1914), Bianchi concludes the poem with a line she apparently supplied as editor: "Finite Infinity."

7. Fame is a: in this poem, ED twice may have written a single poetic line that SD represents as two: "Whose table once a / Guest but not:" and "Flap past it to the / Farmer's corn"; in both cases, the hypothesized lineation would give a 6686, or short meter, stanza and be consistent with ED's pattern of not ending a poetic line with "a" or "the." SD first wrote "Flap past it to the farmers," then began a new line with "Farmers." SD's "Farmers" is emended to "Farmer's."

8. The wind drew: Austria and Italy were sometimes associated with treachery by predominantly Protestant countries, because of their Catholicism. ED may also associate Austria with the tyrannical Albrecht Gessler, who, according to legend, forced William Tell to shoot an apple off his own son's head; see "Tell as a Marksman – were forgotten."

9. I did not: RWF emends SD's transcription to read "waters murmur" in line 30; because it is unclear whether "water murmur" is SD's typographical error or ED's intention, I do not emend.

10. A word made: "In the beginning was the Word . . . and the Word was God"; Jesus was the Word: "and the Word was made flesh, and dwelt among us" (John 1:1 and 1:14). On SD's transcript, the poem is preceded by five lines of prose, or perhaps free verse, separated from the poem by a drawn line: "The import of that Paragraph / "The word made Flesh" / Had he the faintest intimation / Who broached it yesterday! // "Made Flesh and dwelt among us."

11. The right to: SD first wrote "upon the opposite" as the end of a run-on line, then changed "upon" to "Upon" to designate a new metrical line—as it is represented here. RWF emends SD's "tho't" to "thought."

12. Of Yellow was: SD wrote "shewn" (perhaps to rhyme with "hewn"), here emended to "shown"; ED does not use "shewn" in any extant poem.

13. A lane of: in line 6, SD wrote "shew," here emended to "show"; ED does not use "shew" in any extant poem.

14. On my volcano: SD began another transcript (unfinished) with different capitalization: "On my Volcano grows the grass."

15. God is indeed: references to God as "jealous" occur frequently in the Bible, e.g. in Exodus 34:14.

16. Had I known: Matthew 19:30, "many that are first shall be last; and the last shall be first."

17. Her face was: when burned, sperm whale oil gave off a particularly pure light.

18. If all the: MLT indented all even-numbered lines in this poem, a common practice in nineteenth-century poetry; here and in other transcripts where she indented lines, I assume the practice was MLT's and omit it.

19. One crown that: refers to the crown of thorns Jesus was forced to wear during the events leading up to his crucifixion, to mock his authority as "King of the Jews." Pontius Pilate, a Roman prefect, authorized the crucifixion.

20. Proud of my: Jesus was from Nazareth; before his crucifixion, he prayed to God to "let this cup pass from me" (Matthew 26:39), understood in Christian iconology as a cup of suffering; his prayer concludes, "Nevertheless, not as I will, but as Thou wilt." I maintain the archaic "can'st" here, following MLT's transcription.

21. There comes an: the Ten Commandments God gave to Moses repeat the phrase "Thou shalt not" (Exodus 20); "Disciple, call again" is dialogue, not a citation.

22. My life closed: the spelling "befel" may be MLT's mistake (it was emended by RWF), but it may also be ED's anachronistic spelling; it is used by Shakespeare and by Isaac Watts, albeit rarely.

23. Were nature mortal: as published in *Youth's Companion*, 20 January 1898; Lavinia may have supplied the lost manuscript or transcript, through William James Rolfe, a family friend.

24. Fame is a: as published in the *Independent* (New York), 3 February 1898; Lavinia may have supplied the lost manuscript or transcript, through William James Rolfe.

25. The saddest noise,: as published in the *Independent* (New York), 2 June 1898; Lavinia may have supplied the lost manuscript or transcript, through William James Rolfe.

POEMS NOT RETAINED

This section includes poems ED circulated (or probably or apparently circulated), for which, to our knowledge, she did not retain a copy or retained only part of what she circulated as a longer poem. We know that her manuscripts eventually passed into others' hands, but we cannot know whether some of those transfers occurred before or after her death.

1. Awake ye muses: The "*six* true, and comely maidens" of lines 31 and 32 were probably Sarah Tracy, Eliza Coleman, Emeline Kellogg, Harriet Merrill, Susan Gilbert, and ED ("she with *curling hair*"). "Then bear her to the greenwood" may allude to the place of peace and beauty for lovers described in Shakespeare's song "Under the Greenwood Tree" (*As You Like It*).

2. Sic transit gloria: Eudocia Converse copied this poem into her 1848–1853 commonplace book (lost; source text is transcript by Leyda); the error in the Latin in line 3 may be hers, ED's, or Leyda's. This poem alludes to or quotes several stock phrases and works or monuments of popular culture. These references include: a children's poem by Isaac Watts, "How Doth the Little Busy Bee" (1715); Julius Caesar's "*Veni, vidi, vici*" ("I came, I saw, I conquered," as quoted by Plutarch; ED studied Latin); "Peter Parley," the pseudonym under which Samuel G. Goodrich (1793–1860) wrote moral instructional tales for children; "view the Landscape o'er," from Watts's hymn "There Is a Land of Pure Delight" (1707); "The Hill of Science" (1826), a widely reprinted allegorical essay by Anna Laetitia Barbauld; Bunker Hill, the site of a battle against the British in the American Revolutionary War; "Bonnie Doon," from Robert Burns's popular ballad "Ye Banks and Braes of Bonnie Doon" (1791), which ED owned as sheet music; and the Tuscarora, an Iroquois-language people who allied themselves with Americans during the Revolutionary War and in the War of 1812. ED might also have known Fitz-Greene Halleck's popular poem "Red Jacket" (1828), about the "Chief" of the Tuscaroras. William Howland's copy provided the text for the *Springfield Daily Republican* printing, 20 February 1852, as "*St Valentine—'52.*"

3. I have a: this poem concludes the oft-quoted letter beginning "Sue – you can go or stay" (L173). MLT transcribed as prose the stanza sent to the Hollands.

4. Whose cheek is: robins are traditionally said to cover the faces of the unburied dead with leaves.

5. "Mama" never forgets: Jesus claims that God notices even a sparrow's fall, concluding, "Fear ye not therefore, ye are of more value than many sparrows" (Matthew 10:29–31). The phrase "either of her 'sparrows'" alludes to Louisa and her sister, Frances.

6. Is it true,: Toby is a cat. The bottom of the manuscript, containing the last line of the poem and signature, is now missing and has been filled in from the facsimile copy published in *Letters* (1894), edited by MLT.

7. Title divine – is: in the copy to SD, ED added "Tri Victory –" between lines 11 and 12, so the poem reads: "Born – Bridalled – Shrouded – / In a Day – / Tri Victory – / 'My Husband'. . ."

8. Teach Him – when: Mark 10:14, "Suffer the little children to come unto me, and forbid them not: for of such is the kingdom of God."

9. Would you like: what other editors print as the first two lines of this poem are written as prose and represented here as one line; the poem follows a sentence that moves in and out of meter: "We offer you our cups – stintless – as to the Bee – the Lily, her new liquors –" (L229). Sent only to SB, this poem may echo health remedy advertising in his paper, the *Springfield Republican*.

10. Let others – show: Henry Howard, Earl of Surrey (1517–1547), early writer of blank verse, was accused of high treason, convicted in trial, and beheaded.

11. Count not that: DEA presents the lost manuscript as sent to SD.

12. A Mine there: in December 1868, ED's father wrote a letter to SB saying he would rather have been in jail with SB (who had been arrested for libel and jailed for one night) "than to have owned the mines of Potosi." Potosí, Bolivia, was the major supplier of silver to Spain during Spanish colonial rule in South America.

13. He is alive,: apparently given to Samuel and Mary Bowles when they stayed in Amherst, in June 1870. Although the poem appears to have remained in Dickinson family hands, there is no evidence that Emily retained it.

14. The Life we: these lines follow three unrhymed, metered lines that do not seem to belong to the poem: "How fine it is to talk. / What miracles the news is! / Not Bismark but ourselves" (L354), referring to Otto von Bismarck (1815–1898), a Prussian statesman who dominated European affairs from the 1860s until 1890.

15. God made no: Frances Norcross transcribed these lines as prose but her capitalization suggests a couplet in fourteeners, as presented here. RWF capitalized "nor" and "our" to regularize the quatrain in his reading edition.

16. White as an: ED called the Indian pipe "the preferred flower of life," in thanking MLT for a painting of the flowers (L769). An earlier poem begins similarly, "'Tis whiter than an Indian Pipe –."

17. This is the: either ED did not always use line-initial capitals in poems she sent to the Ns in the 1870s and 1880s, or Frances Norcross transcribed them in relatively short lines even where capitalization might have suggested otherwise. I follow her transcription here.

18. Silence is all: last two lines also retained (variant) c. 1873.

19. I saw that: cancelled fragment retained that breaks off in the middle of line 3.

20. When Continents expire: the letter reads, "I am picking you a flower for remembering Sumner – He was his Country's – She [the flower] – is Time's –" (L411). Charles Sumner (1811–1874) led antislavery forces in Congress before the Civil War and Republican policies of Reconstruction after the war.

21. Of Life to: these lines are preceded by two passages of loosely metered prose, in ballad-style mixed iambs and anapests: "Is it Intellect that the Patriot means when he speaks of his 'Native Land'" and "You have experienced sanctity. It is to me untried" (L413).

22. To pile like: may allude to either or both Exodus 33:20, "Thou canst not see my face: for there shall no man see me, and live," and the story of Semele (mother of Dionysus), who asked Zeus to reveal himself to prove that he was her lover; although he revealed himself through the smallest of his lightning bolts and thunderclouds, she was consumed in flame and died.

23. Two Lengths has: retained second stanza (variant); OMC claims that this manuscript was also sent to SD.

24. The Treason of: in copy sent to SD, only the first line remains substantively the same: "The Treason of an Accent / Might vilify the Joy – / To breathe – corrode the rapture / Of Sanctity to be –."

25. I sued the: text of poem follows ED's mention of TWH's *Outdoor Papers* (1863): "It is still as distinct as Paradise – the opening your first Book – It was Mansions – Nations – Kinsmen – too – to me –." The phrase "house not made with hands" is from 2 Corinthians 5:1.

26. The Flake the: ED comments in the letter, "I would love to know your 'Ferns and Grasses'... but it is of Realms unratified that Magic is made. I bring you a Fern from my own Forest, where I pray every Day" (L472). Mary Higginson was suffering a prolonged illness.

27. How know it: in early nineteenth-century New England, a fan for winnowing grain was called a "van"; "van" also designates the front line of an army or fleet of ships or "a wing with which the air is beaten" (Webster's); RWF inaccurately describes the poem as sent with a rosebud.

28. These held their: the copy to Holland follows: "But I intrude on Sunset, and Father and Mr. Bowles" (L544). ED retained the last stanza (variant) c. 1878.

29. "Tomorrow" – whose location: ED anticipated that "Austin will come tomorrow," but apparently he did not (L490).

30. They might not: perhaps one copy retained; the poem was published (variant) in *Youth's Companion*, November 1897, from an unknown source—most likely stemming from ED's sister, Lavinia, through William James Rolfe, a family friend.

31. Whose Pink career: follows "I remember her [TWH's wife] with my Blossoms and wish they were hers" (L503); TWH's wife was ill.

32. Not that he: MLT transcribed these lines as prose but later published them as a four-line stanza of verse; the lack of initial capitals on "who" and "for" in her transcription suggests a fourteener couplet, as presented here.

33. Go not too: preceding the poem, ED quoted John 3:6, "Would it be prudent to

subject an apparitional interview to a grosser test? The Bible portentously says 'that which is Spirit is Spirit'" (L558).

34. We knew not: to TWH, ED writes, "The most noble Congratulation it ever befell me to offer – is that you are yourself – Till it has loved – no man or woman can become itself – Of our first Creation we are unconscious –" (L575); she may have responded to his engagement to Mary Potter Thacher, announced in the *Springfield Republican* on 1 December 1878. This poem varies from the one sent to Whitney only by one dash. Leyda gives an early 1878 date for the letter to Whitney.

35. Spurn the temerity –: references to Jesus's crucifixion ("Calvary," "Gethsemane") in the context of gaiety suggest an Easter message. HHJ wrote on this manuscript, "Wonderful twelve words! H.J." and sent it to TWH.

36. Those not live: in John 3:7 Jesus says, "Marvel not that I said unto thee, Ye must be born again." SD wrote, "To read to friends" at the bottom of this message.

37. "Heavenly Father" – take: in Genesis 3:19 God says to Adam, "for dust thou art, and unto dust shalt thou return."

38. A Counterfeit – a: preceding the poem, ED wrote "In petto" (Italian, "in confidence"; a phrase used by the pope in appointing cardinals); she signed her note "Lothrop." In 1876 Mary Lothrop, the daughter of Amherst minister Charles D. Lothrop, accused her father of mistreating her mother and herself. AD provided the family with informal legal advice. Lothrop sued the *Springfield Republican* for libel, but the court decided against him (April 1879). In July the Amherst parish approved AD's motion to have nothing more to do with the case. SD also supported the daughter's claims.

39. We shall find: in arithmetic, a cube is formed by multiplying any number twice by itself (4 × 4 × 4); according to ED's Webster's, "The law of the planets is, that the squares of the times of their revolutions are in proportion to the cubes of their mean distances"—in other words, scientists believed the cube would provide information about space. ED here uses the language of math to compare two insoluble problems.

40. The Robin is: fragment retained containing versions of lines 1, 2, 11, and 13 (variant), beginning "The Robin is a Troubadour."

41. A Dimple in: these lines finish a sentence that begins: "The route of your little Fugitive must be a tender wonder – and yet / A Dimple . . ." (L641).

42. Could that sweet: a transcription ordered in 1936 by Jake Zeitlin, Inc., before the company put the manuscript (now lost) on sale presents these lines with different punctuation and capitalization.

43. The Stem of: poem begins midsentence and in the middle of a row of print: "Who is 'Today'? 'Yesterday' was a Year ago – and yet, The Stem . . ." (L684); "yet" begins a new row of print.

44. All things swept: follows ED's comment, "It is solemn to remember that Vastness – is but the Shadow of the Brain which casts it –" (L735).

45. No Autumn's intercepting: first two lines retained (lost), transcribed variant by MLT as "No autumn's interceptive chill, / Appalls that Tripoli." The letter to EH responded to a memorial issue of *Scribner's* (then being renamed *The Century Illustrated Monthly Magazine*) honoring her husband, Josiah Gilbert Holland.

46. Not seeing, still: the note begins, "Vinnie asked me if I had any Message for you, and while I was picking it, you ran away" (L741).

47. Now I lay: rewrites a children's bedtime prayer (printed in the *New-England Primer*, 1690) as a mock elegy, alluding to Genesis 3:19, "for dust thou art, and unto dust shalt thou return"; Longfellow comments in "A Psalm of Life" (1838), "Dust thou art, to dust returnest, / Was not spoken of the soul."

48. Elysium is as: in her journal, MLT claimed that after she sang for Lavinia, ED sent in a glass of sherry and this poem, "written as I sang." MLT did not see ED on this or any other occasion.

49. Her Losses make: to Niles, this poem follows a reference to Marian Evans (George Eliot); to SD, it may respond to the death of a cousin on 15 May 1883. ED retained the final two lines: "In vain to punish Honey / It only sweeter grows."

50. No ladder needs: see Matthew 11:28, "Come unto me, all ye that labour and are heavy laden, and I will give you rest," and "Suffer the little children to come unto me" (Matthew 19:14). The poem follows praise of Whitney's interest in the Children's Aid Society. ED uses the last four lines again at the end of a version of "To her derided Home" (c. summer 1883).

51. Candor – my tepid: the note begins: "How inspiriting to the clandestine Mind those words of Scripture, 'We thank thee that thou hast hid these things –'" (L853; Matthew 11:25).

52. Blossoms will run: follows "Blossoms, and Cakes, and Memory! 'Choose ye which ye will serve'! *I* serve the Memory –" (L840); ED quotes Joshua 24:15.

53. Morning is due: follows ED's revision of Revelation 21:21, "every several gate was of one pearl," to the present tense, "is of one Pearl" (L864).

54. Pass to thy: follows several remarkable lines of unrhymed, (mostly) metered prose: "He knew no niggard moment – His Life was full of Boon – The Playthings of the Dervish were not so wild as his – No Crescent was this Creature – He traveled from the Full – Such soar, but never set – I see him in the Star, and meet his sweet velocity in everything that flies – His life was like the Bugle, which winds itself away, his Elegy an Echo – his Requiem Ecstasy – Dawn and Meridian in one. Wherefore would he wait, wronged only of Night, which he left for us – Without a speculation, our little Ajax spans the whole –" (L868).

55. Expanse cannot be: lines 5–8 appear (variant) in the earlier "This Me – that walks and works – must die" (c. 1883) and in the later "The Spirit lasts – but in what mode –" (variant) mid-October 1883.

56. The Spirit lasts –: part of six lines retained (variant) from the middle of the poem. The final five lines (variant) appear in "This Me – that walks and works – must die" (c. 1883) and were sent to Maria Whitney c. summer 1883. The final four lines (variant) appear in "Expanse cannot be lost –," sent to SD c. October 1883.

57. Immured in Heaven!: first two lines retained as "immured in Heaven – what a Cell –."

58. Each that we: these lines of verse are followed in the letter by metered prose: "I work to drive the awe away, yet awe impels the work. I almost picked the crocuses, You told them so sincerely" (L891).

59. There are two: Dickerman's daughter, also Elizabeth, apparently transcribed from memory the poem sent to her mother; Mather passed on the copy she received "by word of mouth" to Georgiana Mills, who made two transcripts from memory.

60. Who is it: in Revelation 21:8, all liars, the fearful, and the unbelieving "shall have their part in the lake which burneth with fire and brimstone."

61. The Auctioneer of: traditionally, an auctioneer indicated a sale by saying, "Going, going, gone" and banging his hammer.

62. Not Sickness stains: follows reference to Simonides's epitaph for the Spartans: "We die, said the Deathless of Thermopylae, in obedience to Law –."

63. The going from: the transcript of this letter has also been lost.

64. In other Motes,: follows the metered phrase "Pursuing you in your transitions," which THJ read as the poem's first line (L937). The poem is complete syntactically without this line and is in a different metrical pattern.

65. Some Arrows slay: ED retained a version of line 1 ("Most Arrows slay but whom they strike –") and a fragment containing the words "Most Arrows."

66. Go thy great: "pointing" was defined as "the art of making the divisions of writing; punctuation" (Webster's). "Punctuation" stems from Latin *punctus* (point). Sent to Kimball with reference to Otis Lord, and to Cooper, "To thank you" (L970).

67. Is it too: the note concludes with a line in meter, apparently not part of the verse, "I give his Angels charge –" (L975); Crowell was about to travel abroad.

68. Of Glory not: sent to TWH as a response to his sonnet, "To the Memory of H. H." (*Century*, April 1886), and to Helen Hunt Jackson's death (August 1885).

69. Those final Creatures,: text from typescript used as printer's copy for *The Single Hound*, edited by Bianchi.

70. That Love is: text from typescript used as printer's copy for *The Single Hound*, edited by Bianchi; this manuscript was lost after 1937.

71. Which misses most –: MLT made a second transcript (variant), perhaps derived from that by Frances Norcross.

Glossary of Correspondents

This glossary includes the names of ED's immediate family members and of correspondents to whom extant manuscripts indicate she circulated one or more poems. It is not a complete list of her correspondents. Names of correspondents to whom ED sent several poems receive abbreviations.

Anthon, Catherine Scott Turner (1831–1917): close friend of SD's who also became a friend of ED's; some have speculated that there was an erotic attachment between them

Bianchi, Martha Dickinson: see Dickinson, Martha

Bowdoin, Elbridge Gridley (1820–1893): Amherst College graduate who practiced law with Edward Dickinson (ED's father), 1847–1855

Bowles, Mary Schermerhorn (1827–1893): wife of SB

Bowles, Samuel (SB; 1826–1878): editor of the *Springfield Republican*; close friend of ED's brother, AD, and his wife, SD, and a friend of ED's; some consider Bowles a candidate for the "Master" to whom ED wrote (but probably never sent) her manuscripts addressed to "Master"

Bowles, Samuel, the younger (1851–1915): son of SB and Mary Bowles; succeeded his father as editor of the *Springfield Republican*

Bullard, Lucretia Gunn Dickinson (1806–1885): ED's aunt; sister of Edward Dickinson

Chickering, Joseph K. (1846–1899): graduate of Amherst College and an English teacher there from 1873 to 1885

Clark, Charles H. (1838–1908): brother of James D. Clark

Clark, James D. (1828–1883): a lifelong friend to Reverend Charles Wadsworth; some consider Wadsworth a candidate for the "Master" to whom ED wrote (but probably never sent) the manuscripts addressed to "Master"; ED corresponded with Clark after Wadsworth's death

Cooper, Abigail Ingersoll (1817–1895): widow of Amherst lawyer James Sullivan Cooper (d. 1870) and mother of an Amherst lawyer and Dickinson family physician

Cowan, Perez Dickinson (1843–1923): great nephew of ED's paternal grandfather; graduated from Amherst College and later became a Presbyterian minister

Crowell, Mary Warner (1830–1903): daughter and wife of Amherst College professors

Dickerman, Elizabeth Street: wife of George S. Dickerman, pastor of the First Congregational Church, which the Dickinsons attended, 1883–1891

Dickinson, Edward, called Ned (1861–1898): ED's nephew; AD and SD's eldest child

Dickinson, Lavinia (1833–1899): ED's sister, who lived with her at the Homestead and also never married

Dickinson, Martha, called Mattie (1866–1943): ED's niece, who married Alexander E. Bianchi and edited ED's writings under her married name, starting in 1914

Dickinson, Susan Huntington Gilbert (SD; 1830–1913): ED's best friend; wife of AD; some have speculated that there was an erotic attachment between SD and ED; SD received far more poems and letters than any other correspondent and may have submitted ED's poems to newspapers for publication in the 1860s

Dickinson, Thomas Gilbert, called Gib (1875–1883): ED's nephew: youngest child of AD and SD; died of typhoid fever at the age of eight

Dickinson, William Austin, called Austin (AD; 1829–1895): ED's brother; an Amherst College and Harvard Law School graduate; lived next door to the Homestead; married to SD

Dwight, Edward (1820–1890): pastor of the First Congregational Church, which the Dickinsons attended, 1854–1860

Flynt, Eudocia Converse: ED's cousin on her mother's side

Ford, Emily Fowler (1826–1893): girlhood friend of ED's who also published poetry; Ford wrote a memoir of their days at the Amherst Academy

French, Daniel Chester (1850–1931): sculptor who resided briefly in Amherst during his childhood, when his father was the president of Massachusetts Agricultural College

Gilbert, Thomas Dwight (1815–894): brother of SD

Higginson, Mary Channing (1820–1877): first wife of TWH

Higginson, Thomas Wentworth (TWH; 1823–1911): critic, essayist, minister, colonel of the first black regiment in the Union army (1862–1864), and outspoken abolitionist and women's suffrage advocate; ED called TWH her preceptor after initiating their correspondence in 1862; coeditor of ED's first books of poems (1890, 1891); visited ED in Amherst in 1870 and 1873

Holland, Elizabeth Chapin (EH; 1823–1896): one of ED's closest friends; married to Josiah Gilbert Holland

Holland, Josiah Gilbert (1819–1881): critic, novelist, poet, physician; an associate editor of the Springfield Republican and later cofounder and editor of *Scribner's Monthly Magazine*; married to EH

Howard, Maria Avery (d. 1893): sister-in-law of SD whom SD visited in Aurora, New York

Howland, William (1822–1880): graduate of Amherst College who studied law with ED's father

Jackson, Helen Fiske Hunt (HHJ; 1830–1885): celebrated poet, novelist, and supporter of Native American rights; a schoolmate of ED's; Jackson grew up in Amherst but attended boarding school elsewhere from the age of eleven

Jenkins, Jonathan Leavitt (1830–1913): pastor of the First Congregational Church, which the Dickinsons attended, 1867–1877; married to Sarah Jenkins

Jenkins, Sarah Eaton (1841–1910): wife of Jonathan and mother of MacGregor and Sarah, who were good friends of Ned and Mattie Dickinson's; MacGregor wrote two memoirs about knowing ED when he was a child

Kimball, Benjamin (1850–1932): cousin of Otis Phillips Lord, with whom ED apparently shared a romantic attachment after the death of Lord's wife in 1877

Loomis, Eben Jenks (1828–1912) and Mary Wilder (1833–1910): parents of MLT

Mather, Ellen Augusta (1847–1898): cousin and second wife of Richard Mather, a professor of classics at Amherst College

Niles, Thomas (1825–1894): editor at Roberts Brothers, a prominent publishing house in Boston that brought out four editions of ED's writing in the 1890s

Norcross, Frances (Ns; 1847–1896): younger cousin on ED's mother's side; sister of Louisa; ED lived with Frances and Louisa for several months while undergoing eye treatment in Cambridge and was very close to them

Norcross, Louisa (Ns; 1842–1919): younger cousin on ED's mother's side; sister of Frances; published a piece in 1904 describing ED as writing and reading poems aloud in the pantry

Stearns, Olive Gilbert (1815–1911): wife of William Augustus Stearns, president of Amherst College, 1854–1876

Sweetser, Catherine Dickinson (1814–1895): ED's "Aunt Katie" on her father's side and a neighbor of the Dickinsons; married to Joseph, brother of Luke Sweetser

Sweetser, Lucy Cornelia Peck, called Nellie (1832–1907): married to John Howard Sweetser, son of Luke and Abby Sweetser, the Dickinsons' neighbors

Todd, Mabel Loomis (MLT; 1865–1932): coeditor of ED's first books of poems (1890, 1891) and editor of the first collection of ED's letters (1894) and a third book of poems (1896); she moved to Amherst in 1881 and began an amorous relationship with AD in 1882

Tuckerman, Edward (1817–1886): professor of botany at Amherst College; married to ST

Tuckerman, Sarah Elizabeth Sigourney Cushing (ST; 1832–1915): neighbor and friend of ED's; married to Edward Tuckerman

Vanderbilt, Gertrude Lefferts (c. 1824–1896): a friend of Catherine Scott Turner Anthon's and SD's

Whitney, Maria (1830–1910): professor of modern languages at Smith College; close friends with SB

Appendix

UNBOUND SHEETS LISTED CHRONOLOGICALLY IN RELATION TO THE FRANKLIN SETS

SHEET OR LEAF NO.	FIRST LINE OF POEM	FRANKLIN SET/SHEET	FRANKLIN POEM NO.	APPROX. DATE OF COPYING
SHEET 1	A Tongue – to tell Him I am true!	Set 1Sh1	673	Second half of 1863
	I could not prove the Years had feet –		674	
	What Soft – Cherubic Creatures –		675	
SHEET 2	You know that Portrait in the Moon –	Set 1Sh2	676	Second half of 1863
	Funny – to be a Century –		677	
	Not probable – The barest Chance –		678	
	When Night is almost done –		679	
SHEET 3	Love – is that later Thing than Death –	Set 4a Sh1	840	Early 1864
	Struck, was I, nor yet by Lightning –		841	
	Patience – has a quiet Outer –		842	
SHEET 4	It bloomed and dropt, a Single Noon –	Set 4b Sh1	843	
	This Merit hath the Worst –		844	Early 1864
	We can but follow to the Sun –		845	
SHEET 5	This Dust, and its Feature –	Set 2 Sh1	866	Early 1864
	I felt a Cleaving in my Mind –		867	
	Fairer through Fading – as the Day		868	
	What I see not, I better see –		869	
SHEET 6	A Coffin – is a small Domain,	Set 3 Sh1	890	Early 1864
	I learned – at least – what Home could be –		891	
SHEET 7	Experience is the Angled Road	Set 5 Sh 1	899	Early 1865
	'Twas awkward, but it fitted me –		900	
	The Soul's distinct connection		901	
	Too little way the House must lie		902	
SHEET 8	A Doubt if it be Us	Set 5 Sh2	903	Early 1865
	Absence disembodies – so does Death		904	
	Split the Lark – and you'll find the Music –		905	
	Light is sufficient to itself –		506	
	That Distance was between Us		906	
	Perhaps you think Me stooping		273	
SHEET 9	That is solemn we have ended	Set 5 Sh3	907	Early 1865
	They ask but our Delight –		908	
	Because the Bee may blameless hum		909	
	Finding is the first Act		910	
	Given in Marriage unto Thee		818	

SHEET OR LEAF NO.	FIRST LINE OF POEM	FRANKLIN SET/SHEET	FRANKLIN POEM NO.	APPROX. DATE OF COPYING
SHEET 10	As Frost is best conceived	Set 5 Sh4	911	Early 1865
	To my quick ear the Leaves – conferred –		912	
	A Man may make a Remark –		913	
	A Door just opened on a street –		914	
SHEET 11	What shall I do when the Summer troubles –	Set 5 Sh5	915	Early 1865
	Drab Habitation of Whom?		916	
	As One does Sickness over		917	
	We met as Sparks – Diverging Flints		918	
SHEET 12	Nature and God – I neither knew	Set 5 Sh6	803	Early 1865
	Be Mine the Doom –		919	
	Each Scar I'll keep for Him		920	
	How well I knew her not		813	
	Snow beneath whose chilly softness		921	
	I could not drink it, Sweet,		816	
	The Sun is gay or stark		922	
SHEET 13	They won't frown always – some sweet Day	Set 5 Sh7	923	Early 1865
	On that dear Frame the Years had worn		924	
	The Lady feeds Her little Bird		925	
	Soto! Explore thyself!		814	
	I stepped from Plank to Plank		926	
SHEET 14	Each Second is the last	Set 5 Sh8	927	Early 1865
	The Bird must sing to earn the Crumb		928	
	I've none to tell me to but Thee		929	
	All I may, if small,		799	
SHEET 15	The Poets light but Lamps –	Set 5 Sh9	930	Early 1865
	An Everywhere of Silver		931	
	Our little Kinsmen – after Rain		932	
	Of Tolling Bell I ask the cause?		933	
	These tested Our Horizon –		934	
SHEET 16	As imperceptibly as Grief	Set 5 Sh10	935	Early 1865
	As Willing lid o'er Weary Eye		936	
	Not all die early, dying young –		937	
SHEET 17	Those who have been in the Grave the longest –	Set 7 Sh1	938	1865
	Be Mine the Doom		919	
	It was a Grave, yet bore no Stone		852	
	Impossibility, like Wine		939	
	So sets its Sun in Thee		940	
	How the Waters closed above Him		941	
SHEET 18	Always Mine!	Set 7 Sh2	942	1865
	I cannot buy it – 'tis not sold –		943	
	A Moth the hue of this		944	
	Good to hide, and hear 'em hunt!		945	
SHEET 19	Dying! To be afraid of thee	Set 7 Sh3	946	1865
	I made slow Riches but my Gain		947	
	Spring is the Period		948	
	Before He comes		949	
	Twice had Summer her fair Verdure		950	

SHEET OR LEAF NO.	FIRST LINE OF POEM	FRANKLIN SET/SHEET	FRANKLIN POEM NO.	APPROX. DATE OF COPYING
SHEET 20	Unable are the Loved to die	Set 7 Sh4	951	1865
	Finite – to fail, but infinite – to Venture –		952	
	Just as He spoke it from his Hands		953	
	The good Will of a Flower		954	
	I sing to use the Waiting,		955	
	Her Grace is all she has –		956	
	When the Astronomer stops seeking		957	
SHEET 21	Absent Place – an April Day –	Set 7 Sh5	958	1865
	Apology for Her		959	
	The Heart has narrow Banks		960	
	When One has given up One's life		961	
	The Veins of other Flowers		798	
SHEET 22	A Light exists in Spring	Set 7 Sh6	962	1865
	Banish Air from Air –		963	
	Like Men and Women Shadows walk		964	
	How far is it to Heaven?		965	
SHEET 23	Truth – is as old as God –	Set 7 Sh7	795	1865
	A Death blow is a Life blow, to Some,		966	
	Two Travellers perishing in Snow		967	
	Fame is the tint that Scholars leave		968	
	Escaping backward to perceive		969	
SHEET 24	The Mountain sat upon the Plain	Set 7 Sh8	970	1865
	Peace is a fiction of our Faith –		971	
	To this World she returned		815	
	Not what We did, shall be the test		972	
	Death is a Dialogue between		973	
	The largest Fire ever known		974	
SHEET 25	And this, of all my Hopes	Set 7 Sh9	975	1865
	Good to have had them lost		809	
	Besides this May		976	
	I cannot be ashamed		977	
SHEET 26	Faith – is the Pierless Bridge	Set 7 Sh10	978	1865
	His Feet are shod with Gauze –		979	
	Love – is anterior to Life –		980	
	Only a Shrine, but Mine –		981	
	If I can stop one Heart from breaking		982	
SHEET 27	Bee! I'm expecting you!	Set 7 Sh11	983	1865
	Satisfaction – is the Agent		984	
	Here, where the Daisies fit my Head		985	
	Where I am not afraid to go		986	
	Her little Parasol to lift		987	
SHEET 28	Said Death to Passion	Set 7 Sh12	988	1865
	Air has no Residence, no Neighbor,		989	
	We'll pass without the parting		503	
	His Bill an Augur is		990	
	To undertake is to achieve		991	

SHEET OR LEAF NO.	FIRST LINE OF POEM	FRANKLIN SET/SHEET	FRANKLIN POEM NO.	APPROX. DATE OF COPYING
SHEET 29	Three Weeks passed since I had seen Her –	Set 7 Sh13	992	1865
	A Sickness of this World it most occasions		993	
	Partake as doth the Bee –		806	
	He scanned it – Staggered –		994	
	The missing All, prevented Me		995	
SHEET 30	I heard, as if I had no Ear	Set 7 Sh14	996	1865
	Not so the infinite Relations – Below		997	
	Somewhat, to hope for,		998	
	Spring comes on the World –		999	
	Lest this be Heaven indeed		1000	
	Just to be Rich		635	
SHEET 31	The Stimulus, beyond the Grave	Set 7 Sh15	1001	1865
	Aurora is the effort		1002	
	Dying at my music!		1003	
	There is no Silence in the Earth – so silent		1004	
	Bind me – I still can sing –		1005	
	The first We knew of Him was Death –		1006	
	Falsehood of Thee, could I suppose		1007	
	How still the Bells in Steeples stand		1008	
SHEET 32	I was a Phebe – nothing more –	Set 7 Sh16	1009	1865
	Knows how to forget!		391	
	'Tis Anguish grander than Delight –		192	
SHEET 33	Crumbling is not an instant's Act	Set 7 Sh17	1010	1865
	Not to discover weakness is		1011	
	Best Things dwell out of Sight		1012	
	No other can reduce		738	
SHEET 34	Superfluous were the Sun	Set 7 Sh18	1013	1865
	This was in the White of the Year –		1014	
	The Fingers of the Light		1015	
	Ideals are the Fairy Oil		1016	
SHEET 35	The Soul should always stand ajar	Set 7 Sh19	1017	1865
	Up Life's Hill with my little Bundle		1018	
	She rose as high as His Occasion		1019	
	There is a Zone whose even Years		1020	
	Which is best? Heaven –		1021	
SHEET 36	A bold, inspiriting Bird	Set 7 Sh20	1022	1865
	Too scanty 'twas to die for you,		1023	
	Did We abolish Frost		1024	
	Were it but Me that gained the Hight –		1025	
	The Hills in Purple syllables		1026	
	To die – without the Dying		1027	
SHEET 37	Who saw no Sunrise cannot say	Set 7 Sh21	1028	1865
	I had a daily Bliss		1029	
	My Season's furthest Flower –		1030	
	Trudging to Eden, looking backward,		1031	
	Far from Love the Heavenly Father		1032	

SHEET OR LEAF NO.	FIRST LINE OF POEM	FRANKLIN SET/SHEET	FRANKLIN POEM NO.	APPROX. DATE OF COPYING
SHEET 38	I knew that I had gained	Set 7 Sh22	1033	1865
	It rises – passes – on our South		1034	
	So large my Will		1035	
	The Products of my Farm are these		1036	
	The Dying need but little, Dear,		1037	
SHEET 39	Bloom – is Result – to meet a Flower	Set 7 Sh23	1038	1865
	My Heart upon a little Plate		1039	
	'Twas my one Glory –		1040	
	Nor Mountain hinder Me		1041	
SHEET 40	When they come back – if Blossoms do –	Set 7 Sh24	1042	1865
	Superiority to Fate		1043	
	Revolution is the Pod		1044	
	We learn in the Retreating		1045	
SHEET 41	What Twigs We held by –	Set 7 Sh25	1046	1865
	We miss a Kinsman more		1047	
	Ended, ere it begun –		1048	
	Myself can read the Telegrams		1049	
SHEET 42	I am afraid to own a Body –	Set 7 Sh26	1050	1865
	The Well upon the Brook		1051	
	It was not Saint – it was too large –		1052	
	Because 'twas Riches I could own,		1053	
	Themself are all I have –		1054	
	To Whom the Mornings stand for Nights,		1055	
SHEET 43	Could I but ride indefinite	Set 6b Sh1	1056	1865
	Embarrassment of one another		1057	
	While it is alive		287	
	To One denied to drink		1058	
SHEET 44	Uncertain lease – developes lustre	Set 6b Sh2	1059	1865
	Noon – is the Hinge of Day –		1060	
	This Chasm, Sweet, upon my life		1061	
	My best Acquaintances are those		1062	
SHEET 45	The Sun and Moon must make their haste –	Set 6b Sh3	1063	1865
	As the Starved Maelstrom laps the Navies		1064	
	Ribbons of the Year –		1065	
	Death leaves Us homesick, who behind,		1066	
SHEET 46	Crisis is a Hair	Set 6b Sh4	1067	1865
	Under the Light, yet under,		1068	
	Away from Home are some and I –		807	
	A Burdock twitched my Gown		289	
SHEET 47	Who occupies this House?	Set 6b Sh5	1069	1865
	The Chemical conviction		1070	
	The Hollows round His eager Eyes		1071	
SHEET 48	A loss of something ever felt I –	Set 6b Sh6	1072	1865
	Herein a Blossom lies –		1073	
	What did They do since I saw Them?		1074	
	As plan for Noon and plan for Night		1075	

SHEET OR LEAF NO.	FIRST LINE OF POEM	FRANKLIN SET/SHEET	FRANKLIN POEM NO.	APPROX. DATE OF COPYING
SHEET 49	Of Consciousness, her awful mate	Set 6b Sh7	1076	1865
	A Cloud withdrew from the Sky		1077	
	Of Silken Speech and Specious Shoe		1078	
	How fortunate the Grave –		1079	
	How happy I was if I could forget		1080	
SHEET 50	Experiment to Me	Set 6b Sh8	1081	1865
	That Such have died enable Us		1082	
	Sang from the Heart, Sire,		1083	
	Fate slew Him, but He did not drop –		1084	
	Who is the East?		1085	
SHEET 51	Nature rarer uses Yellow	Set 6b Sh9	1086	1865
	To help our Bleaker Parts		1087	
	I've dropped my Brain –		1088	
	The Opening and the Close		1089	
SHEET 52	This quiet Dust was Gentlemen and Ladies	Set 6c Sh1	1090	Late 1865
	There is a June when Corn is cut		811	
	To own the Art within the Soul		1091	
	There is a finished feeling		1092	
SHEET 53	The Robin is the One	Set 6c Sh2	501	Late 1865
	'Twas Crisis – All the length had passed –		1093	
	We outgrow love, like other things		1094	
	When I have seen the Sun emerge		1095	
SHEET 54	A narrow Fellow in the Grass	Set 6c Sh3	1096	Late 1865
	Ashes denote that Fire was –		1097	
	The Leaves like Women, interchange		1098	
SHEET 55	At Half past Three, a single Bird	Set 6c Sh4	1099	Late 1865
	The last Night that She lived		1100	
	If Nature smiles – the Mother must		1101	
SHEET 56	Dew – is the Freshet in the Grass –	Set 6c Sh5	1102	Late 1865
	Perception of an Object costs		1103	
	The Crickets sang		1104	
	Of the Heart that goes in, and closes the Door		1105	
SHEET 57	These are the Signs to Nature's Inns –	Set 6c Sh6	1106	Late 1865
	My Cocoon tightens – Colors teaze –		1107	
	The Bustle in a House		1108	
	The Sun went down – no Man looked on –		1109	
SHEET 58	One Day is there of the Series	Set 6a Sh1	1110	Late 1865
	The Luxury to apprehend		819	
	The Robin for the Crumb		810	
	He outstripped Time with but a Bout,		1111	
SHEET 59	This is a Blossom of the Brain –	Set 6a Sh2	1112	Late 1865
	All Circumstances are the Frame		1113	
	A Shade upon the mind there passes		1114	
	It is an honorable Thought		1115	

SHEET OR LEAF NO.	FIRST LINE OF POEM	FRANKLIN SET/SHEET	FRANKLIN POEM NO.	APPROX. DATE OF COPYING
SHEET 60	This Consciousness that is aware	Set 6a Sh3	817	Late 1865
	From Us She wandered now a Year,		794	
	The Sunset stopped on Cottages		1116	
	Ample make this Bed		804	
SHEET 61	Let down the Bars, Oh Death –	Set 6a Sh4	1117	Late 1865
	Reportless Subjects, to the Quick		1118	
	The Definition of Beauty is		797	
	Pain has but one Acquaintance		1119	
	Gratitude – is not the mention		1120	
LEAF 62	Of Paul and Silas it is said	Set 8a L1	1206	1871
LEAF 63	The Voice that stands for Floods to me	Set 8a L2	1207	1871
LEAF 64	"Remember me" implored the Thief!	Set 8a L3	1208	1871
LEAF 65	Somehow myself survived the Night	Set 8a L4	1209	1871
LEAF 66	Because He loves Her	Set 8a L5	1183	1871
LEAF 67	Some we see no more, Tenements of Wonder	Set 8a L6	1210	1871
LEAF 68	Its Hour with itself	Set 8a L7	1211	1871
LEAF 69	My Triumph lasted till the Drums	Set 8a L8	1212	1871
LEAF 70	Like Trains of Cars on Tracks of Plush	Set 8a L9	1213	1871
LEAF 71	Not any higher stands the Grave	Set 8a L10	1214	1871
LEAF 72	The harm of Years is on him –	Set 8a L11	1215	1871
LEAF 73	A Wind that rose though not a Leaf	Set 8a L12	1216	1871
LEAF 74	I worked for chaff and earning Wheat	Set 8b L1	1217	1871
LEAF 75	The Bone that has no Marrow,	Set 8b L2	1218	1871
LEAF 76	Who goes to dine must take his Feast	Set 8b L3	1219	1871
LEAF 77	The Popular Heart is a Cannon first –	Set 8b L4	1220	1871
LEAF 78	It came at last but prompter Death	Set 8b L5	1221	1871
LEAF 79	The pungent Atom in the Air	Set 8b L6	1222	1871
LEAF 80	Immortal is an ample word	Set 8b L7	1223	1871
LEAF 81	Are Friends Delight or Pain?	Set 8b L8	1224	1871
LEAF 82	The Mountains stood in Haze –	Set 8b L9	1225	1871
LEAF 83	Somewhere upon the general Earth	Set 8b L10	1226	1871
SHEET 84	Step lightly on this narrow spot –	Set 9 Sh1	1227	1871
	I cannot want it more –		1228	
SHEET 85	The Days that we can spare	Set 10 Sh1	1229	1871
	'Twas fighting for his Life he was –		1230	
	Frigid and sweet Her parting face –		1231	
	An honest Tear		1232	

SHEET OR LEAF NO.	FIRST LINE OF POEM	FRANKLIN SET/SHEET	FRANKLIN POEM NO.	APPROX. DATE OF COPYING
SHEET 86	I should not dare to be so sad	Set 10 Sh2	1233	1871
	Remembrance has a Rear and Front.		1234	
	Because my Brook is fluent		1235	
SHEET 87	A little Dog that wags his tail	Set 10 Sh3	1236	1871
	Oh Shadow on the Grass!		1237	
	To make Routine a Stimulus		1238	
SHEET 88	To disappear enhances –	Set 10 Sh4	1239	1871
	So much of Heaven has gone from Earth		1240	
SHEET 89	So I pull my Stockings off	Set 11 Sh1	1271	1872
	What we see we know somewhat		1272	
	The Past is such a curious Creature		1273	
	A prompt – executive Bird is the Jay –		1022	
SHEET 90	Now I knew I lost her –	Set 11 Sh2	1274	1872
	The Sea said		1275	
LEAF 91	September's Baccalaureate	Set 15 L1	1313	1873
SHEET 92	The Way to know the Bobolink	Set 12 Sh1	1348	1874
	Not with a Club, the Heart is broken		1349	
SHEET 93	The Mushroom is the Elf of Plants –	Set 13 Sh1	1350	1874
	A Bee his Burnished Carriage		1351	
SHEET 94	A Dew sufficed itself –	Set 14 Sh1	1372	1875
	The Spider as an Artist		1373	
	Winter is good – his Hoar Delights		1374	
SHEET 95	Delight's Despair at setting	Set 14 Sh2	1375	1875
	Which is the best – the Moon or the Crescent?		1376	
	A Rat surrendered here		1377	
	This dirty – little – Heart		1378	
SHEET 96	How News must feel when travelling	Set 14 Sh3	1379	1875
SHEET 97	The last of Summer is Delight	Set 14 Sh4	1380	1875
	The Heart is the Capital of the Mind		1381	
	Not any more to be lacked –		1382	
SHEET 98	After all Birds have been investigated	Set 14 Sh5	1383	1875
	The Mind lives on the Heart		1384	
	That sacred Closet when you sweep –		1385	

Index of First Lines

WITH FRANKLIN AND JOHNSON NUMBERS